The Royal Horticultural Society's
Concise Encyclopædia of
GARDENING TECHNIQUES

EDITOR IN CHIEF: CHRISTOPHER BRICKELL, DIRECTOR GENERAL OF THE R.H.S.

Mitchell Beazley

The Royal Horticultural Society's Concise Encyclopaedia of Gardening Techniques

Editor-in-chief Christopher Brickell
Technical editor Kenneth A. Beckett

This edition first published in 1993
for Aura Books by
Reed Consumer Books Ltd
Reprinted in 1993

The Royal Horticultural Society's Encyclopedia of
Practical Gardening
© Mitchell Beazley Publishers 1981

The Royal Horticultural Society's Concise
Encyclopedia of Gardening Techniques
© Mitchell Beazley Publishers 1983
Revised edition 1988
ISBN 1 85152 399 5

The Royal Horticultural Society's Concise
Encyclopedia of Gardening Techniques was
edited and designed by Mitchell Beazley
Publishers, part of Reed Consumer Books Ltd,
Michelin House, 81 Fulham Road, London, SW3 6RB

Photosetting by Tradespools Ltd, Frome, Somerset
Origination by Culver Graphics Ltd,
High Wycombe, Buckingham
Printed and bound in Spain by
Grafos S.A. Barcelona

Contributors

Tony Biggs, who wrote the section on vegetables, is a former lecturer in horticulture at Wye College, University of London. He now lectures in Australia.

Kenneth A Beckett, Technical Editor of the Encyclopaedia and contributor of the section on growing under glass, is a full-time gardening writer and consultant.

Christopher Brickell, Editor-in-Chief of the Encyclopaedia and author of the chapter on pruning, is Director General of the Royal Horticultural Society's Garden at Wisley, Surrey.

Harry Baker, who writes on fruit, is Fruit Officer at the Royal Horticultural Society's Garden at Wisley.

David Pycraft, who contributed the sections on lawns and ground cover, is Horticultural Adviser at the Royal Horticultural Society's Garden at Wisley.

Phillip McMillan Browse, who writes on propagation, has been a lecturer on the subject for 20 years.

Alan Titchmarsh, author of the basic techniques section, trained as a gardener, then lectured at Kew, then built up a reputation as a TV and radio gardening expert.

Contents

Introduction 1

Gardening can be a relaxing, absorbing hobby, or it can become a chore. Once you have a garden, it is impossible to ignore it: some basic tasks must be undertaken if it is to stay a garden and not become a jungle.

The key to happy gardening is mastery of the central techniques. Over many years and in every season, soil and climate, gardeners have built up a store of ways of doing things: ways of digging without undue fatigue, ways of combatting pests, of pruning a tree so that it gives fruit, of coaxing crops out of difficult ground.

The Royal Horticultural Society's famous and beautiful garden at Wisley is admired by thousands each year, but it is more than a showplace: it is a centre for research into plants and techniques. This *Concise Encyclopaedia* draws upon the RHS resource of practical, common-place expertise. Because it is concerned with methods, with techniques, the *Concise Encyclopaedia* is designed around sequences of step-by-step illustrations with detailed captions. These sequences amplify the accompanying text and provide the gardener with the keys he or she needs to complete – and enjoy – gardening tasks.

The Royal Horticultural Society's Concise Encyclopaedia of Gardening Techniques is a book for the practical gardener. It has been researched, written and edited by experts, specialists in their fields, under the overall supervision of the Royal Horticultural Society.

Using the Concise Encyclopaedia
This book is divided into eight sections – Basic Techniques; Vegetables; Fruits; Lawns; Ground Cover and Weed Control; Propagation; Pruning; Growing under Glass; and Pests and Diseases. Each section contains illustrations for identification as well as the sequences of step-by-step drawings. In this respect the resources of the Royal Horticultural Society's Garden at Wisley were invaluable in obtaining information for illustrating each operation.

The first section of the *Concise Encyclopaedia* is arranged to be of particular help to the gardener who is tackling a new plot or one which is overgrown or neglected. Advice is given on drainage, soil cultivation, modification and enrichment so that the ground can be brought into a fertile and workable state before planting and basic construction begins.

The rewards of vegetable gardening have been justifiably proclaimed many times before. Ecologists, gourmets and health enthusiasts agree, from their different viewpoints, that growing vegetables is a worthwhile pursuit; it can also be extremely enjoyable. The chapter on growing vegetables assumes no prior knowledge and cuts no corners. It reveals what the experts do and why they do it. Each vegetable is dealt with in clear detail from the moment you step outside with a spade to the day, weeks or months later, when you return with a basket of succulent produce.

Few gardeners will deny that one of the most rewarding aspects of gardening is growing and tasting freshly picked sun-warmed fruits. The first pages of this section deal with the practical aspects of fruit growing. The second part concerns soft fruit and the third tree fruit.

A well-maintained lawn is a valuable feature of many gardens, and, as such, it is not only important to tend to the lawn to keep it healthy, its shape should also be considered. The lawns section begins with the preparation of the site then continues with creating a lawn, from seed or from turf, and maintaining it once it has been established.

In recent years gardeners have learned to imitate nature by utilizing the ground covering properties of suitable plants for dealing with those problem areas where little except weeds will normally grow. Not only do ground cover plants keep the ground free of weeds, they also make the area attractive and have the added advantage that once established they require little maintenance. Here we explain how to prepare the site, plant and maintain. Suitable plants are recommended for problem sites; those, for example, that are shady, hot and dry or damp.

Plant propagation, making several new plants from one, has been practised ever since early man abandoned itinerant life and settled down on the land. The techniques of vegetative propagation developed in such ancient civilizations as those of the Babylonians and the Chinese are still relevant and in use in the twentieth century.

In this section is listed the basic tools and equipment you will require. We then discuss environmental control, composts, rooting hormones and fertilizers. Propagation from seeds in containers and the germination and the development of the young plant is examined. The rest of the section then presents a wide range of ways to propagate vegetatively. It starts with a chapter on roots and

Introduction 2

progresses through to sections on stems and leaves. Lastly, there is an explanation on grafting using whip-and-tongue techniques.

Pruning is a skill that is crucial to maintaining an attractive and healthy garden. Yet this basic technique causes much worry to gardeners who are nervous about taking secateurs and saw to their precious plants. This section is carefully written and designed to explain the subtleties of this key gardening art in a practical way. Each stage of pruning is shown, indicating which branch or stem should be removed and how the plant will look after the operation.

When using the step-by-step diagrams remember that your own plant of the species concerned will not be exactly like the one shown. The diagrams are designed to show the basic principles and methods. Different tones of green have been used to designate each year of growth. This enables the gardener to see how the framework of the plant is built up and to identify easily the parts of the plant that should be pruned.

The essential difference between growing outside and under glass is total control of the environment. This element of control is a large part of the appeal of greenhouse and frame gardening, for the plants are completely dependent on the care and skill of the cultivator. Maintaining a temperature regime to meet the needs of a range of plants is the heart of climate control under glass. Many greenhouse owners grow a motley assortment of plants from different countries and climates. Striking a balance might seem impossible, but many plants have wide tolerances and it is surprising how plants from diverse habitats will co-exist satisfactorily—if not to perfection—under the same set of conditions in a greenhouse.

In this section we describe the running of a greenhouse beginning with the importance of hygiene. The growing of plants is covered in the sections on cold and cool greenhouses. Each section begins with an outline of key sowing, flowering and cropping times and routine tasks and then goes on to the cultivation of various types of plants. Finally, there is a section on frames and cloches with detailed step-by-step sequences.

The final chapter of the *Concise Encyclopaedia* is concerned with the identification, prevention and treatment of pests and diseases, particularly those that attack fruit and vegetables.

A glossary of common terms and an index complete the *Concise Encyclopaedia*.

Safety

Accident reports constantly show that the most dangerous place on earth is the home. More accidents occur there than anywhere else. Although this state of affairs is brought about as a result of spending much of the time in and about the house, it is as well to remember that carelessness is the cause of most domestic disasters. It is also the major cause of those that occur in the garden.

There is certainly no need to be frightened of using power tools and chemicals in the garden provided that sensible precautions are taken, but so often familiarity breeds contempt and the gardener takes unnecessary (and foolish) risks.

It is vital to follow the instructions on packages when using garden chemicals.

Remember to wear stout shoes, boots or wellingtons when digging or using soil cultivating equipment. Take special care when using electrical apparatus and make sure that the cables are sound and properly connected. Wear rubber gloves when mixing and applying chemicals and store all such preparations out of the reach of children and animals—under lock and key if necessary. Precautions only seem excessive before an accident.

Common-sense gardening

The soil is rather like a bran-tub—you only get out of it what you put in. It is quite unreasonable to expect an undernourished soil to produce healthy, vigorous plants which are capable of withstanding drought and pest and disease attack. Plants extract nearly all their food from the soil, and on cultivated ground the gardener is responsible for stocking the larder. All manner of living organisms are necessary to keep soil fertile, and it is the addition of organic matter in particular that ensures their wellbeing.

Fertilizers, too, are essential if plants are to be quickly supplied with vital chemical elements, and the sensible gardener will rely both on organic matter and fertilizers to keep his soil "in good heart". Neglect the soil, and all other cultivation techniques and expert knowledge will be of little value.

No-one has ever learned all there is to know about gardening, and that is probably why the craft remains fresh and fascinating. A knowledge of the principles involved and a mastery of the basic skills needed to grow plants will provide anyone with "green fingers". *The Royal Horticultural Society's Concise Encyclopaedia of Gardening Techniques* sets out to do just that.

Soil 1

Soil is the result of organic forces working on the inorganic rock. In a ceaseless process rocks are broken down and living creatures colonize the resulting debris. The nature of the parent rock decides much of the character of the resulting soil.

Soil formation

Several factors are responsible for the development of soil; the most important of these is climate. Rainwater passing over and through the parent rock breaks it down, and repeated freezing and thawing shatters the rock into smaller particles. Organic matter, such as leaves and dead animals, lodges in this rock waste, allowing bacteria and fungi to go into action. Seeds germinate in the resulting mixture. Once plants are established they will contribute organic matter to the soil, so making it capable of supporting other life in the form of more bacteria and fungi, insects, worms and other animals.

Soil profile

A cross-section of the soil (known as a soil profile), can often be seen in the side of a ditch or trench. In most temperate climates there will be five layers or "horizons" (see diagram right). The shallow, topmost layer (a) will consist of humus unless the ground has recently been cultivated, in which case this layer will have been incorporated in the top-soil. The most important layer as far as the gardener is concerned is the top-soil (b). Ideally this should be 2–3 ft deep to sustain a wide range of crops. It should contain adequate supplies of plant nutrients and organic matter, and should be well-drained and aerated. Below the top-soil is the sub-soil layer (c), consisting of partially broken-down rock. It is infertile but can contain useful nutrients. A layer of fragmented rock (d) may occur between the sub-soil and the solid parent rock or bedrock (e). Soil profiles will tend to vary from area to area depending upon the geology, the climate, the history of cultivation and the vegetation cover.

Types of soil

From the gardener's point of view soils are classified according to the amount of sand or clay particles they contain, and according to their acidity or alkalinity.

Clay Clay particles are very small and tend to adhere to one another, making drainage and air penetration slow and cultivation difficult. Clay soils are sticky when wet, hard when dry, slow to warm up in spring and described by the gardener as heavy. They are usually rich in nutrients and, unlike sands, chemically active. To test a soil for clay, squeeze a moist sample between finger and thumb. If the particles slide readily and the soil looks shiny it has a high clay content. A squeezed handful will readily bind together.

The addition of organic matter greatly improves clay soils, for it causes the particles to clump together in larger groups, so allowing water and air to pass between them. Lime, when added to clay soils, also causes particles to bind together by the process of flocculation (forming into compound masses or clumps).

Sand Sandy soils consist of large particles surrounded by air spaces. Water drains through them rapidly and there is ample air for plant roots. They are easy to cultivate and quick to warm up in spring, but they dry out very easily and, due to their rapid drainage, nutrients are quickly washed away. To test a soil for sand, squeeze the particles between finger and thumb. If the sand content is high the particles will both look and feel rough. A squeezed handful will not bind together well.

Soil profile

Improve sandy soils by adding organic matter such as garden compost.

Silt Silty soils have particles intermediate in size between sand and clay. They are sticky and fairly heavy, and can be difficult to cultivate because they are not flocculated and liming is of little help. Improve the texture of silt soils by applying large amounts of humus-producing material.

Loam This is the ideal soil, containing a mixture of clay, sand and silt particles, plus an adequate supply of organic matter and plant nutrients. It is easy to cultivate, retains moisture and nutrients, yet is well-drained. Loam varies and may be classified as light, medium or heavy, depending on the clay-to-sand ratio.

Peat Made up of partially decomposed organic matter, peaty soils are inclined to be acid and poorly drained. The addition of lime, nutrients, coarse sand, grit or weathered ashes, and the construction of artificial drainage systems improves their quality.

Acidity and alkalinity

The amount of lime a soil contains governs its acidity. A soil rich in lime or chalk is said to be alkaline. One which lacks lime is described as acid or sour. The degree of acidity or alkalinity is measured on the pH scale which runs from 0 to 14. A soil with a pH above 7.0 is called alkaline, and one with a pH of below 6.5 is said to be acid. Soils with pH readings above 8.5 and below 4.5 are rare. Most plants prefer a soil with a pH in the range 6.5 to 7.0.

Humus

The dark brown crumbly organic matter within the soil is humus. It consists of plant and animal remains in various stages of decay and ensures the continued survival of bacteria which are essential if a soil is to be fertile. Humus also retains moisture, keeps the soil well aerated and is a source of plant nutrients. On cultivated ground humus breaks down more quickly than it would if left undisturbed, so it is important that the soil is amply replenished with well-rotted manure, compost, leaf-mould or other humus-forming material whenever possible.

Soil life

Earthworms, insects, burrowing animals, slugs, snails, bacteria and many other forms of life all contribute to the organic content of the soil and, unless their presence is a severe nuisance they should be encouraged.

SOIL TESTING

Simple soil testing kits can be bought which allow a rough check to be made on the soil's pH level. Take small random samples of soil from different parts of the garden and shake them up in the solution included with the kit. Allow soil to settle then check the colour of the liquid against the range of colours on the chart in the kit. The pH value is indicated by the depth of the colour of the solution in the tube.

Testing kits are also available which measure mineral levels in the soil and allow deficiencies to be corrected. Alternatively, send a soil sample to one of the educational or commercial laboratories that offer a testing service.

Check the pH level regularly, especially if attempts are being made to modify the soil's pH level.

Soil 2

Plant nutrients

A good soil will contain all the nutrient elements necessary for plant growth. The major ones, required in relatively large quantities, are nitrogen, potassium and phosphorus plus lesser amounts of magnesium, calcium, sulphur, carbon, hydrogen and oxygen. The minor, or trace elements are iron, manganese, boron, molybdenum, zinc and copper.

A plant lacking any of these elements shows certain symptoms. The more common ones are: nitrogen deficiency—slow, stunted growth and pale leaves; phosphate deficiency —stunted growth with red or purple leaves; potassium deficiency—pale yellow or brown leaves; magnesium deficiency—yellowing of older leaves; and iron deficiency—yellowing of young leaves. For details see the Pests and Diseases section (page 244–245).

Drainage

Both water and air are necessary in the soil if plants and soil organisms are to thrive. In poorly drained soils, the roots of plants are restricted to the top few inches of ground where they cannot anchor the plant firmly or search very far for nutrients. Lack of air inhibits the uptake of minerals from the soil.
Causes of bad drainage The structure of the soil may be responsible for poor drainage. Small, tightly-packed-particles of clay or silt may make the escape of water difficult, or problems may be produced by a sub-soil pan (see Box right) or a high water table. The water table is the level in the soil below which the ground is saturated with water. The level is higher in winter than in summer. In bogs and marshes the water table may be level with the surface of the ground; but normally it is to be found within 6–8 ft of the surface. In soils where a high water table inhibits cultivation, some artificial means of drainage must be constructed to move water to a lower level (see pages 8–9).
Natural drainage Under natural conditions, rainwater which lands on the soil is distributed in several ways. Some of it runs off the surface; some is taken up by plant roots and later transpired by the foliage; some evaporates, and the rest drains through the soil.
Artificial drainage This is vital where the

incorporation of organic matter, coarse sand and grit fails to improve the natural drainage sufficiently. Very heavy clay soils, ground where the water table is inconveniently high and land with impenetrable sub-soil all have to be provided with artificial drainage to make healthy plant growth possible. See pages 8–9 for details of drainage systems.
Water retention If all rainwater were carried too rapidly down to the level of free drainage in the soil, plant roots would have little time to absorb water. In most soils, however, the humus content acts like a sponge, absorbing adequate moisture for the plant's needs and allowing excess water to drain away naturally.

Light soils lacking in humus, such as those with a high sand or chalk content, dry out quickly. Frequent applications of well-rotted organic matter—leaf-mould, peat and compost—improve moisture retention without causing waterlogging by creating humus which acts as a sponge.

Adding organics

Dig in organic material to improve soil condition, especially on clay, where organics will encourage particles to stick together.

PANNING

Soil particles rich in elements such as iron and aluminium sometimes form a hard layer, or pan, often only 1 ft or 18 in below the surface. This impairs drainage, makes digging difficult, prevents root penetration and inhibits plant growth.

Continuous ploughing or rotavating at the same level, and compaction caused by vehicles, can also form pans. On small plots, use a sledge hammer and a heavy steel bar to break up the pan. Deep digging will also break up pans formed by cultivation. Over large areas, traverse the land with a tractor fitted with a mole plough. This will break the pan and leave a gully below it into which water can drain. After dealing with a pan, cultivate at different levels to avoid a recurrence of the problem.

The water cycle

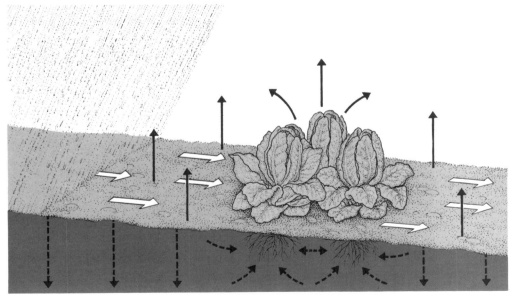

Water in the form of rain or melted snow percolates through the soil and runs off into streams and ditches, is retained in the soil, sinks down to the water table, or is lost through evaporation into the atmosphere. Plants tap the water retained in the soil. This can be up to two-thirds of the rain that falls.

Drainage 1

If a piece of land must be provided with a drainage system, the gardener can choose from a number of alternatives.

Ditches The cheapest way of draining land is to dig ditches to carry the excess water from the cultivated soil to a soakaway, stream or river. Ditches are of particular value on flat, low-lying land where the necessary slope or "fall" needed for tile drains is difficult to obtain. A system of ditches will allow drainage of the water from the soil. Once in the ditches, it will disperse by evaporation or by flowing into a watercourse.

On slightly sloping ground, dig a cut-off ditch at the top of the plot to intercept water from higher ground before it has a chance to saturate the soil further down. Dig another ditch parallel to the first at the foot of the slope to disperse the water received by the slope itself. The top ditch should be connected to the bottom one either by another ditch or by a system of tile drains. The water discharges from the bottom ditch into a soakaway or stream.

Open ditches must be excavated properly at the outset, either by mechanical digger or with a spade. Make them 3–4 ft deep and slope the sides outwards at a 20–30 degree angle to make them stable. The banks of ditches in clay soils will be more stable than those in sand, so they can be steeper.

Clear all ditches of weeds and undergrowth at least once a year and check that there are no blockages which will restrict the flow of water. For safety and efficiency it is a good idea to erect a fence along the ditchside.

Land drains Land or tile drains are short sections of earthenware or longer sections of plastic pipe which are laid end to end, usually in a herringbone system of filled trenches, to collect drainage water and discharge it at a chosen point. The plastic pipes are perforated, flexible and can be bent to avoid obstacles. Concrete drains are a relatively inexpensive alternative.

Dig trenches 2–3 ft deep and about 1 ft wide, taking care to keep top-soil and sub-soil separate. Give the trenches an overall slope of about 1 in 40 to ensure that they can take away water efficiently. The spacing of the side drains (which run into the central main drain) will depend on the nature of the soil—on heavy clay they will need to be closer together than on lighter soils. As a rough guide, space them 15 ft apart on clay, 25 ft apart on loam, and 40 ft apart on sandy soil.

The central drain should consist of 4 in pipes and the subsidiary or side drains of 3 in pipes. Lay the pipes at the bottom of the trench on a 2 in layer of coarse gravel or pebbles and cover them with more rubble or gravel before replacing the top-soil. Discard the sub-soil. The pipes are simply butted together to allow water to percolate between them and the side drains should meet the main drain at an angle of 60 degrees. Cover these junctions with a piece of flat tile to prevent blockages.

Rubble drains On small sites where ditches and tile drains would be impractical, use rubble drains. Take out a single trench across the plot and lead it to a soakaway in an out-of-the-way corner. Make the trench the same dimensions as a tile drain trench and give it a similar fall. Fill it with broken bricks and rubble to half its depth, cap this layer with gravel, then with turf placed upside down and replace the top-soil. Such a system will drain a modest-sized plot adequately and unobtrusively.

Soakaways Tile drains, rubble drains and ditches can all be connected to a soakaway if there is no convenient watercourse into which their water can be discharged.

Dig a hole approximately 6 ft in diameter and at least 6 ft deep (the overall size of the soakaway will be governed by the size of the plot being drained). For best results line the sides with bricks to support the wall of soil and to prevent silting of the soakaway, yet allow the water to seep through. Fill the soakaway with brick rubble or coarse clinker and top with turf, again, to prevent silting.

Mole drains These are constructed by a tractor attachment which pulls a torpedo-shaped steel head through the sub-soil at a chosen depth. The "mole" makes a continuous drain in the sub-soil which allows excess water to disperse. This system of drainage is really effective only when used on land which

Laying a tile drain system

1 Plan ditches in a herringbone pattern, with the main pipe leading to a watercourse or soakaway. Space ditches 15 ft apart on clay, 25 ft on loam and 40 ft on sandy soils.

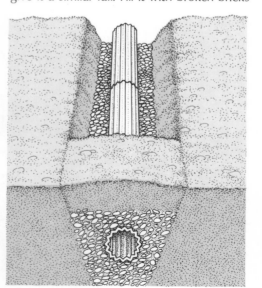

2 Dig trenches 2–3 ft deep with an overall slope of at least 1 in 40. The side trenches should meet the main drain at an angle of 60 degrees.

3 Lay the plastic or clay pipes on a 2 in layer of gravel and add more gravel before replacing the soil. The pipe sections are butted together, not joined.

4 Cover pipe junctions with a piece of flat tile to prevent blockages before replacing first subsoil, then top-soil.

Drainage 2

has clay sub-soil, where it will last for several years. Mole drains should be excavated to the same pattern, depth and fall as tile drains.
Cultivation It is important to keep a careful check on the depth of soil cultivation where underground drains have been constructed. Deep digging or ploughing may break them and create boggy patches.

Draining hard surfaces

Patios and paths can be made impassable by every shower of rain if they are not constructed so that they shed water. When making a paved or concrete area, build in a slight slope so that water is shed and does not stand about in pools. A fall of about 1 in 40 will move water quite quickly either on to border soil (where it can be used by plants), or into a shallow gully which can be led to a soakaway or drain. Construct the gully from half-round ceramic pipes bedded in cement, or from cement which has been trowelled into a similar shape.

If a hidden gully is desirable on a patio or path, lay half-round ceramic pipes down the centre of the area and slope the paving or concrete very gently towards the gully, overlapping the edges. A ½ in gap in the centre will let water run into the channel.

Retaining walls

A reservoir of water will often build up behind a retaining wall if no provision is made for drainage. Not only does the water make the soil inhospitable to plants but it also causes the brick or stonework to become discoloured. To overcome this problem, lay a single row of tile drains, with a suitable fall, immediately behind the wall at its base. Surround the tiles with coarse gravel and lead them to a soakaway or drain. "Weep-holes" are made in the front of the wall to allow more water to escape. Leave one vertical joint unmortared every 5–6 ft along the wall in every second or third course of bricks or stones. Alternatively, insert short lengths of pipe, sloping forwards, at similar intervals to do the same job. Lay a gully of half-round pipes at the foot of the wall if the soil is likely to shed large amounts of water.

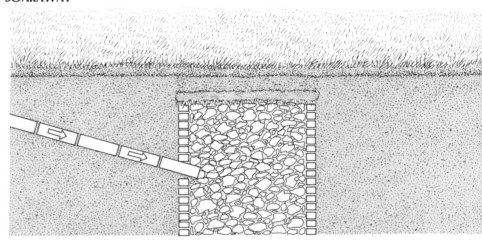

SOAKAWAY

A soakaway must be constructed if there is no suitable watercourse for a drainage system to run to. Dig a hole up to 6 ft deep and across. Line it with unmortared bricks then fill the soakaway with rubble or coarse clinker. Top with turf.

Ditches

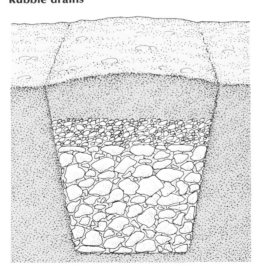

If the land slopes, dig a cut-off ditch across the top of the plot to intercept water from higher ground. Connect it to another at the bottom of the slope by ditches or tile drains.

Rubble drains

Half fill a 2–3 ft trench, dug at the same spacings as tile drain ditches, with broken bricks or rubble. Cap with a layer of gravel then replace the top-soil.

Mole drains

Mole drains are effective in clay soils. They are made by an attachment fitted to a tractor, and can thus only be used on large, open plots.

Retaining walls

Lay a row of tile drains in gravel at the base of the wall. Leave vertical joints unmortared in every third course, 6 ft apart, to allow water to pass through.

Improving the soil 1

As soon as a piece of land is tilled or dug, the process of humus breakdown is speeded up. Added to this, the gardener may discover that the soil is not ideally suited to the crop he wants to grow. This means the soil structure and the organic and chemical content may have to be altered to provide a more satisfactory medium. There are many materials, bulky or granular, organic or inorganic, that can be used to improve soil and turn it into the best possible growing medium for a wide range of plants.

Organic enrichment

Humus is essential in the soil. It helps to retain water and hence nutrients dissolved in it, while at the same time improving drainage (especially in clay). It also helps keep the soil well aerated, maintains soil structure, and it supports the bacteria which break down organic matter into humus. A soil may be rich in chemical fertilizers but if no organic matter is present, most bacteria will not be able to survive. In such impoverished soils plant growth is poor. Humus-rich soils are dark in colour and thus absorb heat more readily than pale soils.

Bulky organic manures have other advantages over fertilizers than the obvious one of improving soil texture and structure by virtue of their consistency. They are often rich in trace elements which may be lacking in fertilizers, and they release their nutrients relatively slowly.

Although each plant has its own particular preferences, it is usually possible to compromise and provide a soil which will suit a number of crops. (See rotation, page 32.)

Most plants thrive in soil that has been dressed with well-rotted manure or compost in the autumn before planting. Fresh manure should not be added to the soil before it has had a chance to decay, because in its fresh state it gives off harmful ammonia. Also, until bacterial decay occurs, nitrogen in the soil is not available to plants.

The nitrogen cycle The nitrogen cycle, by which nitrogen passes from the air to soil to plants and animals and back to the air, involves five basic processes: fixation of nitrogen from the air by micro-organisms and by lightning to form nitrates in the soil; use by plants of these nitrates to make proteins; conversion of proteins into ammonia compounds in decaying plant and animal matter; and finally the recycling of ammonia compounds either into nitrates or into nitrogen gas, which is released into the atmosphere.

THE NITROGEN CYCLE

Organic materials

A wide variety of organic materials can be used to improve soil. The choice is often governed by what is available, but some substances, such as pulverized bark, are easier to store and apply than are manure and garden compost.

Leaf-mould The leaves of deciduous trees, collected in autumn and stacked (in an open position) can be returned to the soil the next year, after they have broken down to a crumbly dark brown mould. Leaf-mould is valued more for its ability to improve soil texture and structure than for the small amounts of plant food it contains. It has the disadvantages of breaking down rather quickly in the soil and may contain weed seeds if weeds have been allowed to grow and seed on the leaf heap. Leaves of the plane, poplar, sycamore and horse chestnut take longest to decompose while those of the oak take a relatively short time. Leaf-mould can be dug into the soil or applied as a mulch. Application rate: 5 lb per square yard.

Animal manures Manure consists of animal droppings, urine and variable amounts of litter such as straw, peat, sawdust, or wood shavings. It must always be stacked before being used so that the litter can be allowed to decompose. Animal manures contain a good proportion of nutrients and many trace elements and are among the best soil conditioners. Horses produce the richest manure, followed by pigs, cows and poultry. Horse manure is quick acting; pig and cow manure break down more slowly. Pig and chicken manure are particularly caustic to plant roots and should not be applied fresh. All are best dug into the soil in autumn or applied as a mulch in spring, where decomposition has occurred during stacking. Application rate: 10–15 lb per square yard.

Peat Peat consists of partially decayed plant remains in which decomposition has been slowed down by the presence of water. Sedge peat comes from lowland marshes in which sedges and reeds predominate and is usually darker in colour than sphagnum peat (also known as moss peat or peat moss) which is from peat bogs in moorland areas. The main ingredient of sphagnum peat is sphagnum moss. Sphagnum is spongier than sedge peat

and therefore more absorbent. Because it darkens the soil, and so helps to absorb heat, peat is valued as a soil conditioner rather than as a fertilizer. Most peats are of an acid nature but when applied at reasonable rates they will not increase the acidity of soil. They are sterile and slow to break down and can be applied as a mulch or dug in. Most commercial peats are blends of different types. Application rate: 10 lb of moist peat per square yard.

Garden compost Garden compost is a valuable alternative to animal manures, which may be difficult to obtain. It may consist of a wide variety of garden and kitchen waste which has been rotted down over a period of several months. (See pages 12–13.) Garden compost is relatively rich in nutrients and a good soil conditioner. It may be applied as a mulch or dug into the soil. Application rate: 10 lb per square yard.

Spent hops A by-product of the brewing industry, spent hops may be available in certain areas. They contain relatively few nutrients but are a good soil conditioner and can be dug in during autumn and winter. Spent hops make a useful mulch. Application rate: 10 lb per square yard.

Hop manure Spent hops with the addition of fertilizers form hop manure. Because it includes artificial fertilizers, it should be used more sparingly than other manures. It can be used as a mulch. Application rate: 1 lb per square yard.

Spent mushroom compost Although they vary considerably in their nutrient value, the spent composts sold off by mushroom growers are well worth using to boost the organic content of soils. They usually contain animal manure, loam and chalk in varying quantities and can be used in all soils except those being used to grow rhododendrons and other lime-hating plants. Application rate: 5–10 lb per square yard.

Seaweed Gardeners in coastal areas may have the opportunity of using seaweed as an organic manure. Spring tides and storms often deposit large amounts of it on beaches. Seaweed contains reasonable amounts of plant nutrients, particularly potash, and it decomposes quickly. It may be dug straight into the ground while wet, or else composted

Improving the soil 2

with garden waste and applied when partially broken down. Dried seaweed meal can be bought from garden suppliers. Application rate of wet seaweed: 10–12 lb per square yard.

Pulverized bark This product is now widely available with or without the addition of fertilizers. The ordinary kind, which does not contain fertilizers, needs nitrogen to break down the bark so it is mainly used as a mulch. Pulverized bark is slow to break down. Use it as a 2–3 in thick mulch.

Shoddy Wool waste or shoddy is a by-product of the textile industry and can sometimes be obtained in industrial areas. It contains a good supply of nitrogen and rots down fairly quickly in the soil. It is best dug in during autumn and winter. Application rate: 11 lb per square yard.

Sewage sludge Dried sludges described as "digested" or "activated" are the safest way to use sewage. Raw sludge, which is sometimes available, may transmit human diseases if applied to ground where salad ("raw") crops are being grown. Sludge-treated land should not be used for "raw" crops for 12 months. Sewage sludge is not particularly high in organic matter, but contains a good supply of nitrogen and some phosphates. It is best dug into the ground in autumn and winter. Application rate: 1½–2½ lb per square yard.

Green manure This is a method of improving soil with organic material by sowing certain crops and then digging them into the ground to enrich the soil. (See pages 12–13.)

Inorganic soil conditioners
On heavy soils the incorporation of inorganic soil conditioners such as weathered wood and fuel ashes, coarse sand, grit, sawdust, wood shavings and pine needles may be of considerable help in making cultivation easier. These materials will open up the soil to some degree, allowing in air, but are best applied in combination with organic matter rather than on their own.

Modifying pH
Although ground limestone will improve the structure of a clay soil by encouraging the soil particles to combine into larger groups, so allowing water to drain away more freely, it is as a means of adjusting the acidity, or

sourness, of a soil that it is of greatest value. This is especially so on light, sandy soils which drain freely and lose lime rapidly by leaching. Some bacteria also will not increase or thrive in acid soils and liming improves the breaking down of organic material.

Some plants find it easier to extract nutrients from an acid soil, others prefer to grow on chalk. While it is generally advisable to grow plants which are suitable on the soil, sometimes this is neither desirable nor practicable. Then the pH, or acid/alkali balance, of the soil has to be adjusted.

A soil with a pH of between 6.5 and 7.0, or neutral, will grow a wide range of crops, and 6.8 is the figure to aim for when correcting acidity. Soil with a pH balance below 6.5 affects the uptake of major and minor plant nutrients. Hydrated lime (calcium hydroxide) is the most effective type to use for pH adjustment as relatively small amounts of it will be needed. It is also more stable than the more expensive quicklime. Ordinary ground limestone or chalk (calcium carbonate), often cheaper, can also be used. An advantage is that it can be used before planting or sowing without damage to the crop.

More lime will have to be applied to acid clay soils, and those containing large quantities of organic matter, than to acid sandy soils. See the instructions on the packet for recommended application rates. Acid soil should be tested annually and suitable amounts of lime added to replace that lost by the soil in the previous season.

Applications of lime are usually made in autumn or early winter. Lime should not be allowed to come into contact with manure or it will react with it, releasing valuable nitrogen into the air. Apply lime and manure in different years, or allow several weeks to elapse between the digging in of the manure and the dusting of the lime. Left on the surface of the soil the lime will gradually be washed in. If necessary, a vegetable plot may be limed in autumn and manured in winter with no ill effects.

Alkaline soils
It is much more difficult to alter the pH of an alkaline soil than that of an acid one. Start by enriching the soil with peat and

other acidic organic matter which will lower the alkalinity to some degree. Then apply flowers of sulphur at the rate of 4 oz per square yard on sandy soils and 8 oz per square yard on heavy soils. Test the soil at monthly intervals to monitor the pH. At below pH 6.5 the availability of nitrogen, phosphorus, potassium and molybdenum decreases while that of iron and manganese increases. On soils with a high pH calcium decreases the uptake of potassium. If the soil is very alkaline, apply flowers of sulphur each year, but also try to grow plants which will tolerate some degree of alkalinity. An efficient drainage system will help to leach some of the chalk out of the soil.

Where iron deficiency is a problem on chalky soils, iron chelates or fritted iron can be watered on to make this nutrient more readily available. Three or four applications a year at the manufacturer's recommended rate should be sufficient.

Fertilizers such as sulphate of ammonia and hoof and horn are acid-reacting and should be used on chalky ground in preference to nitro-chalk and other fertilizers of an alkaline nature.

Types of fertilizer
There are two basic kinds of fertilizer: organic and inorganic, and both are equally valuable in the garden.

All organic fertilizers contain carbon and have been derived from living organisms. Before organic fertilizers can be absorbed by the plant they must be broken down in the soil by bacteria and fungi into inorganic chemicals. It will be seen from this that organic fertilizers actually encourage soil bacteria and so increase fertility. They are released for plant use relatively slowly.

Inorganic fertilizers do not contain carbon. They cannot improve soil texture and do not add any humus, but they are often very quick-acting and, pound for pound, richer in nutrients and are cheaper than organic fertilizers.

The conscientious gardener will use a combination of organic and inorganic fertilizers together with bulky organic soil conditioners to improve his land and keep it in good heart.

All fertilizers are labelled to show their nutrient content in terms of nitrogen (N), phosphoric acid (P_2O_5) and potash (K_2O). Some fertilizers are described as "straight", meaning that they supply just one of these nutrients; others are called "compound" and supply varying quantities of all three nutrients.

Application
Fertilizers may be applied to the ground before sowing or planting (in which case they are known as base dressings) or while the crop is growing, as top dressings.

Apply base dressings to the soil a few days before sowing crops or at the time of planting, working the fertilizer into the top few inches of soil with a fork or rake.

Dust top dressings of fertilizers around growing plants or crops while the soil is moist and hoe them lightly into the top few inches. Where large areas are being fertilized, wheeled fertilizer distributors may be used. These can be adjusted to spread a given quantity of fertilizer evenly over the surface of the soil.

Certain fertilizers are sold in soluble powder or liquid form and can be watered on to the soil or sprayed over plant foliage. These foliar feeds are generally quick-acting and should be applied when the soil is moist. Foliar feeds are best given in dull weather rather than in bright sunshine.

Assessing plant needs
Most plants will be adequately supplied with nutrients if given a base dressing of a compound fertilizer before being sown or planted and one or two top dressings of a similar material during the growing season. Fertilizers containing a large amount of nitrogen can be used to induce rapid leaf and shoot growth where this is lacking. Those containing phosphates will encourage root activity where trees and shrubs are being planted; and fertilizers rich in potash will improve the fruiting ability of a range of crops from tomatoes and beans to apples and pears. The most important requirement, however, is to balance the soil with a mixture of nutrients necessary for a particular crop. Over-application of one nutrient may cancel the effect of others.

Garden compost 1

Animal manure may be difficult to obtain, and proprietary organic soil conditioners are expensive. An alternative source of bulky organic matter is garden compost. A compost heap will cheaply and quickly turn garden and kitchen waste into valuable soil-enriching material.

Principles of compost making

To make good, crumbly compost the heap must be properly constructed so that the organic material can decompose rapidly and not turn into a pile of stagnant vegetation.

Air, moisture and nitrogen are all necessary if bacteria and fungi are to break down the raw material efficiently. Air is allowed in through the base and sides of the heap. Water should be applied with a can or hose if the heap shows signs of drying out, and moisture can be kept in by covering the heap with sacking, old carpet or polythene sheeting. Nitrogen must be provided in the form of

manure, compost activator or a nitrogenous fertilizer. It will aid bacteria and fungi in the breaking-down process.

The heap will be able to function best if it is sited in a sheltered and shady place but not under trees or where tree roots may move into the compost. It must be protected from becoming dried out by the sun and wind. Allow ample time for decomposition.

Compost bins

It is possible to rot down compost satisfactorily by simply stacking it in a spare corner of the garden, but in this way the heap may become untidy and the material on the outside will dry out. Decomposition will take place more rapidly in a home-made or proprietary compost bin which allows air in and retains moisture. For best results, compost bins should not be more than 4 ft high. They can be much longer than wide, for example, 4 × 4 × 8–10 ft is a useful size.

There are many ways of making a compost bin. One of the simplest is to erect a square cage of wire netting, supported by four stout posts driven into the ground. Make the front removable to allow the rotted compost to be easily extracted. For large bins, make a false floor by placing a layer of twiggy branches or brushwood in the base, or support a few short planks on bricks. This will allow air to permeate the compost. Line the inside of the cage with newspaper to prevent excessive drying out. A piece of sacking or polythene can be weighted down with bricks on the top of the heap to keep the moisture in.

A more solid structure can be made from angle-iron posts and wooden boards which are fashioned with gaps to allow in a certain amount of air. The internal structure of the heap is the same as with a wire cage. Brick or breeze-block structures may be used provided that occasional vertical joints are

left unmortared to allow in air. The front of such bays can be equipped with removable wooden slats.

A series of two or three compost bins is very useful, particularly in large gardens. When one bin is full the compost can be left to decompose and another bin brought into use. In this way a cycle of compost production can be kept going.

There are many proprietary compost bins available. Some are equipped with sliding sides to allow the compost to be shovelled out, and with lids to keep in moisture. Check that the bin is robust and large enough for the garden's compost needs, bearing in mind the length of time it takes to decompose.

Compostable materials

Garden and kitchen waste in great variety can be turned into good compost if it is properly mixed. One of the secrets of ensuring rapid decomposition is not to allow large quantities

Building a compost heap

1 Choose a suitable site for the heap, and, if preferred, erect a wire or rigid-sided bin.

2 Spread a 6–9 in layer of compostable material over the base of the heap and firm lightly.

3 Scatter sulphate of ammonia at $\frac{1}{2}$ oz per square yard over the heap, then add more compost material. Keep the heap covered.

4 Continue until the bin is full or the heap is 4 ft tall. Cover finally with a 2 in layer of soil.

Garden compost 2

of one particular material to build up in the heap. All the following materials may be composted if properly mixed together: annual weeds, lawn mowings (unless the lawn has been treated with hormone weedkillers), potato peelings, tea leaves, crushed eggshells, animal manure and urine, torn-up newspapers (but not glossy magazines), soft hedge clippings, dead flowerheads, pea pods, vegetable leaves and stems, tree and shrub leaves. Do not use woody material or any vegetation which has been sprayed with herbicides or is affected by diseases and pests.

Constructing the heap

When the bin has been erected the composting can start in earnest. On top of the false floor, if used, place a 6–9 in layer of compost material and lightly firm it down with the head of a rake or the back of a fork. Scatter sulphate of ammonia over this layer at the rate of $\frac{1}{2}$ oz to the square yard and then add another layer of compost material. Continue in this fashion until the bin is full. Keep a cover over the top of the heap at all times, and if the compost becomes dry, remove the cover and water it to encourage the rotting process.

The layer of sulphate of ammonia may be alternated with one of lime to counteract acidity encouraged by sulphate of ammonia. Never add lime and sulphate of ammonia at the same time. Alternatively, proprietary compost activator may be used between each layer. Animal manure may also be added between the layers of vegetation but it should not come into contact with the fertilizer or lime. If it does, a chemical reaction will be triggered which will result in valuable nitrogen being given off into the atmosphere. When the bin is full a 2 in layer of soil may be spread over the top instead of sacking or polythene. Leave the bin and if possible start to construct a second bin.

Using the compost

In a well-made bin which has been sensibly filled the compost will not need turning, for virtually all the material will decompose sufficiently. Decomposition will be more rapid in spring and summer than in autumn and winter, but a good heap should be ready to use within six months of being completed, sooner in warm weather. Check the heap at intervals and, if possible, shovel out the usable compost from the bottom. The compost should be brown and crumbly, though some of the material may still be recognizable. Unrotted material may be left behind as the basis of the new heap.

Use only very well-rotted compost as a mulch, for partially decomposed material may contain weed seeds that will soon germinate and become a nuisance. Alternatively, dig in the compost during soil cultivations in autumn and winter at the rate of 10 lb per square yard.

Leaf-mould

The leaves of deciduous trees and shrubs may be rotted down on their own to make soil-enriching leaf-mould. A wire bin (similar to that made for compost) makes a suitable container, and 6–9 in layers of leaves can be sprinkled with sulphate of ammonia. A fast space-saving alternative is to pack the layers of leaves and fertilizer in black polythene sacks that have been perforated to allow in air. Filled, tied at the top and stood in an out-of-the-way corner, the sacks of leaves, will form good leaf-mould which can be used in the spring following autumn collection. Leaves in outdoor bins may take rather longer to decay. All leaves of deciduous trees and shrubs can be composted, but plane, poplar, and sycamore take longer to decompose than oak and beech. Leaves of evergreens are not suitable for leaf-mould production. Leaf-mould can be dug into the soil or used as a mulch. See page 10.

Leaf-mould

Fill perforated polythene sacks with dead leaves. Tie the tops and allow the sacks to stand until the leaf-mould is formed.

GREEN MANURE

Seed	Sowing time	Rate/sq yd
Rape	March–June	$\frac{1}{12}$ oz
Mustard	March–August	$\frac{1}{8}$ oz
Vetches	March–May	$\frac{3}{4}$ oz
Annual lupin	March–July	$\frac{1}{2}$ oz

The practice of sowing certain crops and digging the resulting plants into the ground to enrich the soil, provide a source of nitrogen and improve texture is known as green manuring. Rape, annual lupins, vetches, mustard and perennial rye grass may all be used. Broadcast the seed quite thickly over the ground in spring or early summer and then rake it in. The plants will grow quickly; dig them in just before they flower. Apply a dusting of sulphate of ammonia at the rate of 2 oz per square yard when the crop is dug in to prevent any temporary deficit of nitrogen. If there are no plants in the area, the sulphate of ammonia will assist bacteria in the breakdown process by providing nitrogen. Green manure plants are also often sown after a crop has just been cleared from the ground, for example in early spring or early autumn.

TYPES OF COMPOST BIN

Wood slats

Plastic bin

Wire netting

Digging 1

Single digging

a

b
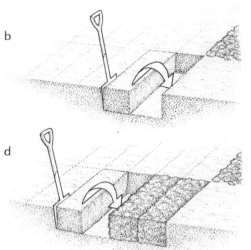

c

d

Double digging

a

b

c

d

Although in nature the soil is seldom disturbed, except by worms and other underground life, man usually finds it necessary to cultivate the ground in which he grows plants for several reasons. These are: to control the growth of weeds; to incorporate manures, composts and fertilizers; to relieve compaction and improve soil texture, so allowing seeds to germinate and young roots to penetrate the soil; and to allow in air, so speeding up the process of humus decomposition and making nutrients available.

Digging

Digging is the most thorough of all soil cultivations because it disturbs the ground to the greatest depth. It is usually carried out annually on the vegetable plot, or on any ground being brought under cultivation for the first time.

As a general rule, digging is best done in the autumn and winter to allow the frost, wind, snow and rain to work on the rough-turned clods of earth and gradually break them down. This action is particularly valuable on heavy soils containing a high proportion of clay. However, never work on any soil when it is frozen or very wet. Digging is difficult in such circumstances and the soil's structure may become temporarily damaged through compaction by feet and tools.

On lighter soils, exposure to frost is not essential, for the clods will be naturally friable. For this reason, light soils can be cultivated at any time during winter and early spring, provided that they are allowed to settle for two or three weeks before the crop is sown or planted.

There are three main methods of digging, which involve cultivating the soil to different depths. See the illustrations above.

Single digging This is the most widely practised form of digging. It is adequate for most ordinary soils of reasonable depth which do not overlay an intractable sub-soil. During single digging the soil is cultivated to the depth of one spade blade or "spit".

Begin single digging by taking out a trench one spit deep and about 12–15 in wide across one end of the plot to be dug (a). Pile the soil removed from this trench at the opposite end of the plot (it will eventually be used to fill the final trench). If the soil is to be manured as it is dug, throw the organic matter into the bottom of the trench at this point and mix it well in. Now take up the spade, starting behind the trench, lift up a comfortable spadeful of soil and throw it forward into the trench, turning it upside-down as you do so (b). This action ensures that any annual weeds are buried. Perennial weeds such as couch grass, dandelions, dock,

bindweed and ground elder should be painstakingly removed. If a portion of root is left, the weed will multiply. If grassland is being dug, the mat of grass can be skimmed off with the spade and thrown into the trench where it should be chopped up.

Work along the first trench throwing the soil over and forwards until another trench has been created (c). More manure may then be added and the operation repeated (d). When the end of the plot is reached, the soil from the first trench is used to fill the last.

If the plot is very wide, divide it in two lengthways and take out the first trench on one half of the plot, depositing the soil at the same end of the other half. Now work down the first strip of land and back up the second, throwing the soil from the first trench into the last one. By dividing the plot into two the chore of barrowing all the soil from one end to the other is avoided.

Double digging or bastard trenching With double digging the soil is cultivated to a depth of two spits. The technique is especially useful on land which has not been cultivated before or where a hard sub-soil layer is impeding drainage and the penetration of plant roots.

To double-dig a piece of land, first take out a trench 2 ft wide and one spit deep at one end of the plot (a). The soil removed is again

positioned alongside the spot to be occupied by the final trench. The plot may be divided in two, as for single digging, if it is very large.

When all the soil has been removed from the first trench, fork over the base to the full depth of the garden fork's tines (b). Compost or manure may be forked into the lower layer of soil or scattered on top of it after cultivation.

When the base of the trench has been cultivated, start to dig and throw forward the soil adjacent to it in the same way as for single digging (c). Make sure that the soil is turned over and perennial weeds are removed. When 2 ft of soil has been thrown forward into the first trench, the second trench will have been created and the base is forked over (d). The cycle continues until the entire plot has been dug to a depth of about 20 in. This method of digging improves the friability of the sub-soil without bringing it nearer the surface, so the richer layer of top-soil is always closest to the young roots of cultivated plants.

Trenching By far the most labour-intensive way of cultivating soil, trenching should only be practised where a deep sub-soil pan is causing problems. During trenching the ground is cultivated to a depth of about 30 in —three spits deep—and manure can be forked into the broken-up sub-soil.

Digging 2

Trenching

Ridging

Divide the plot down the middle and dig down one side and back up the other. Dig a trench one spit deep and 3 ft wide halfway across the plot, and place the soil next to the final trench. Divide the trench base in half lengthways and remove a second spit of soil from the front half of the trench. Deposit this soil at the far end of the plot alongside the top-soil but do not mix the two. The trench will now be "stepped". Fork over the base of the lower half of the trench to the full depth of the fork tines (a), then dig and throw forward the soil from the other half so that it rests on top of the forked strip (b). Fork over the strip of ground just exposed.

Mark out the next 18 in wide strip of top-soil on the plot using a garden line, and throw this soil forward onto the step of second-spit soil in the front of the first trench, inverting it and removing perennial weeds (c). Now transfer the second spit of newly exposed soil to the forked strip alongside it (d), and cultivate the base of the newly created trench with a fork. This cycle of cultivation continues right down the plot—the two piles of soil taken from the first trench being used to fill the second spit and first spit trenches that are left.

Ridging On very heavy soils the type of digging known as ridging may be beneficial, for it exposes a greater surface area of soil to

the elements. Divide the plot in two as described from Trenching above. Then mark out a 3 ft wide strip at one end of the plot to be dug and remove a 1 ft wide trench at one end of this strip. Pile the soil by the final trench (a). Now work backwards along the marked out strip, throwing the central spadeful of soil forwards and turning it upside down (b). The spadefuls of soil at either side of this are also inverted, but are turned inwards so that they lie against the first spadeful (c). In this way a ridge will be built up. Repeat the process (d), working along the first strip, then mark out a second and work backwards along that and so on until the plot is ridged.

Digging sensibly The craft of digging is something that can only be learned by practice, but there are some rules that will prevent it from becoming a back-breaking chore. Firstly, remember to keep the spade vertical; a slanting cut achieves less depth. Drive the spade in at right angles across the trench to free the clod of earth and allow it to be lifted away cleanly. Lift up small spadefuls of soil that are easy to handle. It is possible to dig land faster by taking a greater number of small spadefuls rather than a lesser number of very heavy spadefuls which will tire the gardener rapidly.

Secondly, dig a little ground at a time on a regular basis. Cultivate a yard strip every

day rather than attempting to dig the entire plot at once.

Finally, only dig the soil when it is easily workable, not when it is snow-covered, frozen or very wet.

Forking On very stony or heavy ground which is difficult to penetrate with a spade, a fork may be used instead, and for cultivating the bottom of trenches during double digging and trenching, it is an invaluable tool. The disadvantages of using the fork for the entire digging operation are that it is unable to slice cleanly through surface weed growth, and that light soils may fall through its tines. However, the fork may be used to good effect as a cultivating tool between established plants, and in spring to break down rough-dug land that has been weathered through the winter.

Raking This is an important task but one which is often overdone. The main reason for raking should be to level a piece of ground, either for seed sowing, planting or laying paving materials. Certainly the rake is also used to break down clods of soil to a reasonably fine tilth, but if used to excess it will create a dusty surface that will pan in the first shower of rain. Over-raking will also expose an abundance of stones. As a general rule, it is best to break down the clods of soil with the back of a fork. Then trample the ground to.

firm it and level it with the rake when the particles are reasonably dry. Use long, steady movements of the arms, drawing the rake to and fro and supporting it so that its teeth sweep over the surface and do not dig in. The rake can also be used to lightly cover seeds after broadcast sowing, to replace the soil in drills, and to collect leaves and other garden debris.

No-dig gardening

Some gardeners believe that digging is harmful to the soil as it disturbs the activity of bacteria and earthworms and so upsets the natural balance. Non-diggers prefer to apply thick mulches of well-rotted compost, manure or peat to the surface of the soil and let earthworms and other organisms incorporate this enrichment. Seeds are sown in the compost and subsequent mulches are applied while the plants are growing.

There is no doubt that this technique works and saves labour, but it does require very large quantities of compost or manure so that organic matter may have to be brought in. Digging may be more laborious but it is certainly cheaper and the yield and quality of some crops has been shown in experiments to be markedly improved in land dug to 3 ft. To dig or not to dig is thus more a philosophical than a horticultural question.

Watering 1

If plants are to grow healthily without check, they must have access to a constant supply of water (see water cycle, page 7). For most of the year in temperate climates, the soil contains sufficient moisture to satisfy the plants' needs. But during very dry spells in spring and summer the plants may find it impossible to extract sufficient water to keep them turgid; they will wilt and growth is temporarily halted. If water is not made available to them soon after wilting, their leaves will turn crisp and brown and they will eventually die.

For this reason the gardener must be able to provide "artificial" supplies of water, or irrigate, before the plants wilt.

Timing of applications

The timing of irrigation is particularly important with vegetable crops if they are to develop steadily and produce the maximum yield. Care must also be taken to give plants sufficient water. There must be enough to reach the roots, not just to wet the soil surface.

As a general rule, an inch of water will travel to a depth of 9 in in the soil. To water an acre of land to this depth, a total of 22,650 gallons must be applied. Continuous light applications of water during periods of prolonged drought are not to the plants' best advantage. They will not reach the majority of roots; they will pan the surface of the soil, and they will encourage the plants to produce surface roots, which will suffer in future droughts.

Sandy soils will dry out much more quickly than those containing clay, and will have to be watered sooner during spells of drought. The surface is seldom a good guide as to the state of the rest of the soil, so dig down for 9–12 in with a trowel to see if the soil is moist. If it is dry or only just moist, water.

With vegetable crops in particular the water can best be utilized while the plants are growing rapidly—usually during late spring and early to mid-summer. Shortages of water at this time cause the greatest check and may even result in some crops bolting (prematurely running to seed).

Food crops Later in the summer excessive quantities of water may do real harm to certain vegetables. Melons, for instance, should be kept on the dry side once their fruits are beginning to ripen, otherwise the fruits will split and be spoiled. Late summer rains or irrigation can impair the storage qualities of onions, just when they should be drying off prior to being strung. Beans and peas should be watered at 1–2 gal per square yard per week when the flowers and pods appear. Too much water during early growth encourages leaves at the expense of flowers and crops.

However, for most green crops such as lettuces and brassicas, good supplies of water will keep them cropping, both prolonging and increasing their yields. A rate of 2–3 gal per square yard per week is adequate.

Ornamentals Less research has been done on the water needs of ornamental plants. However, ornamental plants have much the same water needs as food crops. Pot-grown flowers and shrubs are at greater risk than those in open ground. Do not let them dry out.

Planting

Most applications of water to growing plants will be given in spring and summer, rather than in autumn and winter. But this is the prime planting season for deciduous trees and shrubs, and it is a good idea to water them in well unless the ground is extremely moist at planting time. Such watering-in is not necessary so much to keep the plant growing, as to settle the soil particles around the roots in readiness for spring growth.

Susceptible sites

Plants growing in open ground may certainly dry out due to exposure to sun in summer, but they will also receive their full quota of winter rains. Other sites in the garden may not be so well catered for and the gardener should see that they are given extra attention. Beds and borders against walls are particularly prone to drying out and should be enriched with organic matter to make them absorbent. This means that they can readily soak up any rainfall they receive, and also supplies of irrigation water given during dry spells. Soil close to walls is often poor and low in organic matter and can be very difficult to wet once it is dry. The same goes for soil under trees and alongside hedges.

Plants in tubs, pots and particularly hanging baskets will need regular applications of water through the summer because they can dry out very quickly. When filling the container with compost, leave a gap between the surface of the soil and the rim of the container to allow a sufficient amount of water to be applied. Water when the top inch of the container compost dries out. Aim to keep the top inch damp but not sodden. Both over- and under-watering can harm container-grown plants.

Techniques of watering

Water may be applied to the soil or to plants in containers by several different means.

Watering can The simplest method of transporting water to plants is by the use of a watering can. There are several designs and sizes, but a two-gallon can will be found the most useful for general garden needs. Cans larger than this are difficult to lift when full, and smaller ones involve too many journeys to and from the tap. Choose a can with a long spout, good balance when full and a long reach. Steel and plastic cans are available and both have their good and bad points. Steel cans tend to develop leaks after a while, but they can usually be repaired. If handled carefully, plastic cans last many years, but once they start to leak they are

Irrigation and root systems

1 If water is applied in small amounts, the soil surface will harden, and plants will develop surface roots in an effort to reach the moist top layer of soil.

2 Check the moisture content of the soil by digging a hole with a trowel. The state of the soil 9–12 in down is the best guide to watering needs.

3 If the soil is dry, water well to make sure that the moisture reaches the roots of the plants.

Watering 2

useless. Spray heads or "roses" are supplied with most cans. These vary from fine to coarse. Use a fine rose on seeds and seedlings.

When using a can fitted with a rose to water trays of seedlings, begin pouring to one side of the plants then pass the can over them, maintaining a steady flow. Move the can away from the plants before stopping the flow of water. This technique avoids sudden surges of water which can damage tender plants and displace compost.

Hose pipes If a tap is situated in or near the garden, a hose pipe will avoid tiresome journeys with the watering can. It may be left running on a patch of soil and moved around at intervals, or it may be held over a particular plant or group of plants if the gardener has the patience and time to spare. Take care not to allow strong flows of water to wash away soil and expose the roots of plants. On the vegetable garden water can be allowed to run from the hose pipe along furrows made between crop rows. Water applied in this way will quickly get to the roots. Buy a strong hose pipe which will not kink when bent and which will retain its suppleness over the years. Cheap hose pipes will crack and leak, especially if used in cold weather. Hose pipes reinforced with nylon thread are especially strong. A wide range of clip-on connectors and nozzles is available for use with hoses.

Perforated hoses Large expanses of ground are time-consuming to irrigate unless some kind of semi-automatic system is used. Sprinklers are useful because they can be turned on and left to apply large quantities of water to the ground in a fine spray which is easily absorbed. This type of application is to be preferred to flooding because it ensures that the water is more evenly distributed in the soil. The perforated lay-flat hose type of sprinkler is attached to a tap and laid across the land to be irrigated. When the water is turned on, it is discharged at many different angles from the pin-prick holes in the hose. Move the pipe from time to time to provide an even distribution of water.

Sprinklers There are two main types of sprinkler, both of which can be attached to a hose pipe. The oscillating type consists of a perforated tube which rocks backwards and forwards, distributing its water over a square or rectangular area. It can usually be adjusted to cover a chosen part of the garden. The rotating sprinkler ejects water from one or more nozzles which are forced around by the water pressure. This type of sprinkler covers a circular area. Both sprinklers may be controlled to a certain extent by the water pressure—the higher the pressure the larger the area they will cover.

Pop-up sprinklers which oscillate or rotate can be laid in lawns or vegetable gardens and supplied with water by underground pipes. The nozzles sit just below the surface of the soil when out of action (useful on the lawn where mowers can then be used safely) and spring up when the water is turned on.

The evenness of distribution of any sprinkler can be tested by placing jam jars at intervals over the soil being watered. The quantities the jars contain after an hour or so can be compared. The jars will also give an approximate indication of when an inch of water has been applied.

Sprinklers may be less effective on ornamental plants than on vegetables, especially in summer. The foliage of some ornamentals will deflect much of the spray, and heavy blooms and foliage can be weighed down and damaged by the water. Sprinklers are best used on ornamentals not in bloom.

Drip irrigation Lengths of pipe fitted with short drip nozzles, or with longer "spaghetti" tubes that can be directed to individual plants, are particularly useful where water has to be kept off plant foliage. In flower beds, borders and garden frames, and among pots and hanging baskets, such pipes can be fitted to dispense water slowly when the tap is turned on. They keep soil disturbance to a minimum and supply the water slowly enough to ensure instant absorption into the soil and fast take-up by plants.

Use of natural water sources
The diversion of streams and ditches is practised infrequently in temperate climates, but it can be used to advantage, particularly at the start of the growing season. If a stream runs through or past the garden, it is a simple task to pump water from it at any time and apply it to crops. Gravity-fed pumps can be obtained which move a small but continuous amount of water from a spring or stream along a contour line. Power-driven pumps can be used to move water from streams or ponds. Most areas have regulations on the abstraction of water which are enforced by the river authorities. Check the regulations before using water.

Planting

After planting trees and shrubs, water them in well to settle the soil around the roots. This speeds growth.

Containers

When planting in containers, leave a gap between the compost and the rim of the pot to allow for watering. When watering, carefully fill this space.

Watering seedlings

1 Begin pouring to one side of the tray or pot to allow the water to flow steadily.

2 Pass the can across the seedlings, keeping the angle constant, moving it clear of the pot or tray before halting the flow of water.

Basic tools 1

Every gardener should aquire a few basic tools of good quality, rather than a large selection of cheap implements that will be uncomfortable to use, short-lived and of little practical value. Although a good spade or fork is not cheap, with care it will probably have as long a life as its owner.

Shafts and handles

The shafts of tools can be made from several different materials, including wood, metal and plastic. Wood is traditional and long lasting. Make sure that the wood of the shaft is close grained and that the grain runs down the length of the shaft. Check that it is smooth and not likely to splinter.

Shafts made from polypropylene are lightweight yet strong, and lighter tools such as hoes and rakes are often equipped with tubular aluminium alloy shafts which are coated with plastic. All these materials will offer good service if they are not ill-treated.

Spades and forks are fitted with handles in three shapes: 'T', 'D', and 'YD'. If possible try all three when choosing a tool so that the most comfortable is selected.

Spade

Spades are available with shafts of different lengths and blades of different sizes. The standard spade blade measures 11½ in by 7½ in; that of the ladies' spade 10 in by 6½ in, and that of the border spade 9 in by 5½ in. Choose whichever is most comfortable to use and bear in mind that heavy digging will probably be easier with the middle size. Choose a shaft length to suit the height of the user.

The shaft of the spade should have a gentle crank to allow maximum leverage, and the strapped or tubular socket should be securely attached to the shaft. Metal treads welded to the upper edge of the blade make digging heavy soil less painful to the foot.

Spades with stainless steel blades are far more expensive than those equipped with blades of forged steel, but they are exceptionally long lasting and penetrate the soil more easily than ordinary steel spades.
Uses An essential tool for digging and trenching, the spade is also efficient for skimming weed growth off the soil before cultivation

begins. Always hold the spade upright when cutting into the soil prior to lifting it, so that the ground is cultivated to the full depth of the blade. The spade is also useful for planting trees and shrubs, and for mixing compost.

Fork

The fork is just as useful as the spade and is similarly manufactured. The four tines may be square in cross-section, as in the general purpose or digging fork, or flat as in the potato fork which is designed to avoid tuber damage at harvesting time. The head of the digging fork measures 12 in by 7½ in, and that of the smaller border fork 9 in by 5½ in. Stainless and forged steel types are available.
Uses A fork is easier to use than a spade for digging heavy soil, though it cannot be used to skim off weeds. It is essential for breaking down rough-dug soil and for lightly cultivating well-worked ground before seed sowing and planting. The smaller border fork can be used to cultivate the soil among herbaceous plants and shrubs, and the larger fork for moving compost and manure. Both can be used to aerate lawns.

HANDLE SHAPES

T-shape

D-shape

YD-shape

Hand fork

Of the same size as a trowel, the three- or four-pronged hand fork is similarly made.
Uses For transplanting seedlings, for working among tightly packed plants such as alpines in the rock garden, and for intricate planting and weeding, the hand fork is unsurpassed.

Rake

The most popular type of garden rake has a steel head 12 in wide which is fitted with teeth 2 in long. The shaft should be approximately 5 ft long and smooth to allow a good backwards and forwards motion. Larger wooden rakes are useful for raking up leaves, grass and debris, which clog in steel rake teeth. However, wooden rakes wear out faster.
Uses The main use of the rake should be to level soil which has been previously broken down to a reasonable tilth with a fork. Although the rake will make the soil texture even finer, it should not be over-used or the soil will be inclined to pan. Move the rake backwards and forwards over the soil in a sweeping motion, first in one direction and then at right angles to ensure an even finish.

Hoe

There are many different types of hoe but the two most important are the Dutch hoe and the draw hoe. Both are equipped with 5 ft handles and forged or stainless steel blades. The head of the Dutch hoe consists of a horseshoe-shaped piece of metal, across the open end of which is attached a flat 4–5 in blade designed to cut almost horizontally through the soil. The rectangular or semi-circular head of the draw hoe is of a similar width but is attached at right angles to the handle and is used with a chopping or scraping motion.
Uses The Dutch hoe is perhaps the best tool for general weeding, for the operator skims it backwards and forwards just below the surface of the soil while walking backwards. In this way the cultivated ground is not walked over and the weeds (severed from their roots) are left to dry out in the loose soil. The Dutch hoe is also used for breaking up surface pans.

With the draw hoe the operator must move forwards, chopping the soil and pulling it towards him slightly, or scraping the weeds

Using a spade

Keep the blade of the spade vertical when cutting into the soil. This ensures that the ground is dug to the full depth of the spade.

Using a hand fork

Aerate the soil around rock garden plants by the careful use of a hand fork. Hold plants back with one hand.

Basic tools 2

off the surface. The draw hoe (despite its disadvantage of forcing the operator to walk over the cultivated soil) is safer to use among closely spaced plants than a Dutch hoe.

Both types of hoe can be used to draw seed drills against a taut garden line, and the draw hoe is used to earth up vegetables such as potatoes, leeks and celery.

Trowel

An invaluable planting tool, the trowel may have a wooden or polypropylene handle 4–6 in long. Longer-handled versions are available but may be less comfortable to use. If possible buy a trowel with a stainless steel rather than a forged steel blade for it will be much easier to use and less likely to bend.

Uses The trowel may either be used like a shovel or flour scoop and also as if it were a digging claw. Either method may be used depending on the preference of the gardener. Scoop the soil out of the hole. Insert the plant in the hole and refirm the soil around the roots with the hands. Use the trowel for planting bedding and vegetable plants, herbaceous plants and bulbs.

Wheelbarrow

In larger gardens and on the vegetable plot a wheelbarrow can save a lot of time and energy. Always check the weight distribution of a barrow before buying it—as much of the load as possible should be placed over the wheel so that the barrow, and not the operator, takes most of the weight. Barrows are available with large, inflated, ball-shaped wheels, and these are especially useful if the land to be traversed is soft. Small, two-wheeled barrows can be easier to load, unload and push than single-wheeled types. Solid tyre models are adequate where sinkage will not be a problem. Make sure that the chosen barrow is large enough without being too heavy. Two-wheeled trailers can be obtained which can be towed by cultivators or garden tractors. Before purchasing a trailer check the widths of garden paths and gates.

Uses Compost, manure, soil, sacks of fertilizer and all manner of tools and equipment can be moved around the garden with the aid of a barrow. Stand the barrow upright against a wall or under cover when it is not in use to prolong its life.

TYPES OF BARROW

Ball-wheeled

Traditional

Two-wheeled

Using a rake

Level previously dug soil by moving the rake backwards and forwards across the soil surface.

Using a Dutch hoe

Skim the blade of the hoe just below the soil surface while walking backwards. Keep the blade horizontal to cut cleanly.

Using a draw hoe

Use a chopping motion, moving forward and drawing the soil towards the feet.

Use a trowel to make a planting hole

Scoop soil out of the hole, insert the plant and firm the soil with the hands.

19

Cultivation techniques 1

Once the ground has been prepared, the fundamental techniques of cultivation help to keep the soil in the correct state and maximize plant growth.

Hoeing
No gardener can afford to be without at least one kind of hoe to cultivate the soil around his ornamental plants and fruit and vegetable crops. Hoeing serves two useful purposes: it keeps down weeds and so reduces competition for light and nutrients; and it relieves compaction and allows vital air into the soil. It is also claimed that a layer of fine soil on the surface of the ground acts like a mulch and prevents excessive water loss.

There are many designs of hoe to choose from (see pages 18–19). The most popular is the Dutch hoe. It has a flat blade held at the end of two metal arms which allow soil to pass between them. The tool is pushed and pulled back and forth just below the surface of the soil so that it severs the stems of weeds from their roots. If used too deeply the Dutch hoe is less effective at controlling weeds. Pronged cultivators may be used in a similar manner. They are more valuable for breaking down the soil than for weeding.

The Canterbury hoe looks like a three-pronged fork fixed at right angles to the end of a stout shaft. It is used with a chopping and pulling motion and the operator works forwards (instead of backwards as with the Dutch hoe).

Hoes of a similar design but with a solid blade are also available. The draw hoe or swan-necked hoe is a long-handled version. It is the best tool for drawing seed drills and is also very useful for earthing up. The onion hoe is a much smaller version of the draw hoe and can be used effectively with one hand to thin out many crops in the seedling stage—the chosen seedlings are held firm and the rest chopped out with its blade.

Earthing up
The gardener may draw up soil around the stems of plants, or "earth them up", for one of several reasons. Young and tender shoots may emerge too early in spring and a covering of soil will be needed to protect them from frost. This is often the case with potatoes and some herbaceous plants. Pull a little fine soil over the shoots with a draw hoe or a rake.

Brassicas such as cauliflowers, kale and Brussels sprouts will often become top-heavy when nearing maturity. A mound of soil pulled around the base of the stems will give them extra stability. A draw hoe is the best tool to use.

Vegetables grown especially for their crisp, white stems or leaf stalks are surrounded by soil both to keep out the light (a process known as blanching) and to encourage them to extend. With leeks this process can be carried out gradually through the growing season. Celery is earthed up at the end of summer when the plants are almost mature. Hold the leaf stalks together by a tube of paper or card and bank soil up against them with a spade. The paper helps to keep the celery hearts clean.

With potatoes earthing-up prevents the tubers from being exposed to the light, which will cause them to become green and unpalatable. A draw hoe or Canterbury hoe will be found useful for this task, which should be carried out at ten day intervals in the early stages of growth.

Blanching
Blanching aims to prevent light reaching certain vegetable crops so that their leaves, leaf stalks or stems become white instead of

Earthing up

To protect new shoots of herbaceous perennials from frost in spring, pull a little fine soil over them with a draw hoe or rake.

Support tall brassica plants such as Brussels sprouts by forming mounds of soil around their stalks with a draw hoe, helping to prevent wind damage.

Earth up celery every three weeks as the plants grow. Draw soil gently up around the stems with a spade or hoe. Do not let soil fall into the hearts.

Earth up potatoes, using a draw hoe, at ten day intervals during the early stages of growth.

Cultivation techniques 2

green. In such a state certain vegetables have a better flavour and are crisper. The blocking of light prevents the production of chlorophyll—the green colouring in plants. Earthing up, a method of blanching celery and leeks, is described above.

The hearts of endives are blanched to improve their flavour. Place a plastic pot over the plant. Cover the pot's holes to exclude light. The pot will prevent light from reaching the leaves and in a few weeks the endive can be harvested with a crisp, white heart.

Forcing

A number of plants can be coaxed into early growth if they are provided with the necessary conditions. In this way the gardener can produce flowers and food when they are out of season and consequently expensive to buy in the shops.

Most plants that are to be forced require

some heat, but a low temperature of 10°–15°C/50°–60°F will suffice. Greenhouses, frames or propagating cases may be used.

Potatoes and French beans can be potted up in 12 in pots or tubs in December and January and grown on to maturity in their containers. Rhubarb, chicory and seakale require different conditions. To produce the best crops of these three vegetables light must be excluded. When the roots or crowns have been potted or boxed up in compost, put them under the greenhouse staging or in a frost-free place and cover them with a sheet of black polythene supported by wire hoops, or, in the case of pots, place a second inverted, pot on top of the first. Should light enter, the shoots will become yellow and, in the case of chicory and seakale, bitter.

Strawberries potted up in summer may be moved into the greenhouse in January to provide early crops, and container-grown

flowering shrubs may be similarly treated.

Flowering bulbs can be given eight weeks or so in cool conditions to encourage root production and then moved into a greenhouse to bring them into flower early.

Most vegetable plants are best discarded after one forcing, but if necessary they can be planted in the garden and allowed to recover—no crop being taken the following year. Bulbs, too, can be planted outdoors after forcing. Flowering shrubs should only be forced every other year, and forced strawberries should be discarded after use.

Ring culture

Where greenhouse border soil is poor or infected with disease, ring culture offers an alternative means of growing healthy tomato plants. Erect 8 in high boards down either side of the border, flatten the soil and lay a sheet of polythene over it. Pierce the polythene

sheet at intervals with a garden fork to make drainage holes.

On top of the polythene place a 6 in deep layer of coarse gravel, pea shingle or weathered ashes. Tomatoes are best grown in 9 in diameter whalehide or aluminium rings or in 9 in plastic pots with their bases removed. Before planting, space the rings 18 in apart on the bed of gravel and fill them with John Innes No. 3 potting compost. Leave them in position a few days before planting to allow the compost to warm up.

Water the compost after planting to settle the tomatoes in, but apply all subsequent waterings to the gravel. Apply diluted liquid feeds to the compost. This encourages two distinct root systems to develop: feeding roots in the ring and water-absorbent roots in the gravel. Flood the gravel at the end of each season to remove any impurities and disease organisms.

Blanching

Blanch endive hearts by placing an inverted plastic pot on crocks over the plant. Cover the hole to exclude light.

Forcing

Pot up rhubarb, chicory or seakale in compost. Cover the pots with black polythene and put in a frost-free place.

Alternatively, force rhubarb by covering the plants with a bucket or dustbin in mid-January–February. Insulate with straw. Pick 5–6 weeks later.

Ring culture

Place rings on a bed of gravel, ashes or shingle and fill with compost. Water should be applied to the gravel to encourage root growth.

Cultivation techniques 3

There are many gardening techniques which are specifically designed to improve plant performance and yield. They modify the growth and habit of a plant, changing its natural growth pattern in order to satisfy the gardener's requirements.

Thinning

Thinning is practised on the fruits of such crops as grapes and peaches which the plant produces in large numbers. Some fruits are cut out while they are still small to allow a lighter crop to develop more fully. Such action also saves the plants' energy, so increasing the likelihood of their cropping well the following year. Gooseberries can be thinned from late May, when the fruits are large enough for cooking. Remove every second fruit, leaving the remainder to develop into large dessert fruits. Grapes under glass are thinned in June over a 10–14 day period, removing the interior berries first and then the smallest, leaving a pencil thickness between the developing berries. Thin developing fruit and flowers from melons, leaving one fruit per shoot of frame-grown plants.

Apples and pears should be thinned to one or two fruits per cluster, with the clusters 6 in apart. Thin in mid-June and again a month later. Thin plums similarly, leaving them 2–3 in apart. It is essential to thin peaches if good-sized fruits are to be produced. Thin over a period, aiming for fruits 9 in apart.

Pinching

Many plants are naturally bushy and form a well-spaced framework of shoots or branches. The stems of others possess what is known as apical dominance—the shoot at the tip of the main stem will grow vigorously and the growth of all other shoots is retarded. Some plants with this habit tend to become tall, spindly and ugly if not encouraged to bush out. Ornamentals such as fuchsias benefit from pinching and develop an attractive bushy habit. The way to reduce apical dominance is to pinch out the terminal shoot. Other shoots will then develop and the plant will become more shapely. Successive pinching of these shoots may be needed on some plants to maintain a bushy habit.

Vines, cucumbers and melons are pinched at certain stages to encourage fruit development, and chrysanthemums grown for show are "stopped", or pinched back, to obtain a definite number of shoots per plant if large flowers are required.

Disbudding

On plants such as roses, chrysanthemums, dahlias and carnations, the gardener can choose whether he wants a cluster of small blooms or one large one. Exhibitors will invariably attempt to produce the largest bloom possible, allowing only the terminal flower bud to remain on each stem—all the others being pinched out as soon as they are large enough to handle.

Pollination

The transference of pollen from the male stamen to the female stigma of a flower is the first step in seed production and is known as pollination (see pages 102–103). It is essential that most plants grown for fruit are pollinated, and occasionally the gardener must give nature some help—particularly in the greenhouse where natural pollinators

such as bees may not be present at flowering time. Spray the blooms of peaches and grapes with a fine mist of water or dust them with a soft paintbrush or rabbit's tail to transfer the pollen grains. Some flowers may simply be shaken; on those such as melons, which produce separate male and female flowers, detach the male blooms and dust them over the female blooms.

Feeding

Plants both in open ground and in containers must be kept supplied with nutrients to maintain healthy, vigorous growth. Outdoors the rain will leach plant foods from the soil, and the nutrients in container compost are quickly used up by the developing plant.

From March to September all actively growing plants in containers will benefit from being given a fortnightly feed diluted at the recommended rate in water. Only apply such feeds when the soil around the roots is already moist so that the nutrients can be quickly absorbed. There are many proprietary brands, but certain straight fertilizers can be diluted in water and used as liquid feeds (see

Thinning fruit

Thin dessert grapes with scissors, carefully removing interior berries in order to leave a pencil thickness between berries.

Thin wine grapes by bunches, removing surplus bunches to leave the required number per spur.

Thin gooseberries in May, picking every second fruit and using them for cooking. The remainder will be dessert fruits.

Thin apples and pears to one or two fruits per cluster. Thin in mid-June and again a month later.

Cultivation techniques 4

page 11). Plants such as tomatoes grown for their fruits will benefit from being given high potash fertilizer at an early stage of fruit development. Leafy crops will benefit from fertilizers with a high nitrogen content and root crops from those containing a high proportion of phosphates. Different crops have different nutritional needs and therefore these generalized recommendations should be treated with care. The companion volumes in the series, *Fruit* and *Vegetables*, give details.

Liquid feeds may be applied with a watering can or through a special dilutor which can be attached to a hosepipe. This acts as a reservoir for the liquid fertilizer and controls the amount of concentrate mixed with the water.

Certain liquid feeds may be applied to the foliage of plants where they will be quickly absorbed into the sap-stream. Foliar feeds are useful for giving plants a quick boost but they should be used with caution on species with hairy leaves.

Mulching

A 2–3 in thick layer of organic matter spread around plants growing in beds and borders will serve several useful purposes. It will slowly decompose and help to enrich the soil; it will suppress weed growth, and it will conserve soil moisture. Suitable materials for mulching are described on page 10. Mulches are best laid in spring. Remaining material can be forked into the soil in autumn. The soil can then be allowed to weather and absorb the winter rains. It is important to ensure that the soil is moist before applying a mulch. If the soil is dry the mulch slows down the passage of rainwater.

A mulch of black polythene can be used with crops such as strawberries and potatoes. Stretch yard-wide strips across the prepared soil, anchor the edges in shallow trenches and make planting holes with a knife or a bulb planter. The strawberries are planted after the polythene has been laid. Potatoes grown under a plastic mulch do not have to be earthed up, as although they develop on the surface of the soil they are protected from light by the plastic. Although such a mulch will not enrich the soil, it does suppress weeds and retain moisture. It is especially useful where organic matter is scarce.

THINNING SEEDLINGS

Seeds sown where the plants are to grow to maturity will frequently produce dense clusters of seedlings which, if they are not reduced in number, will compete and become weak and spindly. For this reason they are usually thinned out as soon as they are large enough to handle to the distance apart required by the mature crop, or by the growing plants if they are to be further transplanted. Thin seedlings while the soil is damp, pressing firmly on the ground around seedlings to be retained and pulling up and discarding those which are not wanted. Alternatively thin with an onion hoe, which is a tool similar to a draw hoe only small enough to be used with one hand. Hold the seedlings to be retained with one hand and chop away surplus seedlings using the onion hoe. Carefully remove thinnings and put them on the compost heap. Thinnings left lying on the ground may harbour pests and diseases. Water seedlings after thinning.

Pinching

Pinch out the growing tip of plants such as fuchsias to encourage the growth of side-shoots and a bushy habit.

Pollination

Pollinate melons by detaching the male flowers and brushing them against the female flowers.

Transfer pollen from the male stamen to the female stigma using a camel-hair brush.

Feeding

Apply liquid feeds in a watering can (a) or with a reservoir attached to a hose pipe (b).

Mulching

Black polythene can be laid on ground where vegetable crops are to be grown and the plants grown through slits cut in it.

Protecting plants

Staking and supporting

Newly planted trees will be able to support themselves as soon as the roots are established, but require staking initially, particularly in windy places. Other garden plants such as chrysanthemums produce large heavy blooms and need constant support.

Trees Dig the planting hole and check that it is large enough for the tree's roots. Then knock a stake into the soil until one third of its length is buried. The stake should be either a length of 2 in by 2 in timber, treated with a preservative other than creosote, or a larch pole similarly protected. Position the stake to windward of the tree. The top should be just below the lowest branch.

With the stake firmly in place, plant the tree. Then fix one tree tie 2 in from the top of the stake and another 1 ft above soil level. Check the ties regularly and loosen them as necessary.

Another method of staking, used in orchards, is carried out immediately after the tree has been planted rather than before. Knock a stake into the soil at an angle of 45 degrees so that it crosses the tree trunk 2–3 ft above soil level. The top of the stake should point to windward. Bind the tree to the stake with hessian and strong twine.

Alternatively, hold the tree firm with three guy ropes. Fasten these around the trunk and lower branches of the tree and cushion them either with short lengths of rubber hose through which the rope is led, or with hessian. Space the guy ropes equally around the tree and peg their lower ends to the soil.

Flowers Support dahlias, delphiniums and other plants which have top-heavy stems either with stout bamboo canes or 1 in wooden stakes pushed into the ground alongside them. Fasten the stems to the supports with soft twine or raffia. Make sure that the support does not touch the flower or damage may result.

Support bushy herbaceous plants by pushing twiggy branches among them while they are small. As the plants grow they mask the branches but are held steady by them. More permanent herbaceous plant supports include wire hoops on legs. These are available in various sizes and can be adjusted as the plants grow.

Vegetables Among vegetables only beans and peas normally need support. Runner beans can be grown up wigwams of 8 ft canes pushed into the ground in 4 ft circles held together at the top with wire or stout twine. Alternatively, grow the plants up canes or poles spaced 18 in apart. Tie opposite poles together near the top to leave a V-shaped gap. Lay further poles or canes along these gaps and then bind the whole structure together. Support peas with twiggy branches in the same way as herbaceous plants, or with plastic netting on canes.

Wind protection

Wind can cause great damage in the garden, particularly to newly planted trees and shrubs. The plants may be blown over and they may become desiccated, which causes their foliage to wilt and turn brown.

Anti-desiccant sprays These chemicals seal the pores through which the plant loses moisture, and so help it to remain turgid. Spray with diluted mixture at planting time.

Screens may be used to shelter trees or shrubs. For example, a plastic fertilizer sack, slit at the base to make a sleeve, can be held around a shrub with three or four canes. Alternatively nail a sheet of hessian to two posts knocked into the ground on the windward side of the plant.

Frost protection

The crowns of tender perennial garden plants such as globe artichokes, agapanthus, eremurus and gunnera are susceptible to frost. Protect them by laying a piece of wire netting over each crown. Cover this with dry straw or bracken and fasten another layer or netting over the top to make a warm blanket. Protect larger plants and shrubs by surrounding them with a cylinder of wire netting filled with straw or bracken.

Protection from wet

Some alpines are particularly sensitive to excess moisture in winter. In their natural habitat, they are covered with a layer of dry snow which protects them. To prevent them from rotting off, cover each with a pane of glass supported on wooden or wire pegs. Tie the glass down with wire.

Staking

Knock a stake into the planting hole on the windward side of the tree. Ensure one third of its length is below the ground.

Secure the tree to the stake with two tree ties, placed 2 in from the top and 1 ft above soil level.

Supporting flowers

Support top-heavy flowering plants with bamboo canes. Tie the stems to the canes with soft twine or raffia.

Support herbaceous plants by inserting bushy twigs among them. The plants will grow through the branches.

Wire plant supports can also be used to support herbaceous plants.

Wind protection

Use a plastic sack fixed to four canes to keep down the force of the wind.

Moving and storing plants

It is sometimes necessary to move plants, from alpines to large shrubs and young trees, from one part of the garden to another, or to another garden. The technique outlined here is for large plants. The same basic process, with modifications, should be used for all plants. Always insert sacking or plastic sheet under the root ball and never lift a plant by its neck or branches.

Moving trees and shrubs

The operation is best carried out between November and April. First, tie in any spreading branches or wrap the plant in hessian or old sacks to prevent the stems from being damaged and to allow room for lifting. Next, using a spade, cut a vertical slit around the plant. Aim to cut at a distance equivalent to the spread of the top-growth. This cut will sever any side-spreading roots. Using this slit as the inner edge, take out a trench 1ft wide and one spit deep all around the plant, severing any roots that protrude from the ball of soil left around the plant.

Ease away any loose soil around the shoulder of the root ball and then thrust the spade underneath the root ball at an angle of 45 degrees to cut off more roots. The aim should be to retain as large a ball of soil around the roots as can be conveniently handled.

When the plant is movable, ease a sheet of hessian or polythene underneath it and then wrap up the entire root ball to retain the soil and prevent moisture loss. Tie the material firmly in place around the stem or trunk. Transport the plant with care to its new site and dig a hole wide and deep enough to accommodate the root ball with 1ft to spare all round.

Dig a generous helping of rotted manure, peat or leaf-mould into the base of the new planting hole, together with a few handfuls of bone meal to promote fresh root growth. Carefully position the plant. Replace and refirm the soil all round and water it in thoroughly. Spread a 3–4 in mulch of organic matter such as peat, leaf-mould or pulverized bark around the plant.

Considerable amounts of water may be lost by evergreen shrubs and conifers during the move, and an anti-desiccant spray may be applied to the foliage immediately before transplanting to reduce transpiration.

On exposed sites some protection from wind after transplanting will cut down water loss and reduce the likelihood of "wind rock" which will dislodge the roots from the soil and cause them to dry out. Three or four wooden posts can be knocked into the ground around the plant and a screen of hessian or close-weave plastic netting nailed to them. Remove the screen when the plant is established.

Storing plants

Smaller plants can be easily stored in a temporary trench dug in a spare corner of the garden. This technique, called heeling in, should also be used for bare-root shrubs and container-grown plants which are not to be planted immediately. Using a spade, cut a V-shaped furrow at the chosen site. Do this by thrusting the spade vertically into the ground to a spit depth and pulling it back, while still in the earth, to form a trench or slot. Lay the plants against the upright side of the trench and replace the soil loosely.

HEELING IN

Lay bare root plants in a shallow trench at an angle of 45 degrees. Cover the roots with loose, friable soil.

Moving trees and shrubs

1 Tie in any spreading branches to protect the plant during the move. Wrap smaller shrubs in hessian.

2 Cut a vertical slit in the soil around the plant with a spade. Make the slit 1–2 ft away from the stem, depending on size.

3 Take out a trench 1ft wide and 1 spit deep starting from the slit. Sever any roots that protrude into the trench.

4 Thrust the spade under the root ball at a 45 degree angle, cutting the roots. When it will move, ease the rootball on to a sheet.

5 Dig a hole at the new site 1ft wider all round than the rootball. Add leaf mould or peat and two handfuls of bonemeal.

6 Carefully place the plant in the hole. Firm the soil and mulch well. Support with guy-lines if necessary.

Placing plants 1

Having decided on the layout of the garden, it is time to consider exactly which plants will be grown where. It makes sense to start with trees. These will be the largest and most permanent specimens, acting as focal points to which other plantings can lead.

Trees

Site garden trees where their form can be appreciated and where they will have room to develop unhindered. Avoid planting specimens that will outgrow available space. Consider the habit of the tree as well as its flower, foliage and berry colour. In confined spaces fastigiate (columnar) trees are best; where space needs to be filled, those with spreading branches can be chosen. For small gardens choose trees which have several attractive features and which can be enjoyed for much of the year, rather than those which only have a spectacular but brief blossoming period. Evergreen trees provide form and interest all the year round, though many deciduous trees are attractive even when bare. Trees can affect nearby buildings, causing shade and extracting water from the sub-soil, creating the risk of subsidence. Plant large trees away from buildings if possible.

The ground under deciduous trees will have to be cleared of leaves in autumn. For this reason do not position pools or sandpits under their canopy. Evergreens will also lose a proportion of their leaves during the year and these too can be a nuisance.

Shrubs

Once garden trees have been chosen and plotted on a plan, shrubs can be used to build up the framework of the planting scheme. Distribute those which have evergreen leaves over the whole of the garden. This is advisable for two reasons: first, it will give a certain amount of form to the entire plot, and second, it will prevent one particular corner from becoming heavy and unchanging, which might be the case if the evergreens were all planted together. In very small gardens where trees cannot be fitted in, shrubs must take their place, acting as focal points as well as a framework.

When designing shrub and mixed borders, plot in the plants on a plan and number them from one to twelve according to the month in which they are at their best. In this way it is possible to see exactly what will be of interest in the garden at any time of year. Obvious gaps can be filled, or plants repositioned to distribute colour and form more evenly over the garden and over the months of the year. A little careful planning at this stage will help to create a garden for all seasons.

Herbaceous perennials

Strictly speaking, herbaceous perennials are those plants which survive for many years but whose stems and leaves die down each winter and re-emerge afresh in spring. However, some of these plants possess foliage which is more persistent and may be present to a lesser degree through the winter months.

No garden would be complete without herbaceous plants. If shrubs are invaluable as framework then these plants have just as important a role to play as fillers. This is not to say that the plants lack form; some of them are majestic and bold, but their stature is enjoyed only for part of the year.

Plan the herbaceous border in the same way as one devoted to shrubs. In most gardens the two types of plant are inter-mingled in "mixed borders" which are the best solution where year-round form is required.

Plants for walls

House and garden walls, fences, pergolas, arches and ugly buildings can all be improved by training climbers and wall shrubs over their surfaces. All these plants will benefit from good soil preparation and manure enrichment to encourage moisture retention, for the earth at the foot of walls and fences can become very dry. Many of them will need some form of support. Ivy and Virginia creeper will cling on their own, but for the rest some horizontal wires stretched between vine eyes, or sections of wooden trelliswork fastened to the wall will help them to remain upright (see page 85). Most shrubs will need tying in and may need regular pruning to keep them trim and close to the wall.

Make sure that the right plant is chosen for a wall of a particular aspect—the planting lists (page 27) offer advice on suitability.

Single colour schemes

In most gardens colour schemes will involve the use of a wide range of shades, although these should be carefully toned so that they do not clash. However, it is possible to plan beds, borders and even entire gardens with plants having one particular flower or foliage colour. White gardens—where grey-foliaged and white- and cream-flowered plants are grouped together—have been successfully created in the grounds of several English country houses.

In small gardens such schemes are best confined to individual borders if they are not to become overpowering and monotonous. However, if annual flowers are used there is no reason why such a scheme should not be changed from year to year: blues, violets and purples one year; reds, pinks and creams the next; greens and yellows to follow.

Some form of permanent skeletal planting in shades of green and grey can be used to good effect in single-colour gardens. Not only will such plants set off the flowers well, they will also provide interest during the darker months of the year.

Planning

(1) 3 Aster 'Fellowship'. Soft pink, september. 4 ft.

(2) 5 Helenium 'Moerheim Beauty'. Rich crimson, July-Aug. 3 ft.

(3) 3 Echinops 'Taplow Blue'. Metallic blue, July-Aug. 5 ft.

(4) 5 Heliopsis 'Incomparabilis'. Golden orange, July-Aug. 4 ft.

(5) 4 Delphinium 'Blackmore's Glorious'. Mauve, June-July. 5-7 ft.

(6) 3 Aster 'Crimson Brocade'. Deep red, september. 3 ft.

(7) 5 Polygonum Amplexicaule 'Astrosanguin

Plan a border by numbering plants on a plan according to the month they are at their best.

Tree forms

It is important to know the habit of a tree before planting it. Trees can be spreading (a), weeping (b), fastigiate (c) or conical (d).

Check the eventual height and spread of the tree and allow it adequate space when planning the garden.

Placing plants 2

CLIMBERS AND WALL SHRUBS FOR WALLS OF VARIOUS ASPECTS

North-facing walls
Camellia species and varieties
Chaenomeles species and varieties
Cotoneaster horizontalis
Escallonia macrantha
Forsythia suspensa and varieties
Garrya elliptica
Hedera species and varieties
Jasminum nudiflorum
Parthenocissus species
Tropaeolum speciosum

East-facing walls
Celastrus orbiculatus
Chaenomeles species and varieties
Clematis species and varieties
Garrya elliptica
Hedera species and varieties
Hydrangea petiolaris
Kerria japonica 'Pleniflora'
Parthenocissus species
Pyracantha species and varieties
Tropaeolum speciosum

South-facing walls
Actinidia kolomikta
Callistemon species
Campsis species
Ceanothus species and varieties
Clianthus puniceus
Fremontodendron species and varieties
Lonicera species and varieties
Magnolia grandiflora
Rosa species and varieties
Wisteria species

West-facing walls
Abutilon vitifolium
Camellia species and varieties
Carpenteria californica
Chimonanthus praecox
Cytisus battandieri
Fremontodendron species and varieties
Magnolia grandiflora
Passiflora caerulea
Solanum crispum
Wisteria species and varieties

TREES AND SHRUBS WITH COLOURED FOLIAGE

	Height	Colour
Abies species and varieties	20–150 ft	Grey/silver
Acer negundo 'Variegatum'	20–50 ft	Green and white
Acer palmatum 'Atropurpureum'	10 ft	Maroon
Calluna vulgaris varieties	1 ft	Yellow/orange/grey
Catalpa bignonioides 'Aurea'	35 ft	Yellow
Cedrus atlantica 'Aurea'	30 ft	Yellow/gold
Chamaecyparis lawsoniana varieties	1–45 ft	Silver/blue/yellow
Convolvulus cneorum	2 ft	Silver-grey
Corylus maxima 'Purpurea'	10 ft	Deep maroon
Cotinus coggygria 'Royal Purple'	10 ft	Maroon
Elaeagnus pungens 'Maculata'	15 ft	Yellow and green
Gleditsia triacanthos 'Sunburst'	35 ft	Yellow
Juniperus chinensis varieties	3–25 ft	Grey/green/blue
Juniperis horizontalis 'Plumosa'	1 ft	Grey-purple
Juniperus sabina varieties	2–5 ft	Grey/blue
Juniperis virginiana	100 ft	Blue-white
Ilex × altaclarensis 'Golden King'	15 ft	Yellow and Green
Pieris formosa 'Wakehurst'	4–8 ft	Red
Picea glauca albertiana 'Conica'	6 ft	Light green
Robinia pseudoacacia 'Frisia'	30 ft	Yellow
Thuja occidentalis	50–65 ft	Yellow/gold

TREES AND SHRUBS FOR SPECIFIC LOCATIONS

Small gardens

	Height	
Acer palmatum varieties	10 ft	L
Betula pendula 'Youngii'	15 ft	H
Corylus avellana 'Contorta'	10 ft	FS
Gleditsia triacanthos 'Sunburst'	35 ft	L
Malus 'John Downie'	20 ft	FB
Pyrus salicifolia 'Pendula'	25 ft	LH
Robinia pseudoacacia 'Frisia'	30 ft	L
Sorbus aucuparia 'Beissneri'	25 ft	FBL

Fastigiate trees

	Height	
Chamaecyparis lawsoniana varieties	20 ft +	E
Ilex aquifolium 'Green Pillar'	20 ft	EB
Juniperus virginiana 'Skyrocket'	20 ft	E
Prunus 'Amanogawa'	20 ft	F
Prunus 'Spire'	25 ft	F
Sorbus commixta	20 ft	LBF
Sorbus 'Joseph Rock'	25 ft	LBF
Taxus baccata 'Fastigiata Aureomarginata'	15 ft	E

Weeping trees

	Height	
Betula pendula 'Dalecarlica'	40 ft	HL
Crataegus monogyna 'Pendula Rosea'	15 ft	F
Fagus sylvatica 'Pendula'	50 ft +	L
Laburnum watereri 'Alford's Weeping'	15 ft	F
Prunus subhirtella 'Pendula'	15 ft	F
Pyrus salicifolia 'Pendula'	15 ft	L
Salix × chrysocoma	40 ft	LS
Ulmus glabra 'Camperdownii'	15 ft	L

Acid soils

	Height	
Betula pendula 'Dalecarlica'	40 ft	TL
Calluna vulgaris & varieties	1 ft	EF
Erica species & varieties	1 ft	EF
Pernettya mucronata	2–3 ft	EB
Pieris formosa & varieties	10 ft	EF
Rhododendron species & varieties	3–15 ft +	EF

Coastal gardens

	Height	
Arbutus unedo	15 ft	EFB
Choisya ternata	8 ft	FE
Elaeagnus pungens 'Maculata'	15 ft	E
Fuchsia magellanica varieties	6 ft	F
Griselinia littoralis	12 ft	E

Coastal gardens cont.

	Height	
Hebe species & varieties	1–6 ft	EF
Lavatera olbia	6 ft	LF
Phlomis fruticosa	3 ft	LF
Phormium tenax varieties	3–6 ft	L
Pyracantha species & varieties	10 ft	EFB
Senecio 'Sunshine'	5 ft	EF
Sorbus aucuparia varieties	20 ft +	FLSTB
Tamarix pentandra	10 ft	LF

Chalky soils

	Height	
Aucuba japonica & varieties	10 ft	EB
Buddleia davidii & varieties	10 ft	LF
Cistus species & varieties	3 ft	EF
Crataegus oxyacantha	15 ft	FB
Deutzia varieties	6 ft	F
Forsythia species & varieties	6–10 ft	F
Genista species & varieties	1–10 ft	F
Hebe species & varieties	1–4 ft	EF
Helianthemum varieties	1–2 ft	EF
Ilex aquifolium varieties	15 ft	EB
Mahonia aquifolium	4 ft	EF
Philadelphus varieties	8 ft	F
Rhus typhina	15 ft	L
Sorbus aria & varieties	20 ft	FLB

Shrubs for shade

	Height	
Aucuba japonica	10 ft	EB
Buxus sempervirens	1–10 ft	E
Gaultheria shallon	5 ft	EFB
Hypericum calycinum	1 ft	EF
Juniperus × media 'Pfitzerana'	3 ft	E
Mahonia aquifolium	4 ft	EF
Mahonia japonica	3 ft	EF
Pachysandra terminalis	1 ft	EF
Sarcococca confusa	3 ft	EF
Vinca species & varieties	Trailing	EF

Scented flowers or leaves

	Height	
Buddleia davidii & varieties	10 ft	F
Chimonanthus praecox	8 ft	F
Choisya ternata	8 ft	FL
Daphne species & varieties	2–5 ft	F
Eucalyptus species	20 ft +	L
Hamamelis mollis & varieties	12 ft	F
Lavandula species & varieties	1–2 ft	FL
Lonicera periclymenum	8 ft	F
Lippia citriodora	4 ft	L
Mahonia japonica	6 ft	F

Rock gardens 1

Plants from mountain and rocky regions are usually called alpines. They are plants which have adapted to very different soil and climate conditions to those found in the normal garden. If they are to thrive they must be provided with the right site and soil. For this reason the plants are usually grown in specially mixed soil among rocks, which provide shaded root-runs and also form the right background to show off these small plants to best effect. Rock gardens should be planned as garden design features as well as plant habitats and carefully integrated into the overall garden plan. Alpine plants have well-defined soil and site requirements. Many rock garden plants are not true alpines and are easily grown, but the special needs of true alpines must be catered for.

Site Nearly all alpines require an open and sunny spot. Shelter from distant fences or trees is beneficial in cutting down drying winds, but avoid heavy shade from trees, which will shed leaves on to the plants. Roots from trees can penetrate rock gardens and inhibit growth.

Drainage and soil In their natural environment many alpines are covered in a dry blanket of snow through the winter. This protects them from severe frost, then melts away in late spring, watering the plants as it does so. Their growing medium is often less soil than rock waste or gravel. Ideally, therefore, plants should be sheltered from winter rain and grown in a freely-draining medium which can nevertheless retain some moisture. In practice, ideal conditions are not obtainable except in an alpine house. Efforts must be made to avoid the major problems of damp and summer desiccation.

Construction
The traditional rock garden aims at recreating a natural rock outcrop, with the plants growing between carefully bedded stones.

The true rock garden is on a slope, but rock beds can also be built on level ground with rocks and dwarf conifers or shrubs adding height.

The site can be graded to provide a slope, or a depression can be dug and the sides terraced. Top-soil should be removed first and replaced evenly when the re-shaping is complete.

Improving drainage If the site is level, check the soil drainage. If it is at all poor, remove the top-soil to a depth of 12 in, then put down a 6 in layer of rubble. Top this with a 9–12 in layer of loam sand, grit, leaf-mould and peat mixed together to form a suitable rooting medium. Ensure that the drainage of the surrounding area is adequate. Lighter, better-drained soils should be improved by the addition of grit, sand and peat, so that free drainage and adequate moisture retention are ensured. Carefully remove all weeds, and cultivate to a depth of 1 ft.

Rocks Most rock gardens are made from sand-stone or limestone, and occasionally from granite. Choose local stone, which will blend with its surroundings and which may also be available more cheaply. The rock should be of a kind that will weather easily to give a natural appearance. Several large pieces of rock are to be preferred to a multitude of smaller boulders which will tend to give a "plum-pudding" effect. Rock is never cheap so use small quantities wisely. It is usually sold by the ton, which is about 14 cu ft of rock pieces. Specify the largest and smallest sizes required when ordering. Half a hundred-weight is the heaviest one person can comfortably handle.

Mould the ground into the required contours using a fork and a rake and tread the entire site firm before positioning the rocks. Choose the best faces of the rock and bury any newly-broken surfaces which will take a long time to weather. Move the rocks to their sites and position them with their best faces

TYPES OF ROCK GARDEN

Alpines can be grown in spaces between paving stones (a), in traditional rockeries (b), in dry walls packed with soil (c), or in sink gardens or troughs (d).

Construction

1 After clearing and draining, if necessary, fork over and rake the bed, moulding the soil into the required shape.

2 Position the rocks on the site, making sure that the strata run the same way. Adjust until the desired result is achieved.

3 When all the rocks are in place, firm soil around them, taking care to avoid air pockets.

Rock gardens 2

forward and with their strata running in the right direction. Group small rocks around one large piece of stone to give the impression that they are part of it, taking care that the strata correspond. Aim to build up natural-looking terraces, with the layers running horizontally with a slight backwards slope. Rocks do not have to be buried deeply. No more than a quarter of the rock need be below the surface.

Once the rocks are in position they can be let into the soil. Have on hand sufficient mixed soil or compost to create planting pockets between the rocks. Excavate sufficient soil with a spade, manoeuvre the rock into position and then ram the soil firmly behind it. Leave no air pockets. When the rock is positioned it should look and feel firm.

Planting
Once the rocks are laid, lightly rake the soil around them to relieve surface compaction. Plant when the soil is moist but not too wet.

In milder areas planting is best undertaken in early autumn. In colder places and where wet winters are common early spring is a better time, but make sure that spells of early summer drought do not check the plants' root development.

Water the rock garden well before planting. Remove each plant from its pot, having first given it a good watering. Excavate a hole in the required place using a trowel or hand fork. Lower the plant in, refirming the soil so that no air pockets are left and the surface of the potting compost around the plant is level with the surface of the soil on the rootball of the plant. Consider the habit of each plant before positioning it, and allow it sufficient room for growth.

When planting is completed, a 1 in layer of coarse grit can be spread over the surface of the soil. This will ensure that the necks of the plants do not become waterlogged, will show them off well, keeps down weeds and helps to retain moisture. Label each plant.

Maintenance
A grit layer will help to keep down weeds, but any which do emerge should be removed at once. In prolonged dry spells between April and July water the rock garden. To check if watering is necessary, scrape any gravel away and probe the soil with a trowel. When the soil is dry 2 in down it is time to water. Use a sprinkler which will apply a steady and penetrating spray.

Remove all leaves that blow on to the rock garden in autumn and cover any plants that cannot tolerate winter wet with a sheet of glass supported on wire legs. Leave this protection in place from November to February. Top-dress rock garden plants with a mixture of equal parts loam, grit and leaf-mould in early spring. Work a few handfuls around and among each plant. Lightly clip over those alpines which produce untidy seedheads or straggly growth as soon as they have finished flowering. Prune plants which spread too far, using secateurs.

SCREE BEDS

Rock garden plants which require extremely sharp drainage are best cultivated in scree beds, designed to simulate the naturally occurring conditions at the foot of mountain slopes where there is a deep layer of finely broken rock and a certain amount of humus.

A scree bed is essentially a raised bed with much of the soil replaced by stone chippings. Retaining walls of sandstone, brick or broken paving slabs may be used to support the sides of the bed, and these should be given an inward batter to make them stable. Lay the lowest stones on a concrete foundation; the upper courses may be dry or filled with soil to accommodate plants that enjoy growing in vertical crevices (these should be inserted as building progresses) Leave drainage holes in the base of the wall at frequent intervals. The bed should be at least 2 ft high over clay soils to provide good drainage; at least 1 ft high over sandy soil. Place a 4-to-6 in layer of broken bricks and rubble in the bottom of the bed and use the following compost to fill the rest of the space: 10 parts stone chippings, 1 part loam, 1 part peat or leafmould and 1 part sand, plus a slow-release fertilizer. Plant in autumn or spring.

Planting

1 Excavate a hole large enough for the plant's roots. Fill it with water and allow it to drain away.

2 Lower the plant into the hole and firm the soil around the roots to avoid air pockets.

Maintenance

Cover plants that cannot tolerate winter wet with a sheet of glass supported on wire legs. Spread a layer of grit 1 in deep around the plants to keep down weeds.

Hedges 1

Initial pruning of hedges

Group One
Blackthorn (*Prunus spinosa*), box (*Buxus sempervirens*), hawthorn (*Crataegus monogyna*), *Lonicera nitida*, Myrobalan plum, privet (*Ligustrum ovalifolium*), snowberry (*Symphoricarpos* spp), Tamarisk (*Tamarix gallica*): cut each

plant back to 6 in from ground level.

Group Two
Beech (*Fagus sylvatica*), *Corylus maxima* 'Atropurpurea', flowering currant (*Ribes sanguineum*), hazel, hornbeam (*Carpinus betulus*): cut back leading shoots and longer side-shoots by one-third.

Group Three
Conifers and evergreens such as cherry laurel (*Prunus laurocerasus*), gorse (*Ulex europaeus*),' *Griselinia littoralis*, holly (*Ilex aquifolium* and vars), laurel (*Aucuba japonica*), Lawson cypress (*Chamaecyparis lawsoniana* and vars), Leyland cypress (× *Cupressocyparis leylandii*), New Zealand daisy bush (*Olearia* × *haastii*),

× *Osmanthus burkwoodii*, *Osmanthus delavayi*, *Poncirus trifoliata*, *Viburnum tinus*, Western red cedar (*Thuja plicata* especially 'Atrovirens', yew (*Taxus baccata*): cut back untidy laterals, do not prune the leader.

Hedges make excellent garden barriers where walls and fences are undesirable. They provide a natural backdrop to other garden plants and thorny hedges are effective obstacles against domestic and farm animals. The traditional garden hedge is formal, close-clipped to give it a regular outline. But there are many shrubs which will make excellent informal hedges.

Hedges do have two main disadvantages. First, they must be clipped or pruned annually, and in some cases two or three times in one year; second, they use soil nutrients which may be needed by plants growing close to them. The first problem is eased if a powered hedge trimmer is used for clipping, and the second by applying liquid feed or fertilizer each spring to the plants growing alongside the hedge and to the hedge itself. Mulching with rotted manure is beneficial as it makes the hedge's roots less likely to spread in search of food.

Planting

The time of planting will depend on the shrub being used. Deciduous shrubs lifted from the open ground and supplied "bare root" should be planted between November and March. Evergreens and conifers may be planted in September and October or in April and May. If the plants arrive at an inconvenient time or when the ground is unfit for planting, heel them in (see page 25). Container-grown shrubs can be planted at any time of year providing attention is paid to watering in dry spells.

Ground preparation Hedges usually remain in place for a long time, so make sure that ground preparation is thorough. Use bamboo canes and stout twine to mark out the strip of ground to be occupied by the hedge. Excavate a trench 2–3 ft wide and one spit deep along the line that the hedge will take. Fork over the base of the trench, incorporating well rotted compost, manure, peat or leaf-mould. Set aside more of the organic matter to mix with the soil when it is firmed back around the plants. Two or three handfuls of compound fertilizer can be forked into each running yard of the trench.

Choosing plants It is tempting to choose plants which are very large so that an instant

effect is achieved. Avoid doing this. Smaller plants, around 12–18 in high, are not only cheaper but will usually establish themselves much more quickly than older specimens. If immediate protection is needed, erect a post and wire fence alongside the young hedge.

How to plant Plant when the soil is moist and easily workable, not when it is very dry, frozen or muddy. Trim any broken or damaged roots from the plants with sharp secateurs and space them out in the trench at the required distance (see table right). Remove the containers from container-grown shrubs but do not disturb the root ball unless the roots are pot-bound, when they should be gently teased out.

Where hedges of 3 ft or more thickness are required, use a staggered double row of plants. Set the rows 12–15 in apart, against garden lines stretched along the trench.

Spread out the roots of bare-root plants and replace the soil, firming it around the roots with the foot. The old soil mark on the stem of each plant should rest at or just below soil level. Container-grown plants should have their root balls just buried, so that the new soil level is about 1 in above the old. Firm the soil around the stem.

Immediately after planting neatly cut off any ungainly or damaged stems or branches with a pair of secateurs. Prune most deciduous hedges to one third of their height, and hawthorn and privet to 6 in from ground level. Evergreens and conifers may be sprayed with an anti-desiccant solution to reduce transpiration and encourage the rapid establishment of the young plants.

Aftercare

Spread a 2–3 in mulch of moist peat or pulverized bark over the soil at the foot of the hedge in the first spring after planting. Do so immediately in the case of spring-planted conifers and evergreens. Make sure the soil is moist before the mulch is applied.

The hedge must not be neglected after planting if it is to grow unchecked and establish itself rapidly. In dry weather frequent waterings will be necessary. In frosty weather the ground should be refirmed around the plants every day so that the roots do not dry out in the lifted earth.

Planting

Excavate a trench 2–3 ft wide and 1 ft deep where the hedge is to grow.

Fork over the base of the trench, incorporating organics. Add compound fertilizer at 4 oz per yard.

Trim any broken or damaged roots from bare-root plants with secateurs.

Spread out the roots of bare-root plants, place them in the trench and replace soil, firming well.

Initial pruning

Cut plants back on planting to encourage strong basal growth. See chart at top of page.

Cutting

Trim formal hedges at least twice a year. Stretch a garden line taut along the hedge to ensure straight cut.

Hedges 2

Key to hedging plants table

Site
A: suitable for seaside sites
B: suitable for windy sites
C: suitable for chalk soils
D: suitable for heavy soils

Features
1: flowers
2: foliage
3: fruits
4: thorns

Pruning
For pruning groups see list at top of page 48
S: cut with shears
Sh: cut with secateurs

Growth rate
The figures give the number of years taken by the plant to grow to 5 ft.

Clipping and pruning

For most formal hedges twice-yearly clipping is necessary, though privet may need three clips. May and August are the best times to carry out the operation and the shears (or electric trimmer) should be sharp and well lubricated. Aim to create a hedge which is slightly narrower at the top than at the base so that light is allowed to reach the lower portions and snow is shed more easily.

Informal hedges, which are often grown for their flowers, may be pruned to shape with a pair of secateurs immediately after flowering and then left untouched until the same time the following year.

Cut all formal deciduous hedges and small-leaved evergreens with shears or an electric trimmer. For informal hedges and large-leaved evergreens such as laurel and holly use secateurs, which will leave the foliage unmarked and produce a better shape. Shears can be used if the hedge is very long. Remove damaged leaves and stems with secateurs after cutting with shears.

Gather up and burn all the clippings as soon as the job is finished; do not allow them to lie on lawns or among border plants.

Chemical retardants are available to reduce the growth of both formal and informal hedges. They are usually applied in spray form shortly after the spring clipping or pruning. After application, the hedge will retain its shape until the following spring when a further cut and spray will be necessary. Follow the instructions on the label closely and do not apply the retardant to those species listed as being unsuitable for treatment.

Weeds have a tendency to grow unnoticed at the foot of hedges, and leaves and litter may also collect there. Clear out all this rubbish during the winter when it can easily be seen and removed and apply a weedkiller such as simazine to inhibit germination.

Screens and windbreaks

Where strong winds severely limit the types of plant that can be grown in a garden, it is a good idea to establish a row of trees to act as a windbreak. Such barriers may also be useful in hiding an ugly view. Trees make excellent windbreaks for they filter the wind, so slowing it down, rather than stopping it dead like a wall and creating turbulence and damaging eddies. Plant the screen at right angles to the wind. It will cut down the force of the wind on its leeward side for a distance up to 20 times greater than its height.

Suitable upright windbreak and screening trees include: *Chamaecyparis lawsoniana* (Lawson cypress), × *Cupressocyparis leylandii* (Leyland cypress), *Populus alba* (White poplar), *Populus nigra* 'Italica' (Lombardy poplar), *Thuja plicata* and cultivars.

HEDGING PLANTS

		Site	Features	Planting distance	Pruning	Evergreen/ deciduous	Formal/ informal	Growth Rate
Aucuba japonica 'Green hedger'	Laurel	C D	2	24 in	Group 3 S	E	F/I	5
Berberis darwinii	Barberry	C D	1 2 4	18 in	Sh	E	F/I	6
Berberis × *stenophylla*	Barberry	C D	1 2 4	18 in	Sh	E	F/I	5
Buxus sempervirens	Box	C	2	12 in	Group 1 S	E	F	8
Carpinus betulus	Hornbeam	C D	2	12 in	Group 2 Sh	D	F	6
Chamaecyparis lawsoniana and vars	Lawson cypress	D	2	24 in	Group 3 Sh	E	F	5
Corylus maxima 'Atrapurpurea'			2		S	D	F	
Cotoneaster simonsii		A C D	1 2 3	18 in	S	E	F/I	5
Crataegus monogyna	Hawthorn/Quick	A B C D	1 2 4	12 in	Group 1 Sh	D	F	7
× *Cupressocyparis leylandii*	Leyland cypress	A	2	30 in	Group 3 S	E	F	3
Escallonia macrantha		A D	1 2	18 in	S	E	F/I	4
Fagus sylvatica	Common beech	B C	2	12 in	Group 2 Sh	D	F	5
Forsythia × *intermedia* 'Spectabilis'	Golden bells	C D	1 2	18 in	S/Sh	D	F/I	4
Fuchsia magellanica		A C	1 2	12 in	S	D	I	5
Ilex aquifolium and vars	Holly	A D	2 3 4	18 in	Group 3 Sh	E	F	8
Lavandula spica and vars	Lavender	A	1 2	12 in	Sh	E	I	Only 2 ft
Ligustrum ovalifolium	Privet	C	2	12 in	Group 1 Sh	E	FF	4
Lonicera nitida		C D	2	12 in	Group 1 Sh	E	F	5
Metasequoia glyptostroboides	Dawn redwood		2	24 in	Sh	D	F	5
Olearia × *haastii*	New Zealand daisy bush	A C	1 2	12 in	Group 3 S	E	I	7
Poncirus trifoliata			4		Group 3 Sh	D	F/I	
Prunus laurocerasus	Cherry laurel		1 2 3	24 in	Group 3 S/Sh	E	F/I	3
Rhododendron ponticum	Common rhododendron	B	1 2	24 in	S	E	I	5
Rosa rubiginosa	Sweet briar	A C D	1 2 4	18 in	S	D	I	3
Rosa rugosa	Ramanas rose	A C D	1 2 4	18 in	S	D	I	5
Tamarix gallica	Tamarisk	A B	1 2	12 in	Group 1 S	D	I	4
Taxus baccata	Yew	B C D	2	24 in	Group 3 Sh	E	F	8
Thuja plicata 'Atrovirens'	Western red cedar	C D	2	24 in	Group 3 Sh	E	F	5
Ulex europaeus	Gorse	A B	1 2 4	18 in	Group 3 S	E	I	6
Viburnum tinus	Laurustinus	A B C	1 2	18 in	Group 3 S/Sh	E	F/I	5

Crop rotation

Growing the same vegetables in the same piece of ground each year eventually results in a build-up of soil-borne pests or diseases. Such continuous growing of brassicas, for example, favours club-root, and successive crops of onions are likely to cause a build-up of stem eelworm.

Different types of vegetables require different ground preparation and cultivation procedures. Potatoes need a deeply cultivated soil which is continually moved during earthing up. On the other hand, root crops—such as carrots, parsnips and beetroot—need a firm, level soil with a fine tilth which is disturbed very little during the growing season.

Fertilizer, lime and manure requirements also vary. Potatoes respond to large applications of organic manure and fertilizer but they should not be limed. Brassica crops also respond to applications of manure and fertilizer but they require a soil between pH 6.5 and 7.5.

These are the major reasons for practising crop rotation in the vegetable garden. It must be said that rotations are easier to effect on paper than they are on the ground.

Grouping the crops

It is useful to put vegetables together in groups which have similar crop protection, cultivation, manure, fertilizer and liming requirements. Groups are then moved sequentially around the vegetable plot so that, over a period of years, a particular piece of ground grows all the crops. In theory it is better to leave as large an interval as possible between growing a crop again on the same site, but it is rarely possible to leave more than three or four years. Thus three and four year rotations have been devised and a three year plan is considered here. A certain amount of compromise is necessary in order to simplify the rotation. Potatoes are grouped with root crops, even though they benefit from applications of organic manure and root crops do not.

Having divided the vegetables in this way, the groups are moved sequentially around the plot over a three year period. The plot is roughly divided into three equal sized units, but an area should be left at one end on which perennial vegetables, such as asparagus and seakale, are grown permanently.

In year one the potato and root crop unit receives no manure or lime but moderately heavy quantities of fertilizer. The legume and onion unit receives heavy dressings of manure and little fertilizer or lime. The brassicas receive average amounts of manure and fertilizer but heavy applications of lime. Crop rotation therefore ensures that all parts of the plot receive manure, fertilizer and lime regularly while the dangers of pest and disease build-up are minimized.

CROP ROTATION

Year 1
Unit 1 · Unit 2 · Unit 3
Group 1 crops · Group 2 crops · Group 3 crops

Year 2
Unit 1 · Unit 2 · Unit 3
Group 2 crops · Group 3 crops · Group 1 crops

Year 3
Unit 1 · Unit 2 · Unit 3
Group 3 crops · Group 1 crops · Group 2 crops

Year 4
Unit 1 · Unit 2 · Unit 3
Group 1 crops · Group 2 crops · Group 3 crops

Group 1: Celery, Sweetcorn, Spinach, Root crops/potatoes, Leeks
Group 2: Legumes, Florence fennel, Onions
Group 3: Brassicas, Perennial crops

CATCH CROPPING AND INTERCROPPING

Some vegetables grow and mature more quickly than others so there are times of the year when gaps appear in the vegetable plot. These gaps can be used to grow—or catch—a crop of rapidly maturing vegetables. Thus the ground occupied by peas in Unit 2 of the crop rotation plan may not be needed for brassicas until the following spring and can be used for crops such as radishes or endive.

Intercropping Rapidly maturing crops can also be intercropped or grown between slower maturing crops. Spinach can be grown between rows of slow-growing leeks, for example.

Lettuces 1

OUTDOOR LETTUCE
Cabbage types (butterheads)
'Arctic King', 'Buttercrunch', 'Cobham Green', 'Fortune', 'Mildura' (mildew resistant), 'Suzan'.

Cabbage types (crispheads)
'Avoncrisp' (resistant to mildew and root aphids), 'Great Lakes', 'Webbs Wonderful', 'Windermere'.
Cos types
'Little Gem', 'Lobjoits Green Cos', 'Winter Density'.

Lettuce is the salad plant for all seasons. Although an annual that matures naturally during the early summer, the use of suitable varieties, cloches or heated frames, and the correct growing conditions make it possible to harvest lettuce throughout the year.

Types of lettuce
Several different types of lettuce have been bred and they vary considerably in size, form and texture. Three main groups may be recognized although there are intermediates.

Cabbage lettuce These include the butterheads with globular soft-leaved heads, and the crispheads, also round-headed but with crinkly, crisped leaves. They will usually tolerate poorer and drier soils than the other groups.

Cos lettuce The lettuces of this group are upright in growth with more or less oblong heads of crisp leaves. They grow best in rich, moist soils. Modern varieties do not need to be tied to produce a compact heart.

Leaf lettuce These non-hearting lettuces produce masses of curled foliage but no true heart. The leaves can be picked a few at a time and the plants will continue to grow and produce further leaves for later picking. Some varieties of cos lettuce will continue growing in the same way if closely spaced.

Cultivation
Many modern varieties of lettuce have been specially bred to mature at particular seasons and it is important to select those suitable for the crops required. Depending on the weather and the district, summer- and autumn-maturing lettuce is sown successively from late March to early August to mature from June to October. Lettuce sown outdoors in August will mature in November to December if kept under cloches from September. Mildew resistant and forcing varieties such as 'Avondefiance' and 'Kwiek' should be used at this time of year. For eating from January to March, lettuce must be sown and raised in a heated (7°C/45°F) greenhouse from November to January, an expensive and often difficult method for most gardeners. Spring lettuce is obtained from winter-hardy varieties and from lettuces grown with cloche or cold frame protection. Sown from August to September

to mature in early May, hardy varieties stand throughout the winter without protection although a sheltered position is preferable.

Lettuce sown in October under cloches to mature in April has a more succulent flavour and a higher survival rate, however, as well as the advantage of a slight lead in the harvesting date.

Soil and situation All lettuce varieties prefer an open position in a well-drained and fairly rich soil of pH 6.5–7.5. Lettuces require considerable quantities of water during the growing period and the soil must be humus-rich so that it is able to retain and supply moisture for the rapidly growing plants. A soil well manured for a previous crop is ideal, but on poor, thin soils dig in a further dressing of well-rotted compost at a rate of 10–15 lb per square yard when the site is prepared. Apply a balanced general fertilizer at 2 oz per square yard, and before sowing rake the soil to produce a fine tilth.

Sowing To reduce the amount of thinning later, always sow lettuce seed very thinly. Sow in drills $\frac{1}{2}$ in deep at a rate of no more than 10–12 seeds for each 12 in run of drill—hearted lettuces will have a final spacing of 9–12 in apart in the row. Take care not to sow too deeply as this inhibits germination, which should occur within 6–12 days. It is sensible to maintain a regular supply by making frequent sowings with short intervals between, because lettuces, once hearted, do not stand in good condition for very long and soon "bolt" or run to seed.

Spacing
Various spacings and planting patterns are recommended for hearting varieties. The most efficient is to stagger the plants in adjacent rows in a triangular pattern so that the maximum use is made of the land available. Place the plants at 12 in intervals in rows 10 in apart. For dwarf varieties and cloche-grown lettuce spacings of 9 in between the plants and 8 in between the rows may be used. This triangular pattern is particularly valuable for cloche-grown lettuces. If the familiar square pattern with plants opposite one another in adjacent rows is used, the spacings should be 12 in × 12 in, or 9 in × 9 in for dwarf varieties. With conventional leaf-

VARIETIES OF LETTUCE

'Little Gem'

'Webbs Wonderful'

'Buttercrunch'

'Salad Bowl'

'Lobjoit's Green Cos'

LEAF LETTUCE
'Salad Bowl', 'Lobjoits Green Cos', 'Paris White' (cos), 'Valmaine' (cos).

PROTECTED LETTUCE
Cabbage and butterhead types
'Amanda Plus', 'Avondefiance' (mildew resistant), 'Delta', 'Knap', 'Kwiek' (mildew resistant).

Lettuces 2

lettuce of the 'Salad Bowl' type, spacings are similar to those given for hearting varieties. Some cos lettuces, however, will produce good leaf lettuce during spring and summer with only 5–6 in between the rows and 1 in between individual plants.

Thinning and transplanting Direct-sown crops should be thinned as soon as the seedlings are large enough to handle. Never let the seedlings become overcrowded as this will check growth. There is a tendency to grow more lettuce than can be consumed and this is particularly true with sown crops. Trans-planting allows more control. The method of plant raising is critical, however, since any check to growth at transplanting may easily lead to "bolting". "Bolting"—premature running to flower—is induced by high temperatures (over 21°C/70°F) and dry conditions. Lettuce transplants for outside should always be raised in small individual peat pots or blocks and never grown in a seedbed for bare-root planting. Sow lettuce seed in a $3\frac{1}{2}$ in pot every ten days and prick out as many seedlings as necessary into pots or blocks. Do this at the first true leaf stage.

Keep the seedlings cool to produce short, sturdy plants and transplant them when they have four or five true leaves.

Watering The best crops are produced when there has been no check to growth. The quality and size of the crop will be improved greatly by weekly applications of 3–4 gal of water per square yard in dry weather. If this is not possible a single application at the same rate 7–10 days before they are due to mature will increase the size of the lettuce heads markedly in spring and summer. Over-wintered lettuce should not normally need additional watering.

Try to water in the morning, and on sunny, drying days if possible, so that the leaves are dry by nightfall. Lettuces that are wet over-night are more vulnerable to disease.

Pests and diseases

Birds, slugs and cutworms may be troublesome but can be controlled by the methods described on page 249. Leaf aphids may be controlled by the use of systemic aphicides such as dimethoate or by applying derris or pirimicarb as the plants near maturity. Some varieties such as 'Avoncrisp' are resistant to lettuce root aphids but applications of diazinon during the summer may be necessary for other varieties. Mancozeb or thiram sprays may be used against downy mildew which is encouraged by overcrowding.

Botrytis cinerea or grey mould may be a problem on lettuce in damp, cool weather. Affected plants should be destroyed and a preventive spray of thiram or benomyl applied to the remaining plants.

Lettuce viruses show up either as a mosaic or pronounced vein network on the leaves. Burn infected plants because there is no really effective method of control once the symptoms appear. Remove weeds, (groundsel, shepherd's purse) which may harbour viruses, and control any aphids which appear.

LEAF LETTUCE

'Salad Bowl' is the conventional leaf lettuce but certain cos varieties ('Lobjoit's Green', 'Paris White' and 'Valmaine') can also be grown successfully for leafing. Closely spaced, they can produce good leaf in 40–50 days compared with the 60–80 days required for other lettuce. They also have the advantage of growing again from the base to provide a second crop. Grown this way, one square yard of leaf lettuce sown each week from April to mid-May, and again from mid-July to the end of August, will produce lettuce leaves throughout summer and early autumn.

1 April to mid-May. At weekly intervals sow the seed in $\frac{1}{2}$ in drills, 4–5 in apart in the prepared seedbed, allowing 10–15 plants per 12 in of drill.

2 Early May to June. Allow the seedlings to develop unchecked without thinning. Water in dry weather. Spray aphids and diseases as required.

3 Late May to late June. Harvest the leaves by cutting them off near ground level. Leave stumps to re-grow.

Protected lettuce

1 Mid-October. Sow 3–4 seeds $\frac{1}{2}$ in deep at 3 in intervals in drills 8 in apart in the prepared seedbed, and place cloches over the drills.

2 Late October. When the seedlings are $\frac{1}{2}$ in high, thin each group, leaving the strongest plant at each position. Ventilate well during the winter.

3 Late February. As growth begins again thin to 9 in (6 in for dwarf varieties). In dry weather, water the plants 7–10 days before harvesting, March to April.

Lettuces 3

Spring lettuce

1 Late August to early September. Sow the seed thinly in ½ in drills 10 in apart in the prepared seedbed. Cover the drills.

2 Mid to late September. When the seedlings are ½ in high thin to 2–3 in apart. Hoe between the rows once or twice in winter.

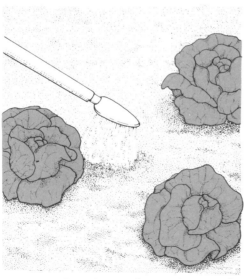

3 Late February to early March. Thin the plants to the full distance for each variety so that they alternate in adjacent rows if possible. Apply a top dressing of balanced fertilizer at 2 oz per square yard.

4 Late April. In dry weather apply 3–4 gal of water per square yard 7–10 days before likely maturity, which should be from early May onwards.

Summer lettuce

1 Late March to early August. In the prepared seedbed take out ½ in drills 10 in apart (8 in for dwarf varieties) and sow the seed thinly. Cover the drill.

2 April to mid-August. When the seedlings are ½–1 in high, thin to 12 in (9 in for dwarf varieties). Alternate the seedlings in adjacent rows.

3 May to September/October. In dry weather apply 3–4 gal of water per square yard each week. Spray against aphids and diseases as required.

4 June to October. Push hearting lettuces gently with the back of the hand to test for firmness. Squeezing between the fingers damages the hearts.

5 June to October. When firm, harvest by cutting the plants below the lower leaves. Alternatively, pull up whole plants and trim off roots.

Growing brassicas

Admirably suited to the climate of northern Europe, the brassicas, such as cabbages, Brussels sprouts, cauliflowers, broccoli and kale, are key plants in any vegetable grower's plot. Certain general principles apply to their cultivation. Most brassicas, except some varieties of kale and Chinese cabbage, should be raised in a special brassica seedbed and then transplanted, usually 5–7 weeks later, to a permanent bed. This saves space, because the main brassica plots can be used for other vegetables while the seedlings are growing. Alternatively, buy young brassica plants ready for planting out.

Brassicas need a fertile soil and they should not be grown in the same plot more than one year in three. Move them around each year, preferably to ground where peas or beans have been grown the previous year (see page 32). Peas and beans leave nitrogen in the soil at a level which suits brassicas. The other reason for keeping brassicas on the move is the danger of previous infections of club-root lingering on in the soil. Another, resistant, vegetable can be grown in a plot which has suffered from club-root. Brassica crops must not be grown again in an affected plot for at least seven years.

Dig the ground early in winter and leave it to consolidate. All brassicas need firm ground. If the area has been dug shortly before sowing or planting, work it over with a three-pronged hand cultivator and firm it down well with the feet. All brassicas need a pH of 6.5–7.5.

The seedbed
The seedbed should be in an open, sunny but sheltered position. Ideally, make a seedbed on soil manured for a previous crop. If this is not possible, in autumn apply well-rotted manure or garden compost (1 bucketful per square yard) and leave the plot to weather over the winter. Before sowing rake in a balanced general fertilizer, such as a brand of Growmore, at a rate of 2 oz per square yard. At the same time apply diazinon to combat cabbage root fly. Firm the soil and rake to produce a fine tilth.

Sowing If the seedbed is dry, water thoroughly before sowing. Use a foot-board to avoid compacting the surface of the bed while sowing. Mark out shallow drills 6 in apart and draw out the drills ¾–1 in deep. Dust the seed with captan or thiram before sowing to control damping-off disease. Mark each row with sticks, placing a label with sowing date

and variety, written in indelible ink. Germination takes 7–12 days. Keep the seedlings free from weeds, and water them during dry weather. Thin the seedlings to 1–2 in apart as soon as they can be handled. Firm back the soil after thinning.

The permanent (planting) bed
Double-dig the permanent brassica plot in winter and dress it with 10–15 lb per square yard of well-rotted manure or compost. Experiments have shown that a marked increase in yield can result from preparing soils deeply for brassicas. The roots of Brussels sprouts, for instance, penetrate 36 in or more into deeply dug soils. Although it is seldom practical to dig the plot to this depth, double-dig it if possible to a depth of 18–24 in. Brassicas are greedy for water, and deep digging allows their root systems to develop and extract more water from lower levels in the soil. It also reduces the uptake of water from the upper soil layers, which remain moist for longer than would be the case with shallower digging.

Transplanting
The young brassicas are ready to transplant 5–7 weeks after sowing, when they have 3–4

leaves and are 4–6 in tall. The day before transplanting, water the seedlings thoroughly so that they lift easily with minimum damage to the roots.

Lift the seedlings carefully so that the roots are disturbed as little as possible. Cover them with sacking or polythene so that they do not dry out before being planted. Dip the roots of the seedlings in benomyl or thiophanate-methyl to control club-root. Plant the seedlings with a trowel or hand fork at the appropriate distance for the brassica concerned. The prepared plot should be watered thoroughly the day before planting takes place. Firm the soil around the roots by hand. Water the plants in, using a rose on the can or, if the weather is dry, prepare planting holes and "puddle" in the young plants. Make sure they are firm by tugging the upper leaf gently. Water them until they become established, placing ¼ pint of water around the base of each plant daily. In hot, sunny weather protect the transplants by covering them with newspaper during the day to cut down transpiration. Within three days of planting-out apply bromophos or diazinon to the soil around the plants as a further insurance against cabbage root fly.

1 Lift the seedlings carefully, taking care not to damage the roots. Dip the roots in calomel paste.

2 Plant the seedlings at the spacing given for each brassica and check they are firmly planted by gently tugging an upper leaf.

3 In dry weather prepare planting holes and puddle in the young plants.

4 Apply bromophos or diazinon to the soil at each plant's base within 3 days of planting. Water until they are established.

Cabbages 1

Cabbage is a biennial plant and the most widely grown brassica. Individual tastes can be satisfied throughout the year with the five types available. Spring cabbage is hardy and is appreciated as an early green vegetable. Summer cabbage provides a welcome alternative to summer salads. Winter cabbage, including savoys, is easy to grow and is hardy. Apart from its pickling qualities, red cabbage is delicious as a cooked autumn vegetable. The increasingly-popular, autumn-harvested Chinese cabbage can be cooked (with little aroma) or used in salads.

Spring cabbage
Spring cabbage is sown or planted in late summer to mature in spring. "Spring greens" are simply closely-planted spring cabbages eaten before they heart up.

Sowing The seed is sown in late July (northern Britain or cold areas) or early August (southern or milder districts) as explained on page 36. The seedlings are transplanted to their final quarters from mid-September to mid-October in rows 12 in apart and with 12 in between the plants in each row if hearted cabbages are required.

Spring greens If space is limited and spring greens are required plant them at 4 in intervals in the rows. The plants can either be left to produce unhearted greens, or two out of every three plants can be removed and used for greens in early spring while the remaining plants, now spaced at 12 in by 12 in, will heart up for use later. Wider row spacings are often recommended but these give a lesser yield.

Firm planting is important and a few weeks after planting it is useful to pull a little soil around the stems to give some additional protection against frost-lifting in the winter. No fertilizer should be given at this stage and, apart from keeping the plot free from weeds, the only attention they need until growth starts the following spring is to firm back plants loosened by frost or other adverse weather.

In early March, if the weather is good, apply and water in a dressing of nitrate of soda or sulphate of ammonia at a rate of 2 oz per square yard. This encourages rapid growth as the weather becomes warmer. Alternatively, in nitrogen-rich soils, a balanced fertilizer can be used at the same rate.

Harvesting
The crop may be harvested as required. In mild seasons spring greens are ready in February while in late seasons hearted cabbages stand until early June. In some cold areas cloches may be used to protect spring cabbages over winter.

Summer cabbage
Summer cabbage is sown between February and May for harvesting from late July until autumn. When deciding how much to grow, remember that it matures at the same time as many other vegetables, including peas and beans. The seedbed and the permanent plot should be well prepared in late February. Sowing in frames during February for planting out in April provides the earliest crops, but seeds are normally sown in the open from March to May.

Sowing Sow the seed thinly in $\frac{3}{4}$–1 in deep drills 6 in apart. Water the drills beforehand to encourage speedy germination and if the weather is warm and dry, dust along the length of the drills with derris or HCH before the seedlings emerge as a precaution against flea beetle. Summer cabbages are very vulnerable to cabbage root fly and it is important to apply appropriate control measures against this and club-root at both the sowing and transplanting stages (see page 36).

Transplanting From April to May dip the seedlings in benomyl or thiophanate-methyl and plant in the permanent bed, at 18 in intervals in rows 18 in apart for large-headed varieties or at 14 in intervals in rows 14 in apart for smaller-headed varieties. Firm the seedlings into their holes and water thoroughly.

When the plants have settled down, and are well-established, apply and water in a balanced fertilizer, such as a brand of Growmore, at 2 oz per square yard. Throughout the growing season, hoe between the rows with a Dutch hoe to keep down weeds and maintain a water-conserving tilth. If necessary spray or dust to control any pests or diseases that occur.

Harvesting
Hearted summer cabbages are ready for cutting from late July until autumn. Cut with a sharp knife just above soil level.

TYPES OF CABBAGE

Winter cabbage

Red cabbage

Summer cabbage

Savoy cabbage

Spring cabbage

Chinese cabbage

Cabbages 2

Spring cabbage

1 July to August. Take out ¾–1 in deep drills, 6 in apart in a prepared seedbed. Sprinkle bromophos along the drills and water them thoroughly.

2 July to August. Sow the seed thinly and dust with derris along the drills. Cover with a fine tilth.

3 Mid-September to mid-October. Prepare holes at 12 in intervals (4 in for spring greens) in the permanent bed and sprinkle bromophos into them.

4 Then, plant the seedlings (previously dipped in benomyl or thiophanate-methyl) and water. Rows should be 12 in apart.

5 About 2 weeks after planting pull up a little soil around the base of each plant to protect against frost-lifting. Firm any plants loosened later by adverse weather.

Spring greens

6 Throughout the growing season hoe between the rows regularly to keep them weed-free and maintain a good tilth.

7 Early March. Spread and then hoe in 2 oz of nitrate of soda or sulphate of ammonia to encourage hearting.

8 April to June. Cut spring cabbages as required. Clear any stumps and roots away.

Mid-March. To obtain spring greens, remove 2 plants out of 3. Those remaining will heart up for later use.

Cabbages 3

Winter cabbage

Winter cabbages are sown in April or May and harvested from late autumn to the following March or April. They include the savoys, which are easily recognized by their dark green, wrinkled leaves. All the varieties are easy to grow and hardy, succeeding better on poor soils than most other brassicas. Apart from the times of sowing, transplanting and maturing their cultivation differs little from that of summer cabbage.

Sowing In May sow the seed very thinly in $\frac{3}{4}$–1 in drills that are 6 in apart. Water the drills before sowing.

Transplanting In July transplant the seedlings to the permanent bed, which should have been enriched with fertilizer a few weeks before (see page 36). Plant the seedlings at 18 in intervals in rows 18 in apart. If the weather is very dry, pour a little water into each hole before putting the plants down. Remember also to sprinkle bromophos or diazinon granules into the holes before setting out the seedlings and firming them in well.

Water the growing plants frequently during the summer and hoe lightly between the rows to keep down the weeds.

Harvesting

From October until early spring, cut the individual heads as they mature.

Red cabbage

Red cabbage is sown in the spring at the same time as summer cabbage but it needs a slightly longer growing season and it is not harvested until the autumn. It can also be treated like spring cabbage—sown in August and transplanted in March to mature in the summer. Before sowing, work out what is needed because a few plants are enough for pickling purposes. Cultivate red cabbage in the same way as summer cabbage. Sow the seed very thinly in March or April and transplant in April or May, 12–15 in each way.

Harvesting

Red cabbage is ready from September onwards. Be sure to cut the mature heads well before there is any danger of severe frost.

Red cabbage can be stored for several months in a cool, frost-free place.

HARVESTING AND STORING CABBAGE

Some types of cabbage, especially the almost white, tight-headed Dutch varieties, can be stored after harvesting in November or December. They will keep until April but should be inspected for blemishes or rot two or three times during the winter.

1 Lift the whole plant up with a fork when the heart is firm to the touch.

2 Cut off the roots and stem and remove the coarse outer leaves.

3 Store cabbages on slatted shelving, in heaps if required, in a frost-free shed.

Chinese cabbage

Chinese cabbage is a versatile vegetable that is easier to grow than other vegetables in the brassica group and has a relatively short growing season. The general principles of brassica growing (page 36) apply. It is especially important to have a moisture-retentive, rich seedbed because Chinese cabbage is not transplanted and matures in the area where it has been sown.

Sowing In July, sow 2–3 of the large seeds at 8–9 in intervals in $\frac{3}{4}$–1 in deep drills, 12 in apart. When the seedlings emerge thin to one plant per station.

Keep them well watered because they may "bolt" in hot summer weather. Do not water, however, if the weather is wet, as this may cause "splitting" of the heads. When the plants begin to heart up in August, tie the leaves together with raffia. This is not necessary with self-hearting varieties.

Harvesting

From September to November cut the heads just above soil level with a knife.

1 Early July. Dribble water into the $\frac{3}{4}$–1 in deep drills, 12 in apart, and sow 2–3 seeds at 9 in intervals.

2 July. Thin each group of seedlings to leave a single plant at each station. Apply bromophos around the base of each plant.

3 August. When the plants begin to heart up tie the outer leaves together with raffia. Keep them well watered.

F₁ HYBRIDS
'Citadel', 'King Arthur', 'Peer Gynt'.

CONVENTIONAL VARIETIES
'Irish Elegance', 'Market Rearguard', 'Winter Harvest'.

Brussels sprouts 1

Brussels sprouts are popular and hardy brassicas, and in Britain they are a traditional ingredient in the Christmas dinner. In recent years F_1 hybrids have been bred, mostly of compact growth, that mature all their uniform "button" sprouts at the same time. While these are ideal for the freezer, most gardeners still grow some of the open pollinated, conventional varieties. With these, the sprouts mature a few at a time on individual plants, so picking may be carried out over a period of several months. This is important for growers without freezers, who may only require a pound or two at a time.

A good selection of varieties will provide harvests of sprouts from September to early March or even April, but the most useful crops are gathered from October to February because few other fresh vegetables are available at this time.

Cultivation

The general principles of brassica growing apply to Brussels sprouts (see page 36). An open position, in full sun but sheltered from strong winds, is most suitable although they will tolerate slight shade. A firm soil is important because Brussels sprouts may grow to 3 ft or more and good root anchorage is essential for them to stand through the winter. In light soils earthing up the stems slightly about a month after transplanting helps to anchor them, but in exposed areas staking is sometimes necessary.

Soil and situation Brussels sprouts grow best on fertile soil that has been deeply dug and well manured the previous winter. As they are not usually planted out until May, another crop is often taken from the same land beforehand. The site should be dug over about a week before planting and a dressing of 2 oz per square yard of a balanced general fertilizer raked in. The seed is sown in the brassica seedbed during March or early April and the seedlings are transplanted in May or early June to the prepared site. March-sown seedlings may need cloche protection if the weather is still very harsh.

Sowing Sow the seed thinly in $\frac{3}{4}$–1 in drills that are spaced 6 in apart. The seed is sown thinly to prevent overcrowding and to encourage strong plants, which are necessary

for the successful growth of this tall, top-heavy vegetable. Brussels sprouts are vulnerable to club-root and cabbage root fly and the same control measures given for cabbages must be applied at both the sowing and transplanting stages. Seeds sown under cloches or frames in February for planting out in April will give an earlier crop. This method is useful for producing sprouts in September in addition to the main crop sown in the open to provide autumn and winter sprouts.

F_1 hybrids If F_1 hybrids to produce button sprouts for freezing are being grown, spacings of 20 in between the rows and 20 in between plants can be used. This provides a good yield from a relatively small area for picking at one time. Remove the growing point and smaller leaves when the lower sprouts are about $\frac{1}{2}$ in across to encourage most of them to mature at the same time.

For the "cut and come again" requirement of most gardeners, spacings of 36 in × 36 in are used. Grown at these distances most varieties produce an excellent crop while allowing easy access for picking. There appears

1 Late May to early June. Dig over the planting site and rake in a balanced, general fertilizer, such as a proprietary brand of Growmore, at 2 oz per square yard.

2 Transplant the seedlings from the seedbed into rows 36 in apart with 36 in (20 in × 20 in for F_1 hybrids) between plants. Plant them firmly with the lowest leaf at soil level.

3 At the same time, puddle in the young plants and check that they are firmly planted by gently tugging each top leaf.

4 June. Apply bromophos or diazinon to the soil at the base of the plants to combat cabbage root fly.

5 June. Continue to water the young plants until they are well established.

Brussels sprouts 2

F₁ HYBRIDS AND CONVENTIONAL VARIETIES

F₁ hybrid

conventional
variety

to be no advantage in closer spacing unless dwarf varieties are used, when spacings of $2\frac{1}{2}$ ft each way are sufficient. Firm planting is essential and the seedlings should be set with the lowest leaves at soil level to help establish a good root system. Water or puddle in the young plants. Check that they are firmly established by tugging gently at the top leaf of each plant.

Although additional watering during the growing season is often beneficial to cabbages, there appears to be no advantage in watering Brussels sprouts regularly unless the weather is very dry. Brussels sprout plants are in the ground for a long period, so regular weeding and hoeing should be carried out and any necessary pest and disease controls should be applied as necessary.

Aphids and cabbage whitefly are often particularly troublesome and if left can spoil the developing sprouts. Aphids must be sprayed as soon as they are spotted, or they will penetrate the sprouts themselves. Wood pigeons may attack the sprouts. A system of stakes carrying netting will protect the growing crop against birds and help to support the plants. Application of a foliar feed or a high potash fertilizer in July is often beneficial, particularly on light soils.

Harvesting
As the sprouts mature, remove any yellowing leaves from the lower part of the stem to improve air circulation. Pick or cut the sprouts when they are still tight and about the size of a walnut. Start picking from the base. When all the sprouts have been picked from a stem, use the Brussels sprout tops as "winter greens".

Aftercare
Surplus leaves can go on the compost heap, but the woody stems should be pulled up with the roots, dried and burned at the end of the season.

Do not leave Brussels sprouts in the ground to flower and seed, because they will continue to draw up nutrients from the soil and leave an unnecessarily large deficit for the crop that follows them.

6 July. In light soils or exposed sites draw up a little soil round the base of each stem. Hoe regularly to keep the plants free from weeds.

7 July. Apply a foliar feed or water in a high potash fertilizer at a rate of 1 oz per square yard. Spray with dimethoate or formothion to control aphid attacks.

8 September onwards. Remove yellowing leaves from the stems, and any "blown" (loose and open) sprouts.

9 As soon as the buttons are firm, gather them as required from the bottom of the stem.

Cauliflowers 1

Gardeners are often confused about the differences between cauliflowers, sprouting broccoli and calabrese and the various times they are in season.

Cauliflowers are distinguished, for practical purposes, by their large heads of tightly packed white, immature flowers known as "curds". Different varieties mature successively virtually throughout the year and they can be divided into three basic groups: summer, autumn and winter cauliflowers. The latter is also known as broccoli or heading broccoli. It is easy to understand how confusion has arisen, but sprouting broccoli is distinct from heading broccoli in that it produces groups of smaller, leafy flowerheads on short stalks and it is these young "spears" of succulent leaves and immature flowers that are eaten.

Broccoli is Italian for "little stalks", so it is better to restrict this term to the purple and white sprouting broccolis that are in season from January to May. Calabrese is structurally intermediate, producing a fairly large central green curd and a number of smaller sprouts that grow once the central head is cut.

Cauliflowers
A favourite among brassicas, the cauliflower is one of the more difficult vegetables to grow successfully because it is demanding in its soil, moisture and food requirements.

Soil and situation A deeply dug, fertile soil rich in humus is essential to obtain crops of good quality. The general principles of brassica growing apply—thorough soil preparation with heavy dressings of manure helping to provide food and retain moisture during the growing period (see page 36). The pH of the soil should be between 6.5 and 7.5 and the site should be open but not exposed. Cauliflowers are less hardy than other brassicas and in severe weather even the over-wintered varieties may be severely damaged or killed. They require ample food during their period of growth and, in addition to the manure dug in during the winter, a dressing of 2–3 oz per square yard of a general fertilizer should be raked into the soil before planting.

Cauliflower seedlings need careful handling and firm planting. They should never be short of water or they will produce small, premature heads of poor quality. Applications of up to 4 gal of water per square yard during dry periods improve the quality and yield. To maintain healthy, vigorous growth a dressing of 1 oz per square yard of sulphate of ammonia should be watered in when the young plants are well established but before the curds start to form. As with other brassicas, club-root and cabbage root fly may be troublesome and the appropriate control measures should be applied as a matter of routine.

Summer cauliflowers mature from June to August and may be raised in several ways depending on the facilities available. The easiest is to sow the seed in the open in March or early April for transplanting in June to crop in August or even September.

Early cauliflowers
Crops in June and July may be obtained by sowing seed in January in gentle heat (13°C/55°F). As soon as the seedlings are large enough to handle they are pricked out into cold frames 3 in by 3 in apart or into 3–3½ in pots of John Innes compost No. 1 (or equivalent) which are then kept in frames or a cold glasshouse. After a few days the frame is ventilated so that sturdy, healthy plants are produced. These are hardened off for planting in their final quarters in March. Alternatively, if no heat is available, seed can be sown the previous September and the seedlings pricked out into frames to over-winter before being hardened off for March planting.

Maximum yield of summer cauliflower is dependent on water supply. If the crop can be watered frequently, the spacing can be as close as 18 in by 18 in. In drier conditions, spacings of 24 in by 24 in are better.

Autumn cauliflowers
Autumn cauliflowers are in season from September to December and are sown outdoors in seedbeds during April and May for transplanting in late June to their final quarters. Their cultivation is similar to that of summer cauliflowers, differing only in their spacing requirements. The large, vigorous varieties are best planted at spacings of 27 in by 27 in but the newer, smaller Australian varieties can be spaced more closely, at 21 in by 21 in.

Summer cauliflower

1 Winter. Dig the soil deeply, incorporating a dressing of 15–20 lb per square yard of well-rotted manure.

2 Late March to early April (frame-raised plants) or early to mid-June (plants raised from seed sown outdoors in March to April). Rake in a dressing of 2–3 oz per square yard of a balanced fertilizer 1–2 weeks before planting.

3 Water the seedlings in the seedbed or frame the day before lifting them for transplanting. Lift them carefully and dip roots in benomyl or thiophanate-methyl.

4 Plant the seedlings at 24 in intervals in rows 24 in apart on the prepared site, watered on the previous day. Water or puddle in the transplanted seedlings. Check that they are firmly planted by tugging the uppermost leaf of each.

Cauliflowers 2

Winter cauliflowers

Winter cauliflowers are not quite so demanding in their soil and moisture requirements as summer and autumn cauliflowers, which do not thrive on dry soils or when moisture is lacking. On heavy soils the problem is often an excess of water because they do not tolerate "wet feet". They are also unlikely to survive periods of prolonged frost, and the early winter varieties, such as those in the Roscoff group, are not fully hardy in Britain and may be killed in severe weather. Depending on the varieties used, winter cauliflowers mature between December and late May or early June. Most gardeners choose to grow varieties that mature from March onwards unless they are in favoured parts of Britain, where home-grown cauliflowers can be enjoyed at Christmas and in the New Year. In cold areas where winter cauliflowers do not thrive, hardy sprouting broccoli should be grown to fill the winter and early spring gap. Cultivation requirements for winter cauliflowers are very similar to those of the summer and autumn varieties, although it is a much slower-maturing crop.

Sowing The seed is thinly sown in prepared seedbeds from mid-April to mid-May and transplanted during June and July into firm ground, well-manured for a previous crop and dressed with 2–3 oz per square yard of a general balanced fertilizer about a week before planting.

Planting distances for winter cauliflowers should be 30 in between the rows with 30 in between the plants. The usual control measures to combat club-root and cabbage root fly should be applied.

Winter cauliflower has a long growing season and needs plenty of nourishment. If growth is slow, further feeding may be necessary. Water in a mixture of 2 oz of superphosphate and 1 oz of sulphate of potash per square yard to improve growth during late summer. The plants must be grown hard to withstand the winter so nitrogen fertilizers that encourage soft growth late in the season should not be given.

As the curds form and begin to swell it is helpful to protect them against hard weather by snapping one or two leaves and bending them over the developing curds.

MINI-CAULIFLOWERS

People with home freezers may want to grow cauliflowers with small curds. Certain varieties of summer cauliflower such as 'Predominant' produce high yields of miniature curds at row spacings of 9 in, with 4 in between plants in the rows.

The seed is best space sown at these distances to provide a uniform crop to pick more or less at one time, but transplanted seedlings can also be grown. Not all varieties of summer cauliflower can be grown in this way, but for the freezer it is well worth selecting suitable varieties.

Apart from spacing requirements, the cultivation of mini-cauliflowers is as for summer cauliflowers.

5 Apply bromophos or diazinon to the soil around the plants to combat cabbage root fly. Continue to water the transplants daily until they are fully established. Make sure they are never short of water because otherwise they will produce small heads.

6 May (frame-raised plants) or July (plants sown outdoors in March to April). Water in a dressing of sulphate of ammonia at 1 oz per square yard before the curds start to form.

7 In dry weather apply water at 4 gal per square yard each week. If this is not possible give a single application at the same rate, when the curds are forming or 2–3 weeks before the crop is due to mature, to improve quality and yield.

8 June to August/September. Cut the mature cauliflowers as needed. The curds are ready for harvesting when they are firm and well developed but not yet beginning to open.

Broccoli and calabrese

Sprouting broccoli

Purple and white sprouting broccoli, with small leafy flowerheads on short stalks, are hardy and extremely useful for cold areas and poor soils where cauliflowers do not thrive. They are also well worth growing for the pleasant flavour of their young, succulent "spears".

Sprouting broccoli matures from January to May, the earliest of the purple varieties being ready to pick in mid-January, or in mild seasons and areas before Christmas. The white varieties, which are usually considered to have a better flavour, do not crop until late February or March and are less prolific.

Cultivation details and the timing of sowing and planting are very similar to those for winter cauliflower. Spacings of 27 in between the rows and between plants in the rows make the best use of the ground, although in very rich soils plants should be given a wider spacing of 30 in by 30 in.

Harvesting

The spears are ready to cut when the small flowerheads are well formed but before the flowers have begun to open. Pick the central spear first, when it is about 4 in long, and continue picking the side-shoots which develop at the same size. If the plants are picked every few days they will continue to provide young spears over a period of two months. It is important to cut sprouting broccoli regularly, both to stimulate further young growth and to prevent flowering. If the flowering shoots are allowed to develop fully the production of side-shoots stops.

Calabrese (green sprouting broccoli)

Calabrese is similar to sprouting broccoli in growth but differs in having a fairly large, compact, central, green flowerhead surrounded by smaller flowerheads that develop once the central head has been cut. It is less hardy than the purple or white sprouting broccolis but has the advantages of a shorter growing season and a delicious asparagus-like flavour. Calabrese takes 12–14 weeks to reach maturity and is in season from August until October, although if the autumn is mild it may continue to crop until severe frost occurs. The general principles of brassica

growing, including pest and disease controls, apply equally to calabrese although it will grow well in relatively poor soils.

Sowing The seed is sown thinly in April or May in prepared seedbeds and the young seedlings are transplanted to the vegetable plot in June or July to follow an earlier crop. If a succession is required, seed can also be sown in June and the seedlings planted out in August for cropping in late September and October. The seedlings should be planted in rows 18 in apart with 18 in between plants in the rows. Closer spacings of 12 in by 12 in may be used provided that ample water is available. This produces smaller spears that are ideal for freezing.

Harvesting

As the central flowerheads mature cut them for use and then water in a light dressing of $\frac{1}{2}$ oz per square yard of a balanced general fertilizer, such as a proprietary brand of Growmore, around the plants. This encourages the growth of side-shoots within 2–3 weeks and, as with sprouting broccoli, picking these every few days when they are about 4 in long will maintain a succession of spears until frosts intervene.

June to July

1 Water the seedlings in the seedbed the day before transplanting. Lift the seedlings carefully. Dip the roots in benomyl or thiophanate-methyl.

2 Plant the seedlings at 18 in intervals in rows 18 in apart and water them in well. Check that they are firmly planted by gently tugging the uppermost leaves.

3 Apply bromophos or diazinon to the soil around the plants to combat cabbage root fly. Water the transplants daily until they are fully established.

July onwards

4 Keep the plants free from weeds. In dry weather apply water at 4 gal per square yard each week or give 1 application at the same rate as the central head forms.

5 When the central heads mature cut them for use. Water in a dressing of $\frac{1}{2}$ oz of a balanced general fertilizer, such as a proprietary brand of Growmore.

6 Cut the side-shoots of calabrese every few days as they mature to maintain a succession.

Kale

CURLY
'Fribor', 'Pentland Brig'.

PLAIN
'Thousand Headed' (very hardy).

RAPE
'Hungry Gap'.

The dark green, crinkly leaves and shoots of kale can be eaten from November to April. As it is extremely hardy it is a most useful vegetable for winter use. Kale is often said to taste bitter, but if the small tender shoots and leaves are used instead of larger coarse foliage, the flavour is very pleasant. It often succeeds where other brassicas will not, because it is tolerant of club-root and cabbage root fly, and it will grow and crop reasonably well on poor soils. It also tolerates harsher climatic conditions than other brassicas. Some varieties, known as rape kales, such as 'Hungry Gap' should remain where they are sown until they mature and not be transplanted. Most other varieties, whether curly or plain-leaved, are grown in seedbeds and transplanted like other brassicas. Kale is planted out later than most vegetables, so space must be set aside for it when planning the vegetable plot. A quick-growing early crop can be taken from the same land.

Some types of kale are ornamental, with coloured decorative leaves. These can be grown in flower beds where they fill the dual purpose of an ornamental and food crop. Perennial kales can be grown but they are less use as a food crop.

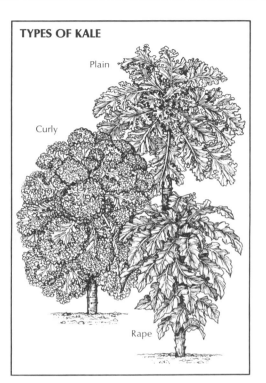

TYPES OF KALE

Plain

Curly

Rape

Cultivation

Although tolerant of poor soils, kale grows most satisfactorily in fertile conditions. Kale will grow in most soils, whether acid or alkaline. The soil must, however, be well-drained. The general rules for brassica cultivation (see page 36) should be followed and the site should be open. Less shelter is needed than for other brassicas, but in areas exposed to cold winter winds some protection will be repaid by better growth. As with Brussels sprouts, firm planting is important, particularly with the tall varieties, because the crop has to withstand winter winds.

The seed of varieties to be transplanted is sown in prepared seedbeds in April and May for planting out from late June to early August. The seedlings should be planted in rows 18 in apart with 18 in between the individual plants in the rows. For dwarf varieties the spacings should be 15 in either way. Early varieties sown in April are ready for picking in November and December, with later varieties continuing until the following April. 'Hungry Gap' and its relatives should be sown very thinly in drills 18 in apart and the young seedlings thinned by stages so that they are 18 in apart in the rows. Alternatively,

2–3 seeds can be sown at stations 18 in apart in the rows. Remove all but the strongest seedling at each station as soon as they can be easily handled. Their cultivation otherwise differs little from winter cabbage (see page 39). Perennial kales are usually propagated by cuttings from established plants.

As with cabbage, avoid nitrogen-rich fertilizers which encourage soft growth and thus increase the risk of frost damage. Earth up around the stems to protect the plants from wind and frost. Kale shows some tolerance of club-root and cabbage root fly, but can be badly affected by aphids, which can be controlled by spraying with a systemic insecticide such as heptenophos or dimethoate.

Harvesting

Kale should be used after other brassica crops have been harvested. It tastes best after frost. Use young leaves and shoots only, pulling off and discarding yellowing or tough old leaves. Further side-shoots will be produced, particularly with varieties such as 'Pentland Brig', and again these should be gathered when young and succulent. Pick the side-shoots from the top downwards. Some varieties produce edible flowering heads.

1 April to May. Sow the seed thinly and $\frac{3}{4}$–1 in deep in a prepared bed. Space the drills 6 in apart.

2 Late June to early August. Transplant the seedlings into rows 18 in apart with 18 in between each plant.

3 Autumn. Earth up each plant to the base of the first leaf as protection against frost and wind.

4 Winter to early spring. Harvest kale by picking the young shoots from the top of the plant downwards.

'Hungry Gap' Varieties

1 May. Sow 3 seeds at 18 in intervals in their final growing position.

2 June. Thin the seedlings to the strongest at each station.

Spinach/New Zealand spinach

SPINACH

SUMMER
'Long Standing Round'.

WINTER
'Green Market' (hardy),
'Long Standing Prickly',
'Sigmaleaf' (bolt resistant).

NEW ZEALAND SPINACH
No named varieties available.

Spinach (*Spinacia oleracea*) is an annual plant. Highly nutritious, it is grown for the use of its leaves which are either cooked or eaten raw in salads. New Zealand spinach (*Tetragona tetragonioides*) is not botanically related to ordinary spinach but is also grown for its leaves. The roughly triangular, blunt-tipped leaves are milder in flavour than those of ordinary spinach.

Cultivation

Ordinary spinach needs a soil rich in organic content and therefore capable of retaining water. When winter digging, add well-rotted compost or manure.

Soil and situation Spinach will not thrive on poor, dry or extremely acid soils. It grows best at a pH of 6.5–7.5. Since it is very fast growing, summer spinach can be cultivated as a catch crop between rows of taller vegetables, such as peas or beans, which provide slight shade in the summer months.

Summer spinach

For a continual supply of fresh leaves throughout the summer, sow the seed at two or three week intervals from March to May. Take out $\frac{1}{2}$–$\frac{3}{4}$ in drills, 12 in apart, and sow the seed very thinly.

Thinning Spinach has a much better flavour if it grows without any check and for this reason both thin sowing and early thinning are important tasks. Overcrowding in the row results in weak plants that run to seed easily. As soon as the seedlings have emerged and are large enough to handle, thin them until the individual plants are 3 in apart. As soon as these plants begin to close in on each other, thin again until they are 6 in apart. These thinnings can be eaten. Hoe between the rows very regularly to keep down weeds.

Watering Spinach must be kept well watered, especially in hot dry weather when there is a risk of bolting. Give the plants up to 4 gal per square yard each week in such conditions, even if they are still very small.

Winter spinach

Late-season sowings can be disappointing if round-seeded varieties are used. For the best results select a bolt-resistant variety of spinach such as 'Sigmaleaf'. Sow the seed in the usual way in late August or September but at this time it is best to choose a sunnier site. Cover the growing plants with cloches from October onwards in cold areas and use a Dutch hoe to remove any weeds around the cloches.

Harvesting

Summer spinach is ready to pick 8–10 weeks after sowing. Up to half the foliage on each plant can be picked at a time.

NEW ZEALAND SPINACH

New Zealand spinach needs a good medium to light soil and an open sunny position. It is not a hardy plant and must be sown indoors in early March for planting out in May or as soon as the danger of frost is past. The seeds are very hard and it helps germination if they are soaked in water overnight before sowing. Sow three seeds together in a $\frac{1}{2}$ in drill with 1 ft between each group of seeds. Thin the seedlings when they emerge, leaving the strongest one from each group of three. New Zealand spinach has a trailing habit and takes up a lot of ground. It does not bolt in hot dry weather although it should be watered well during such spells to encourage growth. Hoe regularly at first to keep down weeds, but later the plants' own thick growth will control them. Pinch out the tips of well-grown plants to produce more branching and young leaves for picking. From June to September harvest New Zealand spinach by picking a few leaves from each plant. Regular picking encourages them to keep on producing.

Winter spinach takes longer to mature and is not ready until about 12 weeks after sowing. Only a few leaves should be taken from each plant at any one time.

Pick the outside leaves while they are young and tender by breaking the stalk by hand. Do not tear the leaf stems away from the plant's base because this damages the plant. If spinach is harvested regularly in this way the plants are encouraged to produce more leaves and the cropping period is longer.

Storing Spinach is best consumed as soon as possible after harvesting, although it can be frozen successfully.

Pests and diseases

Proper thinning of the growing plants and vigilant watering should deter downy mildew. But if it does strike, spray the plants with mancozeb or a copper fungicide.

Summer spinach

1 Winter. Incorporate well-rotted compost into the soil during winter digging.

2 March to July, every 2–3 weeks. Sow the seed thinly

3 When the seedlings begin to touch each other, thin again to 6 in apart. These thinnings can be eaten.

Winter spinach

4 In dry weather apply water at a rate of up to 4 gal per square yard each week. Hoe weeds regularly.

5 Eight to ten weeks after sowing, cut or pick the outside leaves by breaking away their stalks.

October onwards. In cold areas cover the growing plants with cloches.

Asparagus 1

Asparagus is a perennial fern-like plant grown for its young shoots which are cut as fat, succulent spears soon after they come through the soil. Appreciated as a luxury vegetable, asparagus is expensive to buy but economical to grow because the same plants, when established and well-managed, will provide crops for 20 years or even longer. Asparagus is easy to grow and it is a beautiful plant, but it does require time and patience.

Cultivation

Plants may be raised from seed but there is a long, three-year delay between seed sowing and the first crop. The more usual way of starting an asparagus bed is with bought crowns, which can be one, two or three years old. For all ages the period between planting and harvesting is the same. The one-year-old is the best buy because it is cheaper and it establishes a good root system as quickly after planting as does a two- or three-year-old. Order the crowns from the nursery well in advance and ask for delivery in April, which is the best planting time.

Soil and situation Asparagus will grow in most soils but a pH of 6.5–7.5 is preferable and good drainage and freedom from perennial weeds are essential. Dig a dressing of well-rotted manure or compost at 15 lb per square yard into the top spit in the autumn or early winter before planting. Asparagus roots tend to develop laterally so it is best to maintain the food supply in the top 12 in of soil. Asparagus grows best in an open site.

The first year

Never let the crowns dry out; choose a moist day for planting and leave the crowns wrapped until the last minute.

Planting The traditional asparagus bed, which consists of three rows of crowns with access on either side, is more than 5 ft wide. However, if only a single row is planted in each trench, weed control and cutting are easier. In April dig a trench about 10 in deep and 15 in wide for each row. Then lightly fork in a balanced general fertilizer, such as a brand of Growmore, at 3 oz per square yard. In very nitrogen-rich soils dig in 1½ oz superphosphate

SOWING ASPARAGUS

Asparagus seed can be sown outdoors in March or early April.

Sow the seed thinly in ½–¾ in deep drills, 18 in apart. When the seedlings emerge thin them until they are eventually 6 in apart. Keep the bed completely weed-free and water in dry weather. The seedlings can be transplanted to the permanent bed in March or April of the following year.

However, another year in the seedling row will mean that the seed-bearing female plants can be identified and removed before their seeds fall and germinate. In a permanent bed planted with male crowns only there is no seedhead production and constant weeding out of unwanted seedlings will not be necessary. Plant out and proceed as for one-year-old crowns.

The first year

1 Winter. Dig the ground 1 spit deep, incorporating well-rotted manure or compost with a fork and removing perennial weeds.

2 April. Dig a trench 15 in wide and 10 in deep. Lightly rake in fertilizer at 3 oz per square yard. Make a 3 in deep ridge at the bottom of the trench.

3 April. Plant the crowns at 18 in intervals on the ridge with the roots sloping outwards. Cover the crowns with 2–3 in of soil.

4 October. Cut the fern when it has turned yellow. Apply a 2–3 in layer of manure or compost and mound up the soil several inches deep over the row.

Asparagus 2

HOW ASPARAGUS GROWS

and 1 oz sulphate of potash. Make a ridge in the bottom of the trench and place each crown at 18 in intervals on the ridge, with the roots spread outwards over the ridge. Cover them quickly and carefully with fine soil to fill in the trench. If more than one trench is dug the rows should be 4 ft apart.

Once an asparagus bed is established its upkeep is routine. The common reasons for deterioration are lack of weeding, cutting over too long a season and disregard of the need for fern production. Hand weed regularly and never cultivate deeply or dig near a bed because asparagus roots spread out widely and are easily damaged. In the autumn when the foliage turns yellow, cut it down and clear any weeds. Mound up the soil several inches deep over the row.

The second year

In late February or early March top-dress with a balanced general fertilizer, such as Growmore, at 3 oz per square yard.

Do not cut the foliage until it yellows in the autumn. Then clear the bed and apply a 2–3 in layer of well-rotted manure or compost. Ridge up the row with soil if necessary.

Harvesting

Do not cut any spears until the third season after planting. Eventual heavy cropping depends on a slow build-up of crown size, starting with the all important first two seasons, when no cutting should be done.

The cutting season for asparagus is from the end of April to late June, and no longer. Cut all the spears when they are 5–6 in above ground, even if they vary in thickness. In the third year cut for a period of six weeks after the first shoots appear. In the fourth and subsequent years the cutting period is up to eight weeks.

A special asparagus knife is ideal for cutting, but an ordinary sharp knife used carefully will do. By the time a bed is established the crowns will be about 4 in below the soil surface.

Cut the spears obliquely about 1–2 in below the soil surface. An asparagus crown produces many small shoots at different stages of

maturity and it is important to cut the spears cleanly and carefully so that the plant will continue to crop.

Aftercare

From June onwards the ferns must be allowed to grow in order to play their vital role in building up food reserves in the crown for the following year's crop. To encourage this growth apply a general, balanced fertilizer at 3 oz per square yard immediately after the last cutting.

When the fern has turned yellow, and not before, cut it down to ground level. Burn it, because it is too woody for the compost heap. Clear away any debris and tidy the bed after cutting the fern down.

Pests and diseases

If asparagus beetle grubs damage shoots during the cutting season spray the plants with derris. After the cutting season use HCH. If slugs are troublesome control them by the methods described in the section on pests and diseases (see page 249).

The second year

5 Late February to early March. Top-dress the bed with fertilizer at 3 oz per square yard.

6 Autumn. Cut down the yellow fern and apply manure or compost. Ridge up the row with soil if necessary.

Third and subsequent years

7 April to late June. Cut all the spears with a sharp knife when they are 5–6 in above soil level. Cut each spear obliquely 1–2 in below the soil surface.

8 June onwards. Immediately after the last cut, apply a general, balanced fertilizer, such as a brand of Growmore, at 3 oz per square yard to the bed.

Celery

SELF-BLANCHING
'American Green', 'Golden
Self Blanching' (white).

TRENCH CELERY
'Giant Pink', 'Giant Red',
'Giant White', 'Prizetaker'
(white).

Celery is a biennial plant grown for its blanched stalks which are cooked or used for salads. There are white, pink and red varieties, the white producing the finest quality celery. The red varieties are the hardiest and they will stay in good condition well into the autumn months.

Cultivation

Choose an open site with rich, well-drained soil of pH 6.5–7.5. There are two methods of growing celery. By tradition it is grown in trenches which are gradually filled in to blanch the stems. Alternatively, self-blanching varieties can be used which do not require earthing-up but these are less hardy (with a correspondingly shorter growing season) than the trenched varieties. They require much less work and are especially suitable for heavy soils which are laborious to trench and where the trench may become waterlogged with consequent slug damage and rotting.

Trench method Take out a trench 15 in wide and 12 in deep in March or April. If more than one trench is required the centres of each should be 4 ft apart. Fork manure into the bottom of the trench at a rate of 15 lb (1 bucketful) per square yard and return the soil to within 3 in of ground level. The trench should then be left open until planting out time in early summer.

Sowing Use thiram-treated seed if available. In March or April sow the seed thinly in trays in John Innes seed compost or the equivalent, at 13°–16°C/55°–60°F. Do not cover the seed and keep it moist. The seed germinates in 2–3 weeks. Prick out the seedlings when they have two true leaves into boxes of John Innes No. 1 or an equivalent potting compost, spacing them about 2½ in apart. Alternatively, place them singly in 3 in pots. Harden them off gradually for planting out in late May or June. Just before planting rake in a balanced general fertilizer at the rate of 2–3 oz per square yard into the bottom of the trench and apply diazinon to combat carrot fly.

Planting In late May or June plant out the seedlings at 9 in intervals in double-staggered rows 9 in apart in each trench. Water the plants thoroughly. When the plants are about 12 in high cut out any side-shoots at the base and loosely tie the stalks just below the leaves, using raffia or soft string.

As with all leafy crops ample water is essential during the growing season. In dry weather apply 4 gal per square yard. Alternatively, 10–20 days before the final earthing up apply 4 gal per square yard. This improves the quality and size of the crop markedly.

Earthing up As the plants grow, earth up progressively at intervals of about three weeks, leaving plenty of leaf above the soil and taking care not to let soil fall into the hearts. Earth up after rain when the soil is damp, never when it is dry, because the foliage acts as an umbrella and keeps the soil around the roots as dry or as damp as it was when earthed up, for a considerable time afterwards.

Harvesting

From October to February, depending on type and variety, lift celery carefully with a trowel as required. The roots may penetrate very deeply and in such cases it is best to lift with a fork. Bracken or straw placed over the trench assists lifting in frosty weather.

Pests and diseases

Celery leaf miner larvae bore into foliage leaving brown blisters. Pinch out affected leaves and spray with dimethoate or malathion at the first sign of damage. Slugs may be a problem, especially on heavy soils, and so put down slug pellets around the plants. Carrot fly attacks the roots of celery and should be combated by applying diazinon granules before transplanting.

Celery leaf spot can be prevented by using thiram-treated seed or spraying the plants with benomyl or carbendazim as soon as any spots are visible on the leaves.

SELF-BLANCHING CELERY

Sow the seed as for trench-grown varieties but plant out the seedlings on the flat. Prepare the bed in April by digging in well-rotted manure or compost at 15 lb per square yard. Plant out the seedlings during May in a square, not in a row, 11 in apart each way or 6 in each way for a higher yield of smaller sticks.

1 March or April. Dig a trench 15 in wide and 12 in deep. Fork manure into the bottom and return the soil to within 3 in of ground level.

2 March or April. Sow the seed thinly in seed compost at 13°–16°C/55°–60°F. Do not cover and keep moist. After 2–3 weeks prick the seedlings out and gradually harden off.

3 Just before planting, rake fertilizer into the trench bottom at 2–3 oz per square yard. Apply diazinon granules against carrot fly.

4 Late May or June. Plant out the seedlings at 9 in intervals in double-staggered rows 9 in apart. Water well.

5 July. When the plants are 12 in high loosely tie the stalks just below the leaves. Earth up every 3 weeks when the soil is damp to cover the leaf bases.

6 October to February. Lift celery carefully with a trowel or a fork. Place bracken or straw over the trench in frosty weather.

Rhubarb

FORCING
'Timperley Early'.

MAIN CROP
'Hawke's Champagne',
'Prince Albert', 'Sutton',
'Victoria'.

Rhubarb (*Rheum rhaponticum*) is a hardy perennial grown for its delicately-flavoured pink leaf-stalks or sticks, and is therefore classed as a vegetable not a fruit. The leaves contain oxalic acid and are poisonous. Rhubarb is in season from March to July, although earlier crops can be obtained in January and February by forcing plants.

Cultivation
Rhubarb grows best on a sunny site in a fairly heavy, acid soil of pH 5.0–6.0. However, it will tolerate a wide range of conditions and is likely to fail only on very waterlogged soils. The plants will stand for about 5–10 years, so the bed should be thoroughly prepared in the autumn before planting.

Dig the ground deeply, removing all perennial weeds and incorporating organic manure or well-rotted garden compost at a rate of 20–30 lb per square yard. Just before planting rake in a dressing of 3–4 oz of fertilizer.

Propagation Raising rhubarb from seed is a lengthy process which often gives poor results, so either propagate it from root division or obtain offsets of a named variety from a nursery. Propagation should be from established plants at least three years old. Cut the roots into offsets or sets with a spade or knife making sure each set has a bud.

Planting Plant in October to November or February to March, leaving 3 ft between the plants. If more than one row is required, leave 3–4 ft between the rows. The buds should be just below the soil surface. Firm in and water if necessary during dry weather. Cut out flowering shoots as they appear.

Harvesting
Rhubarb can be harvested from March to July. Do not pull at all in the first year after planting and only lightly in the second. Hold the stick near the base and pull up with a twisting movement. Take a few sticks from each crown as required, but always leave 3–4 leaves on each plant to avoid weakening it.

Aftercare In autumn, when harvesting is over and the foliage has died down, clean up around the plants and apply a light top dressing of a balanced general fertilizer at 2–3 oz per square yard. In late winter mulch with well-rotted compost or manure.

Pests and diseases
Stem and bulb eelworm may attack rhubarb, causing poor growth and distorted leaves. Crown rot is the only major disease, the symptoms of which are dull foliage, small sticks and dead buds. There is no cure for either of these problems so dig up and burn affected plants. Do not replant rhubarb on the same ground.

FORCING RHUBARB

Forcing the plants during the winter produces earlier crops of pinker, more tender rhubarb. It can be harvested from February to March if forced *in situ* or as early as January if forced indoors.

Outdoors In mid-January to February cover the plants to be forced with a dustbin, bucket or barrel to exclude the light. Put straw or strawy manure over and around the cover for insulation. The plants should not normally need watering and the sticks will be ready in 5–6 weeks. Do not pick from the plants for at least two years after forcing.

Indoors In October to early November dig up strong clumps and leave them on the soil surface exposed to frosty weather for 1–2 weeks. This encourages rapid growth during forcing. Then pack the roots closely together in a box, cover with a thin layer of soil and water well. Invert another box and place it on top, and exclude light with newspaper or black polythene. Keep in a warm greenhouse or shed at 10°–13°C/50°–55°F. Water the plants occasionally to keep them moist. Pull the sticks in 4–5 weeks. Discard the plants after forcing indoors.

First year

Second and subsequent years

1 October to November or February to March. Cut the roots of an established plant into sets, ensuring each has at least 1 bud.

2 Plant the sets 3 ft apart in well-prepared ground, with the buds just below the soil surface. Rows should be 3–4 ft apart.

3 Summer. Water the plants in dry weather and cut out any flowering shoots.

4 October. Remove old foliage. Apply 2–3 oz of fertilizer to each plant.

5 March to July. Pull sticks by grasping near the base and twisting upwards.

French beans 1

CLIMBING
'Blue Lake', 'Earliest of All'.

CLIMBING PURPLE
'Blue Coco', 'Purple Podded'.

DWARF
'Masterpiece' (prolific),
'The Prince', 'Sprite',
'Tendergreen'.

DWARF YELLOW
'Kinghorn Wax-pod'.

French beans are half-hardy annuals. Dwarf and climbing types are available. They grow best in warm conditions. Early beans can be obtained from plants grown in heated greenhouses or under cloches. The beans are eaten with the pods, which are usually sliced. Green podded types with either flat or cylindrical pods are most common, and there are also yellow, wax-pod varieties. French beans are sometimes known as string beans or kidney beans. Haricot beans, which are the dried seeds of certain varieties of French beans, are grown in the same way. Like other beans, French beans are valuable for their vitamin and mineral content.

Cultivation

French beans grow best in a well-drained, fertile soil of pH 6.5–7.0. A layer of farmyard manure or compost dug in during the winter is sufficient to maintain fertility in most soils. Do not grow French beans in shaded situations. Apply, and work in, a fertilizer such as a proprietary brand of Growmore, at 1–2 oz per square yard a couple of weeks before sowing. Over-rich soils and too much nitrogenous fertilizer encourage soft growth and excessive leaf production. No top dressing should be needed for this crop.

Sowing Do not make outdoor sowings too early. A soil temperature of at least 10°C/50°F is needed for successful and rapid germination. Under good conditions, 75 per cent of the seed should germinate. French beans do not thrive in cold soils and the seeds will rot if conditions are too wet. Raise the soil temperature for early sowings and in cold seasons by placing cloches over the soil 3–4 weeks before sowing. The first dwarf bean sowings can be made outside in early May in most areas. Monthly sowings until July give beans throughout the summer. A late July sowing is often useful in southern districts in Britain, but the plants must be cloched in late

GROWING UNDER CLOCHES

Early sowings of dwarf French beans can be made under cloches at the beginning of April. Put the cloches over the ground for 3–4 weeks before sowing in order to warm up the soil. Picking from early, cloched crops should begin in late June.

1 April. Place cloches over the seedbed to warm up the soil for early sowings.

2 Late April. Rake in general balanced fertilizer at 1–2 oz per square yard 1–2 weeks before sowing.

3 Early May. Sow individual seeds at 2–3 in intervals in 2 in drills, 18 in apart for dwarf, 3–4 in intervals and 2 ft apart for climbing.

4 Throughout summer. Hoe to keep down weeds and then mulch with peat, straw or black polythene to preserve moisture.

French beans 2

September to produce beans in October. Climbing types should be sown in early May.

Sow dwarf beans in rows 18 in apart. Space the seeds 2–3 in apart in 2 in drills. Water the bottom of the drill before sowing to encourage germination. Climbing beans are sown in the same way but with a 2 ft gap between the rows and the seeds 3–4 in apart.

Greenhouse and early cloched beans Very early pickings are possible from dwarf beans grown in a heated greenhouse from an early February sowing. Sow four or five seeds round the edge of a 9 in pot filled with John Innes No. 2 or an equivalent compost. Pre-germinate or chit the seeds by keeping them on moist kitchen towelling in a warm place before sowing. Maintain a temperature of 15°C/60°F and keep the plants well watered once the flowers appear. Ventilate the greenhouse in warm weather to maintain sturdy plant growth. Picking should take place in May.

Cloches can be used to bring forward outdoor sowings of dwarf beans. A sowing can be planned for early April under cloches or polythene tunnels, but stand them on the site for three or four weeks beforehand to warm up and dry the soil.

Growing Climbing types need a support and training system. The plants will grow to 6–7 ft and canes, posts or strings on a post and wire framework all give good support. Stretch the strings at 4 in intervals between top and bottom wires and, if necessary, let two beans climb each string. Canes or poles should also be spaced 4 in apart.

Hoe out any weeds and mulch the plants in June with peat, straw or lengths of black polythene. Once the seedlings are established, do not water until the flowers appear unless the weather is dry. Too much water during early growth encourages leaves to grow at the expense of the flowers.

Water the plants generously once the flowers appear; beans are particularly sensi-tive to moisture-stress at the flower opening and pod swelling stages and it is essential to keep them well watered at these times.

Applications of 3–4 gal per square yard each week markedly increases pod-set, yield and quality. Syringing the flowers to "set" the pods, a traditional practice, is not effective. Organic matter dug in during the winter will help to retain moisture.

Harvesting

Regular picking is essential to maintain a continuous supply of beans. Dwarf beans produce their pods over a relatively short period (hence the successive sowings) but climbing types continue to crop throughout the summer. Pick the beans while they are young and tender. Over-mature pods are stringy and show the beans bulging out the pod walls. Remove the pods carefully so as not to damage the plants; they should snap off the plants cleanly.

Pests and diseases

Aphids (green and black) may feed on the growing shoots, and red spider mites may be found on the under surfaces of leaves. These mites produce yellow dots on the upper surfaces of leaves, which eventually become bronzed and brittle (see p.248–9). Grey mould (*Botrytis cinerea*) can be a problem during wet weather in the picking season. Damaged pods are soon infected and rot on the plant. Spray regularly with benlate or carbendazim during wet or humid conditions.

The bacterial disease, halo blight, may attack French beans (see page 247). It causes dark, water-soaked areas on leaves and pods, and the characteristic "halo" forms a yellow edge around the dark areas. Damp, humid conditions favour the spread of halo blight and fungicidal sprays are usually ineffective against it. Destroy any French beans affected by the disease and never save seed for the next year from them.

5 As flowers appear, carefully apply water at a rate of 3–4 gal per week. Avoid splashing the foliage.

6 July onwards. Pick the pods when they are 5–6 in long. They should snap in half easily and show no stringiness.

SUPPORT SYSTEMS

Climbing French beans must be supported on strings, canes or nets supported by poles and will grow 6–7 ft tall. However, dwarf types of French bean require no support and have a bushy habit with a height of approximately 18 in.

CLIMBING
'Enorma', 'Fry', 'Kelvedon
Marvel', 'Streamline', 'Sunset',
'White Achievement'.

DWARF
'Hammond's Dwarf Scarlet'.

Runner beans 1

Runner beans are perennials that produce small root tubers, but they are usually grown as half-hardy annuals. In temperate zones they may be damaged by frost at the beginning or at the end of the season. The plants are very attractive with different varieties having white, pink or, more usually, scarlet flowers. Their tall habit and dense foliage make them a useful screen plant. A runner bean wigwam makes an attractive centre-piece in an annual flower border.

Cultivation

Runner beans should not be growing while frost is still a danger. When they are sown or planted rapid growth is required, however, and light, well-drained, fertile soils of pH 6.0–7.0 are best suited for this crop. Wet soils cause the large seeds to rot. Careful soil preparation for runner beans is rewarded with excellent growth and yields. Prepare a 2 ft wide, single spade depth trench in early spring. Fork large quantities of farmyard manure or well-rotted garden compost into the bottom of the trench before replacing the soil. These materials retain moisture during the life of the crop and encourage good growth and setting.

Situation Choose a sheltered but open, sunny site for runner beans, because winds can damage the plants and young beans. Still conditions also encourage the insects which are essential for runner bean pollination. One or two weeks before sowing, hoe in 2–3 oz per square yard of a general fertilizer such as a proprietary brand of Growmore.

Plant establishment There are several possible support systems for runner beans and the method of propagation varies with the system. Beans may either be sown or planted. Plants are raised in a cool greenhouse (10°C/50°F) in individual containers. Sow the seed approximately four weeks before the expected planting date. Pre-germinate or chit the seeds first between layers of moistened kitchen towelling kept in a warm place. A germination rate of more than 80 per cent can be expected. Keep the propagation temperature down to maintain strong, sturdy growth. Harden off the plants in a cold frame or under cloches for a few days before planting. Do not plant out until all danger of frost

EARLY CROPS

Early crops can be produced from transplanted plants raised by sowing seeds in pots in a cool greenhouse. Sow the seeds about four weeks before the expected planting date, which must be after the last frost. Make a good-sized hole with a trowel and plant a single bean plant beside each cane, pole or string. Sufficiently long shoots should be twisted around their support and the plants must be thoroughly watered at the base.

has passed. Sowing should take place outside from early May onwards depending on the frost incidence in the area. A soil temperature of at least 10°C/50°F is needed for germination. Cloches can be used to protect sowings made in early areas during April. Use the cloches to warm up the soil for three or four weeks before sowing and sow a single row with the beans spaced 6 in apart. Runner bean seeds should be sown 2 in deep and the positioning in the row depends on the support system.

Support systems

Runner beans are usually grown up supports, although dwarf plants can be grown. 'Hammonds Dwarf Scarlet' is a semi-dwarf variety which needs no pinching, but other varieties can be dwarfed by pinching out their growing point when they are 12 in tall. Pinched or dwarf beans produce slightly earlier crops than supported plants, but the yield is lower and the pods may be soiled. Space the seeds 6 in apart in rows 24 in apart.

Supported beans can be trained up canes,

poles, strings or nets. The plants will grow 8 ft tall, but they can be stopped by pinching out the growing point when they reach the top of the support. Single rows of beans can be grown up any of the supports mentioned. Seeds should be sown at 6 in intervals and the canes, poles or strings should be spaced 6 in apart. If nets are used they should be attached to wires stretched between vertical stakes.

Double row systems use 8 ft canes or poles which are crossed over and wired or tied together at the top to form an inverted V-shape. Sow the beans at 6 in intervals in the rows which should be 24 in apart. If poles are scarce or expensive, two plants can climb each support, but the yield will be reduced. Leave a 36 in path between double rows.

Canes or poles can also be made into wigwam support frameworks. Four to ten supports may be used. A 4-cane wigwam has canes at the corners of a 3 ft square. The canes or poles are wired or tied together at the top. In this case erect the wigwam and sow or plant the beans next to each cane or pole.

1 Early spring. Take out a trench one spit deep and 2 ft wide. Dig a generous supply of farmyard manure or well-rotted garden compost into the bottom and re-fill with the original soil.

2 April. Rake in 2–3 oz per square yard of a balanced general fertilizer. Use cloches to warm the soil in cold seasons.

3 Early May. Sow individual seeds 6 in apart in 2 in deep drills. Two drills 24 in apart are sown for double row growing systems.

Runner beans 2

Growing Gently twist the plants anti-clockwise around their supports to encourage them to climb. Water runner beans only when they are in flower or cropping. Too much water early on encourages leaf growth at the expense of flowers and beans. If the plants become short of water, flowers will drop off and pods fail to develop. Bulky organic manures dug in during the soil preparations help to retain moisture around the roots. Mulch around the plants to eliminate weeds and minimize moisture loss.

Runner beans are insect pollinated and so care is needed when using insecticides. Use low persistence chemicals, such as malathion, and apply them in the evening when pollinating insects have finished working. Pinch out the growing points of dwarf or "pinched" beans at frequent intervals to keep the plants compact.

The first severe frost kills runner bean foliage, which can be cut down and composted if it is disease-free. Diseased foliage should be burned. Dig the small root tubers into the soil because they will add useful

nitrogenous material. Clean and store the canes or poles for next season. Nets and strings should be burned after one season, but plastic netting can be sterilized.

Harvesting

Picking of the cloched and pinched crops starts in July, with the supported crops coming in at the beginning of August. Careful and rigorous picking of dwarf or pinched crops keeps down the number of soil-splashed and bent beans. Harvesting from these crops continues for about three or four weeks.

Supported crops produce beans until the first severe frost kills the plants. Pick them regularly to maintain a continuity of production. At the height of the season, it is necessary to pick every other day.

Pests and diseases

Aphids and red spider mites are the major pests, and grey mould (*Botrytis cinerea*) and halo blight may be problems in wet or humid weather. See page 52 for details of symptoms and treatment.

SUPPORT SYSTEMS AND PINCHED BEANS

Strings, canes or poles are the most usual supports although nets are sometimes used. Plants may be grown in single or double rows. Wigwam supports are formed by joining 4–10 canes or poles together at the top. Unsupported plants—pinched beans—have the growing point removed to produce a dwarf habit.

Supporting a double row

4 June. When the plants are 3–4 in tall erect a double row of crossed 8 ft poles. Space them 6–12 in apart, and train 1–2 plants up each. Place a horizontal pole on top for added stability.

5 June to July. Mulch around the plants once they are established. Use a 3–4 in layer of straw or peat.

6 June to July. Spray against aphids and red spider mites if necessary. Spray late in the evening to avoid harming pollinating insects, such as bees.

7 Late July to early August. Pick young, tender beans with no hint of swollen seeds through the pod wall. Regular picking, every other day if possible, encourages more runner bean pods to form.

AUTUMN
'Aquadulce'.

SPRING
'Colossal', 'Green Windsor',
'Masterpiece', 'The Sutton'.

Broad beans 1

The broad bean is a hardy annual vegetable and the earliest maturing type of outdoor bean grown in Britain. The first pickings are made in June from over-wintered plants sown in the previous November. Special winter-hardy varieties are available today.

For picking from late June, sow under cloches in February. Successive spring sowings provide beans throughout the summer.

Cultivation

Broad beans—in common with other legumes—ideally prefer neutral or slightly alkaline soils, but grow well between pH 6.0–7.0. They tolerate relatively infertile soils but better growth and heavier yields occur on rich, fertile, well-drained soils. Cold, wet soils must be avoided especially for the over-wintered crops. Broad beans have the largest seeds of all common vegetables and they will soon rot in waterlogged soils. Autumn-sown crops do not need fertilizer at sowing time. There should be sufficient remaining from the previous crop. Too much nitrogen at this time encourages soft growth, which is easily damaged by winter frosts. Rapid growth is required in the spring, however, and a top dressing of a nitrogenous fertilizer, such as 1–2 oz per square yard of nitro-chalk, should be applied as soon as growth recommences. Hoe the fertilizer in around the plants. Soil for spring sowings of broad beans should be given a dressing of 2–3 oz per square yard of a balanced general fertilizer, such as Growmore, 1–2 weeks before sowing. No more fertilizer should then be needed.

Sowing Over-wintered broad beans should be sown during the first half of November.

Use varieties recommended for over-wintering and aim to produce a strong 4 in tall plant to withstand the winter. Taller, softer plants will almost certainly be damaged or killed by frosts. Broad bean seeds are very large and there is no need to prepare a very fine seedbed. This is particularly true of over-wintered crops when the soil becomes compacted. Spring sowings of broad beans can begin outdoors as soon as the soil is workable, usually in February or March.

Unlike French and runner beans, broad beans will withstand some frost. The seeds germinate well at soil temperatures of 5°C/39°F. The germination rate should be at least 80 per cent. Successive sowings at monthly intervals will produce beans right into the autumn. Cloched broad bean crops can be sown in February.

1 Early March. Take out drills 18 in apart and 3 in deep. Sow single seeds 5 in apart. For dwarf varieties make the drills 9 in apart and sow the seeds at 9 in intervals. Broad bean seeds are very large so there is no need to prepare a very fine seedbed for them.

2 April. Hammer stakes into the ground at each end of the rows, leaving 3–4 ft above the ground.

3 April onwards. Hoe regularly around the plants and when they are big enough run string around the stakes at 12 in intervals to provide support as they develop.

4 When the plants are in full flower pinch out 4–6 in of shoot to reduce the danger of black bean aphids attacking and feeding on the young shoots in June, and to encourage a more uniform development of pods up the plants.

Broad beans 2

Single and double rows

Broad beans can be grown in either single or double rows. Research has shown that dwarf varieties should be sown 9 in apart with 9 in between rows. Taller varieties should be spaced 5 in apart with 18 in between rows. The seeds may be sown in a 3 in deep drill taken out with a draw hoe. Alternatively, they can be sown at the same depth in holes made with a trowel or dibber alongside a line.

The double row system, which produces the largest yield, is particularly good for cloched crops. Varieties with a dwarf habit, such as 'The Sutton', are also suitable for cloched growing.

Broad beans can also be sown in pots or boxes under glass in January and planted out in March. This system is useful in cold districts.

Hoe between over-wintered crops in the spring to incorporate the fertilizer top dressing and to aerate the soil. Hoeing for weed control is necessary until there is a good foliage cover of beans. Remove the cloches in April when the beans reach the glass. Taller varieties need not be supported. Stakes should be hammered in at the ends or corners of the rows. Leave 3–4 ft of stake above ground and wind successive lengths of string from the stakes all around the plants. Layers of string should be attached at 12 in intervals. Keep the plants well watered during flowering and cropping, but water only in dry spells at other times in the growing period.

Watch for black bean aphids (blackfly) which will attack the plants in June. They feed on the young shoot tips and their arrival usually coincides with the flowering of spring-sown beans. Remove 4–6 in of the growing tips to discourage this pest and to encourage more uniform development of pods up the plant. Spray affected plants with pirimicarb.

Harvesting

Picking begins in June and can continue, from successive spring sowings, into the autumn. Broad beans are usually shelled from the pods before cooking and the stage of picking is critical. The pods should not be tough and fibrous, while the beans themselves must be young and tender. Pods can also be picked when immature (4–6 in long) and either cooked whole or sliced.

After harvesting, cut off the plant tops and dig the roots in. Bean roots contain nitrogen-fixing bacteria which improve the soil fertility for subsequent crops. The roots also make excellent compost.

Pests and diseases

Blackfly can be sprayed with low-persistence insecticides such as malathion, pyrethrum or derris. Spray late in the evening to minimize damage to pollinating insects such as bees. Pea and bean weevils feed on leaves, producing a scalloped pattern round the edge. Nearly all broad bean crops develop dark brown spots or blotches on the leaves and stems, although the pods are attacked only in severe outbreaks. These are the symptoms of chocolate spot fungus caused by a type of grey mould (*Botrytis cinerea*). Poorly grown plants are attacked most severely, with damaged leaves, overcrowding and soft, lush growth contributing to the spread of the disease. It is rarely sufficiently severe to warrant chemical control measures and it is much better to avoid the disease by growing healthy plants.

5 During flowering and cropping, water well to boost crop yield. Do not water before flowering unless the weather is very dry because too much watering during the early life of broad beans increases leafy growth at the expense of flowers and fruit.

6 June to July onwards. Pick young broad beans before the pod walls become tough and fibrous. Shell them from the pods before cooking—the attachment scars of individual seeds should be green rather than black.

7 After harvesting. Cut down the stems to within 4 in of the soil immediately after picking has finished. Compost healthy stem material and dig in the stem bases and roots.

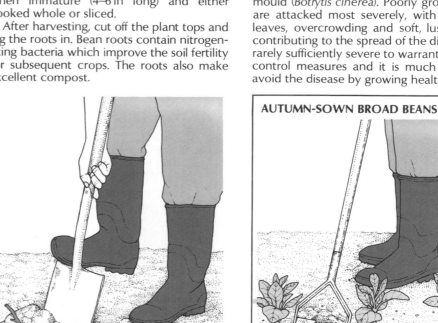

AUTUMN-SOWN BROAD BEANS

Sow broad beans in November in the usual way, using the special winter-hardy varieties available. Do not fertilize, or there will be too much growth which will suffer from winter frosts.

In February, apply a top-dressing of nitrogenous fertilizer, such as nitro-chalk, at a rate of 1–2 oz per square yard and hoe it in around the plants.

Garden peas 1

PEAS
FIRST EARLIES
'Feltham First', 'Hurst Beagle', 'Kelvedon Wonder' (mildew resistant), 'Little Marvel' (heavy yielding), 'Meteor'.

SECOND EARLIES
'Hurst Greenshaft', 'Onward' (hardy).

MAIN CROP
'Lord Chancellor', 'Recette'.

SUGAR PEAS (MANGETOUT)
'Carouby de Maussane', 'Oregon Sugar Pod'.

PETIT POIS
'Gullivert'.

ASPARAGUS PEAS
No named varieties available.

Peas

Garden pea

Asparagus pea

Peas are treated as hardy annuals, and the round-seeded types are the hardiest. These are sometimes sown outside in November to produce peas early the following summer. The wrinkle-seeded types are much less hardy and should not be sown until the spring. Sugar peas (mangetout) and the petit pois of France are closely related to garden peas. The yield depends upon the variety grown. Tall types produce two to three times as many peas as do dwarf types. Peas are usually shelled from the pods before cooking.

Cultivation

Peas must be grown on well-drained, rich, fertile soils of pH 6.0–7.0. Dig in a 2 in layer of farmyard manure or well-rotted garden compost in the winter to improve soil fertility and retain moisture. November sowings should be attempted only in sheltered districts and then only on freely-draining soils. Any hint of waterlogging will rot the seeds. Peas grown on well-manured soils do not require any fertilizers, but crops grown on low fertility soils respond to an application of 1–2 oz per square yard of a low nitrogen compound fertilizer. Incorporate the fertilizer just before sowing the peas.

Sowing Peas are classified as first earlies, second earlies or main crop, according to the time taken from sowing until picking. First earlies take about 12 weeks; second earlies 13–14 weeks and main crop varieties 14–16 weeks. Successive sowings from the beginning of March until the end of April with these various maturity types produce peas from mid-June until August. Further sowings —until the end of June—can be picked until the end of September. A final sowing with a first early variety can be made in early July for picking in early October. It is necessary to cover these plants with cloches if early frosts occur. Cloches can also be used to protect very early sowings made in February. Use a first early, round-seeded variety such as 'Feltham First'. Picking should begin in early June. Seeds germinate at 5°C/39°F, but cold weather after germination and the resulting slow growth can lead to fungal and bacterial disease. Eighty per cent germination is normal. Dust the seeds with an animal repellent before sowing to deter mice.

Peas may be sown in single rows in a V-shaped drill or broadcast in an 8–10 in wide flat-bottomed drill. Experiments have shown that the best yields can be expected from lines of three drills 5 in apart, with 18 in between each group of drills. Space the peas 5 in apart in the drill, which should be 2 in deep. If sowing in a flat-bottomed drill, first make the drill with a broad-bladed draw hoe or with a spade. It should also be 2 in deep. Broadcast the seeds evenly in the drill so that they are about 3 in apart each way. Rake soil back into the drill and firm it lightly by tamping with the back of the rake. The distance between rows should be the same as the eventual height of the mature crops. This varies from 18 in for the dwarf, first early varieties to 4 ft for the later main crop types. These spaces can be used for catch crops of rapidly-maturing vegetables such as radishes early in the season. Birds may dig up the peas unless wire mesh guards are put over the rows of outdoor crops immediately after sowing.

Garden Peas

1 March until June. Use a draw hoe to make drills 2 in deep. Sow the seeds about 5 in apart in the bottom of the drill. For the distance between drills (18–48 in) check the mature height of the variety being grown.

2 March until June. Rake the soil back into the drill after sowing. Firm the soil down on to the seeds (previously soaked in paraffin) by lightly tamping with the back of the rake.

Protecting from birds

3 At the same time, put hoop-shaped, fine-meshed wire netting over the rows immediately after sowing to deter birds from digging up the seeds or eating newly emerged seedlings.

4 When the plants are 3–4 in tall erect the support system. Use a post and wire framework to support the netting up which the peas should climb.

Garden peas/Asparagus peas

Sugar peas and petit pois are sown in the same way but they reach heights of 4 ft and 3 ft respectively.

Growing Peas can be grown without supports but growth and yields are better if individual plants are able to climb and develop off the ground. The traditional method was to use pea sticks—twiggy pieces of hedge trimmings—pushed in alongside and within the rows. These sticks are now difficult to find and wire or nylon netting is more commonly used. Erect a post and wire framework along each row and attach an appropriate width of netting for the expected height of the peas. Put up the supports when the plants are 3–4 in tall.

Watering

Never allow peas to become too dry when they are in full bloom or when the pods are swelling. Too much water before flowering reduces the yield; water only in very dry spells. Mulching the plants with peat, straw or black polythene helps to reduce water loss and keep down weeds.

Harvesting

Picking of garden peas should begin about four weeks after full flower. Regular picking encourages more pods to develop. Pods at the base of the plant are ready first. The pods are the edible portion of sugar peas and it is vital that the peas inside them have not started to swell.

Petit pois must be harvested young or they lose their sweet, delicate flavour and become hard and unpalatable.

Cut down pea plants after harvesting and either put the roots on the compost heap or dig them into the soil, since their nitrogen content will improve its fertility.

Pests and diseases

Thrips (thunder flies) feed on the developing pods and give them a silvered appearance. Control with sprays of dimethoate. The major pest is pea moth. Eggs are laid in the flowers and the resulting larvae feed on the young peas in the developing pods. Crops flowering from mid-June to mid-August are most likely to be attacked. Spray with fenitrothion or permethrin, seven to ten days after flowering begins. Alternatively, avoid the problem by growing those varieties which flower outside the moth's egg-laying period.

Asparagus peas

The asparagus or winged pea is quite different from other garden peas. It is half-hardy and has a bushy habit. The red flowers produce 4-winged fruits, 1–1½ in long, which are eaten whole. In some tropical countries asparagus peas are grown as a fodder crop, but in Britain they are unusual and little grown.

Cultivation

Choose a light, well-drained soil in a sunny position on which to grow asparagus peas. Apply 1–2 oz per square yard of a general, balanced fertilizer, such as a proprietary brand of Growmore, a couple of weeks before sowing or planting the crop.

Sowing Asparagus peas will be killed by frost, so choose a sowing date which takes this into account. Sow outside in early May when the main danger of frost is over. Space the seeds 4–6 in apart in 1 in deep drills, which should be 12 in apart. Water the bottom of the drill before sowing to encourage germination. Alternatively, the seeds can be sown in small pots in a cold greenhouse in early April and planted out at the end of May.

Growing Hoe weeds from around developing plants. Keep them well supplied with water from flowering time onwards. Too much water in the early stages reduces the yield. Asparagus pea plants have a tendency to sprawl and they should be supported by small sticks so as to avoid soiled or bent pods.

Harvesting

It is important to pick the fruits young, when about 1 in long, because they soon become tough and fibrous.

Pests and diseases

Asparagus peas can be vulnerable to the same pests and diseases as garden peas. Control thrips (thunder flies) with dimethoate, but there is no need to take the same precautions against pea moth, as for garden peas.

Asparagus peas

5 A week or 10 days after the first flowers appear spray with fenitrothion or permethrin to combat pea moth. Crops flowering from mid-June to mid-August are most likely to be attacked.

6 Mid-June to October. Pick young and tender but well-filled pods. Regular harvesting encourages more pods to develop.

1 Early May. Sow the seed outside at 4–6 in intervals in the drill. In dry weather water the drill before sowing to aid germination.

2 When 2–3 in high, add stakes to support the plants.

3 Late July to early August. Pick asparagus peas when they are 1 in long, otherwise they soon become stringy and tough.

Sweetcorn

This half-hardy annual grows best in high temperatures and sunshine. Recently introduced varieties have made it a more suitable vegetable for temperate conditions. Male and female flowers are produced in different places on the same plant. Male flowers grow at the top of the plant whereas the female flowers—which develop into the sweetcorn cobs—are found lower down. Expect each plant to produce one or two cobs.

Cultivation

A light, well-drained and fertile soil of pH 5.5–7.0 is essential. Dig in a 2–3 in layer of bulky manure or garden compost during the winter. Avoid shaded sites but choose a sheltered position because the plants can be damaged by wind. Sweetcorn plants need plenty of food and water.

Apply 3–4 oz per square yard of a general fertilizer a couple of weeks before sowing or planting and be prepared to top-dress with 1–2 oz per square yard of nitro-chalk or a general liquid feed in June or July.

Sweetcorn-plants

Sowing Early sowings can be made under cloches at the end of April provided the cloches have been used to warm up the soil beforehand. Outdoor sowings should not take place until mid-May, because a soil temperature of 10°–13°C/50°–55°F is needed for rapid germination. Sow in 1 in deep drills. Place groups of two or three seeds at intervals along the rows, which should be arranged in a block rather than a strip. A block of plants allows wind pollination to take place more readily. Space dwarf plants 12 in apart in each direction, and taller plants 15–18 in apart. Thin to one plant per station after the seedlings emerge. Protect the plants against birds with black cotton.

Better results are obtained with transplanted crops. Sow chitted (pre-germinated) seeds into individual containers or peat pots in a slightly heated greenhouse during April. Maintain a temperature of 13°C/55°F to produce plants for putting out in late May. Harden off the plants for 3–4 days in a cold frame before planting. Take care not to damage the roots, for a check suffered at transplanting reduces yields.

Growing Hoe to keep down weeds but be careful not to damage the young plant stems. Keep the plants moist if dry spells occur. No watering is normally needed until the flowers (tassels) appear, when regular weekly applications of 3–4 gal per square yard (unless the weather is very wet) will improve the quality and yield. In windy positions stake the plants, but raising the soil around the stems is usually sufficient to keep the plants upright.

Harvesting

Pollen is produced from the male flowers from mid-July onwards and falls on to the female flowers. These soon begin to wither, and the cobs should be ready about a month later. The cobs should be firm and well filled and are ready when the silks have turned nearly black. Test maturity by pushing a fingernail into one of the grains. A creamy liquid indicates that the cob is ready. Twist the cobs off the plant and cook or freeze them immediately.

Harvesting

1 Winter. Dig a 2–3 in deep layer of manure or garden compost into the soil of a square plot.

2 April. Scatter seeds on to the surface of a layer of moistened tissue in a container. Place the closed container in a warm place.

3 Two or three days later, sow each seed in individual 3 in peat pots. Keep in a slightly heated greenhouse. Harden off the plants for 3–4 days before planting.

4 Late May. Plant sweetcorn plants in a block 12–18 in apart each way (according to variety). Water regularly after the flowers appear.

5 August. When the silks have withered press a fingernail into 1 of the grains underneath the protective leaves on each cob.

6 If the pressed grain exudes a creamy-white liquid harvest the cobs with a twisting, downward movement away from the plant stem.

Onions 1

ONIONS

AUTUMN-SOWN
'Express Yellow',
'Kaizuka Extra Early', 'Yellow
Globe'.

SPRING-SOWN
'Ailsa Craig', 'Bedfordshire
Champion', 'Hygro', 'Wijbo'.

ONION SETS
'Sturon', 'Stuttgarter Giant'.

PICKLING ONIONS
'Paris Silverskin', 'The Queen'.

SALAD (SPRING) ONIONS
'White Lisbon', 'Winter Hardy'.

The onion is a biennial plant which is grown as an annual. The familiar bulbs are formed from swollen leaf bases. Salad onions (spring onions) are grown for the immature plants and should not produce bulbs.

Cultivation

Onions are easily grown from seed, and the bulb crop may also be grown from sets or be transplanted. Sowings can be made outdoors in February and March, or under glass in January, to mature in late summer and autumn. Sowings made outdoors in August and over-wintered are ready the following summer. Sets planted in March to April mature in August. Sow salad onions in the spring for summer and autumn use, and in July and August for use the following spring. Onion seed germinates very slowly and seedling growth is also slow.

Soil and situation The soil for onion growing should be well drained, reasonably fertile but not freshly manured. The pH should be more than 6.5. Choose a sunny but sheltered site. Soil-borne problems such as stem eelworm and white rot can be serious, so do not grow onions on the same ground each year.

Double dig the land in early winter, working a 2–3 in layer of bulky organic material into the lower spit. Leave the surface rough to allow it to break down naturally during the winter. Spring-sown and planted bulb onions (including sets) should be given a base fertilizer which contains about twice as much potash as nitrogen. Apply 2–3 oz per square yard of such a compound 7–10 days before sowing. Autumn-sown bulb onions do not require fertilizer at sowing time but give them a top dressing of 1–2 oz per square yard of nitro-chalk in February.

Spring-sown crops

Onion seed germinates at temperatures of 7°C/45°F and above. In cold areas it is best to raise seedlings under glass. Sow in January for planting out in April. Sow in February under cloches, and in March in the open. The seedbed is most important. Digging in early winter should ensure that the soil is friable and breaks down easily. Work it down with a cultivator and rake it into a fine tilth, then make it firm and level. Be careful on silt or clay soils, where very fine tilths "cap" over if wet conditions are followed by drying

weather (see page 15). The young seedlings can find it difficult to penetrate the capped surface. Sow the seed thinly in drills 9–12 in apart and ½ in deep. Water the drill gently if the soil is dry. Thin to 2–3 in between seedlings as soon as they have straightened up.

During the summer onions should be kept free from weeds. Additional watering is not usually required except in very dry weather in spring or early summer when applications of 2 gal per 10 ft run may be given each week. Further feeding is unnecessary. As the bulbs approach maturity in mid to late August or September, their leaves begin to yellow and topple over. In wet seasons this may be delayed, and the tops should be bent over by hand to assist the ripening of the bulbs. The leaves of some plants in a row may remain standing and these bulbs often have a wide neck (bull necks). Do not attempt to keep these bulbs as they soon rot in store.

August-sown crops

Onions sown in autumn mature from late June to July, slightly earlier than crops sown in spring. The sowing dates for over-wintering varieties are fairly critical because it is import-

ant to obtain young onions of a reasonable size to withstand the winter, but they should not be so large that they go to seed instead of forming bulbs when growth begins again the following spring. The seed should be sown during August or September in the same way as for spring-sown onions. Onion seed does not germinate well above 24°C/75°F, so in hot weather germination may be erratic. Pre-germination of the seeds at lower temperatures or lowering the soil temperature of the seedbed by frequent light waterings may be necessary in some seasons. It is also useful to prepare the seedbed for August-sown onions about ten days before sowing. This cuts down attacks by bean seed fly which may be troublesome in freshly prepared seedbeds during summer.

If the seed has been sown thinly the young onions should be left to over-winter and thinned to 1½–2 in (3 in for larger onions) in spring (March to April) as growth begins. A top dressing of 1–2 oz per square yard of nitro-chalk or a balanced general fertilizer should be gently hoed in around the young onions after thinning. Autumn-sown onions, particularly the Japanese varieties, should not be

Spring-sown onions

1 February to early March. Apply a balanced general fertilizer at a rate of 2–3 oz per square yard 7–10 days before sowing. Rake it in and tread the soil down to produce a firm seedbed with a fine tilth.

2 Late February to mid-March. Draw out drills 9–12 in apart and ½ in deep. Water the drills if the soil is dry. Sow the seed thinly.

3 April. As soon as the seedlings have straightened up thin them to 1–2 in apart, or 3 in apart if large onions are required. Treat the rows with diazinon granules against onion fly.

4 May to July. Keep the developing onions free from weeds. In very dry weather water at a rate of 2 gal per 10 ft run each week.

Onions 2

transplanted as transplants are liable to bolt.

Spring and summer cultivation is then as for spring-sown onions. Japanese varieties mature in late June, more traditional varieties such as 'Ailsa Craig' in July to August.

Less common onions

A number of other *Allium* species, grown mainly for their curiosity value or in the herb garden, are also excellent for eating and easily cultivated. The tree onion is a perennial plant which forms normal clumps of bulbs at ground level but also sends up tall stems bearing clusters of small onions instead of flowers. These may be used in cooking or to increase the stock by using them as sets. Easily grown on any well-drained soil and providing crops for several years without complications.

The Welsh onion is also a perennial plant and it is a useful winter or spring substitute for the more conventional spring onions. The potato onion, which forms a number of mild-flavoured offsets just below soil level, can do duty for shallots. All are easily grown, providing useful and unusual space-fillers in a small garden.

Pests and diseases

Female onion flies lay their eggs around the bases of young onion plants in late May. They hatch into larvae which tunnel into the developing bulbs, causing the whole plant to turn yellow and die. Young plants must be protected before the larvae attack. Treat the rows with diazinon granules or dust the seedlings with pirimithos-methyl. Stem eelworm causes twisting and thickening of the onion plant. Bulbs become infested and should not be stored. The pest remains in the soil from year to year, so rotate the onion bed around the vegetable garden (see page 32).

Downy mildew can be particularly bad in wet seasons. Grey patches appear on the leaves and turn purple as the disease progresses. Eventually the leaves topple over and collapse. Spray with mancozeb at the first sign of trouble. White rot is another soil-borne problem—this time a fungus. Onions and related crops are attacked. A grey-white growth appears on the basal roots and the leaves turn yellow. Dig up infected plants and do not grow onions on that soil again for 7–8 years. Dust the seed drills with calomel or benomyl to combat white rot.

TRANSPLANTED ONIONS

Early onions and those intended for showing should be transplanted. Sow the seed in trays during January in a heated greenhouse. Keep them at a temperature of 16°C/60°F. Germination is slow, but when the seedlings are large enough to handle they can be pricked out. For exhibition purposes grow each plant in a 3½ in pot containing a proprietary potting compost. For general garden purposes prick out the onion seedlings individually into peat pots or into a seed tray, spacing them 2 in apart each way.

Gradually reduce the greenhouse temperature to 10°C/50°F and harden off the plants in a cold frame or under a cloche for a few days before planting. Plant during early April in rows 12–15 in apart. Space the onions 2–3 in apart in the row. Plant shallowly with a trowel—deep planting hinders bulb development. Water thoroughly after planting.

---

5 Late August to early September. If the leaves have not toppled over naturally by this time, which sometimes happens in wet weather, bend them over by hand to assist ripening.

6 September. Lift the bulbs for drying and storing when the fallen tops have begun to yellow and become brittle.

Autumn-sown onions

1 August to September. Prepare the ground and sow as for spring-sown onions, but do not thin the plants.

2 March to April. Thin the young plants to 1½–2 in apart, 3 in if large onions are required. Top-dress with 1–2 oz per square yard of balanced general fertilizer or nitro-chalk after thinning.

Onions 3

Onion sets

Sets are partly developed onion bulbs. They are stored during winter and replanted in the spring, when they grow away rapidly. Sets are particularly useful for growing onions in places with short growing seasons such as northern Britain. Consistently higher yields are possible from sets or bought-in plants. As the sets have to be bought, it is more expens-ive to grow onions this way. This expense can be avoided by saving some onions from the previous season. The best sets are $\frac{3}{4}$ in in diameter and firm. It is also sensible to buy small sets of this size because they are less likely to bolt than larger bulbs and cheaper per plant.

Planting onion sets

Plant them in late March or early April into a fine tilth. Mark out rows 10 in apart with a garden line and push the sets into the ground at 2–3 in intervals, or at 4 in intervals if larger bulbs are required. There is no point in using the wider spacings sometimes recom-mended because the yield from a given area will be much reduced. Only the nose of each bulb should be visible. Firm the soil around the sets.

Birds may pull up the sets and prolonged frosty weather may also lift them out of the ground. In either case, they should be re-planted immediately.

The remaining cultural operations of water-ing, weed control and harvesting (see pages 60 and 61) are as for spring-sown or trans-planted bulb onions.

SALAD ONIONS

Salad onions, or spring onions, are im-mature onion plants. They are grown close together and eaten as a salad vegetable when the bulb is $\frac{1}{2}$–1 in across. Many of their requirements are the same as for bulb onions. The earliest salad onions are ready in the spring from sowings made at the end of the previous August. Continuity through the summer is then maintained from successive sowings made at two-week intervals from mid-February until mid-June. Salad onions are grown close together in rows 4 in apart to prevent bulbs from developing. Sow the seed reasonably thinly in $\frac{1}{2}$ in drills. The drills should be watered before sowing if the soil is dry. The plants should grow $\frac{1}{2}$–1 in apart in the rows. Pull salad onions before the bases swell. It helps to water them before pulling from dry soils.

1 February to June, every 2 weeks make sowings in $\frac{1}{2}$ in deep drills 4 in apart.

2 Summer. Lift the immature onions with a fork as the bases swell.

RIPENING AND STORAGE

1 July to September. After lifting place the bulbs outside during dry sunny weather to dry and ripen further.

2 In wet weather arrange the bulbs in a single layer under a cloche or frame, or in a shed.

3 Turn the bulbs regularly to prevent diseases developing on the damp skins and wait 3–4 weeks for complete drying.

4 Store well-dried onions in trays with slatted bases and raised corners for good circulation and easy inspection.

Shallots/Garlic

Shallots have a milder flavour than bulb onions and are sometimes grown in preference to onions in smaller gardens, because they keep better and are more easily grown. They are grown from small bulbs (offsets) saved from the previous year's crop. Each newly planted bulb produces a cluster of 8–12 daughter bulbs by the end of the season.

Cultivation

Soil and fertilizer requirements are the same as for spring-sown or planted bulb onions (see page 60). Early planting is very important for shallots, so dig the land as soon as it becomes available.

Planting Save sound, firm bulbs from the previous season, or buy sets. Small bulbs of about $\frac{1}{3}$ oz weight (50 to the pound) are best to obtain maximum yield. Plant the bulbs in mid-February; space them 6 in apart in rows which are 8 in apart. Larger bulbs should be spaced 6 in apart with 12 in between the rows. Push the bulbs into the ground so that only the tips show above the soil surface. Alternatively, the bulbs can be planted in a shallow drill and then covered and firmed. Birds or frost can lift the bulbs out of the soil and it is important to replant them immediately if this happens.

Weeds can be a problem, especially while the crop is young. Hoe carefully around the clusters, but do not damage the developing bulbs or they will not keep. Do not water unless the weather is very dry. Shallots suffer from the same pests and diseases as do onions (see page 61).

Shallots are ready for harvesting earlier than are spring-planted onions. They should be ready in July, and the bulbs will begin to ripen about three weeks before that. Draw away the soil from around the bulbs to encourage quicker ripening.

Harvesting

Dig up the clusters of bulbs when the leaves turn yellow. Separate them into individual bulbs and, in fine weather, leave them on the soil to dry off; dry them under protection in wet weather.

Remove soil and any loose, dry leaves from the ripened bulbs before storing them in nets in a cool, but frost-free place.

Shallots

1 February. Push the bulbs into the ground so that their tops are just visible. Space them 6 in apart in rows 8 in apart.

2 March to June/July. Use a small onion hoe to keep the developing plants weed-free at all times. Remove any difficult weeds by hand.

3 June or July. Remove soil from around the clumps of onions by hand to speed up the ripening process.

GARLIC

Garlic is a member of the onion family. Because of its strong flavour it is used sparingly in cooking. The plant is a perennial with long flat leaves and attractive white flowers. It can be grown in the open, in a pot or window-box, or in a cold greenhouse for early crops. The soil must be rich, moist and well drained.

Garlic grows best in a sunny position, because high temperatures are needed to ripen the bulbs. Before planting prepare the ground as for onion growing. Garlic seed is not readily available and so it is usually grown from bulb segments (cloves) saved from a previous crop or bought from a greengrocer. They are planted in February or March. Split a bulb into cloves. Plant them 1 in deep and 4 in apart with their pointed ends upwards. The rows should be 6–8 in apart. Do not press the cloves into the soil because this inhibits root development. Weed between the young bulbs with an onion hoe.

In late summer the stems and leaves begin to yellow and bend over. Loosen the bulbs gently out of the ground with a fork. Leave the bulbs on the soil surface to dry and ripen off in the sun. Do not handle the bulbs roughly because this may damage their necks and encourage rotting. Store well-dried bulbs of garlic in string bags in a cool but frost-free shed.

4 July onwards. Lift shallots when the leaves turn yellow. Remove soil from around the roots and rub off loose leaves.

5 At the same time, save small bulbs of about $\frac{1}{3}$ oz in weight for next year's propagation material.

6 In fine weather, leave the bulbs in rows in the garden to dry out. In wet weather dry them under protection.

EARLY
'Early Market' 'Lyon-Prizetaker'.

MID-SEASON
'Musselburgh',
'Walton Mammoth'.

LATE
'Royal Favourite', 'Winter
Crop' (very hardy).

Leeks

Leeks are biennial plants grown as annuals. The stem-like collection of rolled leaves is eaten. Leeks have a long growing season and mature from September until May. They are winter-hardy and will tolerate very severe conditions. Leeks grow best in fertile, well drained soils of pH 6.5–7.5. Although they will tolerate slightly more acid or alkaline conditions, they do not thrive in heavy soils which remain wet in winter. Dig the soil well because they must be planted deeply or earthed up to produce the blanched appearance. The ground should be dug well during the winter before planting. Incorporate a 2–3 in layer of bulky organic manure or well-rotted garden compost. Do not give so much fertilizer that the plants become too lush and incapable of standing through frosty winter conditions. Apply 2–3 oz per square yard of a well-balanced compound fertilizer, such as a proprietary brand of Growmore, one or two weeks before planting.

Sowing and planting The germination and early growth of leeks are slow. The seeds need a soil temperature of at least 7°C/45°F to germinate. It is best to transplant leeks, using plants raised under cloches or in a heated greenhouse or purchased from a garden centre.

For early crops, sow in a seed tray in late January to early February in a greenhouse kept at 13°C/55°F. Prick out into other trays when the leaves have straightened up, spacing the seedlings 2 in apart each way. Maintain the temperature until hardening off the plants in a cold frame during March. Plant in late April.

Main crop leeks are sown outside in March to April for transplanting during late May or June. Sow the seed thinly in drills ½ in deep and in rows 6 in apart. June sowings, transplanted in July, produce crops the following spring. Plants can also be raised under cloches.

Planting Leek plants should be planted out when pencil-thick and 6–8 in high. Plant in rows 12 in apart. Make 2 in wide, 6 in deep holes with a dibber at 6 in intervals. After putting a seedling into the hole, do not replace the soil but fill each hole with water. This will settle sufficient soil around the roots.

Alternatively, leeks can be planted on the flat or in 2 in deep trenches and blanched by progressively drawing up soil around the plants during the growing season. Hoe off any weeds with an onion hoe. Water the plants only in very dry conditions, when 2 gal of water per 10 ft row should be applied weekly. Mulch crops grown on dry soils. On poor soils liquid fertilizer can be used, but do not apply fertilizer to leeks late in the summer because soft growth prone to frost damage will be produced. Leeks are relatively free from pests and diseases.

Harvesting
Early varieties are ready before Christmas but most leeks are harvested in mid-winter and spring. Lift them as required using a fork. Leeks are very hardy and they will remain usable until May.

PLANTING ON THE FLAT

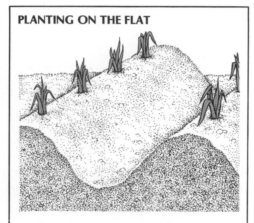

Blanched stems are produced when leeks are planted in holes, as described on the left, but longer white stems can be obtained if plants are earthed up. Plant the leeks 6 in apart in rows 12 in apart. Make holes 2–3 in deep and firm the soil around the base of each plant. Gradually draw up soil around the plants as they develop. Cardboard or paper collars may be tied around them to prevent soil getting into the plant centres.

Continue earthing up until November, when only the tops of the leaves should show above the soil.

Sowing

1 Late March to mid-April. Prepare a seedbed. Sow the seeds thinly in ½ in deep drills 6 in apart.

2 Early May. Thin the seedlings to ½–1 in apart. Firm the soil around the bases of the remaining seedlings.

Planting

3 Late May to early June. Make 6 in deep holes, with a dibber, every 6 in in rows 12 in apart. Drop 1 plant into each. Fill with water.

4 June until harvest. Mulch the crop once the seedlings are established. Water in dry spells.

5 November until April. Lift leeks as required with a fork. Trim off the roots and tips of the leaves. They are very hardy.

Carrots

SHORT
'Amsterdam Forcing', 'Nantes', 'Paris Forcing'.

INTERMEDIATE
'Autumn King', 'Chantenay Red-cored', 'Red Intermediate'.

LONG
'St Valery', 'Scarlet Perfection'.

Carrots are hardy biennial plants grown as annuals for their tasty roots. The long-rooted and intermediate varieties are mainly stored for use during the winter months, but successive sowings of short-rooted varieties produce bunching carrots in 10–12 weeks for use in summer salads from late spring to autumn. A 10 ft row of main crop carrots can yield 10–12 lb, depending on the variety.

Cultivation

Long-rooted varieties need a deep soil but short-rooted varieties are suitable for shallow soils and will grow in heavy conditions.

Soil and situation The ideal soil has a pH between 6.5 and 7.5, is well-drained, stone-free and of medium texture. It should not have been manured for at least a year before sowing. Thorough, deep winter digging is important. An application of balanced general fertilizer at 2–3 oz per square yard about a week before sowing will maintain fertility. Choose an open situation for carrots.

Watering If deprived of water carrots become woody and coarse. In dry weather apply water at a rate of 2 gal per square yard at weekly intervals. If the plants become too wet as a result of applications of water in rainy weather, the development of foliage as opposed to roots is encouraged.

Early carrots In February or March, sow short varieties under cloches or in frames in $\frac{1}{2}-\frac{3}{4}$ in deep drills, 6 in apart. Always sow carrot seeds very thinly and thin the seedlings to $1\frac{1}{2}-2$ in intervals when they emerge. Young carrots mature from mid-May onwards for use in summer salads.

Alternatively, sow the seed outdoors every three to four weeks from March to August. These carrots are ready from June until November. Cover the later crops with cloches from September onwards.

Main crop carrots From April to June, sow intermediate or long varieties very thinly in $\frac{1}{2}-\frac{3}{4}$ in deep drills, with 6 in between the rows. These mature from August to October.

Hoe between the rows, and as soon as the first rough leaves appear, thin the seedlings until the distance between the plants is 2 in for short-, medium- and long-rooted varieties. Water the plants to re-firm them after thinning. The thinnings from larger varieties of carrots can be eaten.

Carrot flies are attracted by the smell of crushed foliage. The females lay eggs around the plants and the resulting larvae eat the roots. Attacks can be minimized by thinning the carrots late in the evening, removing the thinnings and watering afterwards.

Harvesting

Start pulling the early sowings by hand as soon as they are big enough to eat. Young tender roots are the sweetest. Gently ease up carrots for storage, with a fork, in October. Reject any that are unhealthy or damaged.

Remove the soil and foliage from carrots before storing them.

Storing Healthy carrots will last until March or April of the following year if they are stored properly in the right conditions. In particularly favourable districts they can be left in the ground and lifted as they are required. Protect them from severe frost with a covering of straw or similar material.

Pests and diseases

A reddish-brown discoloration of the foliage is often a symptom of carrot fly attack. Drench early crops in May or June and main crops in July or August with a pirimiphos-methyl-based insecticide. Alternatively, apply diazinon granules at sowing time. Spray greenfly with derris or malathion.

1 Winter. Dig the soil early so that a crumbly tilth develops. In spring apply fertilizer at 2–3 oz per square yard.

2 March onwards. Prepare a fine tilth. Sow the seed in $\frac{1}{2}-\frac{3}{4}$ in deep drills 6 in apart. Cover the drills.

3 Thin the seedlings regularly after the first rough leaf appears to 2 in for short-, medium- and long-rooted varieties.

4 Water and firm the rows after thinning. Do not leave thinnings lying about. Hoe between the rows.

5 Throughout the summer. Pull early sowings by hand while they are young and tender.

6 October. Leave carrots in the ground where they have been grown but protect them from frost with a covering of straw.

7 Alternatively, dig up carrots required for indoor storing with a fork. Select healthy roots only and twist off the foliage.

8 Pack the roots in boxes of dry sand, keeping individual roots apart, and store them in a cool frost-free place.

Parsnips

Parsnips are hardy biennial plants grown as annuals for the production of their edible roots. They have a long growing season and are among the first crops to be sown and the last to be harvested.

Cultivation

Parsnips need a well-drained soil of medium texture which must not have been manured for at least a year before sowing. Parsnips have a low nitrogen requirement, take care not to over-manure and do not use nitrogen-rich fertilizers. Avoid stony soil. The best soil is slightly acid or neutral (pH 6.5–7.0) and the best position is open and sunny, although parsnips will tolerate a lightly shaded spot. Deep digging in the winter is essential because parsnips often root down to a depth of 2 ft. Dig the soil one spade deep and if the layer below is too packed for the feeding roots to penetrate easily, loosen it up with a fork. Such

deep digging is not really necessary for short varieties, such as 'Avonresister', however. One to two weeks before sowing apply a balanced general fertilizer such as a brand of Growmore to the soil at 2 oz per square yard.

Sowing Sow parsnip seed in late February or early March, but avoid cold wet weather. A soil temperature of 7°C/45°F is needed. Always use fresh seed because older parsnip seed rapidly loses its ability to germinate. Even with fresh seed, the germination rate is low. Seedlings take up to four weeks to emerge in cold weather, though the normal period is seven to ten days. Take out $\frac{1}{2}$–$\frac{3}{4}$ in deep drills. Keep a 12 in distance between rows for large-rooted varieties. If the soil is dry, water the drill before sowing. Sow the seeds in groups of three or four, with 6 in spacings between groups. Small-rooted varieties should be sown 3 in apart with 8 in between rows.

When the seedlings have their first true leaves carefully remove all but the strongest plant in each group. Weed between the seedlings by hand in the early stages. Carefully hoe between the plants later. If the shoulders of young plants are damaged, parsnip canker or other diseases may enter.

Never allow the soil to dry out. If the soil becomes dry and is then dampened by rain or watering, the parsnips often split. Water at a rate of 2 gal per square yard per week.

Harvesting

Lifting may begin when the foliage begins to die down, usually in late autumn or early winter. Use a fork to dig along the side of the row so as to lift the parsnips without breaking the roots.

Storing Leave parsnips in the ground throughout the winter and lift the roots as required. Frost is said to improve their flavour, although

it is difficult to lift them in a severe winter. Parsnips can be stored in the same way as carrots (see page 65), but they tend to go soft. The remainder of the crop left in the ground can be lifted in March to make way for subsequent vegetables.

Pests and diseases

Young seedlings should be protected from carrot fly. Sprinkle diazinon or bromophos along the row or spray with pirimiphos-methyl when the seedlings are about 2–3 in high.

Parsnip canker develops in the crown of the plants and causes the roots to rot. There is no chemical control—prevention is the only answer—but the variety 'Avonresister' is resistant to the disease. Premature sowing, lime deficient soils and damage to roots by carrot fly larvae or careless hoeing are all likely to encourage the disease and weak or damaged roots are more vulnerable.

EXHIBITION PARSNIPS

For long straight roots prepare the soil well and use a crowbar to make holes 3 ft deep and 6 in in diameter. Fill these conical holes with fine soil or potting compost and sow the seed in the usual way as early as possible. Throughout the growing season weed by hand and mulch with peat or black polythene to retain moisture.

Water regularly, especially when dry weather is forecast, to prevent any cracking of the long roots. Lift them as near as possible to the showing date. Remove the rootlets and cut off the tops. Protect exhibition parsnips from damage by wrapping them in damp cloth.

1 December. Dig the soil 1 spit deep. If the layer below is compacted break it up with a fork.

4 When the first true leaves appear thin the seedlings to leave the strongest plant at each station.

2 Late February. Apply fertilizer at 2 oz per square yard 1–2 weeks before sowing. Apply diazinon against carrot fly.

5 Throughout the summer. Water frequently and hoe weeds regularly, taking care not to damage the shoulders of young plants.

3 Late February–early March. Sow 3–4 seeds at 6 in intervals (3 in for small varieties) in $\frac{1}{2}$–$\frac{3}{4}$ in deep drills 12 in (8 in) apart.

6 Late autumn onwards. When the foliage dies down lift parsnips as needed, using a fork to loosen the surrounding soil.

Turnips and swedes 1

TURNIPS
SUMMER
'Jersey Navet', 'Snowball',
'Tokyo Cross'.

WINTER
'Golden Ball' (very hardy),
'Manchester Market'.

SWEDES
'Bronze Top', 'Chignecto'
(club-root resistant),
'Purple Top'.

Turnips and swedes are biennials grown mainly for their edible roots. Swedes are usually grown as a crop for winter harvesting, but turnips may be eaten all the year round. The young leaves or "turnip tops" are cut in March and April for use as a green vegetable and the roots may be eaten, either young or mature, for most of the year.

Cultivation
Turnips and swedes are brassicas and have broadly similar requirements to cabbages and Brussels sprouts.

Soil and situation They thrive in light, well-drained, firm soils of pH 6.0–7.0, rich in humus and water-retentive during the growing season. Main crop turnips and swedes require much the same methods of cultivation, although sowing dates and plant spacings differ. Soil preparation is identical and both crops are thinned in the seed rows to the appropriate distance and not transplanted.

The roots fork if they are grown in soil that has received dressings of fresh manure and so a site well manured for a previous crop should be used if possible. The site is dug over and prepared as a seedbed. Before sowing rake in a dressing of balanced general fertilizer at 3 oz per square yard to improve fertility. Then apply calomel dust to combat club-root, and bromophos or diazinon to control cabbage root fly.

Watering The size and quality of both turnips and swedes are improved if ample water is available. If they are allowed to become dry at any stage the roots are likely to become woody and less palatable. Experimental work has shown that applications of 2 gal per square yard of water each week in dry weather increase both yield and quality, although flavour is slightly reduced.

Pests and diseases
Turnips and swedes, like other brassicas, are attacked by cabbage root fly, and flea beetle, turnip gall weevil and aphids (with virus as a consequence) may also be troublesome. Swedes are less mildew-resistant than turnips.

Turnips
Turnips are fast-growing and are ready to eat 6–12 weeks after sowing. They germinate within a few days and must never become crowded in the rows. Thinning should take place as soon as possible when the first rough, true leaves appear (at about 1 in high) or the roots will not develop satisfactorily.

The main crop is sown in July or early August for winter use but earlier sowings from February (under cloches) onwards may be made, using early varieties. As these can be used in 6 or 8 weeks from sowing, when they are 1½–2 in in diameter, they are excellent for intercropping. Late sowings in September of winter types will also provide turnip tops as spring greens in March or April.

Swedes
Swedes have a sweeter taste than turnips and they are mainly grown for winter use, although immature swedes pulled in late summer make excellent eating. They should never be allowed to develop to the huge size of field-grown crops, which are often woody and more fitted for cattle than human consumption. They are slower to mature than turnips, taking 20–24 weeks from seed to develop fully, but are hardier and can be dug as required during the winter rather than stored. Cultivation is as for main crop turnips but swedes are sown from mid-May (cold areas) to mid-June in drills 15 in apart and they are finally thinned to 9 in apart in the rows.

PESTS AND DISEASES

Pests	Means of control
Aphids (and viruses)	Dimethoate/heptenophas
Cabbage root fly	Bromophos/diazinon
Flea beetle	Gamma HCH
Gall weevil	Gamma HCH

Diseases	Means of control
Brown heart	Boron (applied as borax)
Club-root	Calomel dust
Mildew	Benomyl

EARLY BUNCHING TURNIPS

Bunched turnips are a good salad or early summer cooked vegetable. They must grow quickly with ample supplies of water. Dig the soil early in the autumn and cover the ground with cloches for 2–3 weeks before sowing the earliest crops which are protected. Prepare a fine seedbed and apply calomel dust against club-root and bromophos or diazinon against cabbage root fly. Then sow short-leaved, early varieties from February onwards, at two week intervals for a succession. Mark out the ground into a 5 in crossed pattern with a stick, making the marks ½ in deep. Sow 2–3 seeds where the marks cross. Alternatively, sow the seed thinly in ½ in drills 12 in apart. Thin out the squared system to leave one plant per station. Row crops should be thinned to 4 in apart. Hoe very carefully in the early stages and never allow the soil to dry out.

Harvesting The roots are pulled like radishes. The first sowings mature during May when the roots are 2 in in diameter.

1 March. Thin grid-sown turnips to one plant per station. Thin row crops to 4 in apart at the same stage.

2 May. Pull the plants up by the leaves when the roots are 2 in in diameter.

Main crop turnips

1 July. Rake in 3 oz per square yard of fertilizer to the prepared seedbed and apply calomel dust, and bromophos or diazinon.

2 Mid-July to early August. Water the seedbed the day before sowing. Draw out drills ½–¾ in deep and 12 in apart. If the soil is dry, dribble water into the drills and allow it to drain away.

Turnips and swedes 2

3 Then, sow the seed very thinly, cover, firm and gently rake over the soil.

4 Late July or August. Thin the seedlings to 3 in apart as soon as they produce their first rough leaves when about 1 in high. Water them if the weather is dry.

5 Dust the seedlings with gamma HCH to combat flea beetle and turnip gall weevil.

6 August to September. Thin to 6 in apart as soon as the leaves of adjacent seedlings touch within the rows. Firm back the soil after thinning.

7 Keep the rows free of weeds. In dry weather water at a rate of 2 gal per square yard each week.

8 Winter. Lift as needed in mild areas. In cold areas lift the roots carefully in late autumn when the leaves have turned yellow. Store them in boxes of sand, peat or dry soil in a frost-free shed.

SWEDE SHOOTS AS GREENS

The roots of swedes lifted in mid-winter, if trimmed and packed closely in boxes of peat or soil and then placed in a garage or shed in semi-darkness, will sprout to produce nutritious, partly blanched growth that can be eaten like turnip tops.

TURNIP TOPS AS SPRING GREENS

In September sow the seed of winter varieties thinly in rows 3 in apart. Leave over winter without thinning. Cut the young leaves in March or April when they are 4–6 in high. If cut frequently they re-sprout several times.

Beetroot

GLOBULAR
'Boltardy' (bolt resistant),
'Crimson Globe', 'Detroit'.

LONG
'Cheltenham Green Top',
'Dobies Purple'.

Beetroots are biennial plants which are grown *as* annuals for their edible swollen roots. They usually have red flesh and the root shape may be round or long and tapering. Beetroots are good for intercropping as a useful catch crop; small beets mature in about 12 weeks.

Cultivation

Beetroot is in season from May or early June and throughout the winter.

Soil and situation Do not grow beetroot on freshly manured ground. Early crops can only be grown on well-drained, fertile soils, prepared in early spring, but autumn-maturing crops will tolerate heavier conditions. Beetroot grows best in soil with a pH of 6.5–7.5. A balanced fertilizer applied at 2–3 oz per square yard is sufficient to maintain growth. An open, shade-free site is preferable.

Sowing Beetroot "seeds" are actually fruits with two or three seeds contained within a cork-like pellet. They do not germinate well below 7°C/45°F, therefore warm spring weather is needed for early crops. To improve germination, soak the seeds for an hour or place them under running water before sowing.

Early crop In late February or early March, space-sow two or three seeds of round, bolt-resistant varieties at 4 in intervals under cloches or frames in rows 7 in apart. For outdoor sowing, the seeds are sown at the same spacing but from late March to early April. The plants are thinned to one per station.

Main crop In May and June, space-sow two or three seeds of round or long varieties outdoors at 4–6 in intervals (depending on the type of beetroot) in rows 12 in apart.

Over-wintered beet In late June and July, sow two or three seeds of suitable round varieties at 3 in intervals in rows 12 in apart.

Watering In hot dry weather, water the plants at the rate of 2 gal per square yard each week, to maintain succulent, juicy growth. Give no more than this, however, because an excess of water may result in much leaf at the expense of root. Use black cotton to keep sparrows off the seedlings.

Hoe around the developing roots with a short-handled hoe. Damaged roots bleed readily so great care is needed.

Harvesting

Round varieties can be pulled as soon as they are large enough. Early sowings are ready from May to July. The main crop matures in August and should be lifted for use or stored.

Lift the young roots and twist off the leaves. Store sound, disease-free roots in boxes of peat, sand or sawdust in a frost-free building. Distinct white concentric rings in the flesh when the roots are cut is a sign of old age. Inspect stored crops regularly and remove any old or diseased roots.

Round, late-sown beetroot is ready from October and in favourable locations this crop can be left in the ground during winter, if protected against frost with a covering of straw or similar material.

Main crop beetroot

1 May or June. Apply a balanced general fertilizer at 2–3 oz per square yard to the prepared seedbed.

2 May or June. Soak the seeds of round or long varieties in water for an hour before sowing to improve germination.

3 Space-sow 2–3 seeds at 4–6 in intervals (depending on variety) in 2 in deep rows, 12 in apart. Water with liquid gamma HCH.

4 At the first true leaf stage thin to leave a single seedling at each station.

5 Hoe very carefully around the developing plants with a short-handled hoe and water at 2 gal per square yard in dry weather.

6 August. Gently lift main crop beetroot with a fork when the roots are large enough to eat. Use immediately or store.

7 For storing, cut off the leaves to 1–2 in above each crown and remove dead or decaying leaves.

8 Arrange the beetroots in a box of sand. The roots should not touch. Keep the box in a cool frost-free place.

Radishes

SUMMER
'Cherry Belle', 'Wood's Early Frame',
'French Breakfast', 'Icicle',
'Red Forcing', 'Scarlet Globe'.

WINTER
'Black Spanish', 'Chinese Rose'.

Radishes are most commonly grown for use in salads but some varieties have much longer roots and these are cooked as a winter vegetable. Salad radishes have red, or red and white, skins and globular or cylindrical roots, whereas winter radishes have white, black or pink skins.

Cultivation
Both radish crops grow quickly and they are often grown as a catch crop.

Soil and situation All radishes require a fairly rich and well-drained, but not freshly manured, soil to grow well. The soil must retain enough moisture to ensure rapid uninterrupted growth but too much moisture, or fertilizer, results in excessive leaf growth. Apply 1 oz per square yard of a balanced general fertilizer before each sowing.

An open situation is preferable for early and late sowings but sowings from June to August should be made in a slight shade between other crops.

Spring and summer radishes
The earliest salad radishes come from sowings made under cloches or frames in January and February. Successive outside sowings, without protection, can start in March and continue until August or September at two week intervals. Radishes are attacked by flea beetles and cabbage root fly. Apply diazinon and gamma HCH to the drills before sowing as a deterrent.

Sow the seed thinly in $\frac{1}{2}-\frac{3}{4}$ in deep drills which are 4–6 in apart. Alternatively, broadcast the seed on to the prepared seedbed and rake it in lightly. When the seedlings emerge, thin, if necessary, until they are 1 in apart.

Keep the roots moist at all times. Dry, hot weather encourages hot-tasting radishes and during such periods apply water each week at the rate of 2 gal per square yard.

Winter radishes
Winter radishes are often 12 in long so a deep, friable soil is required. No fertilizer is needed when winter radishes are grown immediately after another crop, but on poor soils a general fertilizer should be raked in at a rate of 1 oz per square yard before sowing. Sow winter radishes in July or August.

Take out $\frac{1}{2}-\frac{3}{4}$ in deep drills 12 in apart, and before sowing apply diazinon and gamma HCH. Sow the seed very thinly and when the seedlings are big enough to handle thin until they are 6 in apart. Alternatively, the seed can be space-sown in groups of 3–4 at 6 in intervals and thinned to one per station.

The rapid growth of this crop means that it shades out weeds, except in the very early stages when careful hoeing is necessary. Regular watering in dry weather is important.

Harvesting
Pull spring and summer radishes when the roots are about $\frac{3}{4}$ in in diameter and they are firm and crunchy. Over-mature roots are hollow and unpalatable. The time taken to mature varies from 6–8 weeks at the end of the season to 3–4 weeks in midsummer.

Winter radishes are ready within 10–12 weeks of sowing. Lift them in late October, and store in boxes of dry sand for use as required. In mild areas leave them in the ground protected against frost.

EARLY SALAD RADISHES
The first sowing can be made in early January. Put cloches over the ground for 3–4 weeks beforehand to dry it out. Rake the soil into a fine tilth.

Using special short-topped varieties of radish broadcast the seed at $\frac{1}{4}$ oz per square yard or sow it thinly in $\frac{1}{2}-\frac{3}{4}$ in deep drills, 4–6 in apart. Water the seedbed thoroughly and keep the radishes moist throughout their life with regular applications of water.

Ventilate the crop on warm days because high temperatures under the cloche encourage leaf growth at the expense of roots.

Early salad radishes should be ready about eight weeks after sowing.

Spring radishes

1 Late February. Prepare the seedbed, rake in 1 oz of a balanced general fertilizer per square yard and water well.

2 Early March. Draw out $\frac{1}{2}-\frac{3}{4}$ in deep drills 4–6 in apart and apply diazinon and gamma HCH. Sow the seed thinly. Cover and firm.

3 After 10–14 days. Thin the seedlings to 1 in as soon as they can be handled easily. If the weather is dry water them each week.

4 Six to eight weeks after sowing (3–4 weeks in midsummer). Pull the radishes as required when the roots are $\frac{3}{4}$ in in diameter.

Winter radishes

1 July or August. Space-sow the seed in groups of 3–4 at 6 in intervals in $\frac{3}{4}$ in deep drills, 12 in apart.

2 After 7–10 days. Thin the seedlings to 1 plant per station as soon as they can be handled easily. Water after thinning.

3 Late October. Lift the roots carefully. Twist off the leaves and store them in dry sand in a cool frost-free place.

Potatoes 1

FIRST EARLIES
'Arran Pilot', 'Epicure',
'Ulster Chieftain'.

SECOND EARLIES
'Craig's Royal', 'Maris Peer',
'Pentland Dell'.

MAIN CROP
'Desirée', 'King Edward',
'Majestic'.

The potato is the most widely grown vegetable in temperate zones. It is a South American perennial but it is only half-hardy in Europe. Late frost in May kills the emerged leaves of a potato crop, and the first autumn frosts kill the remaining foliage.

The potato is grown for its edible tubers and it is propagated from specially grown tubers ("seed") saved from the previous season. It is possible to save tubers from home-grown crops, but this is not advisable because potato plants and tubers soon become infected by debilitating virus diseases and if infected, crop yield and quality suffer. Virus-free "seed" is produced in areas where aphids that spread viruses are less of a problem. Certified seed potatoes should always be used.

Always use small "seed" tubers because large seed potatoes produce too many sprouts. For the maximum yield and to prevent crowded tubers being forced to the surface and "greening", small seed tubers producing only two or three sprouts are ideal for propagating purposes.

Potatoes are classified according to the time at which they mature. Earlies are ready to eat in June or July; second earlies in August and early September; and main crops mature in September and October.

Tuber skin colour also varies but white or red-skinned varieties are most common; the flesh of potatoes is usually white but occasionally pale yellow.

Cultivation

Soil and situation Potatoes tolerate a wide range of soils but they grow best in deep, fertile, well-drained soils with sufficient bulky organic manure to retain moisture in dry weather. Do not apply lime before planting potatoes because they grow best at a pH of 5.0–6.0 and alkaline conditions favour potato scab disease. Dig in a dressing of 15–20 lb per square yard of well-rotted compost or manure in the autumn.

In spring, fork over the ground and rake in a general fertilizer, such as a proprietary brand of Growmore, at the rate of 4 oz per square yard and apply diazinon to combat wireworm and cutworm. A deep tilth is needed for earthing-up. Plant potatoes in an open site but not in a frost pocket.

Planting Seed potatoes should be about 1 oz in weight, the size of a small hen's egg. Plant the tubers with the "rose" end upwards in 6 in deep drills, with 12 in between early potato tubers and 16 in between second earlies and main crops. Cover the planted drills immediately after planting. Draw up the soil to produce a mound 4–6 in high over each row.

Early potatoes Plant at the end of March in rows 24 in apart with 12 in between tubers.

Second early and main crop Plant from mid- to late April in rows 27–30 in apart with 16 in between the tubers.

Potatoes are usually grown in ridges which are formed gradually during the season by earthing-up (ridging) every two to three weeks. Cultivate and hoe between the initial mounds to provide sufficient loose soil for earthing. Use a draw hoe to pull up soil into ridges around growing plants.

Watering Earlies should be watered at the rate of 3–4 gal per square yard every 10–14 days to increase yield from an early stage of growth. If they are watered at the "marble" stage (when the small developing tubers are the size of a marble, approximately $\frac{1}{2}$ in diameter) and not before, at the rate of 3–4 gal per square yard, they mature earlier.

Main crops should be given 4 gal per square yard at flowering time, which markedly increases yield and depresses scab.

Harvesting

Early potatoes should be ready about three months after planting, in June and July. The potatoes should be ready when the flowers are fully open. Lift as needed.

Second early and main crop potatoes should be lifted from August onwards.

Use a flat-tined fork to avoid too much damage to the tubers when lifting potatoes. Leave the tubers on the soil surface for two to three hours to dry. In wet conditions dry the tubers in a garage, a cold frame or under cloches. Make sure that all the potatoes are lifted so that no disease is carried over to the next year by overlooked tubers.

Storing Store only sound, healthy tubers. Any damaged potatoes should be used or discarded immediately. Store in a frost-free

1 Spring. Fork over the ground and rake in general balanced fertilizer at 4 oz per square yard, and apply diazinon against wireworm and cutworm.

2 March to April. Take out 6 in deep drills, 24 in apart for earlies, 27–30 in apart for later crops (according to the variety being grown).

3 At the same time, place the seed tubers in the drills at 12 in intervals for earlies, 16 in for second early and main crops, with the buds or "eyes" upwards.

4 Use a draw hoe to cover the drills. Draw up soil from both sides to produce 4–6 in high mounds over the planted rows.

Potatoes 2

building. Boxes with raised corner posts are ideal because it is easy to inspect the tubers. Keep them in the dark or cover with black polythene, to prevent the tubers turning green. Large quantities of potatoes can be stored in outside clamps. After lifting leave them to dry out for several hours, having removed the stems. Heap them up underneath straw and leave them to "sweat" for a couple of days before mounding up with earth to form a clamp.

Pests and diseases
Use virus-free seed to avoid the problems of potato virus diseases. To prevent attacks by wireworm and cutworm apply diazinon at planting. Potato cyst eelworm can be avoided by rotating crops. Scab is rarely a serious problem, although it is worse on alkaline soil. Ample watering is a good deterrent.

Potato blight This is the worst fungal disease of the crop and it can be particularly bad in warm, humid conditions from July onwards. The symptoms appear first on the leaves as yellow blotches on the upper surface. A white fungal growth may be seen underneath the leaves. The blotches turn brown and whole leaves are killed in severe attacks. Fungal spores are washed into the soil, where they can also infect the developing tubers. Very regular spraying is the major method of control. Spray the plants with bordeaux mixture or mancozeb at ten day intervals when conditions favour the disease.

5 During the summer, hoe regularly in the furrows between the ridges. Water during dry weather.

6 Hoe the soil from the furrows into ridges around the growing plants at 2–3 week intervals, until the ridges are 12–15 in high.

7 July onwards. At 10 day intervals, in warm humid conditions, spray all the surfaces of the leaves with an appropriate fungicide for potato blight control.

8 June to July. Lift early potatoes when the flowers are fully open, using a flat-tined fork to avoid excessive damage to tubers.

9 August onwards. Lift second early and main crop potatoes when the tops have died down.

10 Store in a frost-free building in boxes with raised corner posts for easy inspection.

Potatoes 3

Place a single layer of tubers—"rose" end upwards—in boxes or trays and keep them in a light, airy place such as a cool green-house. Begin the process in early February so that sturdy shoots about $\frac{3}{4}$–1 in long will have formed prior to planting in late March. Chitted tubers grow away quickly when planted and are particularly useful for early crops which have a relatively short growing period. It may be worth while chitting second early or main crop varieties in areas where late planting is necessary.

Potatoes are normally grown outdoors as described on the previous pages. There are alternative systems, however, for growing out-of-season potatoes or for less intensive cultivation of this basic vegetable crop.

Out-of-season potatoes
Very early potatoes can be grown in a green-house to mature in March or April. Plant chitted seed in a slightly heated greenhouse at a temperature of 7°–10°C/45°–50°F in January and grow in the same way as outdoor crops. Never allow the temperature to get very high or too much foliage will be pro-duced and few tubers. Keep the plants moist.

Growing in pots

Plant 2 or 3 chitted tubers in large pots which are at least 12 in wide and deep, containing good garden soil.

An alternative is to grow the plants in pots. Plant 2–3 chitted tubers in a large box or pot containing good garden soil. Keep the pots in a slightly heated greenhouse and grow as for the greenhouse crop.

Early outdoor plantings can be covered with glass cloches or polythene tunnels to speed development and give protection against frost. Cover the cloches with sacking when frosts are forecast.

Non-cultivation system
Potatoes can be grown without earthing up. Water the ground well before planting. In April, push chitted tubers into the soil and

Growing under black polythene

1 April. Water the ground and push chitted tubers into the soil at the same spacings as for outdoor potatoes.

cover and mound over the drills. Cover with a black polythene sheet to prevent greening and weed growth, to warm the soil and to conserve moisture. Make a slit above each tuber. Bury the edges of the polythene by pushing them into the soil with a spade.

Slugs and wireworms thrive in the con-ditions provided by polythene. Control slugs by scattering methiocarb or metaldehyde slug pellets around the mounds.

When the shoots emerge they begin to push up through the slits in the sheet towards the light. Roll back the sheet to expose the tubers for harvesting or take them out as required through the slits.

2 Cover and mound over the drills. Scatter slug pellets around the slightly mounded ridges.

3 Cover the ridges with a 36 in wide length of black polythene and bury the edges to leave a 24 in wide strip exposed.

4 Make slits with a sharp knife above each tuber where the shoots have pushed against the polythene.

5 May. As the shoots emerge they push up through the slits in the polythene.

6 July. As the tubers develop, roll back the polythene sheeting to expose the potatoes for harvesting.

Tomatoes 1

GREENHOUSE
'Cura' (tomato mosaic virus resistant), 'Eurocross BB' (leaf mould resistant), 'Moneymaker'.

OUTDOOR (BUSH)
'The Amateur', 'Sleaford Abundance'.

YELLOW-STRIPED (GREENHOUSE OR OUTDOOR)
'Marmande' (large irregular fruits), 'Tigerella', 'Yellow Perfection'.

In Britain tomatoes are usually grown in greenhouses, but they can be grown outside in mild, sheltered locations, and the protection of frames or cloches makes it possible to grow them in less favourable areas. There are many varieties of tomatoes, most of which are long-stemmed and crop over a long period. Bush varieties are less common but, because they are short jointed, they do not require staking and trimming. Tomato fruits are usually red, although some yellow-fruited varieties are available.

Raising tomato plants
Tomatoes are transplanted into their final positions, and the same procedure is used for raising seedlings for both greenhouse and outdoor drops. Alternatively, it may be more convenient to purchase the plants from a reliable nursery or garden centre.

Seed sowing
In a heated greenhouse kept at 18°C/65°F it is possible to raise plants for planting in about eight weeks. Outdoor planting does not take place until early June, but cold glass tomatoes can be planted in mid- to late April. Heated greenhouse crops can be planted from mid-February onwards. Sow the seed about eight weeks before the anticipated planting date. Sow thinly into seed trays or pans. Cover lightly with sieved compost and maintain the temperature at 18°C/65°F (see page 161). Germination and emergence occurs in 7–10 days. Do not sow too thickly or damping-off diseases quickly spread. Keep the seedlings evenly moist without waterlogging them.

Pricking out
Carefully remove the seedlings from the tray

GROWING SYSTEMS

Tomatoes may be grown directly in the greenhouse soil but, after a number of years, pests and diseases may build up. These are best controlled by soil sterilization, no easy task in home gardens.

An alternative is to grow the plants in large 9 in pots filled with a proprietary or home-made compost and stand them on the greenhouse soil. The roots eventually come out of the pot bottom, but most of them will be in clean compost.

Ring culture is very similar, except that the pots are placed on a 3–4 in deep bed of pebbles or ashes which is isolated from the soil by a layer of polythene.

It is also possible to grow tomatoes directly into straw bales which stand on a polythene sheet on the greenhouse soil. The bales must come from fields that have not been sprayed with hormone weed-killers, however. Sprinkle 2–3 oz of a nitrogenous fertilizer, such as nitro-chalk, on to the surface of each bale and water it in thoroughly. Allow 2–3 weeks for straw decomposition and fermentation to begin before planting in a small bed of compost on top of the bales.

Growing bags contain peat and permit complete isolation from the greenhouse soil. They are also useful for roof gardens, patios, balconies and outside against sunny walls. Growing bags contain few nutrients, and so correct watering and feeding is critical.

Plant raising

1 Sow the seed thinly in trays 8 weeks before planting. Cover with $\frac{1}{8}$ in of sieved compost and water before covering with glass and newspaper. Keep at 18°C/65°F. Turn the glass daily.

2 Ten to twelve days after sowing, gently remove the seedlings by inserting a small dibber beneath the roots. Fill 3 in peat pots with potting compost, making holes big enough to take the seedlings.

3 Plant each seedling at the same depth as in the tray. Water to firm, then water little and often. Reduce the temperature to 16°C/60°F when the plants begin to shade each other. Liquid feed before planting.

4 Plant tomatoes when they are 6–9 in tall with the flowers on the first truss just opening. Water well before and after planting.

Tomatoes 2

or pan at the true leaf stage. Hold them very gently by the leaves and prick them out singly into individual pots, such as 3 in peat or plastic pots, which contain a proprietary potting compost. Water them gently to firm the compost around the roots. Keep the young plants in the greenhouse at the same temperature (18°C/65°F).

Good light conditions are essential for growing sturdy, healthy tomato plants; shaded, overcrowded conditions must be avoided. Water the plants sparingly—little and often is better than fluctuations between drought and waterlogging—and liquid feed with a balanced nutrient solution as the time for planting approaches. Reduce the temperature to 16°C/60°F when the plants begin to shade each other. It may be necessary to support each plant with a small, split cane if it becomes too tall.

The planting stage
The ideal time for planting is when the flowers on the first truss are opening. The plants should then be 6–9 in tall. Destroy any plants affected by virus diseases.

Tomatoes in the greenhouse
Greenhouse tomatoes are generally liquid fed and it is unusual to use solid fertilizers for them. If plants are grown in the soil then it is important to double dig and incorporate well-rotted organic manure or compost with the lower spit. Water the plants thoroughly before planting and use a trowel to make holes which accommodate the roots without crowding. Plant with the top of each root ball level with the soil surface. Plants raised in peat pots should be planted complete with the pot. Make sure that the peat pot is very wet and, if drying out is likely, tear down one side of the pot wall before planting. Then water in thoroughly and keep the plants moist until the roots are established.

Supporting Whatever the support system, space the plants about 18 in apart each way. Greenhouse tomatoes are usually supported by strings suspended from overhead wires. Attach a length of soft garden string loosely around the stem beneath the lowest true leaf. Tie the other end to a wire attached to the greenhouse and stretched above the row of tomato plants. Twist each tomato plant loosely around the string as it grows upwards. Do not make the string too tight or the tomato stem will be constricted and damaged. Alternatively, the plants can be supported by tying them loosely with soft string to bamboo canes.

Trimming and de-leafing Side-shoots develop in the axils (angles between the leaves and stems) of each leaf and must be removed while they are still small. Otherwise they use up water and nutrients intended for the main plant. Snap off the small side-shoots between thumb and forefinger. This is best done early in the morning when the plants are turgid and the shoots snap off easily. Avoid pulling out side-shoots, because irregular and untidy wounds produce scars into which fungal diseases easily spread. If side-shoots become too large it is best to cut them out carefully with a sharp knife. When the plants are 4–5 ft tall it usually helps to remove the lower leaves up to the first truss. This allows more light into the bottom of the plant and improves the air circulation and, hence, reduces the chance of fungal diseases. Always cut off the leaves cleanly with a sharp knife.

Watering and feeding Watering and feeding of greenhouse tomatoes is critical and requires a great deal of attention. Soil-grown plants are the easiest to manage because the soil acts as a buffer and a reservoir for nutrients and water. Completely isolated systems, such as growing bags, are more difficult because they contain few inherent nutrients and the small volume of peat can only hold a small amount of water. Overwatering growing bags is dangerous and quickly kills off plant roots, causing wilting of the plants. Little and often watering is time-consuming and a nuisance, but it is the only satisfactory method with growing bags which may need watering three or four times during a hot summer day. Mix a well-balanced liquid feed with the water. It is best to follow the instructions, although it is as well to understand that nitrogen encourages vegetative growth of the plant whereas potassium improves fruit quality.

Pollination and fruit setting There is usually no difficulty in getting tomato flowers to set fruit. Occasionally, however, problems occur and fruit setting is improved by vibrating the

Greenhouse tomatoes

Supporting

1 Mid-February onwards Make holes with a trowel and plant tomato plants 18 in apart each way with the top of each root ball level with the soil surface. Water thoroughly.

2 At the same time attach soft string loosely around the stem beneath the lowest true leaf of each plant. Tie the other end of the string to a wire stretched above the row.

3 Snap or cut off side-shoots and basal shoots. Shaking the plants in this way or spraying with a fine droplet spray improves fruit setting by dispersing pollen. Water and feed.

4 When the plants are 4–5 ft tall cut off the lower leaves (up to the first truss) on each plant. Remove yellowing, decaying or diseased leaves on sight.

5 When 6 or 7 trusses have set fruit, or when the plants may be reaching the greenhouse roof, remove the growing points 2 leaves beyond the top truss.

6 Harvest tomatoes in the greenhouse as needed. Pick each fruit with the calyx still attached.

Tomatoes 3

bamboo cane or string, by tapping the flower trusses, or by spraying the plants over with water to disperse pollen.

Stopping Cold greenhouse tomato plants are unlikely to produce more than six or seven trusses in a normal season. It is best, therefore, to remove the growing point of each plant when it reaches the roof of the greenhouse, or two leaves beyond the top (sixth) truss.

Harvesting
Pick the fruits as required. Ripening takes place rapidly once the tomatoes begin to turn orange.

Pests and diseases
Glasshouse whitefly is the most common pest of protected tomatoes. Pyrethrum- and permethrin-based sprays may control the pest, but biological control with the wasp *Encarsia formosa* is preferable.

Fungal diseases such as grey mould (*Botrytis cinerea*) and leaf-mould are particularly troublesome in humid, poorly ventilated conditions. Botrytis is also encouraged when plants are soft or have trimming and side-shooting scars. Remove any yellowing, damaged or decayed leaves immediately.

The foliage of outdoor tomatoes can be attacked by potato blight and must be sprayed with a fungicide in July (see page 72).

Soil-borne pests, such as eelworms, produce yellow and stunted growth and virus diseases, such as tobacco mosaic virus (T.M.V.), cause mottling of the leaves, reduced plant vigour and poor fruit set. Eelworms can be avoided by not using the greenhouse soil, and T.M.V. resistant varieties are the only way of avoiding the virus.

The most common nutrient deficiency is caused by a lack of magnesium. The condition develops from the bottom of the plant upwards and produces a marked yellowing between the leaf veins. Magnesium deficiency can often be corrected by sprinkling a pinch of Epsom salts (magnesium sulphate) around each plant and watering it in.

Outdoor tomatoes
Outdoor tomatoes may be planted from early June onwards in mild temperate loca-tions such as southern England. Frames and cloches can be used to protect young plants and they can also be used to ripen fruit at the end of the season.

Cultivation
Choose a well-sheltered site such as a south-facing wall. Tomatoes do not tolerate cold, windy conditions and it may be necessary to use polythene or netting windbreaks. It is also important that the soil allows rapid, uninterrupted growth. Dig in well-rotted organic manure at 15 lb per square yard in the winter. Incorporate 3–4 oz per square yard of a general, balanced tomato fertilizer before planting in early June. Later in the season it may be necessary to feed the plants with a proprietary tomato liquid feed.

Planting The technique is the same as for greenhouse plants but outdoor tomatoes are usually grown directly in the soil. Alternatively, pots or growing bags can be placed on the soil or on balconies or patios. Soil-grown plants should be spaced 18 in apart in each direction. Warm the soil with cloches for 2–3 weeks before planting or spread black polythene over the soil surface and cut holes through which to plant the tomatoes. The polythene conserves moisture and suppresses weeds as well as warming the soil.

Supporting and training When tomatoes are grown outside they are usually tied to 5 ft bamboo canes but there are proprietary plastic-covered wire supports for use in conjunction with growing bags. Tie the stems to the canes with soft garden string at 12 in intervals. Bush tomatoes are stocky in growth and no supporting or trimming is necessary for them. Side-shoots must be removed from other varieties, however.

Stopping It is unlikely that more than four trusses will ripen outside. Stop the plants when four trusses have set by pinching out their growing points two leaves beyond the fourth truss. Spray against potato blight.

Weed control Weeds can be removed by hand weeding or careful hoeing.

Harvesting
Fruits can be ripened on the plant by laying the stems along the ground on a bed of straw and then covering them with cloches.

Outdoor tomatoes

1 Early June. Before planting apply 3–4 oz per square yard of tomato fertilizer to the soil. Plant 18 in apart each way and water well.

2 Immediately after planting, loosely tie the stems with soft garden string to bamboo supports at 12 in intervals.

Training

3 Remove any side-shoots that develop on tomato plants (except bush varieties).

4 Stop each long-stemmed plant 2 leaves beyond the fourth truss as soon as the fruits begin to swell.

5 Continue to remove any side-shoots induced to grow as a result of stopping. Spray against potato blight. Water and liquid feed regularly.

6 Mid-September. Cut the strings and lay the plants on a bed of straw. Cover with cloches and continue to water without wetting the fruit.

Cucumbers 1

GREENHOUSE
'Sporu' (cold glass, all female flowers), 'Telegraph' (heated or cold glass, male and female flowers).

RIDGE
'Burpee Hybrid', 'Burpless' (mildew resistant), 'Perfection'.

Cucumbers are sub-tropical plants grown for their green-skinned fruits which are used raw in salads. Greenhouse cucumbers are long-stemmed types and produce long, cylindrical fruits, whereas outdoor ridge types are trailing or bushy and usually have shorter, stumpy fruits.

Greenhouse cucumbers

Greenhouse cucumber plants are raised in a heated house with a temperature of 21°–25°C/70°–75°F. It takes about 4–5 weeks from sowing until planting can take place at the end of March. Do not plant in unheated greenhouses until the end of May.

Sowing Cucumber seed has somewhat erratic germination and should be "chitted" before sowing. Place the seeds on moist kitchen towelling in a closed plastic container and keep in a warm place such as an airing cupboard. Germination begins in 2–3 days and the germinating seeds can then be sown into their individual containers. Put single seeds into 3 in peat or plastic pots filled with a proprietary potting compost such as John Innes No. 1. Maintain the temperature at 21°C/70°F. Keep the developing plants well watered and support and tie them to small split canes. Keep the greenhouse atmosphere as humid as possible and liquid feed the plants with a proprietary, balanced general fertilizer to maintain good growth.

Growing systems

Greenhouse cucumbers can be planted directly into the soil but it is better to use growing-bags, pots or straw bales. Straw bales should not have been sprayed with hormone weedkillers and must be treated and fermented before planting. Make a small compost bed, using John Innes No. 3, along the middle of each bale and plant the cucumber into the compost. Growing bags can also be used for greenhouse cucumbers. Allow two plants per bag. Alternatively, grow each plant in a 9–10 in pot filled with a potting compost such as John Innes No. 3.

Growing

Greenhouse cucumbers grow best at high temperatures and high humidities. They grow rapidly and need constant watering and liquid feeding, although the compost must never be allowed to become waterlogged. Plants must be supported and trimmed by twisting them around strings or by tying to bamboo canes (see page 76). Pinch out the growing points when the plants reach the greenhouse roof.

The older greenhouse cucumber varieties have both male and female flowers, but modern introductions have female flowers only. Greenhouse cucumbers are produced without pollination and it is important that any male flowers are removed because the fertilization of female flowers results in bitter-tasting cucumbers. There is a small "embryo" cucumber behind each female flower.

Pinching and trimming

Pinching and trimming is also important. The first cucumbers produced form in leaf axils directly on the main stem. When they have developed, lateral shoots should be allowed to come out from the leaf axils and these, too, produce cucumbers. Stop the laterals after two leaves. More cucumbers will then develop in the axils of the lateral leaves. Use a sharp knife to trim cucumbers and handle them carefully because they snap easily.

Harvesting

From May onwards cut the cucumbers with a sharp knife as they reach the required size. The plants will regulate the number of fruits which they produce and the excess will drop off at a young stage. Do not be tempted to keep too many cucumbers per plant since individual fruit size will be reduced.

Pests and diseases

Glasshouse red spider mite and glasshouse whitefly are likely to be most prevalent. Pirimiphos-methyl may be used to control them. Biological control with the wasp *Encarsia formosa* can be used against whitefly. Powdery mildew is the most common disease. It covers the leaves with a white powdery growth and it is controlled with benomyl or related fungicides.

Chitting

Sowing

1 Late February. Sprinkle cucumber seeds on moistened kitchen tissue in a plastic container. Cover and keep in a warm place (21°C/70°F), such as an airing cupboard.

2 Two or three days later, sow each chitted seed ¾ in deep in 3 in pots of potting compost. Keep at 21°C/70°F. Water and feed, and support with split canes if necessary.

3 Late March (late May in unheated greenhouses). Plant 2 plants into a standard-sized growing bag. Give small amounts of water and liquid feed regularly.

4 April. Support the plants by tying them to bamboo canes and pinch out the growing points when the main stems reach the greenhouse roof.

5 April onwards. Allow the cucumbers to develop sequentially up the main stems. Keep single laterals in each leaf axil and stop them at 2 leaves. Remove male flowers.

6 May onwards. Cut cucumbers with a sharp knife when they reach the required size.

Cucumbers 2

Outdoor cucumbers

Ridge cucumbers and gherkins can be grown outside in cool temperate climates, but earlier crops are obtained if plants are covered with cloches in the early stages. Pollination is necessary for the production of outdoor cucumbers and gherkins so both male and female flowers must be retained. The Japanese climbing outdoor varieties available today produce smoother, longer cucumbers but they require training on netting or wire to a possible height of 6 ft.

Soil A moisture-retentive and fertile soil is essential. Prepare planting or sowing positions by making holes and filling them with a good fork load of well-rotted organic manure or compost. Cover with soil to make a mound.

Allow 36 in between ridge cucumbers and 24 in between gherkins. It is possible to incorporate 1 oz of general purpose fertilizer around each mound but regular liquid feeding of developing plants with a proprietary product is generally more convenient.

Sowing Plants can be raised in the same way as greenhouse cucumbers and then transplanted. This is difficult and laborious, however, and the outdoor types are readily checked by transplanting. Consequently it is better to sow the seed directly outside. Pre-germinate the seeds to ensure 100 per cent success or sow three seeds at each station where a plant is required.

Sow outdoor cucumbers in early May in mild locations such as southern Britain but not until early June in less favourable areas. Push the seeds ¾ in deep into the soil and thin to one per station later if necessary. Germination is quicker if the soil is covered with small individual cloches or jars.

Growing

Ridge cucumbers and gherkins are usually allowed to trail along the ground. Some training and trimming is necessary to keep them within bounds. The plants should first be stopped after five or six leaves to encourage a branched habit. Large numbers of fruits are produced and the plants must be continually supplied with water and liquid fertilizer. Remember that both male and female flowers must be retained.

Use a mulch of black polythene to keep down weeds. As well as raising the soil temperature and helping to conserve moisture, the mulch also keeps the cucumber fruits off the soil, thus considerably reducing the likelihood of rotting.

Harvesting

Ridge cucumbers are shorter and fatter than the greenhouse types and are ready when 6–8 in long, from late July to late August onwards. Cut them as needed.

Gherkins should not be allowed to grow any longer than 3–4 in.

GHERKINS

Gherkins are ideal for salads and for pickling. They can grow outside in the same way as ridge cucumbers, and can also be grown in 9 in pots and trained on to a cane and wire support. Sow two or three seeds in the centre of the pot and keep only the strongest seedling. Stop the plant after five or six leaves. Train the laterals along the support canes and retain all the flowers. Gherkins trained in this way make attractive potted plants for balconies or patios.

Ridge cucumbers

1 Early May to early June. Make holes 12 in wide and deep and fill them with organic manure. Replace the soil to produce mounds, 36 in apart each way.

2 Sow 3 seeds in each mound. Push the seeds ¾ in down into the soil. Cover each seed with a small jar.

3 When the seedlings have produced their first true leaves, thin to leave 1 plant at each mound.

4 Stop the plants after 5–6 leaves and spread out the laterals so that they grow evenly around the main stems. Retain both male and female flowers.

5 Water and liquid feed the plants regularly. Mulch to conserve moisture and keep down weeds.

6 Late July to late August onwards. Cut ridge cucumbers as required with a sharp knife when they are 6–8 in long.

Marrows and squashes 1

MARROWS, SQUASHES, PUMPKINS AND COURGETTES

Courgettes

Custard marrow

Marrow

Pumpkin

Squash

Marrows, courgettes, pumpkins and squashes are closely related with only slight differences in growth habit, and both bush and trailing types are available. The fruits are quite different, however, and can be produced from June (early courgettes) until mid- to late September (pumpkins, squashes and marrows). Marrows and courgettes have similar fruits but courgettes are much smaller (about 6 in long). The skin colour varies from dark green, through stripes to golden yellow. Squashes have globular and spherical fruits with a colour range from yellow to green. Pumpkins produce large spherical fruits.

Soil and situation Well-drained soils are essential and these fruiting vegetables grow best in warm sunny positions.

Make planting holes which are a spade's width and depth. Fill the holes with well-rotted organic manure or garden compost and replace the soil to form a mound over each hole. All these vegetables grow vigorously and there is no need to add any fertilizer. Liquid feeding may be needed, however, especially when the fruits have set and are growing rapidly. Bush varieties should be spaced 36 in apart each way but trailing types must be spaced 5 ft apart.

Sowing For the most part these crops can be sown directly outside. However, it is often more convenient to raise the plants in pots and transplant later, and transplanting is essential for early courgette production under cloches. Sow 2–3 dry or a single "chitted" (see page 77) seed into 3 in peat or plastic pots filled with a proprietary potting compost such as John Innes No. 1. Push the seeds $\frac{3}{4}$ in down into the compost. Keep them at a minimum temperature of 18°C/65°F and in good light to maintain sturdy growth. Allow 5–6 weeks to produce plants which have 3–4 true leaves at planting time. None of these vegetables, apart from the early cloched courgettes, must be planted out while a frost danger remains. Consequently, plants for early June planting should come from a mid-April sowing.

Direct sowing should take place in early to mid-May depending on the location. Sow 2–3 dry seeds or a single "chitted" seed into the top of each mound. Thin to one plant per mound when necessary.

Transplanting Transplant pot-grown plants into the tops of the prepared mounds when all danger of frost has passed. Put down a mulch around each plant while it is still small because it is difficult to get under the leaf canopy when the plants begin to grow rapidly. Keep the plants watered generously and liquid feed as required when the fruits begin to swell. Marrows and pumpkins being grown for exhibition need generous feeding.

Training Bush varieties of courgettes, marrows, pumpkins and squashes do not require stopping or training, but trailing varieties need attention. Each plant produces a number of lateral branches which should be stopped at 24 in. Fruiting laterals are then produced which bear male and female flowers. Both are needed and pollination usually takes place naturally with the aid of visiting insects. Early in the season or in cold weather it may be necessary to do some artificial pollination to ensure good fruit set. The female flowers have a small, undeveloped fruit immediately behind the large yellow flower. Male flowers are smaller and produce only pollen. Remove a male flower when pollen is being released and push it into a newly opened female flower.

Harvesting

These vegetables have a self-regulating mechanism which limits the number of fruits a plant carries. If fruits are grown for exhibition then the number per plant should be artificially limited. Marrows, pumpkins and squashes which mature in September should be kept off the soil to discourage slug attacks and rotting of the fruits. Mulching the plants helps or the developing fruits can be placed on sheets of glass or plywood.

Regular cutting of courgettes ensures continuing production. Cut the fruits with a knife when they are 4–6 in long. Summer marrows are harvested as needed while those intended for winter use—along with pumpkins and squashes—should be cut in September before the frosts and stored in nets or on shelves in an airy, frost-free place.

Pests and diseases

Glasshouse whitefly may be a problem in warm, sunny seasons (see page 77).

Herbs 1

Most herbs are easy to grow and a selection of culinary types provides a variety of flavours to complement home-grown vegetables and enhance the flavour of everyday food. Many of them are perennial plants with invasive habits. Clean up the herb garden each spring to prevent the stronger plants from taking over, and weed it regularly by hand. Once every three or four years replant herbs using fresh stock. It is a good idea to site the herb patch as near to the kitchen as possible. Some of the herbs described on these pages also grow well in containers, provided they have good drainage.

PROPAGATING HERBS

Heel cuttings

1 Strip away a young side-shoot from its parent stem so that a heel, which is a thin sliver of bark and wood, also comes away at its base.

2 Trim the tail on the heel and any leaves near it. Dip the heel cutting in rooting hormone and plant immediately, preferably in a cold frame.

Root division

1 Lift the parent plant to be divided towards the end of the dormant season. Shake off the soil and wash the crown.

2 Cut off a piece with at least 1 developed bud. Dust the cut surfaces with fungicidal powder and replant.

Angelica (Angelica archangelica)

Angelica is a decorative biennial or monocarpic herb, which can sometimes be maintained as a perennial by the prevention of seeding. It is a tall plant and can reach a height of 6 ft. It has large, indented leaves and yellow-green flowerheads which appear in late summer.

Cultivation Angelica grows best in a rich, moist but well-drained soil. It grows in semi-shade or in an open position and it is quite hardy. Angelica is best grown from seed; it can be propagated by division but this often encourages flowering. In late summer (August to September) sow the seed outside, with a cloche over the drill in cold areas. In the following March transplant the seedlings, keeping them 12 in apart. Spring sowings are also possible. Angelica needs to be kept weed-free. Remove flowerheads to maintain growth because if angelica is allowed to seed the plants die. It can be grown in a container although its height is a drawback.

Harvesting Angelica is grown for its stems which should be cut before flowering. They are candied and used for cake decoration.

Basil (Ocimum basilicum)

Basil is a tender plant easily killed by frost when it is grown outdoors.

Cultivation Basil should be grown in well-drained soil which has been enriched with a liberal dressing of well-rotted organic manure. The site should be warm, sheltered and sunny. The best way of plant raising is to sow the seed in a heated greenhouse during March. Keep them at a temperature of at least 16°C/60°F; the seeds germinate quite slowly. Prick off the seedlings into small, individual peat pots and maintain the temperature at 13°–16°C/55°–60°F. Harden off the plants prior to planting in early June. Space the plants 9–12 in apart each way. Do not plant out earlier because the slightest hint of frost kills basil.

Alternatively, the seed can be sown directly outside in late May. The developing seedlings should be thinned to 9–12 in apart in each direction.

Water regularly during the season and remove flower stalks as soon as they appear, to prolong vegetative growth.

Basil is killed by the first frost but plants can be lifted in September and potted into 5 in pots with a rich potting compost. Cut the plants back hard to within 2–3 in of the base, and take them indoors. Re-growth then occurs to provide young leaves for use in autumn and winter.

Harvesting Pick the leaves as required throughout the summer.

Herbs 2

Borage (*Borago officinalis*)

This hardy annual plant grows very readily in cool, temperate climates and has a number of culinary uses. The young leaves taste of cucumber and can be added to salads or used to flavour cool summer punches. The plants have bright blue flowers, which appear from May onwards, and hairy stems and leaves. Borage grows to a height of 3 ft very quickly.

Cultivation Borage tolerates almost any site and soil although the most rapid growth occurs in fertile soils and warm, sheltered sites. Sow the seed outside in February and, as soon as they are large enough, thin the seedlings to 12 in apart in each direction.

Seeds are shed on to the ground by the plants and these germinate in the summer or the following spring.

Harvesting Pick fresh, young leaves as required. The flowers can be used to garnish salads.

Chives (*Allium schoenoprasum*)

This hardy perennial herb is one of the smallest and most delicately flavoured members of the onion family. Chives do not have bulbs like onions but are grown for their narrow grasslike leaves which are chopped and used in savoury dishes, soups and salads.

Cultivation Chives grow well in a rich, slightly alkaline soil. They flourish in full sun but tolerate semi-shade. In March or June take out a $\frac{1}{2}$ in deep drill and sow the seeds. When the seedlings are large enough to handle, thin them out until they are about 6 in apart. Do not cut any of the leaves during the early stages of growth. Later, cut off any flowers and, to ensure a continual supply of leaves throughout the summer, cut back the leaves to 2–3 in several times during the growing season. Water chives regularly and give them a little fertilizer in October and March. The clumps should be divided every two or three years and replanted 6 in apart. They can also be grown indoors in pots.

Harvesting Cut off the leaves with sharp scissors above soil level as required.

Dill (*Anethum graveolens*)

Dill is in the same family as fennel. It is grown for its aromatic leaves, which are used to flavour salads and fish dishes, and for its seeds. Dill vinegar is made by soaking the seeds in vinegar for a few days; the seeds are also used in pickling. The plant has feathery green-blue foliage and tiny yellow flowers arranged in flat umbels.

Cultivation Sunny, well-drained sites are ideal but the plants must never be short of water or the growth becomes weak and straggly. Sow dill directly into the permanent bed because the plants do not tolerate disturbance. Sow successively from April to June for a continual supply of young leaves to harvest.

Thin the seedlings to 12 in apart as soon as possible. Seeds which fall on to the soil germinate in the next season and produce large numbers of self-sown seedlings.

Harvesting Pick fresh leaves as required when the plants are 8 in tall. Harvest the seeds at the end of the season when they are dark brown in colour and the plants have turned purplish-brown. The young leaves can be cut and dried for winter use.

Fennel (*Foeniculum vulgare*)

Fennel is an attractive perennial herb which can grow to 6 ft or more in height. It has feathery, blue-tinged foliage and yellow flowers and it is grown for its young shoots and seeds which can be used in sweet and savoury dishes. Fennel can be grown in pots or as a border plant.

Cultivation Fennel tolerates a variety of conditions but it grows best in a moist, well-drained and slightly acid soil. It needs full sun but it is quite hardy in winter. In February sow the seed in a $\frac{1}{2}$ in deep drill. Thin the seedlings to 12–15 in apart or remove all but the strongest if only one plant is required. Keep the plants weed-free.

Established fennel can be propagated by division. Divide or raise fennel from seed every three or four years to keep vigorous young stock.

Harvesting Pick fresh leaves regularly throughout the summer to maintain a constant supply. Allow the seeds to ripen fully and dry on the stem. In autumn, shake them off the stem and store in a warm, dry place.

Herbs 3

French Tarragon (*Artemisia dracunculus*)   **Marjoram** (*Origanum majorana*)   **Mint** (*Mentha spicata*)   **Parsley** (*Petroselinum crispum*)

French tarragon is a perennial shrub which can grow to a height of 3 ft and it spreads, as does mint, by underground runners. Tarragon has widely-spaced leaves and clusters of white flowers.

Cultivation French tarragon grows well in poor soil but it must be well-drained. It should be grown in full sun. It is very seldom grown from seed and plants are usually acquired by root division, or less often from cuttings. Plant in spring when there is no longer any danger of frost. Leave a distance of 24 in between plants if more than one is being grown. Keep tarragon weed-free.

Renew French tarragon every three or four years by lifting and replanting a few of the vigorous runners. Discard the older portions of the plant. French tarragon can be grown in suitably large containers.

Harvesting Cut the young leaves as needed in July. They may still be suitable in October. Cut the leaves for drying in June to July.

Sweet marjoram is a half-hardy annual. It is grown from seed each year although some forms are perennial. Pot marjoram (*Origanum onites*) is a hardy dwarf shrub which, as the name suggests, can be grown indoors in pots when it will continue to produce leaves for use during the winter.

Cultivation Sweet marjoram can be sown out of doors in mid-May in a warm, sunny site. Thin the plants to 12 in apart each way as soon as they can be handled. Alternatively, sow the seed in seed trays or pans under glass at a temperature of 16°C/60°F in early April. Prick out the seedlings into small individual peat pots and gradually harden off the plants before planting them outside in late May, when the danger of frost is over. Water the plants generously and keep down the weeds, especially in the early stages.

Pot marjoram (*Origanum onites*) is best propagated from heel cuttings taken in May or June. Otherwise, divide established plants in March and pot the plants. Keep them on the patio in summer and take them indoors in winter. Pot marjoram is deciduous and likely to lose its leaves if left outside in the cold months. Cut the plants back hard in March; new growth then appears from the base.

Harvesting Sweet marjoram can be used fresh, or the leaves can be removed and dried for winter use. Cut the shoots when they are about 8 in tall.

Common mint or spearmint (*M. spicata*) is the most popular kind of this hardy perennial herb. Apple or Bowles' mint (*M. × villosa alopecuroides*) is also common and it is considered by some people to have a more subtle and therefore preferable flavour.

Cultivation Mint grows anywhere if the soil is well dug and moist. It does equally well in a sunny or semi-shaded position. Since it is such an invasive plant underground it is advisable to restrict the roots by planting in a bottomless container sunk into the ground. Keep mint free of weeds and pinch out the flower buds when they appear to encourage maximum leaf-growth. Divide the roots each March and replant if possible in a fresh position. Otherwise, incorporate well-rotted compost or manure and a handful of bone-meal into the soil.

Mint is readily grown in pots or containers but should be kept clipped to maintain vigorous young growth.

Harvesting Pick fresh young leaves as required from May until the autumn. If dried leaves are required gather these before the plants begin to flower.

Pests and diseases If mint is attacked by the rust (*Puccinia menthae*), dig up all the roots and burn them. It is best to acquire new stock from a healthy source.

Parsley is a biennial plant which is best grown as an annual, although it will over-winter successfully and provide leaves for winter use if cloched. There are several varieties available, some with flat leaves, but the curly-leaved variety is most often grown.

Cultivation A rich, slightly alkaline, soil is ideal for parsley but poorer soils can be used if they are enriched with some well-rotted compost. Moisture is very important for successful parsley growing, and the plant grows best in a semi-shaded position. If parsley is grown in a sunny place it needs to be watered regularly.

The seed is sown in March. Germination, which is sometimes erratic, may take 6–8 weeks outdoors. This process can be speeded up by sowing the seed indoors in pots. When the seedlings are large enough to handle thin them out until they are 4 in apart. Weed regularly by hand when the seedlings are small and apply a liquid feed occasionally to increase leaf production. In the second year cut off the flower stalks to delay the plants' production of seed.

Throughout the winter parsley can be grown indoors, or in the greenhouse, in suitable containers for continual harvesting.

Harvesting Pick parsley fresh as required.

Pests and diseases Seedlings can be attacked by carrot fly. Before sowing sprinkle bromophos in the seed drill as a deterrent.

Herbs 4

Rosemary (*Rosmarinus officinalis*)   **Sage** (*Salvia officinalis*)

Sweet bay (*Laurus nobilis*)   **Thyme** (*Thymus vulgaris*)

Rosemary is a perennial shrub which is very attractive when in flower. The leaves are needle-shaped and grey-green in colour and the flowers, which appear from March to September, are pale to deep blue.

Cultivation Rosemary grows in any well-drained soil. It does best in a sunny sheltered spot although it may be grown in partial shade. Rosemary can be grown from seed sown in May and June but because seed is difficult to obtain and germination can be very slow, it is best to grow it from heel cuttings taken in early summer. Prune rosemary regularly to prevent straggly growth and to encourage a bushy habit.

Rosemary does well as a pot plant but it should be kept indoors during the coldest part of the winter.

Harvesting Pick fresh leaves and flowers as required but cut shoots for drying in the summer months only.

Sage is a small evergreen shrub 1½–2 ft high. The species most commonly grown, *Salvia officinalis*, may be grown from seed or propagated from heel cuttings.

Cultivation Sage tolerates any well-drained soil but grows best on a chalky loam. It requires a sheltered site in full sun. Sage shrubs grow well in any kind of container. Sow the seed under glass in March. Plant out the seedlings 12–15 in apart when there is no longer any danger of frost. Keep them weed-free and trim regularly when they are fully grown. Cut sage back lightly after flowering is over in July. Renew the shrubs every three or four years.

Harvesting Pick the leaves as required; they are best just before flowering. Cut leaves for drying in the active growing season.

Sweet bay is an attractive evergreen tree grown for its aromatic leaves. It can be grown in containers or in open soil. In some parts of the world it reaches a height of up to 50 ft.

Cultivation Sweet bay grows best in a dryish, well-drained soil which may be acid or alkaline. It grows well in full sun but a sheltered site is preferable because in severe winters the foliage, and occasionally the shoots, may be damaged. Buy a young, well-established tree from a nursery or propagate in late summer or early autumn (August to September) from cuttings of ripe shoots. Protect young trees in harsh weather to prevent the leaves turning brown. Sweet bay grows well in containers and makes a good ornamental tree because it can be clipped into shape and growth is restricted by the pot.

Place pot-grown trees indoors or in a frost-free shed during the winter months.

Harvesting Pick the young leaves as required and dry them slowly in the dark to make sure the colour is retained.

Common culinary thyme is a small perennial bush about 10 in high. It has a beautiful scent and is a useful bee-plant.

Cultivation Thyme prefers a light, well-drained, neutral soil. Common thyme grows best in full sun although it is hardy. However, various other thymes grown mainly for ornament may require some winter protection.

Seed sown outdoors in March germinates fairly readily and the resulting seedlings should be thinned until they are about 12 in apart. Keep the thyme patch weed-free and trim the plants after flowering to encourage compact growth.

The plants should be renewed every three or four years. Propagate thyme by root division or heel cuttings. Common thyme grows well in containers.

Harvesting Pick the leaves for drying or immediate use before the plants flower.

Planning 1

CLIMATE ZONES
Where climate zones are mentioned, the reference is to the Arnold Arboretum system, designed for North America, and its extension to Europe. The zones refer to areas with a consistent average annual minimum temperature. Plants are spoken of as being 'hardy in Zone X'. Most of the British Isles is in Zone 8, though western coasts, from Cornwall to the Hebrides, are in Zone 9.

The planting of tree, bush and cane fruits represents a long-term investment. Once planted there should be no need to move them until the cropping life of that particular plant is over. This could range from 20 to 50 years and more for tree fruits, and about 10–15 years for soft fruits. It is worth while, therefore, before planting to draw up a scale plan so that the plants are correctly sited.

The planner needs to take into account the approximate yield from each fruit to meet the family's requirements in relation to the amount of land available; the correct spacing; and the right aspect.

Yield

The yield depends upon many factors, such as the fertility of the soil, the climate, and the variety and the size of the plant. As a guide, the table below lists approximate yields from reasonably mature plants of the fruits commonly grown outside.

Spacing

The eventual size and yield of a mature fruit plant are influenced by the environment, the variety and, with many tree fruits, the rootstock on which it is grafted. Trees grafted on vigorous rootstocks in time grow larger than trees grafted on dwarfing stocks, even though they may be the same variety. Nowadays, most trees are cultivated for small gardens and are usually grafted on non-vigorous stocks, except for the half-standard or the standard forms. Soft fruits are grown on their own roots.

The spacings given in the table below are intended only as a guide for the planner. For more detail, refer to the relevant fruit pages. Allow a wider spacing on very fertile soils.

Fruit against walls and fences

While in many gardens the bulk of the fruit crop comes from a plot of land specially set aside for this purpose, the use of walls, fences and trellises should not be neglected, particularly where space is limited. Their structure provides support for the plants and also for netting as protection against birds or frosts. Walls and solid fences have the added advantages of giving shelter and, where the aspect is sunny, extra warmth and light is reflected from the masonry or wood. The added warmth improves the quality of the fruits, promotes fruit bud development and makes it possible to grow the more exotic fruits such as peaches, nectarines and figs where otherwise it might not be worth while.

Because wall and fence space is usually limited, use the restricted forms that are kept in shape and contained by summer pruning.

Apples and pears can be grown as cordons, espaliers or fans but stone fruits, such as apricots, peaches and cherries, do not respond to the cordon and espalier methods of training and are therefore grown only in fan-trained form. The climbing fruits, such as blackberries, hybrid berries and grapes, grow well against walls and fences. The grape vine in particular is perhaps the most versatile of all the trained fruits, being amenable to many forms of training against walls, fences or on pergolas but, of course, the aspect must be sunny.

The height of the supporting structure decides the shape or form in which the fruit is best trained.

Walls and fences up to 6 ft high are suitable for the low-trained tree forms such as the espalier, and for cordon and fan-trained gooseberries, red and white currants as well as blackberry and raspberry canes.

With walls and fences 6–8 ft high, it is possible to grow apples and pears (on dwarfing or semi-dwarfing stock) as cordons, fans or multiple-tiered espaliers, the number of tiers depending upon the height of the structure.

TREE FORMS

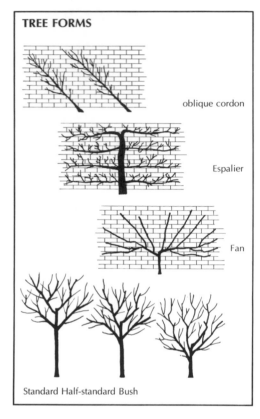

oblique cordon

Espalier

Fan

Standard Half-standard Bush

There is no really dwarfing stock as yet developed for stone fruits, although it is anticipated there will be in the next five years, so the minimum height required for fan-trained apricots, peaches, nectarines, plums, gages and Morello cherries is 7 ft. There are successful peaches on semi-vigorous stocks grown on lower structures than this but they need regular pruning and tying down. The sweet cherry is a vigorous plant and needs a wall or fence of at least 8 ft. Structures can be given extra height by the use of trellis-work.

Aspect

The aspect of the wall, fence or trellis decides the kind of fruit that can be grown. In the northern hemisphere the warmest and sunniest aspect is the south-facing and the coldest and shadiest is the north, with the west and east somewhere between the two.

YIELDS AND SPACING TABLE

APPLES AND PEARS

Tree form	Yield Apples	Yield Pears	Spacing In rows	Spacing Rows apart
Bush	60–120 lb	40–100 lb	12–18 ft	12–18 ft
Dwarf bush	30–50 lb	20–40 lb	8–15 ft	8–15 ft
Dwarf pyramid	10–15 lb	8–12 lb	5–6 ft	6 ft
Espalier (2-tier)	20–25 lb	15–20 lb	10–18 ft	6 ft
Fan	12–30 lb	12–30 lb	12–18 ft	—
Single cordon	5–8 lb	4–6 lb	2½–3 ft	6 ft
Standard	100–400 lb	80–240 lb	18–30 ft	18–30 ft

OTHER TREE FRUITS

Tree form	Yield	In rows	Rows apart
Bush (Morello cherry)	30–40 lb	12–18 ft	12–18 ft
Bush (plum and peach)	30–60 lb	12–18 ft	12–20 ft
Bush, half-standard and standard (sweet cherry)	30–120 lb	15–40 ft	15–40 ft
Bush or small tree (fig)	15–20 lb	18–20 ft	18–20 ft
Fan (all stone fruits)	12–30 lb	12–18 ft	—
Fan (fig)	15–20 lb	12–15 ft	—
Fan (sweet cherry)	12–30 lb	18–25 ft	—
Pyramid (plum)	30–50 lb	10–12 ft	10–12 ft
Standard (plum, peach and apricot)	30–120 lb	18–25 ft	18–25 ft

SOFT FRUIT

	Yield	In rows	Rows apart
Bush (black currant)	10–12 lb	5–6 ft	6 ft
Bush (gooseberry)	6–8 lb	4–5 ft	5 ft
Bush (red and white currant)	8–10 lb	5 ft	5 ft
Cordon (gooseberry, red and white currant)	1–3 lb	12–15 in	5 ft
Blackberry or hybrid berry	10–30 lb	8–15 ft	6–7 ft
Raspberry	1½ lb per ft of row	15–18 in	6 ft
Strawberry	8–10 oz per plant	12–15 in	2½–3 ft

Planning 2

South The southern, south-eastern and south-western aspects are best reserved for the sun-loving fruits, although most fruits would thrive in this situation. The soil at the base of a south-facing wall can become very dry, so ensure there is adequate moisture during the growing season by mulching and watering. This aspect is suitable for figs, peaches, nectarines, apricots, grapes, gages, pears, plums, cherries and apples.

West The western aspect receives the afternoon sun but it is exposed to south-westerly winds and usually receives more rain than do other aspects. It is suitable for peaches, nectarines, apricots, sweet and sour cherries, grapes, gages, pears, plums, apples, raspberries, hybrid and blackberries, gooseberries, red and white currants.

East The eastern aspect is a dry situation receiving the morning sun but shaded in the afternoon. It is open to cold easterly winds. Suitable fruits include the early pears, apples, plums, sweet and sour cherries, currants, gooseberries, hybrid berries, blackberries and raspberries.

North The northern aspect is restricted to those fruits that are able to grow and ripen in cold situations. Suitable fruits are fan-trained acid cherries and damsons, early culinary apples, cordon currants and gooseberries and blackberries. They will ripen later than those in full sun.

Wiring walls and fences

Horizontal wires firmly attached to the wall or fence are necessary to support the framework branches and for tying in the new growth. Use gauge 14 galvanized fencing wire for espaliers and cordons, and gauge 16 for fan-trained trees.

For espaliers, fix the wires so that they coincide with the height of the arms (tiers). Generally the tiers are 15–18 in apart but plant the espaliers first to see where the wires should be placed. The wires for oblique cordons are usually fixed every 2 ft, the highest wire being 6 in below the top of the wall or fence.

Fan-trained trees require horizontal wires every 6 in or two brick courses apart, starting at 15 in from the ground and continuing to the top of the wall or fence. Straining bolts are not necessary on wires for fan-trained trees because the wires are placed closer together, so wire staples will suffice on wooden fences and lead wall eyes on walls.

Buying fruit plants

To ensure healthy new plants, it is best to buy fruit stock from a specialist fruit nursery.

Apart from having a better selection, the specialist is likely to stock varieties of a guaranteed high standard of purity, health and vigour.

In many countries now, there are government-operated schemes for certain fruits, such as those in Britain for apples, pears, plums, black currants, raspberries, strawberries and cherries, whereby each variety is inspected and, if healthy, certified as such.

Healthy, certified stock also has the advantage of being guaranteed true to name.

Also, before choosing any fruit plant check its pollination requirements. Some fruits such as sweet cherries, apples, pears, certain plums and gages must be grown in compatible pairs or they will not produce fruit (see pages 102–103). Select the best varieties from the lists of recommended varieties and descriptions which head each fruit page.

WIRING WALLS AND FENCES

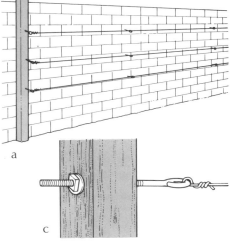

Wires must be held 1½–4 in away from walls by fixing 2 in square wooden battens (or 1½ in × 1½ in angle irons) to the masonry to hold the straining bolts and the ends of the wires (a). Screw or drive in 4 in galvanized or lead wall nails with eyes, or vine eyes (b) every 5 ft to hold the wires between the battens. With the screw type,

drill and plug the wall first. Wires should be kept taut by attaching straining bolts (c) to one end post. Use wire staples (d) to hold the wires on the intermediate and other end posts. Tighten the wires with the straining bolts before driving the staples home. A diagonal post is needed to brace the main post.

Planning a small fruit garden

The above plot is a guide for planning a small intensively cultivated fruit garden. It can be modified to suit individual requirements. It contains: espalier pear (a); loganberry arch (b); espalier pear (c); fan peach (d); grape arch (e); cordon apples (f); gooseberries (g); red currants (h); black currants (i); summer-fruiting raspberries (j); autumn-fruiting raspberries (k).

Soft Fruits

Introduction

Soft fruit is an umbrella term for several low-growing shrubs and perennials that bear soft, juicy fruit. They are not all closely related and they have a variety of growth habits. Botanically the best-known fruits can be placed into two groups: those belonging to the rose family (Rosaceae), including the raspberry, blackberry, loganberry and allied hybrids, and the strawberry; and those classified in the gooseberry family (Grossulariaceae) including the black, red and white currant, gooseberry and Worcesterberry. Three fruits not included in these two families are grapes (Vitidaceae), the melon (Cucurbitaceae) and the blueberry (Ericaceae). However, all the fruits in the soft fruit section have the common advantage of bearing fruit soon after planting—in some cases (such as the melon) within the same year. Also, soft fruits are particularly suitable for the small garden because they need far less room than do tree fruits.

Site

With good basic culture, all the soft fruits are easily grown and, once established, provide annual crops without fail. Although best grown in an open, sunny position, they do reasonably well in partial shade or in a site that gets afternoon sun only. Low-lying areas that are susceptible to late spring frosts should be avoided if possible.

If space in the garden is restricted, use walls and fences for grapes and climbing cane fruits, as well as for gooseberries and red and white currants as cordons or fans (see pages 84–85). Soft fruits such as strawberries, grapes and currants can also be grown in containers, in window boxes or in tubs on a patio, and climbing fruits can be trained over pergolas and arches.

In a small garden the fruits to be grown must be chosen carefully. If there is room, for example, for only six bushes it is tempting to grow one of each of all the main soft fruits. But it is more sensible and profitable to grow a minimum of three bushes of two favourite sorts only. In this way enough fruit can be picked for the family's needs, with some left over for jam-making perhaps, or for freezing.

Personal preference will, of course, dictate the choice of fruits. If only a few sorts can be grown, black or red currants, raspberries and strawberries are a good choice because, apart from their excellent taste, all are good croppers relative to their size and those in shops are seldom as fresh as those picked straight from the garden.

With the use of cloches, cold frames or polythene tunnels the season of some soft fruits (strawberries in particular) can be extended both in the early summer and in the autumn.

Protection against birds

Another advantage of growing soft fruits is the comparative ease of providing protection against pests. Very few gardens escape bird damage to ripe fruit in summer and autumn, or to fruit buds in winter and spring. This means some sort of year-round protection is needed. A permanent fruit cage is highly recommended because it provides both efficient bird protection and allows easy access to the plants for picking, spraying, pruning and top-dressing.

Clearing the site

Although most soft fruits grow well enough in any moderately fertile soil, it is always worth while doing some initial preparation. See pages 6–9 for details of soil preparation and drainage. A first essential is to make sure that all perennial weeds are removed. Nowadays there are selective herbicides for this purpose if necessary, although some gardeners may prefer to double dig before planting which buries the weeds. Clean, cultivated ground needs single digging before planting (see pages 14–15), and hand picking occasional weeds during this operation should usually be all that is needed.

Planting

Strawberry plants are set out with a trowel in much the same way as any bedding plant or young perennial. Raspberry canes and blackberry layers (plants) can usually be dealt with in the same way, depending upon how much root they have. At the most a small border spade is all that is necessary.

Bush fruits generally have a more extensive root system and, because they are a fairly long-term crop, their planting ritual should be more elaborate. Plant bushes from November to March.

Dig a hole which is deeper and wider than the roots when they are spread out. The bottom of the hole should be loosened with a fork and if little or no organic matter was dug into the area initially, a spadeful or two can now be worked in. Use well-rotted manure or garden compost, or peat and bonemeal.

Set the plant in the hole and spread out the roots. Fill in the hole with the soil, occasionally giving the bush a gentle shake up and down so that the soil filters among the roots and makes close contact with them. Firm the soil gently throughout with the feet. When all the plants are in position, rake the site over so that it is level and apply a light dressing of a balanced fertilizer such as a proprietary brand of Growmore.

Strawberries 1

SUMMER-FRUITING STRAWBERRIES
Late May to mid-July

EARLY
'Pantagruella' Good flavour. Scarlet berries. Moderate cropper. Very compact.

SECOND EARLY
'Gorella' Flavour fair. Shiny attractive berries. Heavy cropper. Good for protected cropping.
'Cambridge Vigour' Excellent flavour. Fruit bright red, large and early from 1-year-old plants, size deteriorates in second year. Heavy cropper. Good for protected cropping.

'Tamella' Moderate flavour. Fruits large, dark red, orange flesh. A very heavy cropper.
'Grandee' Flavour good. Dark red with reddish flesh. Very large fruits up to 3 in dia., sometimes with hollow centre. Heavy cropper.

'Royal Sovereign' Early to mid-season. Flavour first class. Fruits brilliant red, flesh pale. Susceptible to diseases and virus infection. Moderate cropper. Forces well under heat.

The strawberry cultivated today has resulted from the interbreeding of a number of *Fragaria* species, principally the North American *F. virginiana* as well as the South American *F. chiloensis*. This intermingling of genetic characteristics has resulted in a fruit of great variety in taste and colour, with a cropping ability and season of such versatility that it can be grown from the Tropics to the cool temperate regions of the world. It is no wonder the strawberry is the most popular soft fruit.

For the purposes of cultivation the strawberry is divided into three categories: the ordinary summer-fruiting strawberry; the perpetual or remontant strawberry that crops in irregular flushes throughout the summer until stopped by autumn frosts; and the alpine strawberry (*Fragaria vesca* subspecies *alpina*), a mountain form of wild strawberry (see page 89).

Summer-fruiting strawberries

The ordinary, or summer-fruiting strawberry, crops once only in the early summer. A few do crop again in autumn and these are called "two crop" varieties, but they are cultivated in the same way as the others.

The expected yield per strawberry plant is about 8–10 oz.

Cultivation

Some gardeners prefer to grow strawberries as an annual crop, planting new runners each year. This method produces high quality fruits but a lower yield than that of larger two- or three-year-old plants.

Soil and situation Most soils are suitable for strawberries, but they should be well drained. On waterlogged land, if a drainage system is not practicable, grow strawberries on ridges 2–3 in high. They prefer a slightly acid (pH 6.0–6.5) light loam in a frost-free, sunny situation. They will, however, tolerate some shade and because many varieties flower over a long period, the later flowers should escape spring frosts. Strawberries are readily attacked by soil-borne pests and diseases and a system of soil rotation should be practised. Do not grow them for more than three or four years in any one site. For this reason, strawberries are best grown with the vegetables rather than with the more permanent fruit plants.

Soil preparation A strawberry bed will be down for three or four years, and the initial preparations should be thorough so that the land is made fertile and free from perennial weeds. In July dig in well-rotted manure or compost at the rate of 14 lb to the square yard. Rake off any surplus because bulky organics on the surface encourage slugs, snails and millipedes. Once applied, no more organics should be needed for the life of the bed. Just before planting, lightly fork in a balanced fertilizer such as a brand of Growmore at 3 oz per square yard.

Planting and spacing The earlier the planting, the better the maiden crop in the following year. Ideally, plant in July, August or not later than mid-September. If planted in late autumn or spring, the plants are unlikely to establish well in the first year, and should be deblossomed. This means losing the maiden crop. Plant the runners in moist soil with the crown of the strawberry just level with the soil surface; planting too deep may result in the rotting of the buds and planting too shallow may cause drying out. Plant with a trowel or hand fork, spreading out the roots well. Replace the soil and firm it. Space the plants 18 in apart in rows 3 ft apart. On a light soil they can be 15 in apart with 2½ ft between the rows. If plants are to be grown for two years only, space them only 12 in apart in the row.

Pollination The flowers are pollinated by bees and crawling insects such as pollen beetles. Imperfect pollination results in malformed fruits. All modern varieties are self-fertile.

Watering and feeding Water regularly for the first few weeks after planting and whenever dry conditions occur during the growing season, but try to keep water away from the ripening berries because this encourages grey mould (*Botrytis cinerea*). The risk is less with trickle or drip irrigation because only the soil is wetted. Damp conditions overnight also encourage botrytis; water in the morning so that the plants are dry by nightfall. At the end of January each year apply sulphate of potash at ½ oz per square yard along each side of the row for hardiness, the development of flowers and flavour. No other feeding is necessary unless growth has been poor. In this case apply sulphate of ammonia at ½ oz per square yard in April, taking care to prevent fertilizer touching the foliage because it will scorch it.

Weed control Weeds compete for nutrients and water. Keep the rows clean by shallow hoeing and tuck any runners into the row to fill gaps. Pay particular attention to cleaning up between the rows before strawing down. Weedkillers may be used.

1 In July, dig in well-rotted manure or compost at a rate of 14 lb per square yard. Rake off any surplus manure.

2 Just before planting, lightly fork in a balanced fertilizer such as a brand of Growmore at 3 oz per square yard.

3 In July or August, plant the strawberries 18 in apart in rows 3 ft apart. Spread out the roots, keeping the crowns level with the soil surface. Firm the soil.

4 For the first few weeks after planting and during dry spells in the growing season, water regularly. Keep water away from ripening berries.

5 When the fruits begin to swell, scatter slug pellets along the rows. Cover the ground beneath the berries and between rows with barley or wheat straw.

6 Protect the fruit from birds with netting stretched over cloches. Or support nets with posts at least 18 in tall. Cover posts with jars or pots first.

Strawberries 2

MID-SEASON
'Cambridge Favourite' The most widely grown. Flavour fair. Fruits large, salmon scarlet. Cropping heavy and reliable.
'Redgauntlet' Widely grown. Flavour fair. Fruits large, scarlet. A heavy cropper. Will give a second crop in the autumn if protected in the spring. Some resistance to red core disease.

'Cambridge Aristocrat' Rich flavour. Highly fragrant. Long conical, crimson fruits. Light cropper.

LATE
'Cambridge Late Pine' Excellent aromatic, sweet flavour. A dull-red fruit. Medium/large fruit. Heavy cropper.

'Domanil' Good flavour. Fruits large, round; orange-red with orange flesh. Heavy cropper. Tall, vigorous plants.

Strawing down When the fruits begin to swell and weigh down the trusses, scatter slug pellets along the rows. Then put straw down around the plants. This is to keep the fruits clean, so tuck the straw right under the berries and also cover the ground between the rows to help to keep down weeds. Do not straw down earlier than this because the straw prevents the heat from the earth reaching the flowers, which may then be damaged by frost at night. Preferably use barley straw (which is soft) or, as a second choice, wheat straw.

Protection from birds One method of protection is to use barn cloches with netting over the framework. Alternatively, make cages using $\frac{3}{4}$ in or 1 in plastic netting, supported by posts and wire or string. The height should be at least 18 in; about 4 ft is the ideal height for picking in comfort. Put glass jars or plastic plant pots over the posts to prevent them tearing the netting.

Harvesting

The best time to pick strawberries is in the morning when the berries are still cool. Pick them complete with stalks; try not to handle the flesh because it bruises easily.

Alternatives to strawing down

If straw is not available, strawberries can also be grown through black polythene. First, prepare the bed by raising a 3 in high ridge of soil. Water it well. Lay 150-gauge plastic over the ridge, tucking in the edges under the soil. Plant the

At the end of the season

Immediately after cropping cut off the old leaves (about 3 in above the crown) and unwanted runners using shears or a sickle. Tuck in runners needed to fill in any gaps in the row. In the second year a matted row can be grown by allowing runners to root in the row and reducing the space available, so that the quantity of fruit is greater but the quality suffers. The space between the rows is kept clear. Defoliation and the burning of the old straw or other debris is good horticultural practice because it is a source of pests and diseases, but it must be done as soon as cropping is over to avoid damaging fresh growth and reducing the crop the next year.

Propagation

Strawberries are easily propagated from runners which the parent plant begins to produce as the crop is coming to an end. The aim is to obtain well-rooted runners for early planting and it is achieved by pegging down the strongest runners so that they make good contact with the soil. In June or July choose healthy parent plants which have cropped well. From each select four or five strong runners. Peg them down either into moist

strawberries through slits in the plastic at 15–18 in intervals. Leave a 6 in run of soil between the plastic to enable rain to permeate to the roots. Alternatively, protection can be provided by placing mats around individual plants like a collar.

open ground or into 3 in pots buried level with the soil. Pot-grown runners are best because they are easier to transplant. Fill the pots with a potting compost such as John Innes No. 3, or a peat-based compost. Peg close to the embryo plant but do not sever it from the parent at this stage. For the pegs, use 4 in pieces of thin galvanized wire bent to a U-shape. Straightened out paper clips are ideal.

In four to six weeks there should be a good root system. Sever from the parent, lift and plant out into the new bed. Keep them well watered.

Planting under mist or in a closed propagating case are other useful ways of obtaining very early runners. With these, sever the embryo plants from the parents at the first sign of roots—root initials—and peg them into $1\frac{1}{2}$–2 in peat pots.

Varieties

Strawberries soon become infected with virus diseases, so it is important to plant only virus-free stock. It is best to obtain plants from a specialist propagator who guarantees healthy stock rather than accept them from a dubious source.

Clearing up the bed

In August, after cropping, cut off the old leaves and unwanted runners with shears 3 in above crowns. Rake off the leaves, old straw and other debris and burn it. Fork up the compacted earth between the rows, leaving the ground weed-free.

PROPAGATION

1 In June to August, select four or five runners from healthy, cropping plants.

2 With U-shaped wires, peg runners into open ground or into 3 in pots buried level and filled with a potting compost.

3 In four to six weeks they should have rooted. Sever from parents close to plants.

4 Lift out the potted runners and knock out from the pot. Plant out into the new bed and water well.

Strawberries 3

'Gento' Flavour good. Berries medium to large, bright crimson. Yields a satisfactory crop in second year. Produces runners.

'Aromel' Flavour first class. Fruits medium to large. Grow as 1-year crop. Produces few runners. Propagated by division or runners.

'Trellisa' Flavour good. Berries medium to large. Grow as 1-year crop. Flowers and fruits freely on runners, useful for training on fences or in strawberry barrels.

'Sans Rivale' Flavour fair. Fruits medium, bright red. Heavy cropper, strong grower. Yields a reasonable crop in second year. Propagate by division.

ALPINES June to October.
'Baron Solemacher' Superb flavour. Masses of tiny dark red fruits. Widely grown. Prefers slight shade.

'Alexandria' Sweet and juicy. Very bright red. Fruits long (over ½ in) and large for an alpine. Good cropper.
'Fraise des Bois' Good flavour. Fruits very small. Bright red. Prolific continuous cropper.
'Alpine Yellow' Strongly flavoured, very small golden-yellow fruits. Not as heavy a cropper as the red varieties.

Perpetual or remontant strawberries

Perpetuals have the characteristic of producing fruit in irregular flushes throughout the summer until stopped by autumn frosts. It is useful to cover the autumn crop with cloches to extend the season, possibly into December. It is best to grow perpetuals for one year only because the size and weight of the crop deteriorate in the second year. Replant with new runners each year.

Cultivation

The basic requirements of soil, spacing, strawing down and feeding are the same as for summer-fruiting strawberries. Perpetuals crop at the hottest and driest part of the summer, so the soil should be highly fertile and moisture-retentive. Be sure to water well.

Plant in summer, autumn or spring and remove the first flush of flowers to ensure a good crop later in the season.

In the autumn, when cropping is finished, for varieties that crop in the second year, clean up the rows, remove the old straw, surplus runners and one or two of the older leaves, and burn the debris. If the plants are grown for one year only, dig them up and burn them at this time.

Alpine strawberries

Several varieties have been selected for garden and commercial cultivation. They make an attractive edging plant, having masses of small white flowers. They bear dark red fruits continuously or in flushes from June until November.

Cultivation

Alpine strawberries are usually grown from seed and kept for no more than two years before re-sowing. There are a few varieties that produce runners, but maintaining virus-free stock is difficult.

Sowing Sow the seeds, preferably in the autumn, and over-winter the seedlings in a cold frame. Alternatively, sow in March under glass. Sow into seed boxes containing a moist seed compost such as John Innes. Maintain them at a temperature of 18°–20°C/64°–68°F. Cover the boxes with glass and shade until the seeds germinate. When two true leaves appear, prick out the seedlings 1 in apart into boxes or peat pots.

Soil preparation, planting and feeding The soil should be rich, well drained and slightly acid (pH 6.0–6.5). Just before planting apply sulphate of potash at ½ oz per square yard. Once the danger of frosts is over, but by the end of May, plant out the seedlings in the prepared, moist soil. Plant in the open or in light shade. Space the seedlings 1 ft apart with 2½ ft between the rows. Water them in dry weather (about 3–4 gal per square yard every 7–10 days). For better cropping, when the flowers appear, feed every two weeks with a proprietary liquid feed for tomatoes.

Harvesting

The fruits are small but prolific and, although rather dry, have a stronger perfume than that of ordinary strawberries. Bring out this flavour by slightly crushing the fruits. Sprinkle with sugar and leave to soak overnight.

PROPAGATION

Some perpetual strawberries produce runners and are propagated in the same way as are summer-fruiting strawberries, but a few varieties do not and these are propagated by division.

From late August to early September, dig up a mature plant and break off the new crowns or buds with as many roots as possible. Transfer them to the new strawberry bed and plant them immediately in the usual way. Do not plant the crowns too deep or they will rot.

1 In autumn in a frame, or in March in the greenhouse, sow into seed boxes of moist seed compost.

2 Cover with glass and shade until germination. Maintain a temperature of 18°–20°C/64°–68°F.

3 When the seedlings have two true leaves, prick out 1 in apart into boxes or individual peat pots.

4 Just before planting, apply sulphate of potash at ½ oz per square yard to moist well-dug soil, forking it in lightly.

5 Once the danger of frosts is over, plant out the seedlings in the prepared bed, 1 ft apart in rows 2½ ft apart.

6 In dry periods, water the plants thoroughly every 7–10 days. For better crops, feed every two weeks with liquid manure.

Raspberries 1

SUMMER-FRUITING RASPBERRIES
Listed in order of ripening

EARLY
'Malling Promise' Flavour fair. Firm fruits when ripe softening soon afterwards. Berries large ($\frac{3}{4}$ in), conical, medium red. Heavy cropper. Canes abundant, vigorous. Susceptible to botrytis. Fairly tolerant of virus infection. Will thrive in poorer soils.
'Glen Clova' Flavour fair. Firm fruits. Berries small to medium ($\frac{1}{2}$ in), round, conical, dull red. Cropping very heavy. Canes numerous and strong. Some resistance to spur blight. Susceptible to virus infection, so best planted on its own.

MID-SEASON
'Malling Jewel' Flavour good, sweet. Firm berries, medium to large ($\frac{3}{4}$ in), red. Frost hardy. An excellent variety. Fairly tolerant of virus infection. A heavy and consistent cropper. Canes vigorous but not prolific. Growth compact.
'Malling Orion' Flavour good. Berries firm, medium to large ($\frac{3}{4}$ in), bright red. Very heavy cropper. Canes vigorous and numerous. Susceptible to spur blight and botrytis. Resistant to some aphids.

The European red raspberry (*Rubus idaeus*) can be found growing wild in cool, moist, hillside and woodland areas, from Scandinavia throughout Europe to central Asia. The stems, or, canes, are biennial, in that they grow vegetatively in their first year, flower and fruit in their second year and then die back to ground level. The root system is perennial and of suckering habit, producing each growing season new replacement canes from adventitious buds on the roots and new buds from old stem bases.

Like the strawberry, the raspberry is one of the quickest fruits to crop, bearing a reasonable amount in the second year and full cropping thereafter. A good average yield is $1\frac{1}{2}$–2 lb per foot run of row.

Cultivation
Most raspberries flower in late spring and the fruits ripen in early to midsummer, depending upon the variety and the weather: such varieties are called "summer-fruiting" raspberries.

Some varieties have the characteristic of flowering on the first year's growth on the topmost part in late summer and of ripening in the autumn. These are called "autumn-fruiting" raspberries and, because their cultural requirements differ in some respects, they are described separately (see page 92).

Soil and situation Raspberries grow best on a slightly acid soil of pH 6.0–6.7 that is moisture-retentive but well drained. They can be grown in dry, sandy and limy soils of low fertility, provided plenty of water is given during dry weather and bulky organic manures are liberally applied. Raspberries will not tolerate poor drainage, and even temporary waterlogging can lead to the death of the root system and subsequent death of the canes. In alkaline soils above pH 7.0, iron and manganese deficiencies may occur (see pages 10–11 for reduction of soil alkalinity and correction of iron and/or manganese deficiencies).

The site must be sheltered because strong winds damage the canes and inhibit the movement of pollinating insects. Preferably, they should be planted in full sun, although they grow quite well in partial shade with a minimum of half a day's sun, provided they are not directly under trees and the soil is not too dry.

Soil preparation Prepare the ground in early autumn by forking out all weeds, particularly perennials. Then dig a trench along the intended row three spades wide by one spade deep. Cover the bottom of the trench with well-rotted manure or compost to a depth of 3–4 in and fork it into the base so that it is thoroughly mixed with the soil. With double-dug grassland there is no need for this operation because the buried turf takes the place of the organic manure. Finally, fill in the trench and fork in a compound fertilizer such as a brand of Growmore at the rate of 3 oz per square yard.

Planting and spacing If possible the rows should run north-south so that one row does not shade another too much.

Plant during the dormant season from November to March. Plant the canes 18 in apart in the rows. If more than one row is planted, space the rows 6 ft apart, or 5 ft apart if using the single fence system. Spread the roots out well and plant them about 3 in deep; deep planting inhibits the production of new canes (suckers).

After planting, cut down the canes to a bud about 9–12 in above the ground. In the following spring, when the new canes appear, cut down the old stump to ground level before it fruits. This means foregoing a crop in the first summer but it ensures good establishment and the production of strong new canes in subsequent years.

Supporting the canes
To prevent the canes bowing over when heavy with fruit and to keep the fruits clean, it is necessary to support the canes. The usual method is a post and wire fence, for which there are various alternative systems. It is easier to erect the fence before planting, although it may be left until the end of the first summer.

Single fence: vertically trained canes This is the most popular method and consists of

1 In early autumn, take out a trench in prepared ground three spades wide by one spade deep. Cover the bottom of the trench with a 3–4 in layer of well-rotted manure or compost and fork in thoroughly.

2 Then, fill in the trench and fork in 3 oz per square yard of a compound fertilizer, such as a brand of Growmore.

3 From November to March, plant the canes at 18 in intervals. Spread the roots out well and plant about 3 in deep. Cut down the canes to a bud about 9–12 in above the ground.

4 In late March, apply sulphate of ammonia at $\frac{1}{2}$ oz per square yard. Mulch with a 2 in layer of garden compost, keeping it well clear of the canes.

Raspberries 2

'**Delight**' Flavour moderate. Berries crumbly, extremely large (1–1½ in), pale orange-red. Very heavy cropper. Fruit laterals long, will collapse in windy sites. Canes vigorous, erect and numerous. Susceptible to botrytis and spur blight. Resistant to some aphids.

'**Malling Admiral**' Flavour good. Berries firm, large (¾–1 in), conical, dark red. Canes vigorous and numerous. Fruiting laterals long and need protection from strong winds. Cropping heavy and prolonged. Some resistance to spur blight, botrytis and virus infection.

LATE

'**Leo**' Flavour good, slightly acid. Berries medium to large (¾ in), bright orange-red. Cropping heavy. Canes very vigorous, stout. Slow to build up, plant two per station. Resistant to spur blight and some aphids. Susceptible to cane spot.

YELLOW-FRUITING VARIETIES
Government-inspected stock of yellow-fruited raspberries is not available, and because there is a chance that they are infected with virus, it is best to grow them away from any virus-tested red raspberries.

The yellow raspberry is not as strongly flavoured as the red.

---

single wires stretched horizontally at heights of 2½, 3½ and 5½ ft. It requires the least space of the various fence systems and is ideal for the small garden. The fruiting canes are tied individually to the wires and thus are secure against winter winds. They are exposed to the sun, which enhances the quality of the fruits and reduces the incidence of fungal disease. The system has the disadvantages that the new canes are at risk of being trampled on during picking and of being damaged by strong winds in July unless temporarily supported by string tied to the lower wires.

Drive in preserved 7½ ft posts 18 in into the ground 12–15 ft apart. Use gauge 14 galvanized fencing wire.

Erect the end posts first and strut them and then drive in the intermediate posts. Finally fix the wires to the posts using straining bolts at one end and staples on the intermediates and at the opposite end.

Double fence: parallel wires The double fence is erected in a similar way to the single fence but because the top wires are not as high, the posts are only 6½ ft tall. Cross bars 2½ ft long by 2 in across to carry the parallel wires are fixed to the end posts and to the intermediate posts. In exposed situations, double posts should be used instead of cross bars. Parallel wires are spaced 2 ft apart at 3 ft and 5 ft from the ground. Stretch wire (or 4-ply fillis string) as cross ties every 2 ft along the wires to prevent the canes falling down in the row.

This method has the advantage of enabling a larger number of canes to be trained in and a greater yield to be obtained from much the same area. Picking the fruits from the centre is difficult, however, and there is a higher risk of fungal diseases because of the more crowded conditions.

In an exposed garden the untied canes may be damaged on the wires, so the canes should be tied to the wires.

Scandinavian system (training in a low "V") This is a double fence system with only one set of parallel wires spaced 3 ft apart at 3 ft from the ground.

Drive two sets of posts 4½ ft long 18 in into the ground, 3 ft apart every 12–15 ft in the row.

The fruiting canes are not tied but woven around the wires to form a "V" when viewed from the end of the row. The replacement canes are allowed to grow up the centre unsupported.

With this method the fruit is presented at a low picking height and the replacement canes are safe within the row. However, there is the risk of fungal troubles because of the crowded conditions of the canes on the wires and in the row. If more than one row is planted, space the rows 6 ft apart.

Single post system This is a method particularly suited to a very small garden. It consists of a single post to which each plant is tied. The posts are 7½ ft long by 2½ in top diameter, driven 18 in into the ground.

Initial pruning
In the first two seasons after planting, the number of canes may be few, but thereafter there should be more than enough.

In the second year thin out the weakest canes in the early summer so that the remainder grow more strongly, and pull out unwanted canes growing well away from the row. Allow about 8–10 canes to a stool.

Pruning and training established plants
As soon as fruiting is over, cut down to ground level the old canes which have fruited. Select the healthiest and strongest of the young canes, retaining about four to eight per stool.

If using the single fence system, tie the canes to the wires, 3–4 in apart. Either tie each one separately with a 6 in twist tie or secure them to the wires by continuous lacing using 4-ply fillis string. Tie the occasional knot as a precaution against the string breaking later on.

With the Scandinavian system the canes are laced around a single wire, equally on each side. Gently bend them over at the point they reach the wire and then twist the canes around the wire. No tying is necessary. Do this in late August or early September when the canes are still supple. Depending upon the length of the canes, this could mean four or six canes being twisted around each other and the supporting wires like a rope. The average number of canes from each stool should be about four to six.

For the single post system the fruiting canes are tied to the posts and the replacement canes looped in as and when necessary.

Tipping the canes (This is not applicable to the Scandinavian system). In late winter, about February, cut the canes to a bud 6 in above the top wire. This removes winter damage to the tips and encourages the lowest buds to break.

For very vigorous varieties grown on the single fence system, where tipping would remove a lot of the cane, loop and tie the canes back on to the top wire and then prune about 6 in off the tips. This method gives extra length of canes, hence more crop, but the top wire must be strong.

Feeding and watering
In late January each year apply 1 oz of sulphate of potash per square yard. Every third year add 2 oz of superphosphate per square yard. In late March apply sulphate of ammonia at ½ oz per square yard. The fertilizers should be applied as a top dressing covering about 18 in each side of the row.

Also, in late March, mulch with a 2 in layer of garden compost, damp peat or manure, keeping the material just clear of the canes. The mulch helps to conserve moisture in the summer and inhibits weed seeds from germinating.

Throughout the growing season keep down weeds and unwanted suckers by shallow hoeing. Be careful not to damage or disturb the roots of the raspberries. If preferred, herbicides can be used.

In dry weather water the raspberries regularly but, to minimize the risk of fungal troubles, keep the water off the canes.

Protect the fruit from birds with netting.

Propagation
Raspberries are easily propagated by forking up surplus canes with as many roots as possible at pruning time. The canes must be healthy and strong. Virus-infected plants should be dug up and burned.

Harvesting
Pick the fruits without the stalk and core, unless the raspberries are required for showing, when they are harvested with the stalk attached, using scissors.

SUPPORT SYSTEMS

Single post system

Drive 7½ ft long 2½ in dia. posts 18 in into the ground at each planting station.

Single fence system

Drive 7½ ft posts 18 in into the ground at 12–15 ft intervals. Stretch gauge 14 galvanized wires between the posts at 2½, 3½ and 5½ ft.

Double fence system

Drive 6½ ft posts 18 in into the ground 12–15 ft apart. Fix two 2 in dia. cross bars 2½ ft long to the end posts and to each intermediate post. Then, stretch parallel wires 2 ft apart between the posts at 3 ft and 5 ft from the ground. Stretch wires or string as cross ties every 2 ft along the wires.

Raspberries 3

'Golden Everest' Sweet, mild flavour. Berries small to medium ($\frac{1}{2}$–$\frac{3}{4}$ in), golden. Cropping satisfactory. Canes medium vigour, numerous. Fruits early in mid-season. Also fruits in the autumn on the one-year-old canes.

AUTUMN-FRUITING RASPBERRIES

'September' Flavour fair. Berries crumbly, small to medium ($\frac{1}{2}$ in), conical, dark red. Cropping moderate. Canes prolific, of weak to moderate vigour. Ripens late August to early September onwards.
'Zeva' Flavour fair. Fruits crumbly, medium to large ($\frac{3}{4}$–1 in) long, conical,

dark red. Often "double-nosed". Cropping moderate to good. Canes prolific, moderate vigour. Ripens early September onwards.
'Heritage' Flavour fair. Berries firm, small to medium ($\frac{1}{2}$ in), round, conical, light red. Cropping heavy. Canes numerous and vigorous. Ripens mid-September onwards. Requires a warm situation.

YELLOW AUTUMN-FRUITING RASPBERRIES
'Fallgold' Sweet, mild flavour. Berries medium to large ($\frac{1}{2}$ in), golden-yellow, conical. Canes vigorous, prolific. Fruits ripen early September.

Pests and diseases

If aphids are present, spray with dimethoate, heptenophos or malathion in spring. A tar oil spray in winter gets rid of the over-wintering eggs. To prevent raspberry beetle grubs feeding on the fruits in summer, spray at dusk with malathion or derris when the first pink berry is seen, and again 2 weeks later.

The most serious diseases of raspberries are viruses, which cause the leaves to become mottled or blotched and the canes to be stunted. Seek expert advice before destroying canes because the symptoms are similar to those caused by raspberry leaf and bud mite. New canes should be planted elsewhere.

Canes affected by cane blight in summer will wilt, snap off easily and die. Cut out and burn affected canes. Spray new canes with bordeaux mixture.

Cut out and burn canes badly affected by cane spot and prevent it by spraying with liquid copper or thiram at bud burst and pre-blossom time, or with benomyl every two weeks from bud burst to petal fall.

Spur blight causes dark purple blotches around the buds and shoots wither in early spring. Cut out and burn affected canes. Spray new canes when they are a few inches high with benomyl, thiram or captan repeating two, four and six weeks later.

Prevent grey mould (*Botrytis cinerea*) by spraying three times with benomyl at flowering and at two week intervals. Remove and destroy infected fruits.

Selecting healthy plants

It is important to buy only Government-inspected stock, wherever possible, to ensure the plants are virus-free, healthy and true to name. Healthy plants should last at least ten years before starting to degenerate from virus infection. When this occurs, remove the plants and start a new row in soil that has not grown raspberries or other *Rubus* species before. If this is not possible, re-soil over an area 2 ft wide by 1 ft deep.

AUTUMN-FRUITING RASPBERRIES

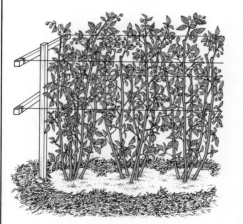

Autumn-fruiting raspberries bear their fruit on the top part of the current season's canes, extending back from the top over 12 in or more, depending upon the variety. The fruits ripen from the beginning of September until stopped by the autumn frosts. They do not come away from the plug or core as easily as some of the summer-fruiting varieties, making picking more difficult. These raspberries are not usually attacked by birds, therefore netting should not be necessary. A good average yield is about $\frac{1}{2}$ lb per foot run of row.

The cultural requirements (soil preparation, planting, spacing, initial pruning and feeding) are the same as for the summer-fruiting kind. Use the parallel wire method of support described on page 91. The fruits are produced when the weather is becoming cooler, so they are best planted in the sunniest position possible, otherwise too few raspberries may ripen before the first frosts arrive.

Pruning established plants Each February cut down all canes in the row to ground level. In the following spring, new canes are produced which crop in the autumn. As the canes are not in the row for more than a year, it is not necessary to thin them unless they are particularly crowded. Pull out any which are growing away from the row.

The first year

1 In spring, when the new canes appear, cut down the old stumps to ground level.

Second and subsequent years

3 In February, cut the canes to a bud 6 in above the top wire. Mulch the plants.

5 When fruiting is over, cut the fruited canes down to ground level. Tie in new canes 4 in apart. If growth is vigorous loop the new canes over to form a series of arches.

2 From June to September, as new canes develop, tie them 4 in apart on to the wires.

4 In midsummer, fruit is carried on laterals from last year's canes. Thin out the weakest new growth to leave strong canes 4 in apart. Pull out new shoots growing away from the row.

6 Each year in late January, apply 1 oz sulphate of potash per square yard as a top dressing 18 in each side of the row. Every third year apply 2 oz superphosphate per square yard.

Blackberries 1

BLACKBERRIES
'Bedford Giant' Flavour fair. Berries round, large, bright black. Fruits ripen July/August. Cropping moderate. Growth vigorous. Not suitable for the small garden.
'Himalaya Giant' ('Theodor Reimers') Sharp, wild blackberry flavour. Berries medium-sized and firm. Fruits ripen

August onwards. Very heavy cropper. Extremely vigorous, with strong thorns. Not suitable for the small garden.
'Oregon Thornless' A thorn-free form of the cut-leaved blackberry (*Rubus laciniatus*). Flavour fair, mild and sweet. Fruit size small to medium. Cropping good. Growth medium to vigorous. Fruits ripen mid-August to September.

Excellent for the medium-sized garden.
'Smoothstem' Flavour sharp. Firm, large, shiny black berries. Heavy cropper. Medium vigour, canes thornless. Fruits ripen from late August onwards. Needs a warm, sunny situation.

The blackberry, or bramble as it is popularly called, is a rambling cane fruit found growing wild throughout the British Isles, northern Europe and in the Mediterranean region. The canes are of arching habit, thick, strong and often aggressively thorned, although there are good thornless cultivated varieties. It is usually deciduous, but not always so in mild winters.

Hybrid berries, of which there are a number of named varieties, have arisen as a result of accidental and deliberate crosses between various *Rubus* species, principally between the raspberry, blackberry and dewberry. As might be expected, they have characteristics that are intermediate between those of the parents. Most hybrid berries are not as vigorous as the blackberry and are, therefore, more suited to the small garden. There are both thorned and thornless varieties of hybrids.

A good average yield from a well-established blackberry or hybrid berry plant is 10–30 lb of fruit, depending upon the size of the plant and the variety.

Cultivation

Cultivated blackberries are much larger and more luscious than are wild varieties. They need little preventative spraying and can be planted in a spare corner of the garden.

Soil and situation Blackberries grow in a wide range of soils and will tolerate slightly impeded drainage. If thin dry soils cannot be avoided, improve their moisture retentiveness and fertility with bulky organics. Hybrid berries are more demanding, and require a well-drained fertile soil, ideally a medium loam not less than 15 in deep.

Blackberries and hybrid berries flower relatively late, from the end of May onwards, and bloom over a long period, and so frost is seldom a problem. They are among the few fruits that can be successfully grown in a frost pocket, although this should be avoided if possible. They will also tolerate partial shade but fare better in full sun (particularly the hybrid berries). Because of their rambling habit, they need some support.

Planting Prepare the ground in early autumn. Fork out perennial weeds. Then, if the ground is poor, apply a 2–3 in deep layer of well-rotted manure, compost or peat over an area 2–2½ ft square at each planting site and dig it in thoroughly. Rake in 3 oz of a compound fertilizer such as a brand of Growmore over the same area.

Plant during the dormant season from November to March, preferably in the early part of the winter while the soil is still warm. Young plants, in the form of rooted tips or one-year-old bedded tips, can be obtained from a nursery. Using a hand trowel or fork, dig a hole wide and deep enough to take the roots spread out well. Plant the canes to the same depth as they were in the nursery. After planting, firm the soil and then cut down each cane to a bud at about 10 in above the ground.

Spacing Plant the canes in rows 6 ft apart. In most gardens one plant, or at the most one row, is sufficient.

Spacing between the plants depends upon the variety and the method of training. For the least vigorous growers, such as the thornless types and the Boysenberry and Tayberry, fan-trained plants should be spaced 8 ft apart; allow 8–12 ft between the weaving and one-way systems. For varieties of medium vigour, such as the loganberry, 'John Innes' and 'Oregon Thornless', the relevant distances are 10 ft between fans and 10–12 ft between weaving and one-way systems. Extremely vigorous growers, such as 'Himalaya Giant' and 'Bedford Giant', should be spaced 12 ft apart when fan-trained and 12–15 ft apart for the weaving and one-way systems.

Support Support is necessary to keep the canes off the ground for easy picking and to keep the plants tidy. Out in the open, a wire fence is necessary with wires every 12 in between 3 ft and 6 ft. Erect the wires before planting the canes.

Training The fruiting canes should be trained to keep them separate from the young replacement canes to facilitate picking and to reduce the risk of the spread of fungal diseases from the old to the new.

The three methods commonly used are the fan, weaving, and rope system trained one way. The fan is best reserved for less vigorous hybrid berries. The weaving system takes full advantage of the long canes of vigorous kinds but there is much handling at pruning time. The one-way system keeps handling to a minimum, but wastes space because young rods are trained along the wires only to one side of the plant. These fruit the following year. When new rods appear they are trained in the opposite direction.

Initial pruning In the first summer after planting, a number of young canes should spring up from the root system. Tie these securely to the lower wires in a weaving fashion. In the second summer these canes should flower and fruit. At the same time new growth springs from the base of the plant. This young growth should be secured and trained in the adopted method.

When fruiting is over, untie the old canes and cut them down to ground level. With the fan and weaving systems the young canes are then trained in to take their place. With the one-way system, the young canes are already tied in. The young growth will fruit in the next year, and so the cycle is repeated.

Subsequent pruning Pruning in the third and subsequent years consists of cutting out the rods that have fruited and replacing them with the new canes. If the replacement canes are few, the best of the old canes can be used again, but the older growth does not yield the best quality berries. Each year in February cut back any winter-damaged tips to a healthy bud.

Feeding and watering In late February apply 2 oz of a compound fertilizer such as a brand of Growmore as a top dressing over one square yard around the base of each plant.

In late March, mulch with a 2 in layer of garden compost, peat or manure, keeping the material just clear of the canes. In dry weather water the plants but, to minimize the risk of fungal troubles, avoid the canes.

If necessary, protect the fruit from birds with netting.

Pollination

All varieties are self-compatible and only one plant is needed.

Harvesting

Blackberries are ready for picking when they are black in colour. Hybrid berries vary from claret red to black. Pick all fruit when it is ripe even if not required, because this helps the later fruit to achieve a good size.

Pests and diseases

Blackberries and hybrid berries are prone to the same pests and diseases as raspberries (see page 92).

PROPAGATION

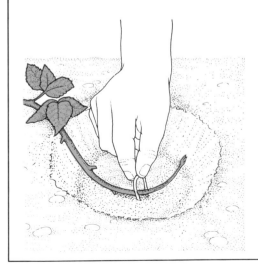

Blackberries and hybrid berries are propagated by tip-rooting. The new canes are tip-rooted in August and September. A 6 in hole is dug with a trowel near the plant, and the tip of a young cane is bent down into it. The soil is then replaced and firmed. As new canes are produced, so more tips can be buried. In the following spring, the rooted tips are severed from the parent plant with about 10 in of stem, and then dug up and planted out in a new position. A few varieties produce spawn (suckers), which should be lifted with as much root as possible and planted out in the new bed.

Another method is by leaf bud cuttings taken in July and August and rooted in a cold frame. This method is useful for rapid propagation when stock is limited.

Blackberries 2

HYBRID BERRIES
'John Innes' Good, sweet flavour. Large, firm, shiny black berries. Heavy cropper. Canes of medium vigour. Few spines. Ripens mid-August onwards.
Loganberry Flavour sharp and distinctive. Berries very large, up to 2 in long, burgundy red. Cropping good. Canes moderately vigorous. Fruits ripen

July/August. There are two good clones, LY59 (thorned) and L654 (thornless).
Thornless Boysenberry Flavour sharp and excellent for jams and cooking. Berries large, conical, ripen to a dark purple-red. Cropping good. Weak to moderate vigour. Ripens July/August. Resists drought well, useful on light soils.

Tayberry Flavour good, mild and sweet. First berries large, smaller later in the season. Similar in shape and colour to the loganberry. Cropping good. Canes moderate in vigour, prolific, slightly thorned. Fruits ripen early July. Excellent for the small garden.

Japanese Wine Berry (Rubus phoenicolasius). Sweet, poor flavour. Seedy, small golden-yellow berries. Cropping light. Fruits ripen August. Canes covered with thin red bristles. Grown mainly for ornament.

Cultivation

1 In early autumn, clear the ground of perennial weeds. If the ground is poor, dig in a 2–3 in layer of well-rotted manure over an area 2–2½ ft square. Fork in 2 oz of compound fertilizer over the same area.

2 From November to March, dig a hole to take the plant with the roots spread out well. Plant to the same depth as it was at the nursery. Firm the soil and cut the cane to a bud 10 in above the ground.

3 In late February, fork in 3 oz of a compound fertilizer such as a brand of Growmore per square yard around the base of each plant.

4 In late March, apply a 2 in layer of garden compost keeping it just clear of the canes. During dry weather, water the plants but keep the water off the canes.

Weaving system

1 In summer, as the young canes appear, tie them to a strong wire support. Weave them in and out of the bottom three wires.

The second year

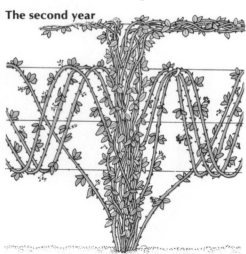

2 In summer, train the new canes up through the centre of the bush and along the top wire. Fruit is carried on laterals of last year's canes.

3 In October, after fruiting, cut out all fruited canes to base. If there are few new canes, retain the best of the old.

4 At the same time, untie the current season's canes and weave them round the lower three wires. In autumn, remove the weak tips from the young canes.

Black currants 1

BLACK CURRANTS
Listed in order of ripening

EARLY
'Boskoop Giant' Juicy, moderately sweet, good flavour. A thin, rather tender skin. Berries very large. Cropping heavy. Bush very vigorous and slightly spreading. Not suitable for the small garden. Susceptible to leaf spot.
'Blackdown' Sweet flavour. Berries firm, medium to large. Cropping good. Bush medium to large, rather spreading. Very resistant to American gooseberry mildew.

MID-SEASON
'Wellington XXX' Sweet, good flavour. Berries medium to large. A tough skin. A heavy cropper. Growth vigorous and spreading, and needs careful pruning to keep upright. Sensitive to lime sulphur.
'Blacksmith' Good flavour. Skin rather thin and tender. Berries large. Cropping heavy. Bush vigorous, large and spread-ing. Not suitable for the small garden.
'Ben Lomond' Flavour good, acid. Berries large, cropping very heavy. Bush upright and compact, spreads a little under the weight of the crop. Flowers late and has some resistance to frost. Carries a good resistance to American gooseberry mildew.

The black currant (*Ribes nigrum*) is a native of central and eastern Europe from Scandinavia to Bulgaria, also northern and central Asia to the Himalayas. It can be found growing wild, generally in damp woody places.

Selection in cultivation has given rise to stronger-growing and highly productive varieties. Black currants are grown on a stool system—that is, many shoots spring from below the ground rather than from a single stem. A well-grown black currant bush may reach 5–6 ft in height and spread and should last 15 years or more before it needs to be replaced. A good, average yield from an established black currant is about 10–12 lb.

Cultivation
It is important to buy only healthy stock because the black currant can suffer from a serious pest called gall mite (big bud mite) with its attendant reversion disease, both of which can badly debilitate the plant. For this reason many countries operate a certification scheme whereby the young stock sold by nurseries is inspected and, if healthy, a certificate to this effect is issued. In Britain only two-year-old certified black currant plants are available.

Soil and situation Black currants can be grown in a wide range of soils. Ideally it should be slightly acid (about pH 6.5), highly fertile, moisture-retentive and well-drained, although black currants will tolerate slightly impeded drainage. Light soils need plenty of bulky organics. Excessively acid soils should be limed to bring the pH up to 6.5.

The site should be frost-free and sheltered from strong winds so that pollinating insects such as bees are not inhibited. Most varieties bloom early in the spring and the flowers are extremely vulnerable to frost. In frost-prone areas, plant the late-flowering or more frost-tolerant varieties and cover the plants on frosty nights. Black currants will tolerate partial shade but prefer a sunny position.

Preparing the soil Prepare the ground in early autumn clearing away all weeds. Apply a 3 in layer of manure or compost over the whole area. If manure and compost are not available, apply a 2 in layer of peat with bonemeal at 3 oz per square yard. If the ground is fairly clean single dig the materials in, but if rough and weedy double dig the area. Rake in a balanced fertilizer such as a brand of Growmore at the rate of 3 oz per square yard.

Planting and spacing Buy two-year-old certified bushes. Select plants with not less than three strong shoots.

Plant during the dormant season from November to March. Space bushes 5 ft apart in the row (6 ft apart for more vigorous varieties), with 6 ft between rows.

Dig out a hole wide enough to take the roots spread out well. To encourage a strong stool system plant bushes about 2 in deeper than they were in the nursery—the soil mark on the stems gives an indication. Fill in the hole and firm.

Initial pruning After planting, cut all shoots to within 2 in of soil level. This encourages the production of strong young shoots from the base, and creates a good stool system for heavy cropping in the future, although it means foregoing a crop in the first summer. If the plants are from certified stock, the pruned shoots may be used as cuttings. They root easily so buy only half the number of bushes required and fill the vacant positions with two to three cuttings to each station.

After the hard initial pruning the young bush should produce three or four strong shoots from the base, each shoot being 18 in or more in length. If growth is poor, they should be cut down again in the winter. Assuming a strong bush has been formed, no pruning is required at the end of the first year; the young shoots are left to fruit in the following summer.

Pruning an established bush Black currants bear the best fruit on the wood produced in the previous summer, although they also crop on the older wood. Prune in early autumn or at any time in the dormant season until March.

The objective with an established bush is to stimulate a constant succession of strong young shoots to carry fruit in the next season. This is achieved by fairly hard pruning, cutting at or as near the base as possible, and by heavy feeding.

It is important to be able to distinguish the young wood from the old. This is fairly easy because the bark of the young shoots is much lighter in colour than that of three years old or more.

There is no need to limit the number of main branches nor to have the centre open. However, about a quarter to a third of the oldest wood should be removed annually. Cut back to a strong young shoot at or near the base or, if there is none, cut out the branch altogether.

Remove any thin mildewed shoots including those suffering from die-back in the centre. Leave a working space between one bush and the next.

Feeding and watering Black currants thrive on heavy manuring and high summer moisture. Each February apply a compound fertilizer such as a brand of Growmore over the whole plantation at 3 oz per square yard. Additionally, in March apply sulphate of ammonia at 1 oz per square yard; on acid soils apply nitro-chalk instead. Follow this with a 3 in thick mulch of manure or compost around each bush.

In dry weather apply $4\frac{1}{2}$ gal of water per square yard every ten days, but keep the water off the stems as much as possible to lessen the risk of fungal trouble. This assists new growth and the developing crop.

Weed control The bushes are shallow-rooted. Do not dig around the plant but keep the weeds down by shallow hoeing or by hand weeding or by using herbicides (see page 155).

Pollination
Black currants are self-compatible and are pollinated mainly by bees.

Frost and bird protection
The flowers are extremely vulnerable to spring frosts which cause the fruitlets to drop. On nights when frosts are likely, drape the bushes with hessian or a few layers of bird netting (see page 97), remove the cover in the mornings. Net the fruits against birds when the first fruits begin to colour.

Harvesting
Pick selectively when the currants ripen but before they begin to fall or shrivel. For show purposes the whole strig should be cut off using scissors.

Pests and diseases
The most serious pests of black currants are aphids, the black currant gall mite, and glasshouse red spider mite. Use a systemic insecticide against aphids, carbendazim for gall mite, and malathion, dimethoate or derris to control glasshouse red spider mite.

Of the diseases, the most troublesome are reversion disease, American gooseberry mildew, leaf spot and botrytis. Bushes affected by reversion should be dug up and burned. Mildew can be controlled by regular spraying with benomyl, carbendazim or thiophanate-methyl; the last two will also control leaf spot. Alternative fungicides are mancozeb or thiram. For botrytis use benomyl, carbendazim or thiophanate-methyl at flowering time.

PROPAGATION

Black currants are propagated from cuttings 8–10 in long about a pencil's width, from well-budded healthy wood of the current year's growth. Take the cuttings in October or November. Make a sloping cut just above a bud at the top and a straight cut just below a bud at the base. Insert the cuttings deeply with only two buds showing above the surface in well-drained light soil. Space the cuttings 6 in apart and firm them in the row.

At the end of the first growing season dig up and plant the rooted cuttings 12 in apart. Cut them down to within 1 in of the ground. This hard pruning should create a stooled bush.

Black currants 2

'Baldwin' (Hilltop strain) The most widely grown variety. Acid flavour, rich in vitamin C. Tough skin. Berries medium and hang well without splitting over a long period. Cropping moderate to good. Bush of medium vigour, fairly compact. Suitable for the small garden.
'Jet' Flavour good, acid. Berries firm, small to medium. Trusses extremely long, hang well, easy to pick. Cropping very heavy. Bush large and vigorous. Flowers very late. Carries some resistance to American gooseberry mildew.

1 In autumn, clear the ground of weeds. Dig in a 3 in layer of manure or compost. Rake in a balanced fertilizer such as a brand of Growmore at 3 oz per square yard.

2 Dig a hole wide and deep enough to take the roots spread out well. Plant the bush 2 in deeper than it was at the nursery. Fill in the hole and firm the soil.

3 After planting, cut down all shoots to within 2 in of soil level.

The second year

4 In November, the severe pruning has resulted in strong new shoots appearing from the base. These will fruit the following year. No pruning is required.

5 In February to March, apply a compound fertilizer such as a brand of Growmore at 3 oz per square yard. A month later, apply 1 oz sulphate of ammonia per square yard.

6 In July, the bush fruits best on last year's wood. New basal growths develop.

The third year

7 In November, thin out weak shoots and any branches that are too low, broken or mildewed.

In subsequent years

8 Every winter, between November and March, remove about one-third of the bush. Cut out badly-placed, damaged wood. Cut back fruited branches to a strong shoot.

Red and white currants 1

RED CURRANTS
EARLY
'Jonkheer van Tets' Good flavour. Thin but tough skin; deep red, large berries. Ripens July. A very heavy cropper. Bush moderately vigorous, fairly upright, spurring freely. Branches may need support in early years against the weight of crop. Short picking period.

'Laxton's No. 1' Good flavour, firm berries, medium to large, bright red. Ripens July. A heavy cropper. Bush vigorous, upright to slightly spreading.

MID-SEASON
'Red Lake' Good flavour, juicy, firm berries. Large bright red fruits. Ripens July to August. A heavy cropper. Easy to pick. Bush moderately vigorous, upright, spurring freely.

Red and white currants are basically derived from two European species, *Ribes rubrum* and *R. spicatum*. The latter species is native to northern Britain. Red currants sometimes occur as garden escapes from bird-sown seed and *R. rubrum* is also found naturalized in many areas.

Cultivation

The fruit buds are produced in clusters at the base of the one-year-old shoots and on short spurs on the older wood. Because of this fruiting habit there is a permanent framework of branches, unlike the black currant for which a succession of young wood is needed.

The red currant is usually grown as an open-centred bush on a 4–6 in stem or leg, rather like a miniature apple tree, with a height and spread of about 5–6 ft. This method of growth makes cultivation around the plant easier and keeps the fruit clear of the ground. The red currant is also grown as a single or multiple cordon, and, more rarely, as a standard or fan. A well-grown bush should yield at least 8–10 lb of fruit and a single cordon about 2–3 lb. Plants should bear well for at least ten years.

The smooth-skinned, glistening red berries are attractive and ideal for jelly, pies, juice and for wine making.

The white currant is a mutation or sport of the red currant and for cultural purposes is treated in exactly the same way. The berries, of somewhat milder flavour than the red, are also useful for jelly and for wine making.

Soil and situation Ideally, the soil should be neutral to slightly acid (about pH 6.7). It is less tolerant of poor drainage than the black currant but, provided the soil is reasonably well drained and not deficient in potash, the red currant is tolerant of a wide range of conditions.

The flowers of the red and white currants are hardier than those of the black currant, so it is a useful plant for north-facing walls and fences and for shaded areas, provided the soil is not dry and overhanging trees do not drip on the plants. It will grow in zones 7–8. A sunny position is preferable if the berries are to acquire their full flavour. The site should be sheltered but not a frost pocket.

Soil preparation Prepare the soil in the early autumn by clearing away all weeds. Apply a light dressing of well-rotted manure or compost about 1½ in thick over the whole area. If farmyard manure or compost are not available, apply a 1 in layer of damp peat. If the ground is fairly clean, single dig the dressing in; but if weedy, double dig the area. Rake in a compound fertilizer, such as a brand of Growmore, at the rate of 2 oz per square yard and sulphate of potash at ½ oz per square yard.

Selection of plants Buy plants from a reliable source because certified stock is not available. One- or two-year-old bushes are usually supplied by the nursery. Select a plant with a clear stem, or leg, of about 4–6 in with a head of about 3–6 evenly balanced shoots. The single (or multiple) cordon may be two or three years old and should consist of one (or more) straight stems with plenty of side-shoots. The standard, rarely seen nowadays, has a clear stem of about 3½ ft.

Planting and spacing Plant during the dormant season between November and March, unless the plants are container-grown, when they can be planted at any time.

Space bushes 5 ft × 5 ft (5 ft × 6 ft on fertile land) and single cordons 15 in apart, or 12 in apart on light soils. Allow 12 in between each stem of a multiple cordon; for example, double cordons should be planted 24 in apart from the main stem at ground level. Cordons should be trained up a vertical cane for straight growth and support. If planting cordons in the open, before planting erect a wire fence with horizontal wires at 2 ft and 4 ft and tie canes to the wires at each planting station.

Next, take out a hole large enough to contain the roots well spread out, and plant the bush or cordon to the same depth as it was in the nursery. Fill in and firm the soil.

Feeding and watering Each February apply a compound fertilizer, such as a brand of Growmore, over the whole plantation at 2 oz per square yard and sulphate of potash at ½ oz per square yard. On light soils also apply a mulch of rotted manure, compost or peat 2 in thick around each bush. If manure, compost or peat are not available, apply sulphate of ammonia at 1 oz per square yard. Water copiously in dry weather.

1 In early autumn, dig in a 1½ in layer of well-rotted manure. Then, rake in a compound fertilizer, such as a brand of Growmore, at 2 oz per square yard and sulphate of potash at ½ oz per square yard.

2 From November to March, dig a hole large enough to take the roots well spread out and plant the bush to the same depth as it was at the nursery. Delay planting if the ground is very wet or frozen.

3 Each February, apply Growmore at 2 oz per square yard and sulphate of potash at ½ oz per square yard. On light soils also apply a 2 in mulch of rotted manure, compost or peat around each bush.

4 During the winter, protect the fruit buds with netting against attack by birds and frost at blossom time. Remove it during the day at flowering time.

Red and white currants 2

LATE
'Rondom' Flavour fair, rather acid, flesh less juicy than other varieties. Firm, medium size, dark red fruits. Ripens August. A heavy cropper. Bush vigorous, intermediate between upright and spreading.

WHITE CURRANTS
'White Grape' Flavour excellent, firm, juicy. Berries large, clear yellow-white. Ripens mid-July. Moderate cropper. Easy to pick. Bush medium vigour.
'White Versailles' Good flavour, sweet, firm. Berries large, pale yellow. Ripens July. Good cropper. Easy to pick. Bush moderately vigorous, upright.

Pruning bush currants

The objective is to create a goblet-shaped bush with about 8–10 main branches growing upwards and outwards on a 4–6 in clear stem with an open centre. Prune in the same way as the gooseberry bush (see pages 99–100) except that the leaders are pruned to outward-facing buds, unless the branches are drooping, when they are pruned to upward-facing buds.

Pruning the single cordon: initial pruning

On planting a one-year-old rooted cutting, shorten the central leader by about one-half to an outward-facing bud. Cut back all other laterals to about 1 in at a bud, and remove any buds lower than 4 in to create a short clear stem. If planting an older pre-shaped cordon, shorten the leader by one-third and prune maiden laterals to one bud.

In late June to early July cut back the current season's side-shoots to 4–5 leaves. Tie the leader to the cane as and when necessary throughout the growing season, but do not prune it.

Second and subsequent years A cordon is pruned in much the same way as a bush. Each summer at the end of June or early in July prune the current season's side-shoots to 4–5 leaves. Do not carry out summer pruning earlier than this or secondary growth may be stimulated. The leader is trained and tied to the cane, but not pruned in the summer until it has reached the required height, usually about 5–6 ft. From then on it is summer-pruned to 4–5 leaves.

Each winter, from November to March, cut all the previously summer-pruned laterals to about 1 in at a bud. Prune the leader to a bud leaving 6 in of new growth. Once the leader has reached the required height, it is also pruned to leave one bud of the previous summer's growth. This helps to maintain the cordon at approximately the same height for some years.

Multiple cordons, such as the double- and triple-stemmed cordon, are pruned in exactly the same way as the single, except that in the early formative years suitably low placed laterals are used to form the main stems.

Weed control

Red and white currants are shallow rooted. Do not dig around the plants but keep the weeds down by shallow hoeing, hand weeding or by using herbicides.

Pollination

Red currants are self-fertile and insect pollinated, so pollination is not a problem.

Frost and bird protection

Red and white currant flowers are fairly hardy, although they will not tolerate hard frosts. Cover them with hessian or two or three layers of bird netting on frosty nights.

The berries are extremely attractive to birds in the summer, as are the fruit buds in the winter. Net the bushes in the winter and at fruit ripening time. Remove the netting at flowering time, because netting inhibits insect pollination.

Harvesting

Red currants are ripe in July or August. Pick whole clusters to avoid injury to the fruit.

Propagation

Propagate new red currant plants in the autumn from hardwood cuttings, which should be 12 in long or more. Before planting the cuttings, remove all the buds except the top three or four. Insert into the soil with the third bud within 2 in of the soil surface and label the cuttings. After they have rooted (in about a year's time) plant out the cuttings. This method produces rooted cuttings with four good branches and a short leg.

Pests and diseases

The most serious pests are aphids (particularly the red currant blister aphid) and, to a lesser extent, sawfly caterpillars and capsid bugs. Control aphids with a systemic insecticide; control caterpillars and capsids with fenitrothion, derris or malathion.

Occasionally leaf spot and coral spot can be troublesome. If leaf spot occurs, apply mancozeb, thiram, benomyl, carbendazim or thiophanate-methyl. Cut back to healthy wood any branches affected by coral spot and burn the prunings.

The first year: Cordon

1 In winter, when planting a one-year-old shorten the central leader by about one-half to an outward-facing bud. Cut back all laterals to 1 in at a bud and remove any lower than 4 in.

2 From late June to early July, cut back the current season's side-shoots to 4–5 leaves. Tie the leader to the cane as it extends but do not prune it.

Second and subsequent years

3 From November to March, prune the leader to a bud leaving 6 in of new growth. Cut all previously summer-pruned laterals to 1 in at a bud. In later years, cut the leader back to one bud.

4 From late June to early July, prune the current season's side-shoots to 4–5 leaves. Tie the leader to the cane as it extends.

Gooseberries 1

GOOSEBERRIES
Listed in order of ripening.

EARLY
'Keepsake' Very good flavour. Fruits medium to large, green-white with a transparent, slightly hairy skin. Crops well. Ripens late but earliest for picking for cooking.

'May Duke' Good flavour when cooked. Fruits medium, oblong, dark red with smooth, downy skin. Early when picked green. Good cropper.
'Golden Drop' Rich flavour. Fruits small, round, dull green-yellow, with downy thin skin. Excellent dessert gooseberry.

The gooseberry (*Ribes uva-crispa*) is a deciduous thorny shrub native to the cooler areas of Europe (zones 7–8).

Like the red currant, the gooseberry bears its fruit on spurs on the older wood and at the base of the previous summer's lateral growth. For this reason the gooseberry is grown with a permanent framework of branches, usually in the form of an open-centred bush on a short stem, or leg, of about 4–6 in. It is also widely grown as a cordon in single or multiple form and occasionally as a standard on a $3\frac{1}{2}$ ft stem or as a fan.

The fruits may be smooth or hairy, yellow, white, green or red according to variety.

A well-grown bush should reach a height and spread of 5 ft and crop well for 12 years or more. A good average yield from a bush is 5–6 lb, and from a cordon 1–2 lb.

Cultivation

One-, two-, or three-year-old bushes can be bought from a nursery. A one-year-old bush should have about 3–5 shoots evenly placed around the stem, a two-year-old about 5–7 and a three-year-old 6–8 primary and secondary branches. Gooseberries are self-fertile and insect pollinated, so they can be planted singly if required.

Soil and situation The soil requirements of the gooseberry are similar to those of the red currant. The soil should not be allowed to become potash-deficient. It tolerates a little impeded drainage, provided it occurs below 18 in. The ideal soil, however, is a slightly acid (pH 6.7), well-drained medium loam.

The gooseberry is tolerant of cool, partial shade, but grows best in an open sunny site, which should be sheltered against strong winds, especially at flowering time in early April. Do not plant it in a frost pocket.

Soil preparation Prepare the soil in early autumn. It is essential to eliminate perennial weeds because the gooseberry is thorny and not easy to weed around. On light soils, dig in a $1\frac{1}{2}$–2 in layer of well-rotted manure or compost over the whole area. On rich soils there is less need for bulky organics because too much of them encourages soft growth prone to snapping and to mildew. Rake in a compound fertilizer such as a brand of Growmore at 2 oz per square yard and sulphate of potash at $\frac{1}{2}$ oz per square yard.

Planting and spacing Plant during the dormant season between November and March, preferably in autumn when the soil is warm.

Dig a hole wide and deep enough to contain the root system with the roots well spread

out. Before planting, clean off any suckers at the base of the plants and any shoots too near the ground, then plant it to leave a clear stem of 4–6 in. Fill in the hole and firm the soil.

Space the bushes 5 ft apart, or on highly fertile ground 5 ft by 6 ft apart, and single cordons 1 ft apart. Allow 1 ft of space for each stem of a multiple cordon. For straight growth and support, train a cordon up a cane. If growing cordons in the open, erect a wire fence with horizontal wires at 2 ft and 4 ft and tie the canes to it.

Feeding and watering Each February apply a compound fertilizer such as a brand of Growmore over the whole plot at 2 oz per square yard and sulphate of potash at $\frac{1}{2}$ oz per square yard. Mulch around the base of the plant with a 2 in layer of well-rotted manure, compost or peat on light soils, but less on medium or fertile soils. In the absence of bulky organics apply sulphate of ammonia at 1 oz per square yard.

Water copiously in dry weather but do not water irregularly or heavily at the ripening stage because this causes the fruit to split.

Formative pruning: Bush

Most varieties have a tendency to form drooping growth and, in order to maintain

an erect bush, counteract this habit by pruning the leaders to inward- or upward-facing buds or back to upright laterals. The centre of the plant is kept open to make picking and spraying easier, to ripen the wood and fruits, and to improve air circulation (which lessens the risk of mildew).

When planting a one-year-old bush, cut back each framework branch by one-half to an outward-facing bud if the shoot is upright, or to an inward-facing bud if the shoot is weeping.

The second year (or a two-year-old bush)
In November, shorten the leaders by one-half. Select well-placed shoots to form further permanent branches and cut back by one-half. Remove any suckers or low-growing shoots growing from the stem.

The third year (or a three-year-old bush)
The bush should have developed a main framework of about 6–8 branches with well-spaced leading shoots; it is at the start of its cropping life. Between November and March, shorten the leaders by one-half to a bud facing in the required growth direction. Cut out shoots crowding the centre and shorten those not required for the framework to about 2 in. Thereafter, prune the bush both in the summer and in the winter.

The second year

1 In early autumn, clear the soil of perennial weeds. Rake in a compound fertilizer such as a brand of Growmore at 2 oz per square yard and sulphate of potash at $\frac{1}{2}$ oz per square yard.

2 From November to March, dig a hole wide and deep enough to take the roots spread out well. Plant the bush so that there is a clear stem of 4–6 in above ground.

3 At the same time, cut back each framework branch by one-half to an inward- and upward-pointing bud. Clean off the suckers at the base and any shoots too near the ground.

4 In November, shorten the leaders by one-half to inward- and upward-facing buds. Select well-placed shoots to form further permanent branches and cut back by one-half. Remove suckers and low stems.

Gooseberries 2

'Careless' Good flavour. Fruits large, oval. Green skin ripening to white, smooth transparent skin. Reliable and good cropper.

'Green Gem' Fair flavour. Medium-sized, round. Deep green with pale green veins. Good cropper. Can be picked early for cooking.

'Lancashire Lad' Fair flavour. Large oblong hairy fruit. Dark red and juicy. Heavy cropper. Some resistance to mildew.

'Langley Gage' Excellent, sweet flavour. Medium, oval, smooth fruit. Pale yellow with transparent skin. Cropping variable.

'Leveller' Excellent flavour. Large oval yellow-green fruit with slightly downy

skin. Very good cropper. Requires a fertile soil.

'Lord Derby' Fair flavour. Large, round dark red fruit, skin smooth with a faint down. Good cropper.

'Whinham's Industry' Sweet flavour. Fruit large, dark red and hairy. Crops heavily. Very vigorous bush.

'Whitesmith' Very good flavour. Medium to large oval fruit. Pale green with a yellow tinge. Heavy cropper.

Pruning an established bush

Each summer, in late June to early July, prune all laterals (that is, the current season's growth) to five leaves. This opens up the bush and removes any mildew and aphids at the tips of the shoots. Do not prune earlier because this might induce secondary growth. Do not prune the leaders unless mildewed.

Each winter, from November to February, cut back the leaders by one-half to a bud facing in the required direction. If the branch is weeping badly and there is a suitably placed upright lateral on it, then cut back to this.

Next deal with the laterals that were pruned the previous summer. Where fewer large dessert fruits are required, cut all of these laterals back to about two buds. Where quantity is required, pruning should be moderated accordingly. Vigorous varieties such as 'Whinham's Industry' and 'Howard's Lancer' should be pruned less severely because this could encourage excessive growth. Cut out dead and diseased wood, and any growth crowding the centre.

As the bushes become older and branches less productive or too spreading, leave in some suitably placed strong, young shoots to replace the old which are then cut out.

Pruning a single cordon
Prune in the same way as the red currant cordon (see page 98).

Weed control
As with most bush fruits, the gooseberry is shallow rooted. Keep the weeds down by shallow hoeing or with herbicides.

Protection against frost and birds
The gooseberry flowers early, during April, and spring frosts can substantially reduce the crop. On frosty nights protect the plants when they are in flower. Cover with hessian or two or three layers of bird netting, but remove it during the day to allow in light and give access for pollinating insects.

The fruit buds are attractive to bullfinches and sparrows in the winter and the ripening fruits to blackbirds and thrushes in the summer. Net the bushes in the winter and when the fruits begin to ripen.

Thinning and harvesting the fruits
For large dessert fruits start thinning the fruits in late May, removing every other one, and use them for cooking.

For small or medium dessert fruits, do not thin the fruits but leave them to ripen and develop their full flavour. Pick gooseberries

for cooking when they are a good size, but still green, from late May.

Propagation
Propagate gooseberries using 12 in hardwood cuttings taken from healthy shoots in late September. First remove the weak tip and all but four buds from the upper part of the cutting. This produces a miniature, open-centred bush on a short leg. Dip the base of the cuttings in a hormone rooting powder. Insert the cuttings in the open ground with their lowest buds 2 in above the soil surface. Leave the cuttings in the nursery bed for the growing season. Lift and replant, exposing more of the stem.

Pests and diseases
The most troublesome pests are aphids, gooseberry sawfly and magpie moth caterpillars. For aphids, apply malathion or a systemic insecticide, and for caterpillars apply fenitrothion, derris or malathion when flowering is over.

The most troublesome disease is American gooseberry mildew. Regular spraying with benomyl, carbendazim or thiophanate-methyl controls it. The diseased shoots should be cut out and burnt.

WORCESTERBERRIES

The Worcesterberry is often described as a hybrid between the gooseberry and black currant, but it is now more generally considered to be a form of the north American species *Ribes divaricatum*.

The fruits, borne singly, are a dull black, and much smaller than the gooseberry, being about ½ in across. They have an acid flavour but make good jam.

The bush resembles the gooseberry in leaf and form, but it is more vigorous and very thorny. In comparison with the gooseberry, it is not very productive. However, it is fairly hardy and disease-free. For cultural purposes, treat it in exactly the same way as the gooseberry.

The third year

5 From November to March, shorten the leaders by one-half to a bud facing in the required growth direction. Cut out shoots crowding the centre. Shorten laterals not required for the framework to about 2 in.

6 In May, when the fruits are large enough for cooking, thin the fruits by removing every other one. Cover the bush with bird netting to protect the fruits from birds.

The established bush

1 In late June to early July, prune all the laterals produced that season to five leaves. This opens up the bush and removes aphids at the tips of the shoots. Do not prune the leaders.

2 From November to February, cut back the leaders by one-half. Cut back laterals pruned in the previous summer to about two buds. Cut out diseased and dead wood and growth that crowds the centre.

Tree fruits

Introduction

Tree fruits (also sometimes referred to as top fruits) form a group comprising all the larger growing fruits which, in the natural state at least, attain tree form. The exceptions to this are the fig, elderberry, mulberry, quince and medlar, which may have several main stems and be more shrub-like in appearance; they are, however, still classified as tree fruits.

Botanically, the most familiar tree fruits are members of the rose family (Rosaceae), including the apple, pear, plum, cherry, peach, apricot, quince and medlar; the mulberry and fig are outsiders belonging to the mainly tropical family Moraceae. Also included in the tree fruit section are the most popular nuts: walnuts, sweet chestnuts, cob-nuts and filberts.

Tree fruits are not difficult to grow provided the soil is well drained but moisture-retentive and of a moderate to good depth (see pages 6–9). The site must be sunny and not prone to severe late spring frosts.

Unlike growing soft fruits, cultivating tree fruits in the garden is a long-term project. Full fruiting capacity is reached by the tree only after several years, but with care it will then continue for a lifetime. However, the fruit grower is compensated by the fact that the fruiting season for tree fruits is much longer than that of soft fruits. Furthermore, if fruits such as peaches or figs are grown in a greenhouse the season can be prolonged.

Rootstocks

Apples, pears, peaches, cherries, apricots and plums can all eventually make sizeable trees if grown on their own roots; some even become too large for most gardens. For this reason they are grafted on to rootstocks which control their eventual size. Usually apples are grafted on to a range of apple rootstocks to produce dwarf or less vigorous trees which are ideal for the small garden (see page 105). Pears are traditionally grafted on to quince rootstocks and this lessens their vigour and ultimate size. A dwarfing root-stock for cherries has proved harder to find but a less vigorous one has now been pro-duced, although it is not as dwarfing as some of the apple stocks.

Pruning and training

For all tree fruits, initial training and sub-sequent pruning is necessary to keep them in good shape and productive throughout their lives. Methods of training, particularly pruning, can seem daunting to an amateur but this need not be so if the instructions with each fruit entry in this book are followed closely. There is also a companion volume on pruning in this series.

Pruning terms The terms used frequently in fruit tree pruning are defined as follows. Maiden describes a one-year-old, for ex-ample, a maiden tree. A scion is a variety grafted on to a rootstock of another tree; the union is where the two join. A branch is a limb that arises from the trunk. Primary branches are the first formed, and secondary branches arise from the primary ones. A leader is a main central stem of a tree or a shoot selected to extend a main branch; a lateral is a side-shoot. Spurs are short laterals that bear flower buds and which can occur naturally or be induced by selective pruning of the laterals. Flowers buds, or blossom buds, are unopened flowers, often referred to as fruit buds. Wood buds open to give rise to a shoot, as opposed to a flower. Suckers are shoots that grow from below the ground or below the union.

Choice of site

The site should be chosen with care and the soil cleared of perennial weeds either with a selective herbicide (see page 155) or by hand weeding during digging. If some weeds still persist, herbicide treatment can be given again after the tree is planted, but take care to choose one which will not damage the tree.

Protection against birds

In areas where bird damage is expected (and few rural or suburban districts are exempt), protection is necessary. For small tree forms, such as dwarf bush trees, cordons or espal-iers, this can be provided by a fruit cage, ideally one with tubular steel or metal alloy poles and netting, although 7 ft headroom is a minimum. It is generally impracticable to protect larger tree fruits against bird damage.

Wall- and fence-trained trees

If there is no room in the open garden for free-standing tree fruits, good use can be made of walls and fences if restricted tree forms such as fans, cordons or espaliers are grown. North-facing walls can be used in this way for Morello cherries. Some plums and gages are even more successful on walls than in the open, ripening well in the sheltered and warmer environment. Figs are invariably best grown on a warm wall (see pages 84–85).

Pollination

Unlike most soft fruits, which will produce an adequate crop even if only one plant is grown, many tree fruits are totally or partially self-incompatible. This means that some varieties cannot produce a good crop of fruit if their flowers are fertilized with their own pollen. In such instances, at least two different compatible varieties must be grown close enough for bees to be able to carry pollen from one to the other. Sweet cherries provide the best example of self-sterility, but practically all the tree fruits set heavier crops if two or three varieties are planted together. They must, of course, flower at the same time and produce plenty of good pollen. Before buying any fruit tree, consult the pollination tables on pages 102–103.

Storage

If it is decided to plant enough apples and pears to provide fruit for the late autumn to winter period, storage facilities are necessary. This can be provided by a cool but frost-free cellar or shed. Late apples and pears finish ripening many weeks after they have been picked, and so they should not be stored with mid-season varieties until this ripening has taken place because the gases given off by the earlier varieties shorten the storage life of the later ones. Deep freezing is suitable for these two fruits only if they are to be used in cooking when thawed.

Fruit under glass

Figs, peaches and nectarines all produce their most luscious fruits under glass in cool areas. Artificial heat is not required although ripen-ing can be hastened by its use early in the season. Wall or roof space not less than 10 ft long is needed for a well developed peach or a fig rooted in the floor of the house. Alter-natively, much smaller trees can be grown in large pots and housed in all but the smallest greenhouse. Space outside should be set aside where hardy potted trees can be plunged up to their pot rims to keep the roots protected during the winter after the fruit has been picked (see pages 238–239).

Pollination 1

Pollination is the transfer of pollen from the anthers or male parts of the flower to the stigmas or female parts of the flower. This results in fertilization and the eventual production of fruit. It is usually carried out by bees or other insects or by the wind. Occasionally, it is necessary to pollinate by hand (see below).

The flowers of most garden fruits contain both anthers and stigmas. Some fruits, such as melons and cobnuts, bear separate male and female flowers on the same plant.

Some fruit trees, such as peaches, nectarines, apricots and certain plums and gages, are self-compatible—that is, they can be fertilized by their own pollen. Others, such as nearly all sweet cherries, elderberries and many varieties of apples and pears, are self-incompatible; they must be grown with another variety of the same fruit that flowers at the same time so that the two varieties can fertilize each other.

Pollination groups

Different varieties of plums, gages and damsons, apples, pears and cherries are divided into pollination groups according to when their flowers are open and ripe for pollination. Those varieties that appear in the same pollination group will cross-pollinate because their flowers are open at the same time. Those in adjacent groups are also acceptable because in most years their seasons of flowering overlap. The most common and popular varieties are listed in the pollination groups below. The pollination groups are listed in order of the flowering season; Pollination Group 1 is the earliest.

Incompatibility groups

Not all varieties of the same fruit can cross-pollinate, even when they appear in the same pollination group. This is called cross-incompatibility. These varieties are divided into incompatibility groups and will not set fruit with their own pollen or that of any variety which appears in the same incompatibility group. They will cross-pollinate with varieties in another group or in adjacent groups (provided they flower at the same time).

Ineffective pollinators

Some varieties of apples and pears, although not strictly cross-incompatible, are ineffective pollinators. This can occur for a number of reasons.

Most varieties are diploid, that is, they have the normal number of chromosomes. A few are triploid, that is they have $1\frac{1}{2}$ times the normal number. Triploids, shown in the pollination groups as (T), are poor pollinators and should be grown with two diploid varieties to pollinate each other and the triploid.

Some varieties of pears are known to be ineffective pollinators and are indicated (IP) in the pollination groups. Also some varieties of both apples and pears flower only every two years (biennially) or irregularly, designated (B) in the pollination groups. These cannot, therefore, be relied upon to pollinate other varieties.

Many triploids, ineffective pollinators and irregular flowering varieties are good varieties in their own right and popular with gardeners. If planting these varieties, remember to plant other varieties near them to provide the necessary pollen.

STRUCTURE OF BLOSSOM (APPLE)

Stigma
Style
Petal
Stamen
Anther
Filament
Ovule
Receptacle

HAND POLLINATION

Some fruits require hand pollination, such as those inaccessible to pollinating insects because they are grown under glass, or those whose flowers open early in the year when few insects are about.

Test to see if the pollen is being shed by drawing the finger-tip over the anthers, which should deposit yellow grains on the finger. Pollinate at midday when conditions for fertilization are best and when the weather has been warm and dry for two or three days. Very gently transfer the pollen from the anthers to the stigmas by using a soft camel-hair brush or a piece of cotton wool on a matchstick.

When male and female flowers are borne separately, as on the melon, another method may be used. Test the male flowers with the finger-tip to ensure that pollen is being shed. Strip the petals off the male flower and press its centre against the centre of each female flower.

Carry out hand pollination every day until flowering is over.

Pollination 2

Apples

No apple tree is completely self-compatible, so more than one variety should be grown.

Pollination Group 1 Gravenstein (T); Lord Suffield; Red Astrachan; Stark Earliest.

Pollination Group 2 Adam's Pearmain (B); Baker's Delicious; Beauty of Bath; Bismark (B); Christmas Pearmain (B); Devonshire Quarrenden (B); Egremont Russet; George Cave; George Neal; Golden Spire; Idared; Irish Peach; Keswick Codlin (B); Laxton's Early Crimson; Lord Lambourne; Margil; McIntosh Red; Melba (B); Merton Charm; Norfolk Beauty; Rev. W. Wilks (B); Ribston Pippin (T); St Edmund's Pippin; Warner's King (T).

Pollination Group 3 Allington Pippin (B); Arthur Turner; Belle de Boskoop (T); Blenheim Orange (TB); Bramley's Seedling (T); Brownlees' Russet; Charles Ross; Chivers Delight; Cox's Orange Pippin; Crispin (T); D'Arcy Spice; Discovery; Duchess Favourite; Emneth Early; Emperor Alexander; Epicure; Fortune (B); Granny Smith; Greensleeves; Grenadier; Holstein (T); James Grieve; John Standish; Jonagold; Jonathan; Katja; Kent; Kidd's Orange Red; Lord Grosvenor; Lord Hindlip; Mère de Menage; Merton Knave; Merton Worcester; Miller's Seedling (B); Ontario; Peasgood's Nonsuch; Queen; Rival (B); Rosemary Russet; Spartan; Stirling Castle; Sturmer Pippin; Sunset; Tom Putt; Tydeman's Early Worcester; Wagener (B); Worcester Pearmain.

Pollination Group 4 Annie Elizabeth; Ashmead's Kernel; Autumn Pearmain; Claygate Pearmain; Cornish Gillyflower; Cox's Pomona; Delicious; Duke of Devonshire; Dumelow's Seedling; Ellison's Orange; Encore; Gala; Gladstone (B); Golden Delicious; Golden Noble; Hawthornden; Herring's Pippin; Howgate Wonder; Ingrid Marie; King's Acre Pippin; Lady Sudeley; Lane's Prince Albert; Lord Derby; Monarch (B); Orleans Reinette; Pixie; Superb (Laxton's) (B); Tydeman's Late Orange; Woolbrook Russet.

Pollination Group 5 Gascoyne's Scarlet (T); King of the Pippins (B); Merton Beauty; Mother; Newton Wonder; Northern Spy (B); Royal Jubilee; William Crump; Winston.

Pollination Group 6 Bess Pool; Court Pendu Plat; Edward VII; Laxton's Royalty; Suntan (T).

Pollination Group 7 Crawley Beauty.

There are no incompatibility groups but 'Cox's Orange Pippin' and 'Kidd's Orange Red' are cross-incompatible, as are 'Cox's Orange Pippin' and 'Holstein'.

Pears

Although the variety 'Conference' is sometimes described as self-compatible, no pear variety is fully self-compatible.

Pollination Group 1 Brockworth Park; Maréchal de la Cour (T); Précoce de Trévoux.

Pollination Group 2 Bellisime d'Hiver; Beurré Alexandre Lucas (T); Beurré Clairgeau; Beurré d'Amanlis (T); Beurré d'Anjou; Beurré Diel (T); Beurré Six; Doyenné d'Eté; Duchesse d'Angoulême; Emile d'Heyst; Louise Bonne of Jersey; Marguerite Marillat (IP); Packham's Triumph; Passe Crassane; Princess; Seckle.

Pollination Group 3 Beurré Dumont; Beurré Hardy; Beurré Superfin; Conference; Doyenné Boussoch (T); Dr Jules Guyot; Durondeau; Fertility; Fondante d'Automne; Hessle; Jargonelle (T); Joséphine de Malines; Laxton's Progress; Merton Pride (T); Roosevelt; Souvenir du Congrés; Thompson's; Williams' Bon Chrétien.

Pollination Group 4 Bristol Cross (IP); Beurré Bedford (IP); Calebasse Bosc; Catillac (T); Clapp's Favourite; Doyenné du Comice; Glou Morceau; Gorham; Improved Fertility; Laxton's Foremost; Marie Louise; Napoleon; Nouveau Poiteau; Onward; Pitmaston Duchess (T); Santa Claus; Winter Nelis; Zépherin Grégoire.

There are two incompatibility groups.

Incompatibility Group 1 Fondante d'Automne; Laxton's Progress; Louise Bonne of Jersey; Précoce de Trévoux; Seckle; Williams' Bon Chrétien.

Incompatibility Group 2 Beurré d'Amanlis; Conference but one way only—'Beurré d'Amanlis' will pollinate 'Conference'.

Plums, damsons and gages

Some varieties are self-compatible and are shown (SC). All cherry plums are self-compatible.

Pollination Group 1 Angelina Burdett; Blue Rock; Heron; Jefferson; Mallard; Monarch (SC); Utility.

Pollination Group 2 Ariel; Brahy's Greengage (SC); Coe's Crimson Drop; Coe's Golden Drop; Curlew; Denniston's Superb (SC); Guthrie's Late (SC); President; Warwickshire Drooper (SC).

Pollination Group 3 Allgrove's Superb; Bryanston Gage; Bountiful (SC); Czar (SC); Early Laxton; Early Rivers; Edwards (SC); Golden Transparent (SC); Goldfinch; Late Orange; Laxton's Cropper (SC); Laxton's Gage (SC); Merryweather Damson (SC); Merton Gem; Opal (SC); Pershore (SC); Purple Pershore (SC); Reine-Claude Violette; Severn Cross (SC); Thames Cross; Victoria (SC); Washington.

Pollination Group 4 Blaisdon Red (SC); Bradley's King Damson (SC); Cambridge Gage; Count Althann's Gage; Early Transparent Gage (SC); Farleigh Damson; Giant Prune (SC); Kirke's; Ontario (SC); Oullin's Golden Gage (SC); Wyedale.

Pollination Group 5 Belle de Louvain (SC); Blue Tit (SC); Late Transparent; Marjorie's Seedling (SC); Old Greengage; Pond's Seedling; Red Magnum Bonum; Shropshire Damson (SC).

There are three incompatibility groups.

Incompatibility Group 1 Allgrove's Superb; Coe's Golden Drop; Coe's Violet Gage; Crimson Drop; Jefferson.

Incompatibility Group 2 Cambridge Gage; Late Orange; Old Greengage; President.

Incompatibility Group 3 Blue Rock; Early Rivers.

There are exceptions to these incompatibility groups. In Incompatibility Group 2, 'Late Orange' and 'President' will set full crops when pollinated by 'Cambridge Gage' or 'Old Greengage', but 'Cambridge Gage' and 'Old Greengage' will set poor crops when pollinated by 'Late Orange' or 'President'. In Incompatibility Group 3, 'Early Rivers' will set a full crop when pollinated by 'Blue Rock', but 'Blue Rock' will set a poor crop when pollinated by 'Early Rivers'.

Sweet cherries

With the exception of the Canadian variety 'Stella', which is self-compatible, all sweet cherries are self-incompatible and considerable cross-incompatibility between varieties also exists. It is essential to check the compatibility of chosen varieties before purchase.

Below is a selection of sweet cherry varieties arranged in compatibility groups in order of flowering, with the earliest first. Provided at least two varieties within any one group are chosen, the pollination requirements will be met. For example, 'Early Rivers' will pollinate 'Noir de Guben' and vice versa, but 'Early Rivers' will not pollinate or be pollinated by 'Merton Glory'.

Pollination Group 1 Early Rivers; Noir de Guben.

Pollination Group 2 Merton Favourite; Merton Glory.

Pollination Group 3 Merton Bigarreau; Roundel.

Pollination Group 4 Governor Wood; Napoleon Bigarreau; Stella (SC); Van.

Pollination Group 5 Bigarreau Gaucher; Bradbourne Black.

Acid and Duke cherries

These are much more straightforward than sweet cherries because some acid and Duke cherries are self-compatible and no cross-incompatibility is known. Sweet cherries are not suitable pollinators for acid and Duke cherries but both acid and Duke cherries can pollinate sweet cherries, although most of them flower too late.

'Ronald's Late Duke', 'Wye Morello', 'Montmorency Morello' and 'Flemish Red' are self-compatible. 'May Duke', 'Royal Duke' and 'Archduke' are partly self-compatible, that is, they set a moderate crop with their own pollen but do better with cross-pollination. 'Reine Hortense', 'Belle de Chatenay', 'Olivet' and 'Coe's Carnation' are self-incompatible.

Other fruits

Most other fruits are self-compatible. Nevertheless, cropping is usually improved when cross-pollination is available.

Two exceptions are blueberries and elderberries, most of which are partly self-incompatible. Two varieties should be planted.

Apricots, peaches, nectarines and melons usually require hand pollination (see opposite). Pollination of cobnuts and filberts can be assisted by pruning during the flowering season, when the shaking of the branches helps to disperse the pollen. Tapping or shaking vine rods during the flowering season helps to pollinate grapes.

Planting fruit trees

Good establishment, healthy growth and eventual successful cropping of a fruit tree depend a great deal on how well it is planted.

Preparation

Before planting prepare the ground in early autumn as described on pages 14–15. Then, for each tree, prepare an area 3 ft square by single digging clean ground and double digging weedy land. Prepare the ground overall for closely planted trees such as those on dwarfing rootstocks. Apply lime if the pH is less than 5.8.

Just before planting, fork in a balanced fertilizer, such as Growmore, at a rate of 3 oz per square yard with bonemeal at 2 oz per square yard.

Time to plant

Plant in the dormant season, from November to March (the earlier the better while the soil is still warm). Container-grown trees can be planted at any time. Do not plant when the soil is frozen hard or very wet.

If the tree arrives from the nursery when the soil conditions are not right, heel it in in a sheltered part of the garden. If the ground is too cold and hard to heel in, keep the tree in an unheated, frost-free place such as a garden shed. Unpack the upper parts of the tree but keep the roots in damp straw wrapped in hessian until planting.

Staking

Mark out the planting position and drive in a stake to a depth of 18 in on heavy soils and 24 in on light. Standard trees require 7½–8 ft posts, half-standards 6–6½ ft and bush 3½–4 ft. Central-leader trees need a stake as long as the height of the tree plus the depth into the soil. A large-headed standard, such as a sweet cherry, is best supported by two stakes 18 in apart with a crossbar (to which the tree is tied) nailed just below the stake tops. The top of the stake should be 2–3 in clear of the tree's head to avoid chafing the lowest branches. Stakes come in a variety of materials.

Trees on very dwarfing rootstocks, for example apples on M9, are best staked permanently. But for trees on more vigorous stocks, the stake can usually be removed

after four or five years, depending on the vigour. Before removing the stake, check by rocking the tree that its anchorage is sound.

Planting

If the roots are a little dry, soak them for an hour before planting. Keep them covered.

On the day of planting, dig out a hole deep and wide enough to take the roots fully spread out. Mound the soil in the centre. Keep the fertile top-soil separate from the lower layers. Fork the bottom and prick the sides of the hole to allow the roots to develop outwards. Dig in into the base rotted-down turf or a bucketful of well-rotted manure, compost or peat. Trim off with secateurs any broken or long tap roots. If planting a container-grown tree, gently tease out the soil and roots around the edge of the rootball.

Place the tree on the mound with the stem 2–3 in away from the stake. Ensure that the lowest branches clear the top of the stake. Plant the tree to the same depth as it was in the nursery, indicated by the soil mark. Keep the union between scion and rootstock at least 4 in above the soil surface to prevent the scion from rooting.

Fill in the holes; this is easier if one person holds the tree while another fills it in. Sprinkle a little of the fertile top-soil over the roots first then return the remaining soil a spadeful at a time. Occasionally shake the tree gently so that the soil falls among the roots. Finally, firm the soil and level off the surface.

Next, mulch the tree with well-rotted manure, compost or peat over an area 18 in in radius to a depth of 2–3 in, keeping the material 1–2 in clear of the trunk to prevent fungal diseases from infecting the base.

Tie the tree to the stake. A one-year-old can be secured with plastic chainlock strapping using a figure of eight tie, but older trees need a more substantial tie with a cushion between stake and tree to prevent chafing. There are a number of proprietary makes, or one can be made.

Bushes require one tie placed 1 in from the top of the stake. Half-standards and standards require two ties, one at the top and one halfway down. Nail the ties to the post to prevent them slipping down.

Where rabbits or other animals are trouble-

some protect the trees with wire netting.

Each year in April, July and October check the tree ties and if necessary loosen them to avoid constriction. Re-tie home-made ties.

Planting against a wall

The soil at the foot of a wall can become very dry and poor, especially if it is protected from rain-bearing winds or is sheltered by overhanging eaves.

Where the soil is poor and the drainage is bad, construct a soakaway or a single line of tiles 3 ft deep to take the water away (see pages 8–9). Re-soil over an area at least 6 ft × 3 ft wide × 2 ft deep with a fibrous, medium chalky loam, if possible made from turves stacked for six months before use. Add rubble to the loam in the ratio ten soil to one rubble. Two weeks before planting thoroughly mix in John Innes base fertilizer at the rate of 8 oz per 2 gal bucketful of soil.

The tree should be planted about 9 in from the wall base. During the growing season, water it when the soil is dry, applying 4 gal at a time around the base of the tree.

(see pages 8–9)

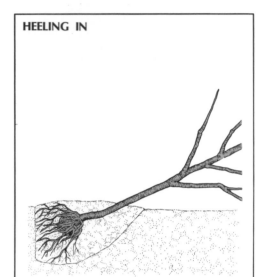

HEELING IN

Take out a shallow trench. Unpack the tree and lay it in the trench at an angle. Cover the roots with moist, friable soil.

1 If the roots are dry, soak them for an hour before planting. Trim off broken or long tap roots with secateurs.

2 Drive in stake. Dig a hole deep and wide enough to take the roots fully spread out. Mound the soil slightly in the centre.

3 Set the plant on the mound 2–3 in away from the stake with the union at least 4 in above the soil surface. Replace the soil, firming gently. Mulch well.

Apples and pears 1

DESSERT APPLES
Listed in order of ripening. (NB The "season" is the eating not ripening period.)
★ Recommended for flavour.

'Gladstone' Pleasantly flavoured. Flesh soft, green-white. Small to medium size, colour green-yellow, almost covered with a dark red flush and a few broken stripes. Cropping regular, light to moderate, spreading. Season late July to mid-August. Tendency to biennial bearing. Hardy.

'George Cave' Refreshing flavour, crisp texture. Medium size fruits. Colour light red flush and stripes over green background. A regular and heavy cropper. Medium vigour, upright and then spreading habit. Season mid-August. Flowers early. Like many early apples tends to drop prematurely. Fairly hardy.

★ 'Discovery' Good flavour, sweet and crisp, much loved by birds and wasps. Small to medium. Green-yellow, almost entirely covered bright red. Cropping regular and good, but can be slow into bearing if not on a dwarfing stock. Growth moderate. Upright and then spreading habit. Season end August to mid-September. Blossom fairly frost-tolerant.

★ 'Merton Knave' Sweet, richly flavoured, crisp texture. Fruits small to medium. Flushed red over-all. Cropping

Introduction and rootstocks

The domestic apple (Malus domestica) is of complex hybrid origin but it has evolved, under human influence, from various species, all of them belonging to the series Pumilae. It has been estimated that up to 1980 there were at least 6,000 named varieties of apples in the world.

Like the apple, the pear (Pyrus communis) has long been cultivated. It is a native of Northern Europe, and can also be found growing wild in parts of Britain.

Site

Ideally, the site should be frost-free, in full sun, and sheltered from strong winds. Pears flower in late April to early May and apples in the first half of May, when they are at risk from spring frosts. The gardener in a frost-prone site should consider growing trees on dwarfing stocks or using the restricted forms whose small size makes it practicable to protect them by covering the trees on frosty nights. With apples, the alternative is to plant varieties that flower late, but this is not applicable to pears because even the later varieties flower in the danger period.

Ample sunshine is important, particularly for pears, if the fruits are to develop their full colour and flavour. Apples will tolerate some shade, provided they receive at least half a day's sun in the growing season. Where there is a choice, allocate the sunniest position for pears and dessert apples, and the less sunny positions for culinary apples, for which colour and flavour are not so critical.

Shelter is essential because both kinds of fruit are insect pollinated and strong winds inhibit the insects' flight, which results in poor pollination. Wind-breaks, either living or artificial, should be provided on exposed sites or, again, choose apples and pears on dwarfing stocks or in restricted forms because they are easier to shelter than are taller trees (see pages 84–85).

Soil

The ideal soil for both apples and pears is a medium well-drained loam, not less than 24 in deep and slightly acid (pH 6.7). They are, however, tolerant of a wide range of soils. Pears and dessert apples require good drain-age, whereas culinary varieties can be grown in heavy soil and marginally poorer drainage, but the soil must never be waterlogged.

Light sandy soils are acceptable provided bulky organics are incorporated and heavy mulching and watering is practised. Thin soils over chalk are unsuitable because lime-induced chlorosis and lack of water and nutrients generally occur. Deep soils over chalk can support apples and pears quite satisfactorily.

Soil preparation

In early autumn, prepare the soil by clearing away perennial weeds over an area 3 ft square. Fork in a compound fertilizer such as a brand of Growmore at 3 oz per square yard.

Planting and staking

In the dormant season, from November to March, plant the tree to the same depth as it was at the nursery, spreading the roots out well (see page 104).

Bush trees, half-standards, standards and spindlebushes require stakes and tree ties. The restricted forms are supported by wall or fence wiring.

Selecting the rootstock

Apples and pears are not grown on their own roots for a number of reasons. Some will not root easily, some are prone to root troubles, and some make large unproductive trees. To overcome these problems, apple and pear varieties are grafted by the nursery on to various rootstocks.

The rootstock is the most important influence on the eventual size of the tree. An apple grafted on to a dwarfing stock, for example, will stay small, whereas on a vigorous stock it will eventually become large. It can also affect how long it is before the tree will fruit and its cropping capacity, so it is important to know the rootstock on which the tree is grafted or, when ordering a new tree, to indicate to the nursery what size of tree is required so that the appropriate rootstock is selected.

The stocks most widely used are listed below in order of vigour. The size of the tree quoted under the rootstock is an estimate only and will vary according to conditions.

ROOTSTOCKS

Apples

M27: Extremely dwarfing Recently released by East Malling Research Station, Kent. It is too soon to comment about its suitability for garden use but first reports are that it will make an ideal tree for growing in pots and in small gardens. It needs careful feeding and watering.

M9: Very dwarfing One of the most dwarfing stocks, M9 is widely used, making a bush tree about 6–10 ft in height and spread. It soon bears fruit, usually from the third year onwards, sometimes even in the second year. It requires good soil conditions and will not tolerate neglect, or competition from grass and weeds. The root system is brittle and as a bush tree it requires staking throughout its life. An excellent stock for the small garden. Used for dwarf bush, spindlebush, dwarf pyramid and cordon.

M26: Dwarfing M26 makes a dwarf bush tree 8–12 ft in height and spread. It tolerates average soil conditions. It soon bears fruit, usually within three or four years of planting. As a bush tree, it requires staking for the first four or five years, longer on exposed sites. Used for bush, dwarf pyramid, spindlebush, cordon and occasionally espalier and fan. It is a suitable stock for the small garden.

MM106: Semi-dwarfing MM106 makes a bush tree 12–18 ft in height and spread. It is tolerant of a wide range of soils. Trees on this stock soon bear fruit—usually within three or four years—and can produce heavily in later years. As a bush tree it requires staking for the first four or five years. Used for bush tree, spindlebush, cordon, espalier and fan.

MM111 and M2: Vigorous Bush trees on these stocks make trees 18–22 ft in height and spread, but their growth varies according to soil and variety. They make large trees on good loamy soils, but only medium-sized trees on poorer sandy soils. Used by nurseries for bush, half-standard and standard trees, espaliers and occasionally cordons and fans. They are slow to fruit in comparison with the more dwarfing stocks, sometimes taking seven to eight years. They are too vigorous for most gardens except where the soil is poor.

Pears

Pears are usually grafted on to quince rootstocks, which make them small to medium-sized trees. Some pears have a weak and spreading habit, and others are vigorous and upright, therefore the sizes given below are only an approximation.

There are three rootstocks: Quince C, Quince A and Pear. Both Quince C and A are suitable for the garden.

Quince C: Moderately vigorous Quince C makes a bush pear tree about 8–18 ft tall. It bears fruit in four to seven years. It is suitable for highly fertile soils and vigorous varieties, but not where conditions are poor. Used for bush, cordon, dwarf pyramid and espalier.

Old stocks of Quince C may be infected with a virus, so where possible obtain stock certified as virus-free. If in doubt, use Quince A because there is not much difference in vigour between the two.

Quince A: Medium vigour Slightly more vigorous than Quince C, it is the stock upon which most pears are grafted. It bears fruit in four to eight years. Bush pears on Quince A make trees between 10–20 ft in height and spread. It is used for all forms of pear tree except standards.

Certain pear varieties are not compatible with quince and these have to be double worked by nurseries. This means a piece of pear graftwood compatible with both the quince rootstock and the pear variety, such as 'Beurré Hardy', is used as an intermediate between the two. Varieties requiring double working include 'Bristol Cross', 'Dr Jules Guyot', 'Doyenné d'Eté' and 'William's Bon Chrétien'. If this is not done, the pear could eventually separate at the graft union.

Pear stock: Very vigorous Pears grafted on to pear rootstock make very large standard trees, too big for most gardens.

Apples and pears 2

regular. Moderate growth. Upright and then spreading habit. Season late August to September. Blossom fairly frost-tolerant.

'Worcester Pearmain' Flavour sweet and perfumed when fully ripe. Texture a little chewy. Fruits small to medium, round, conical. Cropping regular. Growth moderately vigorous. Upright and then

spreading habit. Season September to October. Fairly resistant to mildew, susceptible to scab and canker. Blossom fairly frost-tolerant.

'Katja' Sub-acid, juicy, fair flavour, flesh crisp, yellow. Fruits medium, round, conical with a red flush on yellow-green background. Cropping very heavy and regular, requires thinning. Medium

vigour. Upright and then spreading habit. Season early September to October. Fairly hardy, suitable for the north.

'James Grieve' Excellent flavour, very juicy, flesh yellow, tender, somewhat soft. Fruits medium to large, flushed pale yellow, striped and blotched crimson. Occasionally russet. Cropping regular and good. Medium vigour. Rather upright

habit. Season September to October. Early fruits can be picked green for cooking. Subject to scab and canker. Blossom has some degree of frost-tolerance.

★ **'Fortune'** Flavour sweet, aromatic, flesh firm at first, but later soft. Fruits medium, round to slightly conical. Fruits golden-yellow, flushed and striped bright

Selecting the tree form

Just as important as the correct choice of rootstock is the choice of tree form.

There are two basic types of trees, those that are planted in open ground and pruned in the winter, and those that are grown in restricted form, usually against a wall or fence, and pruned mainly in summer.

Where a gardener has plenty of land and a heavy yield is the main criterion, the unrestricted winter-pruned trees planted in the open are the best choice. Where the gardener has little room, or prefers the neat look of well-trained summer-pruned trees, or wants to fill a blank space on a wall or fence with fruit trees, then the restricted forms should be chosen.

Trees in the open

The tree forms commonly grown in the open are the dwarf bush, bush, the half-standard and the standard. These are all open-centred trees and they differ in appearance only in the length of stem or trunk before the first permanent branch and in the size of the head, or framework.

There is also the central-leader tree, sometimes called the spindlebush, which is widely grown in commercial orchards.

Dwarf bush tree The dwarf bush tree has an open centre and is goblet-shaped with a short stem of about 18–24 in. It is used only for apples because there is as yet no truly dwarfing stock for pears. Dwarf bush apples are grafted on to M9 and, because of their small size, are suitable for any garden. The soil must be very fertile, however, and the trees have to be fed and watered regularly or they will be stunted. Gardeners with less fertile soils should choose trees on the more vigorous stock M26.

Dwarf bush trees are easy to prune, spray and pick, and they soon bear fruit, but obviously their cropping capacity is not as great as that of larger trees. It is best not to plant dwarf bush apples in a lawn because they cannot compete with grass but if this is unavoidable, maintain a grass-free area for at least 2 ft around the base and water the tree regularly.

Bush tree The bush tree has a clear stem or trunk of about 20–30 in before the first

primary branch is reached. Usually, the bush apple is grafted on to M26, MM106, MM111 or M2, and the bush pear on Quince C or Quince A.

Apples on the rootstocks M26 and MM106 develop into moderately-sized trees which bear fruit in about the third or fourth year. Trees on M26 are suitable for the small to medium garden and on MM106 for the medium to large garden. Bush trees on MM111 and M2 eventually become medium-sized to large trees and are best reserved for the larger orchard if this is the size of tree required. They are slow to bear fruit, taking five to eight years depending upon the variety and the growing conditions.

Bush apples and pears are suitable for the medium to large garden and can be planted in a lawn provided the grass does not inhibit the young tree's growth. They are not suitable as shade trees because the head is too low.

Half-standard and standard The half-standard has a clear stem of 4–4½ ft and the standard 6–7 ft. Both are grafted on to vigorous stocks and eventually make very large trees. For this reason they require more pruning and larger equipment than do smaller trees—for example, a long ladder for picking and a fairly powerful sprayer for pest and disease control. Vigorous trees are slow to bear fruit but, because of their large size, they eventually yield heavy crops.

Central-leader tree (spindlebush) The central-leader tree, or spindlebush, is cone shaped. It consists of a central stem on which are carried horizontal branches starting at 2 ft from the ground.

The tree is supported by an 8–9 ft pole and the horizontal branches are achieved by tying them down in the early formative years. During the training it does not look attractive in the garden, but because this kind of tree shape allows plenty of sunlight to reach all parts, it can yield heavy crops.

Apples are grafted on to M9, M26 or MM106 and pears on to Quince A and sometimes on to Quince C.

Restricted tree forms

The restricted tree forms are used where trees have to be contained in some way, for example, against a wall or fence. They are

---

TREES IN THE OPEN: SPACING AND YIELDS

Dwarf bush tree
Spacing Plant the trees 8–10 ft apart.
Yield A good average yield from an established tree is about 40–60 lb.

Bush tree
Spacing Plant bush apples on M26 rootstock 10–15 ft apart; those on MM106 12–18 ft apart; and bushes on MM111 or M2, 18–25 ft apart. Plant bush pears on Quince C rootstock 10–14 ft apart and those on Quince A 12–15 ft apart. Choose the smaller spacing on light sandy soils or with the weak varieties, and the wider spacing on good fertile land or with vigorous varieties.
Yield A good average yield from a well grown bush apple on the less vigorous rootstocks is 60–120 lb and from a pear 40–100 lb.

Spindlebush
Spacing Plant apples on M9 rootstock, or in poor soils on M26, with 6–7 ft between the trees and 12 ft between the rows. If on M26 or MM106 rootstocks on good soils, leave 8 ft between trees and 14 ft between rows. Space pear trees 8 ft apart in the row with 12 ft between rows.
Yield A good average yield ranges from 30–160 lb depending upon the rootstock, variety and the growing conditions.

---

ideal for the small garden or where space is limited. However, because they are restricted, the yield in comparison with trees in the open is relatively small.

The main restricted tree forms for apples and pears are the cordon, the espalier and the dwarf pyramid. The fan is occasionally used.

The cordon is intended for a low fence. If closely planted, many varieties can be grown in a relatively small space and the gardener can more easily meet the cross pollination requirements (see pages 110–111).

The espalier may be planted against a low or high fence, depending upon the number of

arms it is intended to have. Its long horizontal arms require more room than the cordon. It is a handsome form (see pages 112–113).

The fan requires a high wall, the height depending on the kind of fruit grown (see pages 84–85). Unlike the cordon or espalier it cannot be planted against a low fence unless the gardener is prepared to increase the height with trellis work. The fan is used mainly for stone fruits such as peaches, cherries and plums, and for this reason it is described only on those pages.

The dwarf pyramid The dwarf pyramid is a small tree, pyramidal or Christmas tree-like in shape and kept this way by summer pruning. If, like the cordon, it is closely spaced, many trees can be planted in a relatively small area. Close attention to summer pruning is necessary, however, to maintain space between the framework branches and adjoining trees, otherwise a row of dwarf pyramids can soon degenerate into an unproductive hedge.

Although a restricted form, the dwarf pyramid is intended for planting in the open, not against a wall or fence (see pages 114–115).

Varieties

The choice of varieties depends upon the personal preferences of the gardener. Nevertheless, when making the final selection, ensure that the varieties will pollinate each other (see pages 102–103).

Many triploid varieties (see pages 102–103) are very vigorous and are not suitable for growing in restricted form unless grafted on to the dwarfing rootstocks M9 for apples and Quince C for pears.

Those varieties specially recommended for flavour are marked with an asterisk in the descriptions (above). The season refers to the period when the fruit is mature and fit to eat or cook. The picking date and maturity are not necessarily the same; a late apple, for example, is picked in October but might not be ready to eat until December. The season can be considerably affected by locality, climate, cultural treatment and, for stored fruit, the storage conditions. The seasons given are applicable to warmer areas, for example southern Britain, and in the northern areas they will be one or two weeks later.

Apples and pears 3

red on the sunny side. Cropping heavy, but sometimes biennial. Moderately vigorous, spreading habit. Season September to October. Fairly resistant to scab. Blossom fairly frost-tolerant.
'Greensleeves' Pleasant, moderately acid flavour, crisp and juicy. Fruits medium, conical, green-yellow with a trace of russet around the stalk. Cropping regular

and very heavy. Growth habit semi-dwarf to moderate, soon into cropping. Season mid-September to late November. Blossom fairly frost-tolerant.
★ **'Merton Charm'** Flavour excellent, sweet, aromatic, flesh tender crisp, creamy white. Fruits small, skin green-yellow with a slight brown-red flush. Cropping regular. Tree growth moderate

and upright. Season September to October.
★ **'St Edmund's Pippin'** Flavour excellent, crisp and sweet. Fruits tend to be small, with golden russet skin. Regular cropper. Growth dwarfish to moderate. Season September to October. The best early russet.
'Ellison's Orange' Flavour good, with a

distinct aniseed taste, flesh tender, yellowish. Fruits medium to large, skin golden-yellow with crimson stripes and flush. Crops well, but sometimes biennial. Growth medium, upright and then spreading. Season September to October. Fairly resistant to apple scab, but cankers badly on some soils. Blossom fairly frost-tolerant.

Trees in the open
The dwarf bush, bush, half-standard and standard are commonly grown in the open.

Selecting the tree
A nursery can supply one-year-old, two-year-old or three-year-old trees. Trees older than this are not recommended because they may not establish well.

A one-year-old, or maiden, tree consists of a straight stem with or without laterals. A maiden with laterals, called a feathered maiden, is a better choice because if the laterals are suitably placed they can be used as primary branches, and a year is saved in the formative pruning stage. The maiden is the least expensive type, but it requires initial shaping and takes longer to bear fruit.

Trees of two and three years old will have already been partly shaped by the nursery and, being older, bear fruit sooner.

Soil preparation and planting
Prepare the soil in early autumn (see page 104). Plant the tree in the dormant period from November to March, driving in a stake first.

Pruning
Prune in the winter, from November to February, but not when the air temperature is below freezing.
The first winter The work of forming the head begins with the maiden tree.
Unfeathered At planting, shorten the maiden tree to 24 in for a dwarf bush or to 30 in if a bush tree is to be formed. Cut back to just above a bud, making a sloping cut away from the bud and ensuring there are three or four good buds beneath it. This cut stimulates the formation of primary branches the next year.
Feathered Cut back the main stem to a lateral at about 24 in for a dwarf bush or 30 in for a bush, ensuring there are two or three suitably placed laterals just beneath it. Remove all others flush with the main stem. Shorten the selected laterals by about two-thirds to an outward-facing bud.
The second winter (or the two-year-old tree) In the dormant season, select three or four strong leaders to form the primary branches, taking care to select those that are evenly spaced and have formed wide angles with the main stem. The wide angles ensure a stronger

joint; a narrow-angled branch may break off under the weight of the crop later on. Notice the effect of apical dominance, that is, the topmost shoot is the most upright and it is often unsuitable because it is too central and forms a narrow angle with the stem. If this is so, cut it out, heading back to the next branch. Next, shorten the selected primary branches by one-half and shorten the less vigorous ones by two-thirds. Cut each to an outward-facing bud. The remaining shoots are removed altogether.

During the summer, the branch growth following the hard pruning should be strong, with secondary branches forming.

In the third winter (or the three-year-old tree) Select about four more widely-spaced branches. The framework now consists of about eight branches. Shorten these by one-half or, if weak, by two-thirds, cutting back to outward-facing buds. Prune back to about four buds those laterals not required for secondary branches and those competing with the leaders. If the tree is growing vigorously, some laterals on the outer part of the tree can be left unpruned to form flower

buds. Shoots crowding the crotch of the tree should be removed. The centre should be open, but not completely barren of growth. Growth from the main stem lower than the primary branches should be cut off to maintain the clean leg. Protect the cuts.
The fourth winter The tree is entering the cropping phase of its life, but a little more formative pruning is still necessary, as described for the third winter. Weak varieties may need further formative pruning for the next two or three winters.
Winter pruning the cropping tree By the fourth or fifth year the tree should start bearing fruit. From then the pruning guidelines are flexible, exactly how much is pruned depends on the condition of the tree.

Before pruning an older tree, remember that the harder the tree is pruned, the more growth is obtained, but in consequence the less fruit is produced. Thus, a heavily pruned tree will be vigorous but unfruitful, whereas a lightly pruned tree may crop heavily, but the fruit will be small and the framework weak and badly shaped. It is a question of balance between growth and fruitfulness.

Pruning a feathered maiden

1 In November to March, prepare the soil and drive in a stake. Plant a maiden tree to the same depth as it was at the nursery. Tie to the stake. Cut the main stem back to a bud or lateral at about 24 in for a dwarf bush, 30 in for a bush.

The second year

2 In November to March, select four of the primary branches that have formed wide angles to the stem. Cut back vigorous ones by one-half and less vigorous ones by two-thirds. Prune to outward-facing buds. Remove unwanted branches.

The third year

3 In November to March, select a further four well-placed new growths to form permanent branches. Cut back vigorous ones by two-thirds. Prune to outward-facing buds.

Fourth and subsequent years

4 In November to March, the branch framework has now been formed and leader pruning can cease, unless growth is weak. Leave laterals on the outer parts of the tree unpruned. Cut back laterals on the inside to about 4 in.

Apples and pears 4

'Lord Lambourne' Moderately sweet and aromatic, flesh fine, crisp, cream coloured. Fruits medium, skin green-yellow with red flush and darker stripes. Compact tree. Crops heavily and regularly. Season October to November. Some scab-resistance.
★ **'Ribston Pippin'** Rich, sweet flavour, flesh yellow, firm, somewhat dry, crisp

and aromatic. Fruits medium, round, conical, irregular. Colour yellow with dull brown-red flush, a few stripes and russet. A regular, heavy cropper. Growth moderate. Triploid. Season November to January. A parent of 'Cox's Orange Pippin'. Blossom fairly frost-tolerant.
★ **'Egremont Russet'** Good, nutty russet flavour, flesh green-yellow, firm. Fruits

medium, yellow almost covered with russet. Crops well. Moderate vigour, upright. Season October to December. Blossom fairly frost-tolerant.
★ **'Sunset'** Excellent aromatic flavour, flesh creamy yellow, crisp and juicy. Fruits small to medium, round and flattened, regular. Colour golden-yellow with red flush and russet in the eye.

Cropping regular and very heavy, requires thinning. Season November to December. A small tree, which succeeds in many areas where 'Cox's Orange Pippin' grows with difficulty.
★ **'Cox's Orange Pippin'** Generally considered to be the finest flavoured dessert apple. Flesh tender, yellow, juicy, aromatic. Fruits medium, round, conical,

Pruning the cropping tree

Before pruning apple or pear trees that are past the formative stage, it is important to distinguish between the spur-bearing and the tip-bearing varieties. A spur-bearing variety produces fruit buds on the two-year-old as well as on the older wood, where they are carried on short stubby shoots called spurs. Where these shoots become very branched, typically on old wood, they are called spur systems. The spur-bearer is the most common type of apple and pear tree.

A tip-bearing variety produces fruit buds at the tips of slender shoots made in the previous summer. A few spurs are also produced on the older wood, but considerably fewer than on a spur-bearer. The tip-bearer has a more gaunt appearance in comparison. There are also partial tip-bearers, which produce spurs on the older wood as well as fruit buds at their tips. For pruning purposes they are treated as spur-bearers.

Examples of spur-bearing varieties are the apples 'James Grieve', 'Cox's Orange Pippin' and 'Sunset', and the pears 'Conference', 'Doyenné du Comice' and 'William's Bon Chrétien'. Among the tip-bearers are the apples 'Irish Peach' and 'Worcester Pearmain' and the pear 'Joséphine de Malines'. Examples of partial tip-bearers are the apples 'Bramley's Seedling' and 'Discovery'.

There are three basic pruning techniques: spur pruning, renewal pruning, and regulatory pruning.

Spur pruning As mentioned above, spur-bearing varieties form spurs naturally, but they can also be induced to form spurs. Each winter cut back a proportion of maiden laterals to four or five buds. Choose those that have insufficient room to extend as secondary branches.

In the following summer, a lateral so pruned produces one or two shoots from the uppermost buds, but usually the lower buds develop into flower buds by the end of the growing season.

In the second winter, cut back the laterals to the topmost flower bud, thus removing the previous summer's growth. However, where there is room and no risk of the spur overlapping an adjoining branch, extend the spur system by cutting back to three or four

wood buds on the previous summer's growth.

After some years, a spur system may become crowded and complicated and, as a result, the fruits are too numerous and therefore small. Then spur thinning is undertaken by reducing the length of the spur systems, cutting away the weakest buds and those on the undersides of the branches.

Renewal pruning of spur-bearers This also depends upon the tendency of many apple and pear varieties to produce flower buds on unpruned two-year-old laterals. It is best reserved for the strong laterals on the outer part of the tree, where there is room for such growth.

In the winter, select a proportion of strong, well-placed laterals on the outer part of the tree and leave them unpruned. Prune the others as described in spur pruning. During the following growing season, the terminal bud on each unpruned lateral extends to produce a further maiden shoot, while most of the remaining buds develop into flower buds.

In the second winter, cut back the laterals to the topmost flower bud. In the following summer the cut-back laterals produce fruit.

In the third winter, half the laterals that have fruited can be retained as an elongated spur system. The others are cut back to leave a 1 in stub. This severe shortening stimulates the production of a new lateral from the stub, and so the cycle is repeated.

To sum up, at any one time the tree carries a number of one-year-old laterals unpruned, two-year-old laterals pruned back to a flower bud, and three-year-old laterals which are stubbed back to 1 in after fruiting—or left if there is room.

Regulatory pruning This applies to the tree as a whole rather than to specific parts of it as in spur or renewal pruning. Basically it entails keeping the centre open by removing crowding and crossing branches and cutting out dead, diseased and broken wood. There is no need to prune the leaders after the early formative years except with poorly growing varieties, which require the stimulus of hard pruning.

The framework branches, laterals and spurs also should not be crowded. As a rough guide, in an old tree no main branch

should directly over-shade another by less than 18 in, nor should branches be closer than 18 in when side by side. Laterals should be spaced about 18 in apart and spurs not less than 9 in along the framework of branches.

If in later years, as a result of light pruning, the tree over-crops (with consequent small fruit) and growth is weak, adopt a policy of harder pruning to reduce the number of flower buds and to stimulate new growth. Simplify some of the over-long spur systems, and where they are crowded cut out some

of them altogether. Increase the amount of renewal pruning.

Pruning of tip-bearers In the winter, prune lightly on the regulatory system (see above). Leave any maiden shoots less than 9 in long unpruned because they have fruit buds at their tips. Prune longer laterals back to four buds. This induces short shoots in the following summer with fruit buds at their tips—spur pruning in effect.

Always prune the leaders of tip-bearing varieties because this induces more laterals to bear fruit in the following year.

SPUR PRUNING

The first year

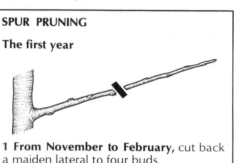

1 From November to February, cut back a maiden lateral to four buds.

The second year

2 From November to February, cut back the lateral to a flower bud.

Third and fourth years

3 From November to February, a spur system begins to form.

RENEWAL PRUNING

The first year

1 November to February, select a strong, well-placed lateral and leave it unpruned.

The second year

2 In November to February, extension growth has occurred. Flower buds have formed on last year's wood. Cut back to the junction between old and new wood.

The third year

3 In November to February, cut back the fruited lateral to leave a 1 in stub.

4 In October, at the end of the growing season, a strong new lateral has been produced from the 1 in stub. This is left unpruned, to repeat the cycle.

Apples and pears 5

regular. Colour golden-yellow with brown-red flush and streaks with patches of russet. Trees medium size, fairly upright, with slender branches which are usually numerous. Season October to December. The blossom is not hardy and the tree develops canker in cold and wet soils. Also very susceptible to scab and mildew. Difficult.

'Laxton's Superb' Sweet and aromatic, can vary greatly in flavour depending upon season and locality. Flesh white, firm and juicy. Fruits medium to large, skin yellow, but flushed dark crimson and streaked grey russet, somewhat like 'Cox's Orange Pippin' but duller. Very heavy cropper, but inclined to be biennial. Vigorous with long whippy shoots. Season November to February.

★ 'Orlean's Reinette' High quality, sweet rich flavour, crisp, very juicy. Fruits medium to fairly large, somewhat flattened, quite regular. Colour golden-yellow with slight red flush and cinnamon russet. Cropping moderate. Growth strong, upright and spreading. Season December to February.

'Spartan' Fairly sweet with a pleasant vinous flavour, flesh white, fine and juicy. Fruits medium, oblong. Skin yellow, entirely covered with deep purple-red and a distinct bloom. A regular and heavy cropper. Tree moderately vigorous, upright and then spreading. Season November to January. Subject to canker. Blossom fairly frost-tolerant.

The central-leader tree (spindlebush)

The success of this form depends upon producing wide-angled branches off the central leader. Therefore buy a feathered maiden, because the laterals on such a tree are naturally formed at the correct angle.

Soil preparation and planting

Prepare the soil in the early autumn (see page 104). A spindlebush requires a long stake to support the central leader. The stake should be 8–8½ ft long by 1½–2 in top diameter.

Drive the stake in first, 18 in deep on a heavy soil and 2 ft deep on a light soil. Plant the tree and tie it to the stake.

Pruning and tying down in the first year (or the one-year-old tree)

During the dormant season from November to February, select three or four laterals to form the first tier of branches starting at not less than 24 in from the ground. Choose strong, well placed laterals coming off the main stem at a wide angle. Prune these back by one-half to an outward-facing bud. Remove the rest or the laterals entirely. Cut back the central leader to the third bud above the topmost selected lateral.

By August the original laterals will have extended and possibly new laterals will have been produced. A new central leader will have grown on. Tie the leader to the stake using a figure of eight tie with soft thick string such as 4-ply fillis. Choose three or four good laterals that form a wide angle with the main stem and gently tie the extension growth of each down to 30 degrees above the horizontal with soft thick string secured to 9 in long wire pegs pushed into the ground. Remove any upright laterals and those directly beneath the central leader.

Pruning in the second winter

Cut back the central leader by about one-third of the previous summer's growth to a bud on the opposite side to that of the previous year. The technique of cutting to an opposite bud is called "zig-zagging" and helps to maintain the more or less straight growth essential in the central leader. Remove any upright laterals and those competing with the leader. Prune each remaining lateral by one-quarter to a downward-facing bud. Check the string ties to ensure there is no constriction and remove any where the branch has set at about 30 degrees.

In August, again tie down suitable new laterals to form branches.

Pruning the cropping tree

In the third and subsequent years a similar procedure is followed. The central leader is pruned by one-quarter (if weak by one-third) to induce the lower buds to produce new laterals. The more vigorous the leader is, the lighter it is pruned. Branches are allowed to grow from the central stem at regular intervals, choosing those with a wide angle. Narrow-angled laterals are removed. The higher placed branches must be kept shorter than those beneath to allow sunlight to reach the lower parts. After the laterals at the very top have fruited, they must be pruned on the renewal system (see page 108). Tying down is discontinued once the branches have set at the required angle. The need for tying down decreases once the tree is cropping because the crop pulls the branches down.

Each winter cut back the extension growth of the central stem to a weaker side branch once it has reached a height of 7–8 ft. Tie up the side branch to the stake and treat it as the new leader.

The second year

1 In November to March, prepare the ground and drive in a stake. Plant the feathered maiden tree to the same depth as it was at the nursery. Tie it to the stake.

2 At the same time, select three or four laterals to form the first tier of branches at about 24 in from the ground. Prune them back by one-half to an outward-facing bud. Remove remaining laterals entirely.

3 Then, cut back the central leader to the third bud above the topmost selected lateral. Protect the pruning cuts with a wound paint.

4 By August, the original laterals will have extended and a new central leader will have grown on. Tie the leader to the stake. Tie down the extension growth to 30 degrees above the horizontal using soft string.

5 In winter, cut back the central leader by one-third of the previous year's growth to an opposite-facing bud. Remove any upright laterals. Prune remaining laterals by one-quarter to a bud.

6 Every year, check the string ties. Remove the ties where the branch has set at 30 degrees. In August, tie down new laterals. Cut back the leader to a weaker lateral. Tie it up as the new leader.

Apples and pears 6

'Golden Delicious' The most universally planted variety. Pleasant flavour but in Britain unlikely to produce the quality comparable with imported fruit. Flesh yellow-white, crisp. Fruit small to medium, round, oblong, slightly ribbed. Skin green-yellow to golden-yellow. Cropping usually regular, occasionally biennial. Growth moderately vigorous.

Season November to February.
★ **'Ashmead's Kernel'** Sweet aromatic flavour, firm, crisp, yellow flesh. Fruits medium, round with somewhat flattened sides. Skin green-yellow with a brown flush and covered with russet. A tendency to light cropping. Trees of moderate vigour. Season December to March. A fruit for the connoisseur.

'Crispin' Pleasant fresh flavour, flesh white, coarse, crisp and juicy. Fruits large, oblong with ribbing. Colour bright green, turning to golden-yellow when ripe. A regular and heavy cropper. Tree vigorous, tip- and spur-bearer, open spreading habit. Triploid. Season end October to February. A culinary and dessert apple.

★ **'Tydeman's Late Orange'** Good flavour, flesh creamy, firm, crisp, but not juicy. Fruits small to medium, round, conical. Skin golden-yellow with orange-red flush and russet patches. Tends to crop biennially. Growth vigorous. Season January to March. Blossom fairly frost-tolerant.

Restricted tree forms: The cordon

A cordon consists of a single straight stem furnished with side-shoots or fruit spurs which are kept short by summer pruning and sometimes by winter pruning. It may be planted and trained vertically or obliquely, usually the latter because it requires less height and its growth is more easily controlled. There are also multiple cordons, with two or more stems.

The cordon is a form that, perhaps more than any other, is suited to the small garden. It is closely planted, so many varieties can be grown in a relatively small space and the gardener can more easily meet the cross-pollination requirements of apples and pears. Cordons can be grown against walls and fences or out in the open on a wire fence.

Choice of rootstock

For apple cordons, the rootstock M9 is the most suitable where space is very limited and the cordons are to be kept down to a height of 5–6 ft. The soil must be fertile, however. If in doubt about the soil, obtain trees on a slightly more vigorous stock. M26 (dwarfing) and MM106 (semi-dwarfing) are widely used and are satisfactory for most situations. MM106 is especially useful for varieties that do not spur easily. The rootstocks M2 and MM111 (vigorous) are recommended where the soil conditions are very poor.

For pears, the cordons must be grafted on to Quince A or C rootstocks.

Selecting the tree

Cordons of one, two or three years old can be planted. If selecting a maiden tree, preferably choose one with plenty of laterals because these are the foundation of the fruit spurs to come. Two- or three-year-old cordons will be quicker to bear fruit, but they must be well furnished with spurs and laterals.

Spacing

Space the cordons 2½ ft apart on medium to good soils or 3 ft apart on poor, shallow or sandy soils with the rows 6 ft apart.

It is best, although not essential, that the rows run north-south.

Support system

Cordons may be planted against a wall or fence or out in the open on a wire fence. On walls and wooden fences erect horizontal wires every 2 ft as described on pages 84–85. Out in the open drive in wooden posts every 12 ft to hold the wires. The posts may be 2½ in x 2½ in oak or 3½ in top diameter in other woods. Set the posts 2 ft deep or 3 ft in sandy soils. The end posts should be strutted. Alternative materials include iron, steel or concrete posts. Erect the wires at 2 ft, 4 ft and 6 ft and use gauge 10 wire for the upper wire and gauge 12 for the other two. Securely tie 8 ft bamboo canes to the wires at an angle of 45 degrees, with the tops pointing towards the north if the rows run north-south, or to the east if they run east-west. Space the canes at 2½–3 ft intervals to correspond with the planting stations.

Planting and training oblique cordons

Prepare the soil in the early autumn (see page 104). Plant in the dormant season, November to March, unless using container-grown plants. Against walls and solid fences, the cordon should be planted 6–9 in away from the structure to allow room for the growth of the trunk. Set the cordon at an angle of 45 degrees with the union above ground and the scion uppermost, and then securely tie the cordons to the cane using thick soft string or plastic chainlock strapping in a figure of eight. If the one-year-old tree has laterals, shorten those over 6 in long to four buds. Thereafter, prune each summer. Do not prune the leader.

It is not wise to allow a cordon to crop in the first year after planting, so in the spring remove any flowers, taking care not to cut the growing shoot just behind the blossom.

Summer pruning: Modified Lorette System

Summer pruning is necessary to confine the growth to the limited space available. It also induces the production of fruit spurs close to the main stem. The Modified Lorette System is the simplest method.

Summer prune in about mid-July for pears and in the third week of July for apples in southern England. Prune seven to ten days later farther north. Cut back to three leaves all mature shoots of the current season's growth that are growing directly from the main stem. Cut back those mature sub-laterals arising from existing side-shoots or spurs to one leaf beyond the basal cluster or rosette of leaves. Mature shoots have a stiff woody base, dark leaves and are 9 in or more long. Leave immature shoots until mid-September. Do not prune shoots that are shorter than 9 in because they usually have fruit buds at their tips.

Pruning the cropping tree

Each May, once the cordon has passed the top wire and reached the required height (usually 7 ft), cut back the extension growth to its origin. Each July subsequently, cut the leader to 1 in. From mid-July onwards the remaining shoots on the cordon are pruned on the Modified Lorette System (see above).

If, later on, there are secondary growths from shoots pruned in July, cut them back to mature wood just before leaf-fall. In areas

The first year

1 From November to March, plant the maiden tree with the scion uppermost, against a cane secured to wire supports at about 45 degrees. Do not prune the leader. Cut back any feathers to four buds.

Second and subsequent years

2 In spring, after a further year's growth spurs will have formed on the cut-back feathers. Remove any flowers as they appear, leaving intact the growing shoot behind the blossom.

3 In late July, cut back laterals longer than 9 in arising directly from the main stem to three good leaves from the base, ignoring the basal cluster. Cut back sub-laterals from existing spur systems to one leaf beyond the basal cluster.

Apples and pears 7

★ **'Suntan'** 'Cox'-type flavour, but more aromatic and acid. Fruits large, flat to conical, skin golden-yellow, flushed heavily with brown-red and faint stripes with some russet. Good cropper. Growth vigorous, upright and then spreading. Season December to March. Triploid. Flowers very late, escapes frost.

★ **'Sturmer Pippin'** Good flavour, flesh yellow-green, crisp and firm. Fruits medium, round to conical. Skin green-yellow, brown flushed. Regular cropper, growth compact. Season January to April. Best left on the tree as late as possible before picking. Requires a light soil and warm situation to develop its full flavour.

'Idared' Fair flavour, can also be cooked. Flesh white, somewhat juicy. Fruits large, flattish and ribbed. Colour yellow with red flush on the sunny side. Cropping regular. Growth moderately vigorous, rather spreading. Season November to May. Stores well.

where secondary growth is prolific after pruning, for example in high rainfall regions, delay pruning until later in the summer. If much secondary growth still occurs, then stop summer pruning altogether and prune in the winter instead, pruning to one bud from existing spurs and three buds on laterals arising directly from the main stem.

Winter pruning

Normally neither the leader nor the side-shoots are pruned in the winter except when a tree makes too much secondary growth, or makes poor growth, or to renovate it.

When a young cordon does not produce sufficient side-shoots, resulting in bare areas of stem, laterals may be induced by pruning the leader (previous summer's growth) by up to one-third of its length. Treat newly planted tip-bearers in the same way.

Neglected cordons can be brought back into shape by winter pruning. Thereafter prune them in the summer. Overlong or complicated spur systems should be reduced to two or three fruit buds.

LOWERING THE CORDON

When the cordons reach the top wire they may be lowered to obtain a longer stem. Lowering also helps to check the vigour of an over-vigorous cordon. Lower carefully five degrees at a time and not lower than 35 degrees, so that there is no risk of breaking the stem. Lowering the angle slows down the movement of sap and limits extension growth while encouraging fruit bud production.

MULTIPLE CORDONS

Cordons may also be formed with two, three or more arms, trained either vertically or at an angle. The training of a multiple cordon is initially similar to the formation of the first horizontal arms of an espalier. Thereafter each stem of the multiple cordon is treated as a single cordon. Vertically trained cordons are generally more vigorous and often less fruitful than those trained at an angle of about 45 degrees. The angle can be reduced further (see Lowering the cordon).

Secondary growths

Just before leaf-fall, if further growth has developed from pruned shoots, cut it back to mature wood. In high rainfall areas, where much secondary growth occurs, stop summer pruning and prune from November to March instead.

The fruiting cordon

1 In May, when the leader has passed the top wire and reached the required height of about 7 ft, cut back the extension growth to its origin.

2 Each July, cut back the leader to 1 in. Cut back to three leaves all mature laterals longer than 9 in growing directly away from the main stem and those from existing side-shoots and spurs to one leaf beyond the basal cluster.

OVERCROWDED SPUR SYSTEMS

From November to February, as the tree matures thin out in the winter by reducing overlong, overlapping or complicated spur systems to two or three fruit buds. Remove buds that are weak on the underside and shaded parts of the branches.

Apples and pears 8

'Emneth Early' ('Early Victoria') Flesh green-white, rather soft. Cooks to a froth. Fruits medium, skin yellow-green. Crops heavily, needs hard thinning. Growth compact, upright, moderate. Season July to August.

'Grenadier' Flesh white, crisp, acid. Cooks to a froth. Fruits large, round, conical, a little uneven. Skin pale green, fading to light yellow, smooth. Crops well. Growth moderate. Season August to September. Resistant to apple scab. A good pollinator for 'Bramley's Seedling'.
★ **'Rev. W. Wilks'** Flesh tender, white, sub-acid. Cooks to a golden froth. Fruits large, flat, conical, slightly irregular. Colour pale creamy-white with light red flush and stripes. Cropping good, but inclined to be biennial. Growth compact and dwarfish. Season September to November. A good apple for the small garden.
★ **'Golden Noble'** Flesh tender, yellow, acid. Cooks to a froth. Fruits medium, round, slightly flattened, regular. Skin clear yellow with light russet. Good, regular cropper. Growth vigorous. Season September to January. Susceptible to scab and canker. Suitable for the north. One of the best cooking apples.

Restricted tree forms: The espalier

An espalier consists of a central stem from which horizontal fruiting arms (tiers) grow at about 15–18 in intervals. The tree is trained in one plane and makes a handsome boundary marker or can be used to cover walls or fences.

Choice of rootstock and spacing

If a small espalier apple is required, for example, against a low fence, the tree should be on the M9 rootstock. This means obtaining a maiden tree and shaping it, because pre-formed espaliers on this stock are not usually available. For more than one espalier, plant 10 ft apart.

For most gardens, espaliers on M26, spaced 10–12 ft apart, or MM106, spaced 12–15 ft apart, are suitable. Where more vigorous trees are required, to clothe a large wall for example, they should be on the vigorous stocks M2 or MM111 spaced 15–18 ft apart. Pears should be on Quince A or C rootstock.

Selecting the tree

The number of horizontal arms or tiers required depends upon the height of the wall or fence. Most nurseries supply two-tier and three-tier espaliers and further arms can be trained in if required. A formed espalier is much more expensive but crops sooner.

Support system

On walls and fences erect the horizontal wires to coincide with the espalier arms (as described on pages 84–85); usually each tier is 15–18 in apart. Out in the open, drive in posts to hold the wires every 12–18 ft, depending upon the spacing of the espaliers. The end posts should be strutted. Plant the espaliers centrally between the posts. Use gauge 10 galvanized wires and strain tight with straining bolts on the end posts.

Soil preparation and planting

In early autumn, prepare the soil (see page 105). Plant in the dormant season from November to March. To allow room for the trunk to grow when sited against a wall or fence, the espalier should be planted 6 in away.

Formative pruning

Formed espaliers may be obtained or the gardener may prefer to start off with a maiden tree and carry out the formative pruning as described below.

The first year Plant an unfeathered maiden tree in the dormant season between November and March. Cut back the stem to within 15 in of ground level, making sure that room for a short leg is left, together with three good topmost buds. The two lower ones should point in opposite directions.

In spring carefully direct the shoot from the top bud vertically up a cane and the others to the right and the left. It is difficult to obtain horizontal shoots in the first year without a check to growth and it is best to train the two shoots initially at angles of about 45 degrees to the main stem. This can be achieved by tying them to canes secured to the wire framework.

During summer the angle can be varied so that a weaker shoot is encouraged to catch up by raising it a little towards the vertical.

In November, at the end of the first growing season, lower the two side branches to the horizontal and tie them to the wire supports. Prune back the central leader to within 18 in of the junction, with the lower arms to coincide with the next wire. The intention is to promote a further three growths—one to continue the central axis and the other two to form a second tier of side branches. Shorten surplus laterals from the main stem to three buds. Prune the two horizontal leaders to downward-pointing buds, removing about one-third of each shoot. If growth has been particularly satisfactory, perhaps because of a good growing season, the leaders can be left unpruned.

Second and subsequent years The next years are a repetition of the first, with subsequent tiers of branches being trained in. In November lower the side branches to the horizontal and secure them to the wire supports. Cut back the central leader to within 18 in of the last tier of arms at the next wire. Cut back unwanted laterals from the main stem to three buds. The horizontal leaders should be cut back by one-third, cutting to downward-pointing buds, if growth has been poor.

Cut back competing growths from the main stem to three leaves during the summer.

The first year

1 From November to March, plant an unfeathered maiden tree. Cut back the stem to within 15 in of ground level just below the wire. Select three good upper buds, the lower two buds pointing in opposite directions.

2 From June to September, train the shoot from the top bud vertically up a cane. Train the shoots from the two lower buds at an angle of 45 degrees to the main stem. Tie them to canes fixed on the wire support.

3 In November, at the end of the growing season, lower the two side branches to the horizontal and tie them carefully to the wire supports with soft string. Cut back surplus laterals on the main stem to three buds.

Apples and pears 9

'Warner's King' Flesh tender, white, acid. Very large, skin pale green to pale yellow. A good cropper. Growth vigorous. Season October to November. Susceptible to scab and canker. Triploid.

'Howgate Wonder' Fair flavour, sub-acid, flesh fairly crisp, creamy. Fruits large to very large. Skin golden-yellow with pale red flush and streaks. Cropping prodigious. Growth vigorous. Season November to February. Often produces a late flush of blossom and so suitable for frosty areas and the north.

★ **'Blenheim Orange'** Culinary or dessert. Fine sub-acid flavour, flesh crisp, yellow. Fruits medium to fairly large, flattened, round and regular. Skin yellow, flushed and striped dull red and fine russet. Cropping sometimes biennial. Growth very vigorous and must be on dwarfing stock to crop early and keep the tree small. Season November to January. Triploid. Suitable for the north. The finest dual-purpose apple.

'Lane's Prince Albert' Flesh tender, green-white, acid, cooks well. Fruits large, round, conical. Skin pea-green with distinct red stripes, smooth and shiny. A most reliable cropper. Habit small, spreading tree. Season January to March. Suitable for the north.

There is a tendency for vertical shoots to grow from the horizontal arms. These laterals are pruned in summer, cutting each back to three leaves above the basal cluster. Do not tie the extension growth of the horizontal arms until the end of the summer because early tying checks growth. In November train and prune both the horizontal and vertical leaders in the same way as before. This regime of winter and summer pruning should continue until the desired number of tiers has been built in.

The number of tiers finally achieved depends on soil, site and inherent vigour, but four or five is usual. Eventually both the central axis and the horizontal arms fill their allotted space. From then onwards cut back the new terminal shoots to their origin each May and summer prune subsequent growth.

The fruiting stage

Each summer The fruits are carried on spur systems on the horizontal arms. The spurs are formed by the summer pruning of laterals on the Modified Lorette System in exactly the same way as for cordons. Regard each arm as a horizontal cordon (see pages 110–111).

Winter After a few years of fruiting, the spur systems may become complicated and should be simplified by removing clusters of weak buds and by cutting back some of the spurs to two or three fruit buds.

Second and subsequent years

4 At the same time, cut back the central leader to within 18 in of the lower arm at the next wire, leaving three good buds to form the central leader and two new horizontal arms. If growth is weak, prune back the horizontal leaders by one-third, cutting to downward-pointing buds.

5 From July to September, train the second tier of branches in the same way as in the previous years (see caption 2). Cut back competing growths from the main stem to three leaves. Cut back laterals from the horizontal arms to three leaves above the basal cluster.

Mature tree

6 In November, cut back the central leader to within 18 in of the lower arm, leaving three good buds to form the new central leader and two new horizontal arms. Cut back surplus laterals on the main stem to 3 buds. Tie down the extension growth of each arm to the horizontal. If growth is poor, prune back the leaders by one-third.

7 In May, when the final number of tiers is produced and the tree has filled its allotted space, cut back the new terminal growths of the vertical and horizontal arms to their origins. From now on prune them each summer as if they were cordons.

Apples and pears 10

★ **'Bramley's Seedling'** Flesh firm, pale yellow, acid, excellent cooker. Fruits large, flat, round. Colour green-yellow, red flush with broad broken stripes. Cropping regular, sometimes biennial. Habit extremely vigorous. Season November to March. Triploid Blossom very hardy, suitable for the north. The most famous of all cooking apples, but unsuited to small gardens unless on very dwarfing rootstocks.

'Edward VII' Flesh extremely firm but yellow, acid, juicy. Cooks dark red and transparent. Fruits oblong, regular, skin pale yellow with faint brown-red flush. Cropping moderate. Growth vigorous. Season December to April. Flowers late. Suitable for frost pockets.

'Annie Elizabeth' Flesh crisp, white, acid. An excellent cooker. Fruits medium to large, oblong, conical, irregular. Skin pale yellow, flushed and striped brilliant red. Cropping regular. Growth vigorous, upright. Season December to June. Fruits tend to drop, primarily because of short stalk. Very good cropper. Very suitable for the north.

The dwarf pyramid

The dwarf pyramid was evolved by commercial fruit growers as an easier method of producing apples and pears intensively. The pear, in particular, when grown on Quince rootstock, responds well to this method of training and in recent years the technique has been extended to plums. With apples and pears the aim is to produce a central-leader tree some 7 ft high with a total branch spread of about 4 ft through the tree, tapering to the top to form a pyramid.

It is essential to keep such a closely planted and compact tree under control. This control is exerted by a combination of summer pruning, early cropping, the complete removal of any vigorous upright shoots, and the choice of a rootstock capable of sustaining the required balance between steady cropping and the renewal of bearing wood.

Choice of rootstock

M9 and M26 rootstocks are suitable for apples in most gardens and either Quince A or the re-cloned Quince C (when it becomes generally available) can be used for pears.

Planting and staking

In early autumn, prepare the soil (see page 105). Plant in the dormant season from November to March. Individual stakes are not necessary unless planting only one or two trees. With a row of trees, support them by erecting two posts at the ends of the row, and stretch two horizontal wires between them, one at 18 in and the other at 36 in. Tie the trees to these, using string or strapping.

Spacing

Space apples on M9 rootstocks at 4–5 ft apart, and apples on M26 rootstocks and pears 5–6 ft apart. Allow the wider spacing on fertile soils. The rows should be 7 ft apart.

Pruning and training

The first year A start is made with a maiden tree, which is cut back to about 20 in on planting during the dormant season from November to March. Prune to a bud on the opposite side to the graft. The result of this initial pruning is the production of four or five strong shoots. The uppermost shoot grows vertically.

The first year

The second year

1 From November to March, at planting, cut back the maiden to a bud within 20 in of ground level.

2 From July to August, four or five strong shoots will have been produced. No pruning is necessary.

3 From November to February, cut back the central leader to leave 9 in of new growth. Cut to a bud that points in the opposite direction to the last pruning. Cut back side branches to downward-pointing buds to leave 8 in of the maiden extension.

4 From July to August, cut back laterals not required for the framework to three leaves or 3–4 in and sub-laterals to one leaf beyond the basal cluster. Leave leaders unpruned.

Apples and pears 11

DESSERT PEARS
Listed in order of ripening.

★ **'William's Bon Chrétien'** Very juicy and sweet with a strong musky flavour, flesh white and transparent. Fruits fairly large, oval, uneven. Skin smooth, golden-yellow with russet dots and faint red stripes. A regular cropper. Growth moderate. Season September. Pick when still green, a few days before ripening. Ripen in store. Susceptible to scab. Needs double working. The best early pear.

'Gorham' Sweet with a musky flavour, flesh white, melting, tender. Fruits small to medium conical with a short thick stalk. Pale yellow with light brown russet.

Cropping regular, but not heavy. Growth moderately vigorous and upright. Season mid- to late September. Pick a few days before ripening.

★ **'Merton Pride'** Excellent flavour, flesh creamy white, firm, juicy. Fruits medium to large, conical. Pale green with brown russet round the eye. Moderate vigour, tends to be biennial. Season mid- to late September. Triploid. First class quality fruits.

★ **'Onward'** Good flavour, flesh creamy-white, melting and juicy. Fruits medium, sometimes large. Skin green, yellow-green when ripe, with pink flush and brown russet. Cropping regular. Habit vigorous. Season mid-September. Only at its best for a limited time.

The second year In the following winter prune the central leader to leave about 9 in new growth, taking care to cut to a bud that points in the opposite direction to the last pruning. This is aimed at keeping the successive stages of the central stem as straight as possible, in a series of zig-zags. It would be easier not to prune the leader at all because the stem would be straighter if left untouched, but such pruning is necessary to stimulate the annual production of side branches during the formative stages. These side branches, perhaps four in number and evenly spaced around the tree, are pruned back to within 8 in of the maiden extension, cutting each to a downward-pointing bud to maintain the horizontal direction.

During the following summer begin summer pruning, starting in mid-July for pears and about the end of July for apples. Cut back laterals (the current season's growth) longer than 9 in arising directly from the side branches to three leaves, and laterals from existing spurs to one leaf beyond the basal cluster. Leave immature shoots until September and then prune them in the same way.

Do not prune the leaders in summer.

Third and subsequent years Prune the central leader in winter. Aim to leave about 9 in of new growth, cutting to a bud that is pointing in the opposite direction from the bud to which the stem was pruned in the previous winter. This stimulates the production of new side branches. Cut back any secondary growth that may have occurred as a result of summer pruning to a mature bud.

Every summer, prune the current season's growth on the side branches using the Modified Lorette System (see page 110), treating each side branch as if it were a cordon. Prune the branch leaders to six leaves.

When the tree reaches 7 ft, further extension growth should be stopped by cutting back the leader to its origin each May. Prune any other shoots that need restriction, such as vigorous upright shoots at the top or branch leaders growing into adjacent trees.

In winter it is occasionally necessary to shorten branches to a downward-pointing shoot in an attempt to maintain the essential horizontal position of the fruiting arms. Trim overcrowded spurs at the same time.

Third and subsequent years

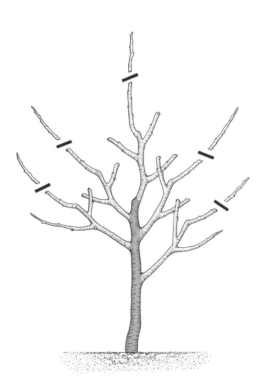

5 From November to February, prune the central leader to leave about 9 in of new growth, cutting to a bud on the opposite side to the previous pruning.

6 From July to August, throughout summer cut back laterals to three leaves or 3–4 in and sub-laterals to one leaf beyond the basal cluster. Prune the leaders of the side branches to six leaves.

7 From November to February, prune the central leader to leave 9 in of new growth. Remove entirely any over-vigorous shoots. Shorten branches to downward-pointing buds as necessary to maintain the horizontal position of the fruiting arms.

THE MATURE TREE

When the tree has reached the required height of about 7 ft, cut back the leader to its origin each May. Thin fruiting spurs as necessary. Maintain the central stem and retain the pyramid shape by close pruning and removal of vigorous shoots.

Apples and pears 12

★ 'Beurré Superfin' Sweet and perfumed flavour, flesh white, melting, juicy. Fruits medium, conical. Skin golden-yellow, patched with fine brown russet. Cropping and growth habit moderate. Season October. Pick early and eat while still firm.
'Louise Bonne of Jersey' Sweet flavour, flesh white, melting. Fruits medium, long.

Colour yellow-green with pronounced red flush and red dots. Cropping regular, growth strong upright. Season October. Blossom fairly frost-tolerant.
'Beurré Hardy' Good flavour, sweet, excellent quality. Flesh white and juicy. Fruits medium to large, conical and uneven. Yellow-green, almost covered with a fine brown russet and occasional

carmine flush. Sometimes a shy cropper and slow to start bearing. Growth vigorous and upright. Season mid- to late October. Pick when hard and ripen in store.
'Conference' Pleasant flavour, sweet, flesh firm, creamy white, very juicy. Fruits medium, long and thin, skin dark olive-green with brown russet. Cropping

heavy. Growth moderately vigorous. Season mid-October to late November. Suitable for the north. A reliable pear.
★ 'Seckle' Excellent flavour, flesh yellow-white, tender, honey sweet and juicy. Fruit small, skin red-brown with prominent white dots. Cropping only moderate, weak growth, making an upright tree. Season October to

Cultivation

Feeding and mulching Apply fertilizers as a top dressing over the rooting area, which is roughly equivalent to the spread of the tree and slightly beyond. Inorganic fertilizers can scorch grass, therefore brush well in and water the grass if the weather is dry. If the soil tends to be acid, with a pH lower than 6.7, sulphate of ammonia should not be applied because it makes the soil more acid. Instead use nitro-chalk, which does not affect the pH.

In early March, mulch newly planted and young trees with well-rotted manure, compost or peat to a depth of 2 in over a radius of about 18 in, but keep the mulch just clear of the stem.

Dessert apples In late January apply sulphate of potash at $\frac{3}{4}$ oz per square yard. Every three years, in late January apply superphosphate at 2 oz per square yard. In late February apply sulphate of ammonia or nitro-chalk at 1 oz per square yard.

Dessert apples in grass See Culinary apples.

Culinary apples The same rates and timings given for dessert apples apply except that extra nitrogen is necessary, so double the application of sulphate of ammonia or nitro-chalk. This also applies to dessert apples grown in grass which need extra nitrogen to compensate for the nitrogen taken up by the grass.

During heavy rainfall in spring and summer, and in high rainfall areas, certain apple varieties ('Cox's Orange Pippin' in particular) suffer from magnesium deficiency (see page 245). At the first signs, apply three foliar sprays at 14 day intervals, using 8 oz magnesium sulphate in $2\frac{1}{2}$ gal water, plus a spreader ($\frac{1}{4}$ fl oz washing-up liquid). To avoid a recurrence, apply the magnesium sulphate as a top dressing, in April, at 2 oz per square yard over the rooting area.

Pears, dessert and culinary Pears benefit from additional nitrogen. Apply all the fertilizers at the same rates and timings as given for culinary apples.

Watering To ensure good establishment and strong growth, young trees (especially newly planted ones) need to be watered in the growing season whenever the soil is dry. As a guide, apply 4 gal per square yard every ten days throughout the dry period.

Cropping trees also respond to irrigation by producing heavier crops of larger and better quality fruit. Lack of water may induce a biennial bearing pattern (see page 118). The total amount of water needed is 4 in (18 gal per square yard) in July, 3 in ($13\frac{1}{2}$ gal per square yard) in August and 2 in (9 gal per square yard) in September.

Obviously, in the cool wet regions these totals will be met by natural rainfall, but in dry areas some irrigation must be applied, the actual amount depending upon the rainfall. Apply 2 in (9 gal per square yard) at a time under the trees, starting in early July. Use a hose and keep the water on the ground rather than on the foliage, irrigating over the rooting area, which is roughly equivalent to the spread of the tree.

Fruit thinning The main purpose of fruit thinning is to obtain larger and better quality fruits. In heavy cropping years if the fruits are not thinned, the resultant crop will consist of small, poor quality apples or pears and, as with lack of water, the strain imposed upon the tree might put it into a biennial habit.

Much depends upon the condition of the trees: trees with healthy foliage and a strong framework can carry more fruit than can weaker trees. Young trees should not be allowed to crop so heavily that the branches are bowed down and the tree cannot make the essential strong growth needed for its framework.

Some varieties naturally shed some of their fruitlets in late June or early July which is called the June drop, but this may not be sufficient. Start lightly thinning before this in mid-June by removing the malformed fruits, and then complete the task after the June drop in about mid-July.

Culinary varieties should be thinned harder than the dessert fruits.

Use sharp scissors or press the fruitlet off with the thumb and finger, leaving the stalk behind. In the final thinning, dessert apples should be spaced on average 4–6 in apart with about one fruit per cluster and occasionally two where there is a good show of supporting leaves. Culinary apples should be spaced on average 6–9 in apart.

With apples, sometimes the "king" or "crown" fruit produced in the centre of a cluster is virtually stalkless and malformed. If this is the case, remove it, but if the apple is well shaped, leave it because the king fruit can be the best in the cluster.

Pears need less thinning than do apples. Start thinning after the natural drop in late June, but not until the fruitlets turn downwards. Thin to two fruits per cluster and occasionally to one where the foliage is poor or sparse.

Supporting heavily laden branches Prop up heavily laden branches well before there is a risk of the branches breaking. Use forked poles or stakes but place a cushion of soft material such as a piece of rubber tyre between the prop and the branch.

Weak branches can be tied to stronger ones with rope or webbing. Small trees can be supported by "maypoling". This involves driving a tall stake into the ground near the stem of the tree and tying rope or thick string from its top to each branch needing support (see page 117 for illustration).

Manuring

1 In January, apply sulphate of potash at the recommended rates. In late February apply sulphate of ammonia or nitro-chalk.

Mulching

2 In early March, mulch newly planted and young trees with a 2 in layer of well-rotted manure or compost over a radius of 18 in.

Watering

3 In summer, apply 4 gal per square yard every ten days in dry periods.

Apples and pears 13

November. Blossom fairly frost-tolerant.
'Packham's Triumph' Good musky flavour, sweet, flesh white, melting and very juicy. Fruits medium, conical and irregular, ribbing on the surface. Skin green with fine russeting, ripening to yellow with orange flush. Good cropper, weak growth. Season November to December.

★ **'Thompson's'** Excellent flavour, flesh white, melting and juicy. Fruits medium to large ribbed. Skin golden-yellow with red flush and russet marking. Cropping moderate. Habit medium vigour, upright. Season October to November.
★ **'Doyenné du Comice'** Excellent flavour, flesh white, melting and juicy. Fruits medium to large. Skin green-yellow

with a brown-red flush. Sometimes a shy cropper. Habit vigorous, fairly upright tree. Season late October to late November. Susceptible to scab. Requires a warm and sheltered site.
★ **'Winter Nelis'** Sweet delicately perfumed flavour, flesh green-white, transparent, very juicy. Fruits small to medium. Skin dull green with dark brown

russet, mainly around the eye. Cropping heavy, growth moderate. Season November to January. Blossom fairly frost-tolerant. One of the best winter pears.

Protection from wasps and birds

Apples and pears (especially the early varieties) sometimes need protection against wasps and birds. The trees can be netted or collars placed around the fruit stalks against birds) but wasps are more difficult to combat. One remedy is to find and destroy the wasps' nests. They can also be trapped in jam jars partly filled with beer and sugar. However, these two methods guarantee only partial control, and the most positive (if tedious) protection against wasps is to enclose each fruit, or cluster of fruits, in a muslin bag or piece of nylon stocking.

Harvesting and storing

The time for picking apples and pears varies according to the season and the locality so it is not possible to give exact picking dates. As a guide, in southern Britain the earliest varieties of apples are ready for picking in late July to early August.

Apples A good test for ripeness is to lift the fruit in the palm of the hand and if it leaves the spur easily with its stalk intact, it is ready.

Another sign is the first windfalls (discounting drops from strong winds and codling moth attack). With the later ripening varieties, the colour of the pips is an indication. They should be beginning to change colour from white to straw-coloured and eventually to brown. With dessert apples in particular the skin of the fruits becomes more brightly coloured.

Early varieties are best picked when slightly immature because they soon go mealy. Pick those apples that have coloured rather than clearing all the apples in one go. Usually those apples in full sun are ready first and those in the middle of the tree last. Handle the fruits very gently because bruised fruits do not keep. Put the fruits carefully into a picking container lined with a soft material and transfer them just as gently into their final container.

Late apples reach maturity in storage sometime after picking, depending upon the variety. Most should be off the tree by the third week of October in Britain, but there are a few varieties which keep better and

acquire more flavour if left on as long as possible, birds and winter gales permitting. These include 'Granny Smith', 'D'Arcy Spice', 'Sturmer Pippin', 'Idared', 'Wagener' and 'French Crab'.

Store only sound fruits (see page 101 for details of storage).

Pears The correct time for picking pears is harder to assess than it is for apples. The best test of readiness is to lift the pear in the palm of the hand and with a slight twist and tug, it should leave the spur with its stalk intact. There is also an almost imperceptible change in the ground colour of the skin from dark green to lighter green.

Early and early mid-season pears (August to September in Britain) must not be left on the tree until they are fully ripe otherwise they may go sleepy, that is very soft, mealy and brown at the centre. Pick them when they are almost ready but still firm, and then let them mellow in the storage house. Their storage life can be extended by keeping them under cool conditions ($3°-7°C/37°-45°F$).

Late pears should be left on the tree until

they leave the spur easily; the first sign of windfalls is an indication. The fruits are hard at this stage but will mellow in storage. Keep them under cold conditions and bring the pears into room temperature to finish ripening whenever required. (See page 101 for details of storage).

Pests and diseases

Apples The most troublesome diseases are scab, mildew and canker and the most troublesome pests are aphids, leaf-eating caterpillars, sawfly and codling moth larvae.

Scab and mildew can be controlled by regular spraying with thiophanate-methyl, benomyl or captan with dinocap starting at bud burst and finishing in July. If canker occurs, cut out the rotting wood and paint the clean wounds with a canker paint. In bad attacks also apply liquid copper sprays after harvest and at 50 per cent leaf-fall, and the following year at bud burst. Check that the soil is not badly drained (see pages 6–9).

Use a systemic aphicide against aphids and fenitrothion or permethrin against caterpillars.

Thinning

4 In mid-June, thin the fruits using sharp scissors or press the fruitlets off with the thumb and finger, leaving the stalk behind.

In mid-July, thin again to leave one or two dessert apples per cluster 4–6 in apart; culinary apples 6–9 in apart. Pears need less thinning; leave two fruits per cluster.

Maypoling

5 On small trees, to support branches with a heavy crop, drive a tall stake into the ground near the stem of the tree. Tie a rope from its top to each branch.

Grassing down the orchard

6 After four or five years, grass down the orchard. Sow a fine lawn mixture at 2 oz per square yard, leaving a grass-free area of 2 ft radius around the base of each tree.

Apples and pears 14

★ 'Joséphine de Malines' Excellent flavour, flesh pink-white, tender, juicy. Fruits small. Skin green-yellow with russet around the stalk. Reliable cropper. Growth weak, moderate, rather weeping. A tip-bearer. Season December to January. Blossom fairly frost-tolerant.

CULINARY PEARS
'Catillac' One of the best pears for stewing, when cooked becoming a deep red. Flesh white, firm and acid. Fruits large and round, skin brown-red flush over dull green, ripening to yellow. Cropping heavy, but irregular. Growth vigorous, spreading. Season December to April. Should be left on the tree as long

as possible. Triploid. Blossom fairly frost-tolerant.

Spraying with HCH, dimethoate or fenitrothion one week after petal fall controls sawfly larvae. Use fenitrothion or permethrin against codling moth caterpillars in mid-June and again at the end of June.

Pears The most troublesome disease of pears is scab and the most troublesome pests are aphids and leaf-eating caterpillars.

For scab spray with captan, benomyl or thiophanate-methyl at bud burst, repeating every two weeks as necessary until late July.

A systemic aphicide controls aphids and fenitrothion or permethrin controls caterpillars.

Propagation

Apples and pears do not come true from seed nor are they satisfactory from cuttings, so they are propagated by budding or grafting on to suitable rootstocks, a task normally performed by the fruit tree nursery.

Biennial bearing

Biennial bearing, or the carrying of a heavy crop one year and little or none in the next, is a common problem with apples and pears. Certain varieties are prone to it, 'Laxton's Superb', 'Bramley's Seedling' and 'Blenheim Orange' for example, although almost any variety can fall into this habit. It is more likely to happen to trees which are starved or receiving insufficient moisture, which makes them unable to carry a heavy crop and at the same time develop fruit buds for the following year. Frost destroying the blossom one spring can sometimes be the start of biennial bearing. Once the tree is into this cropping pattern it is difficult to correct, although there are certain techniques the gardener can try which sometimes improve the situation.

In early spring before an expected heavy crop year, half to three-quarters of the fruit buds are rubbed off the spurs, leaving about one or two per spur. This lessens the burden of too heavy a crop in that year and hopefully enables the tree to develop fruit buds for the next year.

In conjunction with bud rubbing, a policy of more generous feeding and watering should be adopted in "on" and "off" years.

First, clear away grass or weeds from the base of the tree over a radius of at least 2 ft.

Each February apply a compound fertilizer

BIENNIAL BEARING

1 In spring, before a heavy crop year, rub one-half to three-quarters of the fruit buds from the spurs, leaving one or two per spur.

2 Each February, apply 4 oz per square yard of a compound fertilizer, such as a brand of Growmore, and sulphate of ammonia at 2 oz per square yard. Mulch small trees with a 2 in layer of well-rotted manure over a radius of 2 ft.

3 In late August, apply a further 2 oz per square yard of sulphate of ammonia. In dry weather water copiously, giving at least 1 in of water ($4\frac{1}{2}$ gal per square yard) over the rooting area every ten days until rain restores the balance.

such as a brand of Growmore at 4 oz per square yard and sulphate of ammonia (or nitro-chalk) at 2 oz per square yard. Small trees should also be mulched with well-rotted manure or compost to a depth of 2 in over a radius of 2 ft but keep the material clear of the stem.

In late August apply a further 2 oz per square yard of sulphate of ammonia (or nitro-chalk). Throughout the growing season, whenever the conditions are dry, the tree should be irrigated copiously by applying at least 1 in of water ($4\frac{1}{2}$ gal per square yard) over the rooting area every ten days until rain restores the balance.

If bud rubbing does not work, an alternative technique is to induce the tree to crop biennially over half the tree by removing half the blossom. Alternate branches are selected and marked in some way. Half the branches

are designated to crop in the even years (1980, 1982, and so on) and half the branches are designated to crop in the odd years (1981, 1983, and so on). Each spring, those branches not selected to crop in that particular year must be rigorously deblossomed. At first this deblossoming represents quite a task, especially with a large tree, but after the third or fourth year it should be found that the branches have accepted this alternate pattern and very little blossom removal is necessary. However, a careful watch should be kept to see that the tree does not slip back into the full biennial cropping. As with the first technique, generous feeding is recommended.

Grassing down the orchard

After four or five years, grass down the orchard. Grass checks the vigour of the trees

and promotes colour in the fruits, so grass down dessert fruits, but not culinary apples or culinary pears for which size is more important than colour. Delay grassing down if the trees are growing poorly. Once the sward is sown, maintain a grass-free area of 2 ft radius around the base of each tree. Over-vigorous trees should have a smaller area of clean land, but do not grass right up to the stem because the vegetation might encourage the disease collar rot. Where trees are closely planted (cordons, for example), maintain a grass- and weed-free band 3 ft wide down the row.

Sow a fairly fine lawn mixture (but not rye grass because this tends to restrict the growth too much) at 2 oz per square yard. Poor soils should have wild white clover added to the mixture at $\frac{1}{4}$ oz over 10 square yards because it adds nitrogen to the soil.

Plums 1

DESSERT PLUMS
'Early Laxton' Fair flavour. Fruits small, oval, yellow with pink flush. Flesh golden and juicy. Ripens late July to early August. Heavy cropper. Dwarfish growth.
'Victoria' Fairly good flavour. Fruits large, oval, pale red and mottled. Flesh green-yellow and juicy. Ripens late August to early September. Very heavy cropper, sometimes irregular. Moderate growth. Self-compatible. Also suitable for cooking.
'Kirke's' Very good flavour. Fruits large, round, purple-red. Flesh green-yellow and juicy. Ripens late August to early September. Fairly good cropper. Dwarfish, spreading growth.

'Coe's Golden Drop' Excellent, very sweet flavour. Fruits large, oval, pale yellow with red-brown spots. Flesh golden and very juicy. Ripens late September. Light, irregular cropper. Moderate growth.

GAGES
'Oullin's Golden Gage' Moderate, fairly sweet flavour. Fruits large, round, yellow with green dots. Flesh pale yellow and transparent. Ripens mid-August. Slow to bear. Vigorous growth. Self-compatible.
'Count Althann's Gage' Rich flavour. Fruits large, round, dark crimson. Flesh golden and juicy. Ripens mid- to late August. Good cropper. Moderate growth.
'Early Transparent Gage' Excellent flavour. Fruits small to medium, round,

Plums and gages

The origins of the European plum (*Prunus domestica*) are obscure. It is thought to have arisen from hybridization between the sloe (*P. spinosa*) and the cherry plum (*P. cerasifera* or the closely related *P. divaricata*). It may have come from the Caucasus, where these species and hybrids between them occur.

The plum is a deciduous tree, ranging in height from 15–30 ft when mature. The gage is a sweeter, more refined type of dessert plum. Both are usually grown in bush, half-standard or standard forms, or fan-trained against a wall or fence. They may also be grown as pyramids—a very good form for the small garden. They are not suited to such restricted forms as the cordon or espalier.

Damsons and bullaces

The damson (*Prunus domestica* sub-species *insititia*) is a hardier, less vigorous type of plum used mainly for culinary purposes. The fruits are oval, usually blue-black and have a unique, rich flavour. The bullace and the Mirabelle plum also belong to this sub-species. Bullaces are very small, round or oval and may be blue, black, yellow or white. Mirabelle plums are round, small, sweet and golden yellow. All make small, compact, deciduous trees of 10–20 ft in height and spread. They can be grown as bushes, half-standards, standards or pyramids.

Myrobalan plums

The cherry or Myrobalan plum (*P. cerasifera*) is used mainly for hedges and as a rootstock for plums, although when grown as a fruiting tree, it gives a useful yield of small, red or yellow, cherry-like plums that are excellent for jam-making. On its own roots it makes a large tree 20–30 ft in height and spread.

Cultivation

The cultivation of plums, gages, damsons, bullaces and mirabelles is generally the same so, unless indicated otherwise, text references to plums apply to all these fruits.
Yield A good average yield from a plum tree in the open ranges from 30–120 lb and from a fan 20–30 lb.

Soil and situation Plums require a deep, moisture-retentive, well-drained soil with a pH range 6.5–7.2. The plum grows best in clean soil. Control grass and weeds around the tree by shallow hoeing. Avoid deep cultivation because this encourages suckering. Plum varieties on vigorous stocks can be grassed down, but maintain a clean area 2 ft square around the tree.

Plums, particularly the Myrobalan plum, flower early so a sheltered, frost-free site is essential to avoid irregular cropping. Gages and dessert plums need a warm, sunny position to acquire their full flavour. Gages particularly are good plants for a south- or west-facing wall, but they can be grown in the open in milder areas. Culinary plums will tolerate some shade. They can also be grown against an east-facing wall and a few early varieties will grow on a north-facing wall. Damsons are fairly hardy and will crop satisfactorily in regions too cool for plums.

Plums and gages are hardy in zones 4–8; damsons, Myrobalan plums and bullaces in zones 3–8; and Mirabelles in zones 4–8.

Selecting the tree The most suitable rootstock for the garden, both for trees in the open and on walls, is the semi-dwarfing rootstock St Julien A. The relatively new stock Pixy is more dwarfing but it is hard to obtain because propagation is difficult. Rootstocks Brompton and Myrobalan B are too vigorous for all but the largest gardens.

For bush, standard or fan-trained trees, buy a maiden tree or a two- to three-year-old tree already partly trained by the nursery. Plum pyramids are best obtained as maiden trees. A plum on St Julien A or Pixy usually begins cropping in the third to sixth year.
Soil preparation In early autumn, prepare the ground, thoroughly clearing away perennial weeds over an area 3 ft square. Just before planting, fork in a balanced fertilizer such as a brand of Growmore, at 3 oz per square yard and bonemeal at 2 oz per square yard. If the soil is light, also fork in well-rotted manure or compost at one 2 gal bucketful per two square feet.
Planting and spacing Plant in the dormant season from November to March. Trees in

Thinning

1 In autumn, prepare the ground, clearing away perennial weeds. Lightly fork in 3 oz of a balanced fertilizer and 2 oz of bonemeal per square yard.

2 For trees in the open, drive in a stake. For fan-trained trees construct a system of wires on the wall. Plant the tree and tie it to the stake or to the wall wires.

3 In February, apply a balanced fertilizer at 4 oz per square yard. One month later apply sulphate of ammonia at 1 oz per square yard. Mulch the tree with a 1–2 in layer of compost or manure.

4 Thin the fruits when they are the size of hazelnuts and once the stones have formed within the fruits. Repeat when the fruits are twice this size to leave them 2–3 in apart on the branches.

Plums 2

pale yellow with crimson dots. Flesh golden, transparent and juicy. Ripens mid- to late August. Good cropper. Moderate growth. Self-compatible.
'Denniston's Superb' Good flavour. Fruits large, round, green-yellow with dark green streaks. Flesh yellow-green, transparent and juicy. Ripens late August. Heavy cropper. Vigorous growth.

Self-compatible.
'Cambridge Gage' Very similar to 'Old Green Gage'.
'Old Green Gage' Excellent flavour. Fruits small, round, yellow-green with slight red flush and russet dots. Flesh yellow-green and very juicy. Ripens late August to early September. Fair cropper. Vigorous growth.

'Jefferson' Excellent flavour. Fruits large, round, green with russet dots and pink flush. Flesh pale yellow-green and very juicy. Ripens late August to early September. Moderate cropper. Vigorous compact growth.

MYROBALAN PLUM
Cherry Plum Good flavour. Fruits very

small, round, red. Flesh yellow. Ripens late July. Flowers very early. Self-compatible. There is a yellow form.

CULINARY PLUMS
'Early Rivers' Good flavour. Fruits small, round or oval, purple-blue. Flesh golden and very juicy. Ripens late July to early August. Good cropper. Moderate growth.

---

containers can be planted at any time. Dig a hole wide and deep enough to take the roots fully extended. For trees in the open, before planting drive in a stake to reach just below the lowest branches. For fan-trained trees, construct a system of supporting, horizontal wires spaced 6 in apart (see pages 84–85).

Plant the tree to the same depth as it was at the nursery. Return the soil and firm it well. Tie to the stake with a tree tie and cushion or tie in the branches of a fan to the wall wires. Water well.

Trees in the open require staking for the first five or six years. If the site is exposed they require permanent support and a heavy-headed standard needs two stakes and a crossbar.

Space bush, half-standard, standard and fan-trained plum and gage trees on Brompton or Myrobalan B rootstocks 18–20 ft apart and on St Julien A rootstocks 12–15 ft apart. Space bush trees on Pixy rootstocks 10–12 ft apart. Space plum pyramids on either St Julien A or Pixy, 10–12 ft apart. Use the smaller spacing also for damsons and bullaces.

Pruning
Never prune plums in winter because of the risk of silver leaf disease. Always protect the cuts with a wound paint.

Pruning bush, half-standard and standard trees The pruning methods for all these forms are basically the same except that in the first year after planting, the maiden half-standard or standard is cut back to a greater height.

The first year In late February to early March, just as the buds start to break, cut back the central stem of the maiden tree to a bud at 3 ft for a bush, at 4½ ft for a half-standard, and at 6 ft for a standard. It may be necessary to grow the tree on for a further year to acquire the necessary height for a standard before cutting it back. Shorten all laterals to about 3 in to help thicken the stem.

In July or August, select four or five evenly spaced primary branches around the stem at the top. Pinch out the growing points of all others at four or five leaves, including those lower down the main stem.

The second year In late February to early March, select four branches that have formed

wide angles with the stem. Cut back each leader of those selected by one-half to outward-facing buds. Remove the remainder, including the lower laterals left the previous year to thicken the stem.

In the summer, remove any suckers that appear from the ground and remove shoots on the main stem below the head.

The third year Repeat the procedures adopted in the previous spring and summer but allow more secondary branches to develop to fill the increased space, allowing up to eight strong and well placed, outward-growing branches. From late February to early March, cut these back by one-half to two-thirds of the maiden growth to outward-facing buds. Leave shoots on the outer parts of the head not required for leaders. Prune back unpruned laterals on the inside of the tree to 3–4 in.

Little pruning is necessary in subsequent years. The leading shoots of weaker varieties, such as 'Early Laxton', may need cutting back for a further one to two years in February to early March. Otherwise, all that is

necessary is to cut out dead, broken, rubbing and crossing branches and to thin out the head when it becomes too crowded; do this between June and the end of August.

Pruning a fan-trained tree Starting with a maiden tree, the framework of a fan-trained plum is built up in exactly the same way as a fan-trained peach (see pages 125–128). Thereafter the pruning is different because the plum fruits on short spurs on two-, three- and four-year-old wood as well as on growth made in the previous summer. However, the older wood tends to become bare with age and because of damage by frost or bullfinches. The aim in pruning is to encourage spur formation and, when necessary, to replace worn-out branches.

In the early years, extend the framework, as with the peach, to fill in the wall space, then follow the illustrated steps below.

In later years, in the spring, cut out a proportion of the old wood back to young replacement branches. Paint the wounds.

Feeding and watering In February, apply a balanced fertilizer, such as Growmore, at

---

The pyramid plum: the first year

1 In March, cut back the leader to 5 ft. Cut back to the stem all laterals up to 18 in from the ground. Cut back the remaining laterals by one-half.

Second and subsequent years

2 In late July, shorten the new growth of the branch leaders to 8 in to downward-facing buds. Shorten the current season's laterals on the branches to 6 in. Do not prune the central leader.

3 In March, shorten the central leader by two-thirds of the previous summer's growth until the tree has reached about 9 ft, then shorten the central leader to 1 in each May to keep the tree at this height.

4 In Late July, shorten the current season's growth of each branch leader to eight leaves. Shorten the laterals to six leaves. Cut out any vigorous shoots at the top of the tree.

Plums 3

'Czar' Good, acid flavour. Fruits medium, round or oval, dark purple. Flesh yellow-green and very juicy. Ripens early August. Heavy cropper. Moderate growth. Self-compatible. Hardy.

'Pershore' ('Yellow Egg') Fair flavour. Fruits medium, oval, golden. Flesh yellow. Ripens mid-August. Heavy cropper. Moderate growth. Self-compatible.

Hardy. There is also a purple variety.

'Victoria' See Dessert plums.

'Monarch' Fair flavour. Fruits large, oval, purple-red with russet dots. Flesh pale yellow. Ripens end September. Moderate cropper. Vigorous. Self-compatible.

'Marjorie's Seedling' Good flavour. Fruit large, oval, purple-blue. Flesh yellow and juicy. Ripens late September to early

October. Very good cropper. Vigorous upright growth. Self-compatible.

DAMSONS
'Prune' ('Shropshire Damson') Excellent flavour. Fruits small, oval, blue-black. Flesh green-yellow. Ripens September to October. Moderate cropper. Dwarfish growth.

BULLACES
'Langley' Good flavour. Fruits large, oval, blue-black. Flesh green. Ripens late October. Heavy cropper. Vigorous.

MIRABELLES
'Mirabelle Petite' Excellent flavour. Fruits small, round, golden. Flesh golden, dry. Ripens mid-August. Fair cropper. Dwarfish.

4 oz per square yard. In late March, apply sulphate of ammonia, or nitro-chalk if the soil is acid, at 1 oz per square yard. Mulch young trees with 1–2 in layer of well-rotted manure or compost over a radius of 18 in, keeping the mulch clear of the stem.

Water well and regularly in dry weather during the growing season, applying 1 in (4½ gal per square yard) every ten days until rain redresses the balance. Avoid irregular heavy watering which can split the fruits, especially near the ripening stage.

Frost protection
Protect plums on walls and, where it is practicable, trees in the open against frost at blossom time by draping with hessian or bird netting.

Pollination
Plums are one of the earliest tree fruits to flower and those on walls flower about seven to ten days earlier than those in the open when there may be few insects about, so hand pollination is worth while (see page 102).

Some plums and gages are self-compatible (see variety lists above) and can be planted singly, but others require cross-pollination (see pollination tables page 103). Most damsons, bullaces and Mirabelle plums are self-compatible. The Myrobalan plum is self-compatible.

Thinning the fruits
Thin the fruits (if the tree carries a heavy crop) after the stones have formed within the fruits to avoid loss of flavour and the possibility of a biennial pattern of bearing. Thin once when the fruits are about the size of hazelnuts and again when they are about twice this size. Those left on the tree to ripen should be 2–3 in apart, or 4 in for large varieties. Do not tug the fruits off because this might tear away the following year's fruit buds, but cut the fruit stalk with scissors or secateurs.

Supporting the branches
Support for heavily laden branches is essential because they may break and spoil the shape of the tree and increase the risk of

silver leaf or bacterial canker infection. Support individual branches with a clothes prop or forked stake driven into the ground at an angle. Wrap the branch with sacking where it meets the crotch. Alternatively, support laden branches with thin ropes tied to the top of a tall central stake in the form of a maypole (see page 117).

Protection against birds
The fruit buds of plums are susceptible to bird damage in winter and the ripe fruit is also at risk in the summer. Where practicable protect the tree with netting.

Harvesting and storing
Plums ripen from late July to November, depending on the variety and locality. They do not ripen simultaneously and it is necessary to go over the tree two or three times. Pick fruits intended for bottling, jam-making and cooking when slightly under-ripe. Pick all fruits with the stalks intact.

Plums cannot be stored for prolonged periods, but if picked when a little under-ripe

they will keep for two to three weeks in a cool place, at about 6°–7°C/42°–45°F.

Propagation
Plums are propagated by budding or grafting —a task normally carried out by the nursery.

Pests and diseases
Control aphids with a tar oil winter wash and by spraying with dimethoate or heptenophos in the growing season. Spray with fenitrothion or permethrin against caterpillars. Grease banding also helps to reduce infestations. If plum sawfly maggots are troublesome, spray the trees with dimethoate or HCH 7–10 days after petal fall.

Cut back branches affected by silver leaf to healthy wood as soon as the disease is noticed. Paint the cuts immediately with a wound paint. Spray with bordeaux mixture in mid-August, mid-September and mid-October against bacterial canker, if this has been troublesome in previous years. Remove branches dying back with canker. Pick off and burn fruits infected with brown rot.

The plum fan

1 For the first three years, follow the formative pruning steps for the peach fan (see pages 125–128), extending the framework to fill in the wall space. Prune only in spring or summer.

Fourth and subsequent years

2 Each spring, as growth begins, rub out shoots growing directly towards the wall and breastwood.

3 From late June to late July, as new shoots are made, pinch out the growing points of shoots not wanted for the framework when they have made six or seven leaves. This begins to form the fruit-bearing spur system.

4 After cropping, between mid-August and mid-September, cut back the pinched-out shoots to three leaves to encourage fruit buds to form at the bases of the pinched-out shoots the following year.

Sweet and Duke cherries 1

'Early Rivers' Very good quality, of excellent flavour. Fruits very large, round with deep red flesh. Ripens mid-June. Heavy reliable cropper. Very vigorous, somewhat spreading.

'Noir de Guben' Fair, juicy flavour. Fruits large, round dark red-brown to almost black. Dark red, firm flesh. Ripens late June to early July. Moderate cropper. High resistance to canker. Vigorous.

'Roundel' Very good flavour, excellent quality fruit. Fruits very large, round with red shiny skin. Soft, sweet red flesh. Ripens early July. Good regular cropper. Vigorous.

'Governor Wood' Fairly good, juicy flavour. Fruits medium to large. Round, dark red with yellow flesh. Ripens early July. Heavy cropper. Tree vigorous when young but does not make a large head.

'Merton Glory' Good, very juicy flavour. Fruits very large, round, creamy white with red flush. Flesh pale yellow. Ripens mid-July. Heavy regular cropper. Vigorous and spreading.

'Merton Bigarreau' Good quality black

The cultivated sweet or dessert cherry is basically derived from *Prunus avium*. It is a hardy deciduous tree which is cultivated in many areas of Europe and western Asia. It bears clusters of attractive, white flowers in spring and bears fruits, ranging in colour from yellow and pink to almost jet black, from June onwards in cool temperate areas.

The Duke cherry is thought to be a cross between the sweet and acid cherry and it is intermediate in character between the two.

Cultivation

Although this delicious fruit merits a place in any garden, it has one serious drawback—its extreme vigour. Despite the introduction of increasingly dwarfing rootstocks, the cherry remains quite vigorous and is therefore not suitable for a small garden. It is usually grown as a fan on a wall, but the wall must be fairly high. In the open it is grown as a standard and occasionally as a bush or half-standard. By using the less vigorous rootstock Colt, it could be grown as a pyramid (see the plum pyramid pages 120–121). For cultural purposes, treat Duke cherries in the same way as sweet cherries.

Yield The yield from the different kinds of cherry can vary enormously depending, of course, on the size, age and form of the tree and the climate. A good average from a fan is about 30 lb and from a well-grown standard 100 lb.

Soil and situation Cherries grow in any good, well-drained soil but it must be deep, ideally more than $2\frac{1}{2}$ ft. The pH should be between 6.7 and 7.5. Light, sandy and shallow soils are not suitable.

Cherry blossom is susceptible to frost and young trees to wind damage so the site should be sheltered from winds, in full sun and not in a frost pocket.

Soil preparation In early autumn clear away weeds over an area 3 ft square, single digging clear ground and double digging weedy ground. Just before planting, fork in a balanced fertilizer such as a brand of Growmore at the rate of 3 oz per square yard with bonemeal at 2 oz per square yard.

Planting and spacing Plant in the dormant season from November to March. Container-grown trees can be planted at any time. Dig a hole wide and deep enough to take the roots fully extended. For trees in the open, before planting drive in a stake to reach just below the lowest branches. Standard cherries require two stakes and a crossbar. For fan-trained trees, erect a system of horizontal wires on the wall using gauge 14 wire and spaced 6 in or two brick courses apart (see pages 84–85).

Plant the tree to the same depth as it was at the nursery. Return the soil and firm it well. Tie to the stake with a tree tie and cushion, or tie in the branches of a fan to the wall wires.

On Malling F12/1 (vigorous) space fan-trees 18–25 ft apart; half-standards and standards at 30–40 ft apart and bushes 25–35 ft apart. On the rootstock Colt (semi-vigorous), space fans and bushes 15 ft apart and pyramids 12–15 ft apart.

Pruning the fan-trained tree

The sweet cherry fan is pruned as shown in the step-by-step instructions below. Prune in spring as the buds burst and not in winter because of the risk of bacterial canker. If the maiden tree is well feathered use two strong laterals, one to the left and one to the right at the first wire to form the initial ribs. Tie these to canes fixed to the wires at 35 degrees.

Pruning bushes, half-standards or standards

The first year: the maiden tree Prune in the early spring just as the buds begin to open. The head is formed by cutting back to three or four suitably placed buds in the same way as for the apple (see page 107). The objective is to obtain three or four well-placed primary branches by the end of the summer. Pinch out any flowers that are produced. Shoots lower down on the main stem should be pinched back to four leaves. These help to stiffen the stem and should not be removed until the cherry is four years old.

The second year In spring, prune each leader by one-half to an outward-facing bud. Summer prune the pinched-back shoots on the main stem by pinching out the growing points.

Pruning the fan-trained tree: the first year

The second year

1 From November to March, prepare the soil. Dig a hole wide and deep enough to take the roots fully extended. Plant the tree against a wired wall for fan-training (or with two stakes and a crossbar for standards).

2 Each February, apply a top dressing of balanced fertilizer at a rate of 3 oz per square yard over the rooting area. Mulch with a 2–3 in layer of well-rotted manure over a radius of 18 in.

1 In spring, tie two strong laterals to canes fixed to wires at 35 degrees. Head the centre stem back to the uppermost of the selected laterals. Remove all other laterals and protect the cuts.

2 In spring, select suitable buds and shorten each leader to about 12 in. This encourages shoots to develop in the summer which are used as the ribs of the fan.

Sweet and Duke cherries 2

cherry. Very good flavour. Fruits large, purple becoming almost black when ripe. Firm red flesh. Ripens mid- to late July. Heavy and regular cropper. Vigorous.
'Bigarreau Gaucher' Sweet, good quality flavour. Fruits large, roundish. Dark red firm flesh. Ripens mid- to late July. Good cropper, vigorous, upright growth.

'Bradbourne Black' Rich, dark crimson cherry. Fruits large, round with dark red flesh. Ripens late July. Heavy cropper. Vigorous, drooping habit.
'Merton Favourite' Excellent flavour. Fruits large, round, black with dark red flesh. Ripens late July. Good cropper. Tree vigorous but compact.
'Stella' Juicy flavour of good quality.

Fruits large, dark red. Ripens late July. Good cropper. The first self-compatible sweet cherry introduced. Vigorous and upright and then slightly spreading.
'Van' Flavour sweet. Fruits large, bright red shiny. Firm, sweet, dark red flesh. Ripens late July. Good regular cropper. Very vigorous, upright when young, spreading later.

The third year By the third spring six to nine well-spaced leaders should have been formed. Prune them lightly, leaving about 24 in of the previous summer's growth. Prune laterals competing with the leaders back to three buds. Upright laterals in the centre should be cut out because these may grow too vigorously and spoil the shape of the tree. Where there is room, leave other laterals unpruned.

Fourth and fifth years No more leader pruning should be necessary. In the fourth spring clean up the trunk by removing the pinched-back shoots. Protect the wounds.

Pruning an established tree
Very little pruning is necessary while the tree is well furnished with cropping wood and of manageable height. Each year cut out dead, broken, crowded or crossing branches, cutting them flush to avoid any snags. Prune in the spring and protect the wounds.
Grassing down For the first four or five years the soil around trained trees must be kept clear by maintaining a 3 ft wide border along

the length of the wall over the spread of the tree. The border may then be grassed down, if the tree is growing satisfactorily.

Bush and standard trees should also be grassed down after five years. For the grass mixture see page 63. Keep the grass clear of the trunk of the tree.

Feeding and watering In February apply a balanced general fertilizer, such as a brand of Growmore, at 3 oz per square yard as a top dressing over the rooting area. Young trees, both fan-trained and in the open, should also be mulched to a depth of 2–3 in over a radius of 18 in.

Cherries against walls require watering in dry spells during the growing season. Once a good set of cherries has been achieved, water the border soil copiously in times of drought. Apply 1 in (4½ gal per square yard) over the rooting area every seven days (ten for the acid cherry) until rain falls. Keep the tree accustomed to moist soil conditions. Do not suddenly give heavy applications of water after the soil has become dry because this may cause the fruits to split.

Pollination
With one exception (the variety 'Stella') sweet cherries are not self-compatible, in fact, cross-incompatibility occurs. Most Duke cherries are self-compatible and can be planted singly but a few are not, so before making the final selection of varieties, refer to the pollination tables on page 103.

Protection against frost and birds
It is feasible to protect the blossom of a fan-trained tree against frost, but hardly practicable with a tall standard. Drape the fan with layers of hessian or netting. Birds, particularly bullfinches, destroy the buds in the winter and starlings and blackbirds eat the ripe fruits in summer. Where practicable, the best solution is to protect the tree with netting.

Harvesting
Leave the cherries on the tree until ripe unless they start cracking. Pick with the stalk on using scissors or secateurs: if fruits are pulled off and the stalk is left hanging it encourages

brown rot. Cherries should be eaten as soon as possible after picking.

Propagation
Cherries are propagated by budding, or by grafting on to rootstocks, tasks normally carried out by the nursery but which can be done by keen amateurs.

Pests and diseases
Cherry blackfly is the most troublesome pest and occasionally caterpillars attack the foliage. Spray with five per cent tar oil in December or use dimethoate whenever blackfly occurs. Apply fenitrothion or permethrin against caterpillars, except at flowering.

Bacterial canker is the most serious disease, but silver leaf also occurs. Brown rot can affect the fruits. Spray with bordeaux mixture against bacterial canker, in mid-August, in mid-September and finally in mid-October. There is no cure for silver leaf, as yet. Cut the diseased branches back to healthy wood. Fruits affected by brown rot should be picked and burnt as soon as possible.

The third year

3 **In spring,** cut back all leaders to suitable buds, leaving 18–21 in of new growth.

Fourth and subsequent years

4 **In spring,** when most of the wall space has been filled, rub or cut out any breastwood or laterals growing directly towards the wall.

5 **In late July,** cut back to six leaves any laterals not wanted for the framework. When growth reaches the top of the wall, cut back to a weak lateral just below. Or, bend and tie down the shoots.

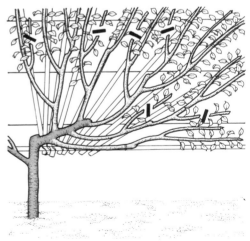

6 **At the end of September,** cut back to three leaves the laterals that were pinched out in July. This encourages fruit buds to form at the base of the shoots in the following year.

Acid cherries

Morello By far the most widely planted and regarded as being synonymous with the acid cherry. Juicy with a bittersweet flavour when fully ripe. Flesh soft, dark red. Fruits large, round, very dark red. Crops heavily and regularly. Moderately vigorous on good soils. Ripens August to September. The clone 'Wye Morello' is grown for making cherry brandy.

'Kentish Red' An Amarelle type. Flavour slightly bitter, acid, juicy. Flesh yellow, softish. Fruits small to medium, round, slightly tapering. Skin shiny, bright transparent, scarlet, cropping moderate. Medium vigour. Ripens early July or into August on a north-facing wall. Good resistance to bacterial canker.

The acid cherry is a culinary fruit derived from *Prunus cerasus*. It is a hardy deciduous tree that is much less vigorous than the sweet cherry and can be grown in a small garden. There are two types of acid cherry: the Morello with dark red, almost black fruits and red juice; and the Amarelle, with red fruits and colourless juice. Both are self-compatible and can be planted singly.

Cultivation
Usually grown as a fan on a wall, or as a bush tree in the open, the acid cherry can also be grown as a central-leader tree in pyramid form.

The acid cherry begins to bear fruit in its third or fourth year. A maiden tree can be planted but a few years are gained if a two- or three-year-old tree already partly shaped by the nursery is obtained.

Soil and situation Provided the soil is well drained, the acid cherry is tolerant of a wide range of soils but it prefers one that is neutral to slightly alkaline (pH 7.0).

The acid cherry flowers early in spring and so should not be planted in a frost pocket. It will tolerate partial shade and can be grown as a fan on a north-facing wall.

Planting and spacing Plant the tree at any time in the dormant season from November to March. Prepare the soil and plant, stake and tie as for the sweet cherry (see page 122). Bush and central-leader trees should be staked for the first four or five years. For fan-trained trees, erect a support system of horizontal wires on the wall before planting. Use gauge 14 wire and stretch the wires at every 6 in or two brick courses (see page 85).

Space bush trees, fans and pyramids on the vigorous rootstock F12/1 15–18 ft apart. On the Colt rootstock, which is less vigorous, space them 12–15 ft apart.

Control weeds and grass by shallow hoeing or use weedkillers (see page 17). Leave a border of uncultivated soil around the tree.

Pruning the fan-trained tree
The formative pruning and training is the same as for a peach fan (see pages 126–128), taking care to cut the leaders back hard in the first three years of training so that a densely-ribbed head is formed.

Pruning the cropping tree is based on the fact that the acid cherry fruits almost solely on the growths made in the previous summer. As with the peach, the aim is to obtain a constant supply of strong new shoots to carry the next season's cherries.

In spring and early summer, thin out the new shoots to about 4–6 in apart along the framework branches. Leave one replacement shoot at the base of each fruit-carrying lateral. Tie the young shoots to the wires while they are still flexible. Do not pinch out the growing points of the young shoots, but let them extend where there is room.

After harvesting in late August, cut out the laterals that have fruited back to the young replacement shoots.

Some acid cherries are relatively weak growing and the fruiting laterals do not readily produce replacement shoots near the base. If these fruiting laterals are left unpruned and no replacements form, they become extremely long with the base and centre of the fan bare and the crop carried only on the perimeter. When this happens, in March, cut out a proportion of the three- and four-year-old branches back to younger laterals to stimulate new growth.

Pruning the bush and pyramid
The initial training for these forms is the same as for the open-centred bush and pyramid plum (see pages 120–121). The leaders are cut back in early spring as growth begins to establish the framework.

Mature trees bear fruit along young wood formed in the previous season. In March cut back a proportion of the older shoots to one-year-old laterals or young shoots so that the old growth is continually replaced.

As the trees become older, the centre may become bare and unproductive. Each August after harvesting, cut back one-third of the main branches to within about 3 ft of the head to produce vigorous young replacement branches. Protect the cuts with a wound paint to avoid infection.

Routine cultivation
For feeding, watering, protection, thinning, harvesting, propagation, pests and diseases see Sweet and Duke cherries (pages 122–123).

Fan-trained tree

1 For the first three years, follow the steps for formative pruning of a peach fan (see pages 127–128), cutting the leaders back hard.

3 After harvesting, in late August, cut out the laterals that have fruited back to the young replacement shoots.

The mature tree

2 In March, cut back some of the older shoots to one-year-old laterals or young shoots to replace the older growth.

Fourth and subsequent years

2 In spring and early summer, thin out new shoots to 4–6 in apart along the framework branches. Tie in young shoots to the wires.

Pyramid tree

1 For the first three years, follow the steps for the initial pruning of a pyramid plum (see page 120). Cut back the leaders in early spring.

3 After harvesting, if the tree is bare and unproductive, cut back one-third of the main branches to within 3 ft of the head.

Peaches and almonds 1

PEACHES
Listed in order of ripening, which is based on fruit on a wall in southern England.

'Amsden June' Good flavour, flesh creamy white. Fruits medium, round, green-white with red flush. Crop moderate. Ripens mid-July. Suitable for growing under glass or in the open.

'Duke of York' Good flavour, flesh tender, pale yellow. Fruits large, rich, crimson. crops well. Ripens mid-July. Suitable for growing under glass or trained against a wall.

'Hale's Early' Good flavour, flesh soft, pale yellow. Fruits medium, yellow with red mottling and flush. Crops well but needs rigorous thinning. Ripens mid- to end July. Hardy, suitable for growing under glass or on a wall.

'Peregrine' Excellent flavour, flesh firm, juicy, green-white. Fruits large, round, crimson. Crops well, ripens early to mid-August. Suitable for growing under glass, on a wall or out in the open in warmer areas. A good garden variety.

Peaches, nectarines and almonds (outdoors)

The peach (*Prunus persica*) is a small deciduous tree with long, tapering light green leaves and attractive pink flowers borne singly in the early spring. Despite its name, the peach did not originate in Persia, but almost certainly in China where it was cultivated for many centuries before being introduced to Europe. The peach is grown throughout the warm temperate regions of the world (zones 8–10).

The nectarine is a smooth-skinned sport, or mutation, of the peach. Generally the fruits are smaller than peaches and often considered to have a better flavour. For most cultural purposes, however, it is treated in exactly the same way as the peach although it is slightly less hardy.

The almond tree is similar in size, habit, leaf form and flower to the peach, but it blossoms even earlier and therefore in cooler areas the blooms are frequently destroyed by frost or affected by cold. For this reason in northern latitudes it is grown largely more for its beautiful blossom than its fruit, nevertheless in frost-free springs moderate yields can be gathered.

There are two types of almond, the sweet almond (*Prunus dulcis dulcis*) and the bitter almond (*Prunus amygdalus amara*). In areas where almonds are grown commercially, there are named varieties, but in Britain it is sold as the flowering almond. It is usually grown either as a bush, half-standard or standard and is grafted on to the same rootstocks as the peach.

The ornamental flowering almonds are closely related and their nuts are edible to a greater or lesser degree, depending upon the amount of hydrocyanic acid in the nut. If growing it for its fruit, choose from the two species mentioned (above).

Cultivation

The peach and the nectarine are self-compatible and single trees can be planted. The almond is only partly self-compatible.

Yield The yield from a peach or a nectarine can vary enormously depending upon the size of the tree and the environment. A good average yield from a fan is about 30 lb and from a bush 30–100 lb.

Planting

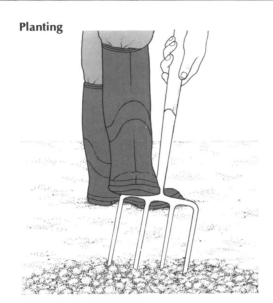

1 Before planting, fork in 3 oz per square yard of a balanced fertilizer, such as a brand of Growmore, with 3 oz bonemeal. Repeat every February.

2 From November to March, plant during the dormant season. A fan should be 6–9 in away from the wall or fence with the stem inclined towards it.

3 After planting, mulch to a depth of 2–3 in with manure or compost for 18 in around the tree. Replenish every year in February.

4 At the end of January, in February and at leaf-fall every year, spray with a copper fungicide against peach leaf curl.

Thinning

5 From early May to August, give the tree 1 gal of diluted high-potassium liquid feed every 14 days. Thin the fruits, starting when they are the size of large peas.

Harvesting

6 From August onwards, pick the fruit when the flesh feels soft at the stalk end. Hold the fruit in the palm of the hand, lift and twist it slightly.

Peaches and almonds 2

'Redhaven' Good flavour, flesh firm, yellow, reddening near the stone. Fruits medium, round, deep red over yellow. Crops well. Season mid-August. Suitable for growing under glass, on a wall or in the open in warmer areas.

'Rochester' Fair flavour, flesh firm, yellow and juicy. Fruits medium, yellow with a deep crimson flush. Crops well. Ripens early August. Hardy, suitable for growing under glass, on walls or out in the open as a bush. The best all-round variety.
'Royal George' Rich and highly flavoured, flesh firm, pale yellow, very red at the stone. Fruits large round, pale yellow with

deep red flush. Crops well. Ripens late August to early September. Suitable for growing under glass or on a wall.
'Bellegarde' Richly flavoured, firm flesh. Fruits large, golden-yellow, almost covered dark crimson with darker mottling. Crops well. Ripens early to mid-September. Suitable for growing under glass or on a wall.

Rootstocks and spacing Three rootstocks are widely used for peaches and nectarines: plum stock St Julien A (semi-vigorous); plum stock Brompton (vigorous) and occasionally peach seedling stock (vigorous). For most gardens St Julien A is adequate.

Fans on St Julien A should be spaced 12–15 ft apart and on Brompton or peach seedling 18–24 ft apart. Space bush trees on St Julien A 15–18 ft and standards on Brompton 18–24 ft apart.

Soil and situation The peach is tolerant of a wide range of soils but it is essential that they are well drained. To improve the drainage of a heavy soil, place brick rubble and chopped up turves in the bottom of the planting hole. The ideal soil is a medium to heavy, moderately limy loam, not less than 18 in in depth with a pH of 6.7–7.0.

The peach is quite hardy, preferring a cold winter and a sunny dry spring rather than a warm, wet winter which causes the buds to open only to be damaged by subsequent frosts. The site must be in full sun and sheltered from cold winds and ideally not in a frost pocket. The peach flowers very early so it is best grown as a fan on a wall or fence with a southerly aspect, where it can be protected against frost at flowering time and benefit from the warmth of the structure. In southern England and further south it can also be grown in the open, usually as a bush and sometimes as a full or half-standard.

Soil preparation Where there are poor soils at the base of a wall, it is worth while preparing the border specially (see page 104).

On good soils, however, it is sufficient to fork in a balanced fertilizer such as a brand of Growmore at the rate of 3 oz per square yard with sterilized bonemeal at 3 oz per square yard over an area of two square yards.

Selecting the tree For a bush tree buy a well-feathered maiden tree. For a fan, obtain a fan already partly formed by the nursery, choosing one with 5–12 shoots (depending upon the age of the tree) that are evenly spaced to form the first ribs of the fan.

Planting Plant during the dormant season from November to March. If planting a container-grown tree, it can be planted at any time. In the prepared soil, dig a hole wide and deep enough to take the roots fully

spread out. Plant the tree to the same depth as it was at the nursery.

A fan must be planted 6–9 in away from the wall or fence to allow for growth, with the stem inclined slightly towards its support structure (see page 104).

After planting, apply a 2–3 in mulch of well-rotted manure, compost, peat or mushroom compost for 18 in around the tree.

A system of horizontal wires is necessary to support the fan. Fix the wires to the wall or fence every 6 in or two brick courses apart, starting at 12 in above the ground (see pages 84–85). Tie canes to the wires where needed with thin wire.

Pruning and training
Stone fruits such as the peach are never pruned in the winter because of the risk of silver leaf disease and bacterial canker. They should be pruned while the sap is rising, from February onwards.

The fan-trained tree
The first year In February, starting with the feathered maiden tree, cut back to a lateral at about 24 in above the ground, ensuring that there are two good buds, or laterals, beneath it, one to the left and one to the right. Cut all remaining laterals to one bud. If there is no suitable lateral, cut back to a wood bud which is slender and pointed. If in doubt, cut to a triple bud which consists of two round flower buds and one wood bud.

In the early summer select three strong shoots. Train the topmost shoot vertically and of the other two, train one to the left and one to the right, choosing those that come from just below the bottom wire. Remove all other buds or shoots entirely.

As the two side-shoots lengthen, tie them to canes at an angle of 45 degrees. When both these shoots are about 18 in long, in June or July, cut out the central shoot entirely. Protect the wound with a wound paint.

The second year In February, cut back the two side-shoots to a wood or triple bud at 12–18 in from the main stem. This will induce new shoots in the coming summer. Protect the cuts with wound paint.

In summer, select four strong shoots from

each arm. One to extend the existing rib, two equally spaced on the upper side and one on the lower side of the branch to give the tree a total of eight ribs by the end of the season. Pinch back all other shoots as they develop to one leaf.

Carefully train each new shoot to a cane to extend the wings of the fan. Keep the centre open at this stage.

The third year In February shorten each leader by about one-third, cutting to a downward-pointing wood bud. Protect the cuts with a wound paint.

In the summer, allow the leading shoot on each of the eight ribs to extend. Also select three more shoots on each branch and train these outwards, tying them to canes on the wires, to fill in the remaining space on the wall or fence. Rub out buds growing directly towards the structure and breastwood. Of the remaining buds, allow young shoots to grow every 4 in on the upper and lower sides of the ribs. Pinch back to one leaf any surplus shoots. Repeat this process as and when necessary throughout the summer. When the selected laterals have made 18 in of growth, pinch out the growing points, unless they are required as part of the framework. In late summer tie them to canes on the wires. Fruit will be borne on these laterals in the following summer.

Fourth and subsequent years From this point onwards the tree must be regarded as a cropping tree. The wall or fence should now be more or less completely covered with framework branches on which every 4 in are fruit-bearing laterals.

The peach carries its fruits on shoots made during the previous summer so pruning is aimed at a constant and annual renewal of young shoots. It follows also that the shoots which have borne fruits are cut out to make room for the new young ones.

Each late spring, about May, remove shoots growing directly towards and away from the wall or fence but leave one or two leaves on shoots which have flower buds at the base. Next deal with the previous summer's laterals which should be carrying both blossom and side-shoots. Select one side-shoot at the base as the replacement, one in the middle as a reserve and one at the tip to extend the

fruit-carrying lateral. Pinch back the remaining side-shoots to two leaves. When the basal side-shoot and the reserve lateral are 18 in long and the fruit-carrying extension lateral has six leaves, pinch out the growing points of each.

Pruning the bush tree The formative pruning is the same as for a bush apple (see page 107) except that the pruning is done in the spring and a few branches in the centre of the tree can be left.

In the cropping years the objective is to encourage plenty of strong new growth each year to carry fruit in the next summer. This pruning should be done in the spring as the young shoots appear. It is occasionally necessary to cut back to young healthy replacements some of the older wood which has become bare. Avoid, however, making large wounds because these encourage bacterial canker to which peaches and nectarines are susceptible.

Feeding and watering In February each year, apply a balanced fertilizer such as a brand of Growmore at the rate of 3 oz per square yard as a top dressing over the rooting area. Replenish the mulch if necessary.

In May start giving a liquid feed every 14 days diluted in a gallon of water at a time, but stop in August when the fruits start to ripen. Use a high-potassium feed such as that sold for tomatoes.

The base of a south-facing wall can become very dry. Once a good set has been achieved, water copiously during dry weather. Apply 1 in, or $4\frac{1}{2}$ gal per square yard, every ten days until rainfall restores the balance. Keep the tree accustomed to moist soil conditions and do not suddenly apply a lot of water near ripening time because there is the risk of splitting the fruits.

Pollination and frost protection
The peach flowers early when there are few pollinating insects about, so it is worth while pollinating the flowers by hand to ensure a full set (see page 102).

Protection of the blossom against frost is also essential from pink bud stage until the danger of frost has passed. Drape the tree with hessian or bird netting. Remove it during the day.

Peaches and almonds 3

'Dymond' Richly flavoured, flesh firm and melting. Fruits large, pale yellow with deep red flush and mottling. Cropping moderate. Ripens mid- to end September.

NECTARINES
'Early Rivers' Rich juicy flavour. Pale yellow flesh. Fruits large, yellow with red streaks. Ripens end July. Suitable for

growing under glass or on a wall.
'Lord Napier' Rich flavour. Flesh white. Fruits large, yellow-orange with a crimson flush. Heavy cropper. Ripens early August. Suitable for under glass or on a wall.
'Humboldt' Rich flavour. Golden-coloured flesh. Fruits medium to large, yellow-orange with a deep crimson flush. Heavy cropper. Ripens mid-August.

'Elruge' Good flavour. Green-white flesh, red near the stone. Fruits medium, round to oval, pale green with a dark purple flush. Ripens end August. Suitable for growing under glass or on a wall.
'Pine Apple' Excellent rich flavour. Yellow flesh. Fruits medium to large, rich crimson red. Ripens early September. Suitable for growing under glass.

Thinning

To obtain good-sized fruits it is essential to thin the fruits. Thin over a period, starting when the fruitlets are the size of large peas and stopping when they are the size of walnuts. Peaches should be 9 in apart and nectarines 6 in apart after the final thinning.

Harvesting peaches and nectarines

The fruit is ripe when it has a reddish flush and the flesh feels soft near the stalk end. Hold the peach in the palm of the hand, lift and twist it slightly. It should part easily from the tree. Store the fruits in a cool place until they are to be eaten. They will keep for up to a week only and for long-term storage they must be bottled or frozen without the stones.

Pruning the fan-trained tree after harvesting

Immediately after cropping, not later than the end of September, cut out the laterals which carried the fruits back to the replacement shoots. Tie in the young shoots and cut out any dead or broken branches.

Once the peach has reached the required height and spread, remove any unwanted extension growth by cutting to a lateral further back along the branch. Cut out bare wood back to strong young replacements. Protect the wounds with a wound paint.

Harvesting and storage of almonds

Harvest the nuts in early October when they fall naturally and the husks split. Remove the nuts from the husks and dry them thoroughly in well-ventilated conditions: in sunshine is ideal, or in an airing cupboard. Keep the nuts off the ground by laying them on wire netting to allow air circulation. Once dry they should be kept in cool and dry conditions.

If squirrels are troublesome, harvest the nuts slightly earlier and dry both husk and nut initially before splitting them open.

Propagation

Peaches, nectarines and almonds are propagated by budding or grafting, a task normally carried out by the nursery, but it can be performed by the keen amateur.

Pests and diseases

The most troublesome pest is glasshouse red spider mite, especially on warm walls. This can be controlled by applying malathion, dimethoate or pirimiphos-methyl. Alternatively, use the predacious mite, *Phytoseiulus persimilis*. Occasionally aphids infest the young shoots; control these by spraying with a systemic insecticide as necessary.

The most devastating disease on peaches outside and almonds is peach leaf curl. To prevent it, spray thoroughly with bordeaux mixture or a liquid copper fungicide at leaf-fall, at the end of January and in mid-February. If it occurs, pick off the infected leaves (provided there are only a few). Give the tree a high nitrogen feed to promote new leaves. Other troubles are bacterial canker, silver leaf and split stone. Split stone can be prevented by hand pollination, the application of lime if the soil pH is below 6.7, and regular watering and feeding.

Varieties

Under glass any of the varieties listed above will ripen. Outdoors it is best to choose those ripening not later than early September in the south and early August in the north.

The fan-trained tree: the first year

1 In February, cut back a feathered maiden peach to a lateral about 24 in above the ground, leaving one good bud on each side beneath it. Cut remaining laterals to one bud.

2 In early summer, select three shoots. Train the topmost vertically, and one to the left and one to the right. Remove all other buds or shoots.

The second year

3 In June or July, tie the lengthening side-shoots to canes set at an angle of 45 degrees. Later that summer, cut out the central shoot and protect the cut with wound paint.

4 In February, cut back the two side-shoots to a wood or triple bud at 12–18 in from the main stem. Protect the cuts with wound paint.

5 In summer, select four shoots on each arm, one to extend the existing rib, two spaced equally on the upper side and one on the lower. Stop other shoots at one leaf.

Peaches and almonds 4

The third year

6 In February, shorten each leader by one-third by cutting to a downward-pointing wood bud. Protect the cuts.

7 In summer, allow the leading shoots on each rib to extend. Train three shoots on each branch outwards, tying them to canes. Allow shoots to grow every 4 in.

8 In late summer, when the selected laterals have made 18 in of new growth, pinch out the growing points of each and tie them to canes on the wires. These laterals will bear fruit the following summer.

Fourth and subsequent years

9 Each year in about May, remove shoots growing directly towards and away from the wall or fence. Leave shoots with flower buds at their base one or two leaves.

10 Select two replacement laterals on each leader: one at the base and a reserve in the middle. Allow a lateral to extend the fruit-carrying lateral. When the basal and reserve laterals are 18 in long and the extension has six leaves, pinch out the growing points. After harvesting, cut the fruited laterals back to their replacements.

Apricots

'Alfred' Good flavour. Fruit medium to large, round and flattened, orange with pink flush; flesh orange and juicy. Ripens late July to early August. Tends to biennial cropping. Flowers early. Vigorous tree.

'Breda' Good, sub-acid flavour and aromatic. Fruit medium to large, squarish, orange with dark red flush and

brown and red dots; flesh orange, moderately firm and juicy. Ripens mid-August against walls and September in the open. Heavy cropping but tends to be short-lived. Flowers mid-early to late. Moderately vigorous tree.

'Early Moorpark' Rich flavour. Fruit round to oval, yellow with crimson flush and darker mottling; flesh deep orange

and juicy. Ripens late July. Heavy cropping. Vigorous when young.

'Farmingdale' Very good flavour. Fruit medium, roundish, orange-yellow with red flush; flesh orange and moderately juicy. Ripens late July. Heavy cropper. Vigorous, fairly disease-resistant tree.

'Hemskerk' Good, very sweet, rich flavour. Fruit large, conical, yellow with

red patches; flesh golden yellow. Ripens early August. Good cropper. Moderately vigorous tree.

'Moorpark' Very popular variety. Rich sweet flavour. Fruit large, uneven round, pale yellow with reddish-brown flush and dots; flesh orange, firm and juicy. Ripens late August. Regular cropper. Moderately vigorous growth. Prone to die-back.

The apricot (*Prunus armeniaca*) is a hardy deciduous tree. It is a native of China and is widely grown in California, around the Mediterranean and in Australia. With care, it can be grown in zones 6–8.

Cultivation

A dwarf tree is best for the garden where space is limited. Even this can reach a height of 8 ft and a span of 15 ft. Buy a two- or three-year-old tree, already partly formed by the nursery, grafted on to a plum rootstock (such as St Julien A) which is less vigorous than other available rootstocks.

Soil and situation The apricot needs a well-drained but moisture-retentive and slightly alkaline soil with a pH range of 6.5–8.0. Light, sandy soils are not suitable.

Warmth in summer is essential and, although the apricot can be grown in the open in warm temperate areas, it thrives best fan-trained against a south- or west-facing wall in the cooler regions. It can also be grown successfully in containers.

Shelter the tree from frost and wind to encourage pollinating insects and to protect the ripening fruit. Keep the soil around the tree clear of weeds and grass so that ample moisture can reach the roots.

Planting In mid-autumn, prepare the ground, clearing away perennial weeds over an area 3 ft square. Dig in well-rotted manure or compost at a rate of one 2-gal bucketful per square yard. Plant the tree (see page 104). Water well and mulch lightly with well-rotted leaf-mould or compost.

Plant fan-trained trees 15 ft apart and 6 in from the wall or fence. Plant bush trees 15–20 ft apart.

Formative pruning and training The formative pruning of the fan-trained apricot is the same as that of the fan-trained peach (see pages 126–128). The formative pruning of the bush apricot is the same as that of the bush plum, but prune it in early spring as growth begins (see pages 120–121).

Pruning the cropping tree Mature fan-trained apricots are pruned in the same way as are fan-trained plums (see pages 120–121). Mature bush apricots are pruned in the same way as acid cherries (see page 124).

The apricot carries the best quality and

most abundant crops on short spurs on two- and three-year-old wood. Extensive pruning is not necessary because it results in a poor crop. Every four to six years, cut out the older shoots that have fruited to make room for new young ones. This means cutting out some of the lateral and sub-lateral branches of a fan-trained tree. Retain and tie in the same number of new shoots to replace them. Do not prune or pinch back these shoots until the second season and then only if required.

Thinning Thin the fruits at intervals from the time they are the size of cherries until they are almost full size. First remove misshapen fruits and those growing towards the wall. Later, thin pairs and clusters so that those left to ripen have 3–4 in between them.

Feeding Root dryness is a common problem with wall-trained trees. Water generously until the root area is soaked, especially if the weather is dry when the fruit is setting or when it starts to swell.

In late winter, sprinkle nitro-chalk around the tree at a rate of 1 oz per square yard and apply a general fertilizer, such as a brand of Growmore, at a rate of 2 oz per square yard. Every four years, if necessary, apply lime to maintain the pH at a little above 7.0. In late spring, mulch the root area to a depth of 1 in with leaf-mould or compost.

Pollination Apricots are self-compatible but, because the flowers open early in spring when few insects are about, hand pollination is sometimes necessary (see pages 102–103).

Protecting the blossom The apricot is highly susceptible to frost damage. Protect it with polythene or netting.

Harvesting

Depending on the variety, apricots ripen from midsummer to early autumn. The fruits are ripe about one week after they have stopped swelling and reached their full colour. Pick the ripe fruit carefully and try not to break the skin. It should come away easily in the hand.

Pests and diseases

Major diseases are silver leaf and bacterial canker; major pests are aphids and red spider mite. See peaches and nectarines (page 128) for details.

1 In mid-autumn, in prepared ground dig a hole large enough for the roots. Plant at the same depth as at the nursery. Mulch well.

The first year

3 In February, shorten each leader by one-third, leaving about 30 in of growth.

The second and subsequent years

5 In spring, rub out buds pointing towards or away from the wall or fence. Prune the leaders by one-quarter.

A three-year-old fan-trained tree

2 Erect supporting horizontal wires 9 in apart on the wall or fence. Tie in the young branches to the canes on the wall wires.

4 In July/August, select and tie in three additional shoots from each pruned leader. Pinch out all remaining shoots.

6 Early in July, pinch off the tips of side-shoots at six leaves. After cropping, cut back these laterals by one-half.

Preparing the site 1

When preparing a site for a lawn begin at least two to three months before the planned sowing or turfing dates. This gives sufficient time for the soil to settle and for weeds to be brought under control. For autumn sowing or winter turfing begin preparations in early summer if levelling or draining the site is going to be necessary, or if there are many weeds present. For spring sowing the draining can be done in autumn but levelling is best carried out during the summer since the soil needs to be dry.

Clearing the site

The first step is to clear away builders' rubble, bricks, discarded gravel and rubbish, if present. Remove any heaps of sub-soil left by the builders—do not spread them over the site. Next, carefully dig out any tree stumps or broken-off roots. If they are left in the soil they may become colonized by fungi, even if the pieces of wood are quite small, and in time produce unsightly and recurring crops of toadstools. If the new site is heavily infested with weeds use the appropriate weed-killers or fallow the land during the spring and summer months (see page 145).

Recently vacated building sites may have been subjected to considerable soil disturbance, and in some cases much of the fertile top-soil will have been lost. First establish the nature and depth of the top-soil by making trial excavations on the nearest accessible undisturbed site. Ideally, there should be at least 9 in of top-soil, but a minimum depth of 6 in is acceptable. If there is less, purchase sufficient top-soil from a local supplier.

Grading

The term grading means the elimination of surface irregularities. This is done by relating site levels to nearby fixed levels such as house foundations, walls or paths. It is not essential to have a perfectly level site; a fall of 1:80 is quite acceptable and has the advantage of assisting surface drainage.

Grading can be expensive and on larger sites need not be necessary since a gentle slope or undulations can be visually quite pleasing.

When grading major irregularities first remove all top-soil and heap it clear of the site. Then even out the level of the sub-soil and replace the top-soil to an even depth.

Minor irregularities can be corrected by adding a little top-soil. Do not, however, take it from higher points on the site since this may leave the top-soil very thin in places which will cause the grass to grow irregularly. Instead, bring in top-soil from elsewhere in the garden.

Where there are steep slopes it is preferable to draw the soil forward to make a single level area since turfed banks can be very difficult to maintain. Alternatively construct two or more terraced lawns with retaining walls and connecting steps (see Box, page 133).

Levelling

Few people may take the trouble to establish the level of the site properly by using a spirit level, straight edge and pegs. Usually they rely instead on a "good eye", or pegs and garden line. However, for finer ornamental lawns and areas where games are to be played it is always advisable to do this task properly. For this, the following equipment is required: a straight-edged board about 7 ft long, a large spirit level, a tape measure or marked cane, a handful of marked pegs and a mallet. Hammer in the master peg at a selected point, leaving about 4 in of the peg above the surface. Then drive in the other pegs at 6 ft intervals to form a grid system. Establish the master peg at the required level then, working from it, adjust the other pegs with the straight edge and spirit level until they align with the master peg. Next, add or remove soil (sub-soil or top-soil) until the soil surface is level either with the top of each peg or to a predetermined peg marking. Where a slope is required, establish across-slope levels in the same manner. Down-slope levels can then be established with pegs and line or, more accurately, with a spirit level, using pairs of marked pegs at each station.

Digging

Digging serves two purposes: it allows improvement of soil texture (and hence aeration and drainage) and it relieves compaction. It is advisable to dig all lawn sites unless, of course, they have recently been ploughed. Lawn sites that have been vacated by builders should be deeply dug because such sites almost invariably are compacted to a considerable depth.

When digging, take out a trench a spit deep, then fork over the bottom of the trench to the full depth of the fork. On heavy soils incorporate gritty material or lime-free, medium-grade sand ($\frac{1}{5}$–$\frac{1}{2}$ mm) to improve soil texture and porosity. Also add well rotted stable manure, garden compost, leaf-mould or moist granulated peat at up to 14 lb per square yard. On sandy soils improve moisture retention and encourage deeper rooting by incorporating similar dressings of organic materials. Dried sewage can also be used at up to 2 lb per square yard.

Break up organic materials when digging them in; if they are left in large lumps, surface irregularities may occur as they gradually decompose. Finely broken organic matter can also be worked into the sub-soil, but do this in moderation, otherwise settling may occur at a later date.

Soil pH

If soils are very acid (low pH) or very alkaline (high pH) some of the nutrients in the soil can become "locked up" and be unavailable to plants. The ideal pH level for most lawn grasses is between 5.5 and 6.0, that is, moderately acid—simple test kits are available for measuring the soil pH. Grasses can grow at higher or lower pH levels and it is not essential for the soil pH to be at this level, but with increasing acidity or alkalinity growth problems occur. Few lawn sites will require the pH to be altered. Possibly some heathland development sites will be too acidic for a lawn, but those developed from agricultural land almost always have a satisfactory pH value.

Where tests show that the soil is strongly acid (below pH 5) apply lime in the form of carbonate of lime (either ground chalk or ground limestone). If there is uncertainty as to how much lime is needed, apply only a moderate dressing of 2 oz per square yard on sandy soils and 4 oz per square yard on clay soils. Lime needs may vary considerably according to the texture of the soil, and very acid soils may need further treatment. Test the soil again after one or two years. Do not

Clearing the site

1 Remove any debris left by builders, such as rubble and bricks. If they have left heaps of sub-soil, remove these as well.

2 Carefully dig up and remove any tree stumps together with all their roots, including those that have broken off.

3 Test the depth of the top-soil and, if necessary, purchase sufficient to bring it up to a minimum depth of 6 in.

Preparing the site 2

over-lime, since this can lead to increased worm activity on humus-rich soils, increase the risk of disease and encourage coarse grass and weeds to establish. If in any doubt, it is preferable to seek professional advice rather than risk over-liming.

On strongly alkaline soils, the incorporation of acid peat materials will benefit early growth of seedling grasses, but it will not appreciably reduce the alkalinity of the soil.

Final preparations
The final stage of preparation is the creation of a firm, even, fine-particled soil surface. If the soil is heavy then digging may have left the surface very rough. However, if it has been subjected to a long period of weathering after digging, or if the soil is light, then the surface should be in a reasonable condition. On larger sites that have been worked with a rotary cultivator there will be few clods to break down, but the soil will have been less

thoroughly prepared than if it were well dug.

For autumn sowing, begin the final preparation of the seedbed during the summer. This will allow several weeks fallowing during which germinating weed seedlings can be killed periodically by light hoeing or spraying with paraquat/diquat. For seed sown in spring, germination will be slower and, although it is still advantageous to prepare the seedbed a few weeks in advance of sowing, the weather conditions may prevent this. In this case it is better to take advantage of favourable conditions and sow immediately after preparation. For laying turf fallowing is less important, but take advantage of favourable weather conditions for early preparation, particularly on heavier soils.

The first step is to break down clods and lumps into fine particles. On smaller sites use a heavy metal rake or a garden fork reversed. On larger sites use a rotary cultivator set to a shallow level of penetration. Breaking down

clods should be done when the soil is fairly dry since this reduces the risk of compacting the soil.

The second step is to firm, or consolidate, the soil. On smaller sites this can be done by light treading. Very short or overlapping steps are taken with body weight mainly on the heels, the ball of the foot providing balance. Alternatively, use the head of a rake. Ensure that uniform pressure is applied over the entire surface so that all soft spots are located and firmed. As with breaking down, do not firm when the soil is wet.

After firming, rake the soil level, remove stones and debris and firm again. If hollows are still present, repeat the process until the surface is uniformly consolidated and heel pressure makes only a slight indentation. Do not allow the soil to become so compressed that surface drainage is impaired. Keep a close check on the level of the site as firming progresses.

Large areas can be firmed by a roller, but this is less satisfactory than treading or using a rake since air pockets may be left, which in time may subside to leave the surface uneven.

Pre-sowing fertilizer
If a site is known to have been heavily manured and fertilized in recent years, a dressing of fertilizer is not essential. However, where there is any doubt regarding soil fertility apply the following dressing: $\frac{1}{2}$ oz sulphate of ammonia, 1oz superphosphate and $\frac{1}{4}$ oz sulphate of potash per square yard. Rake this in thoroughly seven to ten days before sowing, if possible. However, sowing can, if necessary, be done immediately after applying fertilizer. Use the fertilizer at once — if stored it will soon set hard.

If sowing is not done immediately after applying fertilizer, give the site a final raking to remove all small stones and debris so that it is ready for sowing when planned.

Grading major irregularities

1 Dig up all the top-soil from the site and pile it up to one side, leaving just the sub-soil beneath.

2 Even out the sub-soil, filling hollows with sub-soil taken from bumps, and then replace the top-soil.

Grading steep slopes

1 After removing the top-soil from the slope, transfer the sub-soil from the higher half of the slope to the lower half.

2 Level out the sub-soil and firm it. Finally return the top-soil evenly over the surface.

Preparing the site 3

Levelling the site

1 Hammer the master peg into the soil at a suitable point, leaving about 4 in of the peg showing above the surface. Then drive in the remaining pegs at 6 ft intervals to form a square grid system.

2 Adjust the height of the secondary pegs with a spirit level and straight-edged plank or board, working away from the master peg. Continue until the tops of all the pegs lie in the same horizontal plane.

Creating a sloping site

3 Add or remove soil until it is either level with the top of each peg or comes up to a predetermined marking on each peg. Ensure that all the soil has been evenly firmed before removing the pegs.

Establish the across-slope levels as above. The down-slope levels are determined by using a pair of pegs, with the soil being added or removed up to a fixed distance below the top of the down-slope peg, and to the top of the up-slope peg.

Preparing the site 4

Firming the soil

Lightly tread over the site, taking short or overlapping steps and with the weight of the body on the heels. Alternatively, firm the

soil with the head of a rake. Then rake the soil level, remove any debris present and firm again.

TERRACING A STEEP SLOPE

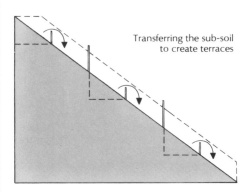

Transferring the sub-soil to create terraces

Finished terraces, with top-soil replaced

The first step is to decide how many terraces are required and to mark out their dimensions. Starting at the lowest terrace, remove the top-soil and place to one side or on the next highest level. Next, stretch a line across the terrace to divide it into an upper half and a lower half. Then move

sufficient sub-soil from the upper half to bring the two halves level. Finally, replace the top-soil. If necessary, construct a retaining wall before replacing the top-soil and beginning work on the next terrace. Do not forget to include a ramp for mowers if needed.

DRAINING

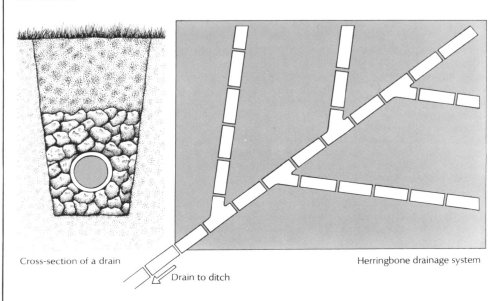

Cross-section of a drain

Drain to ditch

Herringbone drainage system

When constructing a new lawn, a thorough working of the top-soil and breaking up of the sub-soil, with textural improvement where necessary, should ensure that surplus moisture is not held at the surface. If, however, the site is known to be wet in places then some form of drainage should be installed.

For a small lawn or wet corner, a soakaway provides sufficient drainage. To build one, first dig a hole 2–3 ft square by at least 3 ft deep at the lowest part of the lawn. Fill it with clinker, broken bricks or stone to 8 in from the surface and add a 2 in layer of coarse sand, grit, or upturned turves to prevent the soil from washing through to the coarse material below. Finally, fill in the hole by adding a 6 in layer of top-soil.

A more satisfactory method of draining, though not often necessary, is tile draining. On a very wet site a herringbone or grid system may be needed, but usually a single line of drainpipes laid diagonally across the site, or through a wet section and feeding

into a sump, is sufficient. For this, use agricultural clay or 3 in diameter plastic lateral or collector pipes. If several lines are being laid, space them about 10 ft apart on heavy soils, and up to 30 ft apart on light soils. Their depth should be about 2 ft and they should have a fall of between 1:80 and 1:100. A herringbone or grid of lateral 3 in pipes should feed into a 4 in main drain laid at a depth of $2\frac{1}{2}$ ft. This in turn should be connected to a main drain or ditch—check beforehand with the appropriate authorities that this is permissible.

Pipe drainage should be installed only after the site has been levelled. Excavate the soil carefully so that, firstly, the pipes will just fit into the bottom of the hole and, secondly, the top-soil and sub-soil are kept separate. Place a small piece of turf with the grass down over the joints between the pipes, then cover with clinker or gravel to within 8 in of the surface. Finally, add a 2 in layer of coarse sand, grit or fine gravel, then replace the top-soil, discarding the sub-soil.

Lawn grasses 1

Of the many kinds of grasses that exist in nature only a few are suitable for creating lawns. The most important qualities needed in lawn grasses are that they should tolerate close mowing, drought and cold. They should also be resistant to diseases, be hard-wearing and have a naturally low-growing habit. Since no single species of grass possesses all these qualities, lawns almost invariably contain a mixture of different grasses to provide the optimum blend.

Many seedsmen supply good basic proprietary mixtures of grasses, and these are perfectly satisfactory in a wide range of conditions. If, however, problems are experienced in establishing turf from seed on the more difficult kinds of soil it could be worth while studying the qualities and preferences of the main types of lawn grasses and then over-seeding or modifying a proprietary mixture with the appropriate species or strains. New varieties having improved characteristics are introduced from time to time, and the best varieties available should be sought. They are usually the most expensive but are a worthwhile investment. Note that particular named varieties are only available commercially in large quantities.

Seed mixtures
No mixture of seeds is suited to all soils and situations, or for all purposes. The following are basic mixtures that can be used with confidence in a very wide range of conditions, but they should be modified if necessary. Smooth-stalked meadow grass, for example, dislikes wet or acid soils and on such soils can be omitted from the mixtures.

High-quality ornamental turf
80% Chewings' fescue
20% browntop bent
Sow at the rate of 1oz per square yard. The height of cut should be $\frac{1}{4}$–$\frac{3}{8}$ in, but it will tolerate $\frac{3}{16}$ in.

General purpose ornamental turf
30% Chewings' fescue
25% creeping red fescue
10% browntop bent
35% smooth-stalked meadow grass
Sow at the rate of $\frac{3}{4}$ oz per square yard. The

height of cut should be $\frac{3}{8}$–$\frac{1}{2}$ in. This mixture has ornamental quality but is harder-wearing than the first mixture and may be used for play areas.

General purpose turf
20% Chewings' fescue
20% creeping red fescue
10% browntop bent
20% smooth-stalked meadow grass
30% perennial rye grass
Sow at the rate of $\frac{1}{2}$ oz per square yard. The height of cut should be $\frac{3}{4}$–1 in. Since it contains rye grass, this mixture is hard-wearing and suitable for utility areas.

Banks and steep slopes
30% Chewings' fescue
45% slender creeping red fescue
20% browntop bent
5% lesser timothy
Sow at the rate of 1oz per square yard. The height of cut should be to $\frac{1}{2}$ in. These grasses will establish quickly, thereby preventing erosion, and, since they are low-growing, require a minimum of mowing.

Shade
All grasses grow reasonably well in light shade providing the site is prepared adequately and is fed and watered regularly. As the young grasses develop note the extent of poorer growth and, when mowing, leave the grass considerably longer over this area. In heavier shade, or if longer grass is not desired, plant ground cover plants that are tolerant of shade (see page 150).

Types of lawn grasses
Browntop bent (*Agrostis tenuis*) is a dwarf, tufted grass with short rhizomes. Bents (*Agrostis* spp) are the most tolerant of all grasses to close mowing, and browntop bent is found in most fine-lawn mixtures. It will adapt to most conditions, including soils that are acid and tend to be dry. It tolerates close mowing to $\frac{3}{16}$ in.
Creeping bent (*Agrostis stolonifera*) is a stoloniferous species that is sometimes used in turf mixtures for playing fields on heavier alkaline soils. It is a shallow-rooting grass that lacks resistance to drought.

Browntop bent

Chewings' fescue

Chewings' fescue (*Festuca rubra* ssp *commutata*) has a dwarf, densely tufted habit and tolerates poor soils. It can be mown to $\frac{3}{16}$ in.
Creeping red fescue (*Festuca rubra* ssp *rubra*) is a hard-wearing grass with slender creeping rhizomes that is tolerant of wet, dry and cold conditions. It is, however, less tolerant of close mowing than Chewings' fescue. The strain slender creeping red fescue (*Festuca rubra* ssp *littoralis*) is better suited to close-mown turf.

Annual meadow grass (*Poa annua*) is a tufted annual or short-lived perennial weed grass that is found in many lawns. It perpetuates itself by seeding freely and is useful in lawns subjected to hard wear.
Crested dog's tail (*Cynosurus cristatus*) has a tufted, fairly dwarf habit. It is sometimes used in fine turf mixtures, but it does not blend well. Do not mow it closer than $\frac{3}{4}$ in.
Perennial rye grass (*Lolium perenne*) is a broad-leaved species of loose, tufted habit

Lawn grasses 2

Crested dog's tail

Perennial rye grass

Smooth-stalked meadow grass

Rough-stalked meadow grass

that grows well on almost any soil. It is particularly suited to heavier soils and is very hard-wearing. Do not mow closer than $\frac{3}{4}$–1 in, otherwise it will deteriorate. Some newer strains are denser and more tolerant of close mowing.

Smooth-stalked meadow grass (*Poa pratensis*) has a tufted growth with slender creeping rhizomes. It is tough and hard-wearing, but rather slow to establish. It dislikes wet, heavy or acid soils. Do not mow closer than $\frac{3}{4}$ in.

Rough-stalked meadow grass (*Poa trivialis*) has a loosely tufted habit with short, creeping stolons. It is more suited to wet, heavy soils than smooth-stalked meadow grass, but is less tolerant of wear and unsuitable for fine turf. Do not mow closer than $\frac{3}{4}$ in.

Lesser timothy (*Phleum bertolonii*) is a tufted species, with swollen basal internodes and is sometimes stoloniferous. It is hard-wearing and useful in wet, heavy conditions. Do not mow closer than $\frac{1}{2}$ in.

CHOICE OF GRASSES

Grasses having the lowest growth:
Browntop bent
Creeping bent
Lesser timothy

Grasses most tolerant of close mowing:
Browntop bent
Creeping bent

Grasses tolerant of close mowing:
Chewings' fescue
Slender creeping red fescue

Hardest-wearing grasses:
Perennial rye grass
Lesser timothy
Smooth-stalked meadow grass

Seed or turf?

By far the most common methods of creating lawns in the United Kingdom are to sow seeds or lay turf. At one time turf lawns were much more common than seed lawns. However, in recent years there have been considerable improvements in the quality, variety and availability of seed mixtures, and sowing is now an increasingly popular alternative.

A point that is often overlooked when comparing seeding and turfing is that, whichever process is decided upon, the site needs to be prepared thoroughly. In particular, it is not sufficient simply to rake over the site before laying turves.

There are various factors to consider when making a choice between seeds and turf. To help the gardener decide which method to use, the various advantages and disadvantages of each are listed below.

Advantages of seed

The most important advantages that seed has over turf are that it is much cheaper to buy and there is less work involved in sowing than in laying turf. The gardener can choose a mixture of seeds to suit his or her own particular requirements or conditions, whereas with turves, the gardener has much less variety to choose from. A further advantage of seed is that it can be stored easily and will not deteriorate. Unlike turfing, sowing can, therefore, be delayed until the weather conditions are exactly right.

Disadvantages of seed

Seed takes much longer to establish than turf, and it is some months before the lawn can be used: a lawn sown in late summer will not be usable until the following June, and a spring-sown lawn will not be able to tolerate normal wear and tear until late autumn. The soil surface requires a more careful final preparation and, if the site is weedy, it must be left fallow for a time to ensure a reasonable freedom from weed seeds. These may also be carried on to the site by birds and wind, where they quickly become established and compete with the grass seedlings for water and nutrients. A lawn created from seed is more dependent on good weather for successful establishment than is a turfed lawn and, in cold damp conditions especially, is much

more susceptible to disease. There is also the risk of disturbance to the seedbed from birds, cats, dogs or moles to be borne in mind. Lastly, grass seed is sown in either the spring or early autumn, which are often busy periods in the garden.

Advantages of turf

The most obvious advantage of turf is that the lawn can be created and used almost immediately, although it is advisable to allow a period for rooting into the bed before general use. Since laying turf has an instant visual effect, it is a much more attractive proposition than seeding for people moving into a newly built house with a featureless garden. Other points in favour of turfing are that it is easier to achieve a neat, well defined edge to paths and borders with turves than with seed, and turf can be laid in late autumn or winter, at which time it is too late for sowing grass seed. Another advantage of being able to lay turves in the autumn or winter is that there are few other pressing tasks in the garden at this time of year. Lastly, unlike sowing, there are no problems with birds or animals after laying.

Disadvantages of turf

Turfing is more expensive than seeding and good-quality turf is often difficult to obtain. The inexperienced buyer may fail to notice weeds, weed grasses or other defects that may be present in low-quality turf, for example, variations in thickness and shape, which will both require attention before turfing can proceed. Laying to a good standard is much more difficult than sowing, and takes both skill and time. Turf will deteriorate if a long period of bad weather prevents laying, so the operation needs to be planned well in advance. The lawn site should be completely prepared before the turves are ordered and they should be laid within two or three days of delivery, since they may deteriorate rapidly, even if they are stored carefully. Dry weather following laying also causes problems with turves. The grass dies along the joints before the turves can root into each other and the soil. This causes the turves to shrink, and crevices will soon appear between them.

STOLON LAWNS

A common method of creating lawns in warmer countries is to plant stolons. This technique can be used in temperate climates using stolons of creeping bent. To do this, chop the stolons into 2–3 in lengths and scatter them evenly over the site, ensuring that each stolon is no more than 1 in from its nearest neighbour. Cover them lightly with sifted top-soil, then lightly roll—this can be done with a rear-roller mower, holding the blades clear. Keep the site well irrigated with a lawn sprinkler; do not use a hose or watering can because their heavier spray may disturb the surface and dislodge the stolons. Mow as for new lawns raised from seed (see page 18), and when the stolons are established top-dress regularly.

Stolons should be planted in spring or early autumn during cool, moist weather.

Storing turves

Store turves for two or three days by stacking them grass upwards, three or four deep. Rolled or folded strips of turf should be similarly stacked.

For longer periods of storage, lay each turf flat in a shaded position and keep them well watered; failure to do so will cause exposed roots to dry up and shrivel.

Growing lawns from turf 1

Buying turf

Since turves are a relatively expensive means of creating a lawn, they should always be examined carefully before being purchased, and again when they are delivered. Do not hesitate to reject sub-standard turves on delivery. Failure to do so will very likely create problems both with laying the turves and with subsequent care of the lawn.

The most important points to look for are the quality of the grass, the soil and the roots, and whether there are weeds present. The grass should be uniform in appearance, with no broad-bladed coarser grasses present, and it should be suitably mown since long shaggy grass may hide defects. The soil should be loamy, not light and sandy or heavy and clayed. A clay soil, in particular, could adversely affect the lawn later on. The turves should have a good root system and a reasonable level of organic matter. If there is too little organic matter the turf may break up in handling. On the other hand, a high level may give poor rooting, which will subsequently create problems. The turves should be weed-free, or virtually so. If there are many weeds present, it indicates that the turves have been poorly managed. Such turves usually break apart when handled, and if laid, there would be immediate problems with weeds.

The last point to check is that the size and thickness of the turves should be uniform. The size of the turves may be 1ft square, 1½ ft by 1ft, or 3 ft by 1ft. For the inexperienced the smallest size is the simplest to lay. The thickness of the turves should be preferably 1–1½ in. Thinner turf will establish satisfactorily if its quality is good and the roots are well developed, but more care is needed both when laying and with the subsequent lawn. If the turf is thicker or irregular, it will have to be trimmed to an even and satisfactory thickness. To do this lay each turf grass-side down in an open-ended box of suitable depth. Then, using a long-bladed knife, preferably one with two handles, shave off the unwanted soil.

When to turf

The best period for turfing is between October and February, though not when frost or rain is present. The advantage of turfing during this period is that newly laid turf is then rarely subjected to the stress of drying winds or hot sunshine, and it usually inter-roots before such conditions occur.

Lawns may be established satisfactorily at other periods, but in warmer, drier conditions there is increasing need for artificial irrigation. This has the disadvantage that, unless this is very carefully applied, it can affect the level of the lawn and its firmness.

Before laying

Always apply fertilizer before laying, unless the soil is already rich and well manured due to, for example, vegetables having been grown there regularly. The fertilizer encourages the turves to knit together and the roots to establish. Apply either superphosphate at 2 oz per square yard or the following mixture, which also supplies nitrogen and potash: 1 oz superphosphate, ¾ oz bone meal, ¾ oz hoof and horn meal and ¼ oz sulphate of potash per square yard. Apply the fertilizer a few days before turfing begins, and rake it well into the soil.

Lay the turves as soon as possible after they have been delivered. If laying is to be done within two or three days, the turves can be stacked grass upwards three or four deep. Strips of turf are usually rolled or folded, and can be similarly stacked.

If turves cannot be laid within this period, place them flat in a shaded site and keep them well watered otherwise exposed roots will dry up and shrivel. Before laying the turves, check each one and remove any coarse grasses or rosetted weeds.

The final step is to mark out the precise dimensions of the lawn and allow 1–2 in overlap if there is sufficient turf. This can be trimmed back when the turf is well established to leave a neat, sharp edge.

Laying turf

Begin by laying a row of turves along the most accessible side of the soil bed, using a tautly stretched garden line as a guide. Always ensure that each turf is laid as close as possible to the previous one. Lay in straight lines and do not at any time stand on the prepared bed. Work forwards, facing the unturfed area, standing or kneeling on broad planks. Avoid walking on the newly laid turf by using planks as pathways. This spreads the weight and prevents depressions being formed by heavy boots or heels.

Stagger successive lines of turf by using half turves in alternate rows. The turves will then hold together more firmly when mown during the early stages of inter-rooting. If a short piece is needed to finish a row, greater stability is obtained by laying the last whole turf to the edge with the short piece fitted in behind. Keep a constant watch on the soil level and have a bucket of ordinary soil and a rake handy for adjusting minor irregularities or for packing extra soil under thin turves. Never attempt to level a piece of turf by beating it with a spade since this will cause local compaction. Instead, lift the turf, remove a little soil and then re-lay it.

After laying

When the laying has been completed, trim the turf by rolling with a light garden roller. Rolling is not essential but it will help to settle the turves. Alternatively, construct a simple turfing board by attaching a pole, such as a broom handle, to the centre of a 9in by 15in wooden board. Firm the turf, gently pressing down on the turfing board. Then top-dress with a sandy top dressing mixture at 3–4 lb per square yard. This will protect the lawn from drying out and improve the level of its surface. Apply as an overall dressing, working it well into the crevices between the turves with a broom or the back of a rake. If good top dressing materials are in short supply, fill a bucket with a mixture of sand and sifted soil, and top-dress along the crevices between turves, afterwards brushing it in.

Irrigate the new lawn thoroughly and regularly during dry periods—turf laid in the spring or summer is particularly susceptible to drying out and, if neglected, will often deteriorate rapidly.

When the grass begins to grow in spring top with the mower and from then on adopt the programme of maintenance for established lawns given on page 142.

Trimming turves

Place the turf grass-side down in a box of the correct height. Then take a knife whose blade is at least as long as the turf is wide, and pull this along the top of the box to shave off unwanted soil. If possible, the knife should have two handles.

Growing lawns from turf 2

Laying turves

1 Apply a dressing of fertilizer a few days before laying. Do not feed if the soil is already rich and well manured.

2 Rake in the fertilizer, incorporating it well into the soil.

3 Mark out the exact shape of the lawn and allow for the turves to extend an inch or two beyond its edges. This can then be

trimmed back after the turves have been laid and have settled down to leave a neat, sharply defined edge.

4 Lay the turves in straight lines, ensuring that each turf is as close as possible to the preceding one. If a segment of turf is needed to complete a row, lay a whole turf at the end and place the segment behind it. Allow 1–2 in overlap at the edge.

5 Stagger successive rows of turf by laying half turves. Do not walk on newly laid turf; instead lay down planks as pathways. They will spread out the weight and so avoid risk of compaction.

Growing lawns from turf 3

6 Correct irregularities in the soil level as turfing progresses. Have some soil at hand for packing under thin turves.

7 After the laying has been completed roll the lawn with a light garden roller, if one is available.

8 Apply a sandy top dressing mixture at 3–4 lb per square yard. Distribute it throughout the lawn surface.

9 Work the dressing well into the crevices between turves, using either a broom or the back of a rake.

SEEDLING TURF

An alternative to laying turves of established grass is to lay seedling turves. These come in large lightweight rolls, about a yard thick, and are well rooted and of uniform thickness. Seedling turf is raised in special turf nurseries by one of two methods. One method uses long, polythene-lined troughs filled with water. Buoyant soil-less compost is then spread on the water, and on this is laid a thin strip of polyurethane foam upon which the grass seeds are sown. The second method is to grow the turf on a thin layer of soil-based rooting medium over a hard, impenetrable base. In the first method, the turf is held together by the foam, and in the second method by the densely intermingled roots. When laid the foam base gradually disintegrates.

Seedling turf is best laid during cool, moist conditions in spring or early autumn because it is more susceptible to cold and drought than ordinary turf. Also, it needs a period of good growing conditions in which it can quickly establish itself. Do not attempt to lay seedling turf in the summer unless it can be adequately irrigated. Give the turf an initial cut after two or three weeks, and do not cut it closer than 1 in during the first six weeks after laying. Then cut it to the appropriate height for the grass and the time of year.

This technique can be adopted by gardeners who wish to raise small squares of turf for repair work. Line a seed box or a deep tray with polythene, then introduce a $\frac{1}{2}$ in layer of well firmed seed compost and cover with a piece of cheesecloth. Add a second layer of compost and sow grass seeds on the surface at the standard rate (see page 134). Then place the box in a sunny position and keep it constantly moist. Once the seeds have germinated, feed it weekly with a liquid fertilizer. The turf will be ready for laying about three weeks after germination.

139

Growing lawns from seed

Sowing

Seeds may be sown either by hand or by seed drill. For hand-sowing divide the grass seeds into two equal portions, adding dry soil, if wished, to facilitate distribution. Sow half the seeds by traversing the plot lengthways, then sow the remaining half crossways. This method gives a more even coverage than a single application. Divide large areas into smaller sections or small plots marked out in square yards to facilitate accurate sowing.

If hiring a drill first ensure that it can be calibrated to apply grass seeds at the required rate. To check that a drill is applying the correct rate of seeds, mark out two separate square yard areas on concrete or a hessian strip. Scatter $\frac{1}{2}$ oz of seed by hand on one square, then run the drill over the other square. The density of seeds should be equal in the two squares.

Apply the seeds to the seedbed in parallel strips using the previous run's wheeltrack as a guide. Again, sow half the seed lengthways and half crossways. If space allows lay a strip of hessian along the edge of the lawn and over-run since the drill may distribute the seed unevenly when it is being turned.

Sow during a period of calm, dry weather when the surface of the seedbed is dry and soil does not adhere to boots or to the wheels of a seed drill. There should, however, be moisture just below the surface.

After sowing, lightly rake over the seedbed. Do this carefully since the seeds may not germinate if buried too deeply, and it may also make the distribution uneven. Do not roll because this tends to flatten or "cake" the surface. If after a few days there has been no rainfall then irrigate gently but thoroughly with a garden sprinkler. Do not use a hose or a coarse-rose watering can since they may redistribute the seeds. If sparrows or other seed-eating birds are troublesome locally, use seed that has been treated with a bird deterrent. Usually a more serious problem created by birds is dust-bathing. Help to prevent this by stretching black thread 3–4 in above the seedbed. Alternatively, lay some leafless twiggy brushwood lightly over the bed after sowing.

When to sow

The two most suitable periods for sowing grass seeds are early autumn and spring. The best time for autumn sowing is early September in the warmer regions of the United Kingdom, and the end of August in colder parts. During this period the soil temperature is still high and moisture is usually plentiful, both conditions that encourage a quick germination period of seven to ten days. This enables seedling grasses to become well established before the first frosts in October or early November. Do not sow much later than these recommended times since germination may be poor and seedlings will not establish well. They may not then survive prolonged cold or wet weather.

If seed is to be sown in spring do this during April since the soil is beginning to warm up at this time and there is a full growing season ahead. Note that germination is slower at this time of year and there is a greater risk of the weather being dry than in autumn.

After germination

The soil surface is often slightly lifted at germination. Therefore, when the young grasses are about 2 in high (3 in for utility turf) lightly roll when the surface is dry using a light garden roller or a rear-roller cylinder mower with the front roller and blades lifted clear of the grass.

Two or three days later, when the grass has recovered from rolling and is growing vertically again, cut it with a sharp-bladed mower. Remove no more than about a third of the grass growth. It is preferable to use a side-wheel cylinder mower, or rotary mower since they have no front roller to flatten the grass before cutting. If using a front-roller machine, lift or remove the front roller before mowing. After this first mow, autumn-sown turf usually needs no further mowing until the spring. With spring-sown turf progressively reduce the height of cut to the normal mowing height for an established lawn (see page 143 for details).

First season of growth

Use the lawn as little as possible during the first season of growth. If there are any surface irregularities, gradually eliminate them by top-dressing lightly with compost at intervals beginning after the first cut. Feed the lawn regularly according to seasonal requirements, and irrigate as necessary. This will quickly establish a vigorous grass coverage of sufficient density to prevent mosses and weeds from establishing.

Damping-off diseases

Fungal diseases may kill both grass seeds and young grasses. Damping off may cause young seedlings to become yellow or bronze and collapse at or near ground level, or brown shrivelled patches may occur, depending on the species of fungus responsible. At the first sign of attack water with Cheshunt compound at $\frac{1}{2}$ oz in 1 gal water per square yard. In established lawns most weeds can be easily controlled by applying selective lawn weedkillers, combined with appropriate cultural measures. These weedkillers may, if used

Sowing grass seeds

1 Divide the seeds into two halves and, if sowing by hand, broadcast one batch walking lengthways across the site and the other batch walking crossways.

2 If a seed drill is being used, lay a strip of hessian along the edge of the site and over-run. Again, sow half the seeds lengthways and the other half crossways.

3 After sowing, lightly rake over the entire seedbed, taking care not to bury the seeds too deeply, otherwise they may not germinate.

4 Prevent birds from dust-bathing by inserting small twigs or sticks at intervals in the seedbed. Then twine black thread among them 2–3 in above the soil surface.

Weed control in new lawns

on new lawns, damage young seedling grasses before they are well established. For this reason do not use selective lawn weed-killers on newly seeded lawns earlier than three months after germination, and preferably not until at least six months have passed. However, it is important to control weeds in these early stages to prevent them competing with the young grass.

Annual broad-leaved weeds

Seeds of annual broad-leaved weeds are likely to be present on any site selected for a lawn and it is always advisable to deal with them well in advance of sowing to allow for a period of fallowing. Even so, weed seeds may still be introduced to the site unknowingly if fresh soil is used in the final stages of preparation. Seeds may also be carried in on the wind from surrounding areas. A few scattered weeds are no real cause for concern. They can be removed by hand (see below) with little effort, or left to be controlled by the mower—annuals such as groundsel, fat hen and mayweed soon die out once the grass has become strong enough for it to be mown regularly. Where strong-growing annual weeds are numerous they may smother grass growth, particularly where it is slow because of bad weather, or poor and weak because of inadequate preparation of the site. Common chickweed can be particularly troublesome since it grows strongly from very early in the year.

Grass weeds

The most troublesome weeds in new lawns are seedling perennial grasses such as cocksfoot (*Dactylis glomerata*) and Yorkshire fog (*Holcus lanatus*). In high-quality turf, perennial rye grass can also be troublesome. They are checked to some extent by frequent close mowing but tend to persist indefinitely, particularly Yorkshire fog.

Seeds of coarse grasses may be present in grass seed mixtures as an impurity and it is advisable always to purchase seed of reliable quality from a reputable supplier. It is much more likely, however, that seeds were already present in the soil at the time of sowing.

Annual meadow grass (*Poa annua*), a free-seeding annual grass and common garden weed, may also give trouble. It can survive close mowing to seed freely throughout the year, especially during May and June when its pale seedheads can mar the appearance of finely mown turf. Being short-lived its numbers can vary from season to season, at times leaving the turf sparser and more susceptible to invasion by moss and weeds. Thorough fallowing prior to sowing will minimize problems with all grass weeds.

Hand-weed in fine weather when the soil surface is firm, and not soft and wet from recent rain. If hand-weeding causes any serious disturbance to the lawn grasses, irrigate after weeding with a lawn sprinkler to resettle the grass roots.

Perennial weeds

Even after thorough preparation and removal of perennial weed growth, the deeply penetrating roots or rhizomes of some broad-leaved perennials may remain. Suitably deep cultivations during preparation should, however, ensure that little growth appears prior to mowing. Once the lawn has established, close and regular mowing combined with the use of selective lawn weedkillers will soon eradicate such recalcitrant weeds.

Newly laid turf

Do not use selective weedkillers on newly laid turf until it is well established and growing strongly. Purchase only good quality, weed-free turf.

GRASS WEEDS

Cocksfoot

Yorkshire fog

Perennial rye grass

Controlling grass weeds

Remove grass weeds by hand-pulling, using one hand to grasp the weed and the other to press down the soil around the weed and keep it firm. This will prevent the surrounding grasses from being disturbed.

Month-by-month guide

This programme provides a useful indication of the approximate times when particular operations or treatments can be undertaken effectively. It is important for the gardener to decide firstly the precise requirements of his own lawn and secondly when the soil and weather conditions are most suitable for carrying out each operation. This programme does not give the details of these operations. For these, consult the relevant pages elsewhere in the book.

JANUARY
Remove any accumulations of dead leaves.
Check drains if water is standing on the surface for any length of time after rain, and drain persistently wet sites.
Overhaul the mower and other lawn tools before the start of the new season.

FEBRUARY
From February check regularly for signs of worm activity or unhealthy turf following mild spells. Disperse worm casts regularly.
Complete all major turfing work by the end of the month.
Apply a mosskiller in late February if weather is settled; if still cold leave until March.
Top-dress lightly if necessary.
Towards the end of the month, begin preparations for spring sowing if soil conditions and weather are suitable.

MARCH
Scatter worm casts and lightly rake to remove debris; then mow with the blade set high. Roll before mowing if turf has been lifted by frost.
Treat against worms if they become very troublesome.
Re-align ragged lawn edges.
In southern Britain feed in late March if the weather is mild and settled.

APRIL
Increase the frequency of mowing according to the weather and grass growth.
Continue checking at intervals for signs of unhealthy turf.
Apply a spring feed in early to mid-April; a few days after feeding apply a weedkiller if necessary.
Remove patches of coarse grass and re-seed.
Seed-in sparsely grassed areas and new lawns.
Check newly turfed areas and top-dress lightly if necessary to improve levels or fill joins.

MAY
In early May adjust the mower to the summer cutting height.
Continue weedkilling; if very mossy apply a mosskiller.
From May onwards irrigation may be needed in drier periods.
During mid- to late May apply a light dressing of nitrogenous fertilizer.

JUNE
Mow frequently; if patches of creeping weeds are troublesome lightly scarify before mowing.
Continue weedkilling and irrigation as necessary.
Spike, lightly top-dress and irrigate areas that are subjected to heavy wear.

JULY
Mow regularly; scarify patches of creeping weeds and surface-running grasses before mowing.
Feed lightly early in July.
Apply weedkillers and irrigate as necessary.

AUGUST
Mow regularly.
Give a final summer feed in mid- to late August, followed by a final application of weedkiller.
In colder areas sow grass seed during late August.

SEPTEMBER
Modify the cutting height of the mower towards the end of the month, since the rate of growth is now slowing.
Examine the condition of the turf and carry out autumn renovation: scarify to remove matted growth or thatch, spike and top-dress, and seed-in sparse patches.
Apply a lawn sand to control moss. Do not use mosskillers containing sulphate of ammonia at this time of year.
With the onset of cooler, moister conditions check regularly for signs of unhealthy turf and worm activity.
In milder areas seed-in new lawn sites.

OCTOBER
Set the mower to its winter height and mow as the growth dictates during dry periods.
Switch or brush to remove early morning dew and encourage rapid drying if the weather is fine.
Spike and top-dress if unable to do so in September.
Prevent accumulation of fallen leaves because this can create conditions in which diseases may establish.
Treat against worms if they become very troublesome.
Lay turf lawns from this month onwards.

NOVEMBER
A final mow may be necessary, but do not attempt mowing in frosty conditions, nor when the soil is heavy after a recent fall of rain.
Continue clearing up fallen leaves.
Continue turfing when conditions are suitable.

DECEMBER
Apply lime this month if it is needed.
Continue with turfing and leaf clearance where necessary.

Table of operations
This table provides a simplified version, for quick and easy reference, of the month-by-month guide to lawn maintenance given on this page. As stated previously, the exact timings of the various operations depend very much on the weather conditions, the state of the soil and the nature of the lawn.

In this table, heavy shading indicates that the particular operation or treatment will be necessary, or almost always so, during the period concerned. Where the shading is lighter, it indicates that the operation is optional or, in the case of treatment, that it may sometimes be necessary. For example, moss is very likely to occur in the autumn, but it may also be present in the spring.

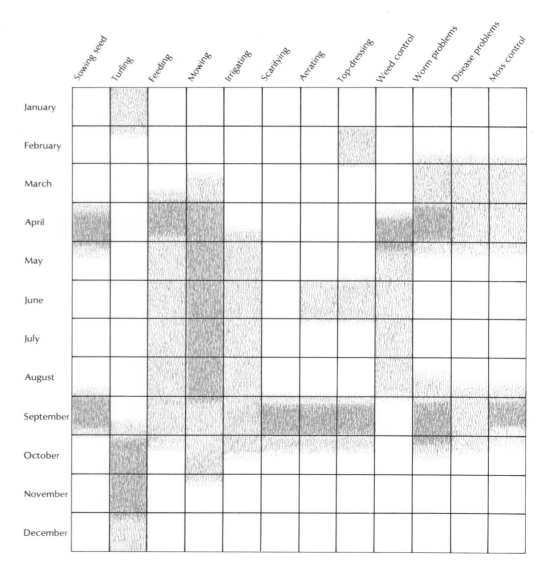

Mowing 1

The purpose of mowing a lawn is to keep the grass short enough to be neat and attractive, but without hindering its ability to grow strongly. Mowing a lawn too close weakens the grass and allows moss and lawn weeds to become established. On the other hand, where lawns are allowed to grow too long, coarser grasses become increasingly dominant and finer grasses deteriorate. The best approach is to mow regularly but not too closely. Apart from keeping the grass to a reasonable length, it encourages tillering, which increases the density of the turf, and deters moss and weed development. Further advantages of this approach are that the yield of mowings is lower and the turf quicker and easier to mow if the grass is mown regularly rather than sporadically.

Height of cut

The most suitable height of cut is determined by the kind of grasses present, the time of year and by the function of the lawn. During late spring to early autumn the finest quality ornamental turf should be cut to $\frac{1}{4}$–$\frac{1}{2}$ in. On average lawns cut the grass to a height of $\frac{1}{2}$ in, on utility lawns with rye grass cut to 1 in and on paddocks and areas of rough grass cut to 1$\frac{1}{2}$–2 in. Leave the grass slightly longer during hot dry weather unless the turf can be irrigated adequately.

During autumn to early spring, when growth is slow, increase the height of cut by $\frac{1}{4}$ in. This leaves the turf less open to moss and weed infestation. Where the soil is moist and soft adjust the height of cutting to compensate for any sinking of the mower's wheels or rollers.

Do not cut any turf to below $\frac{3}{16}$ in because all grasses are weakened when cut below this level. On the other hand, lawn turf should not be allowed to grow longer than 1$\frac{1}{2}$ in since above this height coarser grasses begin to dominate over the finer grasses.

Frequency of mowing

Once the most suitable height of cut has been established, mow with sufficient frequency to keep the grass as close to the desired height as is practicable. Increase or decrease the frequency of mowing according to the rate of growth. This varies from season to season, and may be influenced by factors such as weather conditions, feeding, irrigation, the varieties of grass being grown and the general health of the turf itself.

Fine lawns should be mown at intervals of two to three days. Mow average lawns at least every seven days and preferably at intervals of three to five days. For other turf mow at least once every seven days. Never allow the turf to grow long then cut it very short on the pretext that it saves time.

Removing the mowings

Most gardeners remove the mowings from a lawn, usually by means of a grass-box. There are a number of reasons for doing this. In wetter weather mowings cling to the surface, impeding aeration and becoming increasingly unsightly as they slowly decompose. Seeds of weeds and annual meadow grass are scattered and will infest other areas, as will severed stems of white clover and speedwell. Leaving the mowings on the lawn also encourages worm activity and the mowings make the turf softer and lusher. In milder, moister autumns, this causes the lawn to be more susceptible to diseases, many of which thrive in such conditions.

There are, however, some advantages in leaving the mowings on the lawn. Firstly, mowing is less arduous without a grass-box. Secondly, the mowings act as a mulch, increasing drought resistance and deterring moss. As they decompose, they return nutrients to the soil to give a greener, lusher turf. Nevertheless under normal conditions always remove the mowings from the lawn. Return them only in hot dry conditions when irrigation is not available.

After gathering the mowings do not simply lump them on to the compost heap. Grass mowings contain a high percentage of moisture, and if heaped when they are still fresh they decompose into a green-black glutinous mass. Small quantities can be added to the compost heap when fresh as long as they are layered thinly with other garden waste. Larger quantities should be dried before composting. Do this either by spreading them out thinly, or by making a loose heap of the cuttings and turning it frequently.

HEIGHT AND FREQUENCY OF CUT

This chart indicates the height and frequency to which different quality lawns should be cut for the period late spring to early autumn. The figures given are only a rough guide, and should be varied according to the weather and the state of the turf. Outside this period the height of cut should be increased by $\frac{1}{4}$ in.

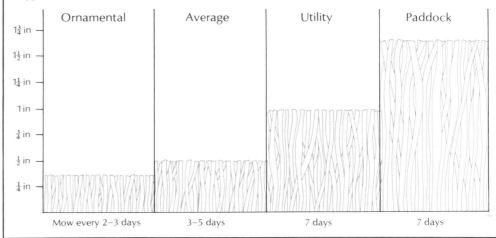

Type of lawn

	Ornamental	Average	Utility	Paddock
	Mow every 2–3 days	3–5 days	7 days	7 days

Chart height markings: 1$\frac{3}{4}$ in, 1$\frac{1}{2}$ in, 1$\frac{1}{4}$ in, 1 in, $\frac{3}{4}$ in, $\frac{1}{2}$ in, $\frac{1}{4}$ in

Composting mowings

Small quantities of mowings can be added to the compost heap in thin layers, which should be alternated with other refuse.

Dry large quantities before composting by spreading them out thinly, or by making a loose heap and forking it over.

Mowing 2

Mowing problems

Ribbing is a series of narrow, parallel strips of alternating longer and shorter grass. This effect occurs with cylinder-bladed mowers that have a low cylinder speed and a low number of blades, which cause them to give few cuts in relation to distance travelled. Ribbing may also occur when the grass is too long for the mower setting; if this is so, increase the height of cut.

The washboard effect is the occurrence of irregular waves or corrugations; the grass alternates from long on the crest of each wave to short between crests. It is caused by the grass always being mown in the same direction and usually occurs where powered mowers are used. Change the mowing pattern and vary the direction of mowing with successive cuts.

Lacerated grass or uneven cutting are caused by having blunt or incorrectly set blades, or by the mower having a damaged bottom plate. Check the mower and adjust or repair it as necessary.

Scalping occurs where there are surface irregularities. Increase the height of cut and improve the level of the lawn: correct minor irregularities by top-dressing and major ones by lifting the turf and adding or removing soil as necessary.

HOW TO MOW

1 Always plan the direction of mowing to minimize overlapping, reversing and abrupt changes of direction, since these will all increase compaction and wear.

2 Mow when dry. Wet mowings clog the machine and grass-box, and lengthen the mowing time. During the autumn and spring mow on sunny days in the early afternoon when the grass has dried. If dew is heavy disperse it two or three hours before mowing using a supple bamboo cane, rake or besom.

3 Scatter worm casts before mowing.

4 During the colder months, do not top when cold winds are blowing. The leaf-tips may be wind-scorched and seared, and remain unsightly until the next cut.

5 If the grass contains weeds or unwanted surface runners, rake it occasionally before mowing to lift unwanted growth.

6 Move steadily forward if using a hand-propelled mower. Repeated backward and forward movements result in an uneven cut.

7 Always mow at right-angles to the line of the previous mow since this helps to control weed grasses and bents and to smooth out irregularities in the mowing.

SEASONAL GUIDE TO MOWING

March: top with the blade set $\frac{1}{4}$ in higher than the summer height of cut.

April: increase frequency according to the weather and growth of the grass.

May–August: adjust to summer heights and frequencies.

August–September: reduce frequency as growth rate slows.

Late September: adjust to the autumn height of cutting.

October–February: occasional topping may be necessary during mild winters.

Producing a banded finish

A neat, banded finish of contrasting light and dark strips can be obtained by using a mower with a rear-mounted roller. Work across the lawn and mow each succeeding parallel strip in the opposite direction to the previous one.

Weed control in lawns

The weeds most troublesome in established lawns are the low-growing perennials of creeping or rosette-type growth, such as clovers, speedwell, daisy and plantain, which can adapt to or are unaffected by regular close mowing.

Sowing or laying clean turves on a thoroughly cleaned and fallowed site will ensure a weed-free start (see pages 130–133). Regular mowing with a grass-box, careful feeding and attention to irrigation will keep the turf densely leaved and healthy, making it difficult for weeds to establish themselves.

Weeds may reach the lawn in various ways: as seeds blown by the wind; carried by birds; brought in on muddy footwear, machinery or tools; or concealed in unsterilized soil or badly made compost used for top dressing. Runners may be introduced on borrowed mowers or fertilizer spreaders, or they may encroach from weedy paths or flower beds.

Always use a grass-box when mowing since this minimizes the spread of lawn weeds. Sections of runners of certain weeds can regrow if not removed from the lawn, while the seeds of lesser yellow trefoil, which seeds freely, are easily scattered.

Hand-weeding with a hand fork or grubbing tool is a useful approach when dealing with scattered weeds, but it is essential to firm the surrounding turf carefully after extracting each weed. Hand-weed only during good growing conditions in spring when the grass will grow quickly to fill in the bare patches. Later in the year, when there are drier conditions, slower grass growth and more weed seeds, there is a much greater risk of bare patches being recolonized by weeds—or moss if a wet period follows a long spell of warm, dry weather. If large numbers of weeds are present in the lawn then hand-weeding is no longer practicable and weedkillers must be used.

Weedkillers

Lawn sands containing sulphate of ammonia and sulphate of iron are occasionally advocated for spot treatment of lawn weeds. They have a burning or caustic effect when sprinkled on flattened leaves and into the crowns of rosette weeds. The high localized nitrogen source also inhibits clovers and trefoils when it reaches their roots. But there is often strong weed regrowth, and lawn sand has now been largely superseded by selective lawn weedkillers.

These do not harm narrow-bladed erect grasses but kill or check broad-leaved weeds. Some weeds can be killed by a single treatment, others may need several.

Most proprietary brands of lawn weedkiller contain two or occasionally three active ingredients, such as mecoprop, MCPA or 2,4-D. A product with two different active ingredients will give control of a wider range of weeds than a product containing a single ingredient. To decide which is best, list the different kinds of weeds in the infested lawn. Then check the proprietary mixtures and choose one that carries the manufacturer's recommendations for use in controlling the listed species.

If some weeds are not killed by the first application, repeat the treatment after four or five weeks. Some weeds may survive a second treatment. If so, confirm their identities then try another means of control. This may, in some cases, involve a change to a different weedkiller or some cultural measure that will help to weaken or check its spread.

Form and methods of application

Most lawn weedkillers are sold in concentrated liquid form, to be applied after dilution with water. Read the product label before buying, and mix and apply strictly according to the manufacturers' recommendations accompanying the product. Some lawn fertilizers incorporate weedkillers in dry form, which allows the two operations of feeding the lawn regularly and weedkilling to be combined into one.

Lawn weedkillers are also available in aerosol or solid stick form for spot-treating isolated weeds. Some aerosols have the advantage that they leave a foam marker which persists for some time after weed treatment. Although spot treatment is a more economical approach than overall spraying where few weeds are involved, there may often be some localized temporary scorching of the grass since it is difficult to gauge the amount being applied.

Apply lawn weedkillers from spring to late summer, ideally during fine warm conditions when the soil is thoroughly moist and grass growth is vigorous. The weedkiller is then rapidly translocated throughout the weed and the vigorously growing grass will fill in the space as the weed dies. Apply a nitrogenous fertilizer one or two weeks before the weedkiller is used to encourage recovery of the turf. Then apply the weedkiller evenly with the aid of canes and twine.

Spot-treating weeds

Spot treatment with a lawn weedkiller in aerosol or solid stick form is a simple and economical method of control if there are only a few isolated weeds present.

HOW TO USE LAWN WEEDKILLERS

Do not apply in the cold earlier months of the year or during drought when there is little growth.

Do not apply immediately before rain, otherwise much of the weedkiller may be washed into the soil.

Do not apply when windy, otherwise the spray may be carried to affect nearby garden plants. If this does happen, spray the plants immediately with large amounts of clean water.

Do not apply immediately before mowing or much of the treated leaf surface may be removed before the weedkiller can reach the roots. Allow three or four days where possible before resuming mowing.

Do not apply at a rate stronger than that recommended by the manufacturer. Too high a concentration may kill weed foliage before the weedkiller can reach the roots, and this would allow the weed to revive. It may also cause the grasses to be badly damaged.

Do not mow immediately before weedkiller application or there will be a much-reduced leaf-surface area to receive and absorb the weedkiller.

Do not use fresh mowings as mulches for at least two weeks following treatment of lawns. Freshly treated mowings can be composted but the compost should not be used for at least six months.

Moss control in lawns

Of the hundreds of mosses found in temperate climates relatively few are troublesome as lawn weeds. Of these the most common are the following. *Hypnum cupressiforme* (and its forms) has yellow to golden-green trailing stems, and often colonizes large areas. *Brachythecium rutabulum*, with bright green, creeping, irregularly branched stems, is common in poorly drained lawns. *Ceratodon purpureus*, with short erect stems and densely tufted growth, is often found on poor, acid, heathland soil. *Bryum argenteum* is a cushion-type moss which has an attractive silvery sheen to its foliage.

Contrary to widespread opinion, the presence of moss in a lawn does not necessarily show the need for lime, for example, mosses such as *Hypnum cupressiforme* var *lacunosum* naturally inhabit chalk grassland. Other species are natural to all forms of grassland. Moss colonizes lawns for various reasons. Poor fertility or weakness of the turf due to attacks by pests or diseases, lack of aeration, bad drainage, excessive shade or mowing too closely will all result in weak, sparse turf that allows moss to establish.

Moss can be temporarily controlled by using mosskillers but, unless the reason for infestation is established and then corrected, moss will return. Examine the lawn and identify factors causing weak growth. Feed regularly if previous feeding has been sporadic. Top-dress regularly to improve moisture retention if the soil is light and sandy; irrigate regularly and thoroughly if the lawn is prone to drought. Aerate if surface drainage is impeded and carry out deep spiking if there is compaction through heavy usage. Watch for signs of waterlogging during the winter months and, if necessary, check and clear existing pipe drainage systems or install a new system. Do not set the mower blades too low; close and frequent mowing can weaken grass, letting weeds and moss establish themselves. On very acid soils a light winter application of lime in the form of ground chalk or ground limestone will slightly reduce acidity and usually discourage the mosses present. First determine by soil testing that liming is likely to be beneficial since excessive use of lime, or use when not required, can improve conditions for coarser

grasses, clovers and other weeds while suppressing growth of the finer-leaved, more desirable grasses. If lime is necessary, apply at 2 oz per square yard (see page 130).

Where moss is troublesome in turf under trees there is often little that can be done. Lifting the tree canopy by removal of the lower branches will let in more light but turf growth may remain poor and sparse if the soil is light, dry and full of roots. A permanent solution to this problem is to replace the turf with ground cover (see page 150).

Moss spores, which are released during the summer, may allow moss to spread on lawns where the grass is weak and sparse. The spore-producing bodies develop well above the level of the moss foliage and on a well mown lawn are unlikely to survive to maturity; mosses can, however, reproduce from vegetative cells and the simple act of mowing or raking can spread moss about the lawn. When mowing always use a grass-box to collect mowings, and rake inwards towards the centre of moss patches.

Mosskillers

Moss grows most strongly during cool moist conditions in the autumn and spring and these are the best periods for applying chemical mosskillers. Lawn sands consisting of sulphate of ammonia, sulphate of iron and lime-free sand have been used to kill moss for many years and are still a useful means of control. Proportions vary in proprietary mixtures. A suitable formula is three parts sulphate of ammonia, one part calcined sulphate of iron and ten parts medium grade lime-free sand (not builders' sand). Apply at 4 oz per square yard during fine weather, ideally on a moist, dewy morning with a fine day ahead. Water the lawn 48 hours later if there has been no rain. One to two weeks later carefully rake out the blackened dead moss. Lawn sand is not a long-term control but it does stimulate grass growth, especially when applied in spring.

Dichlorophen is an effective chemical mosskiller and the active ingredient in some proprietary lawn moss eradicants. It is marketed as a concentrated liquid formulation. Apply it with a watering can as in illustration (a) to wet the moss thoroughly.

Moss control programme: autumn

a

b

In early September apply a mosskiller, using a watering can with dribble bar (a). A week or two later rake out blackened and dead moss. Then apply an autumn turf fertilizer (b), followed by a top dressing of six

parts sand, three parts sandy loam soil and one part granulated peat; apply it at the rate of 4 lb per square yard. If necessary, seed-in bare patches at 1 oz per square yard, then rake in.

Moss control programme: spring

c

d

In mid- to late March, apply a mosskiller during fine weather. One or two weeks later, rake out the dead moss, taking care not to disturb any young, developing stoloniferous grasses (c). Feed the lawn with a general

lawn fertilizer. Then apply a light top dressing at the rate of 2–3 lb per square yard (d). As with the autumn programme, seed-in any bare patches at 1 oz per square yard and rake in.

Preparing the site

Planning

The first step in preparing to plant ground cover is to draw a plan of the site. If the site is large, mark in any variations in soil conditions, exposure to wind and the degree of sun or shade. These can then be more easily taken into account when ground cover plants are being selected.

The choice of plants depends, in the first instance, on whether ground cover is needed to occupy a difficult site where little except weeds will grow, or whether it is needed because the site, though satisfactory, cannot be maintained to an acceptable level of appearance. In the former case the ornamental value of the ground cover is of less importance than its ability to grow satisfactorily under the conditions, and the choice may be confined to a single species, such as common ivy or St John's wort.

With the latter, the less stringent conditions usually allow a considerably wider choice of cover plants, and more emphasis can be placed on their ornamental qualities. Thus groups of plants with contrasting or complementing colours can be grown, for example, heathers that differ in both the colour of their foliage and of their flowers. Variations in height between adjoining groups can also be utilized, as can the contrast between leafy clump-forming plants and those that form a dense carpeting cover.

Weeding the site

The first step in preparing the site is to clear it of weeds. Established annual weeds are mostly shallow rooting and are easily removed when the site is forked over before planting. If the site has been neglected for a year or two, seedling growth after planting may be a problem, in which case a period of fallowing would be helpful.

Perennial weeds are a more serious problem, and it is essential to clear the site of all traces of such weeds before planting. If this is not done, strong-growing perennials such as bindweed, ground elder and couch grass will compete with the ground cover and weaken it. They will also be extremely difficult to eradicate once the ground cover is established. Do not plant until the site is completely free of perennial weeds, even if

this means that planting ground cover has to be delayed for a season or more.

To eliminate perennial weeds it is necessary to kill or remove the underground parts, such as rhizomes. If the weeds are to be dug out, this can be done at any time of the year, but weedkillers are only effective when the weeds are in active growth. The roots of some weeds, particularly bindweed and mare's tail, penetrate too deeply for them to be dug out completely. If they are present, it is better to leave infested plots unplanted and spray in late spring or early summer with glyphosate when the weeds are growing strongly. Even then there may be some regrowth later in the year, in which case, spray again. Mare's tail is very persistent, but control is improved if the weed is crushed before spraying.

Improving the soil

Irrespective of the nature of the site and the choice of plants, thorough and careful soil preparation is essential. The fact that some types of ground cover plant will grow in poor soils and difficult habitats does not mean that they will provide effective cover if they are planted into unprepared soil. The site should

be prepared as thoroughly as for any other kind of plant, since to obtain good cover the plants need to establish rapidly and remain healthy and effective for some years after being planted.

The texture of all types of soil will be improved by digging in a heavy dressing of organic matter or humus. Any type of decomposing vegetation can be used: garden compost, stable manure, leaf-mould or leaf litter, peat, pulverized bark or spent mushroom compost. However, the last of these is usually strongly alkaline and should not be used where acid-loving plants are to be grown. Use well decomposed materials on lighter soils. On heavier clay soils dig in coarser materials since they help to improve the aeration and drainage. A suitable quantity of dressing is roughly one heaped barrowload of manure for every 25 sq ft, dug in to a spade's depth.

Organic manures are rich in trace elements but contain relatively small amounts of major plant foods, and these foods are hardly present at all in peat and pulverized bark. Therefore, to ensure that a sufficient supply of nutrients is available to encourage early

growth, apply a general balanced fertilizer at 1–2 oz per square yard before planting, working it well into the top few inches of soil with a hoe or fork.

Another factor to take into account is the soil pH, although many ground cover plants are tolerant of all but extreme conditions. There are several soil testing kits on the market which will provide a good indication of the soil's acidity. Excessively acid conditions can be modified by dressings of lime, but the improvement is not immediate. Do not apply lime without establishing that it is needed. With alkaline or chalk soils, on the other hand, the pH cannot be reduced appreciably. Digging in acid peat or pulverized bark in quantity will improve the texture, but it will have little effect on the alkalinity. On some neutral or slightly alkaline soils the pH can be reduced by means of chemicals, but the process is slow and complicated. Whether the soil is acid or alkaline, it is simpler to choose plants that are tolerant of a particular type of soil than to attempt to change substantially the basic character of the soil.

Planning

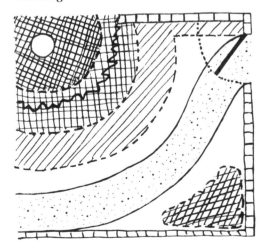

Draw a plan of the site, marking in any areas that are shaded or exposed to wind, and features such as walls, gates, paths, trees and shrubs.

Weeding the site

Remove all traces of weed growth. Dig out shallow-rooted perennial weeds and use glyphosate against deep-rooted ones. Fork over to control annual weeds.

Improving the soil

Dig in organic matter to a spade's depth, at one heaped barrowload per 25 sq ft. Before planting, fork in a general balanced fertilizer at 1–2 oz per square yard.

Planting and spacing

Ground cover plants must be planted carefully and correctly, at the appropriate spacings and at the right time of year, to ensure that they grow away quickly and vigorously.

When to plant
The best period for planting is in late winter to early spring. At this time the soil is beginning to warm up and there is ample moisture available, both of which are conditions that encourage plants to produce new root growth quickly. They will also have a full growing season ahead in which to become well established and are, therefore, less likely to be damaged by severe winter conditions later on. Do not plant during hot, dry summer weather because such conditions may check their growth. Also avoid planting late in the year because the roots may not establish properly and the plants will deteriorate or even die during the winter.

Container-grown plants can be planted out at any time of the year as long as the soil conditions are suitable. The ground should not be heavy with recent rain, bone dry, frosted or covered with snow.

If planting has to be delayed because the soil or weather conditions are not right, the plants must be protected from hot sun and drying winds. Store plants with bare roots by heeling them in. To do this, dig out an angled trench in a cool position in friable soil. Insert the plants close together and cover the roots with earth to the level of the planting mark. This is the point on the stem where there is a slight colour change that indicates the depth at which they were planted. Store container-grown plants by plunging them to the rim in weathered ashes, grit or similar porous material. Alternatively, stand them in a cool, sheltered site and protect the containers with straw or bracken. Check their water requirements regularly.

Even if there is no delay to planting, always cover bare-rooted plants with damp sacking to protect them during site preparation.

How to plant
First, dig out a planting hole that is wide enough to take the roots when they are fully spread out. Where necessary, tease out the roots of container-grown plants that have become compacted. Ensure that the hole is deep enough to allow the plant to be inserted at the correct level. The soil level should be up to the planting mark on bare-rooted plants, or at the point where the roots and shoots meet if they are herbaceous. With container-grown plants the soil level should be the same as it was in the container, or marginally deeper.

Insert the plant carefully. Return the soil around and between the roots and firm it well. Water in evergreen plants. Finally, lightly fork over the soil to give a smooth surface.

Planting distances
It is important to decide the correct planting distance for each kind of ground cover plant in order to achieve 75–100 per cent cover in one or two years. The planting distance is determined by a number of factors. The most important are the natural growth habit of the plant and the soil and climate conditions, all of which influence how quickly it will cover a given area and what its ultimate spread is likely to be.

The size of the plants should also be taken into account. Young, well rooted plants establish faster and grow more rapidly than larger, older plants, and will usually provide good cover by the end of the first season. However, more plants are required and this can be expensive.

The recommended planting distances for individual plants are included in the section on specific plants, pages 152–153.

Planting ground cover

1 Cover bare-rooted plants with damp sacking as soon as they have been lifted. This will protect the roots until they can be planted out.

2 If planting is delayed, store bare-rooted plants by heeling them in up to the level of the planting mark.

3 To plant ground cover, first dig out a planting hole sufficiently deep and wide to accommodate the roots.

4 Tease out the roots of plants if they were raised in a container, since they may have become compacted.

5 After inserting the plant, replace the soil and firm it down well. Then lightly fork over the surface.

Maintenance

One of the main factors to be considered when selecting ground cover plants is that they should not require a high degree of maintenance. However, a certain amount of work is necessary in the early stages to ensure that the plants establish successfully.

Weed control
During the first year after planting it is essential to keep weeds under control, otherwise they will compete with the plants for water, nutrients and light. Clear weed seedlings by hand-weeding or hoeing. Continue hand-weeding to kill weed seedlings as they appear and to remove any perennial weeds that have escaped treatment when the site was being prepared. Alternatively, spot-treat perennial weeds very carefully with glyphosate.

The weedkiller lenacil is used commercially to control germinating weed seeds among many established ground cover plants; simazine is also used professionally, though its range of application is more limited than in the case of lenacil. For gardeners, however, an approach which is both effective in weed control and beneficial to plant establishment and growth is to apply a 2–3 in mulch of peat or pulverized bark. Well rotted garden compost or leaf-mould can also be used, but they may contain viable weed seeds. Apply the mulch between the plants, taking care not to cover the growing shoots if they are herbaceous. Carpeting plants only require a light sprinkling of mulch between the spreading shoots. The mulch suppresses most weed development and, as it breaks down, will provide nutrients for the plants. Mulching encourages carpeting plants to take root and give more rapid cover. It also helps to keep the soil cool and to conserve moisture. Renew mulches each spring until good cover has formed.

Fertilizers
Once the plants are established they should not be neglected completely. Feeding, though not essential, greatly improves their appearance and vigour. Feed every two years in early spring as new growth appears, applying either a balanced inorganic fertilizer or an organic one such as bone meal.

Alternatively, use a slow release fertilizer; these are particularly suitable for ground cover plants since they release nutrients over a period of several months. Apply inorganic fertilizers carefully around the plants to avoid scorching the leaves.

Where plants have suffered a check, or where newly planted ground cover is slow to grow away, apply a foliar feed in late spring or early summer.

Pruning
As with feeding, pruning is not essential, but it does benefit the appearance and vigour of ground cover plants. Remove old flowering stems, dead twigs or damaged shoots when necessary, and examine all plants annually in late winter or early spring.

More severe pruning may be needed to prevent vigorously spreading plants from becoming invasive, and plants such as heathers and vincas from becoming straggly. Do this in January or February for deciduous woody plants, or in April for evergreens. Some young woody plants may need to be pruned back to encourage lower branching.

Tidy up deciduous herbaceous plants in late autumn when the foliage has died down. Cut back old flowering stems and remove dead leaves, but do not harm the crowns of plants that retain some foliage over winter.

PROPAGATION

Many ground cover plants can be easily propagated, either by division, layering, taking cuttings or sowing seeds. Some general points concerning propagation are discussed below. For the methods of propagating a particular plant, see the propagation section on pages 156–187.

One of the simplest methods of propagating a plant is to divide and replant it, or to replant runners that have taken root. However, this inevitably disturbs the existing plants and can check their growth. A better method, though not always possible, is to peg down runners into pots of compost. Once they have taken root they can be severed from the parent and planted out. With clump-forming or suckering plants the only alternative to division is to grow several stock plants in a nursery bed and gradually build up the stock over several seasons.

Another method of propagation is to take cuttings. In most cases these will require two to three years to become sufficiently sturdy to be planted out. Most woody plants can be propagated from softwood cuttings taken in June or July; they will root satisfactorily if placed in a mist unit or a propagator with bottom heat. Others can be rooted from hardwood cuttings taken in autumn and planted in a cold frame or plastic tunnel. Certain herbaceous perennials can be propagated from leafy cuttings taken in late summer and planted under glass.

Many ground cover plants can also be raised from seed, but considerable attention is needed to produce well rooted plants within a few years of germination.

Weeding

Hand-weed regularly to remove weed seedlings as they appear, and any perennial weeds that develop.

Feeding

Feed the plants every two or three years in early spring. Apply inorganic fertilizers carefully to avoid scorching the leaves.

Pruning

Examine plants annually in late winter or early spring, removing any dead foliage, damaged shoots or straggly growth.

Problem sites 1

Shaded sites
A indicates a moist soil
B indicates an average soil
C indicates a dry soil
If a plant prefers one of these conditions, then a letter in bold type is used; a letter in normal type indicates that the plant will tolerate these conditions.

☆ indicates that the plant requires an acid, lime-free soil.

One of the most common reasons for growing ground cover is to utilize those awkward sites in a garden where little other than weeds will grow. This section discusses these sites in turn, the difficulties that they present and points concerning site preparation and planting. For each site, a list of suitable ground cover plants is given, usually in tabular form. If only a few plants can be recommended, they are given within the text.

Shaded sites

One of the most important factors that limits the choice of plants for a particular site is the degree of shade present. Many plants grow poorly in shade and may become distorted by developing only towards the light. The soil conditions at the site may also be extreme, for example, under the canopy of larger trees the soil is often poor and dry, and there may be many tree roots near the surface. On the other hand, in low-lying poorly drained sites or open woodland, the soil may be perpetually moist.

To prepare the site, the first step is to mark out the extent of the shaded area; do this on a sunny day in spring or autumn. Decide on the degree of shade possessed by the site and the nature of the growing conditions there, then choose the appropriate plants accordingly. Plant the ground cover in the autumn because, if the plants are evergreen, they benefit from the moister winter conditions and may receive some winter sunshine. Also, many deciduous plants will begin growing in spring well before the trees come into full leaf.

Prepare the site thoroughly and, after planting, water in evergreens to help their roots settle in the soil; if the weather is dry, water in deciduous plants as well. Mulch the plants in spring and, for at least the first season after planting, keep a close check on them to ensure that they have sufficient water.

If the plants are growing under large mature trees, there will be little change in the soil conditions from year to year. However, under young, rapidly growing trees both the extent and the degree of shade will increase annually. If, in the latter case, existing plants show signs of deterioration, replace them with plants that are more tolerant of the increasing shade and dryness. Where planting under young trees anticipate the change in the shade as the trees mature by choosing plants that possess a greater tolerance to shade than is needed at the time.

Moist sites

With the exception of aquatics, few plants can survive prolonged wet or waterlogged conditions. Therefore, where possible, drain the site if the soil remains very wet or waterlogged for long periods, particularly if this occurs in winter.

Some plants, including a few with good ground cover qualities, can survive in moist to wet soils. Their roots have low oxygen requirements and they can establish and grow in conditions where those of many plants would rapidly decay.

DEGREES OF SHADE

In the list on the right, and in the text that follows, the degree of shade that a plant needs, or tolerates, is indicated by the terms light shade, partial shade, moderate shade and deep shade.

Light shade usually refers to a site that is open to the sky, but is screened from direct sunlight by some obstacle such as a high wall or a group of trees.

Partial shade describes a site where the sun is excluded for all but two or three hours in a day, either early morning or late evening. Note that several hours of sunlight in the middle of the day qualifies a site as sunny.

Moderate shade has little or no direct sun, but there is some reflected or transfused light. It often occurs in woodlands or larger shrubberies.

Deep shade is usually encountered under the canopy of larger deciduous trees that have low branches and dense foliage, for example, sycamore, beech and horse chestnut. This type of shade is also found under clumps of conifers or among overgrown shrubberies.

PLANTS FOR SHADED SITES

Medium or deep shade

GROUP 1

Plant	A	B	C
Galeobdolon argentatum	A	**B**	C
Hedera canariensis		**B**	
Hedera colchica		**B**	
Hedera helix and var hibernica		**B**	
Vinca spp	A	B	**C**
Waldsteinia ternata	A	B	**C**

GROUP 2

Plant	A	B	C
Asarum spp	**A**		
Euonymus fortunei var radicans			**C**
× Gaulnettya wisleyensis ☆	A	**B**	
Gaultheria shallon ☆		**B**	C
Leucothoe fontanesiana	A	**B**	
Lonicera pileata		**B**	
Mahonia aquifolium		**B**	C
Pachysandra terminalis	B	**C**	
Prunus laurocerasus	B	**C**	

GROUP 3

Plant	A	B	C
Acanthus mollis latifolius		**B**	
Brunnera macrophylla	**A**	B	
Hosta spp	A	**B**	
Iris foetidissima		B	**C**
Pulmonaria spp	**A**		

GROUP 4

Plant	A	B	C
Asperula odorata		**B**	
Blechnum spicant	**A**		
Convallaria majalis	**A**	B	
Dicentra formosa	**A**		
Duchesnea indica		B	**C**
Euphorbia robbiae			**C**
Gaultheria procumbens		**B**	
Geranium nodosum	A	**B**	
Geranium phaeum	A	**B**	
Geranium punctatum	A	**B**	
Lamium maculatum	A	**B**	C
Luzula maxima		B	**C**
Maianthemum bifolium	**A**		
Omphalodes spp	**A**	B	
Oxalis oregana	**A**	B	
Rubus spp		B	**C**
Sarcococca humilis		**B**	C
Symphytum grandiflorum	**A**	B	
Tellima grandiflora	A	**B**	C

Plant	A	B	C
Tiarella spp	**A**	B	
Vancouveria hexandra	**A**	B	
Viola labradorica	A	**B**	C
Viola obliqua	A	**B**	C

Light or open shade

GROUP 2

Plant	A	B	C
Arctostaphylos uva-ursi ☆	**A**	B	
Bergenia spp and hybrids	A	**B**	
Cotoneaster spp	A	**B**	C
Cotoneaster 'Gnome'		**B**	C
Erica herbacea		**B**	
Euonymus fortunei f carrierei		**B**	
Hypericum × moserianum		**B**	C
Juniperus conferta		**B**	C
Juniperus × media 'Pfitzeriana'			**C**
Juniperus sabina var tamariscifolia		**B**	C

GROUP 3

Plant	A	B	C
Alchemilla mollis		**B**	
Geranium endressii 'Wargrave Pink'	**A**	B	
Geranium psilostemon	**A**	B	
Geranium sylvaticum	**A**	B	
Geum × borisii		**B**	C
Hemerocallis spp	A	**B**	
Polygonum campanulatum	**A**		

GROUP 4

Plant	A	B	C
Ajuga reptans	**A**		
Campanula spp		**B**	
Cornus canadensis ☆	**A**		
Cotula squalida		B	**C**
Epimedium spp		**B**	
Geranium ibericum	**A**	B	
Geranium macrorrhizum	**A**	B	
Geranium × magnificum	**A**	B	
Geranium platypetalum	**A**	B	
Geranium procurrens	**A**	B	
Glechoma hederacea	A	**B**	C
Lysimachia nummularia	**A**		
Potentilla alba	A	**B**	
Prunella grandiflora	**A**	B	
Vaccinium vitis-idaea ☆	**A**	B	
Viola cornuta		**B**	
Viola garden hybrids		**B**	

Problem sites 2

Moist sites
A indicates moist shade
B indicates cool, damp shade
C indicates a moist sunny site
If a plant prefers one of these conditions, then a letter in bold type is used; a letter in normal type indicates that the plant will tolerate these conditions.

☆ indicates that the plant requires an acid, lime-free soil.

Hot, dry sites
☆ indicates that the plant requires an acid, lime-free soil.

The roots of moisture-tolerant plants are usually rather fleshy, with the plants spreading by means of stolons or rhizomes to form a dense leafy cover. Some are plants of wet pasture or meadowland. Others are native to cool moist woodland or its fringes. They have large soft-textured leaves and pale delicate flowers; they come into growth and flower early in the year before the development of dense overhead leafy cover.

Plants with these qualities and characteristics can be used along the damp margins of streams and ditches where, for most of the year, conditions are too wet for other plants. They can also be used to provide good summer cover in poorly drained, low-lying areas and in damp woodland where deep leaf-mould provides a moist root run throughout the summer months.

Plant in the spring where possible. Autumn planting is acceptable, but even moisture-tolerant plants may deteriorate over winter in very wet conditions when their roots are not well established.

In suitably moist conditions there will be little need for summer watering except in very dry seasons, but, if the site is drier than anticipated, herbaceous plants may die down prematurely during the summer, giving a shorter season of good cover and the possibility of weeds establishing during the late summer or autumn. There may also be some leaf-fall from evergreens, reducing the density of cover and giving rise to similar problems of weed seedling development. In either case, water the plants to prevent this.

For the purposes of the table on this page, a moist soil is defined as one that is uniformly moist, or relatively so, throughout the year. It may, however, become wet occasionally during periods of heavy and extended rainfall. Sites that are very wet in the spring and very dry during the summer do not come into this category. Few if any ground cover plants will provide satisfactory cover in such situations.

Cool, damp shade relates to sites both under trees and in open shade where the soil remains cool and moist throughout the year. Under trees, this is usually due to the presence of a good depth of moisture-retentive leaf-mould or humus.

PLANTS FOR MOIST SITES

GROUP 1			
Galeobdolon argentatum		**B**	C
Vinca spp		**B**	
Waldsteinia ternata	A	**B**	C

GROUP 2			
Arctostaphylos uva-ursi ☆		B	**C**
Asarum spp	A	B	
Bergenia spp and hybrids	A	**B**	C
Calluna vulgaris			**C**
Cotoneaster spp		**B**	C
Daboecia cantabrica			**C**
× Gaulnettya wisleyensis ☆		**B**	C
Leucothoe fontanesiana ☆		**B**	
Pachysandra terminalis		**B**	

GROUP 3			
Brunnera macrophylla	**A**		
Geranium spp	A	**B**	C
Geum × borisii		**B**	C
Hemerocallis spp	A	**B**	C
Hosta spp	A	**B**	C
Polygonum campanulatum	A	B	**C**
Pulmonaria spp	**A**	B	C

GROUP 4			
Ajuga reptans	**A**	B	C
Asperula odorata	A	**B**	
Campanula spp		B	**C**
Convallaria majalis	A	**B**	
Cornus canadensis ☆	A	B	C
Cotoneaster dammeri		**B**	C
Dicentra formosa	A	**B**	
Epimedium spp		**B**	
Gaultheria procumbens		**B**	
Geranium spp	A	**B**	C
Glechoma hederacea	A	**B**	C
Lamium maculatum	A	**B**	
Lysimachia nummularia	A	B	C
Maianthemum bifolium	A	**B**	
Oxalis oregana	**A**	B	
Potentilla alba		**B**	
Prunella grandiflora		**B**	C
Symphytum grandiflorum	A	**B**	
Tellima grandiflora		**B**	C
Tiarella spp	A	**B**	
Vaccinium vitis-idaea ☆	A	**B**	
Viola spp and hybrids	A	**B**	C

PLANTS FOR HOT, DRY SITES

GROUP 1	
Hedera spp (not variegated varieties)	Lonicera pileata
Hypericum calycinum	Phlomis fruticosa
Vinca spp and varieties	Salvia officinalis
	Senecio 'Sunshine'

GROUP 2	
Anthemis cupaniana	
Arabis albida	GROUP 3
Aubrieta deltoidea	Liriope muscari
Aurinia saxatilis	Nepeta × faassenii
Ballota pseudodictamnus	Origanum vulgare
Cerastium tomentosum	
Cistus parviflorus	GROUP 4
Cotoneaster spp	Acaena novae-zelandiae
Cytisus spp	Antennaria dioica
Daboecia cantabrica (not on very dry sites)	Anthemis nobilis
Dianthus spp	Artemisia stelleriana
Dryas octopetala	Centaurea 'John Coutts'
Erica herbacea (not on very dry sites)	Cotoneaster dammeri
Euonymus fortunei var radicans	Geranium 'Russell Prichard'
Euonymus fortunei f carrierei and varieties	Muehlenbeckia axillaris
Genista spp	Phlox douglasii
× Halimiocistus sahucii	Phlox subulata and hybrids
Hebe spp	Potentilla alba
Helianthemum hybrids	Potentilla calabra
Hypericum spp	Saxifraga "mossy" hybrids
Iberis sempervirens	Sedum spathulifolium
Juniperus communis and varieties	Sedum spurium
Juniperus conferta	Stachys byzantina 'Silver Carpet'
Juniperus horizontalis and varieties	Thymus serpyllum
Lithodora diffusa ☆	Veronica prostrata
	Viola labradorica
	Viola obliqua

Hot, dry sites

There is a wide choice of plants for covering dry, sunny sites since there are many that grow naturally in such conditions. The main problem facing these plants is that they tend to lose more moisture through their leaves than they can absorb through their roots. Plants that are native to this type of habitat have had to adapt themselves to overcome this, for example, by having very small or narrow leaves and a dense system of branches, which help to shade the roots from the drying effects of the sun. Other plants have thick-skinned fleshy evergreen leaves, or leaf surfaces that are densely covered with fine hairs, making the plant appear silvery.

In many cases the root systems of such plants have also adapted, becoming extensive and deeply penetrating. This enables them to obtain sufficient moisture from the soil and allows their roots to escape the desiccating effects of summer heat on the upper soil layers. However, this places an important limitation on the type of site on which these plants will grow: it must be well drained throughout the year and, in particular, not become wet and heavy during the winter since much of the root system would die in such conditions. Plants with woolly or hairy leaves are particularly susceptible to this effect because, although they are perfectly hardy to frost, in their natural habitats the

Problem sites 3

Slopes and banks
A indicates a sunny site
B indicates a lightly shaded site
C indicates a deeply shaded site

☆ indicates that the plant requires an acid, lime-free soil.

climate is dry throughout the year. Thus, unless the soil is very well drained they may suffer or even die during a British winter, which typically has alternating periods of cold, frosty weather and mild, wet weather.

Before planting it is important to dig in a dressing of well rotted farm manure, garden compost, leaf-mould or peat, particularly if the soil is light. This is because the plants will have been raised in rich compost and kept well irrigated. They may, therefore, suffer a considerable check to growth and be slow to establish if they are planted into unimproved soil. By digging in a dressing, the ability of the soil to retain moisture will be increased temporarily, and so the risk of early losses will be reduced.

Planting should be done either in the spring or the autumn when the soil is cool and moist. If possible, it is better to plant in the autumn, since this allows the roots to become well established before the following summer, when the site will become hot and dry. Mulch the plants in spring to help them conserve moisture during the summer.

Slopes and banks

Most slopes or banks are, by their nature, well drained, and those in full sun on lighter soils usually become quite dry in the summer. Therefore, when choosing plants, it is usually important to select those that are tolerant of drier, well drained soils.

Gentle slopes (those with an angle of less than 20 degrees) provide few problems and allow a wide choice of plants as there is usually little risk of surface erosion. However, if water drains on to the site from higher ground, choose stem-rooting or suckering plants rather than clump-forming plants.

On steeper slopes, grow either suckering shrubs or plants whose branches or stems take root as they spread, since they will consolidate loose surfaces and prevent erosion. Evergreen plants are also useful since they protect the surface from the impact of heavy winter rains, which can rapidly erode unprotected slopes. Common ivy is a valuable ground cover plant in deep shade where few other plants can survive.

Begin planting at the top of the site and

PLANTING ON SLOPES AND BANKS

On gentle slopes (a) plant in shallow hollows since this facilitates mulching and watering. On steeper slopes (b) create terraces, holding them in place with boards and pegs. On banks of porous rock, plant in pockets chipped from the rock face (c). If the rock is non-porous, either train plants up or trail them down the bank (d) or plant them through matting pegged to the rock (e).

PLANTS FOR SLOPES AND BANKS

GROUP 1	Planting distance	
Hedera colchica	36–48 in	A B C
Hedera colchica varieties	36–48 in	A B
Hedera helix	36 in	A B C
Hedera helix variegated varieties	24–36 in	A B
Hedera helix var hibernica	36–48 in	A B C
Hypericum calycinum	15–18 in	A B C
Vinca major	18 in	A B C
Vinca major var oxyloba	24 in	A B C
Vinca minor	9–12 in	A B C
Also for milder climates:		
Hedera canariensis 'Azorica'	36–48 in	A B C
Hedera canariensis 'Gloire de Marengo'	36–48 in	A
GROUP 2		
Arctostaphylos uva-ursi ☆	15 in	A B
Calluna vulgaris and varieties ☆	9–18 in	A B
Cotoneaster conspicuus 'Decorus'	72 in	A B
Cotoneaster 'Gnome'	18–24 in	A B
Cotoneaster microphyllus	18–24 in	A B
Cotoneaster 'Skogholm'	18–24 in	A B
Daboecia cantabrica and varieties ☆	15–18 in	A
Erica herbacea and varieties	12–15 in	A B
Erica vagans and varieties ☆	12–15 in	A
Euonymus fortunei var radicans	12–18 in	A B C
Euonymus fortunei f carrierei 'Variegatus'	12–18 in	A B C
Gaultheria shallon	36–48 in	A B C
Genista hispanica	24 in	A
Genista pilosa	15 in	A B
Helianthemum hybrids	18 in	A
Juniperus communis, ssp depressa and varieties	24 in	A
Juniperus horizontalis and varieties	18–24 in	A
Juniperus × media 'Pfitzeriana'	48–72 in	A B C
Lonicera pileata	24 in	A B C
Also for milder climates:		
Ceanothus thyrsiflorus repens	36–48 in	A
Juniperus conferta	24 in	A B
Phlomis fruticosa	30 in	A
GROUP 4		
Cotoneaster dammeri	24 in	A B
Luzula maxima	15 in	A B C
Polygonum vacciniifolium	9–12 in	A
Rubus tricolor	36 in	A B C
Stephanandra incisa 'Crispa'	36 in	A
Symphoricarpos × chenaultii 'Hancock'	36 in	A B
Rosa spp and varieties	36–48 in	A

Problem sites 4

work downwards. On gentle slopes dig a shallow hole for each plant with a trowel, drawing the soil forwards. Alternatively, dig a shallow trench across the slope. These holes will help the site to retain mulches and water. If the digging exposes sub-soil, or if the soil is poor, dig out larger planting holes and fill them with richer soil or work in some good planting compost.

On steeper slopes, construct small terraces by drawing soil forwards to create a series of levels. Hold the back of each terrace in place with boards and wooden stakes or pegs; after a year or two, when the plants are well established, these can be removed. Do not use logs to hold the terrace back because they will decay and may become infested with honey fungus which will endanger woody plants in the garden.

On a newly cut bank where the soil is sandy there is considerable risk of erosion. Prevent this by firmly pegging down coconut matting or a similar, decomposable, material before planting so that the surface is held firm. Then make holes in the matting and plant through these with spreading, stem-rooting plants that will root down through the matting as it rots to provide good consolidation against erosion. Alternatively, if the underlying material is porous rock, chip pockets out of it and plant in these.

On very steep banks where erosion is likely to occur and it is virtually impossible to plant, the most satisfactory answer is to construct a retaining wall. Alternatively, plant sprawling climbers at the base of the slope and train them up the face, or plant them close to the crest of the slope to trail downwards. The strong-growing species of ivy are suitable for this, as are certain climbers which, though of little merit as ground cover in general, are very useful in this type of situation. They include *Clematis montana* 'Tetrarose', *Clematis orientalis*, *Lonicera henryi*, *Lonicera japonica* 'Halliana' and *Parthenocissus quinquefolia*.

Large areas

As the cost of maintaining a garden has escalated in recent years, the designs of many larger gardens have had to be modified. This has usually been done by increasing shrub plantings and putting down larger areas to grass. However, both methods have several disadvantages. Shrub plantings may take several years to develop into good cover and, in the interim period, will need regular weeding, mulching and pruning. Unless they are carefully selected and positioned, shrub plantings may grow to blot out attractive garden features. With grass there is the expense of fertilizers, weedkillers and mowing equipment. It also needs regular maintenance throughout the growing season.

A much more satisfactory solution to the problem of large areas is to plant ground cover, since it is visually pleasing and requires little maintenance.

As with any other kind of site, the choice of cover plants must be related to the nature of the site and its soil type, but where the planting is to replace a prominent garden feature, or will occupy a strategic position in a new garden, then strong emphasis should be placed on having attractive plants.

Apart from the ornamental aspects, the two most important factors when choosing plants are their height and planting distances. As stated above in connection with shrub plants, height may detract from other features in the garden. The planting distance will, of course, affect the cost of the ground cover. Before planting, measure the site carefully, then calculate the precise number of plants required by referring to the spacing recommendations. Where large numbers of plants are required, obtain quotations and, if the cost is too great, consider alternative selections. The planting distances may be slightly increased where the soil conditions are good, but this may delay the development of effective coverage for a season.

Exposed coastal gardens

Many plants do not grow well in coastal gardens because their shoots and leaves become badly scorched by the salt present in sea winds, even when they are growing some distance inland. There are, however, a number of plants that have become adapted to this type of habitat. For example, marram grass, sea holly and sea pink can be found close to the high-tide mark, where they are frequently drenched by sea spray during stormy weather. Similarly, gorse, Cornish

PLANTS FOR LARGE AREAS

GROUP 1	Height	Planting distance
Galeobdolon argentatum	6–9 in	24–36 in
Hedera canariensis 'Azorica'	6–9 in	36–48 in
Hedera canariensis 'Gloire de Marengo'	6–9 in	36–48 in
Hedera colchica and varieties	6–9 in	36–48 in
Hedera helix	6–9 in	24–36 in
Hedera helix var *hibernica*	9–12 in	36–48 in
Hypericum calycinum	9–12 in	15–18 in
Vinca major and var *oxyloba*	6–9 in	18–24 in
Waldsteinia ternata	3–4 in	12 in
GROUP 2		
Bergenia spp and hybrids	6–12 in	9–24 in
Calluna vulgaris varieties	6–18 in	9–18 in
Cotoneaster 'Gnome'	3–4 in	18–24 in
Daboecia cantabrica	15–18 in	15–18 in
Erica vagans and varieties	9–18 in	12–15 in
Euonymus fortunei f *carrierei* and varieties	24 in	30 in
Genista hispanica	24 in	24 in
Juniperus × *media* 'Pfitzeriana'	36 in	48–72 in
Juniperus sabina var *tamariscifolia*	15–18 in	24–30 in
Leucothoe fontanesiana	36 in	36 in
Lonicera pileata	18 in	24 in
Pachysandra terminalis	3–4 in	12 in
Prunus laurocerasus varieties	36 in	36 in
Senecio 'Sunshine'	36 in	36 in
GROUP 3		
Brunnera macrophylla	12 in	15–18 in
Geranium endressii 'Wargrave Pink'	18–21 in	12–18 in
Geranium psilostemon	30 in	12–18 in
Hemerocallis spp and hybrids	18–24 in	18 in
Hosta spp, particularly *H. sieboldiana*	12–18 in	15–24 in
Polygonum campanulatum	18–24 in	18–24 in
GROUP 4		
Asperula odorata	4–5 in	24 in
Geranium procurrens	18–24 in	18–24 in
Glechoma hederacea	3–4 in	18 in
Luzula maxima	12 in	15 in
Rosa 'Max Graf'	36 in	48–60 in
Rosa × *paulii*	36–48 in	48–72 in
Rosa 'Temple Bells'	18–24 in	30–36 in
Rosa wichuraiana	12–18 in	60–72 in
Rubus tricolor	12 in	36 in
Stephanandra incisa 'Crispa'	24 in	36 in
Symphoricarpos × *chenaultii* 'Hancock'	24 in	36 in
Tellima grandiflora	6 in	12 in

Problem sites 5

Exposed coastal gardens
A indicates a light sandy soil
B indicates a medium to medium-heavy soil
If a plant prefers one of these conditions, then a letter in bold type is used; a letter in normal type indicates that the plant will tolerate these conditions.

☆ indicates that the plant requires an acid, lime-free soil.

Exposed inland gardens
☆ indicates that the plant requires an acid, lime-free soil.

PLANTS FOR COASTAL GARDENS

Fully exposed sites

GROUP 2	A	B
Arctostaphylos uva-ursi ☆	A	**B**
Calluna vulgaris ☆	A	**B**
Cerastium tomentosum	A	B
Cistus spp	A	
Cotoneaster spp	A	**B**
Cotoneaster 'Gnome'		**B**
Cytisus spp	A	**B**
Daboecia cantabrica ☆	A	**B**
Dianthus spp	A	
Erica herbacea and varieties	A	**B**
Erica vagans and varieties ☆	A	**B**
Euonymus fortunei var *radicans*	A	**B**
Euonymus fortunei f *carrierei* and varieties	A	**B**
Genista spp	A	
× *Halimiocistus sahucii*	A	
Hebe spp	A	B
Juniperus communis and varieties	A	B
Juniperus conferta	A	B
Juniperus horizontalis and varieties	A	B
Potentilla fruticosa var *mandschurica*	A	**B**
Senecio 'Sunshine'	A	
GROUP 4		
Artemisia spp	A	
Cotoneaster dammeri	A	**B**
Potentilla spp	A	**B**
Rosa wichuraiana	A	
Sedum spp	A	B

Less exposed sites

GROUP 1	A	B
Hedera spp	A	B
Hypericum spp (and Group 2)	A	B
Vinca spp and varieties	A	B
GROUP 2		
Arabis albida	A	B
Aubrieta deltoidea	A	B
Bergenia spp and hybrids		B
Dryas octopetala	A	
Helianthemum hybrids	A	B
Lonicera pileata	A	B
Mahonia aquifolium		B
GROUP 3		
Alchemilla mollis		B
Geranium spp (and Group 4)		B
Hemerocallis spp		B
Polygonum spp (and Group 4)		B
GROUP 4		
Campanula spp		B
Euphorbia robbiae		B
Phlox spp and varieties	A	B
Rubus spp		B
Saxifraga "mossy" hybrids	A	B
Stachys byzantina	A	
Symphoricarpos × *chenaultii*		B
Thymus serpyllum	A	
Vaccinium vitis-idaea ☆		B

EXPOSED INLAND GARDENS

The following plants provide good ground cover in gardens that, although inland, are still exposed to severe weather, for example, northerly gardens. The same considerations apply to these plants as to those growing in coastal gardens.

GROUP 1
Hedera helix and var *hibernica*
Vinca major and var *oxyloba*
Vinca minor
Waldsteinia ternata

Iberis sempervirens
Juniperus communis and varieties
Juniperus horizontalis and varieties
Leucothoe fontanesiana ☆
Pachysandra terminalis

GROUP 2
Arctostaphylos uva-ursi ☆
Calluna vulgaris and varieties ☆
Cotoneaster spp and varieties
Erica herbacea and varieties
Euonymus fortunei and varieties

GROUP 4
Cornus canadensis ☆
Gaultheria procumbens ☆
Sarcococca spp
Symphoricarpos × *chenaultii* 'Hancock'
Vaccinium vitis-idaea ☆

heath and thrift survive on sea cliffs, even though they are fully exposed to salt-laden gale-force winds.

Before selecting ground cover plants, study the site carefully and note whether any part of it is protected against the prevailing wind. Also take into account the soil type and growing conditions.

Prepare the site thoroughly before planting by digging in a dressing of well rotted farm manure, garden compost, leaf-mould or peat. This is particularly important on sand, silt or dry chalk soil. On drier soils, dig in fresh moist seaweed at up to 20 lb per square yard. This will increase temporarily the capacity of the soil to hold moisture, and so reduce the risk of early losses and encourage quick establishment.

Plant in the spring to give the ground cover a full growing season ahead in which to become well established before there is any serious risk of exposure to severe weather conditions. After planting evergreens, water them in well to settle the roots. With all plants, whether deciduous or evergreen, apply a good surface mulch after planting.

Rose beds
Rose beds are very susceptible to weeds since the plants are spaced fairly far apart and are often rather gaunt and leafless towards the base. This problem can be overcome by using weedkillers (see page 155), but an alternative approach is to grow ground cover. The use of ground cover does, however, have one serious drawback: it can interfere with pruning and feeding. Roses need feeding regularly in order to maintain their health and vigour. This can be done by using foliar nutrient sprays, but the best method is to apply mulches of farm manure or garden compost. However, these cannot be laid down effectively where ground cover has been planted. A compromise is to use ground cover plants of moderate vigour and height to provide a broad edging to rose beds without letting them encroach within the boundary defined by the stems of the outermost rose bushes. This will allow the roses to be mulched and pruned, while at the same time providing an attractive border.

Suitable plants for such ground cover include *Geranium sanguineum* var *lancastriense*, *Hebe pinguifolia* 'Pagei', *Helianthemum* hybrids, *Viola*, *Nepeta* × *faassenii* and "mossy" hybrids of *Saxifraga*.

If ground cover is to be planted throughout a rose bed, then the choice is limited to low-growing plants with some shade tolerance. On drier soils, suitable plants include *Lamium maculatum*, *Saxifraga* × *urbium* and *Campanula portenschlagiana*. On moister soils plant *Viola*, *Lysimachia nummularia* 'Aurea' or *Prunella grandiflora*.

Bulbs
In most gardens, bulbs are grown on sites that, for most of the year, are bare earth, for example, at the front of shrubberies or flower beds. This has the disadvantage that the site is readily colonized by weeds after the bulb foliage dies down in early summer. Some bulbs have to be grown in open ground since they need a high dormancy temperature, or "baking", to induce flower bud development, but others, particularly spring-flowering kinds, can be grown successfully under ground cover. The cover must not be so dense that it smothers the bulbs, yet it should be vigorous enough to suppress weed growth. The best plant to use for dwarf bulbs is *Cotula squalida*, which has a very low-spreading habit and gives medium density cover. It tolerates dry or moist conditions and full sun or light shade.

With taller, stronger-growing bulbous plants such as daffodils, *Muscari armeniacum* or bluebells, the density of cover is not so critical. Suitable plants for ground cover include *Ajuga*, *Pulmonaria*, *Viola*, *Glechoma hederacea* 'Variegata' and *Lysimachia nummularia* 'Aurea'.

Weed control

A weed is a plant growing where it is not wanted. Thus one of last year's potatoes which comes up in this year's carrots is a weed. Weeds compete with crops for light, water and nutrients and they also create a micro-environment around plants in which grey mould (*Botrytis cinerea*) and damping-off diseases flourish. Weeds also act as hosts for pests, such as aphids and whitefly, and diseases, such as club-root of brassicas.

Annual weeds and perennial weeds
Annuals are plants that complete their life-cycle within a growing season, and they are often able to undergo more than one life-cycle in a season. Annuals are also character-ized by the production of very many seeds so that the weed seed population in the soil is constantly replenished. Perennial plants live from year to year and usually have underground organs—stems or roots—which enable them to survive through the winter. Thus docks (*Rumex* spp) have thick, fleshy tap roots and couch grass (*Agropyron repens*) has underground stems or rhizomes.

Controlling perennial weeds
Weed control begins with winter digging prior to growing the first crops. Cut down any woody perennials, such as brambles (*Rubus* spp), and dig out all the roots. Double dig the whole of the garden in the first instance and remove all perennial weed roots and rhizomes. Burn or dispose of them all and never use them for compost making. Once the land has been cleared of perennial weeds, they should never be a problem again, unless, of course, they are imported with organic ma-terials such as farmyard manure.

Controlling annual weeds
Annual weeds continually reappear, how-ever, and all fertile garden soils have a large reservoir of weed seeds. Weed seeds are also blown in on the wind and carried by birds and by man.

When winter digging, the gardener should skim off annual weeds and dig them into the bottom of each trench along with organic manure or garden compost. Digging brings up annual weed seeds which were buried in previous seasons. Many will germinate, but subsequent cultivations should kill the young weed seedlings that emerge. They will have appeared by the time cultivations take place to prepare the land for sowing or planting. Remove these, and the next flush of weed seedlings will appear with the sown or planted crops.

Hoeing against weeds
Hoeing is the main method of weed control in the growing crop. It is largely a matter of personal preference which type of hoe to use, but in every case the blade must be kept constantly sharpened so that the weeds are severed from their roots rather than pulled up with them.

Choose a warm, drying day so that the weeds wilt and die quickly after hoeing. Care is needed when hoeing closely around crop plants because any damage caused is quickly colonized by disease organisms. Keep the hoe in the upper, surface layers of the soil so as not to bring up more weed seeds to germinate and cause further problems. The dry soil produced by surface hoeing acts as a mulch which in itself inhibits weed growth.

Mulching against weeds
Weeds can also be controlled by using mulches. The use of dry soil as a mulch has already been mentioned but materials such as black polythene, well-prepared compost, or peat can also be used. Black polythene forms a complete physical barrier to weed growth; it also warms up the soil and con-serves moisture. It is usually necessary to bury the edges of the polythene to prevent it blowing away and holes must be cut in it through which vegetables can be planted or sown. As well as eliminating weeds, a black polythene mulch can bring crops forward and hasten their maturity by as much as three weeks but, unfortunately, pests can thrive in the moist conditions produced. Organic mulches, such as peat, perform similar func-tions but have the advantage that they can be dug into the soil at the end of the season, thus improving its structure and fertility. Straw is not recommended as a mulch material because the bacterial action re-quired to break it down can lead to a nitrogen deficiency in certain soils.

Using chemicals against weeds
The amateur's vegetable garden is extremely productive and a large number of crops are grown in a very small area. The danger of spray drift and persistence from chemical weedkillers is therefore considerable. Against annual weeds the non-persistent contact weed-killer paraquat/diquat does have a place, how-ever, but it must be applied at low level with a dribble bar when there is no wind and, there-fore, no danger of drift. It is inactivated rapidly on contact with the soil but kills any green tissues with which it comes into contact so must be handled with care.

More toxic and persistent weedkillers should not be used in the home vegetable garden because the risks involved are too great. Whenever using chemicals always follow the manufacturer's instructions.

Hoeing

Carefully hoe annual weeds, keeping the blade level with the surface layers of the soil. Choose a warm, drying day for hoeing and keep the blade sharp.

Digging perennial weeds

During winter digging remove all perennial roots and rhizomes and burn them.

Mulching

Use black polythene (or organic mulches) to act as a barrier against weed growth, to conserve moisture and to warm up the soil.

Chemical weed control

Use a dribble bar for paraquat/diquat at ground level just on top of each weed. Never apply herbicides on a windy day and follow the manufacturer's instructions.

Tools and equipment

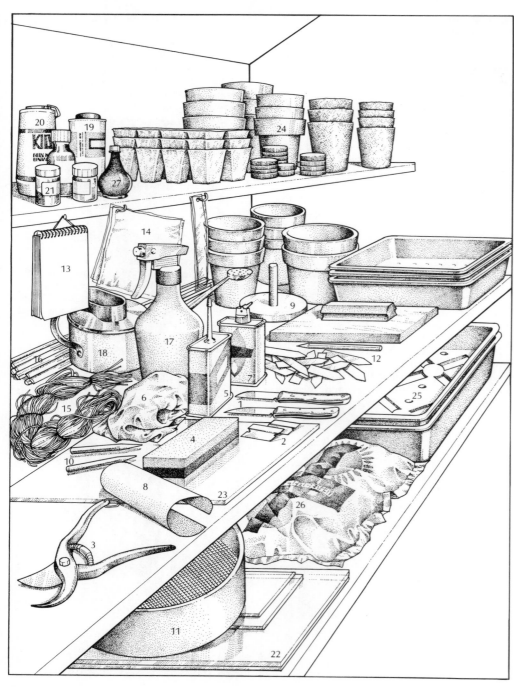

To propagate plants successfully, it is necessary to have a clean and tidy working area, efficient and effective tools and kit and to follow a standardized procedure. Failure in any part of the system leads to frustration and, more importantly, delays that will reduce the probability of success.

Most important of the gardener's special tools and equipment for plant propagation are a sharp knife, a pair of secateurs, a dibber, suitable compost and a selection of pots and seed trays. Not all tools or fancy bits of equipment will necessarily enhance the success of propagation, but the important ones will because they make the gardener's job easier, and if the job is easier it often succeeds more readily.

The use of suitable tools gives the plant material the very best start. To avoid tearing and crushing, for example, always use a sharp knife or razor blade and a clean sheet of glass when preparing a softwood cutting for planting. If the plant material is damaged, it will die and become a site for possible rots to infect the cutting. By the same token it is important

not to push a cutting into the compost; always first make a hole with a dibber of suitable size, and then plant the cutting in that hole. A dibber should be approximately the same diameter as the cutting to be planted.

Although many people will use a kitchen table, draining-board or greenhouse bench, the most suitable place to make cuttings, graft or sow seeds is a bench in the garden shed with a convenient shelf for all the bits and pieces of kit, tools, rooting powders, etc. The height of the bench will be a critical factor to the comfort of the gardener if considerable time is to be spent propagating or potting plants. Incorrectly sited benches will encourage or enhance backaches and cricks in the neck. It is also important to have good lighting placed directly over the work bench itself.

Plant propagation in many ways is akin to surgery, and nowhere is there more routine and standardized procedure than in an operating theatre—where all concentration is centred on the patient.

Therefore the secret of success for a gardener lies in having all the required tools and kit readily to hand and clean and in good working order, so that any technique of propagation can proceed smoothly and all concentration can be centred on the plant material.

After use it is important to clean, service and restore all kit to its correct place so that it is readily accessible on the next occasion.

Basic tools and kit

Knives (1), safety razor blades (2) and secateurs (3)
Sharpening stone (4)
Oil for lubrication (5)
Cleaning rags (6), solvent (7) and emery paper (8)
Pressers (various) for firming compost (9)
Dibbers (10)
Sieve ($\frac{1}{8}$ in mesh) (11)
Labels and soft lead pencil (12)
Notebook for records (13)
Polythene bags and tape (14)
Raffia, twine, etc. (15)
Split canes 12 in or 15 in (16)
Hand sprayer (17)
Watering can (18)
Fungicides (19)
Pesticides (20)
Rooting powders (21)
Panes of glass for covering seed trays (22)
Panes of glass for cutting (23)
Pots (24) and seed trays (25)
Composts (26) and fertilizer (27)

WORK BENCHES

To find the correct height for your work bench, stand up straight, drop your arms to the side; then raise your forearms at right angles to your body and drop your wrists— the bench should be at the height indicated by your fingertips.

Environmental control

The main problem in propagation is to ensure survival of the propagated material (be it seed, cutting or graft) until it establishes as a new young plant. If the correct material has been used at the start, and as long as any treatments or cuts have been made correctly, then success is directly related to the control of the environment. The quicker the regenerative processes can be induced the less chance there is for things to go wrong.

In plant propagation there are two environments: the aerial environment, which can be broken down into humidity, temperature, gaseous balance and light transmission; and the environment of the medium (soil and compost), which covers temperature, moisture status, aeration and its reaction (acidity/alkalinity). Any equipment therefore should be measured in relation to the effect it has on these factors.

An ideal environment is one that allows minimum water loss from the plant material, cool air temperatures, adequate light penetration for photosynthesis, a normal atmospheric balance between compost and air, good drainage and warm soil/compost temperatures with a neutral acidity/alkalinity reaction. The degree to which a particular system of environmental control operates will limit the propagation techniques that can be used successfully within it. In general, the "softer" or less hardy the plant material the greater will be the degree of environmental control needed to achieve success. The vagaries of the normal climate are too great for all but the easiest and hardiest plants to be propagated successfully outdoors.

Cold frames

To provide initial control over the environment, place a box with a lid of glass on ordinary soil. This cold-frame environment helps to increase soil temperatures, reduce temperature fluctuation, maintain humidity and allow light penetration, and it can be used for the propagation of a wide range of hardy plants. Its main disadvantage, which is shared with all enclosed environments, is that air temperatures build up when conditions are sunny. This necessitates either airing the frame to reduce the temperature, and thereby losing humidity, or shading the glass to cut down the light input, and so reducing photosynthesis.

There are many plastics substitutes used in place of glass, but because of their heat/light transmission characteristics they are less satisfactory in the late autumn to spring period as they do not conserve heat so effectively as glass.

The most manageable cold frame to construct is made with "Dutch lights", which are single panes of glass held in separate wooden frames 4 ft 11 in long by 2 ft 6¾ in wide. These can be laid side by side across a base frame with a distance between backboard and frontboard of 4 ft 9 in. For propagation the backboard is best made at a height of about 12 in and the frontboard at 9 in. The slope of the roof should be pitched in a southerly direction. The cold frame can be made more reliable by improved sealing of any cracks in the structure and by double glazing with two layers of "lights"—the lid of a cold frame being called a "light".

Greenhouses

The next step in the sequence of environmental control is the greenhouse, where slightly more sophisticated pieces of equipment for environmental control can be used. Greenhouses can, of course, be of a wide variety of shapes and sizes. Wooden-framed greenhouses are expensive to purchase, maintain and keep clean. Metal greenhouses are less expensive, cheaper to maintain and easier to keep clean, but unless they have an adequate internal structure they are subject to considerable distortion and damage if exposed to high-velocity winds.

A closed case, which is a frame with a lid of glass in a greenhouse, provides a high-temperature system for propagation of house plants and less hardy subjects. Accurate control of temperature can be attained by installing a thermostatically controlled soil-warming cable, which will provide bottom heat, into some sand at the base of the closed case.

Mist propagation units

The ultimate environmental control is provided by a mist unit. This is an open system that automatically maintains the moisture level while allowing the full penetration of light and the use of bottom heat without an increase in air temperature. However, such a system requires both electricity and water in the greenhouse.

Propagators

The alternative compromise is the so-called "propagator". This is a portable unit and can be used either in the greenhouse or indoors provided that adequate light is available. It consists of a glass-fibre base fitted with a thermostat and heating cables and a Perspex-type dome, which provides the closed environment. All sorts of variations are available so make sure that the propagator you buy is sufficiently large for your needs.

Polythene tents and tunnels

At the other extreme is a cheap and simple arrangement that provides a sufficiently effective closed environment for easily propagated plants. Place a polythene bag over the top of a pot or tray, and support it either by one or two canes or by a loop of wire with an end stuck in the compost; seal with a rubber band. Make a polythene tunnel over plants outdoors by supporting some polythene sheeting with wire and then sealing the ends.

Composts

Basically a compost is a soil substitute for propagating and establishing plants. To carry out this function a compost requires certain properties—to be well aerated, to retain water, to hold nutrients and to conduct warmth. Thus in constituting a compost the components used should be chosen to establish these particular conditions as well as maintaining them throughout the life of the compost. In order to prevent the occurrence of pests, diseases and weeds the component materials should also be sterile.

The only component of a compost that is not initially sterile is the loam. To sterilize it place the loam in a broad, flat container such as a meat tin and put in the oven at 82°C/180°F for 30 minutes. Best results are obtained if the loam is dryish and if the tin is covered with foil so that the steam generated encourages the sterilizing effect. Cool and riddle the loam before use.

Cuttings compost

The formulation of a compost for rooting cuttings really only requires two considerations: the retention of sufficient moisture to help prevent desiccation of the cutting, and the provision of an aerating agent so that air can always circulate within the medium.

Conventionally, peat has been used as the water-retentive component and, although various peats are available, sphagnum moss peat is best as it retains a good structure for a long period. For most reliable use and to achieve uniformity it should be riddled through a $\frac{1}{4}$ in sieve.

Sand is used as the aerating agent, and it also allows adequate drainage—peat by itself tending to become waterlogged. In horticultural parlance sand usually means grit, and for these purposes a washed and crushed lime-free grit providing a particle size of between $\frac{1}{8}$ in and $\frac{1}{16}$ in across is the most desirable. The particles should also be "sharp", that is they should not be rounded but have points and corners and thus be irregular in shape.

Although these two components provide the basic compost they can be substituted with such items as sedge peat, well-weathered sawdust, perlite, vermiculite and graded coal dust—in fact by any material that has suitable physical properties, and that is chemically inactive and biologically more or less sterile.

Cuttings composts are usually formulated by evenly mixing equal parts by volume of peat and grit, although it is often difficult to assess how much sieved peat there is in a particular mix. In the end there is no substitute to determining the "feel" of the compost and whether it has the right properties.

Compost for germinating seedlings

The composition of a compost for seedling germination does not differ greatly from that produced for cuttings, except that a little more attention needs to be paid to the nutrient and chemical aspects.

The basic components are peat and sand and for germination pure and simple this is sufficient. However if the seedlings are to remain in the compost for some time, add loam to act as a buffer in holding nutrients and controlling drying out. The amount of sterilized loam required need not be great: a formula of 2 parts by volume peat, 2 parts sand and 1 part loam is satisfactory.

As seeds are much more sensitive to the acidity in such a compost, lime in the form of ground chalk or ground limestone should be mixed in with the sand at the rate of $1\frac{1}{2}$ oz per bushel of compost.

Although it is not usual to include complicated nutrient mixes in seed composts, it is important to ensure that sufficient phosphate is available. Therefore also mix $\frac{3}{4}$ oz superphosphate per bushel of compost in with the sand.

Potting composts for growing on young plants

The formulation of composts for the establishment and growing on of young plants follows on from seed composts in much the same pattern. It is necessary to prepare a compost that allows the development of a root system; contains adequate water to support the plants and sufficient nutrients not to check growth; has a suitable acidity/alkalinity status; and does not dry out too easily.

Nowadays such composts are based on the use of peat, although traditionally the John Innes concepts were based on the use of sterilized loam. The recommendation of loam as a base for composts has had to be discontinued because it is no longer feasible to obtain a standard material on which a recipe can be formulated. Peat is capable of being relatively standardized and so currently forms the basis. It is important, however, to realize that loam has a steadying and controlling influence on both water and nutrient availability that peat does not provide, and so peat-based (that is, loamless) composts require a higher degree of management and maintenance. Therefore it is prudent to use loam as a minor component merely to provide the buffering action and so ease management. In practice the aim is to produce a loamless compost with added loam!

Young plants also need nutrient in the compost and this should be added at the rate of 4 oz fertilizer base per bushel of compost unless the manufacturer recommends otherwise.

There are, of course, many available proprietary brands of peat-based composts, all of which have been tried and tested successfully. Their main disadvantage is their capacity for drying out and the difficulty of rewetting a dried compost, although this latter factor is less of a problem if a wetting agent has been incorporated. Their chief advantage is that they are ready mixed and come packed in handy-sized plastic bags.

If a peat-based compost proves difficult to rewet, then add a small quantity of wetting agent or spreader such as soft soap. Do not use washing-up liquids.

How to mix composts

The important aspect of mixing compost is to obtain an even and uniform end product. Thorough mixing of the ingredients is essential. It is also easier if you have a bushel or half-bushel box on which to base the formula as lime and fertilizers are normally added at a bushel rate. (A bushel is the amount that will fit into a box 22 in × 10 in × 10 in without compacting.)

Evenly layer the ingredients into a pile on a clean concrete floor. The lime and fertilizers should be sprinkled into each sand layer. The whole should then be well mixed with a clean shovel.

INGREDIENTS FOR VARIOUS COMPOSTS
(parts by volume)

Cuttings compost
Equal parts peat (sieved) and sand ($\frac{1}{8}$—$\frac{1}{16}$ in grade)

Compost for germinating seedlings
2 parts peat (sieved)
2 parts sand ($\frac{1}{8}$—$\frac{1}{16}$ in grade)
1 part loam (sterilized)
and $1\frac{1}{2}$ oz ground limestone
and $\frac{3}{4}$ oz superphosphate
per bushel of compost

Potting composts for young plants
JOHN INNES No. 1 POTTING COMPOST
7 parts loam (sterilized)
3 parts peat (sieved)
2 parts sand ($\frac{1}{8}$—$\frac{1}{16}$ in grade)
and $\frac{3}{4}$ oz ground limestone
and 4 oz J. I. fertilizer base
per bushel of compost

LOAMLESS POTTING COMPOST
3 parts peat (sieved)
1 part sand ($\frac{1}{8}$—$\frac{1}{16}$ in grade)
and 4 oz any fertilizer base
and 4 oz ground limestone
per bushel of compost

LOAMLESS POTTING COMPOST WITH LOAM
7 parts peat (sieved)
2 parts sand ($\frac{1}{8}$—$\frac{1}{16}$ in grade)
1 part loam (sterilized)
and 4 oz any fertilizer base
and 4 oz ground limestone
per bushel of compost

For ericaceous composts, omit lime.

SIEVING PEAT

Riddle peat through a $\frac{1}{4}$ in sieve before mixing thoroughly with other ingredients to make the required compost.

Rooting hormones/Wounding

Certain chemicals will promote or regulate growth responses in plants when used in minute dosages, and they are used by gardeners not only for plant propagation but also to achieve a variety of other responses, such as encouraging fruit trusses to set.

These plant-growth regulating substances work at very low concentrations and within very critical limits; a substance that sets fruits at one concentration and produces roots on stem cuttings at another may be used as a weedkiller at yet another. Thus it is exceedingly important to follow dosage instructions exactly in order to obtain the desired results.

It is also important to realize that these chemicals do not constitute a panacea for success: they will not induce rooting responses if the inherent ability of the stem to produce roots is not present. Their action is merely to enhance the innate capacity of the stem to produce its roots both in greater quantities and quicker than might otherwise have been the case. If the stem cutting is propagated from a healthy plant and at the correct season, then the use of such hormones is usually of no advantage whatsoever. They should be used with knowledge, and only as and when they are likely to achieve an effect.

The majority of rooting hormones available on the market are constituted as powders, the base simply being finely ground talc. Talcum powder is used because it is extremely soft and it lacks an abrasive quality, so causing no damage to the cutting. Mixed in with the talcum powder is the rooting hormone. Normally this is a chemical, β-indolyl-butyric acid, known as IBA. Occasionally either IAA (β-indolyl-acetic acid) or NAA (naphthoxy-acetic acid) is substituted. The concentration for hardwood cutting propagation is normally 0.8 per cent IBA in talc; softwood concentrations are usually much less—about a quarter of this figure. All-purpose hormone powders are usually based on NAA.

In many cases fungicidal chemicals are also incorporated into the powders, so helping against any rots that may develop in the cuttings.

Rooting hormones are also made up in liquid formulations, where the chemicals are dissolved either in water or in an organic solvent such as alcohol.

It is important to emphasize that these hormones should not be used on either leaf or root cuttings. For these cuttings chemicals are not yet commercially available to aid regeneration.

How to apply rooting hormones

In order to know how to apply rooting hormones, it is important to understand one or two basic premises. Firstly, that the concentration of hormone applied to induce root formation is not the best concentration to cause root development. Secondly, although the hormone may be absorbed through the bark, most of the hormone will be taken up through the cut base of the stem cutting.

In actually applying the hormone therefore take care to touch only the basal cut surface on to the powder so that no powder adheres to the outside of the stem; do not dip the cutting even as deep as 1 in.

By applying the hormone the roots are induced to form, but if they emerge and come into contact with the hormone still on the bark this may cause the roots to die off. In many cases this does not happen totally, but it may cause losses in some plants or under certain conditions; it is prudent to adopt a system that is suitable for all plants.

If there is difficulty in getting sufficient hormone powder to adhere to the cut surface at the base of the cutting then the cutting should first be dipped in water. This is an especially valuable hint with softwood cuttings, which will benefit from the water anyway.

Make up water-based formulations by dissolving a pill in a specified amount of water. Then stand the base of the cutting in the solution for 12–24 hours. As the concentration of water-based rooting hormones is much lower than powder-based ones, the bark is not adversely affected and so the cutting can be left standing in any depth of the solution.

If an alcohol-based solution is used, dip the base of the cutting in solution and allow to drain so that the alcohol can evaporate, leaving the hormone on the cuttings.

Correct way to apply rooting hormones

Incorrect method

1 Dip the base of a stem cutting into water.

2 Push the base of the cutting on to the hormone powder.

Ensure no hormone powder adheres to the outside of the stem cutting.

WOUNDING STEM CUTTINGS

Since certain chemicals are capable of enhancing root production on a stem cutting, it is possible that other techniques may also cause a surge in natural hormone production that could improve rooting.

In some plants there exists in the stem between the bark tissues and the wood tissues a sheath of material that is capable of inhibiting root development. However, when part of this sheath is damaged, then roots will be produced normally. This damage is achieved by a technique known as wounding.

The commonest method of wounding is to remove a slice of bark from the bottom inch or so of the cutting, using a sharp knife so that the wood tissues are just exposed. Alternatively make three or four 1 in long incisions in the bark at the base of the cutting as deep as the wood tissues.

The technique of wounding can be very effective with rhododendron, daphne and juniper, but it is unwise to use it as a matter of course as it provides another possible site for infection and rotting. It may only be necessary on older, hardwood cuttings; softwood cuttings do not normally require wounding. The need to wound a cutting will only be discovered in the light of experience—a continued failure to root a cutting, which cannot be attributed to any other cause, may then suggest that the cutting may respond to wounding.

Fertilizers

Nitrogen deficiency
Slow, stunted growth;
pale green leaves

Iron deficiency
Yellowing of young
leaves

Phosphate deficiency
Stunted growth; red
or purple leaves

Potassium deficiency
Pale yellow or brown
leaves

Magnesium deficiency
Yellowing of older
leaves

There is much misunderstanding of the role that plant nutrients play in the growth of the plant and hence they are often misused in the propagation and establishment phases of plant production.

The three so-called major elements that are required for successful plant growth are nitrogen, potassium and phosphorus. These materials are needed in addition to carbon, hydrogen and oxygen as the basic building blocks of plant material. At a secondary level elements such as calcium, sulphur and magnesium are needed in fair quantities, while trace elements, which include iron, manganese, boron, molybdenum and cobalt, are used by the plant in small to minute quantities.

Nitrogen is required wherever and whenever plant growth is anticipated. A shortage of available nitrogen is typified by the slow, stunted development of the plant and pale green leaves. It is usually taken up by the plant in the form of either nitrate or ammonium salts. Nitrogen's role in the plant is predominantly as a basic ingredient of protein and it is thus a necessary feature of developing new plant tissue. Often it is referred to as being "important for leafy growth", which is essentially true because leaves constitute a major part of plant tissue; however it is equally a necessary component of stem, root, flower and seed production. As a protein component it is also a vital feature of chromosome development.

The role of potassium in the plant is rather less easily explained. Potash, as it is commonly called, is needed as a catalyst wherever chemical reactions occur. It is especially associated with the food-making process of photosynthesis and with supplying nourishment around the plant. This again explains its general association with "leafy growth". However potash is equally important in virtually all parts of the plant where chemical reactions are occurring. Potassium deficiency in plants is usually manifest when the edges of the leaves turn pale yellow, and as this discoloration moves inwards the outer edges turn brown and appear scorched.

Phosphorus, which is normally used in the form of phosphate, has two major roles to fulfil in plant growth. Firstly it is an essential

component of those very specialized proteins that constitute the chromosomes. Secondly it is the basis on which the energy needed for plant growth and development is collected, transported and released within the various chemical reactions of the plant. A phosphate shortage is much more difficult and uncertain to describe especially when it is only a marginal amount, but generally stunted growth associated with a purple or red leaf discoloration is a typical symptom; however a similar situation often arises with root damage caused by pests or rots.

Most other plant nutrients occur in sufficient quantities as minor components or impurities in the main fertilizers, and they do not specifically need to be applied as individual fertilizers.

The only two nutrients that may cause problems are magnesium and iron. The prime role of magnesium is in the formation of chlorophyll, the green colouring in the plant. A lack of it is typified by a yellowing of the older leaves as the plant transfers magnesium from its older parts to its newly created parts so causing the "chlorosis" in the old leaves.

Iron has a similar function to magnesium but it is not reusable in the plant. Its deficiency causes the young leaves to turn yellow although the veins remain green, and by this characteristic it is possible to distinguish a shortage of this element from a magnesium deficiency.

The correct use of fertilizer

It is important to ensure that sufficient nutrients are available to young plants. If composts are correctly formulated they should contain an adequate amount. However, seedlings, for example, are germinated in a compost containing only phosphate; as soon as they begin to show green leaves they will benefit from feeding with nitrogen and potash to encourage growth.

Although it is possible for the gardener to make up his own soluble feed it is far simpler and much more reliable to use one of the several proprietary brands of liquid feeds that are readily available. If a plant shows signs of, for example, potash deficiency, buy a proprietary brand of liquid fertilizer with a high balance of that particular

nutrient, and not one with only that nutrient in it, and use it as recommended.

Organic fertilizers such as bone meal, dried blood and hoof and horn are too slow acting to have any real beneficial effect on a plant with a nutrient deficiency.

In the closed environment of pot or seed tray, inorganic fertilizers such as nitrate of soda, sulphate of ammonia, sulphate of iron, sulphate of potash and superphosphate should also be avoided as they may have too drastic a chemical effect on the plant and also upset the balance of the other nutrients.

If the gardener is plagued with regular magnesium deficiency substitute magnesian limestone (Dolomite limestone) for ordinary limestone in the compost.

Acid-loving plants and ericaceous ones such as heathers and rhododendrons are liable to have an iron shortage and this can be treated with a chelated iron compound either in the compost or as a foliar feed.

When applying a foliar fertilizer, always follow the manufacturer's instructions exactly. Water the nutrients over the plant's leaves using a fine rose.

APPLYING A FERTILIZER

Make up a non-foliar fertilizer according to the manufacturer's instructions. Then water on to the compost, protecting the plant's leaves with the hand. Alternatively, place the plant pot in a bowl. Pour in a dilute solution of fertilizer. Leave overnight to absorb.

Sowing in containers

To assist with germination and the establishment of a new plant, it is often helpful to soak seeds in water for 12–24 hours before being sown in a compost that will provide adequate aeration, sufficient water-holding capacity, a neutral acidity/alkalinity reaction and sufficient phosphate. Thus a "sowing" or "seed" compost should be used.

Before choosing a pot, pan or tray decide how much seed is to be sown; the container should be large enough to allow the seedlings space to develop to the size at which they are to be pricked out.

Heap the container with compost and then, to ensure it is evenly distributed and there are no air locks, very lightly firm it to the corners and base using the fingers. Do not compact the compost.

Using a sawing action, strike off the compost with a presser board or other piece of wood so that it is level with the top of the container. Then with a presser board that fits into the container, lightly and evenly firm the compost to $\frac{1}{4}$–$\frac{3}{8}$ in below the rim, ensuring that the surface is level.

The container is now prepared for sowing. The seeds should be sown evenly over the surface either by station sowing large seeds or gently shaking small seeds direct from the packet. When shaking, keep the packet low over the compost to prevent the seeds from bouncing and giving an uneven distribution.

If the seeds are very fine it is easier to distribute them evenly, and see where they are sown, if they are mixed thoroughly with some dry fine sand. Sow the seeds by shaking across the container, using about half the seeds; then turn the container through 90 degrees and sow the rest of the seeds in the same way.

Gently shake some compost over the container through a $\frac{1}{8}$ in sieve so that an even and uniform layer covers the seeds. As a general rule seeds do not need to be covered by compost deeper than their own thickness.

Finally label the seeds and water them in by standing the container in a shallow bath of water so that the water moves up by capillary action. Do not stand the container in so much water that it overflows the rim on to the seeds and compost. After watering stand out to drain.

Alternatively water the compost from above, using a watering can with a fine rose. Start pouring the water away from the container and once an even flow is attained direct it over the seeds; similarly, to stop, move the water away from the container and then stop the flow, so that no drops fall on to the compost.

Cover the container with a piece of glass and place in a warm dark place, for example an airing cupboard. Otherwise, cover with glass and a sheet of paper and leave in any warm (21°C/70°F) environment.

1 Soak large seeds in water for 12–24 hours before sowing in compost.

2 Fill a container with compost until it is heaped above the rim.

3 Firm the compost into the corners and base using the tips of the fingers.

4 Strike off the compost using a sawing action until it is level with the rim.

5 Firm the compost lightly to $\frac{1}{4}$–$\frac{3}{8}$ in below the rim using a presser board.

6 Sow half the seeds across the container, keeping hand low to prevent bouncing.

7 Turn container through 90 degrees. Sow the remaining seeds.

8 Cover the seeds by sieving on compost, keeping the sieve low over the seeds.

9 Label the seeds with their full name and date of sowing.

10 Water in the seeds from above the compost, using a can with a fine rose.

11 Cover the container with a pane of glass to keep the seeds moist and warm.

12 Place a sheet of paper over the glass to minimize temperature fluctuations.

The developing seed 1

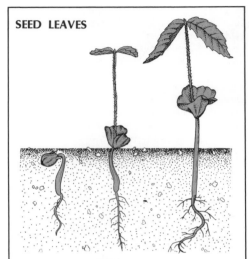

SEED LEAVES

When the seed begins to germinate, the embryo produces a root and seed leaves. These seed leaves are usually different to the true leaves that will follow.

Germination

The germination of seeds covers the entire process, from subjecting a resting seed to suitable conditions to cause it to develop to the stage at which the seedling produces true leaves and establishes as a young plant. If a seed is subjected to the conditions required for germination, and it fails to germinate, despite the fact that it is alive, then the seed is described as being dormant.

Water is vital to allow plant growth to get under way. So, if the seed has not been soaked before sowing, it is important that the compost should be watered immediately after sowing.

Once the seed has sufficiently imbibed, the embryo inside the seed begins to produce root and stem systems, which eventually break out of the seed.

To grow, the embryo uses its food reserves. When oxygen is combined with carbohydrates in these food reserves, the energy necessary for growth is produced. Thus the germinating seed will have a massive oxygen requirement, which can only be satisfied by a well-aerated environment within the compost.

All growth processes within the seed are chemical reactions activated by the addition of water. To develop successfully, the seed needs an increasing quantity of water, and the compost must be capable of holding these amounts.

As all the processes involved are basically chemical reactions they will obey normal physical rules, the simplest of which implies that the higher the temperature is raised, the faster will be the rate of the reaction. In practice, this means that the warmer seeds are kept, the quicker they will germinate. As all these reactions are taking place in a biological context, there are biological limitations as to how high the temperature can be raised. In practice there are also economic considerations, because high temperatures are costly to maintain. Experience suggests that a germination temperature of 21°C/70°F is a reasonable compromise for most flower and vegetable seeds, and this is why an airing cupboard is an excellent place for seeds to germinate.

Protection

To keep seeds moist and warm, cover the container with a sheet of glass so that water condenses on the glass and falls back into the compost. To minimize temperature fluctuations cover the glass with a sheet of paper.

As soon as the seedlings emerge, both paper and glass should be removed. Spray the seedlings regularly with water and place them in a well-lit area, out of strong direct sunlight to avoid scorching.

Spray germinating seeds with Cheshunt compound fungicides regularly or they may succumb to damping-off diseases.

If the seedlings are to be kept in their container for some time they should be given a liquid feed diluted according to manufacturer's instructions, because many seed composts contain only a phosphate fertilizer.

Pricking out

As soon as seedlings can be handled, transplant them into a more suitable compost, leaving enough space for unrestricted

The developing seed

1 Remove the glass and sheet of paper as soon as the seedlings appear. Place in a well-lit area.

2 Spray seedlings regularly with water, but do not allow compost to become waterlogged.

3 Water in a fungicide to prevent or contain any outbreak of damping-off diseases.

Pricking out

4 Knock the sides of the container on the work bench to loosen the compost and seedlings.

5 Loosen the compost further with the dibber, lifting a clump of seedlings.

6 Lift one seedling free of compost by holding its seed leaves and gently pulling.

The developing seed 2

development of the young plants. This is known as pricking out or potting on.

Fill a container with John Innes No. 1 compost or a compost of similar structure (see page 158), and firm to the base with the tips of the fingers. Strike off compost level with the rim. Lightly firm with presser board so that the compost is $\frac{1}{4}$–$\frac{3}{8}$ in below the rim of the container, which is now prepared.

Water the seedlings; then loosen them by knocking the old container so that the compost comes away from the sides. Hold a seedling by its seed leaf and gently lift with the aid of a dibber, keeping its root system intact. Never hold the seedling by its stem.

With the dibber, make a hole in the fresh compost big enough to take the roots. Drop in the seedling and gently firm the compost back round the roots with the dibber. Repeat this operation for each seedling, spacing at 24–40 seedlings per tray.

After the tray has been filled, water in the seedlings and return them to the warm environment (21°C/70°F) so that they can re-establish as quickly as possible.

Hardening off

After the seedlings have been pricked out, they have to be gradually weaned to a stage at which they can be planted out and survive cool temperatures, fluctuating water conditions and the effects of wind without their growth rate being affected. In the plant world this process is generally referred to as hardening off.

Most seedlings will have been germinated in a protected environment during the early part of the year to produce a plant of sufficient size to be planted out as soon as the danger of frost is passed. Because so many seedlings are produced in the early part of the year, and they are not hardy, and in most gardens there is a premium on any space that provides sufficient protection, plants tend to be grown at a high density.

The problem with crowding plants together is that an increase in fungal diseases both on the stems and leaves and in the compost is likely to result; the plants tend to become spindly as they compete for light; and the varying plants have different watering needs

so more day-to-day care and attention are needed, which is of course time consuming.

Once the pricked-out seedlings have re-established, move them to a cooler environment. For this purpose there is no real substitute for a cold frame, which should be kept firmly closed. Over the course of a few weeks increasingly air the frame during the day by raising the lid, until the frame is continually aired during the day and night: indeed the lid may be completely removed during the day if it is warm. Eventually the lid can be discarded altogether.

Frosts as severe as −4°C/25°F are sufficient to penetrate into the cold frame, so, if this level of cold is expected, provide some insulation to protect half-hardy plants. The best and most easily manageable insulation should be light yet thick; coir matting and similar materials are useful and effective.

Regularly check the seedlings in the frame to ensure that they are not drying out excessively. They should not however receive too much water. If anything it is better to err on the side of dryness rather than risk water-

logging. Under these cooler conditions wet composts are increasingly susceptible to fungal root rots. Similarly, the close density of plants creates conditions under which leaf diseases are capable of taking hold.

Another aspect of seedling management is the necessity for feeding. Many pricked-out seedlings will spend several weeks in the potting compost before being finally transplanted, and there is no point in starving them and preventing them developing to an adequate size. Thus the seedlings should be regularly fed using a proprietary liquid fertilizer at the intervals stated on the manufacturer's instructions. Avoid excessive feeding as it will produce over-vigorous plants that will check their growth on transplanting; it will also increase the risk of disease in the cold frame.

Hardening off

7 Hold the seedling in one hand. Make a hole with the dibber in the fresh compost in a new container.

8 Place the seedling in the hole and firm the compost back with the dibber.

9 Water in the seedlings once the seed tray is completed. Place in a warm (21°C/70°F) area.

10 Cover cold frame with coir matting to insulate seedlings against damage caused by frost radiation.

11 Raise the cold frame lid to allow the seedlings to harden off.

12 Water, using a fine rose, to ensure seedlings do not dry out. Add a fungicide and liquid feed regularly.

Root cuttings 1

Some plants propagated successfully from root cuttings

ALPINE PLANTS		Eryngium	Romneya	Rhus (sumach)	Robinia
Anchusa	Morisia	Limonium		Rubus	
Anemone	Primula denticulata	Papaver	SHRUBS		CLIMBERS
Arnebia	Pulsatilla	Phlox	Aesculus parviflora	TREES	Bignonia
Carduncellus	Verbascum	Statice	Aralia	Acacia (mimosa)—some species	Campsis
Erodium		Verbascum	Chaenomeles	Ailanthus (tree of heaven)	Eccremocarpus
Geranium	HERBACEOUS PLANTS		Clerodendrum	Catalpa (Indian bean tree)	Passiflora
Lactuca	Acanthus	SUB-SHRUBS	Daphne genkwa	Koelreuteria	
	Anchusa	Dendromecon	Prunus (plum and blackthorn)	Paulownia	

When to take root cuttings

When propagating plants from root cuttings it is vital to understand how seasonality affects the capacity of root cuttings to produce stem buds.

The subject of "on" and "off" seasons appears to have been virtually unconsidered until the mid-twentieth century. However, recent research has established that fluctuations in the ability of roots to produce stem buds do exist and that it is pointless to propagate while the plant's response is inhibited by adverse seasonal influences.

It is this fluctuation in the capacity to propagate that has probably produced the uncertainty which has led to the propagation of plants from root cuttings being virtually ignored by nearly all gardeners.

It is therefore necessary to determine whether the plant from which root cuttings are required does have different seasonal responses, and, if so, what is the best time to take cuttings.

Without prior guidance, the natural inclination for the gardener would be to take such cuttings in the growing season, but experience has shown that this has met with little success; although results sometimes improved if cuttings were taken very early or very late in the season.

A few plants can produce new plants equally well at any time of the year, but these are relatively uncommon. Perhaps the best example is the horseradish, which can make itself into a pernicious weed by virtue of this characteristic: when the roots are broken, it is capable of establishing itself as a new plant from each root piece.

Virtually all other plants demonstrate a seasonal response. Early observations suggested that plants propagated most successfully during the winter, but experience has shown that, although this is typically true for woody plants, the real feature is not the winter but the dormant season. Many herbaceous plants and more especially alpine plants are not necessarily dormant during the winter. Some alpines, for example the Pasque flower (*Pulsatilla vulgaris*), start growing in the new year and if root cuttings are made after this period they do not respond; success is only achieved during their dormant season, which is in the late summer and early autumn.

Although propagation from root cuttings is likely to succeed throughout a plant's dormant season, it is best to keep to the mid-part of that season, as a maximum response may not exist while the dormancy is still developing or once it is phasing out.

Preparing the plant

Before propagating from root cuttings, it is preferable to prepare the parent plant itself so that it will develop roots that will have a high capacity to regenerate stem buds and so produce new plants.

This ability to produce adventitious stem buds on a severed root is already present in most plants, but it can be enhanced. Lift a healthy plant prior to the growing season and shorten any top growth. Reduce its root system by cutting off the roots close to the crown of the plant, using a knife. Then return the plant to the ground. The pruning upsets the natural root/shoot balance of the plant, and it will grow quickly during the following season to bring the plant back to its normal equilibrium between root and shoot. As a result of this treatment the vigorous, quickly grown roots will exhibit a very high level of ability to develop stem buds.

The roots will have developed fastest at the beginning of the season, and the rate will gradually have declined as the season progressed until, as the dormant season approached, growth will have ceased altogether. At the point where any root started its growth in the spring, and where it grew fastest, will also be where it has the greatest capacity to produce buds; in other words, there is a direct correlation between the rate at which a root grows and its ability to produce stem buds. If, therefore, plenty of root material is available, it is best to take a root cutting only from the top of the root where it began its development in the early spring.

In order to obtain cutting material, lift the parent plant and shorten any top growth. Wash it free of soil either in a bucket of water, or by hosing it down. It is then possible to distinguish the young roots which are suitable for propagation. Cut these close to the crown

Preparing the plant

1 Lift a healthy plant from the ground during the dormant season.

2 Cut back any top growth. Shake any excess earth off the roots.

3 Wash the roots in a bucket of water or hose them clean.

4 Cut off the roots close to the crown, using a sharp knife.

5 Return the plant to its position in the garden.

6 Leave the plant to re-establish during the growing season.

Root cuttings 2

of the plant, at right angles to the root. Return the parent plant to the garden.

Discard the thin root end by slicing with a sloping cut. Slice off any fibrous lateral roots on the cutting to ease handling and planting later on.

The removal of roots from the parent plant for propagation will have had the additional effect of root pruning and so will cause the development of further roots for propagation in the ensuing propagating season.

Size of a root cutting
The size of a root cutting may not be critical if only one cutting is made from each root, but, with roots that regenerate readily and from which it is possible to make more than one cutting, the optimum size of a root cutting becomes very important. It is therefore necessary to determine the minimum size for a root cutting so that maximum use can be made of the available root.

The size of the root cutting depends on two factors. Firstly, the cutting requires sufficient food to initiate and develop a stem bud to the stage at which it produces green leaves and can begin to support itself. Secondly, the cutting requires sufficient food reserves to support itself while this regenerative process is going on.

The size of the cutting, therefore, is made up of the regenerative portion and the survival portion. The size of the survival portion depends on how long the cutting will take to regenerate, and this is reliant on the temperature in which the cutting is propagated: the warmer 'the environment the quicker the stem will develop. A root cutting taken and planted in the open ground during the winter may not produce a shoot until May, but if it had been placed in a propagator in a temperature of 18°–24°C/65°–75°F, it might well have regenerated in about four weeks. The amount of food reserve required for survival between these two temperature environments is dramatically different.

The size of the regenerative portion needed, however, will remain constant whatever the temperature of the propagating environment, so a rule of thumb measurement for the size of a root cutting is based on the variable factor—temperature.

As a plant's roots will have been pruned a year before the cuttings are taken, all roots will show one year's growth and therefore be approximately the same thickness. Thus the cutting length is unaffected.

An open-ground cutting should be at least 4 in long as it will need to survive for some 16 weeks. A cold frame/cold greenhouse provides a warmer environment, and regeneration will occur in about eight weeks and so a smaller survival portion is required and the cuttings need only be just over 2 in long. In a warm (18°–24°C/65°–75°F) greenhouse or propagator, regeneration time is reduced to four weeks, halving the survival time and the required food reserve once again so that in this environment root cuttings need only be about 1 in long.

Recognizing the top of a root cutting
When propagating plants from root cuttings it is very important to notice the "polarity" of the cutting—that it has a top and a bottom and therefore a "right way up". Most people suggest that root cuttings should be planted horizontally because the cuttings have been made in such a way that the top and bottom cannot be recognized, and there is no other way in which polarity can be recognized because roots have no leaves and axillary buds. However, stem cuttings are not planted on their·side, so it is unreasonable to expect root cuttings to be, no matter in what direction their roots subsequently grow. Cuttings planted vertically and the correct way up will usually develop to a maximum level provided that the cuttings were taken from a healthy plant and they were given suitable conditions (see page 40). Cuttings planted on their side rarely achieve more than a 40 per cent success rate.

In order to recognize the top of a root (that is, the end nearest the crown of the plant) so it can be planted the right way up, make a flat cut at right angles to the root where it was severed from its parent; at the bottom end cut away the thin portion using a sloping cut. Always cut roots in this way so, whatever subsequently happens to the root cutting, it will be possible to recognize its correct polarity and so ensure that it is planted the right way up.

Obtaining cutting material

7 Lift the plant in the middle of the dormant season. Cut any top growth.

8 Wash its roots. Then cut off the young roots close to the crown and set aside.

9 Return the plant to its usual position in the garden.

Taking a root cutting

10 Cut off any fibrous lateral roots on undamaged young roots.

11 Make a right-angled cut on a root where it was severed from its parent.

12 Cut away the thin root end at the appropriate length, using a sloping cut.

Root cuttings 3

Treatment
After all the initial aspects have been considered and the root cutting has been made, the next step is to consider the question of what treatment the cutting may need in order to enhance its chances of producing a stem bud and then surviving until the bud develops and establishes as a new plant. At present there are no growth-promoting substances available for root cuttings, so that it is not possible to enhance bud production in this way. The special powders produced for inducing roots on stems should not be used on root cuttings as they will actually depress bud production.

Planting
Root cuttings need to be planted in a medium that will support them, prevent them from drying out, allow adequate aeration and, when regeneration starts, provide basic nutrients. All these features can be found in the ground outdoors and the root cuttings will do well there provided that the soil is reasonably light or they are placed under a cold frame in soil to which peat and grit have been added. However, except perhaps for a few very vigorous herbaceous perennials, it is more convenient to plant root cuttings in a container and then plant them out just as soon as they are established.

Select a container of suitable size for the number of root cuttings to be propagated, allowing 1–1½ in for each cutting. For example, plant seven cuttings in a 3½ in pot. Fill the container with a peat-based compost containing loam, which will act as a buffer to prevent excessive drying and will maintain an even level of nutrients. Strike off the compost with a presser board so that it is level with the rim. Then press the soil down to at least ⅜ in below the rim of the container.

Make a hole in the compost with a dibber and then plant the root cutting. Place the top of the cutting just level with the top of the compost. Firm back the compost around the cutting. Space the remaining root cuttings evenly round the container.

Cover the cuttings with grit. Strike off with a presser board until the grit is level with the rim of the container. This weight of grit tends to compress the compost slightly so causing the tops of the cuttings to be pushed further up into the grit. This will provide almost perfect aeration for the bud that will develop at the top of the root cutting. Do not water. Label the container and stand it in an environment (propagator, cold frame, etc.) that is appropriate to the size of the root cutting (see page 165).

Some plants, for example *Romneya coulteri*, do not like being dug up and having their roots disturbed. Therefore, place only one or two of their root cuttings in a small pot and treat as one plant, disturbing their roots as little as possible when transplanting them once they are established.

Aftercare
Keep watering to a minimum to maintain a well-aerated compost, which encourages bud development and reduces the likelihood of rotting. In fact there is probably no need to water at all if the root cuttings were initially planted in a reasonably moist compost and a humid environment is maintained.

Very often when the bud first develops, it produces a stem and green leaves but no root system. This will grow later from the base of the new stem. Even if the new roots do develop from the cutting, they too will not appear until after the stem and green leaves have grown. Do not water until the roots appear as the cutting is still liable to rot.

Place in a well-lit area once the stem appears. Harden off any young plants propagated in a warm (21°C/70°F) environment before planting out or potting up. Apply a liquid feed, according to the manufacturer's instructions.

Planting root cuttings

1 Fill a pot with compost. Make a hole with a dibber. Plant cutting vertically.

2 Plant remaining root cuttings 1–1½ in apart. Cover the pot with grit.

3 Strike off the grit until level with rim. Label, and leave cuttings to develop.

4 Do not water until the roots have appeared. Then apply a liquid feed.

Tuberous roots

Some herbaceous perennial plants die back to a crown of buds each dormant season, and their roots are modified to store food. These specialized swollen roots are described as tuberous roots. They can be distinguished from modified stems by their structure and from root cuttings by their inability to produce adventitious buds on isolated roots and so grow a new plant.

There are two basic kinds of tuberous roots: those that develop annually, such as on dahlias, and those that are perennial and simply increase in size, such as on begonias.

Annual tuberous roots develop from lateral roots at the crown of the plant. During the growing season, certain of these develop as food stores, swelling up and producing a cluster of such roots. Each year the new shoot system develops at the expense of the food store in the tuberous roots, which eventually die and disintegrate.

Perennial tuberous roots are much simpler in their development. Usually the emerging radicle of the seedling begins to modify as a food storage organ, and this increases in size as and when food is available.

The division of tuberous roots is not a widely used technique as many plants with tuberous roots can be propagated more satisfactorily by stem, leaf and leaf-bud cuttings. Success depends on how well the roots are stored. Lift the plant at the end of the growing season. Clean the crowns and dust with sulphur. Wrap each plant in thick newspaper and place in a frost free environment, below 5°C/42°F.

Just before the growing season, divide the tuberous roots into portions, each with at least one crown bud, from which the new stem will develop. Protect all cut surfaces from rotting by dusting with dry bordeaux powder or sulphur such as Thiram or Captan. Then place the divisions in a warm (21°C/70°F), dry, airy area for a couple of days so that the cut surfaces seal themselves quickly by developing a corky layer of tissue, to give added protection. Pot up the divisions in John Innes No. 1 compost if they are to be transplanted within a month or so; otherwise plant them in John Innes No. 2 compost. Label them; do not water. Place in a frost-free area. Set in the light once a shoot appears.

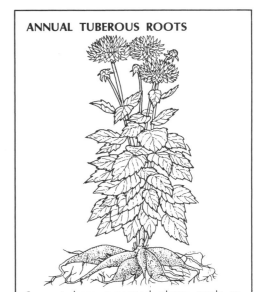

PERENNIAL TUBEROUS ROOTS

Plants such as begonias have only one tuberous root, which is perennial and extends sideways each year.

ANNUAL TUBEROUS ROOTS

Some tuberous rooted plants such as dahlias produce annual storage roots that die and disintegrate after one season.

1 Lift a plant at the end of the growing season. Clean the crowns thoroughly.

2 Dust the entire crowns with a fungicidal powder. Lift on to some newspaper.

3 Wrap up the plant. Store in a frost-free place until the buds begin to swell.

4 Divide the swollen roots into portions, each with at least one crown bud.

5 Dust all cut surfaces with fungicide. Leave in a warm, dry, airy place.

6 Pot up the cuttings once the cut surfaces have formed a corky layer.

Tubers

The name "tuber" in horticultural terms has been much misused and has on occasions covered almost any swollen food storage organ that is chiefly underground.

A tuber is, in fact, a swollen underground stem, modified as a food storage organ. It often is of roundish (usually terminating) growth and is normally annual. The leaves are scaly and membranous, and the axillary buds provide the following year's shoots.

Within these limitations the number of plants producing true tubers is not very great. The commonest is the potato. Those plants, such as Jerusalem artichokes, that produce opposite rather than spirally arranged buds, such as potatoes, often have a knobbly shape. Some water lilies (*Nymphaea* sp.) produce small tuber-like structures that develop from the main rootstock towards the end of the growing season.

Although potatoes are prolific producers of tubers, this is unusual. Normally, plants that develop tubers do so only in very small numbers.

Any increase in numbers must be achieved artificially. As the tuber is normally an organ that allows a plant to survive its dormant period, the season to propagate tubers by artificial division should be just before growth would commence in the spring.

Cut the tuber with a sharp knife so that each piece has at least one good dominant bud or "eye". Then dust all the cut surfaces with a fungicide such as dry bordeaux powder to reduce the possibility of fungal infection. Stand the pieces on a wire tray and keep in a warm (21°C/70°F), dry environment, for example an airing cupboard, for a couple of days. A protective corky layer, which enhances their survival, will then develop. These tuber "seeds" should not be kept in the dry for any longer than necessary, otherwise the tuber itself will desiccate.

Therefore plant them out immediately in a hole twice their depth. They will then quickly produce roots and shoots and establish as a new plant. Label them clearly at all stages of propagation.

POTATOES

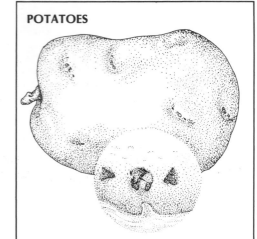

A potato tuber is marked by a scar at one end, where it was attached to the parent plant, and by "eyes", or nodes, placed spirally over its surface.

TUBERCLES

Just a few plants produce very small tubers from the axillary buds. These buds modify into tubers and eventually fall off the parent stem.

1 Cut a tuber into pieces with a sharp knife. Ensure each piece has at least one good "eye".

2 Dust all the cut surfaces with a fungicidal powder. Stand on a wire tray in a warm (21°C/70°F), dry place.

3 Plant the tuber pieces in the open ground as soon as a protective corky layer has formed. Label them clearly.

Rhizomes

A rhizome is a stem that grows laterally at about the soil surface, although in some plants it is underground. Normally, a rhizome stores food, but the degree to which it does this varies from species to species.

A rhizome is a perennial, and it is propagated artificially by division at an opportune season of the year: in most cases this is after flowering, when the rhizome is about to extend and produce new roots.

It has two ways of growing. In one, typified by the German or bearded iris, a terminal bud develops and flowers; the plant sends out extension growth through a lateral bud. The following season, this extension growth develops its own terminal bud, which flowers, and the plant continues to extend through its lateral buds. In the other way of growing, typified by mint and couch grass, its extension growth develops continuously from the terminal bud and occasionally from a lateral bud, which usually produces flower spikes.

In habit, rhizomes may also vary: "crown" rhizomes, such as asparagus, have virtually no extension growth annually and develop as a spreading crown, whereas other kinds of rhizomes, such as mint, couch grass and ground elder, make rapid and continuous growth and spread over large areas of ground in a relatively short time.

Perhaps the most prolific of garden plants to be propagated using rhizomes are bearded irises. The best time to divide their rhizomes and establish new plants is immediately after flowering, when the old root system dies down and a new root system begins to develop. Lift the clump of rhizomes with a fork and knock off as much soil as possible. Cut away and discard any old rhizomes, just leaving the current season's flushes of growth. Cut back their roots to 2–3 in, and shorten the leaf blades to reduce water loss before the new root systems develop. The prepared rhizomes are now ready for planting.

As a general rule, a rhizome should be replanted at the same depth as it was growing; for irises this is more or less in the surface soil. Usually, a rhizome has two rows of roots longitudinally on each side underneath. Therefore, when replanting, dig out two linear shallow trenches and place the roots in these. Firm back the soil over these roots and label the rhizome clearly. If necessary, settle in by watering.

CROWN RHIZOMES

Less easy to propagate are the "crown" rhizomes, such as peony and asparagus, which have what is traditionally referred to as herbaceous perennial rootstock. Fairly massive cuts are needed to divide such rootstock into suitable pieces for propagation: each piece requiring at least one well-developed bud.

Divide crown rhizomes in late winter before the buds enlarge and before the new season's root system begins to develop. Make a few relatively large divisions, unless quick bulking-up is essential, when it is better to plant small divisions in pots filled with John Innes No. 1 compost or similar (see page 12) in order to give them good conditions in which to become established. Dust the cut surfaces thoroughly with a fungicide to prevent bacterial and fungal rots. Leave them in a warm (21°C/70°F), dry atmosphere for the surface to dry out and develop the beginnings of a protective corky layer. Then plant out the divisions. Label them clearly.

1 Divide crown rhizomes in late winter.

2 Dust the cut surfaces with a fungicidal powder.

3 Plant out after two days in a warm, dry area.

1 Divide rhizomes after flowering, when the old root system dies down.

2 Lift a clump with a fork. Knock off as much soil as possible from the roots.

3 Cut away and discard any old rhizomes from the current season's growths.

4 Shorten the leaf-blades and cut back the roots to 2–3 in.

5 Replant each rhizome on a ridge with its roots in trenches either side.

6 Firm back the soil over the roots. Label and settle by watering.

Corms

Some plants that develop corms
Acidanthera
Crocosmia
Crocus
Gladiolus
Ixia
Ixiolirion
Montbretia
Tritonia

Corms look very similar to bulbs and are often confused with them. However, structurally they are very different. A corm consists of a stem that is swollen as a food store and that is shorter and broader than a bulb. The leaves of the stem are modified as thin, dry membranes that enclose the corm and protect it against injury and drying. Each leaf has a bud in its axil, the top of the stem usually develops as a flowering stem, and the roots are produced from the corm's base, which is often concave. In some kinds of corm, several buds at the top of the stem may grow out and flower.

Each year a new corm develops around the base of each stem. Increase, therefore, is

directly related to the number of stems produced by a corm. Normally, most plants developing corms will propagate naturally to give a sufficient increase, but should it be necessary to bulk up supplies more quickly then an artificial technique should be used.

Always buy corms from a reputable specialized grower, because it is vital to propagate from disease-free corms.

Cut a large, healthy corm into several pieces just prior to the season for planting and ensure each piece has at least one bud. Dust the cut surfaces with a fungicidal powder such as dry bordeaux or sulphur, in order to reduce the risk of rotting. Set the pieces on a wire cake-tray and place in a warm, dry environment, such as an airing cupboard, for 48 hours. This will cause the cut surfaces to seal. Then plant singly in a pot or in the ground, and label clearly.

If the corm is too small to cut up satisfactorily, then the lateral buds can be induced to develop more readily by removing the main stem either by snapping it off or digging it out with a knife. Then dust the cut surface with fungicidal powder and plant out the corm in the ground. During the growing season it will produce several shoots, which will eventually become new plants.

Propagation by division

1 Cut a corm into several pieces, each with at least one bud, just before planting in autumn.

2 Dust the cut surfaces with a fungicidal powder. Set pieces on a wire tray. Leave in a warm, dry place.

3 Plant each piece in a pot or in the open ground once it has developed a corky layer. Then label.

Propagation by inducing lateral buds

1 Lift the corm in autumn. Snap off the main stem or dig it out using a pointed knife.

2 Dust all the cut surfaces with a fungicidal powder.

3 Dig a hole twice the depth of the corm in the open ground. Plant it out immediately and label.

CORMELS

Cormels are miniature corms that are produced as offsets between the new corm and the old disintegrating corm. The quantity produced is very much a varietal feature—gladiolus developing up to about 50 cormels.

The level of cormel production will be influenced by the depth at which the main corm is planted; the deeper the corm is in the ground, the more cormels produced.

Collect the cormels when the corm is lifted from the ground before winter and store them below 5°C/41°F in a dry, frost-free environment with air circulating round them. Soak any cormels that become dry in tepid water for 24 hours before planting the following season. Plant them outdoors close together and label. They will normally take two years to reach flowering size.

Bulblets and bulbils

Bulblets

Bulblets are tiny bulbs that develop below ground on some bulbs.

Plants that produce bulblets can be artificially induced to increase their bulblet production. This is done by removing the flower stem, and burying it until bulblets develop in the leaf axils.

Dig a trench 6 in deep; slope one side up to ground level. Pinch out any buds or flowers on the stem and then twist it out of the bulb, which should remain in the ground. Lay the stem in the trench along the slope, leaving part of it sticking out of the ground. Spray the stem with a liquid fungicide to prevent disease. Then fill the trench with sand or a light compost and label.

By autumn, bulblets will have developed in the leaf axils at the lower end of the stem. These can be detached and planted straight into the ground at twice their own depth or be left *in situ* for a year.

This is a surprisingly easy method of producing bulblets, and the only difficulty that is likely to arise is the potential rotting of the stem before the bulblets are produced.

Bulbils

Bulbils are tiny bulbs that grow on a stem above ground. This natural process is an extremely prolific way of increasing stock.

A number of lily species such as *Lilium candidum* can be artificially induced to produce bulbils by disbudding the plant just before flowering. Bulbils will develop in the leaf axils during the remainder of the growing season. Collect them as they mature.

Fill a pot to the rim with John Innes No. 1 compost or similar (see page 158). With a presser board, strike off the excess compost and then firm gently to within $\frac{3}{8}$ in of the pot rim. Set the bulbils 1 in apart on the compost surface and gently press them so they make contact with the compost. Cover generously with grit. Strike off the grit level with the rim of the pot. Label and place in a cold frame. Leave for at least twelve months, until autumn of the following year. Then transplant into the open ground.

Certain other plants can also be artificially induced to produce bulbils; some of the ornamental onions will develop them in the flower heads.

Bulbil propagation

1 Disbud a suitable plant stem just before it begins to flower.

2 Pick off any bulbils as they mature in the leaf axils on the stem.

3 Set them 1 in apart in a compost-filled pot. Cover with grit and label.

Bulblet propagation

1 Pinch out any buds or flowers on a suitable plant.

2 Twist the stem out of the bulb, leaving the bulb in the ground.

3 Lay two-thirds of the stem along the sloping side of a trench 6 in deep.

4 Spray the stem with a liquid fungicide such as copper or Benomyl.

5 Fill the trench with sand or a light compost. Label clearly.

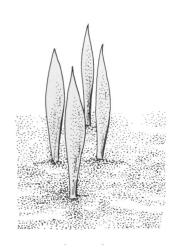

6 Leave during the summer. Detach the bulblets in autumn and replant.

Division 1

Herbaceous plants with fibrous crowns

Dividing a plant is a common way to propagate many herbaceous perennials, and it is also used to rejuvenate favourite plants and keep them in a vigorous condition. Propagation by division is also successful with shrubs, such as sumach, that produce suckers; with semi-woody perennials, such as New Zealand flax, that produce a crown of offset shoots; and with most plants with modified stems, such as bearded iris (see pages 168–171).

Herbaceous plants with fibrous crowns

The commonest method of propagating plants by division is that used for herbaceous perennials, such as chrysanthemums, with fibrous roots and a relatively loose crown. Normally, the central part of the crown becomes woody over the course of two or three years. As this woody area does not produce many shoots and generally loses vigour, it is discarded and the remainder of the clump is divided into suitable-sized portions for planting out and re-establishing a new crown.

The only variable feature of this form of propagation is the time at which division is carried out. As a general rule, the most opportune time to divide such plants is directly after flowering, as this is when the new vegetative shoots are being produced and the new root system is developing. In very late-flowering subjects, this would be the following spring.

Lift the parent plant and shake off as much soil as possible. Then wash the crown in a bucket, or hose it clean of any residual soil. The plant can be divided without this preliminary preparation, but it is much easier to deal with clean plants, especially if the soil is wet and muddy. Shorten any tall stems above the ground to prevent unnecessary water loss, especially if the division takes place in summer. Break off a piece with at least one good "eye" from the periphery of the crown, where the young shoots are generally produced; avoid the central woody crown, which is of no value and should be discarded. If the piece proves rather intractable to remove, cut it off, using an old carving knife or similar blade. Plant out the new clump as quickly as possible to the same depth as it was growing previously. When replanted it should be labelled and watered in—indeed "puddled" in would be more appropriate.

1 Lift the plant that is to be divided directly after it has flowered.

2 Shake off as much soil as possible.

3 Wash the crown and its roots in a bucket, or hose it clean.

4 Shorten all tall stems above the ground to minimize water loss.

5 Break off a piece with at least one good "eye" from the edge of the crown.

6 Divide any intractable pieces with an old carving knife or similar blade.

7 Make a hole and replant the new clump at once. Firm the soil and label.

8 Water very thoroughly, using a watering can with a spray attachment.

9 Keep the new clump free of weeds.

Division 2

Herbaceous plants with fleshy crowns

Many herbaceous plants, such as hostas, develop a compact, fleshy crown that is not easy to pull apart.

The best way to propagate these plants is by division towards the end of their dormant season, when buds will begin to shoot, indicating the most vigorous areas.

Lift the parent plant and shake off as much soil as possible. Wash the crown thoroughly. With a convenient-sized knife, cut the crown into pieces. The size of divisions will depend on preference, but must include at least one developed shoot. Avoid latent buds, which do not always develop satisfactorily. Dust the cut surfaces with dry bordeaux powder to reduce chances of fungal rots. Do not allow the divisions, especially from really fleshy rooted plants such as hostas, to dry excessively. Therefore replant the divisions either in the ground or in a pot as quickly as is feasible. Label them clearly.

Naturally dividing alpines

There are a number of alpine plants, such as campanulas, which lend themselves to propagation by division because their crowns separate naturally into individual new plantlets each season.

After flowering, or in the spring if the plant flowers in the autumn, as does *Gentiana sino-ornata*, lift the plant and tease apart the divisions. Replant as soon as possible. Label and water in well.

This is a very simple but effective system of increasing plants. If the crowns are lifted and divided fairly frequently the rate of increase can be quite dramatic. However, plants left *in situ* for a long period tend to produce only a few large divisions.

Semi-woody herbaceous plants

Some perennials with upright, sword-like leaves, for example *Phormium*, increase in size by producing a sort of offset that develops into a large crown of individual shoots, each with its own root system.

To propagate these plants, it is best to divide them in the spring, although it can be done at any time of the year. Lift them and shake out the soil, if necessary hosing or washing the crown clean. Pull the various pieces apart. Cut the clump with a spade or hatchet if it is hard and woody in the middle, and replant the divisions fairly quickly to avoid the roots drying.

Woody shrubs

There are a few woody shrubs, such as blackthorn, that produce suckers, which then develop into individual clumps of stems. Lift these plants in the dormant season and wash thoroughly. Divide the clump of stems into convenient-sized portions. Normally the main core of the clump will be woody and will carry few roots. This will be of little value for propagation purposes, so take the new pieces from the younger, more vigorous growth on the outside of the clump.

Cut back the branches fairly drastically to reduce water loss, as the buds will break in the spring before sufficient roots have been produced. Replant the divisions back in the ground as soon as possible and label.

Lift relatively isolated suckers individually in the dormant season and use to establish new plants.

If the plant has been grafted—as may happen with Japanese quinces—then it is the rootstock, not the cultivated variety, that is divided.

IRISHMAN'S CUTTINGS

Plants, such as Michaelmas daisies, that produce particularly loose crowns can be propagated by separating off single stems on the periphery of the crown so that each has an adventitious root system. These single stem portions are described as "Irishman's cuttings", and they should be planted at once.

Herbaceous plants with fleshy crowns

1 Lift the plant to be divided towards the end of its dormant season.

2 Wash the crown well. Cut off a piece with at least one developed bud.

3 Dust the cut surfaces with a fungicidal powder. Then replant immediately.

Woody shrubs with suckers

1 Remove isolated suckers from woody shrubs during the dormant season.

2 Cut back part of the roots and top growth.

3 Replant immediately; label and water in well.

Offsets/Runners

Offsets

An offset is a plantlet that has developed laterally on a stem either above or below ground: the stem arises from a crown bud and usually carries no other buds.

Most plants, such as sempervivums, that produce offsets first grow a miniature plant with only minimal roots. A root system will not fully develop until late in the growing season.

To speed up this process of propagation, pull away the offset from its parent, usually in spring. Either plant out in the garden or pot it up, using a cuttings compost with added grit, which will drain freely and so ensure good root development.

Where offset development is poor, it is possible to stimulate offsets by removing the plant's growing tip. This has the same effect as removing a terminal bud.

Although the term offset is normally used for a plantlet that is separated from its parent during the growing season, it is also used to describe slower-developing shoots that are produced by mainly monocotyledonous plants such as yuccas. Eventually these shoots should be sufficiently mature to be separated from the parent and planted on.

A pineapple plant produces offsets that can be used for propagation once its fruit is nearly mature. These offsets are variously described as slips, ratoons or suckers. Cut them off the plant close to the crown and plant out.

Many corm and bulb plants, such as fritillarias, each year produce miniature reproductions of themselves from the bases of the newly developing corms or bulbs. These are known as cormels (see page 170) and bulbils and bulblets (see page 171).

1 Pull an offset away from the parent plant, preferably in spring.

2 Plant the offset in a pot filled with a cuttings compost with added grit.

Cut off pineapple slips close to the crown and plant out individually.

Runners

A runner is a more or less horizontal stem that arises from a crown bud and creeps overground. The leaves are normally scale-like, and rooting may occur at the nodes. The lateral buds develop as new plants, and eventually the stem of the runner deteriorates, leaving a new isolated plant. The classic example of this kind of natural vegetative reproduction occurs in the strawberry plant.

New plantlets usually root down and produce new plants quite successfully. However, unless controlled, a mat of new plants tends to develop, and these are not easily lifted and separated without damage, so thin out the runners regularly.

To produce large, well-established individual plants, dig in plenty of good compost for rooting; in early summer, thin out some of the runners, and pin down the rest into the compost, evenly radiating them around the plant. This method will induce early rooting, but the rate of development will not be quite as fast as for pot-grown runners.

These are obtained by placing a pot under each runner.

Dig a hole in the ground beneath a developing plantlet. Set a pot containing good compost into it and then push back the soil to keep the pot in position. Pin down the runner, using wire bent in the shape of a staple, so that the plantlet will root in the pot.

1 Thin out some runners in early summer to encourage strong growth.

2 Fill a pot with John Innes No. 1 compost. Firm to within $\frac{3}{8}$ in of the rim.

3 Dig a large hole in the ground beneath a plantlet. Set the pot in the hole.

4 Pin down the plantlet in the middle of the pot, using a wire staple.

5 Pin down any other plantlets in a star-shaped pattern round the parent plant. Sever their connecting stems once they are fully established.

Layering/Simple layering 1

Layering is one of the oldest techniques used by gardeners to propagate woody plants. A stem is encouraged to develop roots before it is removed from the parent plant. This method is easy as it avoids any complicated environmental control to ensure the stem survives while the root system is developing. The early gardeners had probably observed this process when it occurred naturally under certain conditions. To do it artificially they just repeated the conditions and modified the technique.

As with any method of propagation, it is necessary to consider both the stem from which the layer is to be made and what soil is suitable to encourage rooting.

The condition of the stem will have a significant affect on the eventual success of propagating by layering. For greatest success, the gardener should develop vigorous, rapidly grown stems with their high capacity to produce roots. Certain methods of layering, such as stooling, encourage this capacity in stems as part of the normal system of management, but in others, such as simple layering, it is necessary to prepare the stems by pruning the parent plant well before propagation can take place. When pruning bear in mind that, with most methods of layering, the branches to be layered will have to be brought down to ground level.

The soil around the parent plant will also require preparation so that it will induce the stem to form roots. Rooting will be encouraged primarily by the exclusion of light, but also by the availability of oxygen and the presence of sufficient moisture and warmth.

The exclusion of light from the stem, that is blanching it, is extremely important when encouraging roots to start growing. The sooner light is excluded from the stem, the more effective is the response. So, the earlier a stem is buried or earthed up the more likely it is to root. This effect cannot be overemphasized, as lateness in earthing up is probably the commonest reason why a stem fails to produce roots, provided that it is basically vigorous and capable of producing roots.

The soil for layering must have a good water-holding capacity, good aeration and adequate drainage. Thus, especially if plants are to be layered in an ordinary garden border as opposed to a purpose-developed layer bed, the soil must be dug deeply to provide good drainage and so reduce the chances of waterlogging. It can be further lightened and improved by the addition of peat and/or grit, depending on the heaviness of the soil.

Warmth will improve rooting, so ensure the layered stem and soil are placed where they will receive adequate sunlight. However, warmth will only be effective if the soil is moist, so water the layered stems during dry periods.

In most methods of layering, the soil should be carefully forked away from the layer once it has rooted, so it can be lifted. Do not allow the roots to dry out, otherwise they will die.

Layers that may have difficulty rooting successfully should be well established before they are lifted. To encourage this, sever the newly rooted layers from the parent plant about three to four weeks prior to lifting and replanting.

This weaning can be further enhanced by pruning the stems so that there is a greater balance of root to stem.

Simple layering

Simple layering is perhaps the easiest and most effective method of layering a wide variety of woody plants, and it is a technique that can be carried out with minimum disturbance to the parent plant.

A stem is buried in the soil behind its tip so that roots are induced in this area. Once the root system is established, the stem can be severed from the parent. The roots are encouraged to develop because the plant foods and hormones are restricted where the stem is buried. To be successful, the gardener must use stems that have a high capacity to produce roots, and they should also be near ground level.

Twelve or more months before layering, rigorously prune a low branch or branches on the parent plant so that young, rapidly grown shoots are produced. These will be more amenable to the bending and manipulation involved in the actual layering operation, and because of their rapid growth will have the required capacity to produce roots.

Layering is normally done in late winter/early spring, as soon as the soil can be worked down to a tilth.

As the technique is likely to be carried out in the garden and not in a purpose-prepared nursery bed, it is important to prepare the soil both thoroughly and effectively. Dig as deeply as possible. Then add peat and grit in sufficient quantities to convert the existing soil into a rooting medium with good water-holding capacity, good aeration and adequate drainage.

Trim a rapidly grown stem of side-shoots and leaves for about 4–24 in behind the tip. Pull the stem to ground level and mark its position on the soil 9 in behind its tip. Dig a trench from that point, with one straight side about 4–6 in deep and the other sloping up to ground level near the parent plant.

The secret of inducing root formation is to restrict movement of food and hormones in the tissues of the stem: this is usually achieved by bending the stem at least at a right angle. However, in plants that are particularly difficult to root, the stem should first be girdled by cutting into the stem with a knife or by binding the stem tightly with a piece of copper wire at the bend.

Bend the stem at right angles 9 in behind its tip and set it in the trench against the straight side with its tip exposed above the trench. If the stem is whippy, peg it down with heavy wire staples. Bury the stem with soil, firm in and water well.

Keep the soil reasonably moist, especially in dry periods. Rooting will normally occur during the growing season.

In autumn, sever the layered stem from the parent plant so that the new plant can accustom itself to an independent existence.

About three to four weeks later, cut off the growing tip to encourage the roots to establish. Pot up or plant out the layer and label it. If rooting is not well advanced by autumn, leave the layer to establish for a further year before lifting and transplanting it.

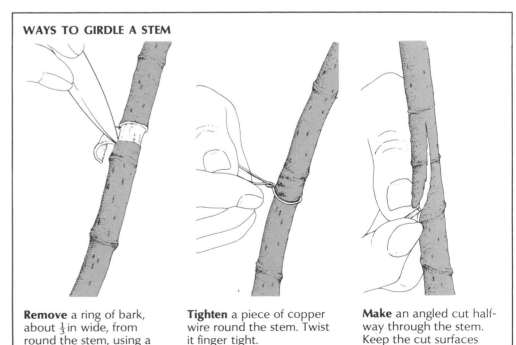

WAYS TO GIRDLE A STEM

Remove a ring of bark, about $\frac{1}{3}$ in wide, from round the stem, using a sharp knife.

Tighten a piece of copper wire round the stem. Twist it finger tight.

Make an angled cut halfway through the stem. Keep the cut surfaces apart with a matchstick.

Simple layering 2

1 Prune some low branches off the parent plant during the dormant season to induce vigorous growth.

2 Cultivate the soil well round the plant during the following late winter/early spring. Add peat and grit.

3 Trim the leaves and side-shoots off a young, vigorous stem for about 4–24 in behind the growing tip.

4 Bring the stem down to ground level and mark its position on the soil 9 in behind its tip.

5 Dig a trench from that point. Make one straight side 4–6 in deep. Slope the other towards the plant.

6 Bend the stem at right angles 9 in behind its tip. Peg it down in the trench against the straight side.

7 Return the soil to the trench to bury the stem. Firm it in well.

8 Water well, using a watering can with a coarse rose. Keep the soil moist, especially in dry periods.

9 Sever the layered stem from its parent plant in autumn.

10 Cut off the growing tip from the rooted layer about three to four weeks later.

11 Lift the layered stem if its roots are well advanced. Otherwise, leave for a further year.

12 Replant either in the open ground or in a pot and label. Leave to establish.

Tip layering

Some plants responding to tip layering
Blackberry
Boysenberry
Loganberry

Rubus phoenicolasius
(Japanese wineberry)
R. thyrsoideus 'Plenus'
R. ulmifolius bellidiflorus
Veitch berry

Tip layering is a specialized technique used for the various members of the genus *Rubus*, such as blackberries and loganberries. If the growing tip of such a plant is buried in the soil, it will naturally swell, develop roots and establish itself. This phenomenon is modified to suit the gardener.

Tip layering is an invaluable technique for propagating a few plants, as it can be carried out in the garden on one part of a plant without disturbing the flowering or fruiting ability of the rest of it.

The members of the genus *Rubus*, especially the fruiting varieties, are prone to virus infections, and they should be propagated only from known virus-free stocks.

Select a new strong stem as it develops from the crown of the plant during the spring. As soon as it reaches 15–18 in long, pinch out the tip to encourage branching. The growth of these stems is rapid and vigorous, and soon the stems can be pinched out again. Continue to do this until midsummer, when about six to eight tips should be well developed.

It is at this stage that the stems can be layered. However, as the roots of these particular plants are fine, fibrous and easily damaged, the soil for layering should be well prepared so that once the layers have rooted they can be lifted with minimum damage to their root system.

Dig and cultivate the soil thoroughly, if possible dig in a deep layer of organic matter to conserve moisture and prevent the roots drying. Improve the top 6 in by adding some peat and grit.

Pull down a stem and make a mark where its tip touches the ground. Start digging a trench at this spot, making it 4 in deep. Give it smoothed vertical sides except for one which should be sloped towards the parent plant. Smoothed vertical sides will help any shoots to grow vertically and so produce a manageable plant.

Place the tip in the deepest part of the trench and pin it down with a heavy wire staple. Replace the soil, firm and water.

In about three weeks, shoots should appear above ground level.

In September cut back the original stem at the crown of the parent plant, so that the layer can establish as an independent plant.

Cut off the rest of the original stem and shorten the growing tip before lifting the rooted layer in autumn after leaf-fall. Replant the layer immediately and label it.

Protect any layers that cannot be replanted straight away by wrapping their roots in damp newspaper, which is then placed in a plastic bag. Close the bag and tie the neck tightly so the roots will not dry out.

Propagation by tip-layering in this way can be repeated each year.

1 Pinch out the tip of a 15–18 in basal shoot of the current year's growth.

2 Continue to pinch out the tips until six to eight tips have developed.

3 Cultivate the soil well. Add peat and grit to the top 6 in of the soil.

4 Pull down a stem. Dig a trench 4 in deep where its tip touches the ground.

5 Place the tip in the deepest part of the trench. Pin it down with a staple.

6 Replace the soil, firm and water, using a can with a coarse rose.

7 Cut back the original stem at the crown of the parent plant in September.

8 Cut off the rest of the stem once the rooted layer has dropped its leaves.

9 Shorten some of the top growth that the layer may have made.

10 Lift the layer very carefully to avoid damaging its fine, fibrous roots.

11 Plant the rooted layer at once in well-cultivated soil. Label it clearly.

12 Place layers that cannot be planted at once in damp newspaper in a plastic bag.

Making a stem cutting 1

Some plants suitable for propagation by leaf-bud cuttings
Aphelandra
Camellia
Clematis

Ficus elastica (rubber tree)
Haberlea
Ivy
Mahonia
Ramonda
Vine

Leaf-bud cuttings

Leaf-bud cuttings can be taken from any type of stem—soft wood, green wood, semi-ripe wood, hard wood or evergreen. Each cutting consists of a leaf, a bud in its leaf axil and a very short piece of stem. The leaf supplies food to support the cutting and the regenerative processes; the bud provides the basis for the new stem system; and the piece of stem is where the first roots are produced.

To be successful, the gardener must use stems that have a high capacity to produce roots. Therefore, prune the parent plant rigorously should it be a woody plant. This will encourage new stems, which will grow rapidly and so have a high rooting potential.

For leaf-bud cuttings, select one of these new stems with an undamaged leaf that is fully expanded and mature. If the leaf is immature, the cutting will complete leaf growth before it starts producing roots, and this increases the chances of peripheral problems, such as rotting. Also, ensure that there is a viable bud in the leaf axil. (For example, some virginia creepers do not have a bud in every leaf axil.)

Make the cuttings with a razor blade, knife or secateurs, depending on the hardness of the stem. Cut close above the bud so that as small a snag as possible is left. This minimizes the likelihood of rotting and die-back, which might endanger the bud.

Make the basal cut about 1–1½ in below the top cut so that sufficient stem is available to anchor the cutting firmly in the cuttings compost. This is especially important with plants that have big leaves and are liable to rot.

Plants with big leaves are also difficult to plant at a realistic spacing, so reduce their leaf area either by removing some of the leaf or by rolling the leaf and placing a rubber band round it so that it takes up less room. Dip the cutting in a rooting hormone.

In a pot filled with cuttings compost make a hole with a dibber. Plant the cutting with its bud about level with the compost surface. Firm sufficiently to prevent rocking. Label and water in. Place hardy cuttings in a cold frame and less hardy cuttings in a well-lit, more protected environment, such as a mist unit or closed case.

DOUBLE LEAF BUDS

1 Cut a stem with leaves that grow opposite each other just above a bud and again 1–1½ in below it.

2 Split the stem down the middle, using a sharp knife, to make two cuttings.

OR Remove one leaf. Dip the cutting in a rooting hormone. Then plant and label clearly.

Leaf-bud cuttings

1 Prune the parent plant, if suitable, to encourage new stems with a high rooting potential.

2 Select a new stem with an undamaged mature leaf and a viable bud in its axil, later in the season.

3 Make an angled cut just above the bud.

4 Make a straight cut 1–1½ in below the top cut.

5 Roll up or cut a large leaf. Dip the leaf-bud cutting in a rooting hormone.

6 Plant in a pot with its bud about level with the compost surface. Firm well. Then water in a fungicide.

Making a stem cutting 2

Heel cuttings

The taking of heel cuttings is a traditional way to propagate plants from stem cuttings. It is a widely used method of removing a stem cutting from a plant, and it is quite possible to make heel cuttings of softwood, green-wood, semi-ripe, hardwood or evergreen stems.

A young side-shoot is stripped away from its parent stem so that a heel, that is a thin sliver of bark and wood from the old stem, also comes away at the base of the cutting.

The reason for taking a stem cutting with a heel is to give the cutting a firm base so that it is well protected against possible rots. It also exposes the swollen base of the current season's growth, which has a very high capacity to produce roots.

Heel cuttings are often used for stem cuttings that take some time to develop roots, for example those that are planted in autumn and have to survive through the winter before rooting, or those hardwood cuttings that are planted in a cold frame. Heel cuttings are also made from softwood and greenwood stems that are left to develop in partially controlled environments, such as a propagator. Heel cuttings can be taken at any time of year.

Hold the bottom of the side-shoot between the thumb and forefinger and pull down sharply so it comes away with a long tail.

If the side-shoot does not pull off readily, place a knife blade in the angle close against the parent stem and cut away the side-shoot with a heel.

Trim the tail on the heel and any leaves near it. Remove some of the tip on semi-ripe and hardwood cuttings. Dip the cutting in a rooting hormone.

Plant hardwood cuttings straight into the ground; semi-ripe and sub-shrub cuttings in a cold frame; and less hardy cuttings in the protected environment of a propagator. Label and water them in with a fungicide.

Mallet cuttings

Mallet cuttings have a hardwood plug at the base of each cutting to guard against rotting organisms. Their use is restricted to semi-ripe and hardwood cuttings, and they are es-pecially successful for many *Berberis* when propagated in the autumn and planted in cold frames.

Mallet cuttings are most successfully made from stems with a feathered habit, that is from a stem with small side-shoots.

Prune back the parent plant in winter to encourage vigorous stem growth, which has a high capacity to produce roots.

Take mallet cuttings from these new stems in the later part of the growing season. Cut horizontally with scissor-type secateurs across the parent stem immediately above a suitable side-shoot. It is important to make this top cut as close to the side-shoot as possible because the longer the snag the greater the likelihood of die-back and hence potential rotting.

Make a further horizontal cut about $\frac{3}{4}$ in below the top cut so that the side-shoot is isolated with a small "mallet" of parent stem. Split this piece of mallet with a knife if it is thick. Trim any leaves at the bottom.

Dip the base of the mallet stem in a root-ing hormone. Make a hole large enough to take all the mallet and part of the side-shoot with a dibber. Plant semi-ripe cuttings in a cold frame and hardwood cuttings in the open ground. Label and water with a fungicide.

Heel cuttings

1 Hold the bottom of a side-shoot between the thumb and forefinger. Pull down sharply.

2 Neaten the long tail on the heel and any leaves near it. Dip the basal cut in a rooting hormone.

3 Make a hole in the soil or compost. Plant the cutting. Label it and water with a fungicide.

Mallet cuttings

1 Cut horizontally with secateurs across the parent stem just above a side-shoot.

2 Make a basal cut about $\frac{3}{4}$ in below the first cut. Remove any leaves at the bottom.

3 Dip the basal cut in a rooting hormone. Plant the cutting and label it. Water with a fungicide.

Soft woods 1

Soft wood is the most immature part of a stem, and, when propagating, it is the most difficult kind of cutting to keep alive. However, soft wood does have the highest capacity of all kinds of stems to produce roots: the younger and the more immature the cutting, the greater will be its ability to develop roots, and so propagate successfully.

Soft stem growth is produced continuously at the tip of any stem during the growing season. As it matures, the stem gradually hardens and becomes woody. The faster the growth at the tip, the more stem without wood will be present.

Softwood cuttings, then, are taken in spring from the fast-growing tips of plants. Growth when the buds first break is remarkably rapid, and, if cuttings are made as soon

as there is sufficient growth, the highest rooting potential will be available. Tips of plants taken slightly later in the season, around the beginning of June, will be slower growing, more mature and have a lower capacity to root, and they are referred to as greenwood cuttings.

It is possible to obtain softwood cuttings later in the season by forcing the plant, that is by increasing temperatures well above the norm, which will accelerate growth. This can be done, for example, by placing deciduous outdoor plants in the warmth of a greenhouse, or by placing house plants in a temperature of about 29°C/85°F. The very highest capacity to produce roots can be achieved by pruning the parent plant vigorously in winter, which will encourage rapid

growth; by increasing the temperature around the plant in spring; and by then taking the cutting as soon as sufficient tip growth is available.

Softwood cuttings are extremely susceptible to water loss. Their immature leaves have not fully expanded and so have not completely developed their own mechanisms for reducing water loss. Even a relatively minor water loss will hinder the roots developing. By the time a cutting is wilting all root development will have ceased.

The secret of success is to collect the cuttings in small batches and to maintain them in a fully turgid condition before planting them.

Fill a container with cuttings compost and firm to within $\frac{3}{8}$ in of the rim.

Take a cutting in early morning when the stem is fully turgid. By mid-afternoon normal water loss from the plant will exceed uptake, and the plant will be under water stress.

If the stem has grown less than 4 in since bud-break, remove it with a heel, that is with the swollen portion at the base of the stem that had the very fastest growth when the new stem started to develop at bud-break.

Place the cutting in a polythene bag or a bucket of water immediately. Keep the polythene bag shaded to avoid "cooking" the cutting—a major cause of failure.

Plant the cutting as soon as possible. If it cannot be dealt with quickly, keep it cool in the salad-box area of a domestic refrigerator, where the low temperature will prevent excessive water loss.

1 Prune woody plants hard in winter to promote stems with a high capacity to produce roots.

2 Fill a container with cuttings compost. Firm to within $\frac{3}{8}$ in of the rim.

3 Cut the fast-growing tip off a stem in the early morning in spring.

4 Place the cutting at once in the shade in a polythene bag or a bucket of water.

5 Cut the base of the stem $\frac{1}{8}$ in below a leaf joint if the cutting is more than 4 in long.

OR Trim the tail if the cutting was taken with a heel.

Soft woods 2

If there is more than 4 in between the tip and the base of the cutting, place the cutting on a sheet of glass and make a nodal cut—that is a cut at the base of the stem just ($\frac{1}{8}$ in) below a bud or leaf joint. This provides as hard and solid a surface as possible and will help prevent rotting.

If the cutting was taken with a heel, neaten the tail that will also have come away with the stem.

Remove the leaves on the bottom third of the cutting, which will be reliant on the remaining leaves to produce sufficient food to keep it alive until its roots are fully established.

Dip the base of the cutting in a proprietary hormone rooting powder containing a fungicide such as Captan to protect it against rotting, although softwood cuttings do not need to be treated with a rooting hormone.

Make a hole with a dibber and plant the cutting up to its leaves in the compost, taking care not to damage the base of the cutting. Plant cuttings so their leaves do not touch. Label and firm them in by watering from above the compost, using a watering can with a fine rose; pressing by hand may damage the cuttings.

Place the cuttings as quickly as possible in a well-lit propagating environment such as a mist unit, a closed case or a polythene tent that will conserve moisture within the cuttings.

The advantage of a mist unit is that it keeps the top of the cuttings cool, whereas air temperatures are high in a closed case or polythene tent. A high aerial temperature will force the cuttings to grow upwards, and food will be diverted from the important function of root initiation. If the cuttings are shaded to reduce the aerial temperature, then the light intensity penetrating to the leaves of the cuttings is decreased, and this reduces food production and hence the rate of regeneration.

The problem then becomes a vicious circle that is not easy to resolve without a mist unit, which maintains both a cool, aerial environment and high water status within the cuttings.

Softwood cuttings, because they are the immature part of a plant, are susceptible to all the vagaries of their environment: so the longer they take to root, the greater are the chances of them succumbing to some outside influence. Thus the speed with which they regenerate is vital. The rate of root production will be dependent on the temperature surrounding the base of the cuttings; in general, the higher the temperature, the faster the roots are produced. Best rooting will occur with a temperature around the base of the cuttings of 21–24°C/70–75°F.

Harden off the cuttings once they have rooted successfully, gradually weaning them from their controlled environment; finally pot them up in John Innes No. 1 compost or similar (see page 158) and label.

6 Remove the leaves off the bottom third of the cutting. Dip the basal cut in a powder fungicide.

7 Make a hole with a dibber in the compost. Insert the cutting up to its leaves. Plant any more cuttings.

8 Label the cuttings clearly. Water from above the compost. Place in a well-lit protected area.

9 Harden off the cuttings gradually when they have rooted.

10 Pot them in John Innes No. 1 compost once they are weaned and label.

Green woods

The essential but subtle distinction between softwood cuttings and greenwood cuttings is their speed of growth. Externally they may appear to be very similar, but greenwood cuttings are taken from the soft tip of the stem after the spring flush of growth has slowed down. The stem is, then, slightly harder and woodier than for softwood cuttings because the tip is not growing away from the hardening stem so fast as it was in the spring. In fact, as the season progresses greenwood cuttings become harder and harder. However, it should be emphasized that greenwood cuttings require just as much environmental control as softwood cuttings.

Use greenwood cuttings to propagate a wide range of trees and shrubs, such as gooseberries, that will root easily, and the majority of herbaceous plants, such as chrysanthemums. However, plants that are difficult to root should be propagated from softwood cuttings and not from greenwood cuttings, which have a slightly reduced ability to develop roots.

Prune back woody plants rigorously in winter to encourage rapidly grown stems with a high capacity to root, which can be used for propagation in the growing season.

Take cuttings from these stems once their growth rate has begun to decline, which will usually be about the beginning of June for most outdoor plants.

Fill a container with cuttings compost and firm to within $\frac{3}{8}$ in of the rim.

Take a cutting from a fully turgid stem with all its current season's growth, early in the morning. Place the cutting immediately in a bucket of water or a polythene bag in a shaded position, because it is vitally important to maintain the turgidity of a greenwood cutting. If it suffers water loss, its rooting will be hindered.

Place the cutting on a pane of glass and with a knife reduce the cutting to about 3–4 in. The cutting's length will very much depend on the amount of soft growth available. Discard the leaves from the bottom half of the cutting. Dip the base of the cutting in a rooting hormone powder of "softwood" strength containing a fungicide.

Make a hole in the compost and plant the cutting up the leaves. Label it and water. Place in a closed case, mist unit or polythene tent, to prevent excessive water loss and wilting. Ensure the cutting receives adequate light to make the food needed for root production, as

the cutting has little or no food reserves.

Rooting should take between three and eight weeks. Take the rooted cutting out of the propagating environment but keep it well

protected, gradually hardening it off. Then repot in John Innes No. 1 compost or similar (see page 158), and label clearly.

 1 Prune woody plants in winter to encourage strong, vigorous stems with a high capacity to root.

 2 Fill a container with cuttings compost. Cut off all of a vigorous stem early in the morning.

 3 Place the cutting at once in a bucket of water in the shade.

 4 Place the cutting on a pane of glass. Reduce to about 3–4 in, using a sharp knife.

 5 Trim the leaves from the bottom half of the cutting, slicing them flush with the stem with a sharp knife.

 6 Dip the base of the cutting in rooting hormone containing a fungicide.

 7 Make a hole with a dibber in the compost. Insert the cutting up to its leaves. Label the container.

 8 Water with fungicide. Place in an environment that will control water loss and give shaded light.

 9 Harden off the rooted cutting. Repot and label as soon as it has established.

Semi-ripe woods

During the late summer, annual stem growth slows down and plant stems become harder. Cuttings taken at this time are called semi-ripe cuttings. As they are thicker and harder than softwood cuttings, they are more capable of survival. However they are still susceptible to the same problems of water loss because the cuttings carry leaves.

Semi-ripe cuttings have relatively high levels of stored food and can therefore survive and produce roots in poor light.

Many deciduous plants, such as deutzias, that root fairly easily are propagated from semi-ripe cuttings, and some evergreen plants can also be increased in this way.

Prune the parent plant at the start of the dormant season, so that strong, fast-grown stems are available for propagation the following season. These will have a greater ability to produce roots than unpruned stems.

Prepare the soil in the cold frame by digging deeply. Add peat and grit to improve drainage and its water-holding capacity. Cover the surface with a 1 in layer of fine (builder's) sand to make a better rooting medium. If only a few cuttings are to be taken, fill a container with cuttings compost and cover with a 1 in layer of fine sand.

Take semi-ripe cuttings from a main stem with all the current season's growth or from side-shoots if the main stem has feathered growth, that is a series of small side-shoots growing on the main stem.

Remove the tip of the stem if it is soft, but leave it if the apical bud has set and growth has ceased for the year. Shorten the cutting with secateurs to 4–6 in long, depending on the vigour of the particular plant.

Cut off the lower leaves flush with the stem so that about 2 in of stem is clear at the base.

Treat the basal cut surface with a rooting hormone powder containing a fungicide. The strength for semi-ripe cuttings is 0.4 per cent IBA.

Make a hole with a dibber in the soil in a cold frame. Plant the cutting about 1½ in deep, so its base just enters the soil below the sand layer. Space the cuttings as close as is feasible, but this is not likely to be much less than 3–4 in apart. Label them clearly.

Water in the cuttings; this also firms the sand around the cutting. Close the frame tightly and shade it to prevent the leaves from scorching. Air the cold frame from the lower end if the temperature rises above 27°C/80°F. Water sufficiently to rewet and develop high humidity within the frame again should conditions become dry.

As semi-ripe cuttings are usually deciduous, they will drop their leaves in autumn. At this stage remove all the fallen leaves from the frame so that they do not rot.

Insulate the frame with matting once the leaves have fallen to protect the cuttings against frost in winter. Once the cuttings have no leaves, light is not necessary for the plants to manufacture food and so the matting can be left in place all the time.

Rooting may start fairly quickly if the weather is mild; otherwise it will occur during the late winter or spring.

Leave the rooted cuttings *in situ* during the following growing season. Feed them regularly with a liquid fertilizer and water when dry. Remove insulation and air the cold frame by raising its lid during the day as soon as the danger of frost is over. Eventually remove it altogether. Lift the new plants and transplant them after leaf-fall in the autumn. Label the new plants clearly.

1 Prune the parent plant at the start of the dormant season to encourage strong stems to grow.

2 Prepare the soil in the cold frame by digging deeply. Add peat and grit. Cover with 1 in fine sand.

3 Cut off a shoot with all its current season's growth in late summer. Remove the tip only if it is soft.

4 Shorten the cutting to 4–6 in. Cut the leaves off the bottom 2 in of the stem.

5 Treat the basal cut surface with some rooting hormone. Dibble in a cutting 1½ in deep.

6 Plant the remaining cuttings 3–4 in apart. Label and water. Seal and shade the frame.

7 Rewet the soil if it dries. Remove any fallen leaves. Insulate the cold frame with matting.

8 Remove the insulation and air the frame once the danger of frost is over. Apply a routine liquid feed.

9 Lift the new plants and transplant them once their leaves have dropped in autumn. Label them clearly.

Leaf-petiole cuttings

Some plants responding to propagation by leaf-petiole cuttings
Begonias—other than
  Begonia rex
Peperomia caperata
P. metallica
Saintpaulia

The simplest and most reliable way to produce new plants from leaf cuttings is to use a complete leaf with its stalk. The disadvantage of this method is that it develops only a few new plants from each leaf.

Rotting and disease are the main causes of failure so always use clean tools, containers and composts.

Leaf-petiole cuttings can be taken at any time of year provided a new, fully expanded leaf is available.

Make up a cuttings compost of equal parts sifted peat and grit. Fill a container that is large enough to take the leaf-petiole cuttings. Firm the compost to within $\frac{3}{8}$ in of the rim of the container.

Slice a suitable leaf cleanly through the leaf-stalk, using a sharp knife or a safety razor blade to ensure the least possible damage. Leave about 2 in of the leaf-stalk attached to the leaf-blade.

Make a small hole with a dibber in the compost to a depth just sufficient to hold the cutting. Plant at a shallow angle so that the leaf-blade is almost flat on the compost. The shallower the base of the stalk is planted into the compost the more the air can circulate around it, which will encourage a quick response. Then firm the compost around the stalk. When the cuttings are all planted, label them and water in, using a fine rose to avoid damaging them.

Place the cuttings in an environment that maintains a steady high humidity, so that the cuttings do not dry out. The temperature, especially for house plants, needs to be relatively high, and this is best provided by using a propagator that is heated at the bottom—ideally at about 20°C/68°F.

Expose the cuttings to sufficient light for them to manufacture food and develop the new plantlets. Too much sunlight may scorch the cuttings. In general, light shade is the best compromise.

The new plantlets will develop on the cut surface of the leaf-stalk within five to six weeks, and several may appear at this point. Leave them until they can be handled and separated into individual plants, potted on and hardened off. If it is likely to be some time before they are large enough to be potted on, then liquid feed the plantlets.

1 Fill a container with equal parts sifted peat and grit.

2 Slice an undamaged leaf that has recently expanded fully away from the plant.

3 Cut through the leaf-stalk about 2 in from blade, using a sharp knife.

4 Make a shallow hole and insert the cutting at the angle shown.

5 Firm the compost gently round the cutting. Plant the remaining cuttings.

6 Label and water in, using a fine rose.

7 Place the cuttings in light shade in a propagator that is heated from below.

8 Apply a liquid feed once the new plantlets have started developing.

9 Pot on the plantlets once they can be handled. Label and harden them off.

Foliar embryos

A few plants are capable of developing isolated groups of simple cells in certain areas of their leaves. As a result these cells, or foliar embryos, are capable of developing into new plantlets. Given certain growing conditions some of these plants, such as *Mitella*, have foliar embryos that develop naturally into plantlets. Other plants such as *Cardamine* will only respond in this way if the leaves are separated from the parent plant.

The position on the leaf of these embryos is fixed according to each plant's characteristic and it is not influenced by the way the actual plantlets develop. The plantlets in *Kalanchoe* leaves, for example, arise between the jagged edges of the leaves; in *Mitella* and *Cardamine*, the plantlets appear at the junction of the leaf-stalk and leaf-blade. *Sedum*, however, produces only one plantlet and this is at the base of each sessile leaf.

Collect the plantlets from those plants that produce them naturally. With some of these plants, such as *Kalanchoe*, the plantlets fall off once the roots begin to develop. Plant them in cuttings compost in a labelled seed tray. Repot them separately once they have established properly.

Although other plants such as *Asplenium* and *Cystoperis* develop foliar embryos naturally, it is best to remove the leaf together with the plantlets to allow them slightly longer to become established before separating them from the parent leaf. Place the leaf flat on some cuttings compost in a seed tray. Pin it in position with a light wire staple if it does not sit flat on the compost. Label and leave on a shaded greenhouse bench. Ensure that the parent leaf does not become desiccated. Separate the plantlets and pot on once they have rooted and established. This should take seven to eight weeks.

Some plants, such as *Tiarella*, will only be stimulated into developing plantlets from foliar embryos if their leaves are severed. Cut off a leaf as soon as it has expanded fully. Set it on some cuttings compost in a seed tray. Label; then place in a warm (21°C/70°F), humid, shady environment such as a polythene tent until the plantlets develop and establish (five to seven weeks); then separate and pot on. Succulents, such as *Sedum* and *Kalanchoe*, can be left on an open bench in a greenhouse to develop their plantlets. Certain *Kalanchoe* respond best if the leaves are stimulated in spring to produce plantlets.

Establishing naturally produced plantlets

1 Cut off a leaf together with its plantlets. Fill a container with some cuttings compost and firm.

2 Pin the leaf flat on the compost with a wire staple. Label and place on a shaded greenhouse bench.

3 Ensure the leaf does not dry out. Separate the new plantlets and pot on once they are rooted.

Stimulating plantlet development

1 Cut off a leaf as soon as it has expanded fully. Fill a container with some cuttings compost.

2 Set the leaf on the compost. Label. Place in a warm (21°C/70°F), humid, shaded environment.

3 Leave until the plantlets develop and establish. Then separate, pot on and label.

WHERE FOLIAR EMBRYOS CAN DEVELOP

Kalanchoe   *Tolmiea menziesii*   *Sedum*

Grafting/Whip-and-tongue 1

Grafting is a technique of joining two parts of different plants together in such a way that they will unite and continue their growth as one plant.

One part, called the scion, is usually a stem from the plant to be propagated. This is grafted on to a root system from another plant, which is called the rootstock (also, the stock or understock). All the various techniques of joining plants are called grafting, although, when buds only are joined to the rootstock, it is sometimes called budding.

There are two basic grafting positions: apical grafting, in which the top of the rootstock is removed and is replaced with the scion; and side grafting, in which the scion is grafted on to the side of the rootstock and the rootstock above the graft is not removed until after a union is achieved.

Because time-consuming preparation work is necessary before two plants can be joined, grafting is superficially a less attractive technique than other relatively easy methods of vegetative propagation, such as taking stem cuttings or layering. However, some plants such as witch-hazel are not easily propagated by any other vegetative method if selected forms are required, and so they are grafted on to rootstocks.

Perhaps the most useful reason for grafting is to transfer the benefits of a particular rootstock on to another plant. Various fruit-tree rootstocks, for example, have been developed to control both the size and fruiting vigour of other varieties of fruit tree. Other advantages that a rootstock might possess are resistance to pests and diseases; toleration of high soil-moisture levels and salt concentrations; and toleration of high alkalinity levels in the soil. The more rootstock incorporated into a new plant, the more influence the rootstock will have.

Another advantage of grafting is that more than one scion can be joined on to a plant. This is particularly useful with fruit trees as a suitable pollinator variety can be grafted into a tree or bush already grafted with another variety, or it may allow a decorative stem to be grafted on and then be top worked with another variety.

There are a number of problems associated with grafting. The main one is ensuring two plants are compatible. This limitation determines which variety and species of plants can be grafted on to which rootstocks; in general, it is normal to graft varieties on to their own species or very closely related ones.

To graft successfully, it is vitally important to position the various tissues of the stem correctly so that the stem can make a quick and continuous union. The cambium is the actively growing part of the stem that lies just under the bark. This cambium layer on both the scion and the rootstock must be positioned so they are absolutely adjacent to each other, or at least in as much contact as possible.

The successful formation of a graft also depends on making and matching cuts quickly and cleanly: the cut surfaces must be placed in contact with the minimum of delay. Should the surfaces dry out, the tissues will die and so make an effective barrier to the development of a successful union.

The making of a graft union is only partly due to successful carpentry. Much also

THE ADVANTAGES POSSESSED BY VARIOUS ROOTSTOCKS

Rootstock	Advantage	Plant
East Malling series (EM)	Controls vigour	Apple
Malling Merton series (MM)	Resists woolly aphids and controls vigour	Apple
Colt, F12/1	Controls vigour	Cherry
East Malling quince	Controls vigour	Pear
Brompton, Pixie, St Julien A	Controls vigour	Plum
Rhododendron 'Cunningham's White'	Tolerates up to pH7	Rhododendron
Rosa chinensis 'Manetti'	Tolerates soil moisture and salt concentration	Roses (pot-grown)
Rosa laxa	Does not produce suckers, has few thorns and has long hypocotyl	Roses

Whip-and-tongue grafting

1 Select a plant that will be suitable as rootstock. Plant it outdoors. Label and leave for a growing season.

2 Select a plant that is suitable as scion material. Cut off some vigorous hardwood stems for scions.

3 Bundle these scions together. Heel them into the ground in a well-drained, cool place. Label.

4 Trim the bottom 12–15 in on the rootstock of all branches just before the leaf-buds break.

5 Cut back the rootstock to where the scion is to be grafted. Make a 1½ in sloping cut at the top.

6 Lift the scions from the ground. Make a top cut just above a bud about four buds from the base.

Grafting/Whip-and-tongue 2

depends on providing suitable conditions for the tissues to develop and grow to form a successful union. In effect, this means that water loss must be prevented and warmth must be provided round the grafted parts by carefully covering them until they have joined together.

Traditionally, the grafted parts have been covered and tied together with raffia, but most grafts are now enclosed by ½ in wide clear polythene strip. This has the advantage of completely surrounding and sealing the cut areas, so reducing water loss to a minimum. The graft union on indoor grafted plants is taped with rubberized strip before being placed in a humid atmosphere to develop.

Once the grafted parts have successfully united, the development of the new plant depends on preventing any further competition from the rootstock. Therefore, always remove all subsequent growths from anywhere on the rootstock.

Although it is theoretically possible to graft at almost any time of the year, the best season for most grafting is in the spring.

Shield-budding, however, must normally wait until midsummer when the bark lifts easily from the wood on the rootstock.

Whip-and-tongue grafting
Whip-and-tongue grafting is commonly used to propagate fruit trees, although the technique can be employed successfully for trees and shrubs with tissues that will also readily unite at relatively low temperatures.

Select a plant that will be suitable as rootstock and plant it outdoors. Label it and leave it to establish for one growing season.

In mid-winter, select a plant that is suitable as scion material. From it take some hardwood stems with all their previous season's growth. Bundle these scions together and heel them in 6 in of soil in a well-drained cool position. Firm back the soil and label them. When the scions are eventually grafted in spring, they will be less developed than the growth on the rootstock.

Prepare the rootstock once its sap has started to rise; this is usually just before the leaf-buds break. Trim to make a single stem with no branches.

Fruit trees (especially apples) are grafted at 9–10 in above soil level to avoid problems such as collar rot. Ornamental plants, on the other hand, are grafted as close to the ground as feasible, to avoid unsightly bulges that may occur with certain rootstock/scion combinations.

Cut back the rootstock to the appropriate height with a pair of sharp secateurs. Then make a 1½ in sloping cut across the top, using a sharp knife.

Lift the scions from the ground. Select one that has a similar diameter at its base to that of the rootstock top. Take a sharp knife and make a top cut close above a bud about four to five buds from the scion base. Then make a sloping 1½ in cut across the base of the scion, ending it just below a bud; ensure the cut is at the same angle as the rootstock cut.

This is a splice or whip graft. To provide rigidity, add a tongue to the cuts.

The tongue is made from single cuts on both the scion and rootstock. From one-third of the way down the sloping cut on top of the rootstock, make a shallow, single ½ in slice down into the rootstock.

Make the scion tongue by cutting for ½ in from one-third of the way up the scion sloping cut, keeping the knife blade at the same angle as the tongue on the rootstock.

Slip the scion into the rootstock so they interlock. If the rootstock is thicker than the scion, move it to one side until there is good contact between the two cambial layers. Bind with clear polythene grafting tape to hold the join firmly. Seal the top of the scion with tree paint and label.

For a wide range of trees and shrubs, including apple and pear trees, the grafted parts can then be left to unite. Cherry trees, however, should have their scion and grafted area covered with a polythene bag, which is then tied just below the union—the increased temperature hastening development.

Remove the grafting tape and polythene bag as soon as the cut surfaces start callusing, which means the two grafted parts are beginning to join.

Cut off any growth that the rootstock may produce and, if required, reduce the scion shoots to just one to promote a single-stemmed tree or shrub.

7 Make a 1½ in basal cut at the same angle as the rootstock cut. End it just below the bottom bud.

8 Make a shallow, single ½ in slice into the rootstock from one-third down the sloping cut.

9 Make a shallow, single ½ in slice into the scion from one-third up the scion sloping cut.

10 Slip the scion into the rootstock so they interlock.

11 Bind the join firmly with clear polythene tape. Dab the top of the scion with tree paint. Label.

12 Remove the polythene tape once the cut surfaces start callusing. Cut off any rootstock growth.

Roses: introduction

Most people grow at least a few roses in their garden or against the walls of their house, but to many gardeners the correct way to prune roses remains a complicated and mysterious process.

Roses in the wild produce strong new shoots from near to the base of the plant each season. In subsequent years the secondary, or lateral, growth from these shoots becomes progressively weaker. When strong new shoots appear, the food taken in by the roots is directed to this new growth and the original shoots are gradually starved out. Eventually the old shoots die and remain as dead wood before falling to the ground—a natural but long-winded method of pruning. The purpose of pruning is to short-circuit nature by cutting away the old worn-out shoots and so encourage the production of vigorous, disease-free new growth and the optimum number of flowers for the rose concerned.

Pruning is a simple operation, but as roses range in size from miniatures, which are less than 1ft tall, to vigorous climbers, which may reach 30–40ft, they require a variety of pruning techniques to keep them healthy, free flowering and within bounds.

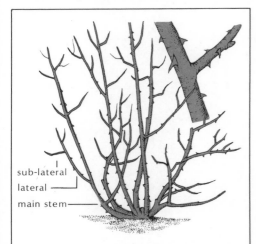

Rose "eyes" or growth buds are located in the axils of the leaves. If the leaf has fallen they can be seen just above a leaf-scar. Always cut close to a bud.

There are certain general principles that apply to pruning all kinds of roses.

1 Always use sharp secateurs and a knife, as a ragged cut caused by blunt tools may cause the shoot to die back (a). The cut must not be more than $\frac{1}{4}$in above the eye and must slope gently away from it (b). If you cut too high the snag will die back (c); a cut too low may damage the eye or allow disease spores to enter the wound (d). A cut in the wrong direction allows moisture to gather by the eye (e).

2 Cut back into healthy wood. If the pith is brown or discoloured cut back the shoot until healthy white pith is reached.

3 Cut to an outward-pointing eye to encourage an open-centre habit. With roses of spreading habit it is sometimes useful to prune some branches to inward-pointing eyes to obtain more upright growth.

4 Vigorous modern roses may often produce two or three shoots from one eye after pruning. As soon as possible reduce these to one shoot by pinching out the young growth. Never allow more than one shoot to grow from a pruning cut.

5 Cut out completely any dead and diseased stems (a) and weak, spindly growth (b). This may mean cutting it out to ground level or, with a lateral growth, to the junction with a healthy stem. Where two branches cross, cut one back below the point where they cross (c). With shrub and climbing roses this is not always easy, but wherever possible at least prevent branches rubbing against each other or on their supports.

6 Keep all branches well spaced to allow free air-flow through the plant and to allow light to reach the leaves. This lessens the likelihood of such diseases as black spot, rose mildew and rose-rust, which all thrive under stagnant air conditions.

7 Burn prunings to reduce the possibility of spreading disease.

You may not know to which group the roses in your garden belong, particularly if you moved house in late autumn or winter and there are no labels on the plants. If you are not sure how to deal with them, confine your winter pruning to the points made under general principles. Next summer you can see from the way they flower to which group they belong and prune accordingly. Pruning techniques may vary slightly in different conditions, and with experience you will quickly learn how to deal with them to suit your own local soil and climate.

SUCKERS

Most roses are budded on to the selected rootstock of a wild rose species. During the growing season shoots may arise from below the budding point. These are sucker growths from the rootstock, which can quickly weaken, and eventually replace, the rose variety concerned. They must be removed as soon as they are seen.

Trace the sucker back to the root from which it springs and pull it off at the point of origin. Never cut it off at ground level; this only encourages basal buds to produce several more suckers.

With standard roses, which are budded at the tops of stems of wild rose rootstocks, shoots may arise from below the budding point on the stem. These are treated as suckers and carefully pulled off, or pared away with a sharp knife.

Time of Pruning

Time of pruning differs to some extent with the group of roses concerned and further details are given in each section.

Winter pruning

Winter pruning is best carried out between mid-February and mid-March, depending on locality, season and prevailing weather conditions. Earlier pruning from December to January can lead to precocious growth and this is often damaged in severe weather. Later pruning in April often involves wasting the plant's energy by cutting off young growth already produced. The best guide is to prune, weather permitting, when the growth buds about halfway up the most vigorous stems are beginning to swell.

After winter pruning put a good mulch of well-rotted compost or manure around the bases of your roses. Pruning encourages a constant supply of young, vigorous shoots and these will only be produced if sufficient food is available.

Frost damage may occur in some seasons, particularly with fluctuating spring weather of warm spells followed by frosty periods. If new shoots are damaged by frost the main shoots must be cut back to dormant eyes.

EXHIBITION PRUNING

Rose-growers who exhibit at National and local shows aim to provide high-quality blooms for a given date. This involves considerable experience and an intimate knowledge of individual rose varieties. It is not the purpose of this book to attempt to provide a guide for would-be exhibitors. Suffice it to say that it usually involves harder initial winter pruning to limit the number of shoots produced and, for Hybrid Tea roses, disbudding to only one flower per stem.

Summer pruning

Summer pruning is confined to the removal of flowers or flower clusters and is carried out through the flowering season.

Some roses, such as 'Scarlet Fire' and *Rosa*

Hybrid Tea

Correctly cut Hybrid Tea inflorescence
Cut back to a strong outward-facing shoot or eye below the inflorescence.

Floribunda

Correctly cut Floribunda inflorescence
Remove the whole truss by cutting back to the first strong outward-pointing eye or shoot.

moyesii are grown for their autumn display of brightly coloured hips as well as their flowers. With these roses the flowers should be left, but with most roses it is best to remove all flower clusters as soon as they fade. This

Incorrectly cut Hybrid Tea inflorescence
The stems are cut too long and will weaken the plant.

Incorrectly cut Floribunda inflorescence
The individual flowers in the truss have been cut off leaving weak stems.

prevents the plant wasting food on unnecessary seed production, removes a possible source of disease from the decaying petals (particularly in wet weather) and encourages fresh growth and bloom in repeat-flowering roses.

Cut back to the first convenient strong eye or young shoot below the flower stem or flower truss. Normally this should be an outward-pointing eye, but occasionally it may be inward pointing to maintain a well-shaped plant. If only the flower and its stalk are removed weak stem buds just below the inflorescence will grow and produce thin, straggly shoots.

Never cut a flower stem longer than is really required and never take more than one or two long stems from a single bush. Leaves manufacture much of the plant's food so cutting off too many when it is in active growth will weaken the plant.

In late summer the removal of faded flower clusters should be discontinued or kept to a minimum to avoid stimulating further growth shoots, which may be damaged in winter.

BLIND SHOOTS

Some varieties of Hybrid Teas and Floribundas and climbers produce a few shoots that are "blind" and do not flower. These blind shoots should be cut hard back as soon as they are seen, to encourage vigorous growth from buds lower down on the shoot, otherwise the flowering potential of the plant is diminished.

Autumn pruning

In very windy areas it is worth shortening any very long growths by 6–12 in during November. This lessens the risk of damage by wind-rock to the roots.

Hybrid Teas and Hybrid Perpetuals

Hybrid Teas and Hybrid Perpetuals are pruned in the same way. The aim is to encourage the production of strong basal growths to form an open-centred, cup-shaped plant with an evenly spaced framework of shoots.

Hybrid Teas and Hybrid Perpetuals flower on the new (current) season's growth and most benefit from a moderate to fairly severe annual pruning. This keeps the plants bushy and ensures a constant supply of strong young shoots. Annual pruning is from mid-February to mid- or late March. Some variation will occur depending on local soil conditions and the prevailing weather at pruning time.

Very vigorous roses, for example 'Peace', should be pruned only lightly as severe pruning stimulates very robust but often flowerless shoots. Other vigorous cultivars, such as 'Chinatown' and 'Uncle Walter', produce their flowers on tall, 5–6 ft stems. An alternative method of growing these cultivars is to peg down the stems horizontally. A different pruning technique is required.

The first year

First-year (newly planted) Hybrid Teas or Hybrid Perpetuals are usually received in autumn from the nursery with 3–4 strong shoots. Cut back main shoots slightly if not already done and prune long, coarse or damaged roots before planting. In late February to mid-March cut back each shoot to 2–4 eyes or 6 in from ground level. This encourages strong basal growths to be produced. If the soil is very sandy and lacking nutrients, more moderate first-year pruning to 4–6 eyes or 9 in is undertaken, followed by more severe pruning in the second year.

Second and subsequent years

In the second and subsequent years Hybrid Teas and Hybrid Perpetuals should be moderately pruned. Cut back the strongest (thickest) shoots to 4–6 eyes or 9 in and the less vigorous shoots to 2–4 eyes or 6 in. This method of pruning gives the best all-round results. As the plant becomes older, one or two old stems should be cut out to the base.

The first year

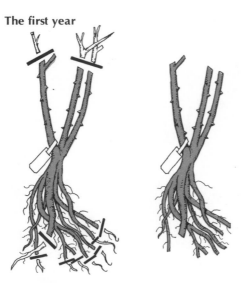

1 Autumn. Open-ground bush as received. Cut back main shoots slightly if not already done. Prune long, coarse or damaged roots before planting.

Second and subsequent years

4 Mid-February to mid- or late March. Cut out dead or diseased wood. Cut out weak stems. Cut out crossing stems. Cut out inward-growing stems.

2 Mid-February to mid- or late March. Cut back each shoot to 2–4 eyes or 6 in from ground level. By June or July new shoots will have grown.

5 At the same time, cut back strong stems to 4–6 eyes or 9 in and less vigorous stems and remaining laterals to 2–4 eyes or 6 in.

3 September to October. At the end of first season's growth, tip back flowered stems and cut out any soft, unripe shoots.

6 September to October. At the end of the season's growth, tip back flowered stems and cut out any soft, unripe shoots.

Floribundas

Floribunda roses are more vigorous than most Hybrid Teas and Hybrid Perpetuals and produce a succession of large clusters of moderate-sized flowers. It is sometimes difficult to prune Floribundas to obtain the optimum number of blooms. Severe annual pruning, as used for Hybrid Teas and Hybrid Perpetuals, can weaken Floribundas within a few years, while light pruning creates large bushes filled with weak, spindly growth.

Moderate pruning of each shoot to 6–8 eyes or 12–18 in is often recommended and proves reasonably successful, particularly in windy areas. It does not, however, always produce the almost continuous summer display which can be achieved, and some of the older wood tends to die away without replacement basal shoots forming.

A combination of light pruning of some shoots to produce early flowers and harder pruning of other shoots to encourage renewal of basal growths and provide later flowers has proved the most satisfactory method.

Annual pruning is from mid-February to mid-March. Variations will occur depending on local soil and weather conditions.

The first year
First-year Floribundas are usually received with 3–5 strong shoots and often weak, spindly laterals. Between mid-February and mid-March cut back each strong shoot to 3–5 eyes or 6–9 in and remove all weak shoots.

The second year
In mid-February to mid-March of the second year all the main one-year-old basal (or near-basal) shoots must be shortened by approximately one-third of their length and any remaining laterals cut back to 2–3 eyes or 4–6 in. Strong shoots from older wood (pruned back at planting to 3–5 eyes) must be cut back to 3–5 eyes or removed completely to keep the centre of the bush open.

Third and subsequent years
In the third and subsequent years this renewal programme is continued between mid-February and mid-March. Prune back strong one-year-old shoots lightly by one-third and cut back two-year-old wood to 3–5 eyes or 6–9 in from ground level. If the bush is crowded cut out some old growths to base.

The first year

1 Autumn. Open-ground bush as received. Cut back main shoots slightly if not already done. Prune long, coarse or damaged roots before planting.

2 Mid-February to mid-March. Cut back all growths to 3–5 eyes or 6–9 in from the base. Remove all weak shoots. By April or May new shoots will begin to form.

3 October. Growth at end of first season. Tip back main growths and cut out any soft, unripe shoots.

The second year

4 Mid-February to mid-March. Cut out dead or diseased wood, weak stems, crossing and inward-growing stems. Prune back one-year-old basal shoots by one-third. Cut back older wood to 3–5 eyes or 6–9 in and remaining laterals to 2–3 eyes or 4–6 in.

5 October. Growth at end of second season. Tip back main growths and cut out any soft unripe shoots.

Third and subsequent years

6 Mid-February to mid-March. Cut out dead or diseased wood. Cut out weak stems. Cut out crossing stems. Cut out inward-growing stems.

7 At the same time, prune back all main one-year-old basal shoots by one-third and their laterals to 2–3 eyes or 4–6 in. Prune older wood hard to 3–5 eyes or 6–9 in from ground level and, if the centre of the bush is crowded, cut out some old growths to base.

Climbers and Ramblers 1

Climbing and rambling roses either bloom freely in glorious unruly tangles or produce only a few poor-quality flowers. However, with pruning and training they will provide a regular abundance of good-quality blooms.

For convenience, the ramblers and climbers have been divided into five groups, but these should not be taken as rigid divisions and some overlap of pruning techniques occurs.

Wherever sufficient space is available it is always advantageous to train new extension shoots of climbing roses as near to the horizontal as possible, provided allowance is made for the need to create a balanced plant, and if the natural growth of the rose allows it. Vertically placed shoots will frequently form only a few flowering laterals at the tips. Horizontally placed shoots will produce flowering laterals along most of their length and create a far better display.

The provision of new shoots depends on adequate feeding, particularly in Group 1, where virtually all the old wood is removed annually. To avoid wind breakage and make training into a balanced framework easier, make sure that all new long growths are tied in as they develop.

Group 1 includes the true ramblers, varieties such as 'Dorothy Perkins' and 'Excelsa',

derived from *Rosa wichuraiana*. They flower in June and July on laterals of long, flexible, basal shoots (canes) produced the previous season.

The first year
Prune all vigorous shoots back to 9–15 in from the base at planting and remove completely any weak growth. This hard initial pruning encourages vigorous, balanced growth during the first season, but no flowers are produced until the following year.

Second and subsequent years
Pruning of established plants consists of cutting to the base all the shoots that have bloomed. This should be done soon after flowering, usually between August and September. The developing young basal growths are tied in to replace the old shoots, and the young shoots will produce flowering laterals the following summer. Where the site allows, train most of the new shoots as near to the horizontal as possible to encourage maximum development of flowering laterals.

Sometimes only a few basal growths are produced. If this happens, retain a proportion of the strongest old shoots and cut back their laterals to 2–3 eyes or 4–6 in from the main stem after flowering.

The first year

1 Autumn. Plant as received with 3–4 shoots about 4–5 ft long. Prune back shoots to 9–15 in and trim uneven and coarse roots before planting. **Spring.** New shoots begin to develop.

2 June to September. Strong shoots have developed from the pruned growth and from the base of the plant. Train them into place.

Second and subsequent years

3 June to July. Plant flowers on lateral shoots produced on previous year's growth. Young basal shoots develop; train these more or less horizontally and tie in.

4 August to September. Cut out flowered shoots to base leaving one or two to fill in framework if required. Cut back laterals to 2–3 eyes or 4–6 in. Tie in all new growth.

5 October. Shoots fully trained in at end of the second season's growth.

Climbers and Ramblers 2

Group 2 includes many well-known vigorous rose varieties such as 'Albertine' and 'Chaplin's Pink'. They flower once in summer on the laterals of long shoots produced the previous year. They differ from true ramblers in producing very few basal shoots each season, most of the new growth coming from higher up on the old stems. The aim of pruning is to remove old wood in proportion to the new.

The first year
Newly planted varieties in this group are treated in the same way as Group 1.

Second, third and subsequent years
Pruning of established plants takes place soon after flowering. Cut away completely one or two old growths and train in their place any basal shoots that have started to develop. If no basal shoots are forming cut back one or two old growths to 12–18 in from the base.

Cut back old wood higher up on the plant to a point where a vigorous new leading shoot has started to grow. Keep leading shoots at full length and train them as near to the horizontal as possible. Any shorter laterals should be cut back to 2–3 eyes or 6 in.

The second year

1 June to July. Plant flowers on lateral shoots produced on previous year's growth. One or two basal growths develop and some leader shoots develop higher up.

2 August to September. Cut back old growth to main replacement leaders. Cut back flowering laterals to 2–3 eyes or 6 in.

Train replacement leaders as near to the horizontal as possible. Cut back weak leaders to 2–3 eyes or 6 in.

Third and subsequent years

3 June to July. Flowers are produced along last year's leaders and spurred back laterals. New leaders begin to develop.

4 August to September. Repeat the pruning operation in Caption 2. Cut back one or two old shoots to 12–18 in from the base to encourage replacement basal growth.

Climbers and Ramblers 3

Group 3 contains those ramblers and climbers that produce their blooms on the current season's growth, and includes climbers of Hybrid Tea style and climbing sports of Hybrid Teas and Floribundas. Most, although by no means all, of the roses in this group are repeat-flowering. Their long, flexible shoots make them ideal for training against walls and fences and on pergolas.

The first year
Newly planted roses in this group should not be pruned back at planting, although the roots should be trimmed and any damaged tips and very weak growth removed. This is because many are climbing sports from bush varieties and hard pruning at planting may cause them to revert to bush form.

It is essential to build up a strong, evenly spaced framework of branches, as roses in this group do not readily produce vigorous basal growths once established, but develop most of their young shoots higher up on existing main stems. Horizontal or angled training of new leader shoots at an early stage will help to prevent the base of the plant becoming too bare.

Second and subsequent years
Apart from maintaining the plant within its allotted space, pruning and training of mature roses in this group is restricted to summer pruning flowering laterals during the growing season as the flowers fade. Diseased, dead and weak wood should be cut out in late autumn or winter before any growth occurs. At the same time train new growths into gaps in the framework and trim all flowered laterals back to 3–4 eyes or 6 in.

With old plants it will occasionally be necessary to cut back weak and exhausted shoots to a few inches from the base. This should encourage one or two vigorous basal shoots to be produced.

The first year

1 Autumn or early spring. Plant as received with 3–4 shoots 4–5 ft long. Trim any uneven and coarse roots. Tip back slightly any unripe or damaged growths. Do not prune except to cut out any weak side shoots. Begin to train shoots.

2 July to August. Tie in framework of new shoots as they develop. Some flowers are produced at the tips of new growths and on laterals. New shoots develop and should be tied in. Summer prune.

Second and subsequent years

3 October to March. Prune back flowered laterals to 3–4 eyes or 6 in. Cut out weak wood and tie in leading shoots.

4 July to August. Flowers appear at tips of new growths and on laterals. Summer prune. Tie in new shoots as they develop.

5 October to March. Prune back flowered laterals to 3–4 eyes or 6 in. Cut out weak wood. Tie in leading shoots from main stems of framework.

Climbers and Ramblers 4

Group 4 includes pillar roses, which are repeat-flowering and produce their blooms on the current season's wood. They differ from roses in Group 3 in their more moderate, usually upright growth and seldom exceed 8–10 ft in height. Their shoots are generally less flexible and, as their name indicates, they are suitable for growing against pillars or for training in positions where limited horizontal space is available.

The first year

Newly planted varieties in this group are treated in the same way as Group 3. Before planting, trim the roots and remove any damaged tips and weak growth. In view of their naturally upright habit do not train the leader shoots at an angle as in group 3.

Second and subsequent years

Pruning of mature pillar roses involves routine removal of all flower trusses as they fade in summer. In late autumn or early winter, cut away weak, diseased and dead wood and shorten some leaders and laterals on main growths just sufficiently to maintain a symmetrical shape. To stimulate growth at the base of the plant, cut back the lower leaders by two-thirds of their length. In old plants where growth is crowded, cut out one or two of the oldest stems to ground level.

The degree of trimming differs with the rose variety and the space available. Some of the more vigorous varieties of pillar rose, which have flexible growth, particularly of the lateral shoots, may require more severe restrictions.

VIGOROUS CLIMBERS

Group 5 includes climbing species, or near-species, and hybrids of tremendous vigour, often producing flexible 20 ft growths each season. These roses are typified by the exuberant *Rosa filipes* 'Kiftsgate' and the Banksian roses. If grown unrestricted in trees it is impractical and quite unnecessary to prune or train them at all, except for the removal of dead, diseased and weak wood where this is possible.

When they become too overwhelming the renovation procedure as illustrated on page 20 should be employed.

Initial planting and training is as for Group 3, but laterals need only very light pruning.

HORIZONTAL TRAINING

Many climbing roses can be trained horizontally along the ground, instead of on a wall or other support.

A similar method is used with vigorous Hybrid Tea, Hybrid Perpetual and shrub roses. The flexuous trailing shoots of varieties derived from *Rosa wichuraiana* are admirably suited for this kind of training, to cover banks and other areas where fairly dense ground cover is required. The effect is dramatic, but needs a large area of ground.

The shoots are pegged down close to ground level and the same pruning methods are used as when these varieties are grown more conventionally as climbers.

The first year

The second year

1 Autumn to early spring. Plant with shoots tied into a post or pillar.

2 June to August. Plants flower on laterals of the old growth. New growth has developed from previous year's stems and from the base. Summer prune.

3 November. Cut back flowered laterals and some new leaders sufficiently to maintain the symmetry of the plant.

4 At the same time, cut out weak, diseased and dead wood. Tie in new shoots.

5 June to August. Plants flower on laterals of the old growth. New growth has developed from previous year's stems and from the base. Summer prune.

6 November. Cut back flowered laterals and some new leaders sufficiently to maintain the symmetry of the plant.

Species and Shrub Roses 1

Shrub and species roses are grown less often than Hybrid Teas and Floribundas, but are increasing in popularity. Grouped together or planted singly in shrub or mixed borders, shrub roses are extremely rewarding during summer and autumn, particularly in informal settings, where modern bedding roses may look out of place.

It is often recommended to leave shrub roses entirely unpruned, "to grow naturally", or suggested that only very minor trimming is necessary. Generally shrub and species roses left to their own devices will grow and flower well for a few years, but this *laissez-faire* approach, although an appealing one, will not always provide the optimum possible display.

To obtain the best results it is necessary to carry out a certain amount of pruning annually, even though it may be no more than a gentle manicure.

In order to simplify the process as much as possible three groups have been recognized, but the divisions are arbitrary and not rigid. Inevitably overlap occurs and slight modifications of pruning techniques may be needed for a few individual roses that do not fit neatly into the groups defined here.

Pruning shrub and species roses involves exactly the same general principles that apply to other roses (see page 188): that is, to encourage strong basal, or near-basal growths and to replace older stems that have lost their vigour and flower sparsely.

It is important also to take into account that the flowers of some varieties may be produced on the current season's growth late in the year as well as on laterals and sub-laterals from older growth; flowers of some varieties are produced mainly during June and July in one flush, but others may be repeat-flowering, producing bloom until the autumn; attractive fruits (hips) may be a feature of some varieties and therefore do not need their spent flowers removed.

The following general points always apply:
1 No initial pruning is required when planting, apart from the removal of coarse and damaged roots and the shortening of unripe or damaged shoots.
2 A sturdy framework of well-spaced shoots should be built up and thin weak growth removed after flowering; dead and diseased wood is cut out as seen.
3 Regular pruning to remove spent flowers is desirable unless dealing with varieties grown for their fruits. Repeat-flowering shrub roses, such as the hybrid musks, benefit considerably from this "manicuring" as their energy is put into producing new flowering laterals rather than fruits.
4 Slight tipping back by a few inches of all vigorous shoots in winter will encourage further flowering laterals and sub-laterals the following summer. It also helps by removing a source of disease, as the thin or soft tips are often mildewed.

Group 1 brings together the following kinds of rose, which require only minimal pruning for many years:
Species roses (other than climbers) and their close hybrids
Rosa spinosissima, the Burnet rose, and hybrids derived from it
Rosa rugosa, the Japanese rose, and hybrids derived from it
Gallica roses
Hybrid musk roses.

Almost all of these roses are of a fairly dense, bushy habit and flower mainly on short lateral and sub-lateral shoots produced from second-year or older wood. They do not regularly produce vigorous basal growths once established.

The first and second year
In the first year and second year after planting pruning is more or less confined to points 1 to 4 mentioned in the introduction to this section. Occasionally a badly placed shoot may need to be cut out to the base.

Third and subsequent years
In the third and subsequent years one or two older main growths, which only flower sparsely, may be cut out in winter to encourage basal replacement shoots and to maintain a sturdy vigorous framework. More drastic treatment may occasionally be necessary with very old bushes. In winter cut out several old and poorly placed main branches to leave a well-spaced framework.

The second year

1 February to March. Tip back all vigorous shoots. Cut out to the base any badly placed shoots. Basal shoots have developed.

2 June to August. Plant flowers on laterals of old wood, new basal shoots develop.

3 September. Summer prune. After flowering cut out thin, weak growth. Cut out dead and diseased wood.

Third and subsequent years

4 February to March. Tip back all vigorous shoots and laterals if required. Cut out one or two older main shoots that have flowered sparsely.

5 July to August. Plant flowers on laterals of old wood, new basal shoots develop.

6 September. Summer prune. After flowering cut out thin, weak growth to maintain a well-spaced framework. Cut out dead and diseased wood.

Species and Shrub Roses 2

Group 2 consists of roses that flower mainly on short lateral and sub-lateral shoots produced from second-year or older wood. This group includes "old roses" such as the Albas, Centifolias, Moss roses and most Damasks. A large number of modern shrub roses, which do not repeat-flower but have one main flush of bloom in midsummer, are also included.

The first year

First-year roses are treated in the same way as those in Group 1. Tip back unripe or damaged shoots and remove coarse or damaged roots.

Second and subsequent years

Mature roses in Group 2 differ from those in Group 1 by their regular production of vigorous basal, or near-basal, shoots, which may reach 5–8ft in one season. In the second year these long shoots produce an abundance of flowering laterals, which often weigh them down so that the shoots are almost resting on the ground and in danger of breaking.

This growth habit necessitates a different pruning technique from Group 1 so that the natural habit is maintained while preventing the top-heavy flowering shoots from snapping or dragging their blooms in the mud.

In addition to the general points 1–4 of the introduction to this section all the vigorous, long shoots of the current year are pruned back by up to one-third of their length and laterals on older main growths are cut back to 2–3 eyes or 6in from the stems during the winter. Care must be taken not to shorten these long shoots too much or the elegant arched habit can be lost and the potential to produce an abundance of flowering laterals is much reduced.

This annual pruning, together with the removal each year of one or two old spent growths, should keep all roses in this group flowering profusely and growing strongly for many years.

The second year

1 February to March. Cut back long new basal growths by up to one-third. Cut back laterals on flowered shoots to 2–3 eyes or 4–6in. Cut out any badly placed shoots.

2 June to August. Plant flowers on cut-back laterals of old wood. New basal shoots develop. Summer prune.

Third and subsequent years

3 September to November. Tip back extra-long growths to minimize wind-rock. No other pruning is required.

4 February to March. Cut back long new basal growths by up to one-third. Cut back laterals on flowered shoots to 2–3 eyes or 4–6in. Cut out to base any badly placed and old shoots that flower sparsely.

5 June to August. Plant flowers on cut-back laterals of old wood. New basal shoots develop. Summer prune.

6 September to November. Tip back extra-long growths to minimize wind-rock. No other pruning is required.

Species and Shrub Roses 3

Group 3 can be regarded as a minor variant of Group 2 and includes most of the China roses and a number of modern shrub roses such as 'Fountain'. Of the "old roses" many Bourbons, such as the well-known 'Zephirine Drouhin' and 'Mme Isaac Pereire', also come into this group. Certain very robust Hybrid Teas and Hybrid Perpetuals can be included in this group and treated as shrubs for borders.

The first year
First-year plants in this group are treated in the same way as those in Group 1.

Second and subsequent years
Mature roses in Group 3 differ from those in Group 2 in flowering more or less recurrently throughout summer and autumn on both the current season's shoots and on laterals and sub-laterals from second-year or older wood. Many also produce long, flexuous or robust growths, either from the base or higher up the plant on strong, established stems. These new shoots often develop sprays of flowers at their tips during the current season, unlike the roses in Group 2.

Severe, or moderately severe, winter pruning of all these roses produces vigorous but sometimes sparsely flowering or even non-flowering shoots. Inevitably the display is delayed and intermittent rather than continuous. Light pruning is needed to achieve the best results.

Group 3 roses tend to produce fresh flowering laterals and sub-laterals all summer and they quickly build up into dense twiggy birds'-nests. Dead-head and thin slightly during the flowering period. This treatment helps to maintain continuity of flower. Otherwise winter pruning is similar to that of Group 2 with more emphasis on removing twiggy growths that have lost their vigour.

The second year

1 February to March. Cut back very long, new basal or near-basal one-year shoots by up to one-third. Take care to maintain the arching habit. Cut back laterals on shoots which flowered last season to 2–3 eyes (3–6 in). Cut out weak or badly placed shoots.

2 June to July. Plant flowers on laterals from previous season's wood. Basal and near-basal shoots are developing. Summer prune.

Third and subsequent years

3 August to September. Flower is produced on laterals from current season's growth. Twiggy sub-laterals have developed from summer-pruned growth.

4 October. Tip back extra-long growths to minimize wind rock.

5 February to March. Cut back very long, new basal or near-basal one-year-old shoots by up to one-third. Take care to maintain the arching habit. Cut back laterals on shoots that flowered last season to 2–3 eyes (3–6 in). Cut out to base any old, badly placed or weak shoots. Mulch well.

6 June to July. Plant in flower on laterals from previous season's wood. Basal and near-basal shoots are developing. Summer prune.

Standard Roses

Hybrid Tea and Floribunda roses are frequently grown as standards, or half-standards, to give height among bedding roses in the garden, where they can be extremely effective, particularly if used in a formal context. They are usually budded on stems of *Rosa rugosa* or common briar, but have become less popular in recent years as the head is often frequently top-heavy and the slender stem requires careful staking to maintain the formal habit. Initial pruning, and subsequent treatment, is similar to that given to the same varieties when grown as bushes.

Light pruning leaves a fairly large head on a standard which is liable to wind damage, particularly in exposed gardens. Moderately severe pruning appropriate to the variety should be practised.

With Hybrid Teas cut back strong shoots to 3–5 eyes or 6 in. With Floribundas cut back one-year-old growth to 6–8 eyes or 10 in and two-year-old shoots to 3–6 eyes or 6 in.

BUDDING STANDARD ROSES

Standard roses are best propagated by inserting growth buds each side of the stem in order to obtain an even head; if only one bud is used one-sided growth normally occurs, so before you buy a standard make sure it is double-budded.

Weeping standards

Climbing roses are budded on tall stems of *Rosa rugosa* or common briar so that the long trailing growths hang down.

Weeping standards of rose varieties in Group 1 of ramblers and climbers (page 192) can be most attractive when grown correctly. Pruning is quite simple. In August to September cut out entirely the two-year-old shoots that have flowered and leave the vigorous young shoots to flower the following season. If insufficient young growths are produced leave a few of the two-year-old shoots in appropriate positions and cut back their laterals to 2–3 eyes or 6 in.

Varieties in Group 2 of ramblers and climbers (page 193) are less satisfactorily grown in this way and are now seldom seen. Pruning should be confined to cutting out surplus older wood and cutting back laterals to 2–3 eyes or 6 in after flowering. Tie down any vigorous young growths as they appear.

The first year

1 February to March. Cut back strong stems to 3–5 eyes or 6 in.

2 October to November. At the end of the season's growth, tip back main stems and cut out any soft, unripe shoots.

Second and subsequent years

3 February to March. Cut out dead, diseased, weak and crossing stems.

4 At the same time, cut back new shoots to 3–5 eyes or 6 in and remaining laterals to 2–4 eyes or 4–6 in.

Shrubs: introduction 1

A commonly held, but quite incorrect, belief is that all shrubs should be pruned, and pruned hard, each year. Often this takes the form of a "haircut" or involves slaughtering the branches to keep the plant within bounds. Both treatments result in a misshapen ugly specimen with little or no flower.

The other extreme of leaving the shrub entirely unpruned is to be preferred. Many deciduous and most evergreen shrubs will grow satisfactorily and give adequate flower without being pruned at all, provided there is ample room for them to develop and the soil is reasonably fertile.

There are, however, several groups of shrubs where correct pruning is beneficial in producing regular and abundant flowers together with healthy vigorous growth and foliage. These same species left unpruned may still flower fairly well, but the quality and quantity of bloom and growth is poor compared with correctly pruned specimens.

An understanding of the basic principles behind pruning and knowledge of the growth habit and method of flowering of the plant concerned is important, particularly the age of the wood on which flowers are borne.

Placing the shrub in the garden also has a bearing on pruning. Never try to fit a shrub which naturally grows to a large size into a position where limited room is available and constant pruning is necessary. This may seem obvious, but frequently one sees large shrubs cut back several times a year to fit a particular position. The result is an ugly plant with a mass of growth and virtually no flowers. So, if you want to grow a *Philadelphus* in a site where only a 4 ft spread is possible choose 'Manteau d'Hermine' (3 ft× 3 ft) or 'Erectus' (5 ft× 3 ft) which will fit, not 'Burfordensis' (12 ft× 6 ft) which is far too large.

Feeding and watering are also important if the shrub is to be pruned so that it produces healthy vigorous growth over a number of years.

When pruning any shrub try to obtain the optimum decorative effect whether it is grown for the flowers, fruit, foliage or the beauty of its winter stems. The pruning technique will vary with the shrub concerned and the effect required.

In some circumstances shrubs may be pruned by different methods to obtain different effects. The purple-leaved varieties of the smoke bush, *Cotinus coggygria*, for example, may be left virtually unpruned to form large 10–12 ft shrubs valued for the coloured foliage and smoke-like plumes of flowers. Alternatively, young plants may be cut back hard each spring to form smaller shrubs with masses of long unbranched stems with large bright purple leaves.

Try also to create and maintain a well-balanced and attractive overall shape and

appearance for the plant. Many shrubs are naturally neat and symmetrical in outline and require no more than the removal of the occasional awkwardly placed shoot that destroys this symmetry.

Others are unruly and may grow unevenly, presenting a lop-sided aspect with weak, twiggy growth on one side and strong healthy branches on the other. They require pruning to restore them to a reasonable shape. Strong shoots should be lightly pruned (a), which will result in moderate growth, while the weak wood (b) should be cut back hard to stimulate vigorous shoots, which will help to balance the shape (c). Do not cut back the strong shoots hard (d) and leave the weak unpruned (e) so that the overall height is the same. This will result in further strong growths being produced from the hard-pruned side but not from the unpruned growth, so accentuating rather than correcting the lack of balance (f).

Pruning should, in many but not all shrubs, also encourage the production of vigorous, basal or near-basal shoots to maintain the vitality of the plant and provide replacement growth for the older, worn-out branches. It also ensures an even distribution of flowers over the plant and prevents it becoming thin at the base and overcrowded at the top. The exceptions are such shrubs as the Japanese maple, witch hazel, and most evergreens.

Shrubs: introduction 2

Shrubs must be kept in a healthy condition. This involves the three "D's" mentioned on page 3—the removal and burning of all dead, diseased and damaged growth as soon as possible. It is obligatory for all plants.

Pruning cuts. All pruning cuts should be made correctly as shown. Incorrect cuts can result in die-back and disease problems. Cuts should be made just above an outward-pointing bud or shoot or above a strong pair of opposite buds so that the resulting shoots will be well placed in relation to the other new growths.

Reversion. Occasionally branches of shrubs with variegated foliage may revert to the original green-leaved form of the species concerned. If this occurs it is most important to remove the non-variegated branches completely as soon as they are seen. They are frequently more robust than the variegated shoots and if allowed to remain will, like suckers, gradually become dominant. Eventually the shrub almost reverts to its green-leaved form. Examples include *Elaeagnus pungens* 'Maculata' and *Kerria japonica* 'Picta'.

Newly planted shrubs. When received from the nursery or garden centre any shrub should be well shaped and bushy with a strong root system (a), and not one-sided (b). Most evergreens should need no pruning at planting apart from removing a damaged shoot or tipping back a wayward branch.

With such deciduous shrubs as *Deutzia* there may be some weak growth present and this should be cut out completely to encourage strong basal growths. Terminal growth should also be shortened slightly to a strong bud or pair of buds. Sometimes more drastic initial pruning is required. Details are given in the appropriate group.

Suckers. Although most modern shrubs are propagated vegetatively from cuttings and are on their own roots, a few are still budded or grafted on to stocks. These may occasionally produce sucker growths from the rootstocks and it is important to remove these as soon as they are seen. The sucker shoots should be traced back to their point of origin and carefully cut or pulled off so that the dormant buds at the base of each sucker are removed at the same time. Cutting them off at ground level merely results in a further cluster of suckers from these dormant buds. If the suckers are left they will gradually take over and replace the grafted plant.

Early training. Most shrubs produce a number of vigorous basal shoots during the first year or two after planting. These shoots will form the basic framework of the shrub and it is important to make sure that they are evenly spaced. Often they may be too close or crossing and, if left, will spoil the balance and overall symmetry of the shrub (c). If shoots are ill-placed or surplus, cut them out (d).

It is particularly important to do this with shrubs that do not naturally renew their growth from basal replacement shoots when older, but form a permanent, woody framework on which both extension growth and flowers are borne on the periphery. Examples of shrubs which come into this category are

magnolias, *Hamamelis*, and many evergreens, including rhododendrons and camellias.

In many cases it is desirable to keep deciduous shrubs open in the centre to allow free air circulation. This avoids stagnant conditions, which favour the spread of disease.

A number of deciduous shrubs such as the Japanese maple, *Acer palmatum,* naturally form an intricate network of crossing branchlets. Apart from the removal of dead or diseased wood, pruning, after the initial year or two, is unnecessary and undesirable as it may ruin the natural habit of the plant. Pruning of crossing branches should be confined to early training with shrubs of this habit.

Root pruning. This is seldom practised with ornamental shrubs, but is occasionally useful to check excessive top growth and more particularly in preparing large shrubs for transplanting.

Deciduous Shrubs 1

Group 1 consists of a considerable number of deciduous shrubs that do not regularly produce vigorous replacement growths from the base or lower branches of the plant. Their extension growth is produced on the perimeter of a permanent framework of older branches. The growth habit, therefore, may be likened to the crown of an oak tree without its trunk.

They require the minimum of pruning once established, but for the first few years after planting it is important to build up a framework of sturdy branches, removing weak, crossing and misplaced shoots in the dormant season so that a symmetrical and balanced plant results. Open-centre plants in this group, such as *Hamamelis* and *Magnolia* × *soulangiana*, may need the occasional removal of misplaced or crossing shoots or branches.

Pruning of the mature shrub is restricted to removing any dead, damaged or diseased growth as seen and to maintaining the overall symmetry of the shrub by pruning back weak and wayward growths.

Occasionally vigorous shoots will be produced from near the base or on the framework of mature plants. These may be used as replacement growths for old branches in the framework if suitably placed, but more usually they are produced in an awkward position and should be cut out completely.

When old branches are removed always use a wound paint on the cut surfaces to protect the plant from such diseases as coral spot, which can be troublesome, particularly with maples.

The first year

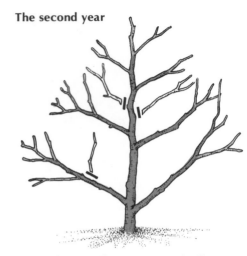

The second year

1 November to April. *Magnolia stellata* at planting. Remove weak shoots and crossing branches. Create a balanced framework by removing any unruly growths.

2 March to April. Cut out any badly spaced extension growth and laterals produced during the first growing season. If they are well-spaced leave them alone.

Third and subsequent years

3 March to April. Minimum pruning is now required. Allow the plant to develop its natural habit, but always remove the dead, diseased and damaged wood.

4 April. The mature plant in flower.

JAPANESE MAPLE

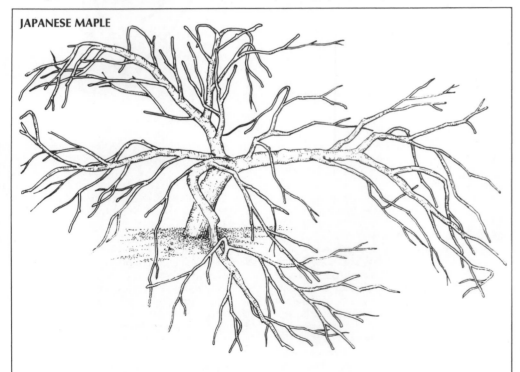

An intricately branched form of *Acer palmatum* (Japanese maple). Note the basic framework branches. After the initial framework is formed no further pruning is carried out except the removal of dead, diseased and damaged shoots as seen. The normal habit should be maintained and the crossing branches left.

Deciduous Shrubs 2

Group 2 includes
Buddleia alternifolia
Cytisus scoparius and its hybrids
Deutzia
Dipelta
Forsythia
Hydrangea × macrophylla
Kerria
Kolkwitzia
Neillia
Philadelphus
Ribes sanguineum
Spiraea × arguta
Spiraea thunbergii
Stephanandra
Tamarix (spring-flowering)
Weigela

Group 2 includes those deciduous shrubs that flower on shoots produced during the previous growing season. The flowers are formed either on short laterals produced from this one-year-old wood (*Deutzia, Philadelphus, Ribes sanguineum*) or directly from the one-year-old branches (*Forsythia*). Many spring and early summer-flowering shrubs also belong to this group. They require renewal pruning to maintain them at a reasonable height and to ensure a regular supply of strong young shoots from low down on the plant each season. Unpruned shrubs in this group quickly form many twiggy branchlets, often becoming ungainly with fewer flowers of poor quality at the top of the stems.

The first year
The plants will usually be two to three years old on receipt from the nursery. Pruning when planting is limited to cutting out weak and damaged growth and cutting back main shoots a few inches to a strong bud or pair of buds. This ensures that during the first growing season the plant's energy is concentrated on producing a strong basic framework of branches. Little flower is produced the first year. Immediately after flowering cut back any flowering laterals to a strong developing shoot and remove thin weak growths.

The second year
Flowers will be borne either on short lateral branchlets or direct from the stem. One or more strong growths will develop below the flowering branchlets. Once the flowers have faded remove all the one-year-old wood that has produced flowers. Cut back the branches to the lowest (usually also the strongest) of the developing new shoots, provided this does not spoil the balance and symmetry of the plant. If the flowered wood is not pruned away immediately after flowering, numerous weaker shoots develop from lateral buds.

Third and subsequent years
Branchlets that have borne flowers should be cut out immediately after flowering, in the same way as during the second year. In addition cut out completely to the base one-quarter to one-fifth of the old stems, taking care to balance the shape of the plant.

Deutzia provides a typical example of a shrub in group 2. The time of pruning will differ slightly, depending on the flowering period of the shrub. Prune immediately after flowering.

The first year

1 Autumn or early spring. Young *Deutzia* at planting. Cut out all weak growth and tip back the main shoots to a strong pair of buds (or an outward-pointing bud for shrubs with alternate buds). Add a good mulch of manure.

4 July. Immediately after flowering cut back the stems that have flowered to vigorous young growths developing lower down on the main stems. Remove any weak growth. Make sure the overall balance and symmetry of the shrub is maintained.

2 October to November. A few strong basal growths and many laterals from the main branches have developed during the first season. Cut out any weak shoots or misplaced shoots to maintain a symmetrical framework. Mulch well in early spring.

5 October to November. The vigorous young shoots have grown several feet and produced laterals on which the following season's blooms will be borne. Mulch well in early spring.

The second year

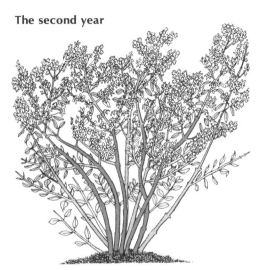

3 June to July. Flowers are produced from short laterals along many of the upper shoots which grew last season. As the flowers fade strong shoots are produced from the base of the plant and from low down on the main stems.

Third and subsequent years

6 July. Immediately after flowering cut back the stems that have flowered to vigorous young growths developing lower down on the main stems. Remove any weak growth. If the main stems are becoming crowded cut out to the base one-quarter or one-fifth of the oldest stems. Mulch well each spring.

Deciduous Shrubs 3

Kerria

Group 2 also includes a few shrubs such as *Kerria*, which produce almost all of their new growth from ground level. They flower on one-year-old wood, but require a slightly different pruning technique. Immediately

The first year

1 Autumn or early spring. Young *Kerria* at planting. Cut out any thin weak growth. Leave the vigorous stems and their laterals as these should flower this season.

Hydrangeas

Hydrangeas are included in group 2. Pruning the Hortensia hydrangea (*H. × macrophylla*), which includes the familiar Mop-head and Lace-cap kinds, frequently causes difficulties. They flower late in the season and there is a tendency to prune them hard each spring in the belief that the resultant strong growths will flower in late summer or autumn. Unfortunately this does not occur.

As a young plant only cosmetic pruning is needed and plants left unpruned will usually flower quite freely. They tend to produce a good deal of twiggy growth if left entirely unpruned, however, and, with plants three or more years old, a proportion of the older wood should be cut out to the base in early spring to encourage a constant supply of vigorous young replacement shoots each season. Do not remove the previous year's flower heads in winter as these provide some protection to the growth and flower buds, which may be damaged in severe weather. Remove them in early spring.

after flowering the shoots that have flowered should be cut out to the base or occasionally to a point low down on the shoot where vigorous young growth is appearing. If flowering wood is left most of it will die back naturally by the following winter, but it is unsightly.

2 May. Cut out the flowered shoots to the base or, with very strong stems, to points low down where vigorous young shoots are forming. Basal growths develop. Mulch well.

1 Late March to April. Cut out one-third to one-quarter of the older exhausted shoots to the base. Cut out any weak thin shoots still remaining. Cut back the old flower heads to a strong pair of buds.

Second and subsequent years

3 May. Cut out the flowered shoots to the base or, with very strong stems, to points low down where vigorous young shoots are forming. Basal growths develop. Mulch well.

2 September. The upper growth buds on the pruned shoots have grown and the strongest have produced flower heads. New vigorous basal shoots have developed but will not flower until next season.

BROOMS

Many brooms (*Cytisus scoparius* and its hybrids) are included in group 2. They are deciduous shrubs, although the bright green young stems make them appear evergreen. They flower in May and June along the length of the previous season's wood.

No pruning is required at planting. Once the blooms have faded cut back the flowered wood by two-thirds of its length to where young growths are developing. The pruning principle is the same as for *Deutzia* and similar shrubs, but brooms should not be cut back hard as shoots do not grow very well from old wood. It is essential, therefore, to prune even one-year-old plants after flowering to prevent them becoming leggy and top heavy.

1 June to July. In second and subsequent years, immediately after flowering, cut back the flowered wood by two-thirds to vigorous young growths developing near the base of the previous season's wood.

Deciduous Shrubs 4

Group 3 includes those deciduous shrubs that bear their flowers on the current year's growth. When pruned back hard in early spring they produce vigorous shoots, which flower in summer or early autumn. If left to their own devices they soon develop into unkempt, twig-filled bushes, which gradually deteriorate in the quality and quantity of flower produced.

It is convenient also to include in Group 3 a small number of deciduous shrubs, typified by *Prunus triloba*, which flower early in the year on the previous season's wood. They also respond to hard pruning in March or April, by which time they will have flowered already, producing long, wand-like shoots which bloom the following spring. The pruning technique is exactly the same.

The basic requirement is to prune early in the year so that the maximum time is available for the flowering wood to develop. This may simply consist of cutting out all growth to ground level between March and April of each year for small sub-shrubby plants, such as hardy fuchsias, *Leycesteria* and *Perovskia* or allowing a framework of woody branches to develop to the required height and then cutting back the growths close to the framework each spring, as with *Buddleia davidii*. Variation in the height of the growth and flowers on a single plant can be achieved quite simply by pruning a few shoots in the basic framework higher or lower than the remainder. This is useful in a position where the plant is only being seen from one side and allows a greater surface area of flower to be presented to the viewer. This hard pruning is carried out in March to early April each year just as the growth buds begin to swell and the position of the new shoots can be seen.

In windy areas it may be necessary to trim back the flowered growths in late autumn to minimize wind-rock, but normally only the spring cut-back is required.

It is most important to feed shrubs pruned by this method to ensure that adequate healthy growth is produced each season.

The first year
Initial pruning is aimed at building up a strong well-spaced framework of branches. In the first season pruning is usually less severe than in subsequent years so that the root system is able to become well established. Remove all weak and damaged growth at planting. Cut back the remaining growths by one-quarter to three-quarters of their length in March to April, the more vigorous shrubs such as *Buddleia davidii* being pruned more severely than less robust species, such as *Perovskia* and the deciduous *Ceanothus*.

The second year
In March to April cut back hard the previous year's growth to developing buds just above the older wood. With fuchsias, *Leycesteria* and similar sub-shrubs which may not develop a woody basal framework cut back almost to ground level. In mild areas these sub-shrubs may become woody and are then treated on the framework principle. Apply a good mulch of compost or manure around the base of the plant to encourage vigorous new growth.

Third and subsequent years
The pruning sequence is exactly as in the second season. After a number of years the basic woody framework may become congested and slight thinning of the old woody stumps may be needed. Always apply an annual basal mulch to ensure continued vigorous growth.

In view of the slight variations in the degree of pruning needed to form the initial framework three examples are provided of shrubs in this group which require marginally different techniques. Failure to feed regularly may result in weak spindly growth.

This method is suitable for deciduous shrubs such as *Ceanothus, Caryopteris, Spartium junceum* and other shrubs in group 3 which are less vigorous than *Buddleia davidii* (see page 207). It is important to let them grow unchecked during the first season, apart from the removal of weak growth and badly placed shoots that will spoil the symmetry of the plant, so that a sturdy natural branching system is developed. If they are cut back hard at planting they may produce only weak growths or die back completely.

The first year

1 March to early April. Cut out any damaged or very weak growths. Tip back main shoots by 1–2 in to strong outward-pointing buds. Cut out entirely any badly placed shoot.

2 August to September. Strong shoots have grown from upper buds on last season's growths and these will flower during late summer.

The second year

3 March to early April. Cut back all last season's growths by one-half to strong outward pointing buds. Remove entirely any weak straggly shoots.

Third and subsequent years

4 March to early April. Cut back all last season's shoots to within one or two buds of the previous season's growth. The basic framework of woody stems is formed.

Deciduous Shrubs 5

Group 3 includes such shrubs as *Perovskia* (Russian sage), *Leycesteria formosa*, hardy fuchsias and *Ceratostigma*, which may not develop a woody framework and are cut back almost to ground level.

The first year

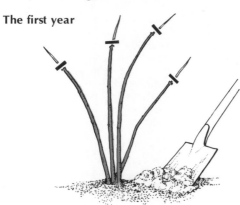

1 March to April. *Perovskia* as planted. Cut back any weak, thin tips by a few inches to a pair of strong buds. Add a good mulch to the base of the plant.

2 November. Basal shoots have developed during the summer and last year's shoots have produced lateral growths. The grey stems remain attractive in winter.

The second year

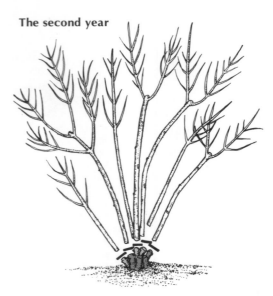

3 March to April. Cut back all stems almost to ground level, above strong pairs of buds.

4 September. Strong growths have developed to a height of 2–3 ft. Laterals are produced towards the top of each shoot. Flowers are borne on laterals and shoot tips.

Third and subsequent years

5 March to April. Cut back all stems almost to ground level, above strong pairs of buds.

Take care not to leave snags that will die back during the year.

CREATING A FRAMEWORK

If required *Perovskia* can be grown on a framework of woody basal shoots. Early training and subsequent pruning is exactly as shown under deciduous *Ceanothus*.

Deciduous Shrubs 6

Group 3 includes vigorous shrubs such as *Buddleia davidii* that should grow on a frame-work of woody branches, which is allowed to develop to the required height.

The first year

The second year

1 March to early April. *Buddleia davidii* as planted. Cut back all main shoots by one-half to three-quarters of their length to points where vigorous shoots are developing or the buds are swelling. Cut out remaining weak growth entirely. Mulch well.

2 July to August. Long wand-like growths have been produced from the pruned branches and also from the base. These will flower near the tips in late summer.

3 March to early April. Cut back new shoots hard to within one or two pairs of buds of the previous year's growth. Cut back any basal or near-basal growths that have developed the previous season to the required height. Mulch well.

4 October. The plant has flowered on terminal shoots and upper laterals of the current season's shoots. In windy gardens cut back all main shoots by one-third to minimize wind rock.

The third year

Fourth and subsequent years

5 March to early April. Cut back as in caption 3. The main framework is now formed. Any basal or near-basal shoots that develop in future years may be used to fill gaps in the framework or cut out if not required. Mulch well.

6 March to early April. Carry out normal pruning. When the framework becomes very woody and congested remove any badly placed "stumps", leaving the remainder as well spaced as possible. Train in any new shoots as required to replace the old framework wood that has been cut out.

Deciduous Shrubs 7

Group 4 includes
Cornus alba
Cornus stolonifera
many Salix species
Rubus cockburnianus
Cotinus coggygria
Corylus maxima 'Purpurea'
Sambucus (Golden-leaved and purple-leaved forms)

Group 4 includes shrubs that are pruned hard in early spring each year so that the maximum decorative effect is obtained from their foliage or the bark of their stems in winter. The technique is very similar to that described in Group 3. Most of the shrubs included here would flower on wood produced the previous year, but pruned by this method do not bloom at all. With appropriate feeding the foliage of variegated or purple-leaved variants of such shrubs as *Cotinus coggygria* and *Cornus alba* or of those such as *Rhus typhina*, grown for the autumn foliage colour, will be two or three times larger.

Many shrubs with beautifully coloured bark, such as the red- and green-stemmed dogwoods, some willows and the white-stemmed brambles, also react well to this drastic pruning, producing vigorous, un-branched new growth with more pronounced colour than unpruned specimens.

As with Group 3 the basic framework can usually be varied in height to suit the position of the shrub. The exceptions are species such as the white-stemmed brambles, which do not build up a woody framework but sucker to produce cane-like growths from the base of the plant.

Cotinus coggygria

This method is used to increase the decorative value of those shrubs in Group 3 that have coloured or variegated foliage, such as the purple-leaved smoke bush, *Cotinus coggygria* 'Foliis Purpureis'. It is also very effective with the golden elder and purple hazel, and useful in small gardens, where the same plants left unpruned would be too large.

The technique is very similar to the method of pruning *Cornus alba* (see page 209), but the plant is allowed to develop a woody stem or group of stems to the required height before being pollarded.

The first year

1 March to early April. *Cotinus coggygria* 'Foliis Purpureis' at planting. Cut back all main growths to 12–18 in to create the base framework. Cut out any weak basal growths. Mulch the plant well.

2 July to August. Vigorous unbranched shoots have developed with larger and more handsome foliage than that of an unpruned bush.

The second year

3 March. Cut back hard the previous season's growths to above a bud within 1–2 in of the framework. If a higher framework is required cut back these growths to the appropriate height. Remove any surplus or weak growths to ensure that the framework branches are well spaced.

4 July to August. The established plant with a strong, basic, woody framework and numerous vigorous growths.

Deciduous Shrubs 8

Rubus cockburnianus

This method is suitable for such shrubs as *Rubus cockburnianus* and its relatives, the white-stemmed brambles. These are grown for the effect of their white, branched stems in winter. They do not form a woody framework but sucker from the base to produce annual replacement shoots like the related raspberry.

Pruning simply consists of cutting all growths down to ground level between March and April each year. If the previous season's growths remain they will flower in summer, but they are not particularly decorative and it is better to remove them before active growth starts. The plant's energy is then diverted into producing vigorous new growths instead of being shared between flower production and shoot production.

Where growth is poor one or two of the previous year's shoots may be left at pruning time, this provides food for the plant early in the season and helps to stimulate basal growth during the summer.

The first year

1 March to April. White-stemmed bramble at planting. Cut out all growth close to ground level. Mulch well.

2 October. Vigorous shoots branched towards the top have grown during spring and summer. In autumn the foliage falls and the stems remain attractive during winter.

Second and subsequent years

3 March to April. Cut out all growth close to ground level.

Cornus alba

This method is applicable to *Cornus alba* and many willows grown for the coloured bark of the young shoots. They usually withstand hard pruning immediately after planting.

The first year

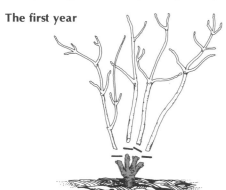

1 March to early April. *Cornus alba* at planting. Cut back hard all main shoots to within a few inches of the base. Cut out any weak basal growths. Mulch the plant well.

2 October. Vigorous whippy, usually unbranched shoots have grown during spring and summer. Once the leaves have fallen the coloured stems form an attractive feature throughout the winter.

The second year

3 March to early April. Cut back hard all main shoots to within a few inches of the base. Cut out any weak basal growths. Mulch the plant well.

POLLARDING

If required the willows and *Cornus* can be allowed to develop a single woody stem or stems to the required height and then pruned back in the same way. This method of pruning is usually known as pollarding.

Evergreen Shrubs 1

Group 5 includes the evergreen shrubs, most of which are naturally bushy and reasonably compact in habit. Provided sufficient room is available they should be allowed to develop with only minor pruning. This usually amounts to no more than the removal of spent flowers or wayward shoots and branches that affect the overall symmetry of the shrub if allowed to remain.

Dead, diseased and misplaced shoots can be removed at any time of year while any winter-damaged growth is best cut back between April and May, just as the growth

buds are beginning to swell. This gives the maximum period for new shoots to ripen before winter. Pruning earlier in the year renders the plant liable to wind and frost damage, while summer and autumn pruning will produce soft growth. This will almost certainly be damaged or killed during the following winter.

A small number of evergreen shrubs or sub-shrubs benefit from harder pruning to maintain a compact habit or increase their flowering potential. This may involve cutting such plants as cotton lavender (*Santolina*)

almost to ground level each spring or shearing over old growths of the rose of Sharon (*Hypericum calycinum*) and *Mahonia aquifolium*, in spring when grown as ground cover.

Early training

Early training is confined to shortening slightly any lateral growths which spoil the overall symmetry. Occasionally the leader shoots of young evergreen shrubs such as camellias may be spindly, rather weak and lacking any lateral branchlets. In these circumstances the leader should be cut back a few inches at

planting to encourage laterals to break from lower down. The uppermost new lateral should be trained in to replace the leader. Take care not to cut the leader back more than a few inches as this may stimulate too much lateral growth and no adequate replacement leader shoot may develop. If the weak leader shoot is left, a plant which is bushy at the base and thin at the top will develop.

The pruning and management of *Eucalyptus* differs from that of other evergreens because of its unusual growth characteristics and is described separately.

Training

April to May. A young camellia with a well-developed leader. Cut back the uppermost vigorous lateral slightly; if left, unbalanced growth may result.

April to May. A young camellia with a weak leader and few laterals. Prune back the weak leader to a strong bud to stimulate vigorous lateral growth.

June to July. Lateral growths have formed. The uppermost lateral is trained in as the replacement leader.

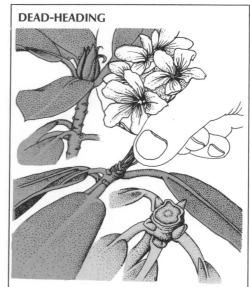

DEAD-HEADING

Some evergreens, particularly rhododendrons, flower and seed abundantly. Unless seed is required to increase stock the spent flower trusses should be removed as soon as possible. This prevents the plant forming seed pods and diverts its energy into producing strong new shoots and flower buds for next season's display. Dead-heading should be carried out immediately after the flowers fade and before seed pods begin to form. Carefully snap off the spent flower truss between finger and thumb. Take care not to damage the growth buds, which are present in the leaf axils immediately below the flower truss.

Evergreen Shrubs 2

Lavender

Unpruned lavenders develop into woody, gnarled shrubs with bare lower stems sparsely topped by grey foliage. It is not worth while trying to rejuvenate mishapen or unkempt plants as they seldom produce satisfactory young growth if cut back into the old wood. It is far better to replace them with young plants, which should be pruned hard in April to establish a low bushy habit.

Pruning then consists of clipping over the bushes every April, removing an inch or so of the previous season's growth to stimulate fresh young shoots that produce flowering spikes later in the season. Tidy gardeners will remove the old flower stems in early autumn to maintain a neat appearance; others will prefer to remove them the following April when undertaking annual pruning. In cold climates it is worth leaving these old flower stems until the April pruning as they help to protect the foliage from severe weather conditions.

Do not prune immediately after flowering as is sometimes recommended. This only stimulates late young growth that is liable to winter damage.

Heathers

Tree heathers (*Erica arborea* and its allies) do not require regular pruning. The removal of awkwardly placed or wayward branches is, however, occasionally necessary. This should be carried out in April. Renewal pruning in April to May can be successful with tree heathers and some larger species and hybrids.

Most summer- and autumn-flowering heathers (*Calluna vulgaris, Erica ciliaris, E. vagans, Daboecia cantabrica* and their variants) benefit from regular trimming. If left unpruned they usually become leggy with shorter, less attractive flower heads.

Trimming should be carried out between March and early April as the russet or bronze colouring of the old flowers is attractive during the winter months. The old flower spikes of those heathers, which are grown for their brightly coloured winter foliage, should be trimmed after flowering in October. They may require a further trim in March to early April.

Winter-flowering heathers are naturally compact or spreading in habit, and when they have finished flowering in April can be gently trimmed to remove the old flower heads. No further pruning is required.

1 March to early April. Trim back the previous season's flower head to a point just below the lowest flowers on the spike. Use shears (or scissors on young plants), taking care to follow the natural growth habit of the individual plants. Avoid the flat "table-top" cut by varying the angle at which the blades of the shears are held.

2 August to September. *Calluna vulgaris* in flower; a compact plant with long flower spikes. Do not trim the old flower heads as they are attractive throughout winter.

The first year

1 April. Young lavender as received 9 in tall. At planting prune hard to remove straggly shoots and encourage new growth.

2 September. Vigorous bushy growth is produced during spring and summer. A few flower spikes develop during the first season.

Second and subsequent years

3 April. Clip over the bush removing all old flower spikes and 1in of the previous season's growth. Follow the natural outline of the plant with the shears so that a flat "table-top" appearance is avoided.

4 September. Old plant after flowering showing the form that should be created by regular pruning.

Climbing and Wall Plants: introduction

House walls and fences add an extra dimension to gardening by providing suitable positions to grow a wide range of climbing plants and trained shrubs. Many people grow a climbing rose or a clematis against the house, but seldom is the available wall or fence space used effectively.

All house walls, fences, the sides of sheds and garages—whatever their aspect—could and should be clothed with plants. Apart from the obvious advantage of masking some of the hideous products of the construction industry it is a method of merging house and garden, creating the single living unit that in Mediterranean countries is achieved by the vine-covered patio that links them together. In addition, walls and fences provide shelter for slightly tender plants that are not hardy in the open garden.

It is also possible to create additional vertical growing space by means of pergolas, arbours, pillars and other devices or to plant climbers to scramble through trees or, occasionally, hedges.

When considering the pruning of the many plants that can be used in these positions it is important to bear in mind the growth habits and the details of basic cultivation that can affect the training and subsequent pruning of climbers and wall shrubs.

The plants used can be divided into various groups based on their growth habit.
1. The natural clingers, such as ivy and Virginia creeper, which support themselves by aerial roots or sucker pads. No support system is needed.
2. The twiners, a large group, including honeysuckle, clematis and wisteria, which climb by means of curling or twining leaf-tendrils, leaf-stalks or stems. A support system to which they attach themselves is required.
3. The scramblers and floppers, which clamber through other plants in the wild using hooked thorns (roses) or by rapid elongation of their willowy shoots (Solanum crispum). A support system is needed to which the growth can be easily tied.
4. Shrubs which are slightly tender and benefit from the protection of a wall or fence. They may either be lightly pruned if space allows or trained and hard-pruned if space is limited. Examples include the evergreen

Ivy, showing aerial roots

Clematis, showing leaf-tendrils

Ceanothus, Carpenteria californica and Fremontodendron. If trained close to the wall they require support systems to which the growths can be tied.

Many hardy shrubs can be trained against walls or fences in the same way and it is particularly useful to do this in small gardens, where space does not allow such large plants as Philadelphus and Forsythia to be grown in the open.

Select a plant to fill the allotted area comfortably without the need for constant restriction to keep it within bounds. A rampant Virginia creeper on a bungalow, however attractive initially, will require constant and prompt attention to prevent its questing growths from dislodging tiles and damaging the gutters. A well-trained clematis, Ceanothus or pyracantha is much more satisfactory in the same position.

The dullest fence can be enlivened and the hard, straight edges lost by growing Clematis montana vertically to the top of the fence and then training and pruning the growth horizontally along the upper 6–12 in as far as is required. Even the difficult areas of low walls beneath windows can be clothed with trained shrubs such as Caryopteris, Daphne odora or variegated Euonymus if correct initial training and pruning is carried out.

Aspect is very important in deciding what plants to grow. It is no use planting sun-loving Ceanothus on a north-facing wall or fence. They may grow but will seldom thrive, often becoming straggly and unkempt, whereas pyracanthas will grow, flower and fruit well.

Never plant directly against a wall or fence, always leave 9–12 in between the plant and its support system. The soil close to the wall is usually very dry. There may be difficulties with poor growth, die-back or sparse flowering.

Unless the plant climbs naturally by suckers or aerial roots some artificial system of supporting it against a wall or fence is required. Make certain the support system, which should be erected before planting, is adequate to support the plant in strong winds or heavy snowfalls. Careful training and pruning can be ruined in a very short time by failure to provide a strongly anchored support system of wire, chain-link or trellis.

Initial training and subsequent pruning

All the precepts of good pruning apply equally as much to climbers and wall plants. In particular the 3 D's, the removal of all dead, damaged and diseased wood, should be carried out regularly.

The gardener prunes to obtain the maximum coverage and the maximum effect of foliage, flower and fruit. This necessitates restricting the natural habit of the plants concerned, and particularly where space is limited pruning must be directed, in part, to maintaining balanced and not excessive growth, which would require fairly drastic annual pruning of very vigorous species.

The importance of early training to establish a sound basic framework of branches cannot be overemphasized. Gardeners will often be reluctant to cut back vigorous growth on young plants, but in some situa-

tions this is essential to obtain maximum coverage of the wall or fence and to avoid the problem, particularly prevalent with wall shrubs, of excessive growth outwards from the supports. The aim of the gardener must be to maintain growth as close to the wall or fence as possible.

Initially this involves considerable directing and tying in of shoots to cover the area of wall or fence concerned and cutting back outward-pointing growth (breastwood) to encourage lateral (sideways) growth.

The pruning of established plants will vary to some extent with the mode of growth. Some climbers such as ivies and Virginia creeper which cling with aerial roots or sucker pads will require no more than the removal of wayward shoots. With other shrubs regular annual pruning is needed to keep the plants neat, within bounds and free-flowering.

Generally follow the rules for pruning shrubs. Those plants which flower on the previous year's wood before midsummer, for example Ceanothus impressus, Forsythia suspensa and Clematis macropetala, are pruned immediately after flowering. Those which flower after midsummer on the current season's shoots are pruned either in late winter (Clematis × jackmanii) or in early spring (Ceanothus × burkwoodii and Ceanothus 'Autumnal Blue').

Some plants require a more complicated regime if they are to flower profusely. Summer pruning—cutting back laterals and breastwood to form flowering spurs—is used. The leading shoots are trained in as required to fill space in the framework, while the lateral and breastwood shoots produced during the growing season are cut back leaving only 2–5 leaves on the shoots, the severity of pruning depending on the plant concerned.

This technique is particularly applicable to the Japanese or flowering quinces (Chaenomeles) and Wisteria. They both need firm control to prevent unruly overvigorous growth, which, if left, results in a limited number of flowers. Summer pruning encourages flower bud formation on the spurred-back laterals, the food being channelled into forming flower buds on the spurs rather than into forming long growth shoots.

Clematis 1

The complicated instructions for pruning *Clematis* that are often found can be reduced to three categories based on the age of the growth on which the flowers are produced.

Some *Clematis* flower entirely on the current year's growth, while a number of spring-flowering species and hybrids produce all their bloom on short shoots from the previous year's wood. A third group, which includes many well-known hybrids such as 'Nelly Moser', produce flowers from last season's growth during early summer and a further display of rather smaller flowers in late summer and autumn from the current year's young shoots.

Vigorous species such as *Clematis montana* can be grown through trees and left unpruned unless they become completely out-of-hand. If this occurs it is simple to renovate them by cutting the old stems hard back to within 2–3 ft of ground level in late winter or early spring. In most instances dormant buds on the old, woody stems are stimulated into growth and within a few seasons they should be flowering freely. As with all renovation techniques it is important to feed and water the plants well.

Left unpruned most *Clematis* develop into tangled masses of growth, bearing their flowers high up above the bare woody stems. The aim with all the following techniques is to provide the maximum coverage and flower in the space available at a reasonable height.

Pruning at planting is important but often overlooked. Many *Clematis*, particularly the larger-flowered hybrids, will tend to grow rapidly upwards on a single stem during the first season after planting unless checked at an early stage.

At planting the stem should be cut back to the lowest pair of strong buds to encourage the plant to produce further basal growth. The two stems produced from these buds can be stopped again to increase the number of basal shoots, but this is usually unnecessary.

This initial pruning applies to all *Clematis*, whether planted dormant in January or February or in leaf during spring or early summer. Most *Clematis* species will break naturally to form bushy, well-furnished plants, but it is as well to prune them at planting to ensure that this occurs.

Group 1 contains all the *Clematis* species and hybrids that flower in summer and autumn entirely on the new growths produced during the current season. If left unpruned they begin growth in the spring from where they flowered the previous season and rapidly become bare at the base with flowers at the top only.

Pruning is very simple and consists of cutting back the whole of the previous year's growth virtually to ground level in late January or February. The pruning cuts should be made immediately above the lowest pair of strong buds on each stem.

Examples of *Clematis* in this group are C. *orientalis*, C. *tangutica*, C. *texensis* hybrids such as 'Gravetye Beauty' and 'Étoile Rose', C. *viticella* and its derivatives; and among the large-flowered hybrids C. × *jackmanii*, 'Ernest Markham', 'Hagley Hybrid' and 'Perle d'Azur'.

The first year

The second year

1 January to February. A newly planted *Clematis*. Cut back to the lowest pair of strong buds. Mulch well.

2 May to June. Train in the strong young growths and any basal growth. Flowers may appear in late summer.

3 January to February. Cut back all growths to the lowest pair of strong buds on each stem. Mulch well.

Third and subsequent years

4 May to June. Train in young growths and further basal growth as it develops.

5 July to September. Flowers are produced on the current season's growth.

6 January to February. Cut back all growths to the lowest pair of strong buds on each stem. Mulch well.

Clematis 2

Group 2 consists mainly of vigorous spring-flowering species, which flower between April and June on short shoots from growth produced the previous summer.

Examples of species in this group are *Clematis montana* and its forms, *C. chryso-coma*, *C. alpina* and *C. macropetala*.

The first two species are very vigorous and attempting to restrict them to limited areas on a wall or fence usually results in a good deal of work. They are best given ample space on a house wall or in a tree and left unpruned or merely sheared over after flowering to keep them tidy. If left unpruned they may require rejuvenation after a few years. This involves cutting them to near ground level in winter.

The first and second years
Initial pruning at planting will encourage vigorous growth that can be gently guided to cover the area available and to form the basic framework over a two-year period.

Third and subsequent years
Once this has been achieved the pruning of mature plants consists of cutting away all the flowered wood to within a few inches of the main framework immediately after flowering.

This stimulates vigorous long growths that can be trained or guided in as required, or allowed to cascade naturally. This growth will provide next season's flowering display and must not be winter-pruned.

The first year

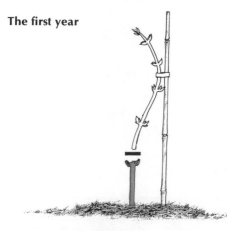

1 January to February. A newly planted *Clematis* with a single main stem. Cut back the stem above the lowest pair of strong buds. Mulch well.

2 May to June. Train in the strong young growths and any further basal growths that may have developed.

The second year

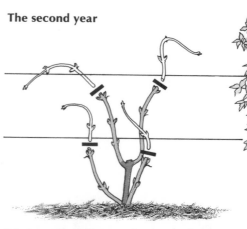

3 January to February. Cut back all the main growths trained in the previous summer by one-half their length to a pair of strong buds. Mulch well.

4 April to June. Train or guide the new shoots as required. Prune back any laterals that have flowered low down on the plant to one or two pairs of buds from the base.

5 July to September. Train or guide in new growth as required.

Third and subsequent years

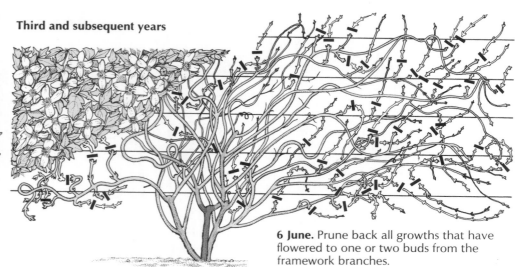

6 June. Prune back all growths that have flowered to one or two buds from the framework branches.

Clematis 3

Group 3 contains all the hybrids that provide large, sumptuous flowers from May to July on the previous year's wood. While the flowers are being produced on side-shoots from the old wood new growth is being formed. This produces further crops of medium-sized blooms during late summer and early autumn.

Popular varieties in this group include 'Lasurtern', 'Nelly Moser', 'The President', 'Henryi', 'Mme le Coultre', 'William Kennett' and the double-flowered 'Duchess of Edinburgh' and 'Vyvyan Pennell', which may produce single blooms late in the season.

The growth habit of Group 3 *Clematis* makes them difficult to prune satisfactorily without a good deal of work, and they may be left entirely unpruned or only lightly pruned until they become straggly and out of control. Then the rejuvenation process described in the introduction can be applied. Alternatively they may be treated as Group 1 and pruned back hard to base each January to February, but then they will only flower in late summer.

Neither of these treatments allows the full flowering potential of these *Clematis* to be exploited, but a simple renewal system can be instituted with mature plants to provide the maximum flower during summer and autumn. It involves the same basic training as Group 1, but mature plants are renewal-pruned with one-quarter to one-third of the old shoots being cut to within a foot or so of the base. This is done between May and July, depending on the variety, immediately after the first flush of bloom has been produced on the previous season's growth. Alternatively the renewal pruning can be carried out annually in January or February, but this means a lesser display of flowers in early summer.

Strong shoots arise from the pruned-back stems and will grow vigorously during summer and possibly provide a few autumn blooms. Ample feeding to maintain vigour is required, but using this method the gawky "bird's-nest" effect so commonly seen is avoided.

This renewal system works more easily with wall- or fence-grown plants, where the shoots can be spaced out evenly. On pergolas or grown amongst shrubs *Clematis* in this group are best left unpruned or trimmed after the initial flowering as it is difficult to disentangle the cut-back stems.

The first year

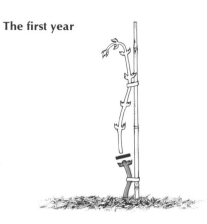

1 January to February. A newly planted *Clematis* with a single main stem. Cut back the stem to above the lowest pair of strong buds. Mulch well.

2 May to June. Train in strong young growths and any basal growths which develop. A few flowers may be produced in late summer.

The second year

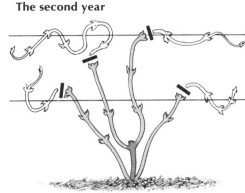

3 January to February. Cut back all the main growths trained in the previous summer by one-half to a strong pair of buds. Mulch well.

4 June to September. Train or guide in new growths as required. The basic framework has been established. Some flower will be produced in summer and autumn on the new growth.

Third and subsequent years

5 June to July. Plant will flower on old wood. Immediately after flowering cut one-quarter to one-third of the mature shoots to within a foot or so of the base. Water and feed well.

6 August to September. Plant flowers on young shoots. Guide into place basal shoots that develop from the cut-back stems.

Wisteria 1

The pruning of *Wisteria* baffles most gardeners as the tremendous vigour of their whip-like summer shoots seems almost impossible to control. It is, however, quite practicable to keep them restrained and trained into a reasonably confined space, although they are capable of clambering a hundred feet or more up a tree or along a wall. Successful control demands a good deal of attention from the gardener as pruning needs to be carried out twice during a season to ensure adequate flowers and to confine the plant's naturally robust growth.

The first year

A young *Wisteria* planted in winter or early spring will normally produce one or two vigorous basal growths that increase rapidly in length. Few or no lateral shoots develop naturally at this stage. If the plant is to be grown in espalier form to cover a wall or fence the main shoot must be cut or tipped back to 2½–3ft from ground level at planting.

This stimulates two or three lateral buds to develop and these new shoots should be trained into the positions required. Tie in the upper shoot vertically and the other growths at an angle of approximately 45 degrees. If the laterals are trained in a horizontal position initially their growth may be checked. At this stage the branches are flexuous and easily positioned on the support system.

The second and subsequent years

The following winter cut back the leading shoot leaving 2½–3ft of wood above the uppermost lateral. Bring down the laterals to a more or less horizontal position. At the same time cut back the horizontal leaders of those laterals by about one-third of their length.

This stimulates further lateral growth and a similar training process is carried out during the subsequent years to form a new vertical leader and further well-spaced horizontal laterals to form the arms of the espalier.

Train in a new horizontal leader for each pruned-back lateral and cut back surplus laterals or sub-laterals in early August to within 6–9in (4–5 leaves) of the main framework branches to form flowering spurs.

This process is continued annually until the desired number of well-spaced lateral branches is obtained. The aim should be to produce an espaliered plant with horizontal branches not less than 15–18in apart. This allows the long pendulous inflorescences to hang down gracefully from the spurs without crowding those on the branches below.

Further basal growth that develops should be cut out completely as seen.

The first year

1 Winter to early spring. Young *Wisteria* at planting. Prune or tip back the strongest growth to 2½–3ft from ground level. Stake this main shoot. Remove to base any surplus shoots that are present.

2 June to early August. Two or three vigorous shoots develop from lateral buds. Train in the uppermost vertically. Tie in other laterals on the support framework at approximately 45 degrees. Remove any new basal growths. Tie in further extension growth. If sub-laterals are produced, cut them back in early August to 6–9in.

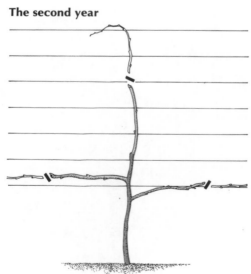

3 December to January. Cut back the vertical leader to within 2½–3ft of the uppermost lateral. Bring down the laterals trained at 45 degrees to a horizontal position and cut back their leaders by one-third.

4 June to early August. Vigorous shoots develop from lateral buds on the vertical leader. Train in the uppermost vertically as the new leader. Tie in other laterals on the support framework at an angle of about 45 degrees. Remove any further basal growth. In early August cut back any surplus laterals and sub-laterals to 6–9in.

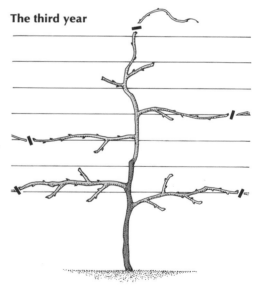

5 December to January. Cut back the vertical leader to within 2½–3ft of the uppermost lateral. Bring down the laterals trained at 45 degrees to a horizontal position and cut back their leaders by one-third. Cut back last season's growth of leaders on horizontally trained branches by one-third.

Wisteria 2

The mature plant
Once the basic framework of branches has been trained to fill the area available any further extension growths, which may reach 10–12ft in a season, and lateral growths are pruned back in early August to within 6in (4–6 leaves) of the main branches to form flowering spurs. This summer pruning is followed by a further shortening of these spurs in winter (December and January) to 3–4in leaving only 2–3 buds on each spur shoot. The following season's flowers are borne on these spurs. In winter the plump flower buds are easily distinguished from the flattened growth buds so the flowering potential is readily observed.

A more laborious procedure to provide more flower buds involves pruning back the extension growths to 6in at two-week intervals during the summer. This stimulates further laterals to form and constant pinching back produces more congested spurs.

Wisteria can, however, be grown in a number of ways and trained not only as espaliers but as fans, as low-standard shrubs or semi-informally against walls or fences. The same pruning technique is used for mature plants, but the initial training will differ slightly with the method used. Wherever possible it is best to train the main branches more or less horizontally as the maximum display is obtained from plants trained this way.

6 Early August. Prune all extension growths back to 6in (4–6 leaves).

7 December to January. Prune the same growths back to 3–4in (2–3 buds).

Ceanothus and Honeysuckle

The shrubby evergreen *Ceanothus* species and hybrids are suitable for training as wall plants, where their abundant blue, powder-puff flower heads show to the best advantage. Most *Ceanothus* flower in May on growth produced the previous summer, but a few, such as 'Autumnal Blue' and 'Burkwoodii', flower on both last season's and the current year's growth and require slightly different pruning treatment.

The first year
Ceanothus should always be planted in spring as pot-grown plants. Training consists of tying in the main shoot vertically as it grows and fanning out the laterals to fill the available space as evenly as possible. Growth is rapid and it is important to tie in the young shoots regularly during spring and summer to ensure that they are guided in the direction required. If left they will tend to grow away from the support structure and become difficult to manage as the growth ripens. Breastwood is produced abundantly and, if not suitable for training into the framework, should be clipped over once in June to encourage dense, tight growth and to maintain the plant close to the wall or fence.

Second and subsequent years
Continue training and tying in extension growth until the space allocated has been filled. Immediately after flowering clip over the previous season's growths, which will normally have flowered during May, to within 2–4 in of the framework. The dense growth produced during the summer provides flower the following spring.

It is important to prune a wall-trained evergreen *Ceanothus* regularly each season so that a compact mat of growth is maintained against the support structure. If it is left unpruned it will quickly grow away from the wall or fence and is liable to be damaged by strong winds or snow. *Ceanothus* resent hard pruning into old wood and it is difficult to maintain the neatly tailored look which is so attractive with well-grown specimens if regular training is not carried out.

Pruning of the few evergreen *Ceanothus*, which flower mainly on the current season's growth, is carried out in April. The initial training and method of pruning is the same. Pruning in early spring means the loss of any early bloom, but ensures that the plant maintains a tight habit and flowers generously in summer and autumn.

The first year

1 April to May. Tie in the leader vertically. Spread out and tie in lateral growths. Cut out badly placed shoots and trim back breastwood to 2–3 in.

2 June to July. Rapid extension growth has occurred. Tie in leader and lateral shoots. Trim breastwood to 3–4 in from the supports.

The second year

3 June. A few flowers have been produced on last year's side-shoots. Cut back breastwood to 3–4 in from the framework.

HONEYSUCKLE

The climbing honeysuckles can be divided into two groups for pruning purposes, based on their flowering habit.

The first group, typified by *Lonicera japonica*, the rampant Japanese honeysuckle, produces flowers in pairs in the axils of leaves on the current season's growth. The only pruning necessary is to restrict the exuberant growth. This involves clipping away any unwanted growth in March or April each season. This stimulates fresh young growth which quickly covers the sheared surface and will flower later in the season.

The second group includes the much more popular Dutch honeysuckle *L. periclymenum* 'Belgica' and a number of related species and hybrids such as *L.× americana*, *L.× brownii*, *L. sempervirens*, *L.× tellmanniana* and *L. tragophylla*. These bear flowers on laterals produced from the previous season's growth.

If space allows they may be permitted to clamber through old trees or on walls and left completely unpruned so that the growth wanders and cascades at will in a natural manner. They tend to form "birds'-nests" on bare stems (like some *Clematis*) and if they are to be grown in positions where tangled growth and bare stems will be unsightly, mild pruning is required immediately after flowering each season. This simply involves cutting back some of the old weak growths and some of the shoots which have flowered to a point where vigorous young growth is developing. The young growth can be tied in to the framework as it develops, but is more effective if left to cascade down so that an informal curtain of flowers is produced.

Third and subsequent years

4 July to September. Tie in leader and main lateral shoots as they develop.

5 June. Cut back all breastwood that has flowered to within 4–6 in of the framework. Tie in extension shoots as they develop.

Chaenomeles and Pyracantha

Most varieties of the common "Japonica" or "Flowering Quince" are excellent plants for training against walls or fences. They flower well even on northern and eastern aspects, where they are particularly useful for early spring colour.

The first year
Although *Chaenomeles* can be trained formally as espaliers or fans a less precise system than that described for *Wisteria* suits their growth habit better.

The basic framework is built up by training in a leader and spacing out more or less horizontally any laterals against the wall or fence. If several basal shoots are present on the young plant these can be spaced out evenly against the support structure as it is not essential for a main leader to be established unless a formal espaliered plant is required.

Most *Chaenomeles* produce laterals and sub-laterals freely without the need to stop the main shoots. These are trained in as required to complete the basic framework. Very little flower is produced during the first year or two after planting.

Cut back any outward-pointing shoots (breastwood) or sub-laterals not required to form part of the framework to 4–6 leaves from the base after they have made their initial summer growth.

Further sub-laterals usually develop on these cut-back shoots and these should be pruned to 2–3 leaves in late summer so that a stubby spur system is formed.

Second and subsequent years
After flowering in spring vigorous extension growth is produced. Unless any shoots are required to train in to fill gaps in the framework summer-prune all new growths to 4–6 leaves from the base in June to July. Cut back any secondary shoots produced from this summer-pruned growth in early autumn, again to 2–3 leaves. This summer pruning builds up flowering spurs that are covered in bloom the following spring. In time these spurs may become congested and some will require to be thinned out each winter to maintain a balanced plant. This winter thinning may be carried out annually on established plants, pruning back all the summer growth originally cut to 4–6 leaves to two buds in winter if required. It produces a neater plant, but specimens which are only summer-pruned with an occasional winter-thinning of spurs flower equally well.

PYRACANTHA

Pyracantha is ideal for covering walls and can readily be trained to form almost any pattern of growth around the windows and doors of houses. It also lends itself to formal training as an espalier, cordon or fan and is particularly valuable for northern and eastern aspects.

The first year
If a formally trained plant is required, the training is similar to that used for espalier apples. Usually it is more convenient to use the less formal system described for *Chaenomeles*, making sure that the basic framework branches are well spaced and that excess lateral growths and breastwood are cut back in July or early August to form spur shoots and to maintain growth close to the wall or fence.

Mature plant
The bunches of white flowers, which are followed by red or yellow berries, are formed in the leaf axils of short spur growths on the previous year's shoots. After flowering growth shoots appear during late June and July, hiding the young berries. On mature plants these need to be summer-pruned so that the fruit can be seen to full effect. Cut back the young growth as soon as the berries begin to ripen in mid- or late July or August to within 3–4 in of the main framework. Secondary growth often occurs and a second trimming in early September can be given if needed. This pruning not only exposes the fruits so that they ripen well and can be seen but also produces the next season's flowering spurs.

The first year

1 October to March. Train in the leader vertically. Space out laterals more or less horizontally. Cut out any awkwardly placed shoots that cannot be trained.

3 August to September. Train in late growth. Cut back any breastwood or surplus laterals to 2–3 leaves.

5 August to September. Cut back summer growth (sub-laterals) to 2–3 leaves from base.

2 Late June to July. Train in the leader, lateral extension growths and new basal shoots to form main framework. Cut back breastwood or crossing shoots to 4–6 leaves.

Second and subsequent years

4 June to July. Train in the leader, lateral extension growths and new basal shoots to form main framework. Cut back breastwood or crossing shoots to 4–6 leaves.

Mature plant

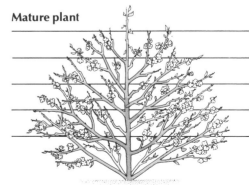

6 March to April. When the allotted space is filled stop the leader and main laterals.

Introduction/Hygiene 1

Of all the branches of horticulture, growing under glass is the most specialized. Not only is the constant maintenance of the plants necessary, but environment must be controlled to give acceptable growing conditions.

The ideal environment The basic aim should always be to create an ideal environment for healthy growth, but perfection is seldom possible—and never possible if a mixed collection of plants is grown, for plants have differing needs. In theory at least, the fully automated greenhouse can be programmed to provide the correct levels of heat, light, humidity and ventilation whatever the conditions in the outside world. But in practice this is rarely the case. Freak weather conditions, a breakdown of equipment or a simple power failure can quickly upset the automated system. In the end, it is the skill of the gardener that counts. Automatic equipment can at best only work to fairly wide tolerances and has the disadvantage of providing the same levels of water, heat and so on for all the plants in the greenhouse. It is most important to get to know the limitations of the individual greenhouse and the degrees of tolerance of the plants being grown. This knowledge goes to build up the intuitive skill which all good growers have, to know when to water and ventilate, when to damp down, shade or feed for the very best results. All this takes patience and practice and the beginner must be keen enough to spend time with his plants, noting what happens to them under different conditions.

Record keeping There is much to be said for keeping a greenhouse diary or notebook. Record in it the daily maximum and minimum temperatures, when seeds are sown or cuttings taken, when plants are potted, fed, staked, and stopped. In addition, comments can be made from time to time on the vigour, appearance and health of the plants. Over the seasons, a valuable record of the prevailing conditions is built up.

The daily routine

It is important to establish a regular daily routine when gardening under glass. To fail to do so is likely to lead to the disappointments of poor-quality plants and frequent failure of seedlings and young plants.

Summer A routine for an imaginary summer day could be as follows. Once the morning sun is fully on the greenhouse, check the temperature. If it is 5.5°–9°C/10°–15°F above the desired minimum temperature for the plants being grown, open the ventilators by half to two-thirds. If temperatures continue to climb, open up fully around mid-morning. Damp down, shade if required and check that there are no dry plants (but leave the main watering operation until later). In early afternoon, go over the watering thoroughly and damp down again if conditions are hot. If it is not particularly hot, damp down in late afternoon. As soon as direct sunlight is off the greenhouse the blinds can be rolled up and when the temperature drops back to the 5.5°–9°C/10°–15°F above minimum, shut down the ventilators. During a warm spell the temperature may not drop so low even after nightfall and the greenhouse can then be left open day and night. All depends on the minimum temperature being maintained.

Cleaning the greenhouse

In late summer, scrub the framework of the greenhouse to remove pest and disease organisms. First empty the greenhouse. Use a dilute sterilizing agent.

Winter Much the same procedure is followed in winter, but if the weather is cold and temperatures do not rise, ventilation and damping will not need to be carried out and watering will be minimal.

While this sort of routine is ideal for the plants, it is not easily carried out by the gardener, who may have to be away all day. Happily, it can be modified and compromises made. Full ventilation and essential watering can be carried out just before leaving in the morning and the main watering and damping down done on arriving home. Damping down during the day, while desirable for most plants, is not essential. Automatic watering and ventilation help to optimize conditions in greenhouses left unattended during the day.

In the winter a daily check over in the morning or evening is enough. If automatic ventilators and capillary watering are installed, then a weekly check over should suffice in winter.

In autumn, wash the glass thoroughly using a non-toxic detergent. Remove dirt and algae from glass overlaps with an alloy plant label.

Hygiene

Along with the right environment and routine care, a good level of hygiene must be maintained to ensure healthy, vigorous plants. The need to keep the greenhouse and particularly the glass clean is often overlooked. It is surprising how much dirt can settle firmly on to a sheet of glass in the open, even in areas where air pollution is low. This considerably cuts down light intensity, the effects of which are particularly noticeable in winter. Plants which need good light, such as tomato, lettuce and freesia, look thin and pale and lack substance.

Glass should be washed thoroughly in autumn, using one of the approved non-toxic detergents. Where the glass overlaps, dirt accumulates and algae flourish, forming a dark band. Remove this dirt with an alloy plant label or a sliver of sheet metal. Glass washing should be carried out at intervals during the winter, especially in areas of air pollution. At other times of the year it is

At the same time, scrub surfaces such as paths and walls to remove algae, using a dilute solution of a proprietary algicide.

Introduction/Hygiene 2

usually not so important and in summer the layer of grime can even be beneficial, acting as partial shading.

At least once a year the framework of the greenhouse should be scrubbed to remove pest and disease organisms such as over wintering red spider mites and spores of fungal diseases. To do the job properly the greenhouse should be empty so that a sterilizing agent, a chemical fluid, can be added to the washing water. Late summer is a good time to wash the greenhouse, when all but the tenderest plants can be stood outside.

In a humid greenhouse a film of green algae can form on all moist surfaces including walls and floors, and can become slippery. All such surfaces should be scrubbed, using one of the proprietary algicides in the water.

Hygiene should not stop at keeping the greenhouse clean. All used pots and seed trays should be thoroughly washed and scrubbed before re-use to minimize the spread of disease. Remove any "tide-marks"

of soil or chemicals around the insides of the pots. Soak clay pots in water to ensure cleanliness. Perhaps the chief cause of infection of compost-borne rots is the use of dirty containers for propagation. It is of great importance to ensure that containers are clean.

In order to avoid cross-infection, always remove containers and spent compost from the greenhouse when not in use. Spent compost provides ideal conditions for the multiplication of both damping-off fungi and sciarid flies. It is important to wipe tools clean after use to ensure they do not become a potential source of infection.

It is futile to go to great lengths to sterilize compost, or to go to the expense of buying sterile composts, if they are left lying about open to the elements. All composts and their components should be kept bagged and covered to maintain their reliability. Do not attempt to re-use spent compost, even if sterilized, as the chemical balances will be out of proportion.

After use, wash and scrub seed boxes and pots to minimize the spread of disease. Store containers neatly and do not allow debris to build up. Compost should be kept in a bin with a tight-fitting lid to avoid staleness and possible contamination. Remove spent compost from the greenhouse after use.

PEST AND DISEASE CONTROL

Good greenhouse hygiene, as outlined in the previous section, is an essential starting point in the avoidance of pests and diseases. However, problems will inevitably occur because it is impossible to avoid introducing infected material into the greenhouse. The following pages detail pests and diseases met with in the greenhouse and prescribe remedies. On this page methods of control are discussed.

Control methods

Because the greenhouse is a closed environment it is often easier than in the open garden to control pests and diseases. Some pests, such as snails, can be removed by hand, but most greenhouse problems will have to be dealt with by chemical means. Some biological control is possible for a few greenhouse pests (see below). Good growing practice is the first line of defence, for healthy sturdy plants are less susceptible to disease than sickly ones.

Applying chemicals Choose an effective chemical which will not harm the plants being grown. Remove any plants likely to be harmed, or cover them with plastic sheeting secured with string or elastic bands. Carefully follow the instructions given on the next page for the use of chemicals in the greenhouse. When spraying, open all ventilators and the door. Many pesticides are also available as dusts which are applied from a puffer pack. Use dusts or smokes on flowers and on plants sensitive to moisture on foliage.

Fumigation Chemicals can also be applied in smoke form, a process called fumigation. First check carefully that none of the plants present will be damaged by the fumigant to be used. The manufacturer's instructions will contain a list. Remove any such plants from the greenhouse. Fumigants are available as simple pyrotechnic smokes which resemble fireworks, or as chemicals which are vaporized on electric elements. Fumigants should be applied at a rate depending upon the cubic capacity of the greenhouse. Measure this by the formula length × breadth × average height. Fumigation can be used against specific pests or as a general hygiene measure every six months. Apply fumigants in the evening, then leave the greenhouse closed overnight. Seal

any leaks and close all ventilators before application. To sterilize the greenhouse, empty it of plants and burn sulphur at the rate of 1 lb per 1000 cu. ft. Burning sulphur produces sulphur dioxide gas, which is highly poisonous. Leave the greenhouse as soon as the sulphur is ignited.

Biological control

In the open, many pests are kept under control by predators and parasites. In the closed greenhouse environment, such natural balances break down, leading to pest problems. In an effort to avoid over-use of chemicals, biologists have investigated the possibility of biological control. This means introducing a predator or parasite to attack concentrations of harmful pests. Some of these are available commercially. A predatory mite, *Phytoseiulus persimilis*, controls glasshouse red spider mite. A ladybird, *Cryptolaemus montrouzeri*, can be used against mealybugs; a parasitic wasp, *Encarsia formosa*, for greenhouse whitefly; and a bacterium, *Bacillus thuringiensis*, attacks caterpillars.

If biological control is used most insecticides are ruled out until the predators have had a chance to work, which limits its application if other pests are found. Predators are a cure rather than a prevention: they cannot work until their prey, the pest, is present. The critical time to introduce predators is when the pest first appears. The predator can then breed and build up a large enough population to eradicate the pest. Predators will only breed faster than the pests when daytime temperatures exceed 21°C/70°F and light intensity is good.

While biological control avoids chemical build-up on plants, a point especially to be borne in mind with food crops, it is a less certain and more complicated method of pest control than the use of chemicals. The use of predators has to be carefully timed. This involves investigating sources of supply well before the trouble arises and taking swift action once the pests are noticed.

The year in a cold greenhouse 1

The year in a cold greenhouse
This calender details sowing and harvesting times for basic cold greenhouse crops and lists planting, sowing and potting on times for ornamentals.

Regular tasks such as watering, feeding, damping down, shading and ventilating are not listed every month. The timing of these procedures is to a large extent dependent upon day to day conditions and on the crops being grown. Follow the instructions given under individual crops, and act according to the basic principles discussed in the first two sections of this book.

Pest and disease control is another regular task that must be attended to whenever problems arise. The worst period for pests is from April to October, but problems such as whitefly and red spider mite can appear in any of the 12 months. For the control of pests and diseases, see page 221; for the specific types, see pages 244–249.

Using a cold greenhouse
A cold greenhouse is one which possesses no form of artificial heat. It is, in effect, no more than a protective covering against extremes of cold, wet and wind. A cold greenhouse can form a vital and interesting adjunct to the garden provided its limitations are recognized and the plants to be grown carefully selected.

The most important limitation of the cold greenhouse is that of temperature. In winter, if the outside temperature drops to around 7°C/20°F it is likely that there will be several degrees of frost inside the greenhouse. It is wise to recognize this and to avoid trying to over-winter plants which are not frost-hardy. It is possible to give protection against frost by plunging pots and covering plants with polythene or sacking, but these methods provide limited defence against severe frosts.

Conditions and choice of plants
A cold greenhouse will suit those plants that are hardy outdoors, and will in most cases allow them to be grown better. It also suits annuals, including fruits and vegetables, which are half-hardy outdoors. A cold greenhouse can extend the growing season at either end, allowing crops to be taken earlier and later than outdoors. Ornamental annuals and biennials can be raised from seed in the predictable conditions a cold greenhouse offers, and various propagation techniques carried out.

Despite the lack of artificial heat, the gardener has various techniques available to allow him to alter the environment of a cold greenhouse. The basic principles explained in the section on Running the Greenhouse (pages 220–221), apply here, though with the narrow tolerance of many cold greenhouse plants extra care is needed.

Ventilation The most effective method of temperature control available is ventilation. In very cold conditions it can be colder in the greenhouse than outside if the doors and lower ventilators are not opened for a few hours in the middle of the day. Cold air is heavy and collects in a pool at ground level, but will flow out if given the chance.

Most ventilation is concerned with trapping solar heat. Once outside temperatures start to rise in spring, ventilators should be opened a little in the morning and closed some hours before sunset. This regime may well cause the thermometer to rise 5°–9°C/10°–20°F above normal; this heat surplus not only acts as a cushion against the rapid drop in temperature as night falls, but also improves the growing atmosphere. Some of the surplus heat is absorbed by the soil, paths and structure generally, moderating night temperatures as it is given off into the cooling air. This mechanism is exploited by several solar heating systems.

At all times the aim is to produce a buoyant atmosphere, one in which the air within the greenhouse is moving up and around rather than lying stagnant.

Air movement The circulation of air is a vital factor in cold greenhouse management. Even in a closed-up cold house in winter, imperfections in glazing can allow air to escape sufficiently fast to give two complete air changes per hour. In high summer well-ventilated greenhouses can have 120 air changes per hour, which helps to keep internal temperatures close to those outside. If through a deficiency in ventilation air changes drop to 30–40 per hour, summer greenhouse temperatures can rise as high as 43°C/110°F, to the detriment of plants.

January
Plan the year's crops and order seeds and seedlings. Ventilate the greenhouse on sunny days.
Sow onions for transplanting. Sow early radishes in soil borders or peat pots.
Bring in plunged bulbs to flower in the greenhouse (*Babiana, Chionodoxa, Crocus,* daffodils, *Fritillaria, Iris, Leucojum, Ornithogalum*).
Bulbs which have finished flowering can be planted out into frames.
Sow lily seed. Begin sequence of chrysanthemum cuttings later in the month.

February
Ventilate as necessary. Water sparingly.
Sow lettuce, early bunching turnips, carrots, parsnips and early beetroot (until March), bulb onions (until April). Sow tomatoes in heat later in the month.
Bring potted strawberries in to crop in late spring.
Bring in remaining plunged bulbs to replace those which have finished flowering.
Pot on and divide ferns if necessary.
Pot on over-wintered coleus, fuchsias and pelargoniums.
Sow and place in a propagating case: *Abutilons,* tuberous and fibrous begonias, *Coleus, Celosias, Gloxinias, Streptocarpus.*
Pot on annuals sown in autumn.
Re-pot evergreen azaleas.

March
Sow lettuce, celery, carrots, mustard and cress.
Sow in heat: aubergines, sweet peppers, dwarf French beans, tomatoes if not sown in February. Prick out lettuce seedlings. Pot out late in month.
Sow for transplanting: broad beans, runner beans, brassicas, leeks, celery, peas, sweetcorn, chives, thyme.
Continue to bring in pot strawberries.
Sow half-hardy annuals and alpines.
Pot on over-wintered annuals. Take pelargonium and dahlia cuttings.
Plant out rooted cuttings taken in winter. Plant hippeastrum bulbs in pots.

April
Sow according to needs: lettuce, radish, mustard and cress, beetroot, endive, parsley. Sow sweetcorn, celeriac, dwarf French beans, cucumbers.
Plant out tomatoes late in month/early May.
Harvest early radishes and lettuce, chicory, seakale and rhubarb.
Complete sowing half-hardy annuals. Sow biennials for spring flowering under glass. Prick out March-sown seedlings. Begin to harden off bedding plant seedlings. Take fuchsia cuttings, pot rooted dahlia and other cuttings. Pot up tuberoses for flowering. Start feeding camellias.

May
Plant aubergines, sweet peppers, okra and cucumber, melons.
Harvest early carrots, early bunching turnips, beetroot.
Harden off bedding plants and plant out after frosts have ended. Take cuttings from regal pelargoniums. Sow *Calceolaria, Freesia, Schizanthus* for winter flowering.

June
Harvest lettuce, radish, endive, mustard and cress, French beans, parsley.
Tie in cucumber plants.
Continue to sow biennials. Pot on cyclamen seedlings.
Take cuttings of pinks. Plunge azaleas outside and feed every 14 days.

The year in a cold greenhouse 2

Excessive summer temperatures can be reduced by damping down floors and walls with mains water, which rarely rises above a temperature of 10°C/50°F. Damping down also promotes a degree of humidity enjoyed by most plants. Excessive transpiration caused by too dry, hot conditions gives a severe check to plant growth. Shading, used in conjunction with ventilation, is also important in controlling summer conditions.

Thus the management of a cold greenhouse is an amalgam of attention to ventilation, atmospheric moisture, warmth and light. Holding the environmental balance is a complicated art in which experience is an important factor.

Plants for the cold greenhouse

Most annuals, biennials and shrubs, provided they are hardy, can be successfully over-wintered in a cold house. The advantage of doing so is that they flower two to three weeks earlier than plants grown outdoors. Their condition, not having had to contend with winter weather, is better than that of outdoor plants. Blooms are more spectacular as wind and rain damage is not a problem.

Alpines and similar plants can also be grown in an unheated greenhouse, but they require conditions which preclude the growth of many other plants.

Many food crops can be grown in a cold house, providing cash saving over shop prices and often produce of a higher quality. Tomatoes, the most popular crop, are covered in detail on pages 228–229. The following pages also detail the cultivation of fruits and other salad and vegetables. Another aspect of garden food production that a greenhouse can assist is the raising of seedlings for transplanting outdoors. This frees the gardener from dependence on commercially raised plants, and makes the growing of unusual vegetables, and the more obscure varieties of common ones, possible. As with flowers, the quality of crops grown under glass will be higher than those grown outdoors, due to the lack of weather damage. This is especially true of salad crops and strawberries.

Over-wintering Successful over-wintering is more likely if certain precautions are taken. During the coldest spells, plants must be kept on the dry side. It is best that the roots do not freeze for these are often more tender than the tops. Ground level beds should be deeply mulched with bracken or straw and the bases of shrubs and climbers lagged. Large pots and tubs must be lagged either with straw, glass fibre, or any other approved insulating material that can be secured in place with netting or hessian and wire twine. Smaller pots are best plunged in peat or sand.

Winter sets limitations on what can be grown permanently in the unheated greenhouse. From about mid-spring to late autumn the full range of cool greenhouse plants thrive happily. From late spring to early or mid-autumn even warm greenhouse plants succeed. With a heated propagating case, such plants can be over-wintered.

Flowering plants from seed

A wide range of hardy and tender annuals and biennials is readily available to provide colour and interest in the cold greenhouse for a large part of the year. These plants can be used as the main display or to fill in gaps between non-flowering permanent plants or fruit and vegetable crops. Hardy annuals can be sown in late summer or early autumn. They will over-winter well in a cold greenhouse and flower late the following spring, well ahead of their normal season. This technique can be used for hardy biennials, but these need to be sown in early summer and may be grown outside or in an open cold frame until late autumn. Routine seed sowing and pricking off into boxes or pans is all that annuals and biennials initially require (see pages 162–163). Thereafter place the young plants singly into 5 in pots, or space three out into 6 or 7 in containers. A fairly rich compost is recommended, a John Innes potting No. 2 being very satisfactory. Once the young plants are 3–4 in tall, pinch out their tips to encourage branching and a more bushy habit. As soon as they are growing more strongly, in late winter or early spring, commence liquid feeding and repeat at 10–14 day intervals. At about this time, insert twiggy sticks or canes for support.

July
Harvest sweet peppers, lettuce, radishes, mustard and cress, parsley, tomatoes (late in month).
Pinch out cucumbers, stop laterals, remove male flowers.
Take hydrangea cuttings.
Take half-ripe cuttings.

August
Sow lettuce, radishes, mustard and cress, winter endive.
Harvest lettuce, radishes, mustard and cress, tomatoes, sweet peppers, aubergines, okra, melons, cucumbers.
Sow cyclamen seeds. Take fuchsia cuttings, pot on half-ripe cuttings.

September
Sow lettuce, radishes, mustard and cress, alpine strawberries.
Plant late in month: apricots, peaches, grape vines.
Harvest lettuces, parsley, radishes, mustard and cress, tomatoes, peppers, aubergines, okra, cucumber, melon.
Lift seakale roots late in month, pot up and blanch.
Sow hardy annuals for spring flowering under glass.
Pot on hardy biennials for spring flowering.
Bring in evergreen azaleas, pot-grown chrysanthemums. Plant bulbous irises and hyacinths in pots.

October
Sow lettuce for crops in spring.
Plant fruit trees.
Harvest lettuce, tomatoes, peppers, aubergine, okra, melon.
Continue to pot up and blanch seakale.
Bring in tender bedding perennials for over-wintering.
Repeat sowings of annuals. Prick out annuals sown in September.
Pot on biennials. Sow sweet peas.
Over-winter chrysanthemum stools and dahlia tubers.

November
Sow onions for transplanting.
Box up rhubarb crowns, chicory and remaining seakale. Insulate boxes if necessary.
Bring in pots of herbs for winter supply.
Plant grape vines.
Cut back chrysanthemums to 6 in after flowering to encourage growth for cuttings. Prick out October-sown sweet peas. Pot on annuals. Bring plunged bulbs into the greenhouse as shoots appear.

December
Harvest chicory.
Bring in remaining plunged bulbs for spring flowering.
Take advantage of quiet period to do cleaning and maintenance jobs on greenhouse and equipment.

Ornamentals 1

Growing annuals from seed

To gain good benefit from the protected environment that the cold greenhouse affords, sow seeds of annuals in autumn for flowering in spring and early summer. Choose from the many available according to personal preference. Annuals can also be grown in a cool greenhouse where they will be protected from frost. In a cold house, plunge the pots in sand or ashes to prevent the roots freezing.

Sowing In September and October prepare boxes of sterilized seed compost. Broadcast the seed thinly, cover it with ⅛ in of sieved compost and water it in using a watering can fitted with a rose to prevent disturbance. Until the seedlings emerge, light is not necessary, but once germination has occurred, put the boxes on a bench or shelf where they will receive good light, but do not risk being scorched by any late summer sunshine. Keep the seedlings well watered and ventilate the house as the weather allows, taking care to make sure that seedlings become hardened but are not damaged by unexpected frost.

Pricking out and potting on When the seedlings are sturdy and large enough to handle, prick them out into peat blocks or trays filled with John Innes No. 1 or a similar potting compost. Continue to water and apply dilute fungicide, and to ventilate the greenhouse during the daytime. By late autumn the seedlings should be large enough to be potted on. Depending on the eventual size of the plants, place between one and three seedlings in each 3 in pot. After this first potting on, and throughout the winter, water the plants sparingly to prevent the compost becoming over-damp and to minimize the risks of disease. Ventilate the house as much as air temperature allows, which will depend on the severity of the winter. In February or March, carry out the final potting on, planting specimens singly or in groups, depending on the ultimate size, in labelled 4–5 in pots filled with John Innes No. 2 or an equivalent compost. If necessary, provide plants with support in the form of canes, pea sticks or wire netting. Increase ventilation and watering as air temperatures rise in spring to help provide a good display of blooms.

Bulbs

The word bulb is a generic term often used in gardening to include plants that also grow from other vegetative storage organs such as corms and tubers. Many such plants are ideal for the cold greenhouse and a planned succession will provide colour nearly all the year round. Once in flower, bulbs can be left in the greenhouse or taken indoors. Select bulbs from the suggestions given, but consult the catalogues and reliable nurseries for a wider choice of named varieties.

Winter and spring flowering bulbs

When growing bulbs for winter and spring flowering, remember that only those that have been specially treated are suitable for forcing. Untreated bulbs will flower satisfactorily under glass, but later than prepared forcing bulbs. This special treatment is applied, for example, to hyacinths and some tulips, narcissi, and bulbous irises, but not to crocuses, which will not flower if forced too quickly. Hyacinths, tulips, narcissi, grape hyacinths, the attractive bulbous irises and crocuses all lend themselves well to cultiva-

Annuals for spring flowering

1 September–October. Make two or three repeat sowings in sterilized seed compost.

2 When seedlings appear, place on the bench or a shelf. Water, shade and ventilate carefully.

3 When they are large enough to handle, prick out seedlings into peat blocks or trays of well-drained compost.

4 Late autumn. Pot on into 3 in pots, placing 1–3 seedlings, depending upon the variety, in each pot.

5 Winter. Water carefully and sparingly and provide ventilation whenever air temperatures allow.

6 February. Pot on into final pots, using John Innes No. 2 compost. Provide supports, using canes, pea sticks or wire netting.

Ornamentals 2

tion in the cold house, although cultural details differ slightly. All these bulbs can be planted in autumn for winter and spring flowering. For hyacinths, set each bulb in potting compost so that it is half exposed, then plunge the pot in a frame (see also page 241). When shoots appear six to eight weeks later, remove pots to a shady place in the greenhouse for a week before placing them in full light. Keep the house well ventilated but make sure that the ventilators are closed during very cold weather to maintain as high a temperature as possible. Return the plants to a shady spot after flowering, and allow the foliage to die away naturally. Bulbs should not be forced two years in succession. Plant forced bulbs in the open garden after one season under glass.

The requirements of narcissi and tulips are similar except that bulbs should be planted with only their 'noses' above compost level while bulbous irises and grape hyacinths are best completely covered. When planting crocus corms, give them a 2–3 in covering of compost. Crocus cannot be forced. If given heat, the flowers abort.

Summer and autumn flowering bulbs

The ambitious gardener can use his cold house to grow many unusual and spectacular summer and autumn flowering bulbs. For a lengthy show of colour, plant *Agapanthus*, *Hippeastrum*, *Tigridia* and *Polianthes* in spring. *Nerine* in August and *Ixia* from October to November. All these bulbs differ slightly in their needs, but all will need good ventilation, even watering, and a compost such as John Innes No. 2. After flowering allow the leaves to die down then lift the vegetative underground organs and store them in a dry and, if necessary, frost-free place. *Agapanthus* and others with fleshy roots should be plunged in their pots in frames and watered sparingly.

Camellias in containers

Most camellia varieties provide a good display if grown within the protected environment of the cold house as they flower earlier in the year and outdoors their blooms are often spoiled by frost. In very large greenhouses camellias can be planted out in the soil, but for the amateur, containers which restrict plant growth to manageable proportions, are best. Containers can be moved outside in summer to free greenhouse space. Place them in a sheltered spot with light shade. If the pots are plunged, camellias can be left outside until late autumn.

Soil Camellias in and out of containers need an acid, lime-free loam-based compost made up, by volume, of 7 parts medium loam, 3 parts moss peat and 2 parts coarse acid sand. This should be mixed with a well-balanced fertilizer at the rate of 4 oz to the bushel. A slow-release fertilizer is a useful addition.

Potting on When a camellia plant is bought from a nursery, check whether it needs potting on. If a tight mass of roots is visible when the plant is removed from its container it needs a pot 2 in larger in diameter. Prepare the new pot by crocking it well to supply good drainage. Place a layer of compost in the base of the pot, put in the plant and fill in with compost all round the roots. Shake the pot, top it up, then press the compost down round the sides. Give the pot a sharp tap on the greenhouse bench to help settle the compost. Water by immersion to ensure that the rootball is thoroughly soaked.

Watering and feeding Care must be taken not to overwater the plants. Equally it is essential to make sure that the rootball does not become too dry in the centre. Water by immersion to maintain evenly moist compost. Because the plants dislike lime, try to collect rainwater for them, particularly in hard water areas. Give liquid feed only between April and August, choosing a formula high in nitrogen in April to June and one high in potash for the remainder.

Ventilation and shading Good ventilation is essential for camellias. Even in winter the greenhouse ventilation should be left open during the day. In summer, if the air temperature in the house exceeds 27°C/80°F the glass on the south side of the house should be painted with shading paint to prevent scorching, and in hot weather the plants will also benefit if the house is damped down every day. Move pot-grown camellias outside in summer if possible. Place them in slight shade and water well.

Care after flowering Any repotting and pruning should be carried out after plants have flowered.

Bulbs

1 Early autumn. Choose equal-sized hyacinth bulbs and pot in potting compost so that the bulb is half-exposed. Use half pots or ornamental containers.

2 After potting, plunge the bulbs in the greenhouse or in a frame by covering with peat, grit or weathered ashes. Keep the compost moist.

3 Six to eight weeks later, when shoots appear, remove from the plunge bed and stand the pots in a cool, shady frost-free place such as beneath the staging.

4 A week later, move into full light. Flowering will take place in early spring. After flowering, keep the bulbs cool and slightly shaded while the foliage dies away.

Ornamentals 3

Evergreen azaleas
Many evergreen azaleas can be grown in pots in the cold greenhouse to provide colour in winter and early spring. Many early flowering varieties are now available and it is wise to consult a catalogue or visit a well-stocked nursery before deciding which ones to choose.

Compost Like camellias, azaleas need lime-free compost. Proprietary peat composts can be used for azaleas, but remember to check that they contain no lime. Alternatively, the gardener can make up his own compost using equal parts by volume of leaf mould, fibrous peat or moss peat, and coarse sand. Add a balanced slow-release fertilizer.

Care of plants Azaleas grown in pots can be plunged in the garden in a sheltered partially shaded place during the summer months after their flowering season is over. If the garden soil is not lime-free, plunge in sand. They should be watered regularly and given liquid feed every fortnight. In September, bring the pots back into the greenhouse to protect plants from winter cold and damp. Keep the greenhouse well ventilated during the day except during the worst weather, and water the plants regularly, preferably with rain water which is almost guaranteed lime-free. Make sure that the compost never dries out completely as it is almost impossible to get peat-based composts thoroughly wet again once they have become dehydrated.

After flowering, remove withered flowers and re-pot plants into slightly larger pots. Tease out some of the old compost from the edges of the root ball and re-pot into fresh compost. Carefully work the compost around the roots and gently firm it with the fingers. After potting, immerse the plants in water. Keep the plants in the greenhouse until the danger of frost has passed, then plunge them outdoors in a sheltered partially-shaded place for the summer months.

Fuchsias
The cold greenhouse is an excellent place to grow fuchsias as their blooms are easily spoilt by bad weather. Pendulous species such as *Fuchsia triphylla* and its varieties are also attractive planted in hanging baskets in the cold house.

Cultivation Fuchsias can be grown from rooted cuttings taken in April and planted in 3 in pots containing John Innes No. 2 or a similar compost, then potted on, using John Innes No. 3, into 5 or 6 in pots in which they will flower. Throughout the spring and summer keep the greenhouse well ventilated but damp it down once a day in hot weather to increase the humidity. In summer, shade the glass with shading paint, or put plants in the shade of larger specimens of other genera. Water the plants well and take care that they do not dry out as this may cause the buds to drop. After flowering, reduce watering so that the compost is kept barely moist until growth restarts in spring. Ventilate the house during the day. Plunge the pots in sand or ashes to protect them from frost, and cover the plants with polythene if frost is forecast.

Pelargoniums
Hundreds of different varieties of pelargoniums—popularly known as geraniums—are available for the greenhouse gardener to choose from and all make excellent shows of colour from spring to autumn. Regal pelargoniums, which flower in early spring, need heated greenhouse conditions. In March, take cuttings of plants over-wintered in greenhouse or frame. Insert individual cuttings in 2½ in pots filled with John Innes seed compost or a mixture of equal parts by volume of peat and sand. Place the pots in a propagating case or a closed frame on the greenhouse bench. When the cuttings have rooted, pot them on into 4 in pots filled with John Innes No. 2 compost.

During the growing season, keep plants well watered and shade the greenhouse glazing once the air temperature exceeds 13°C/55°F. Give plants good ventilation. After flowering, cut the pelargoniums back and leave them in their pots or plant them in boxes and store them in a frost-free frame to save space (see page 241), or on the greenhouse benching. In winter, cut down the amount of water given, but allow as much ventilation as the weather permits. In very cold weather it is essential to provide a little artificial heat to prevent plants from being damaged by frost. Take fresh cuttings in March and repeat the cycle.

Evergreen azaleas

1 After winter flowering is over remove the withered flowers and re-pot the plants. Use larger pots if the plants are in 3, 4 or 5 in pots.

2 Scrape away some of the old compost and remove the old drainage crocks from the base of the plant. Work fresh compost around the roots, firming it well.

3 Water the plants by immersion in rain water so that the peaty compost in which the plants are grown never dries out.

4 Plunge plants outside in their pots from June to September in a partially shaded position. Water regularly. Plunge in sand if soil contains lime.

5 Feed plants once every 14 days in spring and early summer, reducing to every 3–4 weeks in mid-summer. Stop feeding in mid-August.

6 Return plants to the greenhouse in September to flower during the winter. Ventilate freely and water well, if possible with rain water.

Fruits

A cold greenhouse can be used to grow a variety of fruit crops, the best choice being melons, strawberries, grapes, peaches, apricots and nectarines. The more stable environment of the greenhouse, and the protection it affords, allows the production of earlier, more reliable fruit crops compared with outdoor culture, especially in districts with cooler than average summer temperatures. The greatest limitation of the cold greenhouse for growing fruit is that many of the crops, but particularly grapes, peaches, apricots and nectarines, take up a great deal of space. If possible, it may be best to devote a whole greenhouse to fruit culture but if this is not practical, select fruit that will not occupy the whole house or block light from other plants. Alternatively, cultivate plants in pots to restrict their growth to manageable proportions.

Choosing a greenhouse

For small-growing crops such as melons and strawberries a house of conventional dimensions will be suitable but a larger house is necessary to accommodate other fruit adequately unless they are grown in pots. When choosing a greenhouse for growing fruit remember that a vigorous grape vine will need a border at least 8 ft long and that a peach, apricot or nectarine will require a greenhouse with a wall or glass sides at least 12 ft high. When selecting a greenhouse for fruit growing ensure that it is well ventilated. Fruit trees should be grown against a south-facing wall.

Planting

Vines, peaches and their relations and melons can all be planted direct into the border soil of the greenhouse, which should be prepared according to the individual requirements of each crop. Strawberries, however, are best cultivated in pots or barrels. If space is limited it is also possible to cultivate grapes, peaches, apricots and nectarines—and even plums, apples, pears and cherries—in pots, although for the last four of these it is essential to select varieties grown on dwarfing rootstocks. Container culture has the added advantage that it is possible to provide exactly the right type of soil but it is important

to give plants the maximum possible light. It will be difficult for plants to thrive, and for fruit to ripen, if plants in pots are shaded by a thick vine or a vigorous peach.

Training and support Except for strawberries, all the types of fruit suggested for the cold greenhouse will need some system of wires on which they can be trained and this should be combined with a support system. Always remember to arrange the training system before planting because inserting wires behind growing plants is not only difficult but can lead to damage.

Ventilation

The exact needs of fruit crops vary in detail but good ventilation is essential. Peaches, for example, ideally need ventilation from the roof and sides of the house. When growing a crop that takes up a good deal of space in the greenhouse always make sure that the growth of the plant does not interfere with the ventilation system or make windows difficult to open.

For full details of cultural practices see pages 84–129.

CULTIVATION

Grapes Construct a training system of horizontal wires 9 in apart and 15 in from the glass. Plant in November in well-drained porous border soil containing loam, peat and grit with added base fertilizer and ground chalk. Water to give a thorough soaking in early spring. Mulch. Keep the soil thoroughly damp, watering every 7–10 days in hot weather, and reduce watering as fruit ripens. Ventilate from January to March then close the vents until May or when the air temperature exceeds 18°C/64°F.

Peaches, apricots and nectarines Construct a training system of wires placed 10 in apart and 10 in from the glass. Plant in October in border soil enriched with peat and add lime at 1 lb per sq yd. Mulch. Water well after planting and from the time growth starts. Ventilate during the day only after fruit has set. Close the house at night.

Melons

1 Before planting prepare the house by stretching wires at 1 ft intervals along the house sides 15 in from the glass. Tie in two canes per plant, one from soil to eaves, the other from the eaves to the house ridge.

2 As the plants grow tie stems to canes and laterals to the horizontal wires. Pinch out the growing point when plant is 6 ft tall. Pinch back side shoots to two leaves beyond each flower. Increase ventilation.

In May, plant seedlings raised in heat 15 in apart in a compost of loam with 2 oz steamed bonemeal and 2 oz compound fertilizer to a 2 gal bucket of soil placed on top of the border soil, in a ridge 1 ft high.

3 Thin the fruit to four of the same size per plant when fruits are walnut-sized. Water the plants very well and liquid feed them every 7–10 days. As fruits enlarge support them with netting slings.

Tomatoes 1

Tomatoes are an excellent choice of crop for a cold greenhouse for they are tender plants that profit greatly from the protection glass affords. A heated propagating case can be used in a cold greenhouse to provide the added heat necessary for raising plants from seed. All greenhouse-grown tomatoes need careful attention to watering, feeding and care in controlling pests and diseases.

Raising tomato plants
Without the use of a heated propagating case it is usually best to purchase tomato plants rather than raise them from seed. Buy plants in April from a reliable source.

Seed sowing Seed may be sown in a heated propagating case in mid–late February for planting eight weeks later. Sow seed thinly in John Innes No. 1 compost placed directly in the case or in trays or pans which are placed in it. Seeds sown too thickly are likely to suffer from damping off diseases. Set the propagator thermostat to 18°C/65°F. At this temperature germination and emergence should take place in 7–10 days. Keep the seedlings evenly moist but not waterlogged.

Pricking out When the seedlings have developed their first true leaves 10–12 days after sowing, carefully prick them out singly into individual 3 in peat or plastic pots filled with a proprietary potting compost. Insert a small dibber beneath the roots of each seedling and hold the seedling by its leaves to prevent damage. Use the dibber to make a hole big enough to take each seedling without restricting its roots. Water the seedlings gently to firm the compost round their roots and replace them in the propagator.

Temperature control Keep the seedlings at 18°C/65°F until they begin to shade each other, then turn the thermostat down to 16°C/60°F. About a week before planting, reduce the temperature to 10°C/50°F. Apply a balanced liquid feed and support plants with a small split cane if they become too tall to support themselves.

Planting
While seedlings are maturing, decide which growing system will be used. The main choices are between greenhouse soil, ring culture, 9 in pots placed directly on greenhouse soil, growing bags or straw bales (for full details see page 74). If plants are to be grown directly in greenhouse soil, double dig and enrich the lower spit with well-rotted compost or manure. For pot or ring culture fill pots with rich home-made compost or John Innes No. 2 or 3. Plant tomatoes when the young plants are 6 to 9 in tall. This is usually when the flowers on the first truss are just opening. Immediately before planting, water plants thoroughly and destroy any plants that show signs of disease. Make a hole in the chosen growing medium big enough to accommodate the roots without crowding. Place the top of each root ball level with the soil surface. Plants raised in peat pots should be made thoroughly wet before planting (tear down one side of the pot wall if necessary to prevent drying out) and planted complete with the pot. Space plants about 18 in apart each way. Give planted tomatoes a thorough watering in and keep them moist to make sure the roots become well established.

Support In the greenhouse tomato plants are usually best supported on soft garden string tied to a horizontal wire near the greenhouse roof at one end and to the stem of the plant, under the lowest true leaf, at the other. Each plant is then twisted loosely round the string as it grows. Take care not to damage the plant stem by pulling the string too tight. Alternatively, plants in pots or grown directly in greenhouse soil may be loosely tied to bamboo canes for support.

Watering and feeding
The success of greenhouse-grown tomatoes depends on meticulous attention to watering and feeding throughout the life of the plant. Plants will be damaged by drying out which causes flower drop, or waterlogging which is a particular hazard for plants grown in isolated systems such as growing bags, for it quickly kills off plant roots. Plants in growing bags will only thrive if the growing medium is kept uniformly moist, which may mean watering three or four times a day in hot weather. Ring culture also demands much water because drainage is very rapid. The most stable water supply is achieved with plants grown directly in greenhouse soil. In all systems, irregular watering will cause fruit to split.

Raising from seed

1 Mid–late February Sow 2–3 seeds per sq in in propagator filled with sieved compost. Sprinkle over $\frac{1}{8}$ in layer of compost and cover with newspaper.

2 Prick out seedlings 10–12 days after sowing using a small dibber. Transfer to 3 in pots filled with John Innes No. 1 potting compost or equivalent.

Planting

3 Place pots in propagator and set thermostat to 18°C/65°F. Water sparingly but often. Liquid feed before planting.

4 Mid–late April When flowers on first truss are just opening water plants well. Remove plants from pots and place 18 in apart in chosen growing medium.

Tomatoes 2

Greenhouse grown tomatoes should be liquid fed with a proprietary fertilizer mixed with the water according to the manufacturer's instructions. A well balanced feed will provide nitrogen to encourage vegetative growth and potassium to improve quality.

Trimming and de-leafing

As tomato plants grow they develop side shoots in the junctions (axils) between leaf and stem. These must be removed while they are small or they will use up water and nutrients needed by the productive parts of the plant. Snap off each side shoot cleanly between finger and thumb, preferably in early morning when the plants are turgid. Avoid pulling which leaves scars that are easily invaded by disease-causing fungi.

When plants are 4–5 ft tall, remove the lower leaves up to the first truss. Use a sharp knife and cut cleanly leaving no snags. De-leafing allows more light to reach the plant base, improves air circulation and helps to combat fungal diseases. As the trusses crop make sure any yellowing or diseased leaves are removed.

Pollination and fruit setting

If fruit setting is a problem it can be improved by assisting pollen dispersal. Spray the plant with a fine droplet spray, shake the plant gently or tap the flower trusses.

Stopping

In a cold greenhouse tomatoes will not usually produce more than six or seven fruit trusses per season so it is best to snap off the growing point two leaves beyond the sixth or seventh truss. Continue to remove further side shoots, which will often be stimulated into growth by the stopping process.

Harvesting

Ripe fruit should be ready for picking in late June or early July from seed sown in mid-February. Harvest fruit as it is needed, leaving the calyx on each. Feed at the recommended intervals until the last truss of fruit is set.

Pests and diseases

Greenhouse tomatoes are notoriously susceptible to pests and diseases which are described on pages 247–249.

Support

1 Bamboo canes can be used for support. Tie the plant on loosely with soft garden string so that stems are not damaged.

2 Snap off side and basal shoots between thumb and forefinger. If possible de-shoot in early morning when the stems are turgid.

3 Spray the flowers with a fine droplet spray or shake the plant gently to disperse pollen and improve fruit setting.

4 Liquid feed growing plants following manufacturer's instructions. Water them as necessary.

Stopping

5 Snap off growing point 2 leaves above top truss when 6–7 trusses have set fruit. Remove any lower leaves that turn yellow.

6 Pick ripe fruit by snapping the stalk, leaving the calyx on the fruit. Ripe fruit left under hot sun will soon lose its firmness.

TRAINING SYSTEMS

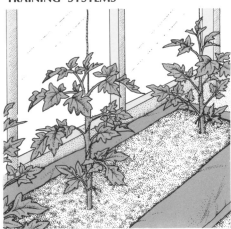

Vertical training Plants are carefully twisted round soft string attached below lowest true leaf and to a horizontal wire 6–8 ft above ground level.

V-training Plants are twisted round strings set alternately at 60° to the ground. This system is good for straw bale culture with plants placed closer than 18 in.

Vegetables and salads 1

The cold greenhouse can be used very successfully for growing salads and vegetables, from the conventional tomatoes and cucumbers to more unusual crops such as seakale, peppers and aubergines. The greatest advantage of the cold house in salad and vegetable growing is that it can be used to extend the growing season at both ends of the year. With good planning it can provide food for the kitchen almost all the year round. It is also very useful for raising young vegetable plants which are later planted out into the garden.

The most significant limitation of the cold house is implicit in its description—because it is unheated, the gardener must wait until the house temperature reaches a suitable point before certain seeds can be sown. Equally, the winter temperature in the cold house precludes the growing of many out of season crops. When considering which crops to grow, make maximum use of space. Catch crops such as carrots and beetroot can be grown between tall crops, such as tomatoes and cucumbers, before they develop.

Leaf crops
Good choices for the cold house include salad greens, seakale and herbs.

Lettuce Sow lettuce seed in pots then prick them out into peat blocks or pots before planting them in greenhouse soil. If seed is sown in small quantities at fortnightly intervals from early spring until autumn, a constant supply can be assured. To prevent diseases, particularly botrytis, it is important to ventilate the house well in all but the worst weather. The crop needs adequate light and attention to watering. Give fewer, thorough waterings rather than many small ones. The crop will be improved by a thorough soaking about 10 days before harvesting.

Mustard and cress As long as the greenhouse temperature is 10°C/50°F or above, mustard and cress can be sown at weekly intervals. Sow seed on a moist tissue in a shallow dish and place it in the dark under a bench, lightly covered with a dark cloth or newspaper if necessary to exclude light. Once the seeds have germinated, move the dish up into a lighter place and keep the seeds well watered.

Winter endive Sow seed as for lettuce in late August to early September and put in a well-lit position. Ventilate the house and water the seedlings regularly. When plants are fully grown, tie them round loosely with raffia and place a large plastic pot over selected plants to blanch the leaves. Cover the drainage hole of the top pot and support it on crocks to allow free air circulation.

Seakale From late September to late October, lift seakale crowns from the garden and trim off the side roots and any yellowing foliage. Trim the main roots to about 6 in. Allowing 3 crowns per pot, plant the crowns in 9 in plastic pots filled with rich compost such as John Innes No. 3. Cover each pot with another of the same size turned upside down and place under the greenhouse staging. Ideally the crowns need a temperature of about 10°C/50°F, so if the house gets too cold insulate the pots with newspaper or sacking.

Herbs Many herbs will continue growing through the winter if plants are potted up and brought into the cold house for protection during winter. Herbs that benefit most from such protection include parsley, chives, mint, French tarragon, pot marjoram, rosemary, thyme and sage. Water plants well and ventilate the house during the day in all but the worst weather. In spring, begin sowing seeds of annual and biennial herbs as soon as the greenhouse temperature is right.

Root crops and bulbs
Small quantities of root crops can be raised in the cold house for harvesting weeks before the main outdoor crops. Seed sowing can begin in February–March in peat pots or direct into slightly acid greenhouse border soil prepared according to crop requirements. If the vegetables are to be eaten really young and tender, make more sowings at three or four week intervals. Thoroughly water and well ventilate the house once the temperatures begin to rise in April.

Pods
Select dwarf varieties of French beans for cold greenhouse cultivation and make two sowings, one in spring for early summer cropping,

Lettuces

1 February Sow seed in 3½ in pots filled with John Innes No. 1 potting compost. Cover the seeds lightly and water using a fine rose. Repeat sowings every 2 weeks.

2 Early March Prick out as many seedlings as required into small individual peat blocks or pots. Water well and increase the ventilation according to the weather.

3 Late March When plants have 4–5 true leaves plant the peat blocks or pots 8 in apart into the greenhouse border soil. Water well and ensure good ventilation.

4 April Harvest lettuce by carefully pulling up whole plants and trimming off the roots, or cut plants below lower leaves. Remove discarded matter from greenhouse.

Vegetables and salads 2

FRENCH BEANS
'Masterpiece', 'Sprite',
'Kinghorn Wax-pod' (yellow).

CUCUMBERS
'Sporu', 'Telegraph', 'Baton
Vert' (ridge), 'Burpless'
(ridge).

SWEET PEPPERS
'Canape', 'New Ace'.

AUBERGINES
'Long Purple', 'Short Tom'.

the other in July for autumn harvesting. Pregerminate the seeds and sow four or five seeds round the edges of a pot filled with John Innes No. 2 or equivalent compost. For the spring sowing wait until early April or germinate the seeds indoors. Water the plants well once flowers appear and ventilate the house in warm weather.

Vegetable fruits
Cucumbers, sweet peppers and aubergines, as well as tomatoes whose culture is described in detail on pages 228–229, can all be grown in the cold greenhouse.

Cucumbers Pre-germinate cucumber seeds then sow them singly in 3 in pots filled with John Innes No. 1 or a similar compost. Allow 4 to 5 weeks from sowing to planting and time the operation so that planting can take place in late May, if necessary germinating the seeds indoors. Preferably, plants should be planted in growing bags (2 plants per standard bag) or singly on straw bales. At planting time or before, erect a system of supporting strings tied to horizontal wires near the greenhouse roof, or insert bamboo canes on to which plants can be loosely tied. Developing plants should be well watered and given liquid feed but the atmosphere in the house should be kept as humid as possible. Pinch and trim the plants as shown in the illustrations and remove any male flower.

Sweet peppers These vegetable fruits are best grown in the cold greenhouse in pots. Because the seed needs a temperature of 21°C/70°F for germination, seeds must be germinated in a propagating case and the seedlings hardened off, or the gardener can buy plants from a nursery. Allow 10 to 12 weeks between sowing and planting in late May. Sow seed thinly on moistened compost covered with $\frac{1}{8}$ in of compost and then with glass and newspaper. When seedlings are large enough to handle, prick them out into 3 in pots filled with John Innes No. 3 compost or plant 3 plants in a standard sized growing bag. Place pots 18 in apart on the border soil or greenhouse staging. When plants are about 6 in tall, remove the growing point to encourage bushy growth, and support and tie them to bamboo canes if necessary. Keep plants well watered and liquid fed and venti-

late the house in warm weather. Watch for aphids and red spider mites. Spray with malathion or derris if pests are seen.

Aubergines These need very similar cultural conditions to peppers, and plants can be raised from seed in the same way or purchased from a nursery. Aim for planting in early May and allow two plants to a standard size growing bag. Pinch out the growing points when plants are 9–12 in high and allow only 5 or 6 fruit to develop on each plant. Remove any extra fruits, leaving the remaining ones well spaced, and pinch off any extra flowers that form. Water and feed often but sparingly and ventilate the house in hot weather. Watch out for pests and spray against those that appear as for peppers.

Raising seed
Seeds of many vegetables can be raised in the cold house for planting out once the weather is suitable to provide earlier, more reliable crops. Sow seed in peat blocks or pots for easy planting later on and keep house well ventilated.

CHICORY

In November, lift chicory roots from the garden and cut off the leaves to within $\frac{1}{2}$ in of the crown. Trim the roots to 9 in and take off any side shoots. Store the roots horizontally in boxes of dry sand outside under a north wall until they are needed. From mid-November onwards

plant 3 or 4 chicory roots at weekly intervals in a 9 in plastic pot filled with sand so that each crown is $\frac{1}{2}$ in above the top of the soil. Water sparingly and cover with pot to keep out light. Place under bench and keep well ventilated. The chicons will be ready after 4 weeks.

Cucumbers

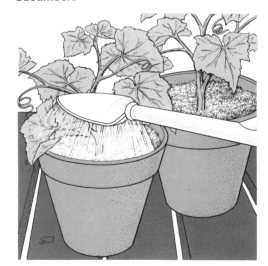

1 Late May Plant seedlings raised in heat in 9 in pots filled with John Innes No. 3 potting compost. Water and liquid feed regularly. Keep the greenhouse humid.

2 June–July Tie growing plants to canes for support. Pinch out growing points as main stems reach the roof. Ventilate frequently, but carefully, as humidity is important.

3 June onwards Keep single laterals in each leaf axil and stop them at 2 leaves. Remove male flowers if appropriate. Harvest by cutting the stems with a sharp knife.

The year in a cool greenhouse 1

A cool greenhouse, one provided with a heating system that ensures that temperatures do not fall below 4.5°C/40°F, provides an environment suitable for a vast range of plants. Nearly all the plants from the world's temperate zones can be cultivated, and the choice extends into those from the sub-tropical and tropical regions. A distinction is made between those plants that can be grown in winter in a cool house, such as salads and chrysanthemums, and those such as sub-tropical bedding plants which are dormant at cool greenhouse temperatures but survive the winter undamaged, when they would die in the open garden or an unheated house. In addition, all those plants which will tolerate cold greenhouse conditions can be grown in a cool house. In many cases their growing seasons will be longer. It is possible to raise a wider range of out-of-season food crops and ornamentals given the minimum temperature of a cool house.

To many gardeners, the cool greenhouse is the norm and a cold or warm house is a deviation from it. When gardening literature and catalogues are consulted, it will be noticed that "greenhouse plants" tends to mean those to be grown in a cool house.

While there are very many plants to choose from for growing in a cold house, it is often worth experimenting to try to widen the range still further. Plants rarely have an absolute minimum temperature which kills them, unless it be frost level which, by freezing the cells, can cause physical damage. Many plants thought to need higher temperatures than the cool house minimum can in fact be acclimatized to the prevailing conditions. A lot depends upon avoiding extremes and sudden changes. If the balance of the environment—heat, humidity and ventilation—is carefully watched, plants thought tender may survive and go on to flourish. Among those worth experimenting

with are the many house plants available, and sub-tropical flowering plants such as those fostered by Victorian conservatory gardeners for winter blooms.

Management

The principles of cool greenhouse care are those outlined earlier in this book for the running of any greenhouse. The one main difference in the running of a cool house is the need to manipulate the heating system.

An inefficient heating system is undesirable for three reasons. First, if the system is not running correctly it will not be able to maintain the necessary temperature and plants will suffer. The second reason is that inefficiency in the use of fuel will lead to rapidly escalating bills. Heating a greenhouse is expensive, and if the system used keeps the temperature unnecessarily high, or burns fuel inefficiently, the cost will be magnified. Third, certain kinds of heating system, those

which burn gas or oil, can harm plants if they are not adjusted correctly. Badly set wicks and burners can cause the heater to give off poisonous fumes.

Thermostats The sensible management of a heating system centres around the use of thermostats. These devices sense temperature changes and act as switches, turning the heating system on and off as required. They are most often used with electrical systems, which are easily controllable and capable of producing heat quickly. Gas and oil systems can also be fitted with thermostats—as are domestic central heating boilers.

A thermostat is only useful if the system it controls has sufficient capacity. The heaters must be capable of maintaining the desired temperature without running constantly. The specialist suppliers use formulae designed to calculate the size of heating installation necessary. Once a large enough system has been installed, thermostatic control will

---

January

Check draught-proofing, insulation (if fitted) and heating system. Set thermostats to night minimum of 4.5°C/40°F. Water plants in flower, water others sparingly. Maintain a dry atmosphere to discourage mildew.
Sow canna, fuchsia, pelargonium. Bring in bulbs for flowering as they show growth.
Take cuttings of winter-flowering chrysanthemums and carnations.

February

Ventilate when possible and gradually increase watering. Day length will increase. Maintain minimum temperature.
Sow bedding plants with long germination/growing periods, half-hardy annuals, sweet peas, begonia, calceolaria, salvia, schizanthus, and germinate in a propagating case.
Continue to take chrysanthemum cuttings.
Sow brassicas and onions for transplanting outdoors. Sow early bunching turnips, carrots, parsnips, beetroot, okra, tomatoes, cucumbers.
Plant tomato plants from middle of the month.
Begin repotting of ferns and palms.
Bring in more bulbs for flowering.

March

Increase watering, ventilate well on sunny days and maintain a more humid atmosphere. Be alert for and combat insect pests such as aphids.
Sow sweet pepper, courgette, half-hardy annuals, tomato, bedding plants, basil.
Transplant rooted cuttings taken in winter.
Repot orchids and other perennials as necessary.
Begin to take softwood cuttings.
Pot up tuberous begonias.

April

Pay attention to ventilation and watering as temperatures increase. Keep heating switched on, setting thermostat for minimum night temperature.
Sow cucumbers, marrows, courgettes, pumpkins, squashes, dwarf French beans, runner beans for transplanting outdoors, primulas, half-hardy annuals such as stocks and zinnias, and Campanula pyramidalis.
Continue repotting and potting on.
Move bulbs which have flowered to a frame. Move over-wintering pot plants outdoors into a sheltered position.
Transplant seedlings from seed sown earlier in the spring. Take further softwood cuttings.
Dust tomato flowers to encourage pollination.
Move half-hardy plants into a frame to harden off.

May

Water freely, shade as necessary in sunny weather and encourage a more humid atmosphere.
Sow cineraria, primula. Plant chrysanthemums and move outside. Pot on carnations, zonal pelargoniums, tuberous begonias, annuals raised from spring-sown seed. Feed all plants in active growth. Continue taking precautions against pests throughout the summer. Pinch out young fuchsias when 4–5 in high.
Remove cucumber laterals and all male flowers.
Tie in tomato plants and pinch out side shoots.

June

Turn off and overhaul heating system. Ventilate freely, shade whenever necessary and damp down and spray to raise humidity. Water as required, twice a day if necessary.
Sow calceolaria, Primula malacoides, zinnia, all for autumn and winter flowering.
Feed tomato plants and all other plants in growth. Pot on plants raised from seed as necessary.
Plant out bedding plants into their flowering positions in the open garden.
Plunge azaleas, hydrangeas and other pot plants which have finished flowering.
Cut back shoots of regal pelargoniums.

The year in a cool greenhouse 2

ensure that it only operates when the temperature falls below the pre-set level. The heater will raise the temperature, triggering the thermostat again and cutting off the system. Thermostats must be placed away from draughts and cold spots, where they will give an artificial reading.

Balance While the main stress of cold greenhouse management is on maintaining the winter minimum, thought must be given to the other components of greenhouse management. Shading, ventilation and humidity control are all crucial, especially in summer. Just as plants have a minimum temperature for healthy growth, so they have maximum levels of temperature which will harm them. Problems caused by high air temperatures are often magnified by failure to ensure adequate humidity. If there is not enough water vapour in the atmosphere, plants will transpire—give out water from their leaves into the air—too quickly. Increase

humidity by regular damping down and the installation of damp sand beds under benches.

While summer heat and winter cold have to be countered by active management, the most difficult times of the year for the running of the cold greenhouse can be spring and autumn. During these seasons the sun has power to quickly heat the greenhouse, while the nights are cool. Cold daytime temperatures can easily occur due to sudden weather changes. This combination can be particularly trying in the late winter and early spring. Sun heat is becoming more powerful, and the effect of the sun combined with artificial heating can quickly raise the temperature, often above the level required, unless ventilation is promptly given. Under these conditions automatic ventilators will begin to show their worth. A cold house will not suffer so much from this problem because it does not have the reservoir of artificially generated heat that a cool house has. More

sun heat is thus needed to raise the temperature to unwanted levels.

Growing plants

The following pages deal with the cultivation of ornamentals, including bedding plants which are covered in detail, and food crops. All the ornamentals and food crops covered in the preceding cold greenhouse section, such as annuals, tomatoes and salad crops, can be added to the list. The difference comes mainly in timing of sowing and cropping. Tomatoes, for instance, can be planted from mid-February onwards in a cool greenhouse, while in a cold house late April is the earliest possible date. Annuals will flower earlier in the spring in a cool house than in a cold one. Lettuce, radish and other salad crops can be sown in late summer and autumn for autumn and winter cropping.

Other plants Many more plants than those described in detail on the following pages can

be grown in a cool greenhouse. The plants chosen, especially those illustrated in the step-by-step sequences, are the most rewarding for the relatively inexperienced and/or those which illustrate a key growing principle. The information given can be adapted to cover the cultivation of many other plants.

There are other categories of plants of interest which are less popular but still worth considering if greenhouse space is available. For example, many shrubs can be grown in containers under glass and brought into flower earlier than outside. Examples are lilac, forsythia and hydrangea. Fruits such as citrus can be grown in tubs in cool greenhouse conditions. Most citrus trees will tolerate a winter minimum of 7°C/45°F, though the lime needs 10°C/50°F. Summer temperatures should be maintained at 13°–16°C/55°–61°F for successful cropping. Full details of the cultivation of warm temperate fruits are given in *Fruit* in this series.

July

Maintain a moist atmosphere and attend to watering. Ventilate well and shade as required. Sow salpiglossis and make a repeat sowing of *Primula malacoides* and calceolaria.
Take hydrangea cuttings.
Pinch out tomatoes to encourage bushy growth. Pinch out cucumber laterals.
Stake plants, especially annuals growing in pots, and train climbers.
Pot on pelargoniums reared from spring cuttings and plunge outdoors. Pot on carnations, and repot freesias.
Harvest cucumbers and tomatoes regularly.

August

Continue summer shading, watering and damping down regime. Watch for cool nights towards the end of the month as days shorten.
Sow annuals for spring flowering, cyclamen, cineraria.
Prick out calceolarias and other seedlings from earlier sowings.
Take cuttings of pelargoniums.
Pot on primulas, cinerarias.
Plant bulbs for winter and spring flowering, such as freesias, tulip, hyacinth, narcissi.
Top-dress tomatoes and feed plants in flower with a liquid fertilizer.
Feed chrysanthemums standing outdoors and water well.
Repair any structural damage to the greenhouse and repaint if necessary.

September

Reduce watering and damping down as temperatures drop.
Restart the heating system to check it and switch on if necessary towards the end of the month.
Check winter fuel supplies if necessary. Reduce shading.
Sow more annuals for spring flowering.
Pot up remaining bulbs.
Bring in azaleas, camellias, chrysanthemums and other pot plants that have spent the summer in the open. Clear tomatoes from the house, removing all debris and cleaning pots, rings, etc.
Pot on cyclamen, cinerarias and primulas into final pots and move on to greenhouse shelves.
Take cuttings of bedding plants before they are discarded, and of coleus, heliotropes and fuchsias.

October

Switch on the heating system and set the thermostat to maintain a minimum night temperature of 4.5°C/40°F. Ventilate freely on warm days but exclude fog and damp. Reduce watering and remove shading completely.
Pot up the last of the bulbs.
Feed cyclamen, cinerarias, primulas and camellias.
If possible, remove all plants and fumigate the house against fungal diseases.
Scatter pellets to combat slugs.

November

Maintain minimum winter temperature as October and ventilate sparingly. Further reduce watering of all except plants in flower.
Pot on annuals. Keep in good light and give minimum water.
Bring in the first batch of bulbs for winter flowering.
Prune shrubs.
Sow lettuce.
Bring in fuchsias, begonias and hydrangeas and store under the staging. Keep almost dry.

December

Fit insulation to greenhouse sides if possible and stop up all draughts. Cover the house with sacking or mats in very severe weather.
Protect tender plants with paper, polythene or sacking if severe frost is forecast. Cut watering to the minimum.
Ventilate a little when possible and run a fan heater to circulate the atmosphere.
Bring in more bulbs.
Box up seakale and chicory for forcing.
Cut down chrysanthemums after they have flowered and start to take cuttings of soft growth.
Keep cineraria, cyclamen, primulas and other plants required for Christmas flowering in a warm part of the house. Water them with care, avoiding the foliage.
Clear debris, dead leaves and used pots from the greenhouse. Clean all pots, trays and propagating equipment.

Bedding plants 1

The cool greenhouse is an ideal place for raising summer bedding plants. Using the greenhouse in this way shortens the propagation period and, as long as plants are properly hardened off and precautions taken against disease, ensures the production of sturdy plants. The other advantages to the gardener of raising his own plants from seed compared with buying plants direct from the nursery are that he knows exactly what he is growing and that there is less risk of plants being damaged as they do not have to be transplanted from overcrowded seed trays.

Seed sowing

One of the most critical aspects of raising bedding plants from seed in the greenhouse is timing. As a general rule, the sequence of sowing is determined by the speed at which seeds germinate and by the growth rate of the developing seedlings. For this reason slow-growing species required for summer bedding are sown in January and February and a monthly sowing plan adopted according to the scheme shown above. Even with the artificial heat provided by the cool greenhouse, development of seeds sown in the first two months of the year is slow because of low winter light intensity.

Seeds of bedding plants may be sown in trays or pans (dwarf pots). Fill the chosen containers with a proprietary seed-growing compost, which should be damp. There is no need to avoid peat-based composts, with their low nutrient reserves, because the seeds will germinate relatively rapidly in the frost-free environment of the greenhouse. Once the containers are full, press down the compost with the fingers or a presser board to within $\frac{1}{4}$ in of the top, but be careful not to press too hard as this will restrict the drainage and tend to encourage damping off diseases and attack by sciarid flies.

The best seed sowing method depends on the size of individual seeds. For small seeds such as those of *Begonia semperflorens*, mix the seeds with fine dry sand in the seed packet then sow them by broadcasting, keeping the hand close to the compost surface. Larger seeds can be broadcast in the same way, but without the addition of sand. The larger seeds, such as those of zinnias—and small seeds that have been pelleted—are best planted singly by hand. Cover sown seed with compost but be careful not to make this covering layer too thick. Label the container clearly then water in the seeds with Cheshunt compound fungicide as a protection against damping off disease. Take care to use a rose on the watering can so that seeds are not dislodged from their planting positions by the water.

Germination

Even in a cool greenhouse, developing seeds, particularly those sown in January and February, will benefit from extra warmth. This is best provided by a propagating case. When using such a case, place the seed containers inside it and set the thermostat to 21°C/71°F. If a propagating case is not available, either take the seed containers indoors and put them in a warm place or cover them with a sheet of glass. A piece of newspaper may be placed on top of the glass as light is not important until after germination.

As soon as the seeds germinate (this may take one to three weeks depending on temperature and the species) remove any covering and put the containers in a well lit place but be careful that they do not risk being scorched by strong sunlight. Water with dilute Captan to combat damping off and other seedling diseases. If possible maintain the temperature at 21°C/70°F to promote speedy development. The seedlings also need good ventilation and the greenhouse ventilators should be opened for at least an hour a day except in very severe weather conditions.

Pricking out

Seedlings should be pricked out as soon as they are large enough to handle. If left in their original containers they will become overcrowded and their roots will become so entangled that the gardener will be unable to avoid damaging them when they are removed. Prick out seedlings into individual pots or trays filled with John Innes No. 1 or a

Growing bedding plants from seed

1 Fill a seed tray with seed-sowing compost. Firm the compost with the fingertips or a presser board to within $\frac{1}{2}$ in of the top.

2 Sow the seeds thinly. Small seeds can be mixed with fine dry sand and broadcast onto the compost to make sowing easier.

3 Sieve compost over medium-sized or large seeds so that they are just covered. Do not cover small seeds.

4 Water the seed tray with Cheshunt compound to combat damping off.

Bedding plants 2

similar potting compost, taking care to handle them by one leaf and between finger and thumb. Use a dibber to prise out the seedlings and to make a hole in the compost big enough to accommodate each plant. If seedlings are pricked out into trays, allow at least 1½ in between them each way to prevent overcrowding. Firm the soil round each seedling with the dibber, label and give another watering with Cheshunt compound to guard against damping off.

Even in ideal conditions the seedlings will suffer some check to their growth after pricking out but careful handling and transplanting when the root system is small and unbranched will help to reduce this to a minimum. After pricking out the temperature can be reduced to 18°C/65°F but good ventilation is still essential to healthy seedling development. When seedlings are big enough and when there is no chance of frost, seedlings should be hardened off in a cold frame (see page 240) or by turning off the greenhouse heating system and gradually increasing the ventilation first by day and then at night.

Propagation

While most bedding plants are raised from seed, several important plants can be propagated by cuttings or division. Full details of these methods of propagation are given on pages 164–187.

Cuttings can be taken in autumn when the plants are lifted, or in spring from tubers kept dormant over the winter. Pelargoniums are one of many bedding plants that can be propagated by cuttings. Keep the cuttings at a minimum temperature of 4°C/40°F over winter, and water sparingly. Pot on as necessary into 4 or 5 in pots, harden off and plant out in the normal way.

Over-wintering

Some bedding plants can be over-wintered in a cool house for re-use the next season. Lift the plants in autumn and pot or box up. Cut back the foliage by about one-half, water very sparingly and ventilate freely to guard against grey mould. Plenty of light is necessary to avoid the production of drawn, weak growth. Plant out as normal in spring.

PEAT BLOCKS

Larger seeds can be sown in peat blocks formed from damp peat-based compost with a blocking device, or in peat pots. Both have the advantage of being planted with the young plant in the flowering position. The seedlings are therefore not subject to the disturbance of pricking out. Sow 2–3 seeds in each block and water well. Provide the conditions described in the caption sequence below. When the seedlings have reached first true leaf stage, thin to the strongest per block.

PLANTING OUT

When seedlings are ready to be planted out and have been hardened off in a frame or being placed outside during the day, plant in the flowering positions. If possible, remove both plants and compost, allowing the roots to be gently teased out and the young plants to be inserted with an adequate rootball. Make planting holes with a trowel and water well after firming in. Water well until the plants have become established. Pot-grown greenhouse perennials can be used as pot plants.

5 Place the tray in a propagating case at 21°C/70°F, or in a warm place indoors if a case is not available.

6 As soon as the first seedlings emerge, place the tray in good light. Keep the temperature at 21°C/70°F.

7 Spray seedlings with Cheshunt compound to combat damping off disease. Ensure that ventilation is adequate.

Pricking out

8 Prick out seedlings into trays, boxes or individual pots as soon as they are large enough to handle.

Ornamentals 1

The frost-free environment of the cool greenhouse is ideal for growing many popular ornamental plants including cyclamen, primulas, cinerarias and winter-flowering chrysanthemums.

Cyclamen

Greenhouse cyclamen are only slightly tender and may be grown successfully with the minimum of heat. They may be grown from seed or, much less frequently, from corms and with care will bloom regularly each autumn and winter for many years.

Raising from seed Although commercially it is possible to flower cyclamen from seed in 6–8 months it will normally take 12–14 months for seed-raised plants to reach flowering size. The seed should be sown between August and November to flower the following autumn and winter. Soak the seed for 12–24 hours in water to assist germination. Then sow thinly in containers filled and firmed to within $\frac{3}{8}$–$\frac{1}{2}$ in of the rim with John Innes seed compost and cover the seed with $\frac{1}{8}$–$\frac{1}{4}$ in of the same compost. Water carefully and cover the container with a pane of glass. Place in a propagating case or on the greenhouse bench at 18°C/65°F, keep moist. Germination is slow and sometimes erratic.

Pricking out Prick out the seedlings into small peat pots or trays of John Innes No. 1 compost when the first leaf is well developed. Keep them at 18°C/65°F for a few days before reducing the temperature to 15°C/60°F. When the seedlings have 3–4 leaves they will need to be potted on into 2½–3 in pots again using John Innes No. 1 compost, making sure that the young corm is just proud of the surface of the compost. A second potting on, into 3½–4 in pots of John Innes No. 2 is needed in April then finally into 5–6 in pots of John Innes No. 3 in May or early June.

A temperature of 10°–13°C/50°–55°F should be maintained and ample ventilation provided. Shading may be needed in summer to avoid leaf-scorch. Water carefully at all times preferably around the rim of the pot so that the corm is avoided. Feeding is usually unnecessary but a high-potash liquid feed may be given as the flower buds develop in late summer. Remove any odd blooms that appear before the main flush.

Care after flowering After cyclamen have flowered growing conditions should be maintained for at least 4–6 weeks before the leaves are allowed to die down by gradually withholding water. Then place plants in a light well-ventilated position in the greenhouse or plunge them in a frost-free frame. Keep them dry until July when they should be re-potted in John Innes No. 3 compost and brought into the greenhouse at 10°–13°C/50°–55°F. Water sparingly until the first leaves develop and then maintain an even watering regime while the plants are in growth.

Primulas

Tender primulas such as *P. malacoides*, *P. obconica* and *P. sinensis* bloom in the cool house during winter and early spring. They are usually treated as annuals.

Sowing seed Sow thinly in May or early June in containers filled and firmed to within $\frac{3}{8}$ in of the rim with John Innes seed compost. The seed is very small and should not be covered in compost. Immerse the container in water to moisten the compost. Cover the container with a pane of glass and place it in a propagating case at 16°–18°C/60°–65°F.

Pricking out It is important to prick out the seedlings as soon as the first true leaf has developed as primula seedlings are very prone to damping off. Use small peat pots or trays of John Innes No. 1 compost. When the leaves begin to overlap in the tray (or the peat pots are filled with roots) the seedlings should be potted on into 3 in pots of John Innes No. 2 compost and in early autumn moved into 5 in pots of John Innes No. 2 potting compost for flowering.

Care of plants As flower buds form, a liquid feed may be given but is usually not required. Throughout their life primulas should be grown in light, cool, airy conditions at 7°–10°C/45°–50°F and during hot spells adequate ventilation and shading will be essential. Even watering is also important, preferably by immersion. If can watering is used apply water around the edge of the pots.

Chrysanthemums

Chrysanthemums for autumn and winter decoration in the greenhouse may be grown from seed or cuttings of named varieties.

Raising cyclamen from seed

August. Sow the large seeds in trays or shallow pots of seed-sowing compost. Cover seeds with $\frac{1}{4}$–$\frac{1}{2}$ in of moist sieved peat. Place in propagating case at 18°C/64°F.

January. Transplant the seedlings into individual 2½ in pots of John Innes No. 1 compost. Keep moist and lower temperature to 15°C/61°F.

March–April. Pot on into 5 in pots of John Innes No. 1. Make sure that the embryo corm is just below the compost surface.

Summer. Keep the plants lightly shaded, well ventilated and moist in a greenhouse or better still in a frame from which the lights are removed in mild weather.

Ornamentals 2

Charm chrysanthemums Sow in February in John Innes seed compost and germinate at 16°C/60°F. The sowing technique is similar to that used for bedding plants (see page 234). Prick out the seedlings into seedboxes in John Innes No. 1 and pot on into 2½–3 in pots also using the John Innes compost. At the 3-leaf stage pinch out the growing point. After potting on in late spring into 5 in pots of John Innes No. 2 move the plants to cold frame, and in June or July pot into John Innes No. 3 in 8 or 10 in pots to bloom. In late summer bring the plants into the greenhouse at a temperature of 7°–10°C/45°–50°F to flower. An occasional liquid feed may be needed whilst the plants are in the frames. Pinch back over-vigorous growths to maintain the neat rounded shape required.

Light, airy conditions are again the key to successful cultivation. The plants may be discarded after flowering and further stock raised from seed the following February or cuttings may be taken from particularly good plants using basal shoots as they develop during early winter.

Winter-flowering chrysanthemums

The late-flowering large-flowered florist's spray chrysanthemums are grown as pot plants outdoors during the summer and transferred to the greenhouse to flower in November and December at 7°–10°C/45°–50°F. There are many different types, varying considerably in colour and form of flower, which may be obtained from specialist nurserymen in February or March as rooted cuttings; or cuttings may be rooted annually from existing plants.

Propagation Chrysanthemum stools, cut down after flowering, will produce new basal shoots that can be rooted at 7°–10°C/45°–50°F as softwood cuttings (see pages 180–181) in February or March.

Growing on Pot on the rooted cuttings into 3–3½ in pots using John Innes No. 2 compost and keep at 7°C/45°F. Give ample ventilation and light and keep the compost evenly moist. Higher temperatures will often result in soft, drawn growths. By late March or early April pot on the plants into 5 or 6 in pots of John Innes No. 3. Once established in these pots, harden them off in a cold frame, closing the

frame only in frosty or bad weather. In early June they will need transferring into their final 8 or 9 in pots again using John Innes No. 3 compost. Stand the pots outside in a sheltered but open site and stake the plants.

Training Naturally chrysanthemums form a single bud at the stem apex (the break bud). Normally this does not develop (or produces a poor flower) and a number of lateral shoots will develop beneath it. Each will produce terminal or "crown buds" that flower if left. Other lateral buds develop and their shoots form secondary crown buds.

In order to produce a small number of large blooms on each plant it is necessary to limit the number of shoots and flower buds by the process known as "staging". This involves removing the original break bud at an early stage of development, usually when the laterals below it are an inch or two long, and allowing each of the first crown buds to remain and eventually form large individual blooms by pinching out any small flower buds that form around them. This is disbudding. Usually six to eight blooms per plant are required (only 3 for exhibition) and in many varieties sufficient laterals are formed below the break bud for these to be produced without further stopping. Some varieties, however, may not produce more than 2 or 3 laterals (and hence first crown buds) so each lateral may need to be stopped to produce several further laterals which then flower.

The timing of stopping varies from variety to variety but normally begins in about mid-April, with the second stopping during June. During the late summer further laterals will develop and those should all be removed as soon as they can easily be handled. Similarly flower buds, other than the crown buds or secondary crown buds, should be removed as they appear if large blooms are required.

Flowering Bring the pots of chrysanthemums into the greenhouse in mid-September. They should be well-spaced and given light, well-ventilated conditions with a minimum temperature of 7°C/45°F. First crown buds bloom in November, the second a month later.

Care after flowering After flowering cut back the plants to about 2 ft. In January cut the old stems down to 2–3 in from soil level and begin the process of propagation again.

Winter-flowering chrysanthemums

1 February–March. Take cuttings of new growth from existing stools. Root in a propagating case. Pot the rooted cuttings into 3 in pots.

2 March–April. Pot on into 5 in pots of John Innes No. 3. Move the plants to a cold frame to harden off, closing the frame only in frosty or bad weather.

3 June. Transfer plants to 8 in pots and stand in a sheltered place outdoors and stake each plant. Fix stakes to a frame to prevent wind damage.

4 September. Bring the plants into the greenhouse and place in a well-lit spot. In November and December the plants will flower.

Fruits and vegetables 1

The cool greenhouse can be used to best effect in growing food crops if it is used to cultivate not only tomatoes, cucumbers and the other vegetable fruits described on pages 228–231 but also more tender vegetables such as okra. Melons and early strawberries are also good subjects for the cool house and so, if space allows, are peaches and nectarines which often fail to do well in the open.

Early strawberries

The cool house will enable the gardener to pick crops of strawberries in March or April.
Propagation In late June, peg down the runners of plants growing in the open garden into 3 in pots filled with John Innes No. 1 potting compost buried with their rims level with the soil surface. After four to six weeks, when the new plants are well established, sever them from the parents and place the pots on well-drained soil or in an open cold frame. Water them well and as plants grow pot them on into their final 6 in pots using John Innes No. 2 or an equivalent peat-based compost. Until September, liquid feed the plants once a week and water frequently.

Leave the plants undisturbed until November then bury the pots up to their rims in peat or well-drained soil to prevent frost from reaching their roots. Ideally, this should be done in a cold frame but a sheltered corner of the garden (not a frost pocket) will suffice if necessary. If there is any risk of frost damage, close the frame or cover the plants with straw.
Greenhouse cultivation In mid-December take the pots into the greenhouse and place them well apart on a sunny shelf to allow good air circulation and maximum light. For a fortnight keep the temperature just above freezing then raise it to 7°C/45°F. Do not be tempted to turn the heating up any higher as this will create too much foliage at the expense of fruiting capacity. When the flower trusses appear in February, raise the minimum temperature to 10°C/50°F and ventilate the house a little during the daytime if the greenhouse air temperature exceeds 21°C/70°F. At this stage plants will benefit if the house is damped down once a week and if they are given a high potash liquid feed twice a week.

When the flowers are open, increase the minimum temperature to 13°C/55°F but do not open the ventilators until the temperature reaches 24°C/75°F. As the flowers open, carry out a daily pollination routine, transferring pollen from flower to flower with a small paint brush. During this pollination period do not damp down the house as this may prevent fruit from forming. To obtain fewer, but larger fruit, remove the smallest flowers as soon as their petals have fallen off and leave eight to ten fruits on each plant.

Once fruit begins to set, resume the damping down routine and water the plants very well in sunny weather. Continue feeding until the fruits begin to turn pink in order to improve fruit flavour.

Melons

In the cool house, melons can be cultivated as described for the cold house on page 227 except that by maintaining a minimum springtime temperature of 21°C/70°C fruit will be produced much earlier. In the cool house melon seed can be planted in February and March to give earlier fruit in June and July respectively. Remember to damp down the house well except during pollination and when the fruits start to ripen.

Okra

Also known as gumbo and ladies' fingers, okra are unusual vegetable fruits particularly good for cooking in curries and other oriental dishes. They are not hard to grow but being tropical plants they need fairly high temperatures, particularly for germination and plant raising.
Raising from seed Sow seed thinly in a seed tray filled with moist compost or sow them singly in peat pots from February onwards. Cover the seeds with a thin layer of compost, water them in, then cover the pots or trays with a sheet of glass and one of newspaper. Turn the glass once a day and maintain a temperature of 18°–21°C/65°–70°F. The seeds will take from one to three weeks to germinate, depending on the temperature. As soon as they are big enough to handle, prick out the seedlings into 3 in peat or plastic pots filled with John Innes No. 1 potting compost.
Greenhouse cultivation In early spring, plant out okra direct into the greenhouse border soil or transplant them into 10 in pots of

Early strawberries

1 Mid-December Bring rooted plants in 6 in pots into the cool house. Make sure they are well spaced. Keep the temperature just above freezing. Liquid feed twice a week.

2 Two weeks later raise the temperature to 7°C/45°F. When flower trusses appear raise it to 10°C/50°F. Ventilate and damp down when the temperature exceeds 21°C/70°F.

3 When the flowers open stop damping down and increase the temperature to 13°C/55°F. Ventilate the house at 24°C/75°F. Pollinate the flowers daily with a brush.

4 When fruit has set resume damping down. Support fruit trusses with forked twigs inserted in the pots. Stop feeding when fruit begins to colour.

Fruits and vegetables 2

John Innes No. 2 compost. Whichever method is chosen, plants should be provided with canes for support and placed 21–24 in apart in each direction. Throughout the growing season, water plants well and when they are 9–12 in high, pinch out the growing points to encourage a bushy habit and a good succession of flowers and fruit. Watch out for signs of whitefly and red spider mite.

Okra should be harvested when they are young and the seeds inside their pods still soft. Harvest between June and September.

Peaches

In a large greenhouse, especially a lean-to, it is possible to grow a fan-trained peach or nectarine. Both these fruits will crop more reliably in the cool house than in the garden. The best sort of peach to choose for a cool house is the common plum rootstock St Julient A which is semi-dwarfing and so more manageable.

Soil The border soil of the greenhouse can be used but should be enriched with plenty of organic matter before a peach is planted. Alternatively, the border soil may be re-placed with a preparation made from turves of fibrous chalky loam stacked for six months then mixed with one part of rubble to every ten parts of loam. A fortnight before planting in spring, mix in 8 oz of John Innes base fertilizer to every 2 gal bucketful of soil.

Care of plants A peach will need a minimum temperature of 7°C/45°F from late winter until fruit is formed. Only ventilate the house when the temperature rises above 18°C/65°F. Until the flowers open, damp down the house on sunny days and spray the foliage with clean water daily. In early summer, mulch plants well with rotted manure or garden compost and apply a liquid tomato feed every 10 days from bud burst to the start of fruit ripening.

When the flowers open hand pollinate them with a small paint brush and when fruitlets form thin them to about two per cluster when they are about ½ in long. Thin again at the 1 in stage to leave fruits evenly spaced 8–10 in apart.

Care after harvesting After the fruits have been picked, open the ventilators and leave them open until spring.

Okra

1 March Transplant young plants raised in heat direct into greenhouse soil or transfer them to 10 in pots. Space plants 21–24 in apart and provide canes for support.

2 Pinch out the growing points to encourage bushy growth and a good succession of fruits when plants are 9–12 in tall. Guard against pests.

FAN-TRAINED PEACH

If space allows a fan-trained peach may be grown against the back wall of a lean-to greenhouse or under the roof of a double or single-span cool house. Ideally an area of 15 ft × 10 ft is needed. Plant the tree direct into greenhouse soil enriched with organic matter and provide wires 6 in apart for support. For early fruiting maintain a minimum temperature of 7°C/45°F from late winter until fruits are formed and ventilate only when the temperature exceeds 18°C/65°F.

3 Through the growing period water plants regularly. If necessary spray against red spider mite using malathion or a similar low-persistence pesticide.

4 June onwards Cut young pods as soon as they are ready, using sharp scissors, to give a long cropping period. Remember that old pods are stringy and unpalatable.

Using frames 1

SOWING PLAN FOR FRAMES

JANUARY
Heated Broad beans 'The Sutton', 'Green Windsor'; cauliflower 'Alpha', 'Snowball'; carrots 'Amsterdam Forcing', 'Amstel'; lettuce 'Kwiek', 'Delta', 'Magnet'.
Unheated Radishes 'Saxenne', 'Short Top Forcing', 'French Breakfast'.

FEBRUARY
Heated Beetroot 'Boltardy', 'Arca Farly'; cauliflower as January; Leeks 'Early Market', 'Lyon-Prizetaker'; lettuce as January; spring onions 'White Lisbon'.
Unheated Broad beans 'Colossal', 'The Sutton'; cabbage 'Hispi', 'Golden Acre'; carrots as January; peas 'Kelvedon Wonder'; radishes 'French Breakfast',

'Red Forcing', 'Cherry Belle'; turnips 'Early White Milan', 'Tokyo Cross', 'Jersey Navet'; swedes 'Chignecto'.

MARCH
Heated Celery 'Golden Self Blanching', 'American Green', 'Giant White', 'Lathom'; cucumber 'Sporu', 'Telegraph', 'Fernspot', 'Fernden', 'Butcher's Disease Resister'; runner beans 'Streamline', 'Harbinger', 'Prizewinner', 'Enorma'.
Unheated Globe artichokes ("suckers") 'Gros Camus d'Aners'; beetroot as

A frame is a versatile piece of equipment which can be used as an extension of the greenhouse or on its own. A frame is particularly useful for a gardener without a greenhouse, especially if it can be heated, for given the restrictions in size, a heated frame can be used for most of the plants that can be grown in a greenhouse. Both heated and unheated frames can be used for raising new plants, including early vegetables; for extending the growing season; for hardening off greenhouse-grown plants before they are planted out in the garden; for overwintering plants such as chrysanthemums and for plunging potted bulbs that will later be taken indoors to bloom. The soil, compost or other growing medium placed in the frame will depend on the exact use to which the frame will be put. Several different shapes and sizes of frames are available. The frame should be deep enough to accommodate the plants that are likely to be grown in it.

Siting

A frame can be placed abutting a greenhouse or on its own. If one wall of the frame is placed against the greenhouse wall the frame will benefit from improved insulation and reduced heat loss. Another advantage is that the heating system of the greenhouse can usually be extended to serve the frame. Place a frame that is to be used on its own in an open, sunny, easily accessible position that affords plenty of light and some shelter from high winds. Never place a frame in a corner of the garden known to be a frost pocket.

Heating

A cold frame, that is a frame with no form of heating, is less useful than a heated frame which will allow a wider range of plants to be grown. In a heated frame, early vegetables will be ready for cropping sooner and there is less chance of tender plants failing to survive the winter. A heating system for a frame works by heating the soil and/or the air. Soil heating can be provided by electric cables or, if the frame is abutting a heated greenhouse, by hot water pipes. The air in a frame can be heated by electric cables or hot water tubes placed round the walls. Whichever heating system is chosen it should always include

an accurate thermostat to aid careful regulation of the growing conditions within the frame.

Insulation To help conserve the heat built up in a frame during the day, the frame lights can be covered on cold nights with hessian sacking or a roll of old carpet. Place blocks of wood carefully on top of the sacking or carpet to prevent it from blowing away. Alternatively, buy a special sheet with eyelet holes and tie it to wooden pegs placed in the soil. The sides of the frame can also be insulated by lining them with bales of straw encased in chicken wire.

Ventilation

Plants grown in heated and cold frames need good ventilation to encourage free air circulation. Poor ventilation increases air humidity within the frame and encourages the growth of disease-causing organisms. Make sure that the lights of the frame can be opened at several different levels and that they can easily be removed altogether. For ventilation the lights may be propped open with a block of wood, a brick or a ratchet, or pushed back off the frame and placed at an angle over the frame with one end on the ground, as long as they will not blow away. In very windy weather secure the lights with cord wound round cleats screwed to the frame surrounds, or by hooks and eyes.

Watering

To water the plants in a frame the lights can simply be lifted or removed. Always water plants with a rose fitted to the watering can or hose so that soil is not washed away from around plant roots. Semi-automatic watering with a perforated hose or capillary watering as used in the greenhouse (see pages 16–17) are also effective and time-saving. In the capillary system, water is supplied via a trickle irrigation line which ensures a slow, steady water supply to the growing medium in the frame. When the frame is not in use and in the summer, remove the lights so that the soil can get a good natural watering from the rain. This will also help to prevent a damaging build-up of mineral salts in the soil.

Growing early carrots in a heated frame

1 January Dig garden soil in the frame. Place heating cables in the frame and cover them with 6 in of good garden soil.

2 Rake in 2–3 oz of general fertilizer then water well. Close the frame.

3 A week later Sow seed in drills 4 in apart or broadcast at $\frac{1}{12}$ oz per square yard. Set thermostat to 18°C/65°F. Keep frame shut.

4 February As seedlings develop thin (if necessary) to 1–1½ in apart. Remove all thinnings. Water to firm. Replace lights.

5 As weather warms open lights on sunny days but close them at night. Plants will now need more water.

6 April Remove lights completely when all chance of frost is past. Store lights in a safe place. Harvest carrots as needed.

Using frames 2

February; French beans 'The Prince', 'Masterpiece', 'Tendergreen'; Brussels sprouts 'Citadel' (F₁), 'Winter Harvest', 'Perfect Line' (F₁); cabbage as February; carrots as February; cauliflower 'All the Year Round', 'Little Gem', 'Mildura', 'Webb's Wonderful', 'Salad Bowl'; parsley; peas 'Onward', 'Hurst Greenshaft'.

APRIL
Heated Celery as March; courgettes (seedlings) 'Zucchini', 'Golden Zucchini'; cucumbers as March; tomatoes (outdoor) 'The Amateur', 'Sleaford Abundance', 'Alfresco'.
Unheated Runner beans as March; celeriac 'Alabaster', 'Marble Ball'; ridge cucumbers 'Burpless', 'Perfection', 'Baton

Vert'; marrows 'Golden Delicious', 'Improved Green Bush'; sweet corn (F₁) 'Earli King', 'Northern Belle'.

MAY
Heated Aubergines (seedlings) 'Long Purple', 'Short Tom'; sweet peppers (seedlings) 'Canape', 'New Ace', 'Outdoor'.
Unheated Okra 'Long Green'; melons (seedlings) 'Dutch Net', 'Tiger'.

Light and shading
To ensure maximum entry of light, keep frame lights clean at all times and renovate and clean them in summer. As in the greenhouse, plants in a frame risk being scorched and badly damaged by hot sun. To prevent this, apply a shading compound to the inside of the frame lights as necessary, or place a sheet of muslin or small mesh plastic netting over the frame on hot, sunny days. The covering can be rolled back in cloudy weather.

Raising seed
Seed of all kinds can be sown in a heated or unheated frame in pots, boxes or trays or directly into prepared soil. Turn on the heating system, if there is one, for a day or two before sowing to warm the soil. Seeds of hardy plants can be sown in a heated frame as early as January or February, seeds of tender plants from February to March. For an unheated frame, add on another month to six weeks in each case, and more if the spring is a cold one. Seedlings in pots or boxes are best placed in the frame on a 3 in layer of gravel or weathered ashes to allow good

drainage or, if a capillary watering system is used, on a 2 in layer of coarse sand placed on a thick sheet of polythene. Note that seeds planted in pots or boxes will need more care in watering as they dry out more quickly than those planted direct into the soil. Seedlings of tender or half-hardy plants raised in a heated frame will also need hardening off before they are planted out into the garden.

Early crops in a heated frame
Carrots, radishes, lettuces, beetroot and spring onions are among the many vegetables that can be grown in a heated frame for early cropping and for eating when young and tender. Months of planting for heated frames are shown in the list above.
Soil Most early crops can be sown in the frame direct into good well-dug garden soil enriched with well-rotted manure, compost or peat, plus 2–3 oz of a general well-balanced fertilizer per square yard. If the garden top soil is very stony or shallow, it may be preferable to replace the top 1–1½ ft with new good-quality top soil or to replace the soil completely with sterilized compost placed

on a perforated polythene sheet placed in the frame. If necessary, make provision for any particular needs of the crop to be grown —lettuces for example do best in humus-rich soil while carrots prefer soil that has not been freshly manured.
Care of seedlings Freshly sown seed of most vegetable crops will germinate best at a temperature of 18°C/65°F so this is the ideal thermostat setting for seed planted in late winter or early spring. On cold nights, insulate the frame with sacking or similar material. The frame should be ventilated during the day as long as the weather is not very cold or windy. In bad weather ensure maximum entry of light by washing all debris off the lights regularly. As the weather warms the lights can be opened wider during the day and closed at night. Once all risk of frost is past and plants are well established, the lights can be removed altogether, cleaned and stored and the heating system turned off.

Crops in a cold frame
For vegetables, a cold frame provides similar protection to cloches (see page 243) but re-

tains heat better and is cooled less by the wind. Vegetables sown in a cold frame will still crop earlier than those sown outdoors with no protection. Among the best crops for the cold frame are ridge cucumbers, courgettes, melons, marrows and outdoor tomatoes. Cucumber and similar seeds are best pre-germinated at a temperature of 21°C/70°F before being planted in the cold frame in early May. Ventilate the frame as necessary during the day and close it down at night until plants are established then remove the lights in June.

For outdoor tomatoes, raise seeds in heat and plant them out in the cold frame in May or early June. Ventilate the frame as necessary but do not remove the lights completely until the plants are well established, by which time they will have probably outgrown the height of the frame. The lights can be replaced at the end of the season to help ripen the last fruits and combat frost.

Cuttings
Cuttings of all types can be grown in a frame. Use a heated frame for cuttings of tender

Hardening off in an unheated frame

1 Spring As air temperature rises, place boxes or pots of greenhouse-reared seedlings or cuttings in the frame.

2 During first week (weather permitting) leave lights half open during the day for ventilation but close down each night.

3 During second week leave lights open a little at night. Towards end of week remove lights completely except in windy weather.

4 In third week remove plants from the frame and plant in their permanent positions in the garden.

JUNE
Unheated Aubergines and sweet peppers as May.

AUGUST
Unheated Lettuce 'Avondefiance', 'Kwiek', 'Amanda Plus'; winter endive 'Broad Leaved Batavian', 'Winter Lettuce-Leaved'.

SEPTEMBER
Unheated Winter endive as August; corn salad 'Broad Leaved English'.

OCTOBER
Unheated Lettuce 'Winter Density'; cauliflower (seedlings) as January.

Using frames 3

plants such as fuchsias and pelargoniums taken in March (wait another six weeks for a cold frame) and dahlia cuttings taken in April. Softwood shrub cuttings can be planted in a cold frame in June, semi-hard ones in July and August. See pages 178–185 for details.

Hardening off
Many tender or half-hardy plants raised in the greenhouse need to be put through a "toughening-up" process called hardening off before they are planted out into the garden. A cold frame is ideal for this purpose. In spring, when there is no risk of tender or half-hardy plants being exposed to frost, once they are in their permanent positions in the garden, take pots or boxes of young plants from the greenhouse and place them in the frame. For one week leave the lights open during the day (as long as the weather is not cold or windy) but close them at night. During the second week, leave the lights open a little at night. Towards the end of the second week open the frame as wide as possible at night. In the third week the plants can be planted in their permanent positions in the garden.

Overwintering and storage
A frame can act as a useful protected storage site for plants during the winter and, at the same time, save valuable space in the greenhouse. A heated frame will be needed for tender plants such as pelargoniums and fuchsias which should be placed in the frame in September. In the same month, freesias can be potted up and placed in a heated frame. Outdoor chrysanthemums can be overwintered in an unheated frame after they have been cut back and boxed in proprietary potting compost. The frame should be well ventilated except in very severe weather to help prevent diseases such as botrytis, which are encouraged by stagnant air.

Storage A cold frame can be employed to store dormant bulbs and tubers that are susceptible to frost damage. After lifting dahlia tubers, for example, pack them in boxes of dry peat before storing them in a heated frame. Store bulbs in a cold frame loosely packed in wooden boxes with plenty of room for air to circulate between them. Make sure the frame is well ventilated but guard against damp which can cause rot.

The plunge bed
A plunge bed is a bed of damp sand, peat or a mixture of gravel and weathered ashes about 1ft deep into which pots are buried or plunged up to their rims. A plunge bed in a cold frame is useful for accommodating plants throughout the year. From spring onwards, as alpines finish flowering in the alpine house, transfer them to the plunge bed. Plunge the pots up to their rims and keep the bed damp but never let it become dry or waterlogged. The cool moist environment of the plunge bed will produce good strong growth. Similarly, pot-grown greenhouse plants can be plunged in summer, which will prevent them from drying out too quickly. During the summer there is no need to place the lights on the frame.

Bulb forcing In winter, use the plunge bed for forcing bulbs. Plant bulbs in pots, plunge them and cover the pots with a 3in layer of peat. Place the lights over the frame, leaving them open a little for ventilation. After eight weeks the bulbs will have formed good root systems and can be taken indoors in succession for flowering.

OVERWINTERING
Heated and unheated frames are very useful for storing and protecting flowering plants in winter, so freeing valuable greenhouse space. Use a heated frame for tender plants such as pelargoniums. Lift plants from the garden in autumn, cut them back and plant in boxes before placing them in the frame. Similarly, make chrysanthemum "stools" by cutting back plants to within 4–6in of the ground before boxing them up and placing them in an unheated frame. Ventilate well.

Plunging bulbs in an unheated frame

1 October Fill frame with a 1ft layer of sand, peat or a mixture of gravel and weathered ashes. Water and allow to settle.

2 Plant hyacinth bulbs in pots then plunge up to their rims in the frame. Cover with a 3in layer of peat to exclude light.

3 Place lights over frame to protect pots from heavy winter rainfall. Keep the frame well ventilated.

4 After eight weeks Remove pots from frame and take indoors in sequence for flowering.

Using cloches

Cloches provide plants with virtually the same protection as cold frames, except that they retain heat rather less well and that the air inside them is cooled more quickly by the wind. The advantage of cloches is that they are more mobile and versatile to use. Cloches can be employed in many ways—to warm the soil before seeds are sown; for raising seedlings, especially half-hardy annual bedding plants and vegetables to extend the growing season at each end of the year; to protect individual plants, particularly alpines, from cold and wet and to save blooms from splashing and spoiling by mud; to provide shelter from cold and wind and to ripen off onions and similar crops in poor weather. Cloches can also be used to spread the season of cut flowers. Rows of gladioli, for example, tend to flower at the same time, but if half is cloched, the cutting period is lengthened.

Using cloches
Cloches should be placed in an open position away from the shade of trees. Never put them in a very windy place where they will cool quickly and risk being damaged or blown over. Any cloches likely to be overturned by strong winds should have fittings to anchor them to the ground or should be secured with string tied to pegs placed in the ground. Leave plenty of room between rows of cloches for easy access and watering.

Ventilation
Ventilation is essential to prevent the build-up of stagnant, over-moist air that encourages disease. If single cloches are placed in rows, always leave a small gap between each one if the cloches have no built-in ventilation system such as adjustable top or sides. In the case of a polythene tunnel the side can be lifted and supported with a pot or wooden block. The gaps between the cloches can be increased if necessary to let in more air, but to avoid too much draught, and consequent heat loss, close the ends with purchased cloche ends or with a sheet of glass or thick plastic held in place with a wooden stake.

Soil preparation
Before placing cloches in position, prepare the soil for the plants or crop that is to be protected according to its specific needs and make sure that the same crop is not grown in the same soil two years running. Before sowing seed or planting out seedlings raised in a greenhouse or heated frame, put the cloches in position and leave them for two to three weeks to dry and warm the soil. A dressing of balanced fertilizer can be raked in before cloches are positioned.

Watering
Cloches need only be removed for watering if they are covering small seedlings which need a very even sprinkling of water. Otherwise, water can be applied to cloches from overhead with a watering can or hose if there is insufficient rain. The water runs down the sides of the cloches and is absorbed into the soil, reaching the roots of the plants which grow naturally towards sources of food and water. For long rows of cloches it is also possible to supply water via a sprinkler or irrigation tubing placed between the rows. On light soil make a shallow channel on the outside of each cloche in which water can easily collect and drain into the soil.

STORING CLOCHES

Store cloches not in use by stacking them on their ends in a sheltered corner of the garden where they will not get broken or blown over by strong winds.

Year-round uses for cloches

1 January Place cloches over soil prepared for seed sowing. Leave for 2–3 weeks to dry and warm soil. Do not close cloche ends.

2 Early spring Use cloches to protect newly sown seed and seedlings. Close cloche ends but ventilate well according to type.

3 Autumn In rainy weather place harvested onions under cloches to dry out before storage. Ventilate well. Leave ends open.

4 Winter Single cloches can be put over alpines such as cushion plants susceptible to rotting in wet soil.

243

Pests and diseases: fruit 1

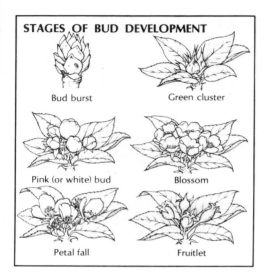

STAGES OF BUD DEVELOPMENT

Bud burst · Green cluster · Pink (or white) bud · Blossom · Petal fall · Fruitlet

Correct cultivation and weed control help to prevent trouble with pests and diseases, although chemical control may be necessary.

Types of chemical control

Fungicides and pesticides are used to prevent, and sometimes control, infection or to treat infestation.

There are various kinds of pesticides and they act in different ways. A contact spray such as derris affects the insect itself. Ovicides such as tar oil washes kill the eggs. These take effect on contact, so it is important to cover all plant surfaces.

A third group, systemic insecticides such as dimethoate and heptenophos, are taken up through the roots and leaves of the plant into the sap. They are thus very effective against sap-sucking pests. Complete coverage is preferable but not essential because the chemical is transported within the leaf to a limited extent.

Most fungicides only check or prevent attacks so they should be applied before the disease first appears. The partly systemic fungicides such as benomyl and thiophanate-methyl are slightly absorbed into the plant's tissues only but are effective for a short period even after symptoms are visible. However, resistant strains of the fungus may develop if systemic fungicides are used too frequently.

Precautions

Always follow the manufacturer's instructions when mixing and applying chemicals. Wash hands and equipment after using chemicals. Do not use the fungicide and pesticide sprayer for weedkillers.

Some chemicals must be treated with extra caution, HCH, malathion and thiram should not be used on fruit that is to be preserved. Thiram may irritate the eyes, nose and mouth; wear a mask and goggles if susceptible to allergic reactions. Do not use sulphur on sulphur-sensitive varieties.

DISEASES AND DISORDERS

American gooseberry mildew Affecting gooseberries and currants, it forms a white, powdery coating on young leaves, shoots and fruits, later turning brown and felted. The shoots may be distorted at the tips.
Treatment: Cut out and burn diseased shoots in late August or September. Spray with benomyl, carbendazim or thiophanate-methyl as the first flowers open, repeating two, four and six weeks later. Keep the bushes open by regular pruning and avoid excessive nitrogen feeding.

Apple canker It affects apples and pears. Sunken discoloured patches appear on the bark, becoming extended ellipses surrounded by concentric rings of shrunken bark. White fungus spores are visible on the sunken bark in summer. The branch becomes swollen above the canker and it may die.
Treatment: Cut out and burn diseased branches and spurs. On branches without die-back, cut out and burn diseased tissue. Paint the wounds with canker paint. Spray with bordeaux mixture or liquid copper after harvest but before leaf-fall. Repeat when half the leaves have fallen.

Apricot die-back The shoots and branches die back. It is usually caused by fungi but occasionally by adverse cultural conditions.
Treatment: Cut back all dead wood to healthy tissue and paint the wounds. Give adequate feeding, watering and mulching.

Bacterial canker Round brown spots appear on the leaves of apricots, cherries, peaches, plums, gages and damsons, later developing into holes. There are elongated, flattened, oozing cankers on the branches. The buds do not develop the following spring or they produce small, yellow leaves which curl, wither and die. The branches also die back.
Treatment: Remove badly cankered branches and dead wood. Paint the wounds with a wound paint. Spray with bordeaux mixture in mid-August, repeating one and two months later.

Bitter pit It affects apples, causing sunken pits on fruit skins, brown spots in the flesh and a bitter taste.
Treatment: Prevent it by watering and mulching the tree during dry weather. Spray with calcium nitrate at 1oz per 2 gal of water in mid-June. Repeat ten days later. Ten days after that spray with 2 oz calcium nitrate per 2 gal of water and repeat at least three times at ten day intervals.

Boron deficiency The pear fruits on most branches are distorted and have brown spots in the flesh. The leaves are small and misshapen. There is some die-back of shoots and the bark is roughened and pimply.
Treatment: Apply 1oz of borax (mixed with sand for even distribution) per 20 square yards.

Brown rot Affects apples, peaches, pears, plums, nectarines and quinces. The fruits are brown with soft, decaying flesh, later becoming covered with rings of greyish spores.
Treatment: Remove and burn affected fruit.

Cane blight It affects only raspberries. A dark area can be seen on the canes just above ground level. The canes become very brittle and the leaves wither.
Treatment: Cut back diseased canes to below soil level and burn. Disinfect tools. Spray new canes with bordeaux mixture as they develop.

Cane spot It affects raspberries, loganberries, hybrid berries and, rarely, blackberries. Small purple spots appear on the canes in May to June, later enlarging and turning white with a purple border and then splitting to form pits or small cankers. The tips of shoots may die back, leaves may be spotted and the fruit may be distorted.
Treatment: Cut out and burn badly spotted canes in autumn. Spray raspberries with liquid copper or thiram (but not on fruit for preserving) at bud burst and just before flowering. Or spray with benomyl or thio-phanate-methyl at bud burst and repeat every two weeks until the end of flowering. Spray loganberries with bordeaux mixture, liquid copper or thiram (but not on fruit for preserving) just before flowering and when the fruit sets.

Coral spot Red currants are very susceptible, but other currants and figs are also affected. The branches die back and coral red pustules appear on the dead shoots.
Treatment: Cut out affected branches several inches below the diseased tissues. Paint the wounds. Burn infected shoots and any other woody debris in the garden.

Crown gall A walnut-size gall can be seen at ground level on cane fruits or there is a chain of small galls higher up.
Treatment: Destroy diseased canes.

Fireblight Affects pears and occasionally apples. The shoots die back and the leaves become brown and withered. Cankers form at the base of the diseased tissue and ooze in spring.
Treatment: Cut out diseased shoots to 2 feet below diseased tissues.

Grey mould (*Botrytis cinerea*) Strawberries, cane fruits, currants and grapes are among the many fruits affected. The berries rot and are covered with grey-brown fluff.
Treatment: Remove and destroy infected fruits if possible. Spray with benomyl, carbendazim or thiophanate-methyl as soon as the flowers open, repeating two, four and six weeks later. For greenhouse crops fumigate with tecnazene smokes.

Honey fungus It affects all fruit crops. White, fan-shaped patches of fungus appear beneath the bark on roots and on the trunk just above ground level. There are blackish growths on the roots and honey-coloured toadstools grow at the base of the tree in autumn. Sudden death of the plant may occur.
Treatment: Dig out affected plants with as many roots as possible and burn them.

Leaf spot of currants and gooseberries Dark brown spots can be seen on the leaves, later coalescing and turning the leaves brown. Premature leaf-fall results.
Treatment: Collect and burn all diseased leaves. Spray with mancozeb or thiram after flowering, repeating every 10–14 days, as necessary. Or spray with thiophanate-methyl

Pests and diseases: fruit 2

as the flowers open, repeating two, four and six weeks later. Or spray with benomyl before the flowers open, repeating two, four and six weeks later. Feed the bushes well to help overcome the disease.

Lime-induced chlorosis All crops in chalky soils are affected but it is most serious on raspberries. Yellow or white bands develop between the veins of leaves.
Treatment: Dig in humus and reduce the alkalinity of the soil. Apply a chelated compound or rake in fritted trace elements (see pages 6–9).

Magnesium deficiency Orange, red or brown bands develop between the leaf veins, especially of apples, grapes and raspberries.
Treatment: Spray at petal fall, or when the trouble shows, with magnesium sulphate at 8 oz per $2\frac{1}{2}$ gal of water. Repeat twice at 14 day intervals.

Peach leaf curl Reddish blisters appear on the leaves. Later, the leaves swell and have a powdery white covering of spores. Premature leaf-fall results.
Treatment: Spray with bordeaux mixture or liquid copper in January or February. Repeat 10–14 days later and just before leaf-fall.

Pear stony pit virus The fruit on some branches is pitted and deformed at maturity. Stony cells form in the tissues making the fruit difficult to cut and inedible.
Treatment: Destroy affected trees.

Plum rust Small, bright yellow spots can be seen on the upper surfaces of leaves, with pustules on the undersides containing brown or orange spores which later turn dark brown or blackish. Leaves may turn brown and fall prematurely. Plum rust is troublesome only on weak trees.
Treatment: Rake up and burn fallen leaves. Good feeding, watering and mulching should prevent a recurrence of the disease.

Powdery mildew Apple, grape, melon, peach and quince are affected. A white powdery coating of fungus spores appears on emerging shoots and young leaves. Apple and pear shoots are stunted, the fruits fail to set or develop brown patches, and the leaves fall. The skins of grapes become discoloured and shrivel and split.
Treatment: Remove silvered shoots at pruning. Cut off infected shoots of apples, peaches

and quinces in spring and summer. Spray all crops at first signs of disease and repeat at least three times at fortnightly intervals, using benomyl, carbendazim or thiophanate-methyl. Ventilate the greenhouse and avoid overcrowded conditions.

Quince leaf blight Dark red irregular spots appear on leaves, later becoming blackish. The leaves may turn brown or yellow and fall prematurely and the fruit may be spotted and deformed. Shoot tips die back.
Treatment: Rake up and burn fallen leaves. Cut out dead shoots in winter. Spray with bordeaux mixture as first leaves open in spring, and repeat in summer if necessary.

Raspberry virus diseases These are very troublesome; loganberries, blackberries susceptible to viruses and related organisms, and other cane fruits may also be affected. Yellow blotching or mottling is visible on the leaves. Poor growth and a reduced crop result.
Treatment: Remove and burn all affected plants at the same time. Plant new canes certified as healthy in a new site 50 ft away or change the soil on the old site to a depth of $1\frac{1}{2}$ ft × 2 ft wide.

Reversion This affects only black currants and is spread by big bud mite. Mature leaves on the basal shoots are narrow with fewer than five pairs of veins on each main lobe. The flowers are bright magenta-coloured and there is a reduced fruit yield.
Treatment: Control big bud mite (see page 246). Destroy all diseased bushes at the same time. Plant new certified bushes on a fresh site.

Scab Affects apples and pears. Brown or black scabs are visible on the fruits which are sometimes misshapen and cracked. Olive green blotches develop on the leaves and they fall prematurely. There is a general loss of vigour and a reduced crop. Pimples on the young shoots later burst the bark and become cracks or scabs.
Treatment: Rake up and burn all leaves in autumn. Cut out cracked and scabby shoots at pruning. For both apples and pears, spray with benomyl, carbendazim or thiophanate-methyl at bud burst, repeating every two weeks as necessary until late July.

Shanking Grapes fail to ripen, become sour and watery due to shrivelling of the berry stalks.

Treatment: Good soil conditions and cultural treatment should prevent this trouble. Cut off affected berries.

Shothole Affects cherries, peaches and nectarines, plums and gages, causing brown spots on leaves which later become holes. Only weak trees are affected.
Treatment: Proper feeding should prevent a recurrence but if not, spray with copper fungicide at half strength in summer and at full strength just before leaf-fall.

Silver leaf It can affect most tree fruits, currants and gooseberries, but it is most troublesome on plums, appearing as silvering leaves which may turn brown. There is progressive die-back of branches and a purplish fungus grows on the dead wood, later turning white or brown. Inner tissues are stained brown or purple.
Treatment: If there is fungus on the trunk, destroy the tree. Otherwise, cut back dead branches to 6 in behind the staining of inner tissues. Paint the wounds. Sterilize all tools after use on diseased trees.

Soft rot (collar rot) of melons The stem rots at soil level causing the plant to collapse.
Treatment: Remove decayed tissues and dust with dry bordeaux powder. Keep the stem dry.

Split stone Affects peaches and nectarines. Fruits crack at the stalk end producing a hole through which earwigs can enter. The stone is split and the kernel (if formed) rots.
Treatment: Hand pollinate the flowers. Lime the soil if necessary. Pay strict attention to watering.

Spur blight This affects raspberries and sometimes loganberries. Dark purple blotches appear around the nodes on canes. They later enlarge, turn silver and become covered with minute black dots. Buds wither and die or produce shoots which die back in spring.
Treatment: Cut out and burn diseased canes. Spray with benomyl or thiram when the new canes are a few inches high. Repeat two, four and six weeks later. Or spray with thiophanate-methyl at bud burst, repeating ever two weeks until the end of flowering. Or spray with bordeaux mixture or liquid copper at bud burst, repeating when the flower tips are just showing white.

Strawberry leaf blotch Large brown blotches

surrounded by purple and yellow may appear on the leaves. Leaf and flower stalks blacken and rot. The leaves die and the fruit withers.
Treatment: Remove and burn affected leaves. Spray the following season with mancozeb just after growth begins, repeating two weeks later.

Strawberry mildew Purple patches are visible on leaves, which curl upwards. Greyish fungal spores develop on the undersides and spread to flowers and berries.
Treatment: Dust with sulphur or spray with dinocap just before flowering. Repeat every 10–14 days until two weeks before harvest. Or spray with benomyl, carbendazim or thiophanate-methyl just after flowering, repeating two and four weeks later. After harvest, cut off old leaves and spray with one of the above.

Strawberry virus diseases Various diseases cause stunting or death. The symptoms are most obvious from April to September. The leaves become dwarfed and puckered with yellow edges and yellow or purple mottling. A virus-related organism causes old leaves to turn red and young leaves yellow. The flowers have green petals and the fruits fail to ripen. Eventually the plant dies.
Treatment: Destroy all affected plants at the same time. Do not take runners. Plant certified strawberries in a fresh site or change the soil on the old site to a depth of 1 ft × $1\frac{1}{2}$ ft wide.

Verticillium wilt It affects melons. Lower leaves turn yellow and wilt and then the whole plant wilts and collapses.
Treatment: Destroy diseased plants and sterilize the soil.

Walnut leaf blotch Irregular brown blotches appear on the leaves which wither and fall prematurely.
Treatment: Rake up and burn fallen leaves. Spray young trees in spring with bordeaux mixture, or other copper fungicide, or mancozeb, repeating two weeks later.

PESTS

Aphids (Greenfly) Aphids suck sap from the leaves and shoots of most tree, bush, cane and other soft fruits, causing leaf curling and distortion, reddish discoloration, stunted growth and black sooty mould. They spread virus diseases.

Pests and diseases: fruit 3

Treatment: Spray with a tar oil wash in December (but not strawberries or myrobalan plum) to kill over-wintering eggs. Use a systemic insecticide, such as dimethoate or heptenophos, in the spring if aphids are present, repeating as necessary.

Apple sawfly Caterpillars tunnel into the fruitlets, causing them to fall in June. A ribbon-like scar forms on the skin of damaged fruits that remain.

Treatment: Spray with HCH, dimethoate or fenitrothion one week after petal fall. Pick up and burn infested fruitlets.

Big bud mite A pest of black currants. It lives inside buds, making them swollen and rounded (instead of narrow and pointed) and they fail to develop in spring. The mites spread reversion disease (see page 245).

Treatment: Pick off and burn big buds during the winter. Spray with carbendazim at the first open flower and again two and four weeks later. Destroy badly infested bushes and replant with virus-free stock in the autumn.
replant with virus-free stock on a fresh site.

Capsid bugs Affect currants, gooseberries and apples. Capsids suck sap from shoot tips, leaves and fruits. Leaves at the shoot tips develop with tattered holes. Mature apple fruits have corky scabs or bumps on the skin.

Treatment: Spray with a systemic insecticide such as dimethoate shortly after flowering has finished.

Caterpillars Caterpillars feed in the spring, causing damaged and ragged buds, leaves and blossoms.

Treatment: Spray with fenitrothion or permethrin as the young leaves appear. Place a sticky greaseband around the trunk in late October to trap emerging wingless female winter moths. Keep bands sticky and in position until late March.

Codling moth Caterpillars tunnel into the mature fruit of apples and sometimes pears.

Treatment: Spray with fenitrothion or permethrin in mid-June, repeating three weeks later. Place bands of sacking around the trunk and larger branches in late July to trap over-wintering larvae. Remove and burn them in November.

Fruit tree red spider mite A tiny, sap-feeding pest of apples and plums. It causes a yellowish mottling of the leaves, which can dry up and fall early.

Treatment: Check the mite with a dinocap spray or use a systemic insecticide such as dimethoate in summer if it persists. Give two or three applications at 7–10 day intervals.

Glasshouse red spider mite These mites can attack all cane and bush fruits, strawberries, peaches and vines, especially plants grown under glass or against warm walls. They cause a fine mottled discoloration of the foliage and early defoliation.

Treatment: Spray three or four times at seven day intervals with malathion, pirimiphos-methyl or a systemic insecticide such as dimethoate. Alternatively, use biological control by introducing a predatory mite, *Phytoseiulus persimilis*. Maintain a high humidity for greenhouse plants.

Glasshouse whitefly Affects mainly greenhouse fruits such as vines, melons, Cape gooseberries and citrus fruits. Small, white, moth-like adults and their scale-like larvae suck sap and foul the foliage with honeydew and sooty mould.

Treatment: Early treatment is necessary because heavy infestations are difficult to control. Spray with permethrin, pirimiphos-methyl or pyrethrum when adults are first seen, repeating at four day intervals as necessary. Alternatively use biological control by introducing a parasitic wasp, *Encarsia formosa*.

Gooseberry sawfly These caterpillars are up to 1in long, creamy-green with black dots. They can completely defoliate gooseberry and red currant plants.

Treatment: Spray with derris or malathion as soon as caterpillars are seen, repeating as necessary, between late April and the end of summer.

Mealybugs Sap-feeding pests of greenhouse plants, especially vines. The small white-pink insects can be seen in the leaf axils covered with a white fluffy wax.

Treatment: Scrape off loose bark from woody plants such as vines in December to expose the mealybugs. Then spray or paint the rods with tar oil. Control summer infestations by spraying with malathion two or three times at two week intervals.

Pear leaf blister mite A minute pest causing pale green or pink blotches on the leaves in May which later turn brown or black.

Treatment: No chemical controls are currently available to amateur gardeners but it is not a serious pest. Remove and burn badly affected leaves or shoots.

Pear midge Its grubs attack the fruitlets, causing them to blacken and fall in June.

Treatment: Spray with HCH or fenitrothion at the white bud stage. Pick off and burn affected fruitlets. Keep the ground cultivated beneath infected trees.

Plum sawfly Its grubs tunnel into the fruitlets and cause them to fall in June.

Treatment: Spray with fenitrothion or dimethoate at 7–10 days after petal fall.

Raspberry beetle The maggot-like larvae damage the ripening fruits of raspberry, blackberry, loganberry and similar fruits.

Treatment: Prevent damage by spraying at dusk with derris or malathion on raspberry when the first pink fruit is seen; on loganberry when flowering is almost over; and on blackberry when flowering starts.
and on the blackberry when flowering starts.

Scale insects These are sap-feeding pests with shell-like coverings which are attached to the bark. Mussel scale attacks apples and brown scale attacks greenhouse fruits such as vines, peaches and figs.

Treatment: Control with a tar oil wash in December or apply malathion in late May and again in late June for mussel scale; treat in early July for brown scale.

Slugs These damage fruits on strawberries.

Treatment: Scatter methiocarb pellets among the plants when strawing down. Keep the garden clear and tidy in winter to reduce numbers.

Strawberry seed beetle A medium-sized, shiny black beetle that eats the seeds from the exterior of the fruits.

Treatment: Trap them in jam jars sunk up to their rims in the soil. Put down methiocarb pellets just before strawing down. Keep the bed free of weeds because weed seeds feed the beetles at other times of the year.

Suckers These aphid-like sap-feeding pests attack the blossom and foliage of apples and pears and foul pear foliage with honeydew.

Treatment: Tar oil winter wash controls the over-wintering eggs of apple sucker but pear suckers overwinter as adults and are less affected. Apply a systemic insecticide such as dimethoate at the green cluster stage of bud development on apples or three weeks after petal fall on pears.

Vine weevil Grubs feed on the roots of grapes and strawberries, sometimes destroying the plants. The adult beetles eat irregular shaped notches from the leaf margins at night but this is less serious.

Treatment: Drench the root area with HCH.

Wasps These feed on the ripe fruit of apples, pears, plums and grapes.

Treatment: Enclose fruit trusses in bags made from muslin or old nylon tights. Destroy wasp nests by placing carbaryl dust in the entrance at dusk.

Woolly aphid This aphid sucks sap from cracks in the bark and young shoots of apples. The colonies can be recognized by their fluffy white waxy coating.

Treatment: Spray or paint the colonies with a systemic insecticide such as dimethoate or heptenophos when the aphid appears in May to June.

Pests and diseases: vegetables 1

Strong, healthy plants are less susceptible to disease and better able to withstand damage from pests. However, despite correct cultivation, vigilant weed control, crop rotation and the increasing availability of disease-resistant varieties, damage due to pests and diseases occurs even in the most carefully managed vegetable gardens. It is therefore important to be able to make rapid and accurate diagnosis of problems so that the right action, often involving the use of chemicals, can be taken as soon as possible.

The use of chemicals

Always follow the manufacturer's instructions precisely, especially concerning dilution, the time of application and the period which must elapse between the final application and harvesting. Always store chemicals, sealed and labelled, out of reach of children, pets and wild animals. Never transfer them to soft drinks bottles. Do not spray on windy days or allow spray to drift on to other crops or neighbouring gardens, ponds, rivers, ditches or water sources. Never use containers previously used for weedkillers when mixing or applying other sprays and do not mix up more material than is required because it is difficult to dispose of the excess safely. Wash hands and equipment thoroughly after spraying.

Some chemicals must be treated with extra caution. For example, calomel dust is poisonous and protective gloves should be worn. Thiram may irritate skin, eyes, nose and mouth; wear gloves, mask and goggles if susceptible to allergic reactions.

Not all insects and other animals in the garden are harmful to vegetables and some are beneficial. They can be killed by the chemicals used to control pest so never use pesticides indiscriminately or excessively.

Types of pesticides and fungicides

Fungicides are used to prevent infections and pesticides to treat infestations. There are various kinds of pesticides and they act in different ways. Contact types such as derris affect the insect itself and it is important to cover all the plant's surfaces for maximum kill. They remain effective for a relatively short period after application. Systemic types such as heptenophos and dimethoate are absorbed into the plant and spread through the sap. They are very effective against sap-sucking insects. Complete coverage of the plant is not essential and most systemics can be applied as a root drench. Most fungicides only check or prevent disease and should therefore be applied before signs of disease are seen. A few partially systemic fungicides such as benomyl are now available. These are absorbed slightly into the plant's tissues and are effective for a short period even after disease symptoms are visible.

Methods of application Chemicals are available as dusts, sprays, pastes, pellets, wettable powders and aerosols. Not all chemicals are in all forms, however, and not all forms of a chemical are effective against the same range of pests or diseases.

Most chemicals are listed in this book according to their active ingredient and not by their trade name. Use products that contain the appropriate active ingredient which is given on the label or in the instructions issued by the manufacturer.

DISEASES

Blackleg of potatoes is caused by the bacterium *Erwinia carotovora* var. *atroseptica*. Early in the season the foliage of an affected plant turns yellow and the shoots collapse because of blackening and rotting of the stem bases, although occasionally one or two healthy stems develop. The plant may die before any tubers form but any which have already developed show a brown or grey slimy rot inside starting at the heel end. Destroy affected plants. If severely infected tubers are stored they will decay, but those only slightly infected may show no symptoms and, if planted, will introduce the infection the following season.

Chocolate spot disease causes discoloration on the leaves and stems of broad beans and can seriously affect over-wintered crops. Plants grown in acid soils or which have become soft through excessive applications of nitrogenous fertilizers are more susceptible to attack. Sowing the seeds thinly, applications of potash at $\frac{1}{2}$ oz per square yard before November sowing and the maintenance of a pH of 6.5–7.0 will cut down the likelihood of infection. Where the disease is endemic spray the young foliage with a copper fungicide before any symptoms are seen.

Club-root distorts the roots and badly affects the growth of all brassicas. The disease is more prevalent in acid soils so where necessary raise the pH to 6.5–7.5 by applying ground chalk or limestone at 14 oz per square yard and maintain the pH level with smaller dressings as required in subsequent years. Four per cent calomel dust raked into the soil before sowing at $1\frac{1}{2}$ oz per square yard helps to control club-root, and also has some combative function against cabbage root fly. Seedlings may also be dipped in calomel paste or a solution of benomyl or thiophanate-methyl to protect them from attack.

Common scab of potatoes occurs most frequently in dry soils lacking in humus and is also prevalent on alkaline soils. A soil pH of 5.0–6.0 and improvement of the soil humus content will cut down the incidence of the disease. Potatoes should also be kept well watered, particularly during dry spells. No available chemical control measures are effective against it.

Damping off diseases of seedlings are encouraged by overcrowded, stagnant conditions and the use of garden soil rather than sterilized soils or compost for raising seedlings under glass. Affected seedlings rot and collapse at ground level. Thin sowing in sterilized compost will cut down the incidence of damping off. Slight attacks may be checked by watering with Cheshunt compound after removing dead seedlings.

Downy mildews may affect lettuce, onions, spinach and young brassicas. Thin sowing and early thinning of seedlings will cut down incidence of these mildews but if seedlings are attacked, remove the affected leaves and spray with mancozeb. Bordeaux mixture on brassicas, onions and spinach and thiram on lettuce are also effective.

Foot and root rot is caused by several different fungi which kill the roots and bases of the stems of young plants. A seed dressing of captan may help to avoid this trouble but at the first signs of this disease, water the crop with a solution of Cheshunt compound. Mound sterile compost around the bases of affected tomatoes. Burn badly affected plants.

Grey mould (*Botrytis cinerea*) may affect most vegetables at some stage in their lives. It is encouraged by overcrowded, stagnant conditions and affected stems, leaves or fruits rapidly rot and become covered with a grey-brown fungal growth. To cut down attacks sow seeds thinly and keep seedlings and plants well spaced. Provide good ventilation under glass and make sure that dead or dying material is removed and burnt. Spray over-wintering plants with thiram. Should the disease occur on any type of plant growing under glass, fumigate with tecnazene smokes.

Halo blight is a seed-borne bacterial disease which appears as spots on the leaves of beans. The spots are surrounded by a light-coloured ring or halo. There is no adequate control and the plants should be burnt once the crop has been picked.

Leaf spot Brassicas, spinach beet and beetroot are among those crops susceptible to leaf spot fungi which usually affect older leaves, causing round brown spots. Sometimes affected tissues fall away, leaving holes. Leaf spot is most troublesome in wet seasons, particularly among overcrowded plants and on brassicas grown too soft as a result of heavy dressings of nitrogenous fertilizers. Affected leaves should be removed and destroyed. Proper thinning and crop rotation are important factors in the prevention of leaf spot infections.

Neck rot fungus (*Botrytis allii*) can cause considerable loss of stored onions. A grey mouldy growth develops on or near the neck of an affected bulb, which subsequently becomes soft and rotten. Later, large black resting bodies of the fungus develop on the rotting tissues. Store only hard, well dried bulbs in a cool, dry place where there is free circulation of air around them. Examine bulbs frequently and remove rotting onions as they are seen. The disease can be seed-borne, therefore buy good quality seed which has been treated against neck rot, or sets from a reputable grower, and dust seeds and sets with dry benomyl before sowing or planting.

Parsnip canker causes rotting of the shoulder tissues of parsnips. There are no satisfactory control measures although the incidence of the disease can be reduced by growing par-

Pests and diseases: vegetables 2

snips on a fresh site each year in deep well-worked soil of pH 5.5–7.0. 'Avonresister' is a variety resistant to parsnip canker.

Potato blight is a serious disease of potatoes and is also liable to infect tomatoes. Foliage, stems and tubers of potatoes can be affected and destroyed. Deep planting of healthy tubers in drills at least 5 in deep and timely earthing up minimize infection. Main crop potatoes should also be sprayed from July onwards with mancozeb or bordeaux mixture to control the disease. Cut off and remove the haulms before lifting. A few varieties are resistant to potato blight and can be grown in areas where this disease is prevalent. Potato blight can be controlled on tomatoes by spraying each season with one of the chemicals recommended for potatoes, as soon as the tops have been pinched out of most of the plants in midsummer. In cool wet seasons the spray should be repeated every 2–3 weeks as a precaution.

Powdery mildews occur on marrows, outdoor cucumbers and some other vegetable crops, particularly if they become dry at the roots. The leaves and stems become covered with a white powdery coating. Control by spraying with benomyl, dinocap or thiophanate-methyl as soon as the first symptoms appear, and repeat if necessary.

Sclerotinia disease can attack the roots or stem bases of several vegetables including carrots, cucumbers, Jerusalem artichokes and roots or tubers in store. Any infected plants must be burnt to avoid further soil contamination from the large resting bodies that form if diseased plants are allowed to remain. There is no practical chemical control. Good hygiene and rotation of affected crops are the only practical methods of control.

Violet root rot of asparagus is caused by the soil-borne fungus, *Helicobasidium purpureum*, which kills the crown and roots. It grows on them as violet web-like strands. Small round masses of fungal threads may also appear. With the death of the roots the top growth turns yellow and dies, and a gap develops in the asparagus bed as the disease gradually spreads outwards. Where only slight infection has occurred, isolate the diseased area by sinking sheets of thick polythene into the soil to a depth of 12 in. In

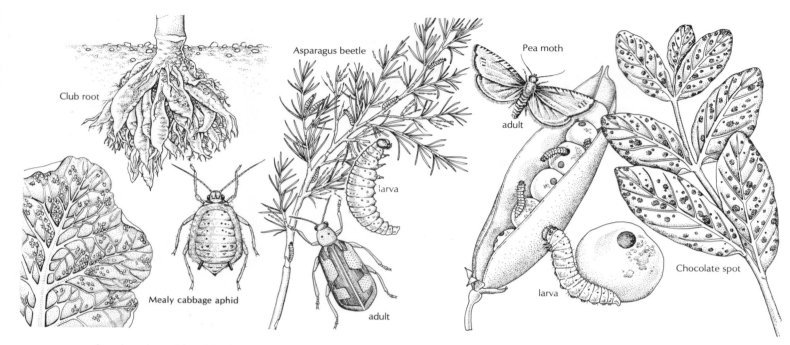

Club root

Mealy cabbage aphid

Asparagus beetle

larva

adult

Pea moth

adult

larva

Chocolate spot

severe cases abandon the infected bed and make a new one on a fresh site.

Viruses causing leaf mottling and distortion and often stunting of the plants can affect marrows in particular, celery, cucumbers, tomatoes and several other vegetables. They are spread by aphids or eelworms and so control of these pests and removal of weeds that may act as hosts for both the viruses and their vectors is important. There is no cure for virus-affected plants, which should be burnt once the trouble has been diagnosed. Always wash hands and tools after handling virus-infected plants.

White rot of onions appears as a fluffy white growth at the bases of onions and quickly affects and kills the foliage. Affected plants should be burnt as soon as the disease is seen. Control may be obtained by applying four per cent calomel dust or benomyl to the drills prior to sowing, or spraying with the recommended rate of benomyl when the plants are approximately 7–8 in high.

PESTS

Aphids (greenfly and blackfly) will infest most

vegetable crops. Apart from the damage caused by the aphids themselves, they are carriers of virus diseases and vegetables should be checked regularly for their presence. Infestations should be dealt with at an early stage by spraying with dimethoate, derris, heptenophos, malathion, or pirimicarb. If plants are to be harvested within one week of applying the spray use derris. Cucurbits are also best sprayed with derris, pyrethrum or permethrin to avoid damage. Beans, if in flower, should be sprayed at dusk with pirimicarb because bees, the main pollinators, are relatively resistant to it.

Root aphids may also be troublesome on beans, lettuce and artichokes. Attacks are not usually noticed until the plants are infested. A malathion drench may check heavy infestations but soil treatment with diazinon granules prior to sowing or planting should prevent attack. Some lettuce varieties such as 'Avoncrisp' are resistant to root aphids.

Asparagus beetle Small yellow, red and black beetles and their grey-black grubs can defoliate the plants during the summer. Control by spraying with derris, HCH or pirimiphos-

methyl as soon as these pests are seen.

Bean seed fly maggots can prevent germination of all types of bean seed and they can also damage onions. Damage usually occurs in cold, wet seasons when germination is slow. The use of cloches to warm the soil early in the year encourages more rapid germination and cuts down attacks. Treating the seed row with diazinon, bromophos or phoxim granules gives some protection.

Birds Damage to vegetable crops by birds, mainly wood pigeons and sparrows, can occur throughout the year. Scaring devices and bird repellent sprays are of limited value in deterring birds. In some instances they may be effective for short periods, but where birds are a persistent problem some form of vegetable cage or netting is essential to produce worthwhile crops.

Cabbage root fly maggots can devastate brassica seedlings and young plants. The seed rows and transplanting sites should be treated with diazinon, phoxim or bromophos prior to sowing or planting. Attacks on established plants can be checked with a pirimiphos-methyl drench.

Pests and diseases: vegetables 3

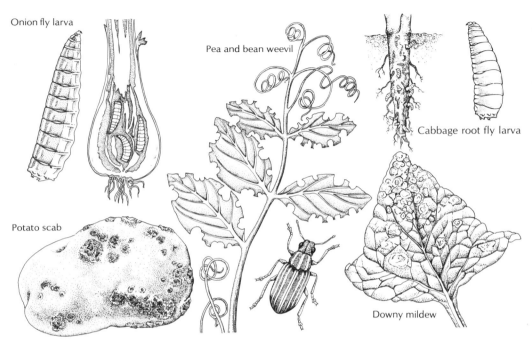

Onion fly larva

Pea and bean weevil

Cabbage root fly larva

Potato scab

Downy mildew

Carrot fly is the most damaging pest of carrots and also attacks parsley, parsnip and celery. Growth is stunted and secondary rots may develop in damaged carrots. Careful spacing of pelleted seed or very thin sowing to cut down the need to thin carrots will help to minimize damage because female carrot flies are strongly attracted to the aroma of carrot foliage bruised when thinning. Sowings made after the end of May normally miss the first generation of maggots but carrot fly is such a widespread pest that treatment of the seed drills with diazinon, phoxim or bromophos is advisable to give protection for 6–8 weeks. Carrots that are not lifted until autumn should also be sprayed with pirimiphos-methyl in early August.

Caterpillars are troublesome on cabbages and should be controlled before they penetrate the hearts, where they are difficult to reach. Hand picking with a small number of plants or treatment with carbaryl, HCH, fenitrothion or permethrin is effective.

Celery leaf miner lives in the leaves of celery, parsnip and lovage. Heavy attacks can be controlled by spraying with malathion or di-

methoate. Light infestations of celery leaf miner can be overcome by hand picking and burning affected leaves.

Cutworms are soil-dwelling caterpillars of various moth species. They feed on roots and the bases of stems and attack most vegetables at an early stage, causing them to wilt and die. Control is by treating the soil with phoxim, diazinon or bromophos before sowing or planting crops.

Flea beetles Heavy infestations of these tiny beetles, which eat small holes in the leaves of brassica seedlings, can be controlled with derris, HCH, or pirimiphos-methyl. Damage seldom occurs once the plants have developed beyond the seedling stage.

Glasshouse red spider mite is a common pest of all vegetables grown under glass, causing leaf discoloration and affecting growth adversely. A damp atmosphere helps to check this pest which thrives under hot dry conditions but spraying with malathion, dimethoate or pirimiphos-methyl at seven day intervals is needed to control infestations. Care is needed when applying chemicals to cucumbers because they may damage the foliage.

Biological control (see p.221) is a safe alternative. Spray in the evening when it is cooler and make sure that the plants are not dry at the roots.

Onion eelworms mainly attack members of the onion family but can also damage carrots, parsnips and beans. They are microscopic, worm-like creatures that live inside the stem and leaves. The tissues become soft and swollen, and infested plants usually rot off and die. There are no chemical controls available to amateur gardeners and infested plants should be burnt. Host plants, which include some weeds, should not be grown in ground infested by onion eelworms for at least two years.

Onion fly attacks all members of the onion family. Young plants may be killed by the maggots, and the bulbs of older onions are tunnelled and made useless for consumption. Soil treatment with diazinon, phoxim or bromophos granules when sowing or planting will control this pest during the vulnerable early stages.

Pea moth caterpillars badly damage peas, eating the green peas and spoiling the crop, particularly of late-maturing varieties. Early-maturing crops usually escape damage because they flower before the pea moth lays its eggs. Peas which flower between mid-June and mid-August should be sprayed with fenitrothion or permethrin 7–10 days after flowering starts.

Pea and bean weevils feed by eating notches from the leaf margins of pea and broad bean plants. Control measures, using HCH or pirimiphos-methyl dust, are necessary only if seedlings are being attacked.

Pea thrips (thunder flies) are tiny, thin, brown-black or yellow insects that suck sap from the leaves and the pods. This causes a silver-brown discoloration and damaged pods may be distorted and only partly filled with peas. Heavy infestations are more likely in hot, dry summers and damage can be prevented by spraying with dimethoate, permethrin or fenitrothion.

Potato cyst eelworms live in the roots of potato and tomato plants and the foliage is often killed by midsummer. The yield is therefore much reduced. There are no chemicals available to amateurs that will control these eelworms. Crop rotation helps to reduce infes-

tation but it may be necessary to stop growing potatoes on land badly affected by these pests. Some potato varieties are resistant to one species of eelworm (*Globodera rostochiensis*) but none, so far, has immunity to *G. pallida*.

Slugs, snails, woodlice and millipedes can destroy seedlings and attack many developing vegetable crops. Slugs can be controlled by using methiocarb or metaldehyde pellets along the rows. Methiocarb gives some control of woodlice and millipedes, but where they are troublesome dusting the young plants with HCH may be necessary.

Whitefly Brassicas, cucurbits, tomatoes and other vegetables are attacked by various whitefly species that may cause a black deposit of sooty mould on the leaves. Cabbage whitefly is a distinct species from the glasshouse whitefly that affects tomatoes and cucurbits, but both may be controlled by three or four sprays with pyrethrum, permethrin or pirimiphos-methyl at seven day intervals. Under glass, biological control with the wasp *Encarsia formosa* avoids the problems of pesticide residues and resistance.

Wireworms may occur in large numbers in grassland or weed infested areas. They attack the roots or many vegetables and may seriously affect the quality of potatoes. Soil dressings of diazinon, phoxim or bromophos at planting or sowing will control infestations.

249

Glossary

Abort Failure to develop properly; usually refers to flowers or their parts.

Acid Describes soil with a pH of below 7.

Adventitious buds Growth buds that arise without any direct relation to the leaves, usually in response to a wound.

Adventitious roots Roots that develop from stems.

Aeration The process of spiking a lawn in order to allow air into the soil and relieve compaction.

Alkaline Describes soil with a pH over 7.

Annual A plant that completes its life-cycle within one growing season.

Anthers The pollen-producing structures at the apices of the stamens of a flower.

Anti-desiccant Chemicals used as a spray to reduce water loss when transplanting trees and shrubs in the dormant season. Especially useful with evergreens and conifers.

Apex The tip of a stem, hence apical bud, the uppermost bud on the stem, and apical shoot, the uppermost stem on a system of branches.

Apical bud The bud on a shoot.

Apical dominance Used of a terminal or apical bud which inhibits the growth of lateral buds and grows more rapidly than they do.

Axil The upper angle between a leaf, or leaf-stalk, and the stem from which it grows.

Bacterial Parasitic or saprophytic single-celled micro-organisms. Many are beneficial but some cause diseases.

Bark-ringing The removal of a ring of bark from the trunk of an unfruitful tree to check shoot growth.

Bare-root plant A plant lifted from the open ground (as opposed to a container-grown plant).

Bare rootstock Rootstock lifted from the open ground to be used for bench grafting.

Base dressing Fertilizer applied immediately before sowing or planting.

Bedding plant A plant used for temporary garden display.

Bench grafting Grafting on to a rootstock that is movable—that is, a pot-grown or a bare rootstock.

Biennial A plant that completes its life-cycle over two growing seasons.

Biennial bearer A tree bearing a good crop of blossom or fruit only in alternate years.

Blanching The exclusion of light from a plant to whiten the shoots.

Blindness A condition in which a shoot or bud fails to develop fully and aborts.

Bloom Either a blossom, or a natural white powdery or waxy sheen on many fruits and leaves, or an abnormal white powdery coating of fungus on galled leaves.

Bolting Producing flowers and seed prematurely.

Bonemeal Bones ground to a powder and used as a fertilizer.

Bottom heat The warmth, normally provided artificially, from under the compost in, for example, a propagator.

Bract A modified, usually reduced, leaf that grows just below the flowerhead.

Branched head A branch system on a tree in which there is no central leader shoot.

Brassica The cabbage, cauliflower and turnip genus of the Cruciferae.

Break The development of lateral shoots as a result of pruning a shoot to an auxillary bud.

Breastwood Shoots growing forward from plants trained against support structures.

Broadcast To distribute seed evenly over the entire seedbed, as opposed to sowing in rows.

Bud The embryo shoot, flower or flower cluster, hence growth bud, flower bud.

Budding A method of grafting using a single growth bud rather than part of a stem with several buds.

Bulb An underground storage organ that consists of layers of swollen fleshy leaves or leaf bases, which enclose the following year's growth buds.

Bud burst The period at the end of the dormant season when new buds begin to swell and produce leaves or flowers.

Bulbil A small bulb, formed in the leaf axil on a stem or in the inflorescence.

Bulblet Very small bulbs that develop below ground on some bulbs.

Bush tree A tree pruned to give a dwarf form with about 2–2½ ft of clear stem.

Bushel An Imperial measure of volume equal to 1.28 cu ft; for example, the amount of compost that will fit into a box 22 in × 10 in × 10 in without compacting.

Calyx The outer whorl of a flower, consisting of sepals which may be free to the base or partially joined, as in tomato flowers.

Canker A sharply defined diseased area on a woody stem, which often has malformed bark.

Cap A hard crust on the soil surface.

Capillarity The process by which water will rise above its normal level.

Carpeting plant A plant whose stems take root as they spread; also known as a carpeter.

Catch crop A rapidly maturing crop grown between harvesting one vegetable and sowing or planting the next on the same ground.

Central leader The central, vertical, dominant stem of a tree.

Chard The young stems of salsify, seakale, beet or globe artichokes.

Chelated Describes a special formulation of plant nutrients, which will remain available in alkaline soils.

Cheshunt compound A proprietary fungicide made up of 2 parts by weight fine copper sulphate and 11 parts by weight ammonium carbonate. The compound should be used at the rate of 1 oz to 2 gallons of water to prevent damping off in seedlings.

Chitting The germination or sprouting of seed prior to sowing.

Chlorophyll The green pigment present in most plants, by means of which they manufacture carbohydrates.

Climber A plant that climbs by clinging to objects by means of twining stems with hooks or tendrils, or more generally, any long-stemmed plant trained upwards.

Clone A plant propagated vegetatively, with identical characteristics to its parent.

Clump plant A deciduous plant that grows in spring from clusters of buds or an over-wintering rosette at the top of a rootstock.

Compost, garden Rotted organic matter used as an addition to or substitute for manure.

Compost seed and potting Mixtures of organic and inorganic materials, such as peat, sand, and loam, used for growing seeds, cuttings and pot plants.

Compound fertilizer One which contains all three major constituents needed for healthy growth, ie nitrogen, phosphorus and potassium.

Conifer A plant that bears its seeds in cones.

Contact insecticide An insecticide that kills pests by direct contact.

Contractile roots Roots of bulbs and corms that contract in length, thereby pulling the organ deeper into the soil.

Copper naphthenate A liquid timber preservative which is harmless to plants once it is dry, unlike creosote.

Coppicing The regular pruning of a tree or shrub close to ground level resulting in the production of a quantity of vigorous basal shoots.

Cordon A normally branched tree or shrub restricted by spur pruning to a single-stem.

Corm A solid, swollen stem-base, resembling a bulb, that acts as a storage organ.

Cotyledon A seed leaf; usually the first to emerge above ground on germination.

Crocking The use of small pieces of clay flower pot placed concave-side down in a pot or container over the drainage hole to facilitate drainage.

Crown Either the basal part of an herbaceous perennial plant from which roots and shoots grow, or the main branch system of a tree.

Cultivar see Variety.

Cultivator A tool used to break up the soil surface to improve its texture. A rotary cultivator, or rotavator, has revolving tines or blades and is power-driven.

Current year's growth/wood The shoots which have grown from buds during the present growing season.

Cutting A separated piece of stem, root, or leaf taken in order to propagate a new plant.

Deciduous Describes a plant that loses all its leaves at the end of the growing season.

Dead-head To prune the spent flowers or the unripe seedpods from a plant.

Dibber A tool that is pushed into the soil to make a hole in which to plant a seedling, cutting or small plant.

Dicotyledon A flowering plant that produces two seed leaves at germination.

Die-back The death of branches or shoots, beginning at their tips and spreading back towards the trunk or stem.

Disbudding The removal of surplus buds or shoots that are just beginning growth.

Dot plant Bedding plant used to give height or contrast to carpet plant arrangements.

Double leader Two shoots competing as leaders on a tree, each trying to assert apical dominance.

Dressing A material such as organic matter, fertilizer, sand or lime that is incorporated into the soil. A top dressing is applied to the surface only, without being dug in.

Dribble bar A sealed, perforated tube attached to a watering can spout that enables weedkiller or other liquid to be dribbled on to the plants or soil.

Drills Straight furrows, narrow and shallow, in which seeds are sown.

Dwarf pyramid A tree pruned to form a pyramid-shaped central-leader tree about 7 ft high.

Earth up Mounding earth around the base and stems of a plant.

Epiphyte (epiphytic) A plant that grows on another but gets no nourishment from it; e.g. an orchid growing on a branch of a tree. Other examples are lichens, mosses and some ferns.

Espalier A tree trained with a vertical main stem and tiers of horizontal branches.

Etiolation The blanching of a stem caused by the exclusion of light.

Evergreen A plant that retains its foliage for more than one year.

Eye Used to describe a growth bud, particularly of roses and vines.

F₁ hybrid A plant that is the result of a cross between two parent strains, usually with the best features of each. It does not breed true in further generations.

Fallowing Allowing land to remain uncropped for a period.

Family A group of related genera. For example, the genera *Poa* (meadow grass), *Festuca* (fescue) and *Agrostis* (bent) all belong to the family of grasses, Graminea.

Fan A shrub or tree in which the main branches are trained like the ribs of a fan against a wall, fence or other support system.

Fertilizer Material that provides plant food. It can be organic, i.e. derived from decayed plant or animal matter, or inorganic, i.e. made from chemicals.

Flowers of sulphur Pure yellow sulphur in finely powdered form, used to correct the pH of alkaline soils.

Flushes Irregular successive crops of flowers and fruit, as on perpetual strawberries.

Foliar feed A liquid fertilizer sprayed on to, and partially absorbed through, the leaves.

Foot The base of the main stem of an herbaceous plant.

Forcing The hastening of growth by providing warmth and/or excluding light.

Friable Describes a fine, crumbly soil with no hard or wet lumps.

Fritted trace elements A special formulation of plant nutrients, which will remain available to plants in alkaline soils.

Frost-lifting The loosening and lifting of plants in the soil after hard frost.

Fungicides A substance used for controlling diseases caused by fungi and some bacteria.

Fungus Any member of a group of non-flowering plants that, since they have no green colouring (chlorophyll), cannot manufacture their own food. Therefore, they are incapable of surviving independently and live on either another living organism or on decaying organic matter.

Gall An abnormal outgrowth of plant tissue.

Genus (plural genera) A group of allied species in botanical and zoological classification.

Germination The development of a seed into a seedling.

Grafting Propagation by uniting a shoot or single bud of one plant—the scion—with the root system and stem of another—the stock or root stock.

Growth bud A bud that gives rise to a shoot.

Growing point The extreme tip of roots or shoots.

Habit The natural mode of growth of a plant.

Half-hardy A plant unable to survive the winter unprotected but not needing all-year-round greenhouse protection.

Half-standard A tree grown with 3–4 ft of clear stem.

Harden off To acclimatize plants raised in warm conditions to colder conditions.

Hardy Describes a plant capable of surviving the winter in the open without protection.

Heeling in The storing of plant material, upright or inclined, in a trench which is then filled in with soil and firmed.

Herbaceous perennial See Perennial.

Glossary

Herbicide Synonym for weedkiller.

Hormone weedkiller Chemicals which, when applied to weeds, affect their growth, often causing the stems to extend rapidly before the plant collapses and dies.

Host A plant that harbours, or is capable of harbouring, a parasite.

Humidity The amount of water vapour in the atmosphere. Relative humidity is the amount of water in the atmosphere, relative to it being saturated, at a particular temperature. (Warm air will hold more water than cool air.)

Humus Fertile, organic matter that is in an advanced stage of decay.

Hybrid A plant produced by the cross fertilization of two species or variants of a species.

Incipient roots Roots that develop from stems; they frequently abort.

Inflorescence The part of a plant that bears the flowers.

Insecticides Substances used to kill injurious insects and some other pests.

John Innes Compounds Standard soil mixes that can be easily reproduced to give good results. Developed at the John Innes Horticultural Institute in 1939. Revolutionized the growing of plants in pots.

Lanceolate Describes a leaf that is much longer than it is wide, and is shaped like the head of a lance.

Larva The active immature stage of some insects. The larva of a butterfly, moth or sawfly is known as a caterpillar, a beetle or weevil larva as a grub, and a fly larva as a maggot.

Lateral A side growth that develops at an angle from the main stem of a tree.

Layering Propagating by inducing shoots to form roots while they are still attached to the parent plant.

Leader shoot The shoot that is dominating growth in a stem system, and is usually uppermost.

Leaching The removal of soluble minerals from the soil by water draining through it.

Leaf Axil See Axil.

Leaf-mould Well rotted leaves, which can be used as a mulch or added to the soil to improve its texture.

Leaf-fall The period when deciduous plants begin to shed their leaves.

Light The glass or plastic covering of a cold frame.

Lime A compound that contains calcium and/or magnesium, added to the soil to reduce acidity.

Line out To plant out young plants or cuttings in temporary positions.

Loam A fertile soil with balanced proportions of clay, sand and humus.

Long Tom A pot about half as deep again as a normal pot.

Maiden A one-year-old tree or shrub.

Manure Bulky material of animal origin added to soil to improve its structure and fertility.

Mature A plant that can produce flowers and, hence, reproduce sexually.

Mechanical digger See Cultivator.

Microclimate The climatic conditions in a particular small area.

Micro-organisms A microscopic animal or plant organism that can cause plant disease. Micro-organisms are beneficial when decomposing plant and animal residue to form humus.

Mole plough A plough pulled through the soil to form a drainage tunnel. Used on clay soils.

Monocotyledon A flowering plant that produces only one seed leaf.

Mosaic A patchy variation of normal green colour; usually a symptom of virus disease.

Mound layering An alternative term for stooling.

Mulch A top dressing of organic or inorganic matter, applied to the soil around a plant.

Mutant or Sport A plant that differs genetically from the typical growth of the plant that produced it.

Naturalized Describes plants grown in natural surroundings where they increase of their own accord and need little maintenance. Also plants established in an area, although they are not native to it.

Nitrate A nitrogen-containing fertilizer that can be natural, such as potassium or sodium, or synthetic, such as calcium nitrate.

Nymph The active, immature stage of some insects and mites.

Offsets Small bulbs produced at the base of the parent bulb; also a young plant developing laterally on the stem close to the parent.

Organic matter Matter consisting of, or derived from, living organisms. Examples include farmyard manure and leaf-mould.

Ornamental A plant grown for its decorative qualities.

Over-winter Refers to the means by which an organism survives winter conditions.

Pan A hard layer of soil beneath the surface.

Parasite An organism that lives on, and takes part or all of its food from, a host plant; usually to the detriment of the latter.

Pelleted seeds Small seeds coated to make them easier to handle for space sowing.

Perennial A plant that lives for more than three seasons.

Perlite A natural, sterile, granular medium derived from volcanic rock. Used as a rooting medium and an ingredient of potting and seed-sowing composts.

Pesticides A chemical used to kill pests; also generally for chemicals used to control pests and diseases.

Petiole The stalk of a leaf.

pH The degree of acidity or alkalinity. Below 7 on the pH scale is acid, above it is alkaline.

Phosphatic fertilizer Fertilizer with a high proportion of phosphorus.

Photosynthesis The process by which a green plant is able to make carbohydrates from water and carbon dioxide, using light as an energy source and chlorophyll as the catalyst.

Pinching (or Stopping) The removal of the growing tip of a shoot.

Planting mark The slight change in colour on the stem of a bare-root plant, indicating the depth at which it was formerly planted.

Plunge outside To bury container-grown plants up to the pot rims in ash, peat or sand bed to protect the roots from frost in winter.

Pollination The transference of pollen from the male to the female parts of a flower.

Pot-bound The condition reached by a pot plant when its roots have filled the pot and exhausted the available nutrients.

Potash (K_2O) Also called sulphate of potash. Essential for plant growth. Present in all balanced fertilizers.

Presser board A piece of flat wood with a handle used to firm and level compost.

Pricking out The transplanting and spacing out of seedlings.

Propagation The production of a new plant from an existing one, either sexually by seeds or asexually, for example by cuttings.

Proteins Organic nitrogenous compounds synthesized by plants from simple substances. An essential component of living cells.

Quicklime chalk or limestone which has been burnt in a kiln. It is caustic and will burn foliage and skin, so the milder hydrated lime is usually employed in correcting soil acidity.

Rambler Roses producing long, flexible basal canes, trained on walls, fences and screens.

Reaction The degree of acidity or alkalinity in soil or compost. Reaction is measured on the pH scale.

Recurrent flowering The production of several crops of flowers during one season more or less in succession.

Regulatory pruning Pruning to remove crossing, crowded and weak shoots and branches.

Relative humidity See Humidity.

Renewal pruning Pruning to maintain a constant supply of young shoots.

Repotting Replacing of some of the compost around the roots of a pot-grown plant with fresh compost.

Resistant Describes a plant that is able to overcome completely or partially the effect of a parasitic organism or disorder. It also describes a pest or disease that is no longer controllable by a particular chemical.

Rhizome A creeping horizontal underground stem that acts as a storage organ.

Rhizomorph A root-like mass of fungal threads, by means of which certain fungi spread through the soil.

Riddle To sieve soil, compost or leaf-mould.

Ring culture A method of growing plants in bottomless pots known as rings. Nutrients are absorbed by the roots of the plant from the compost in the ring and water is taken up from the sand or pebbles on which the ring stands.

Ring pattern Circular areas of chlorosis, the centre of each remaining green. It is a symptom of some virus diseases.

Rod The main, woody stem of a vine.

Rootball The soil or compost ball formed among and around the roots of a plant.

Root cutting A piece of the root of a plant used for propagation.

Root-pruning Severing some or all of the main roots of a tree to reduce vigour.

Rooted tips The shoot tips of plants such as blackberries that have been buried in the soil and taken root to form a new plant.

Rootstock See Grafting.

Rose (spray head) The watering can or hose attachment producing a fine spray.

Rosette A small cluster of overlapping leaves, often close to ground level.

Rotavator See Cultivator.

Runner A rooting stem that grows along the surface of the soil, as in strawberries.

Run-off When spraying, the point at which a plant becomes saturated, and further liquid runs off on to the surrounding area.

Sap The fluid in living plants that transports nutrients to various parts of the plant.

Scab A roughened, crust-like, diseased area.

Scarifying The process of vigorously raking a lawn in order to remove thatch.

Scion See Grafting.

Scramblers Climbing plants that do not twine or bear tendrils, clambering up by pushing through surrounding trees and shrubs, e.g. the so-called climbing roses.

Seedcoat The tough, protective layer around a seed.

Seed dressing A fine powder applied to seeds before sowing to protect them from pests or diseases.

Seed drill A machine for sowing at regular intervals in rows.

Seedheads Faded flowerheads that have been successfully fertilized and contain seeds.

Seed leaf (syn. cotyledon) The first leaf or leaves produced by germinated seed.

Self-sterile Describes a plant whose pollen cannot fertilize its own female parts.

Semi-evergreen Describes a plant intermediate between evergreen and deciduous. It bears foliage throughout the year, but loses some leaves during the winter.

Sepal The outermost, leaf-like structures of a flower.

Sets Whole or part bulbs or tubers used for propagation.

Shrub A perennial plant with persistent woody stems branching from the base. If only the lower parts of the branches are woody and the upper shoots are soft and usually die in winter, it is known as a sub-shrub.

Silt Very fine soil formed from clay.

Snag A short stump of a branch left after incorrect pruning.

Soakaway A pit into which water drains.

Soil profile Used to describe a cross-section of soil from surface to bed-rock, showing layers such as sub-soil, top-soil.

Species A group of closely related organisms within a genus. Abbreviations: sp. (singular) or spp. (plural).

Spit The depth of a normal digging spade, roughly equal to 10 in.

Spore A reproductive body of a fungus.

Sport See Mutant.

Spot-treat To treat a small defined area or a particular plant, usually with weedkiller, fungicide or pesticide.

Spreader A substance added to a spray to assist its even distribution over the target.

Spur A slow-growing short branch system that usually carries clusters of flower buds.

Stamen The male reproductive organ of a flower, comprising a stalk with an anther.

Standard A tree or shrub grown with 5–7 ft of clear stem.

Station sowing The individual sowing of seeds at a predetermined spacing in the site in which they will grow until pricking out or harvesting.

Stock See Grafting.

Stool The base of a plant, such as a cane fruit, that produces new shoots.

Stopping See Pinching.

Strain A distinct group within a species of fungus or eelworm.

Strike To take root, usually of cuttings.

Strike off To remove excess compost above the rim of a pot or seed tray.

Sub-lateral A side-shoot growing from a lateral shoot.

Sub-shrub See Shrub.

Sub-soil See Top-soil.

Sub-species A category intermediate between a variety and a species.

Glossary/Acknowledgements

Succulent A condition in certain plants that has developed as a response to a lack of readily available fresh water. A succulent plant is capable of storing relatively large quantities of water.

Sucker A shoot growing from a stem or root at or below ground level. Also a type of sap feeding insect.

Suckering plant A plant that spreads by means of underground shoots, suckers or stolons.

Sump Syn. for soakaway.

Syn. Abbreviation for synonym.

Systemic fungicide or insecticide A chemical which permeates a plant's sap stream and kills some diseases or sucking insects.

Tap root The primary vertical root of a plant; also any strong-growing vertical root.

Terminal bud, shoot, flower The uppermost, usually central, growth on a stem. (See Apex.)

Thatch On a lawn, a layer of dead or living organic matter, along with debris, found between the roots and foliage of the grass.

Thin To reduce the number of seedlings, buds, flowers, fruitlets or branches.

Tilth A fine crumbly surface layer of soil. It is produced by weathering or careful cultivation.

Tine The prong of a fork, rake or other tool.

Tolerant Describes either a plant that can live despite infection by a parasitic organism, or a fungus that is unaffected by applications of a certain fungicide.

Top dressing See Dressing.

Top-soil The upper layer of dark fertile soil in which plants grow. Below this lies the sub-soil, which is lighter in colour, lacks organic matter and is often low in nutrients.

Transpiration The continual loss of water vapour from leaves and stems.

Trace elements Food materials required by plants only in very small amounts.

True leaves Leaves typical of the mature plant as opposed to simpler seed leaves.

Truss A cluster of flowers or fruit.

Tuber A swollen underground stem or root that acts as a storage organ and from which new plants or tubers may develop.

Turgid Plant material that contains its full complement of water and is not therefore under stress.

Union The junction between rootstock and scion or between two scions grafted together.

Var Abbreviation for the botanical classification *varietas* (variety); it refers only to naturally occurring varieties.

Variegated Describes leaves with coloured markings, usually white or cream, due to an absence of chlorophyll.

Variety A distinct variant of a species; it may be a cultivated form (a cultivar) or occur naturally (varietas).

Vegetative growth Leaf and stem growth as opposed to flowers or fruit.

Vermiculite A sterile medium made from expanded mica. It is light, clean and moisture retentive and is used in seed, cutting and potting composts.

Virus Disease-causing organism, not visible to the naked eye, that may live in plants and less often in the soil.

Watering-in To water around the stem of a newly transplanted plant to settle soil around the roots.

Water shoot A vigorous, sappy shoot growing from an adventitious or dormant bud.

Water stress A variable condition of wilting in which plant material is losing water faster than it can take it up.

Water table The level in the soil below which the soil is saturated by ground water.

Weedkiller, contact action A weedkiller that kills only those green parts of plants with which it comes into contact.

Weedkiller, residual A weedkiller that acts through the soil and remains effective for a period ranging from a few weeks (short-term residual weedkillers) to several months (long-term residual weedkillers).

Weedkiller, selective A weedkiller that kills only certain types of plant, leaving others unharmed.

Weedkiller, translocated A weedkiller that is absorbed through the leaves and stems and is rapidly carried via the sap-stream to kill the whole plant.

Wetting agent A chemical added to a liquid that is to be sprayed, in order to improve the spray's adherence to a plant.

Wind-rock The loosening of a plant's root system by strong winds.

The Royal Horticultural Society and Publishers can accept no liability either for failure to control pests, diseases or weeds by any crop protection methods or for any consequences of their use. We specifically draw our readers' attention to the necessity of carefully reading and accurately following the manufacturer's instructions on any product.

Acknowledgements

Some of the artwork in this book has been based on photographs specially commissioned from the Harry Smith Horticultural Photographic Collection.

The publishers also wish to thank the many companies, academic institutions, public bodies and individuals who supplied illustration references.

Artists

Arka Cartographic Ltd, Nick Bartlett, Janet Blakeley, Lindsay Blow, Linda Broad, Paul Buckle, Ray Burrows, Charles Chambers, Harry Chlow, Pamela Dowson, Chris Forsey, Tony Graham, William Giles, Vana Haggerty, Eric Howley, Roger Hughes, Edwina Keene, Roman Kowalczyk, Terri Lawlor, Alan Male, Sandra Pond, Ed Roberts, Colin Salmon, Mike Saunders, Anne Savage, Bob Scott, Paul Stafford, Ralph Stobart, Stonecastle Graphics, Rod Stutterby, Cynthia Swaby, Lorna Turpin, Venner Artists, West One Arts, Alan White and John Woodcock.

Index

Index

Index

Index